D1559520

Confronting Evil

Confronting Evil

Engaging Our Responsibility to Prevent Genocide

James Waller

To FRED—
THE DEDICATION AND
ANKNOWLEDGMENTS SAY
IT ALL — MY LIFE WAS
CHANGED BECAUSE OF YOU.
REST WELL MY FRIEND,

Jim Waller
7/22/16

OXFORD
UNIVERSITY PRESS

OXFORD
UNIVERSITY PRESS

Oxford University Press is a department of the University of Oxford. It furthers
the University's objective of excellence in research, scholarship, and education
by publishing worldwide. Oxford is a registered trade mark of Oxford University
Press in the UK and certain other countries.

Published in the United States of America by Oxford University Press
198 Madison Avenue, New York, NY 10016, United States of America.

© Oxford University Press 2016

Library of Congress Cataloging-in-Publication Data
Names: Waller, James, 1961- author.
Title: Confronting evil : engaging our responsibility to prevent genocide /
James Waller.
Description: Oxford ; New York : Oxford University Press, [2016] |
Includes bibliographical references and index.
Identifiers: LCCN 2015030195 | ISBN 9780199300709
Subjects: LCSH: Genocide—Prevention. | Social action.
Classification: LCC HV6322.7 .W353 2016 | DDC 364.15/1—dc23
LC record available at http://lccn.loc.gov/2015030195

9 8 7 6 5 4 3 2 1

Printed by Edwards Brothers Malloy, United States of America

To my friends and colleagues at the Auschwitz Institute for Peace and Reconciliation, and to our many global partners who share our mission of building a world that prevents genocide and other mass atrocities.

CONTENTS

Preface: "Done to Death"   *ix*

Acknowledgments   *xvii*

Introduction: "Offend Every Precept of Our Common Humanity"   *xxi*

PART I: Naming and Defining Genocide   *1*

1. "A Crime without a Name"   *3*

2. "By Their Rightful Name"   *41*

3. "By Our Words and Actions"   *99*

PART II: A Continuum of Prevention Strategies   *133*

4. Upstream Prevention Strategies: Avoiding "A Path to Hell"   *135*

5. Midstream Prevention Strategies: "Sometimes
   We Must Interfere"   *211*

6. Downstream Prevention Strategies: "This Is for Those
   Who Want Us to Forget"   *279*

PART III: Never Again?   *351*

Conclusion: "Thus Have We Made the World ...
   Thus Have I Made It"   *353*

Index   *369*

PREFACE: "DONE TO DEATH"

In his provocative essay on the politics of language, the literary critic George Steiner writes of "scholars who were first promoted when their Jewish or Socialist teachers had been done to death" during the reign of Nazi Germany.[1] Although there are certainly many critics of Steiner's work on the relationship between language and inhumanity, I have always found that particular phrase—"done to death"—poignantly descriptive of the destruction of a civilian population. I appreciate how the phrase does not sound like the distancing euphemisms often used by perpetrators in describing their own atrocities—"final solution," "ethnic cleansing," "liquidation," "bush clearing," "special treatment," "resettlement," and "special installations," among many others. Rather, "done to death" evokes an active sense of destruction. Death did not come randomly or as a matter of chance. Death was not agentless or passive. Death did not docilely "move into the vicinity" as Dragan Obrenovic, senior officer and commander in the Bosnian Serb Army, evasively admitted during his guilty plea to crimes against humanity.[2] Death was done to a people. Death, not simply abuse or persecution or torture, was the endpoint. Someone, on the basis of a real or presumed social identity, was identified as a threat—to racial purity, stability, progress, safety, or any myriad reasons concocted by the perpetrators—and they were done to death.

This book is about the times that groups of people have been "done to death" by state or nonstate actors in power over them. Being done to death transcends broader human rights issues of whether a group of people can claim the right "to have" something—equality, freedom from discrimination, free movement, marriage and family, belief and religion, education, adequate living standard, and so on. Certainly many of these rights, which today we recognize as universal, are trampled in the process of destruction.[3] Being done to death also goes beyond forms of repressive, terrorist, or political violence that seek to negotiate with, tame, or repress a targeted group.[4] Rather, being "done to death" is an assault on the most fundamental of human rights—the right "to be."[5] This is an intentional decision to take away the right "to be" for a group of people. It is a decision to murder a group of people because they share an identity, however construed and conceived by the perpetrators, making them unworthy of life; it is an effort to be rid of a group once and for all.

The decision to exterminate a group of people is the extreme end of a continuum that lies beyond proclamations that they cannot live, worship, or love as they see fit and beyond decisions to ghettoize them or force them out of your country. In his landmark work on the Holocaust, Raul Hilberg writes of this continuum in the destruction of the European Jews: "The missionaries of Christianity had said in effect: You have no right to live among us as Jews. The secular rulers who followed had proclaimed: You have no right to live among us. The German Nazis at last decreed: You have no right to live."[6]

In the twentieth century this form of destruction would come to be called "genocide," but it is not a modern phenomenon. The human reality of genocide predated its semantic taxonomy. As Leo Kuper, one of the pioneers in genocide studies, said, "The word is new, the concept is ancient."[7] From the Hittites to the Greeks to the Romans to the Mongols to the Albigensian Crusades to the witch hunts in Europe to colonial destructions of indigenous peoples throughout the world, human history has been replete with cases of mass destruction.[8] In modern times, however, we have gotten very good—in a morally inverted sense of the word—at committing genocide. As historian Omer Bartov argues, since the late nineteenth century and the emergence of the nation-state, the nature and scale of genocide have dramatically changed.[9] Aptly dubbed the "Age of Genocide," the past century saw a massive scale of systematic and intentional mass murder coupled with an unprecedented efficiency of the mechanisms and techniques of mass destruction. Genocidal death rates worldwide—7,700 per 100,000—were an eight-fold increase over the previous 69 centuries.[10] On the historical heels of the physical and cultural genocide of North American indigenous peoples during the nineteenth century, the twentieth century writhed from the near-complete annihilation of the Hereros by the Germans in Southwest Africa in 1904; to the brutal assault on the Armenian population by the Turks between 1915 and 1932; to the implementation of Soviet manmade famine against the Ukrainian Kulaks in 1932–1933 that left several million peasants starving to death; to the extermination of two-thirds of Europe's Jews during the Holocaust of 1939–1945; to the massacre of approximately half a million people in Indonesia in 1965–1966; to genocide or mass killings in Bangladesh (1971), Burundi (1972), Cambodia (1975–1979), East Timor (1975–1979), Argentina (1976–1983), Guatemala (1980s–1990s), Sri Lanka (1983–2009), Iraq (1987–1988), the former Yugoslavia (1992–1995), and Rwanda (1994).

Although this list is not exhaustive, it certainly suggests the universality of the potential—perhaps even the ubiquity of the reality—for genocide. It is clear that genocide cannot be confined to one culture, place, or time in modern history. Even the most restrictive of definitions estimates that at least 60 million men, women, and children were victims of genocide and mass killing in the past century alone.[11] On the upper end, political scientist Rudolph Rummel argues that close to 170 million civilians were done to death in the twentieth century.[12] Even for those who survive, genocide is a collective trauma, a redefining destruction that shatters their assumptive world and transforms societies for generations.

Unfortunately, the first decades of the twenty-first century have brought little light to the darkness as a variety of international watch lists suggest that close to 20 countries are currently "at risk" for genocide. As former U.S. Secretary of State Hillary Rodham Clinton suggested, the "wood is stacked" in those countries and we cannot passively wait for the "match to be struck."[13] Because once the firestorm of genocide is at full blaze, history shows us that death comes in conflagrations of hundreds of thousands and the options for responding are difficult and costly. To borrow the words of Kofi Annan, former Secretary-General of the United Nations, genocide and other large-scale attacks on civilians are "problems without passports."[14] That is, they are global problems that transcend not only countries and regions, but the capabilities and resources of any one nation or sector. In many regards, being done to death can take rightful claim as the most pressing human rights problem of the twenty-first century.

The question of why you should read a book about such inhumanity is parallel to why I would write such a book. An even deeper question is why I and so many others would be drawn to a field such as genocide studies. When I have conversations about this question with colleagues, students, and community members, I am struck that there are three factors that seem to draw us to this work—what we can learn about human capacities in situations of extremity, what we can learn about making a difference in a world that seems intent on tearing itself apart, and what we can learn about our capability for connection when we broaden our world beyond ourselves. I believe that these three "learnings" not only help explain our interest in the field of genocide studies, but also serve as justifications for the field of study itself.

First, to study genocide is to recognize the psychological spectrum of human capacities in situations of extremity. Genocide is a "stress test" that shows how ordinary people are transformed, in a wide variety of ways, by extraordinary circumstances. These transformations do not imply that we are unwitting victims of the situations in which we find ourselves; rather, they are manifestations of our agency and free will, however limited, in situations of extremity. In studying the reactions of victims and survivors, we see the deep human capacity for resilience, even in the grip of the most dehumanizing and debilitating of conditions. In studying the motives of those who resist and rescue, we see the hope of what we can be in the face of inhumanity to our fellow humans. Often, though, we have to look deep into our inhumanity to find our humanity. So, it is in studying the behavior of perpetrators that we stare into the abyss of the deep human capacity for evil and find that the abyss looks back into us. Perhaps most telling, though, is how the silence of bystander behavior reminds us of our deepest capacity of all—our capacity for stifling indifference in the face of human suffering. Everyday life provides us with glimpses into our capacities for resilience, good, evil, and indifference, but the study of genocide—human behavior *in extremis*—brings us into a deeper awareness of who we are and of what we are capable.

Second, to study genocide is to provide us with a window into the pragmatic avoidance of future replications. Indeed, this book is grounded on the belief that genocide prevention is an achievable goal and that genocide is a human problem with a human solution. In writing about the Rwandan genocide, journalist Philip Gourevitch says: "The best reason I have come up with for looking closely into Rwanda's stories is that ignoring them makes me even more uncomfortable about existence and my place in it. The horror, as horror, interests me only insofar as a precise memory of the offense is necessary to understand its legacy."[15] It is only in trying to extract the comprehensible from the unthinkable—the precise memory of the offense—that we can begin to recognize the myriad ways in which we can prevent genocide from ever taking place, prevent further atrocities once genocide has begun, and prevent future atrocities once a society has begun to rebuild after genocide.

Finally, to study genocide is to transform our capability for empathy and compassionate action. As Haig Manuelian, a second-generation survivor of the Armenian genocide, says: "We must know each other's stories. We must consider ourselves one constituent element of a symphony."[16] Although this particular symphony of suffering is certainly hard on the ears, and even harder on the heart, it is part of our collective story. And to know these stories is to reach beyond ourselves to a more expansive awareness of the world in which we live. In his acclaimed work on social intelligence, psychologist Daniel Goleman frames it this way: "In short, self-absorption in all its forms kills empathy, let alone compassion. When we focus on ourselves, our world contracts as our problems and preoccupations loom large. But when we focus on others, our world expands. Our own problems drift to the periphery of the mind and so seem smaller, and we increase our capacity for connection—or compassionate action."[17] If we allow empathy and compassion to be done to death by our own self-absorption, then there remains little hope for repairing a broken world. Studying genocide, as difficult as it may be, can offer an antidote to self-absorption by nurturing our capability to understand the suffering of others and, more importantly, activating our responsibility for transformative compassionate action in the face of such suffering.

Although I believe that these reasons help justify a study of genocide, it is not to say that the same justification somehow makes the study easy. Working in this field, even reading this book, exposes us to a type of secondary trauma that can numb and paralyze our pursuit of understanding. We will encounter realities that shut us down and push us away from active engagement with these issues. I was reminded of this during a May 2013 workshop on genocide and mass atrocity prevention in Arusha, Tanzania at which I was a participant. One of the panelists, Dismas Nkunda, a journalist and refugee rights activist from Uganda, shared recollections from his first visit to Rwanda, just days after the genocide began in 1994. He spoke of coming across a killing site and hearing the wails of a 4-month-old baby who was futilely sucking at the breast of a mother who had died 4 days earlier. Later, at another site, a Catholic Church in Nyarubuye, he and his team found a 12-year-old girl, grievously wounded by machete hacks, who had survived over 3 weeks by eating the raw flesh of the victims who had fallen around her. Rather than capturing life as it is lived, he was struck with death as it was done.[18]

I was surrounded at the workshop by government officials who, in many cases, had spent much of their professional and personal lives in zones of conflict. I have done fieldwork interviewing those who perpetrated, and were victimized by, collective violence in Germany, Israel, Northern Ireland, Rwanda, the former Yugoslavia, Argentina, Tanzania, and Chile. As we listened to Nkunda, however, it was clear that each of us—for at least a moment—was brought back to that gaping void of incomprehensibility. The visual traumas to which he had been exposed became our shared traumas. We closed down, averted our gaze, and protected ourselves through any number of well-rehearsed coping mechanisms. Our minds turned away from the horror, drawing a curtain. We surrendered to the incomprehensibility— emotionally, empathically, and philosophically—of what we were studying.

This is what anthropologist Inga Clendinnen has described as the Gorgon effect—"the sickening of imagination and curiosity and the draining of the will which afflicts so many of us when we try to look squarely at the persons and processes implicated in the Holocaust."[19]

In Primo Levi's renowned *Survival in Auschwitz*, he recalls an encounter with one of the guards at the camp. Levi, suffering from thirst, noticed an icicle through his cell window and reached to grab it. The guard snatched it out of his hand. When Levi asked why, the guard replied, "Hier ist kein warum." Here there is no why.[20] Claude Lanzmann, the director of *Shoah*, a nine-and-a-half-hour cinematic epic, insists that not wanting to understand was always his "iron rule" and has even claimed that "the search for why is absolutely obscene."[21] For those of us who work in this field, however, and for many of you who read this book, we recognize that there has to be a why—along with a who, what, when, and where. We accept the fundamental challenge to step beyond the curtain of incomprehensibility, however tentatively, and toward the comprehension of genocide. There will be times of head-shaking submission in which we are bludgeoned into incomprehensibility. We cannot, though, give genocide the benefit of our ignorance. We cannot afford to be petrified into silence about these atrocities. We are all engaged in a slow, but urgent, journey toward comprehension that is pivotal in our hopes for genocide prevention. It is only by unpacking genocidal pasts that we can prevent genocidal presents.

As philosopher Hannah Arendt wrote in 1950: "Comprehension does not mean denying the outrageous, deducing the unprecedented from precedents, or explaining phenomena by such analogies and generalities that the impact of reality and the shock of experience are no longer felt. It means, rather, examining and bearing consciously the burden which our century has placed on us—neither denying its existence nor submitting meekly to its weight. Comprehension, in short, means the unpremeditated, attentive facing up to, and resisting of, reality—whatever it may be."[22] Rather than focusing on genocide as a molar *event* that overwhelms, we must face up to it as a molecular *process* that can, and, indeed, must, be understood. With that perspective, we can see how compelling it is to study something so important and, even more so, how necessary it is to apply the lessons we have learned.

The dream of a nonfiction writer is to write a book as significant as its topic. The topic of this book—genocide—is arguably the greatest scourge facing humankind today. So, undoubtedly, I have to give up any pretension of writing a book that will end up being as significant as this particular topic. As I writer, I have to mirror my aims as a teacher—earn your trust, stir your curiosity, and engage your willingness to partner with me in discovering what can be understood about preventing genocide. Even then, I have to write in humility and recognize that whatever I write in these pages will be weighed, measured, and found wanting in respect to the problem of genocide. That humility, though, is balanced by a hope that, to at least some small degree, this book can encourage you to think more deeply about your role, and responsibility, as a citizen—whether as an academic, lawyer, policymaker, or member of the global civil society—in a world in which far too many civilians live in fear of being done to death. If each of us can begin to see our brothers and sisters in the world community, no matter how far outside our doorstep, as a priority in our values and life choices, then, perhaps, we can ensure that "Never Again" means far more than "never again will Germans kills Jews in Europe in the 1940s."[23]

ACKNOWLEDGMENTS

This book was born on a muggy May afternoon in 2008 in a former prisoner's barracks on the grounds of Auschwitz-I. There, in a place of suffering temporarily transposed into a place of education, I participated as an instructor in the inaugural Raphael Lemkin Seminar sponsored by the fledging Auschwitz Institute for Peace and Reconciliation (AIPR). A bold experiment from the philanthropic mind of Fred Schwartz, who had gained more than a minor note as a celebrity throughout the New York region in the 1970s and 1980s as "Fred the Furrier" (a 2004 retrospective piece in *The New York Times* referred to him as an "urbane, avuncular, silver-tongued spokesman"), the seminar aimed to expose mid-level government officials from around the world to the importance of their bureaucratic role in genocide prevention. To do so on the grounds of Auschwitz, the world's largest cemetery, was to capitalize on the "power of place" in enhancing the seminar experience.

Fred and I met at a conference of the International Association of Genocide Scholars in Sarajevo the previous year and, interested in my work on the psychology of perpetrator behavior, he invited me to join a small group for a dinner and night of conversation at Pod Lipom in the beautiful Old Town city center near the Baščaršija. There, and in subsequent conversations, Fred challenged me to reframe some of my thinking on perpetrator behavior into more of a preventive focus. By the time the seminar at Auschwitz became a reality the following year, Fred had brought me to the cusp of a new professional direction. That inaugural seminar was the first chapter of my next academic life and, if 90% of writing really is thinking, the writing of this book actually began on that long plane ride home from Krakow, Poland in 2008.

Eight years and countless Raphael Lemkin seminars later, I continue to be involved with AIPR, now as its Director of Academic Programs. So, it is more than fitting that my acknowledgments begin with Fred Schwartz, who pulled my head up from what it was buried in and pushed me to think more broadly about my work, and Tibi Galis, whose extraordinary leadership of AIPR, as skilled as it is, pales in comparison to the depth of appreciation I have for his friendship. In some very real ways, the dual imprint of Fred and Tibi are on each of the pages in this book. The opportunities given to me by my work with AIPR to engage in genocide prevention efforts throughout the world—Latin America, Poland, the United States, the Great Lakes Region of Africa, and Bosnia-Herzegovina—have been invaluable learning opportunities. I am also deeply indebted to my other incredible colleagues at AIPR—Stephanie Alvarez, Samantha Capicotto, Maria Eugenia Carbone, Andrea Gualde, Eli Mandel, Jack Mayerhofer, Michael Otterman, Clara Ramirez-Barat, Rob Scharf, Ashad Sentongo, and Gosia Waligora. As Samantha would say, big hugs to each of you!

The AIPR umbrella is a big one and includes many additional acknowledgments. AIPR board member Owen Pell has been wonderfully supportive of our work and is always a fascinating, a lively, conversationalist. Our partners at the UN Office of the Special Advisers on Genocide Prevention and the Responsibility to Protect, as well as the Stanley Foundation, continue to help shape and share a vision of genocide prevention that is making a world of difference. Over the course of planning dozens of Lemkin seminars, I have had the uncommon pleasure of being able to hand-select instructors from every corner of the world and, although there are too many to list here, each of them has shaped my thinking in some very direct ways. Finally, I acknowledge the more than 1,700 participants in our seminars from over 70 countries around the world, you are my heroes—coming from every sector of government life, you have shown me the rainbow at the end of the storm. Certainly, though, the saddest part of the journey has been the recent loss of AIPR's great friend and supporter, Sheri Rosenberg. Sheri was a leading scholar in the field of international law and mass atrocity, as well as a long-time instructor in our seminars. More personally, she always had the right question at the right time to veer my thinking in a different, or deeper, direction, and I know generations of her students at the Cardozo Law Institute in Holocaust and Human Rights at Yeshiva University received the same gift.

My early work with AIPR was so fulfilling that it drove me to begin a new chapter in my "real job" as a college professor. In 2010, I applied for, and was fortunate enough to receive, an endowed professorship in Holocaust and Genocide Studies at Keene State College (KSC). KSC, a public liberal arts institution in beautiful southwestern New Hampshire, is home to one of the nation's longest-standing Holocaust resource centers, now known as the Cohen Center for Holocaust and Genocide Studies, and, since 2010, home to the nation's only undergraduate department and major in Holocaust and Genocide Studies. It is a testament to the College's commitment to the field that my position, the Cohen Professor of Holocaust and Genocide Studies, was the first endowed professorship in the College's 100-year history and one of the very few in the world specifically devoted to Holocaust and Genocide Studies. The Cohen family, particularly Rick and Jan, have been incredible supporters of our work at KSC and, quite literally, none of us would be doing what we are doing at the College without their long history of generosity and even longer history of friendship.

The opportunity to teach full-time in my specialty area of interest has opened up myriad routes of personal growth as a teacher-scholar in genocide studies and I am very appreciative to the students and colleagues who have helped in that growth along the way. Paul Vincent and Hank Knight have been wonderful partners with whom to negotiate the journey of understanding the "and" in Holocaust and Genocide Studies, as have my other departmental colleagues—Nona Fienberg (formerly Dean at my hiring) and Alexis Herr. Novelist Stephen King has said the only thing a writer's room needs is "a door which you are willing to shut."[24] To that, however, I would add that you also need colleagues who are willing to respect that shut door and I thank each of mine for their patience over these past 2 years as I have been actively writing.

My thinking has also benefitted from a wealth of other talented KSC faculty and staff—among them, Larry Benaquist, Pat Dolenc, Lisa DiGiovanni, Len Fleischer, Renate Gebauer, Patricia Pedroza Gonzalez, Michele Kuiawa, Jamie Landau, Sander Lee, Irina Leimbacher, Dottie Morris, Emily Robins-Sharpe, Kim Schmidl-Gagne, Therese Seibert, John Sturz, Patricia Whalen, Tom White, and Debra White-Stanley. Each of these people has made KSC a wonderful place to be and each reminds me daily of how fortunate I am to be surrounded by so many gifted people with similar interests, commitments, and passions. I have enjoyed nothing but warm collegiality and support from these colleagues at KSC. Because of that, KSC has felt like "home" from the moment I stepped on campus and the mission of the institution, and our unique department, rings true with what I am discovering to be my authentic self, professionally as well as personally—a journey that Alan Moulton helped launch as I sat in his Introductory Psychology class in 1979 and in which, more recently, Jeff Frykholm, Eric Peterson, Pam Praeger, and James Roubos have been indispensable partners.

The late William Zinsser first introduced me to the economy and symmetry of writing. I hope that at least a few of the paragraphs in this book stay true to those principles. This is the third book I have published with Oxford University Press and Abby Gross and the editorial staff, particularly Courtney McCarroll, continue to demonstrate the professionalism, vision, and patient guidance that make Oxford the leading university press in the world.

I am fortunate to have a very large classroom—including global government officials attending our AIPR seminars as well as the thousands of students who have worked with me in classes over the years. In addition, I also have the privilege of giving about two dozen invited campus or community lectures each year and each of those opportunities gives me a chance to think out loud, and most importantly, clarify that thinking by hearing, not simply listening, to other people's reactions. In this enormous classroom, I am a student as much as I am a teacher—particularly in the ways I have benefitted from the committed and exacting work of my international colleagues in the field of genocide studies, many of whom are cited in these pages. I have also been inspired by the frontline fieldwork of activist-educator friends devoted to genocide prevention, many of whom dedicate their lives to working in situations of continuing fragility; in that long list, particularly notable are Vahidin Omanovic and Mevludin Rahmanovic of the Center for Peacebuilding in Sanski Most, BiH; Lina Zedriga Waru Abuku, a former Magistrate now working as a full-time activist to end social exclusion and all forms of discrimination against vulnerable groups, especially women, in Uganda; Debbie Stothard of the Alternative ASEAN Network on Burma, a grassroots movement for human rights and democracy in Burma; and, my sister, Jan Rogers, who continues to inspire with her undying commitment to educating generations of high school students in North Carolina on the importance of making "Never Again" a reality.

Finally, there seems to be an authorial pattern of saving the most important acknowledgments to the very end, when, in truth, they are too important to place there, but also too important to be relegated to the beginning or the middle—rather, they are woven throughout the entirety. So, in the beginning, middle, and to the end, my deepest appreciation and love to my wife, Patti, of whose strength and commitment I am daily in awe, and to our children—Brennan, Hannah, and Noah—who could do nothing to make us love them more and nothing to make us love them less. As parents, we are so deeply grateful for, and fulfilled by, your *being*.

J.W.
February 5, 2016
Keene, NH

INTRODUCTION

"Offend Every Precept of Our Common Humanity"

The decline of Cold War rivalries between the United States and the Soviet Union in the early 1990s brought a cautious optimism that the world was becoming a safer place for civilians. Over the course of the decade, proxy wars fought around the globe decreased, as did the number of interstate conflicts and the global refugee population. A near doubling in the number of democracies led to increased security and sustainable peace. World military spending fell by about a third. The emergence of preventive diplomacy as a tool for achieving durable peace offered the promise of long-term stability. Three times more peace agreements were negotiated and signed during the first decade of the post-Cold War era (1990–2000) than in the previous three decades combined. At the United Nations (UN), more peace operations were mounted in the decade of the 1990s than in the previous four decades combined.[25]

In spite of these global peace dividends, we witnessed in the 1990s some of the most egregious cases of civilian populations being "done to death." Although fewer borders were violated, more people were. In 1994, in Rwanda, more than 800,000 Tutsi and moderate Hutu were slaughtered by Hutu extremists in the space of just 100 days. Three hundred and thirty-three and a third murders occurred per hour. Five and a half lives terminated every minute, a rate of death nearly three times the rate of Jewish dead during the Holocaust. The following July more than 8,000 Bosniaks (Bosnian Muslims), unarmed men and boys, were massacred by Serb forces in and around the town of Srebrenica in Bosnia and Herzegovina. The bodies of the victims—three generations of males, including some as young as 10 years of age—were then dumped into mass graves or thrown into the Drina river. To conceal the extent of the massacre, Serb forces later scattered the remains of many of the victims in secondary or tertiary mass graves. To date, the remains of around 1,100 or so of the victims have yet to be found.[26]

In both cases of genocide, while civilians were being slaughtered in the thousands, the world watched and did not intervene. There were no shields of ignorance behind which to hide. Both Rwanda and the violence that marred the break-up of the former Yugoslavia were well chronicled by international print and television media, activist organizations, and government agencies. Well aware of the inexorable creep toward destruction, the UN proactively deployed an assistance mission in Rwanda (UNAMIR) and a protection force (UNPROFOR) in the former Yugoslavia. In the United States, even casual observers would have noted a *Time* magazine cover, dated August 17, 1992, depicting Muslim prisoners behind barbed wire fencing in a Serbian detention camp, strikingly reminiscent of black-and-white images from the Holocaust, asking: "Must it go on?" The world's deafening silence clearly indicated that, yes, it would go on, not only in the former Yugoslavia for nearly 3 more years but also in Rwanda less than 2 years later. On May 16, 1994, another *Time* cover pictured a Rwandan mother and child at a refugee camp near Ngara, Tanzania and stated: "'There are no devils left in Hell,' the missionary said. 'They are all in Rwanda.'" Devils aside, the suffering in Rwanda, as well as that in Srebrenica, is a compelling reminder that the intimate reality of genocide is humans killing other humans in large numbers and over an extended period of time—while even larger numbers of humans, thinking themselves free of any moral obligation to be a voice for the voiceless, stand by and allow it to happen.

The lack of response to both Rwanda in 1994 and Srebrenica in 1995 left the international community wrestling with its role in the face of genocide. Although the UN did establish tribunals in 1993 (the International Criminal Tribunal for the former Yugoslavia) and 1994 (the International Criminal Tribunal for Rwanda) to prosecute individual perpetrators—the first such courts since the Nuremberg and Tokyo tribunals after World War II—proponents of intervention criticized Member States of the UN for idly sitting by while hundreds of thousands died during the genocides. They argued that the international community has the right to intervene in a country for humanitarian purposes, particularly when civilian lives are at risk. Conversely, critics of intervention defended inaction on the grounds that intervention was an unacceptable violation of state sovereignty that especially leaves small and weak states vulnerable to the manipulative influence of larger and stronger states. They upheld a state's sovereignty over its own affairs as an unconditional and unassailable right.

UN Secretary-General Kofi Annan, in his report to the 2000 Millennium General Assembly, the largest-ever gathering of Heads of State and

Government, addressed this growing tension with the following challenge: "If humanitarian intervention is, indeed, an unacceptable assault on sovereignty, how should we respond to a Rwanda, to a Srebrenica—to gross and systematic violations of human rights that offend every precept of our common humanity?" I take Annan's challenge as the grounding introduction to the focus of this book. How, indeed, are we to respond to events, such as genocide, that offend every precept of our common humanity? Equally important, what is the role of the international community in assisting states to prevent such events or, failing to do so, rebuilding societies in their aftermath?

In recent years there has been an explosion of interest in the new academic field of genocide studies, particularly in addressing how best to respond to those violations that offend every precept of our common humanity. We have seen the professionalization of the field through the emergence of two organizations, the International Association of Genocide Scholars in 1994 and the International Network of Genocide Scholars in 2005.[27] Each organization gave birth to new scholarly journals, *Genocide Studies and Prevention* and the *Journal of Genocide Research*, respectively, both of which expanded the more Holocaust-centric focus of the longer-standing *Holocaust and Genocide Studies* journal. In March 2014, the Institute for Genocide and Human Rights Studies (a division of the Zoryan Institute in Toronto, Ontario, Canada) launched yet another professional journal, *Genocide Studies International*. The 2010 publication of *The Oxford Handbook of Genocide Studies* legitimized the field of study as it testified to a robustness of work that justified the compilation of a comprehensive handbook. On-line encyclopedias, discussion groups, and blog sites reveal the extent to which both scholars and educated laypeople continue to wrestle with the concept, and, more importantly, the ongoing reality of genocidal violence.

In addition, we have seen a corresponding explosion of growth in higher education curricular programs related to genocide studies. Previous programs focusing on the Holocaust have expanded to include genocide studies. My home institution, Keene State College, a public liberal arts institution in New England, offers the only undergraduate major in Holocaust and Genocide Studies in the nation and is in frequent conversation with other institutions from around the world that are interested in developing similar programs. Attesting to the professionalization of the field, several graduate programs in genocide studies have emerged, separate and distinct from more general programs in peace and conflict studies, including some on-line certification programs in genocide studies and prevention. Seeking to promote international interuniversity cooperation and networking in the field, the United Nations Educational, Scientific and Cultural Organization (UNESCO) Chairs Programme has recently established a Chair on Genocide Prevention at Rutgers University, Newark, New Jersey (2012) as well as a Chair on Genocide Education at the University of Southern California (2013).

We have seen similar emergent awareness and activity in the legal and public policy arena. In 2000, against the background of the failure of the international community to respond to the Rwandan genocide and "the outbreak of conflicts involving immense human suffering" in Africa, the African Union's Constitutive Act incorporated the right to intervene in a member state to protect civilians from war crimes, genocide, and crimes against humanity.[28] The following year, the independent International Commission on Intervention and State Sovereignty, established by the Government of Canada, released a report, *The Responsibility to Protect*, outlining the obligation of states toward their populations and toward all populations at risk of genocide and other large-scale atrocities.[29] At the UN level, in 2004, then Secretary-General Annan established an office of the Special Adviser on the Prevention of Genocide and advocated for the "right of humanitarian intervention" in the face of mass atrocity. A 2005 UN World Summit affirmed that the international community has a "responsibility to protect"—the duty to intervene when national governments fail to fulfill their responsibility to protect their citizens from atrocious crimes. On July 25, 2012, UN Secretary-General Ban Ki-moon released a report upholding the need for a collective response to protect populations from genocide, war crimes, ethnic cleansing, and crimes against humanity.[30] Most recently, in March 2014, the Stanley Foundation—in collaboration with the governments of Switzerland, Costa Rica, Tanzania, Denmark, and Argentina—hosted participants from about 50 countries at the launch of the Global Action Against Mass Atrocity Crimes (GAAMAC) initiative.

Internationally, regional and state mechanisms for genocide prevention have developed across the globe. Regionally, the Organization of American States (OAS), the Union of South American Nations (UNASUR), the European Union (EU), the Organization for Security and Cooperation in Europe (OSCE), and the Association of Southeast Asian Nations (ASEAN) have taken initiatives to strengthen frameworks for the prevention of genocide, war crimes, ethnic cleansing, and crimes against humanity. Other regional coalitions of emerging powers such as BRICS (Brazil, Russia, India, China, and South Africa) and IBSA (India, Brazil, and South Africa) offer additional possibilities for genocide prevention initiatives. In Africa, the most conflict-ridden continent, the African Union (AU), the Economic Community of West African States (ECOWAS), the Intergovernmental Authority on Development (IGAD), and the International Conference on the Great Lakes Region (ICGLR) have developed viable programs on early warning and genocide prevention. Domestically, partnering with civil society, the government of Argentina has institutionalized a very robust National Mechanism for Genocide Prevention as has Tanzania, Kenya, Mexico, the Central African Republic, the Democratic Republic of the Congo, Paraguay, and Uganda. Even the world's newest nation, the Republic of South Sudan, born on July 9, 2011, instantiated a National Committee for the prevention of genocide, war crimes, crimes against humanity, and all forms of discrimination in September 2013, several members of which I have had the pleasure to work with at training workshops.[31]

The U.S. Government, somewhat late to the game and frustratingly more reluctant than its international counterparts to partner with civil society, has found its own recent flurry of activity related to genocide prevention. The Genocide Prevention Task Force, chaired by former Secretary of State Madeline Albright and former Secretary of Defense William Cohen, issued a wide-ranging report on December 8, 2008 that made a series of recommendations about steps the U.S. Government could take to be better prepared to prevent or halt genocide and mass atrocities.[32] In the wake of that report, Director of National Intelligence Dennis C. Blair went on record, in congressional testimony, to state his fears concerning the growing potential for outbreaks of mass killing and genocide throughout the world. On December 15, 2010 the U.S. State Department issued a Quadrennial Diplomacy and Development Review in which, for the first time ever, it was made clear that preventing and responding to genocide and mass atrocities is in the national security interest of the United States. Just a week later, on December 22, 2010, U.S. Senators voted unanimously in favor of a groundbreaking act "recognizing the United States national interest in helping to prevent and mitigate acts of genocide and other mass atrocities against civilians, and supporting and encouraging efforts to develop a whole government approach to prevent and mitigate such acts."[33] Most recently, on April 23, 2012, a standing interagency Atrocities Prevention Board, stemming from the issuance of a Presidential Study Directive (PSD-10) by President Obama the previous August, was established with the authority to develop genocide and mass atrocity prevention strategies for the United States.

Finally, a spirit of citizen-activism was renewed by civil society in the face of genocide in Darfur, the western region of Sudan. After the genocide began in 2003, from the Save Darfur Coalition to the Genocide Intervention Network to Amnesty International to Human Rights Watch, millions of global citizens, young and old, pledged a commitment to raise public awareness about, and mobilize a massive citizen campaign in response to, the atrocities in Darfur.[34] The burgeoning antigenocide movement—largely U.S. based and fueled by the advocacy of human rights groups and key public voices such as Nicholas Kristof of *The New York Times* and Eric Reeves of Smith College (MA)—generated meaningful political results and reminded us of the power of citizen-activism in marshalling a united front in the face of mass atrocity. Although the peace in Darfur remains fragile, there are many who believe that it has been the response of citizen-activists, and global civil society, that has played the largest role in the cessation of hostilities in Sudan. The atrocity prevention community continues to nurture a global network of citizen-activists committed to the ideal of "never again." Genocide Watch (United States) and the Combat Genocide Association (Israel), for instance, joined for a 2014 launch of the Never Again Coalition, an international movement committed to intervention and prevention.

So, there is a clear interest in genocide studies at many levels—from academics (scholars and students) to law (lawyers and jurists) to policymakers (international and domestic) to global civil society citizen-activists. Although the literature has tried to keep pace with the interest, the field of genocide studies remains a young and, at times, fractious discipline, in search of theoretical and conceptual maturity. There is a clear and compelling need for a mapping of the field—a timely and relevant synthesis of what we know, to date, about the causes of genocide, its consequences, and how that knowledge can be used to prevent genocide.

I have a colleague who insists that every book must be build on a central argument. So, here it is. I was born the same month the Communist government of East Germany began to build the Berlin Wall (events that my Mother assures me had no direct causal relationship). I grew up in a generation drilled in diving underneath school desks in case of nuclear attack from the Soviet Union. Although, physically, such drills would be futile in the face of such an attack, psychologically, they seared into our minds a fearful world divided between good guys ("us") and bad guys ("them"). As a college freshman, I crammed in a too-small dorm television room with dozens of friends to watch the "Miracle on Ice" as the U.S. hockey team beat the Soviets in the 1980 Winter Olympic Games. To a person, we thought that night illustrated the best we could hope for, in a geopolitical sense, for the rest of our lives . . . an occasional symbolic victory over the Soviet menace—the bigger the stage, the better. We were sure the Berlin Wall would always be there. Until it wasn't. When, as a young college professor just beginning my academic career, the Berlin Wall fell in November 1989, it was more than a geopolitical shift. It was a psychological awakening that the world my generation inherited did not have to be the world we passed on to our children. It was an awakening that took on a physical reality when, the following summer, on June 22, 1990, as a visiting professor at the Technical University of Berlin, I stood with tens of thousands of others to witness the dismantling of Checkpoint Charlie.

My central argument in this book is that the world as it is now is not the world as it has to be. As ubiquitous as genocide seems, it is a human problem and, as such, has a human solution. This is not a quixotic utopian statement about human perfectibility. It simply is a statement that we can, at least in large part, undo a problem that we have created. Genocide is not a problem that came to us from another world or was ingrained in our behavioral genetic repertoire. At its root, genocide happens because we choose to see *a people* rather than individual people and then we choose to kill *those people* in large numbers and over an extended period of time. In the midst of that bad news, the good news is that we can make another choice; we can find constructive, rather than destructive, ways to live with our diverse social identities.

Preventing genocide is an achievable goal. As the Genocide Prevention Task Force argued: "There are ways to recognize its signs and symptoms, and viable options to prevent it at every turn if we are committed and prepared. Preventing genocide is a goal that can be achieved with the right organizational structures, strategies, and partnerships."[35] This book aims to join a growing literature outlining the ways in which we can prevent genocide in the belief that such knowledge will help shape our will do to so.

The goal of this book is to present an analysis of genocide in the modern world that draws out the lessons to be learned in preventing genocide from ever taking place, preventing further atrocities once genocide has begun, and preventing future atrocities once a society has begun to rebuild after genocide. I do not aim for the book to be an encyclopedic recounting of the history of genocide; a number of well-respected comprehensive histories of genocide already dot the landscape of the field.[36] Rather, I want the book to be representative of the best of what the rich field of genocide studies has to offer in terms of preventing and confronting the evil of genocide. I hope the book will appeal, and serve as a valuable resource, to a broad range of audiences in academia, law, policy-making, and global civil society.[37] I also, though, want to bring nonspecialists and general readers into a vital conversation by writing a book that serves as an interface between the intellectual and the activist spheres, between being well informed and being well involved, and between being a bystander and being an upstander in the face of genocide.

My reach may certainly exceed my grasp. Where some audiences will find that particular chapters of the book plow new ground for them intellectually, other audiences will find in the same chapters familiar echoes of what they may already know—but, hopefully, with some useful amplification. I aim to provide a highly informative synthesis that both summarizes the best of existing research as well as contributes a thought-provoking interpretation of that work. In that pursuit, this work is an integration of a vast expanse of interdisciplinary thought and practice that offers an avenue for a wide range of audiences—most of whom seldom interact with each other face-to-face—to think more deeply and more broadly about a human rights issue for which there are no sidelines, only sides. As our Native friends say, "it is a great honor to work together on behalf of the sacred" and there can be no more sacred cause than working together on behalf of protecting civilians who live under fear of being done to death.

Part I ("Naming and Defining Genocide") of the book reviews the birth of the neologism "genocide" and the process by which genocide became a crime under international law. It also includes an examination of how more than six decades of advances in international and domestic humanitarian law—as well as the fruit of academic, policy, and civil society discussions—have helped clarify many of the questions raised by the original conception of the word. Moreover, Part I of the book contextualizes genocide within the broader definitional nexus of mass atrocity—including war crimes, crimes against humanity, and ethnic cleansing—as well as the emergent international norm of the responsibility to protect.

Chapter 1, "A Crime without a Name," recounts the story of a young Polish student, Raphael Lemkin, who would become immersed in the study of "race murder" and would soon become obsessed with the pursuit of establishing international law against this crime. With Lemkin's fascinating story as backdrop, we examine the historical, political, social, religious, technological, and cultural ethos surrounding the development of the word "genocide." The chapter contextualizes Lemkin's pursuit—from a rejected proposal at an international law conference in 1933 to the naming of the crime as "genocide" in 1944 to the successful adoption of a United Nations treaty in 1948 making genocide an international crime—in the broader global issues of modernity, nationalism, and the rise of the nation-state; related developments in human rights norms and legislation; and deliberations of race, politics, and the Cold War. In addition, we will see that Lemkin's pursuit informs several enduring debates that remain as relevant today as they were in his time—for example, the question of a state's right to nonintervention of external actors in internal state affairs (that is, state sovereignty).

Chapter 2, "By Their Rightful Name," tries to bring some clarity to the essentially contested concept of genocide by delving deeper into three conceptual areas that framed much of the discussion in Chapter 1. First, we examine how *protected groups* are defined in the Convention and ask if those groups are the only groups to which the Convention could or should be applied. Second, we explore the defining characteristics of the *acts defined as criminal* in the Convention and unpack the meanings of "intent" and "in whole or in part" in determining criminality. Third, we survey *jurisdictional responsibility* and trace the process by which universal jurisdiction for the crime of genocide—that is, the notion that any country could try any perpetrator, regardless of their nationality or where the atrocities were committed—came to be a recognized part of customary international law.

Chapter 3, "By Our Words and Actions," argues for the value of understanding genocide in the broader context of an umbrella conceptual framework of mass atrocities that also includes war crimes, crimes against humanity, and—in subsumed form—ethnic cleansing. Although these categories of mass atrocity are not mutually exclusive, they are individually distinguishable in some important conceptual, and practical, features. The chapter then continues with an introduction to, and critical review of, a new international norm meant to overcome the world's demonstrated reluctance to engage in the prevention of civilians being done to death— the responsibility to protect.

Part II ("A Continuum of Prevention Strategies") of the book builds on the recognition that prevention is the single most important dimension of the responsibility to protect by focusing on the preventive measures that can be applied to protect civilians from being done to death. This continuum of strategies includes preventing genocide from ever taking place, preventing further atrocities once genocide has begun, and preventing future atrocities once a society has begun to rebuild after genocide. Following a population-based health model in which the aim is the prevention of the disease of genocide and other mass atrocities, Part II of the book is structured around three stages in a continuum of prevention strategies— upstream ("before"), midstream ("during"), and downstream ("after").

Chapter 4, "Upstream Prevention Strategies: Avoiding 'A Path to Hell,'" focuses on the "before" analysis of the longer-term structural factors that leave a country at risk for genocide and other mass atrocities and the inoculation avenues open to mitigating those risk factors. The chapter begins by examining the role of social identity—"we-identities" tied to memberships in groups—as a source of violent or genocidal conflict. Although not all social identity conflicts end in genocide, social identity matters deeply in understanding the etiology of how people are done to death in genocidal conflict—particularly in its interaction with a range of underlying structural conditions that put states at risk for such conflict. In this chapter it is argued that, like genocide itself, upstream prevention is a process, not an event. It is a long-term strategy of building societal and state durability related to governance, the interpretation of conflict history, economic conditions, and social cohesion. Upstream genocide prevention is built on sustained efforts to increase the capacity and resilience of societies to protect themselves from the risk of mass atrocity.

Chapter 5, "Midstream Prevention Strategies: 'Sometimes We Must Interfere,'" examines the immediate, real-time relief efforts that are direct crisis management tactics to slow, limit, or stop the continuation or escalation of genocidal violence. Understanding the factors that accelerate and trigger an at-risk country's descent into crisis—the transformation of possibility into probability—is an important step in understanding how a society at risk of genocide becomes a society trapped in the deadly grip of genocide. Bridging the gap between substantial early warning and an equally substantial early response involves knowledge about the use, and effectiveness of, preventive response tools (political, economic, legal, and military) that can be applied as levers of change at the sign of rapidly growing risks and first indicators, or at the onset of genocide itself.

Chapter 6, "Downstream Prevention Strategies: 'This Is for Those Who Want Us to Forget,'" reviews the "after" efforts to foster resiliency by dealing with the acute long-term consequences of mass violence through pursuits of justice, truth, and memory to help stabilize, heal, and rehabilitate a postgenocide society. These are important transitional justice mechanisms of social repair. They are paths that cleave a trail to societal reconstruction. Although States carry the primary responsibility for such repair, the international community (including international and regional organizations, neighbors, states, private companies and businesses, and civil society) has a responsibility to assist States in building the capacity to carry out that repair—a lengthy, likely generational, process of deep and fundamental societal transformation that inoculates a society against future genocidal violence.

Finally, Part III ("Never Again?") of the book concludes with a look to the future as revealed in present warning signs and drivers of violent or genocidal conflict. This conclusion, "Thus Have We Made the World. . .Thus Have I Made It," argues that regardless of whatever language we use to invoke the phrase "never again," our collective response to the protection of civilian populations under duress from violent or genocidal conflict has been far less than adequate. Indeed, it seems that our words of "never again" most often translate into actions leading to "again and again," "ever again," and "here we go again." The world that we have made is not the one, however, for which we must settle. In this crucial moment of moral conscience, each of us, playing the role of global citizen in the best sense, has our own unique points of leverage to leave an indelible positive impression in the making of a better world.

Each chapter closes with endnotes. These notes should be a helpful next step for those wishing additional study in any of the thematic issues or genocides addressed in the book.

The experience I will bring to bear in this book is built on two different, but complementary, arenas in which I have had the privilege to work. First, I draw from over two decades of work as a teacher-scholar in the field of genocide studies, including extensive travel to, and research in, postatrocity societies around the world. This primary source research has included work with archival material (original documents such as diaries, speeches, letters, official government records, newspaper articles, audio recordings, and artifacts) as well as interviews I have collected with a range of actors from the event involved. I have the fortunate privilege of holding an endowed professorship in Holocaust and Genocide studies, giving me the unique opportunity to focus my teaching and scholarship full time in this emerging field and engage with some of the best and brightest students at our institution. Second, I complement that academic work with my additional involvement with the Auschwitz Institute for Peace and Reconciliation, an international nongovernmental organization devoted to genocide prevention. In my leadership work with their training programs, I have benefitted, and learned, from frontline engagement with a range of actors from academic, governmental, civil society and nongovernmental organizations, military, security sector, and humanitarian agencies, each of whom has challenged, shaped, and clarified my thinking.

The personal experiences from which I draw are buttressed with the most current and respected scholarship in the field of genocide studies— being particularly sensitive to the nuances and controversies that mark our field of study. Consistent with my lifelong commitment to liberal arts education, I rely on core secondary source scholarship from an ever-burgeoning base of disciplinary perspectives throughout the book— including political and social psychology, sociology, anthropology, political science, international relations, peace studies, gender studies, feminist studies, art, memory, performance studies, economics, literature, philosophy, law, and thanatology. This not only broadens my understanding of the topic beyond my limited disciplinary scope, but also provides multiple entry points from which to approach the subject matter.

Zalman Gradowski, a Jew from Luna in the district of Grodno, on the border of Lithuania and Poland (present-day Belarus), arrived in Auschwitz on the morning of December 8, 1942. Upon arrival, his mother, wife, two sisters, brother-in-law, and father-in-law were taken immediately to the gas chambers. Gradowski, an able-bodied man, was assigned to the *Sonderkommando* squad, the prisoners who serviced the crematoria by pulling out the bodies, plundering the corpses, burning the remains, and disposing of the ashes. There, "living at the very bottom of hell," Gradowski became one of the organizers of a prisoner revolt in Crematorium IV at Auschwitz-Birkenau.[38] Having learned that the SS was going to liquidate much of the squad, the prisoners blew up and set the crematorium on fire. It would never again be used for gassing. Three SS officers were killed and 12 were wounded. Four hundred and fifty-one members of the *Sonderkommando* were killed in the rebellion and its aftermath, including Zalman Gradowski, who was cruelly tortured and then hung.

On March 5, 1945, the Soviet Commission for the Investigation of Nazi War Crimes found a manuscript buried in an aluminum canteen near Birkenau's ruined crematoria. The journal had 81 numbered pages and its author, Zalman Gradowski, attached a letter dated September 6, 1944, one month before the rebellion. Having lost all hope of surviving, Gradowski wrote that he had buried the journal "under the ashes, the most certain place where one will excavate in order to find traces of the millions of murdered people."[39] A second manuscript by Gradowski was found among the ruins of the ovens in the summer of 1945 by a Pole.[40]

Today, in a permanent Jewish exhibition recently opened in the original brick, two-story former barracks of Block 27 of Auschwitz I, visitors are confronted in the entranceway with these words from Gradowski's unearthed testimony: "Come here you free citizen of the world, whose life is safeguarded by human morality and whose existence is guaranteed through law. I want to tell you how modern criminals and despicable murderers have trampled the morality of life and nullified the postulates of existence." It is not an easy story to tell, nor is it an easy story to hear. It is, though, a story that must be told and heard if we are to have any hope of reclaiming the morality of our collective lives and the very postulates of our shared existence.

NOTES

1. George Steiner, "The Hollow Miracle: Notes on the German Language," *The Reporter* (February 18, 1960): 41.

2. The transcript of Obrenovic's guilty plea statement was accessed October 6, 2014 at http://www.icty.org/sid/219.

3. On December 10, 1948, the General Assembly of the United Nations adopted and proclaimed the Universal Declaration of Human Rights (UDHR). The complete document, accessed June 6, 2013, can be found at http://www.un.org/en/documents/udhr/.

4. See Scott Straus, "Identifying Genocide and Related Forms of Mass Atrocity," Working Paper for the U.S. Holocaust Memorial Museum (October 7, 2011).

5. I am indebted to Colin Tatz for originally drawing my attention to the "to have-to be" distinction in his *With Intent to Destroy: Reflecting on Genocide* (London, England: Verso, 2003), 173.

6. Raul Hilberg, *The Destruction of the European Jews*, Revised and Definitive Edition (New York, NY: Holmes & Meier, 1985), 9 (Volume I).

7. Leo Kuper, *Genocide: Its Political Use in the Twentieth Century* (London, England: Penguin, 1981), 9.

8. See Frank Chalk and Kurt Jonassohn, *The History and Sociology of Genocide: Analyses and Case Studies* (New Haven, CT: Yale University Press, 1990), 57–220.

9. See Omer Bartov's "Introduction," in Dan Eshet (primary writer), *Totally Unofficial: Raphael Lemkin and the Genocide Convention* (Boston, MA: Facing History and Ourselves, 2007), ix–xiii.

10. Eric B. Larson and Reva N. Adler, "Preventing Genocide," *The Seattle Times* (June 19, 2005).

11. See Roger W. Smith's "Human Destructiveness and Politics: The Twentieth Century as an Age of Genocide," eds. Isidor Wallimann and Michael N. Dobkowski, *Genocide and the Modern Age: Etiology and Case Studies of Mass Death* (Syracuse, NY: Syracuse University Press, 2000), 21.

12. R. J. Rummel, *Death by Government* (New Brunswick, NJ: Transaction, 1994).

13. Hillary Rodham Clinton, *Remarks at the U.S. Holocaust Memorial Museum Forward-Looking Symposium on Genocide Prevention* (July 24, 2012), accessed June 7, 2013 at http://www.state.gov/secretary/rm/2012/07/195409.htm.

14. Kofi A. Annan, "Problems Without Passports" (September 1, 2002), accessed January 16, 2014 at http://www.foreignpolicy.com/articles/2002/09/01/problems_without_passports.

15. Philip Gourevitch, *We Wish to Inform You That Tomorrow We Will Be Killed with Our Families: Stories from Rwanda* (New York, NY: Picador, 1998), 19.

16. Quote accessed September 16, 2014 at https://www.facinghistory.org/get-to-know-us/stories/remembering-armenian-genocide-survivor-voices.

17. Daniel Goleman, *Social Intelligence: The New Science of Human Relationships* (New York, NY: Bantam Books, 2006), 54.

18. An earlier written account of Dismas Nkunda's comments, published in a Ugandan newspaper on December 4, 2008, was accessed July 2, 2013 at http://www.observer.ug/index.php?option=com_content&view=article&id=1796%3Adismas-nkunda-we-have-sunk-lower-than-animals&catid=93%3Acolumnists&Itemid=96.

19. Inga Clendinnen, *Reading the Holocaust* (New York, NY: Cambridge University Press, 1999), 4.

20. Primo Levi, *Survival in Auschwitz: The Nazi Assault on Humanity* (New York, NY: Touchstone, 1996), 29.

21. Der Spiegel, "Shoah Director Claude Lanzmann: 'Death Has Always Been a Scandal,'" accessed June 27, 2013 at http://www.spiegel.de/international/zeit-geist/shoah-director-claude-lanzmann-death-has-always-been-a-scandal-a-716722-3.html.

22. Hannah Arendt, *The Origins of Totalitarianism* (New York, NY: Meridian, 1951), vii.

23. Quoted material taken from David Rieff, "The Persistence of Genocide," *Policy Review* 165 (February 2011), accessed June 10, 2013 at http://www.hoover.org/publications/policy-review/article/64261.

24. Stephen King, *On Writing: A Memoir of the Craft* (New York, NY: Scribner, 2000), 155.

25. Kofi A. Annan, *"We the Peoples:" The Role of the United Nations in the 21st Century* (New York, NY: United Nations, 2000), 43, 48.

26. See Scott Anderson, "Life in the Valley of Death," *The New York Times Magazine* (June 1, 2014), accessed August 8, 2014 at http://www.nytimes.com/interactive/2014/05/29/magazine/srebrenica-life-in-the-valley-of-death.html?_r=0.

27. At present, conversations continue about the oft-delayed merger of the International Association of Genocide Scholars (IAGS) and the International Network of Genocide Scholars (INOGS). Currently, like most in the field, I maintain membership in both professional organizations, serving on the Advisory board of IAGS as well as being a member of the senior editorial team for *Genocide Studies and Prevention*.

28. The Nordic Africa Institute, "The African Union and the Challenges of Implementing the 'Responsibility to Protect,'" *Policy Notes* (2009/4): 1. See also Tim Murithi, "The Responsibility to Protect, as enshrined in Article 4 of the Constitutive Act of the African Union," *African Security Review* 16 (2008): 1424.

29. International Commission on Intervention and State Sovereignty, *The Responsibility to Protect* (Ottawa, Canada: International Development Research Centre, 2001).

30. UN Secretary-General Report, *Responsibility to Protect: Timely and Decisive Response* (A/66/874–S/2012/578), July 25, 2012.

31. For a broader view of South Sudan's vision in this area, see South Sudan Human Rights Commission, *2012–2015 Strategic Plan* (South Sudan Human Rights Commission, 2012).

32. Madeleine K. Albright and William S. Cohen, *Preventing Genocide: A Blueprint for U.S. Policymakers* (Washington, DC: U.S. Holocaust Memorial Museum, The American Academy of Diplomacy, and the Endowment of the United States Institute of Peace, 2008).

33. Senate Concurrent Resolution 71 of the 111th Congress of the United States (2009–2010).

34. In July 2011, The Save Darfur Coalition and the Genocide Intervention Network, along with STAND and the Sudan Divestment Task Force, merged under the new title of United to End Genocide, the largest activist organization in America dedicated to preventing and ending genocide and mass atrocities worldwide.

35. Madeleine K. Albright and William S. Cohen, *Preventing Genocide: A Blueprint for U.S. Policymakers* (Washington, DC: U.S. Holocaust Memorial Museum, 2008), xvi.

36. See, for example, Israel Charny's two-volume *Encyclopedia of Genocide* (Santa Barbara, CA: ABC-CLIO, 1990), Ben Kiernan's *Blood and Soil: A World History of Genocide and Extermination from Sparta to Darfur* (New Haven, CT: Yale University Press, 2007), and Adam Jones' *Genocide: A Comprehensive Introduc*tion (New York, NY: Routledge, 2011).

37. Civil society includes "non-governmental organizations (NGOs), networks, social movements, diaspora communities, the global media, and even key individuals engaged in global debate." Taken from Iavor Rangelov, "The Role of Transnational Civil Society," eds. Adam Lupel and Ernesto Verdeja, *Responding to Genocide: The Politics of International Action* (Boulder, CO: Lynne Rienner, 2013), 136–137.

38. Quoted material taken from Saul Friedlander's *Nazi Germany and the Jews, 1933– 1945* (New York, NY: Harper, 2009), 359.

39. Hermann Langbein, "The Auschwitz Underground," eds. Yisrael Gutman and Michael Berenbaum, *Anatomy of the Auschwitz Death Camp* (Bloomington, IN: Indiana University Press, 1998), 501.

40. Nathan Cohen, "Diaries of the *Sonderkommando*," in Gutman and Berenbaum, *Anatomy*, 522–534.

PART I

Naming and Defining Genocide

CHAPTER 1

"A Crime without a Name"

The German invasion of the Soviet Union, code-named Operation Barbarossa, began on Sunday morning, June 22, 1941. More than 3 million German soldiers, reinforced by half a million auxiliaries from Germany's allies, had attacked the Soviet Union across a broad front, from the Baltic Sea in the north to the Black Sea in the south. Special action squads—organized by Reinhard Heydrich, Chief of the Reich Security Main Office—followed the German forces as they advanced east. These squads, the Einsatzgruppen, included four battalion-sized operational groups, with a total strength of about 3,000 men.

With the Einsatzgruppen, a new stage in the Nazi process of destruction began. The Einsatzgruppen were mobile killing units charged with the murder of anyone in the newly occupied Soviet territories whom the Nazis deemed racially or politically unacceptable. These included Soviet political commissars and other state functionaries, partisans, prisoners of war, Roma (Gypsies), and Communist Party leaders. Specifically targeted for annihilation were Jews. Under cover of war and confident of victory, the Nazis turned from the forced emigration and imprisonment of Jews to outright mass murder—one-on-one shooting of hundreds of thousands of victims into "antitank ditches, natural ravines or pits freshly dug by Russian prisoners of war."[1]

Less than a month after the invasion began, British cryptographers, having broken the latest Enigma code, were decoding regular reports from the Einsatzgruppen.[2] These reports, meant for Berlin, gave detailed accounts and specific numbers of those killed in mass executions. Although Prime Minister Winston Churchill could not reveal the extent of the detailed knowledge about these killings, lest he undermine the British intelligence objectives, he felt compelled to describe the barbarity being inflicted by the German forces.

On August 24, 1941, nearly 2 weeks after a 3-day Atlantic sea meeting with President Franklin D. Roosevelt, an embattled Churchill returned to England and made a live radio address on the BBC. In his moving address, he spoke of ". . . awful and horrible things I have seen in these days. The whole of Europe has been wrecked and trampled down by the mechanical weapons and barbaric fury of the Nazis . . . This frightful business is now unfolding day by day before our eyes." He went on to claim that ". . . whole districts are being exterminated. Scores of thousands—literally scores of thousands—of executions in cold blood are being perpetrated by the German police troops [that is, Einsatzgruppen] upon the Russian patriots who defend their native soil. Since the Mongol invasions of Europe in the sixteenth century, there has never been methodical, merciless butchery on such a scale, or approaching such a scale." In his famous baritone delivery, Churchill then said: "We are in the presence of a crime without a name."[3]

If anything, Churchill's speech would end up underestimating the extent of brutality inflicted by the Einsatzgruppen. When the first sweep of killing was completed toward the end of 1941, the mobile killing units would have killed around 100,000 victims a month. The second sweep of killing began in the Baltic area in the fall of 1941 and spread through the rest of the occupied territory during the following year. All told, in towns and villages having "no architecture of destruction," about 1.3 million Jews and hundreds of thousands of other innocent people were killed, one by one, by the Einsatzgruppen, their support troops, local police, and collaborators.[4]

It was, though, Churchill's evocative phrase, "a crime without a name," that struck a chord with a young European scholar who already had become immersed in the study of "race murder." That scholar's name was Raphael Lemkin and he would soon become obsessed with the pursuit of giving this crime a name.

The biographical facts of Raphael Lemkin's life have been well chronicled, buttressed by various versions of his incomplete and unpublished autobiography.[5] These facts, though, must be contextualized in the larger frame surrounding the first half of the twentieth century in which Lemkin was born and lived. His was an unparalleled time of sweeping historical, political, social, religious, technological, and cultural evolutions. Lemkin's obsessive pursuit to name, and criminalize, Churchill's "crime without a name" is inseparably twinned with many of the challenges raised by these transitions. It is a pursuit that touches on, and is touched by, global issues of modernity, nationalism, and the rise of the nation-state; related developments in human rights norms and legislation; and deliberations of race, politics, and the Cold War. It is a pursuit whose footsteps still echo today as it informs several enduring debates that remain as relevant, and as pressing, for us as they were in Lemkin's time.

There is a geography underlying Raphael Lemkin's biography, a "power of place," that is essential to understanding the sense of precariousness that marked much of his life. Lemkin was born in 1900 on a farm 14 miles from the city of Wolkowysk. Now in Belarus, the Wolkowysk of Lemkin's youth lay, in Lemkin's words, "between ethnographic Poland to the west, East Prussia to the north, Ukraine to the south, and Great Russia to the east."[6] The second of three children, he was a precocious young boy, mastering nine languages by the age of 14 years. As soon as he could read, he would "devour books on the persecution of religious, racial, or other minority groups."[7] A bibliophile, Lemkin seemed particularly impacted by Henryk Sienkiewicz's *Quo Vadis*, a novel of Nero's persecution of Christians in 64 CE. As part of a traditional Jewish family, homeschooled by his mother, a young Lemkin's reading of far-away suffering was all too often translated into real-life experiences of exclusion, extortion, persecution, and even nearby pogroms—including a violent outburst against Jews in 1906 in Bialystok, about 50 miles away. Forced to temporarily flee their home during World War I, his family was driven into the forest where his younger brother, Samuel, died of pneumonia and malnourishment. Lemkin, marginalized as a Jew and a Pole, certainly "identified with 'small nations' caught between rival empires."[8] Never secure in the Poland of his birth, Lemkin internalized these experiences—both the read and the lived—so deeply that he "sometimes . . . felt physically the tension of blood in [his] veins."[9]

In 1920, Lemkin enrolled at the University of Lvov in Poland (present-day Ukraine) to study philology. While there, Lemkin came across the story of Soghomon Tehlirian. Tehlirian was a survivor of the Armenian massacres in which, from 1915 to 1923, up to a million and a half Armenians perished at the hands of Ottoman and Turkish military and paramilitary forces and through atrocities intentionally designed to eliminate the Armenian demographic presence in Turkey. In 1915, on a death march, Tehlirian had witnessed the rape of his sisters, the beheading of his brother, and the murder of his parents and had escaped only by being mistakenly left for dead in a pile of corpses.[10] Tehlirian, as part of the radical wing of the Dashnak Party, and to avenge his family, assassinated Talaat Pasha, one of the Ottoman leaders who were architects of the Armenian genocide, on March

15, 1921 in the Charlottenburg district of Berlin. "This is for my mother," he told Pasha as he shot him.[11] Tehlirian, in what was a sensational trial for its time, was eventually acquitted on the grounds of "psychological compulsion," or what today would be called temporary insanity, rooted in the soul-wrenching trauma he had endured and continued to suffer.

The then 21-year-old Lemkin, in conversation with his professors at the University of Lvov, asked a deceptively simple question: "It is a crime for Tehlirian to kill a man, but it is not a crime for his oppressor to kill more than a million men? This is most inconsistent."[12] His professor cited the banner of state sovereignty—the right of every state to conduct its internal affairs independently. That is, states and statesmen could do as they pleased within their own borders. His professor continued: "There was no law under which he [Talaat] could be arrested . . . Consider the case of a farmer who owns a flock of chickens. He kills them, and this is his business. If you interfere, you are trespassing."[13] Lemkin's response, that "sovereignty cannot be conceived as the right to kill millions of innocent people," was a moral-threshold moment that anticipated his subsequent transfer to the Lvov law school, where he began to search for legal codes that would punish and prevent the mass murder of civilians.[14]

Lemkin's resolve would be reinforced in 1926 with the trial of Shalom Schwarzbard, a Jewish tailor whose parents had been murdered in a pogrom in Ukraine in 1918. Schwarzbard had assassinated the alleged overseer of those pogroms, Symon Petliura, and, like Tehlirian, was acquitted on the grounds of temporary insanity. Again, however, Lemkin was struck by the incongruity in the fact that an individual could be tried for a single homicide but there was no international law to hold a government responsible for the destruction of entire groups of people. After the trial, he wrote an article in which he "deplored the absence of any law for the unification of moral standards in relation to the destruction of national, racial, and religious groups."[15]

Following graduation, working as a public prosecutor in Warsaw, Lemkin's next step in what would become a lifelong crusade toward making such a law came when he developed a proposal that would commit the Polish government and others to stopping the targeted destruction of ethnic, national, and religious groups. He was scheduled to present the proposal, arguing for the establishment of an international law, at a League of Nations conference for the unification of criminal law in Madrid, Spain in October 1933. At the last minute, the Polish minister of justice denied Lemkin the travel visa necessary to attend the meeting. The denial was explained on the basis that Lemkin's proposal was "anti-German propaganda" and there was concern that Lemkin might give the wrong impression to other governments about Polish foreign policy. An influential antisemitic Polish newspaper also denounced Lemkin for being concerned solely with protecting his own race.[16]

Undeterred, Lemkin found a delegate who agreed to present his proposal.[17] The proposal—titled "Acts Constituting a General (Transnational) Danger Considered as Offences Against the Law of Nations"—called for a new type of international law to legislate against "general (transnational) danger [that] threatens the interests of several States and their inhabitants."[18] His proposal addressed three conceptual areas that reappear as recurring threads in the development of international law against the destruction of groups—which groups would be protected, what acts would be defined as criminal, and who would have the jurisdictional responsibility to prosecute individuals accused of those criminal acts.

In terms of protected groups, Lemkin's Madrid proposal focused on "acts of extermination directed against the ethnic, religious or social collectives."[19] His proposal also, though, addressed political motives for extermination, implying that the target group itself may be defined in political terms. In his insistent use of the word "collectivity" throughout the proposal, it seems clear that, at this point, Lemkin was thinking in the broadest possible terms about protected groups. The "offences against the law of nations" are described as "attacks carried out against an individual as a member of a collectivity," and the delineation of that collectivity in the Madrid proposal seems less important than the definition of the attacks themselves.[20]

In outlining the criminal activity, Lemkin included "acts of barbarity" as one type of "offence against the laws of nations." He defined "barbarity" as "acts of extermination directed against the ethnic, religious or social collectivities . . . to endanger both the existence of the collective concerned and the entire social order." Lemkin also identified "acts of vandalism" as another type of offense and defined such acts as "systematic and organized destruction of the art and cultural heritage in which the unique genius and achievement of a collectivity are revealed in fields of science, arts and literature." Lemkin proposed that these acts should be declared "offences against the law of nations" alongside piracy, counterfeiting, slavery, and trade in women, children, narcotics, and obscene publications.[21]

Finally, in addressing jurisdictional responsibility, Lemkin suggested a principle of "universal repression" (the precursor to what is today called "universal jurisdiction") in which a perpetrator of "offences against the law of nations" could be brought to justice "in the place of where he is apprehended, independently of where the crime was committed and the nationality of the author . . . this is because such a perpetrator is regarded as the enemy of the whole international community and in all States he will be pursued for crimes universally harmful to all the international community."[22] Any country could try a perpetrator, regardless of where the atrocities were committed.

Lemkin's paper was presented, in his absence, and tabled. Delegates were not given the opportunity to accept or reject the proposal. Samantha Power, now U.S. Ambassador to the United Nations (UN), points out that some delegates believed that these crimes happened too seldom to legislate and most were skeptical about the "apocalyptic references to Hitler," appearing even as early as October 1933.[23] Moreover, nearly all seemed to be in agreement that state sovereignty trumped mass atrocities against a state's own citizens. Sovereignty holds that states should enjoy political independence and autonomy without outside interference. That is, states have the right to govern and control without external interference, the right to nonintervention of external actors in internal state affairs. International law, such as that proposed by Lemkin, should never usurp the sanctity of state sovereignty. As a dogged Lemkin noted, however, the lawyers at the conference "would not say yes, but they could not say no."[24] In Power's words: "They were not prepared to agree to intervene, even diplomatically, across borders. But neither were they prepared to admit that they would stand by and allow innocent people to die."[25]

Lemkin was prescient in his recognition that conflict in modern times had taken a brutal, and perhaps irrevocable, turn. Even before the storm of the Holocaust, Lemkin saw the gathering clouds through the windowpanes of the twentieth century. Although not unique to modernity—as noted French philosopher Jean-Paul Sartre wrote, "The fact of genocide is as old as humanity"—the notion of exterminating whole peoples loomed more ominous in a modern world in which states had the power and capacity to plan and carry out the destruction of groups.[26] As Philip Spencer points out, the problem confronting Lemkin's century was not conspiracies by groups of people against the state, but, rather, conspiracies by states against groups of people.[27] Crowds, riots, and popular uprisings as causal factors of violence were supplanted by repressive, organized state apparatuses.

This qualitative transformation was the culmination of a journey with eighteenth-century origins. In the course of its revolution in the late eighteenth century, France began to substitute adherence to the nation for fealty to a monarch. Styles of dress, usage of words, anthems, and flag design all were impacted by France's new "nationalism." The resulting spread of nationalism—described by some as "the most important force in world politics in the past two centuries" and "an ersatz religion"—would change the world forever.[28]

Nationalism sees the word as divided into distinctive "peoples," however defined, with a concomitant desire to maintain and protect that distinctiveness. Now, large numbers of people came to be categorized as belonging to the same group, whether because of their ethnic or racial origins, or because of their social and political affinities. Nationalism carried with it the notion that every "people" deserved its own government, with likes ruling over likes. Nationalism is a "psychological bond," not necessarily requiring historical accuracy, joining a people and differentiating it; it is "the essence of a nation."[29] According to historian Michael Ignatieff, "nationalism is the claim that while men and women have many identities, it is the nation that provides them with their primary form of belonging."[30] Political scientist Stuart Kaufman goes even further: "For the nationalist, the nation is a god—a jealous god—to whom one pays homage, venerating its temples (monuments), relics (battle flags), and theology (including a mythical history); and receiving in return a sort of immortality as a participant in what is conceived as an eternal nation."[31]

The political corollary of the rise of nationalism in Europe was the emergence of a new normative form of political organization—the "nation-state"—replacing empires, dynastic kingdoms, tribal confederacies, and city-states.[32] A "nation" refers to a sociocultural identity, a union of people who share a sense of national identity, usually built on similar cultural, linguistic, historical, and religious characteristics. A "state" refers to the legal political identity, a defined territory controlled by a recognized government. The boundaries of some states enclose several nations and divide others. The modern nation-state refers to a group of people, sharing a sense of national identity, joined together in a formal political union—thus merging a sociocultural ("nation") and political ("state") identity. The nation-state emerged from states that defined themselves as the political expression of a certain nation. Nation-states were more cohesive and stronger political units than the old monarchies or empires that they replaced. The identity of monarchies or empires was defined by their rulers; their populations—often of varied religious, ethnic, and racial origins—were merely the subjects of their monarch and emperors.[33] In modern nation-states, however, the identity of rulers and ruled was fused. "Subjects" became "citizens" and states acquired "national interests." Popular passions were now placed at the service of the state's bureaucracies.[34]

This emerging international system, built on nation-state actors pursuing national interests, brought to Lemkin's century an inherently competitive and violent world. As sociologist Andreas Wimmer has pointed out, violence was often related to the creation of the nation-state itself and, later, to the struggle over which "people" would hold power in the newly established state.[35] Moreover, nation-states often sought to expand their geographic boundaries to include others who shared the same sense of national identity. In reaction, the boundaries between states became increasingly rigid even as interstate rivalry and conflict increased. The size and intensity of wars amplified dramatically, often animated by a desire to wrest control of an emerging nation-state's affairs from its former colonial and imperial masters. Historian Mark Levene even argues that it was ". . . through the extension of the Western-created concept of the nation-state to all hemispheres, and with it of the embrace of the entire world's population as citizens of such states within its international nation-state framework" that genocide became a truly global phenomenon.[36] As historian Mark Mazower warns us, however, we should be careful about a Eurocentric vision obsessively focusing on "an overtly state-dominated understanding of mass violence," particularly as it excludes the nature and consequences of colonization. Indeed, as he points out, the state "was often virtually absent in settler colonies, leaving settlers to battle it out with indigenous people for control of land and resources."[37]

What is it about the nation-state that makes it such a lethal polity? As historian Dirk Moses reminds us, "empires were racist, hierarchical and often practiced retributive genocide when challenged, but they were inclusive if subject nations, peoples and cities towed the line. They were not inherently genocidal."[38] Part of the answer for the genocidal lethality of the nation-state, relative to empires, certainly lies in the animating spirit of nationalism. Modern nation-states, in the course of their development, relied on the unifying power of nationalism in order to survive and prosper. Although nationalism can be a source of liberalism and democracy, it can also be manipulated and exploited for more nefarious ends. In psychiatrist Vamik Volkan's words: "While the idea of nationalism may be linked to liberty and universalistic ideals, it also sometimes led to particularism, racism, totalitarianism, and destruction."[39]

The success of the nation-state required a continual reinvigorating of nationalism as a unifying sentiment that solidified commitment to something larger than a family, a tribe, or a local region. In so doing, nationalism sometimes became a lethal exercise in self-definition—as much concerned with identifying who is not a member of the national community as it was with who is a member. Nationalism, a manifestation of what international studies scholar Benedict Anderson has called "imagined communities," can exaggerate differences between peoples to a point that they assume a disproportionate significance. In Anderson's words: "It is imagined because the members of even the smallest nation will never know most of their fellow-members, meet them, or even hear of them, yet in the minds of each lives the image of their communion."[40] As genocide scholar Alex Alvarez points out, such exaggerated nationalist "images of communion" also align with "a spirit of elitism and exclusiveness that teaches that one's own people are not only different, but superior to other groups as well."[41] As a result, nationalism means both voluntary and enforced inclusion of people in the new nation, and often violent exclusion of other groups from it.[42] In this sense, nationalism goes beyond love for one's nation and, in practice, becomes merged with antagonism toward other nations. Although it may promote unity within states, nationalism can also promote disunity among them.

Nationalist sentiments, widespread by the early nineteenth century, joined with several other modern factors to increase the lethality of intergroup relations by the late nineteenth century. As outlined by historian Omar Bartov, there was a "growing interest in science, biology, anthropology, evolution, and the 'origins of man'" that impacted how we viewed the malleability, or lack thereof, in human nature—particularly in regard to racial qualities and characteristics. In addition, in the late nineteenth century there was "a vast expansion of colonial empires in which people of European origin came to dominate, exploit, and often destroy large groups of non-Europeans." This wave of Western colonization exaggerated notions of innate racial superiority and inferiority. Finally, "the late nineteenth century saw an extremely rapid expansion in military and industrial technology." Such technological advances enhanced the state's ability to control its population and exert power beyond its borders.[43]

Genocide was not an inevitable consequence of the advent of nationalism, the rise of the nation-state, or any of the other influences of modernity outlined by Bartov. Certainly, genocide had occurred in premodern societies and before the birth of the modern nation-state. As Martin Shaw reminds us, even modern genocides have their premodern components (e.g., the slaughters carried out by the Einsatzgruppen during the Holocaust).[44] Broadly speaking, however, modernity changed the calculus of mass murder by providing new means and justifications. Genocide, as argued by religious studies scholar Richard Rubenstein, now fell well within the capacity of any modern state and, as a political strategy, would become even more tempting as expanding populations pushed against limited resources.[45] For Bartov, modernity "presents mass murder as a necessary and legitimate undertaking . . . that finds support among intellectuals, academics, spiritual leaders, and others who would normally oppose the murder of individuals."[46] According to the social anthropologist Nancy Scheper-Hughes, genocide is an endemic feature of modernity.[47] In this argument, genocide is not an antithesis of modernity, but the dark side of it; is not a deviation from the straight path of progress, but a consequence of it.[48] Genocide is a paradox of progress and destruction.[49]

Although the modernity thesis has drawn its fair share of critics, it remains difficult to argue with the summation offered by Alvarez: "In the twentieth century the state has posed the greatest threat to life, both the lives of its own citizens and those of other populations."[50] Indeed, we cannot turn a blind eye to the fact that, in the twentieth century, mass violence took a brutal turn as the nation-state became, at times, a deadly form of social organization. In his writings, Lemkin—ever the exhaustive cataloger—never fully nuances the comparative distinction between genocide as a "modern" crime and as a universal feature of humankind throughout history. The spirit of his work, however, clearly intuited a sense of compelling urgency about an impending epoch of "moral atrocity."[51] In this, he would be proved right—again and again—and perhaps even sooner than he dared fear.

After being dismissed by the Polish government for refusing to curb his criticisms of Hitler, he opened a private law practice in Warsaw in 1934, focusing on the international ramifications of tax law. Lemkin's practice thrived and he refocused his scholarly efforts on the drafting of a treatise on exchange control regulations.[52] Not to be dissuaded by the cool reception his proposal received in Madrid, Lemkin continued to push his agenda over the next several years at law conferences in Budapest, Copenhagen, Paris, Amsterdam, and Cairo.

With the Nazi invasion of Poland on September 1, 1939, however, Lemkin soon become an internally displaced refugee. Fleeing the bombing of a train on which he was a passenger, Lemkin was forced to retreat to the woods outside of Warsaw. There, he witnessed further bombing attacks and the death of many from starvation, disease, and exhaustion. After 6 months of this nomadic existence, he decided to flee and failing to persuade his family to join him, Lemkin escaped to then-neutral Lithuania before receiving a visa to Sweden where he taught at the University of Stockholm. Cleared for immigration to the United States in 1941, he made an arduous 10,000 mile journey across the Baltic Sea, Siberia, Japan, the Pacific Ocean, Canada, and the continental United States. In

April 1941, Lemkin finally arrived in Durham, North Carolina to teach at Duke University. There, and later at Yale University, Lemkin continued to sharpen his 1933 Madrid proposal. After the United States entered the war in late 1941, Lemkin joined the ranks of public service, first as a consultant to the Board of Economic Warfare (later to become the Foreign Economic Administration) and later as a special advisor on foreign affairs and international law to the War Department.[53]

In 1942, Lemkin sent a carefully worded memo to President Roosevelt in which he suggested the adoption of a treaty to make the mass destruction of civilians an international crime. He urged "speed" and that "it was still possible to save at least a part of the people." Several weeks later, Roosevelt responded with his own urging—"patience." In his autobiography, a frustrated Lemkin writes: "'Patience' is a good word for when one expects an appointment, a budgetary allocation, or the building of a road. But when the rope is already around the neck of the victim and strangulation is imminent, isn't the word 'patience' an insult to reason and nature?"[54]

Realizing that he "was following the wrong path" and that, indeed, "statesmen were messing up the world," Lemkin turned his attention to publishing his collection of documents on Nazi laws and decrees of occupation. He saw in this work a "picture of the destruction of peoples" that, he held, would give people "no choice but to believe."[55] In November 1944, the Carnegie Endowment for International Peace published Lemkin's manuscript as *Axis Rule in Occupied Europe*.[56] The major part of the 721-page book dealt with detailed commentaries of laws and decrees of the Axis powers, and of their puppet regimes, for the government of occupied areas.

One chapter, however, was devoted specifically to the subject of genocide. Lemkin restated his 1933 Madrid proposal to outlaw the targeted destruction of groups and urged the creation of an international treaty that could be used as a basis for trying and punishing perpetrators. Most importantly, however, it was in this chapter that Lemkin proposed the term "genocide," which he had coined the year before and briefly introduced in the preface, from the ancient Greek word *geno* (race, tribe) and the Latin *cide* (killing). As he defined genocide, it meant "a coordinated plan of different actions aiming at the destruction of essential foundations of the life of national groups, with the aim of annihilating the groups themselves. The objectives of such a plan would be disintegration of the political and social institutions, of culture, language, national feelings, religion, and economic existence of national groups, and the destruction of the personal security, liberty, health, dignity, and even the lives of the individuals belonging to such groups . . . Genocide is directed against the national group as an entity, and the actions involved are directed against individuals, not in their individual capacity, but as members of the national group."[57] As historian Thomas Butcher argues, Lemkin's conception of genocide was multifaceted; it was a "synchronized attack" that was part of a complete, integrated policy.[58] For Lemkin, the concept of genocide would protect the right to life of national groups, just as the concept of homicide protects the right to life of individuals. Lemkin broke from the nationalist ideology that national groups were defined by language, blood, and territory; for Lemkin, national groups were "families of mind" who shared common beliefs and sentiments and whose identities were mutable and constantly changing.[59] Although one scholar critiques Lemkin's preliminary conception of genocide, as articulated in *Axis Rule*, as "extremely vague, confused, and, when illustrated by empirical referents, invalid," Lemkin had, at least, finally given the crime a name.[60]

Lemkin now turned his attention toward making international law against the crime of genocide. In 1945–1946, he left his position with the War Department to become an unofficial advisor to U.S. Supreme Court Justice and U.S. Chief of Counsel at the International Military Tribunal (IMT) in Nuremberg, Robert Jackson. As legal scholar John Q. Barrett has demonstrated, although only nominally affiliated with Jackson's staff, "Lemkin's intellectual work was known to and influenced Jackson and his staff."[61] Although the word "genocide" does not appear in the Tribunal's Charter, it does appear in the drafting history of the Charter, as well as in Count Three (War Crimes) of the IMT indictment, and was spoken for the first time in a courtroom litigation proceeding when the Nuremberg trial began on November 20, 1945. On June 25, 1946, a British deputy prosecutor, Sir David Maxwell-Fyfe, read the definition of genocide directly from Lemkin's book during a cross-examination of defendant Konstantin von Neurath. On July 27, Sir Hartley Shawcross, the British chief prosecutor, spoke in his closing argument of the defendants' crimes of genocide, as did French deputy prosecutor Charles Dubost in his closing argument.

Although progress was made in the use of the word "genocide" during the trial, the word does not appear in the final judgment on October 1, 1946. A disappointed Lemkin wrote: "The Allies decided their case against a past Hitler but refused to envisage future Hitlers. They did not want to, or could not, establish a rule of international law that would prevent and punish future crimes of the same type."[62] More disconcertingly for Lemkin, the IMT maintained that states and individuals who did *not* cross an international border were still free under international law to commit genocide. In other words, the Allies did not question Germany's absolute authority over its internal affairs before the war. As legal scholar William

Schabas points out, "although there was frequent reference [during the trials] to the preparation for the war and for the Nazi atrocities committed in the early years of the Third Reich, no conviction was registered for any act committed prior to September 1, 1939."[63] In essence, had the Nazis killed only German Jews, they would not have been liable for any international crime. Later, Lemkin was to call the Nuremberg judgment "the blackest day of my life"—a rather high bar, given Lemkin's life to that point.[64] (As a minor victory, however, it should be noted that several of the 12 subsequent Nuremberg Trials that followed the IMT did include genocide as a separate charge. In addition, the Polish Supreme National Tribunal adopted Lemkin's framework and convicted Amon Goeth, Rudolf Hoess, and Artur Greiser of genocide under Polish law, becoming the first state to use the word "genocide" in its domestic criminal proceedings.[65])

By 1946, Lemkin's work took on a new, distinctly personal, urgency. He had lost 49 relatives, including his parents—likely gassed at Treblinka—to the Holocaust. The only European members of his family to survive the Holocaust were his brother, Elias, and Elias' wife and two sons. In a draft preface to his autobiography, Lemkin wrote of his reaction to this enormous personal loss: "When I have conceived the idea of outlawing genocide, I hardly could imagine that it will affect me personally. During the war 49 members of my family perished from Genocide, including my parents. Suddenly I felt that the earth is receeding [sic] from under my feet and the sense of living is disappearing. But soon I have transformed personal disaster into a moral striking force. Was I not under a moral duty to repay my mother for having stimulated in me the interest in Genocide? Was it not the best form of gratitude to make a 'Genocide pact' as an epitaph on her symbolic grave and as a common recognition that she and many millions did not die in vain? I redoubled my efforts and found temporal relief from my grief in this work."[66] Impacted by these personal losses, and stung by the disappointment of Nuremberg, Lemkin would be transformed from a "crusader" into a "zealot" for making international law against the crime of genocide.[67]

Outside legislative circles, Lemkin's new word caught on quickly. A December 3, 1944 *Washington Post* editorial (written at Lemkin's urging) claimed that "genocide" was the only word that properly described the murder of Jews at Auschwitz.[68] On January 21, 1945, a full-page review of *Axis Rule in Occupied Europe* appeared on the lead page of the *New York Times Book Review*. The word "genocide" resonated in ways that "race murder," "mass murder," "denationalization," "barbarity," "vandalism," "terrorism," and other descriptions had not. In his unpublished autobiography,

Lemkin recounts a 1946 conversation in which Judge Abdul Monim Bey Riad of Saudi Arabia said: "It [a convention against genocide] is a beautiful concept. It is something worth living for. The word 'genocide' has so much appeal, so much force."[69] By 1950, the word had made its first appearance in the Merriam-Webster English dictionary. In the United States, the word quickly became so commonplace that, in 1962, Governor Ross Barnett of Mississippi, in defending his reactionary decision to prevent the enrollment of James Meredith at the University of Mississippi, could state publicly "we will not drink from the cup of genocide"—with near certainty that his fellow white supremacists would grasp well the meaning of the word.[70]

Still searching for international legislative weight to back the new word, Lemkin devoted himself tirelessly, and even more obsessively, to a single-handed campaign to make "genocide" an international crime. He looked to the newly established United Nations (UN) organization (founded October 24, 1945) to construct an international law that did not link the destruction of groups to internationally recognized cross-border aggression. First written by Lemkin "on a soft sofa in the Delegates' Lounge" of the UN offices in Lake Success, New York—and supported with sponsorships from Panama, Cuba, and India—a draft resolution was prepared for presentation at the first session of the General Assembly, in late 1946.[71] In requesting the inclusion of the resolution on the agenda, the Cuban delegate, Ernesto Dihigo, reminded the Committee that "at the Nurnberg trials, it had not been possible to punish certain cases of genocide because they had been committed before the beginning of the war. Fearing that such crimes might remain unpunished . . . [Dihigo] asked that genocide be declared an international crime. This was the purpose of the resolution."[72] Clearly, the initial Nuremberg trial's failure to recognize the criminality of atrocities committed in peacetime left a lingering dissatisfaction within the international community. Vulnerable emerging states of the underdeveloped world were particularly invested in developing an instrument to protect them from repressive acts and atrocities that could be committed against them in peacetime.[73] There was a legal gap to fill and codifying the crime of genocide was seen by many as a legal, and moral, necessity.

The resolution forwarded to the General Assembly, Resolution 96 (I), condemned genocide as "a denial of the right of existence of entire human groups . . . Many instances of such crimes have occurred, when racial, religious, political and other groups have been destroyed, entirely or in part."[74] The brief resolution analogized genocide to the crime of homicide. The phrase "other groups" implied a nonexhaustive list of protected groups. As legal scholar Howard Shneider has stated: "Just as the key element of homicide is the taking of another human being's life, regardless of who that human being is, the Resolution argued that the key element of genocide is the taking of a human group's life, regardless of the characteristics that bind the group. As such, the identity of the victim group is not significant in concluding whether genocide occurred."[75]

Perhaps most significantly, Resolution 96 (I) went beyond a mere symbolic declaration and also tasked the Economic and Social Council, one of the six principal organs of the UN, with drafting a convention on the crime of genocide, to be submitted to the next regular session of the General Assembly in 1947. On December 11, 1946, the General Assembly of the UN unanimously passed the resolution, without debate.

The subsequent drafting process would go through three stages, and end up taking 2 years, with Lemkin's direct involvement varying throughout.[76] The first stage of the drafting phase began in May 1947 with UN Secretary-General Trygve Lie inviting Lemkin to join Henri Donnedieu de Vabres, professor at the University of Paris Law Faculty and a former judge at the Nuremberg Tribunal, and Vespasian Pella, a Romanian law professor and President of the International Association for Penal Law, in the initial delineation of concepts central to the treaty. (Interestingly enough, both de Vabres and Pella were cited in Lemkin's 1933 Madrid proposal—two of only three citations included in the document.) The following month, the three experts submitted the Secretariat draft (UN Document E/447), articulating definitions and punishable offenses related to the crime of genocide.

Although there are many legal nuances in the 85-page Secretariat draft, central are the three conceptual areas outlined in Lemkin's original Madrid proposal—which groups would be protected, what acts would be defined as criminal, and who would have the jurisdictional responsibility to prosecute individuals accused of those criminal acts.

Notable in this initial draft was the continuing inclusion of racial, religious, and political groups among the protected identities, as well as the additions of national and linguistic groups to clarify the nebulous "other" category from Resolution 96 (I). Lemkin, sensing the controversy it would engender, was willing to exclude political groups from the listing, but de Vabres favored their inclusion and Pella believed the General Assembly should decide this question.

The crime of genocide, mirroring much of Lemkin's 1933 Madrid proposal, was divided into three categories—physical, biological, and cultural (though Lemkin's *Axis Rule* had also included five other categories—political, social, economic, religious, and moral). Physical genocide involved acts intended to cause the death of members of a group or injury to their health or physical integrity. Biological genocide was characterized by systematic restrictions on births, without which the group cannot survive. Cultural genocide was referenced as the destruction of the specific characteristics of a group—language, religion, traditions, and so on. Both de Vabres and Pella saw cultural genocide as an "undue extension" of the notion of genocide, but Lemkin prevailed—at least for now—in his argument that "if the diversity of cultures were destroyed, it would be as disastrous for civilization as the physical destruction of nations."[77]

Also mirroring Lemkin's 1933 proposal, the Secretariat Draft included "universal enforcement," the notion that contracting parties could "punish any offender . . . within any territory under their jurisdiction, irrespective of the nationality of the offender or of the place where the offence has been committed."[78] For Lemkin, such universal enforcement was consistent with international law related to trafficking in women and children, counterfeiting currency, and so on.

Subsequent UN committee deliberations regarding the Secretariat Draft proceeded slowly, often stalled by obstructionists bent on destroying the convention. Additionally, it became clear that not all Member States would have submitted their observations on the Secretariat Draft in time for consideration at the second regular session of the General Assembly in 1947. In response, on November 21, 1947, the UN adopted General Assembly Resolution 180 (II). This resolution reaffirmed Resolution 96 (I) and (re)tasked the UN Economic and Social Council to submit a draft of a convention on the crime of genocide to the third regular session of the General Assembly in 1948.

The second stage of the drafting phase occurred the following spring between April 5 and May 10, 1948. The Economic and Social Council convened an Ad Hoc Committee with the task of reworking the Secretariat draft of the previous year. The committee was composed of seven delegates representing China, France, Lebanon, Poland, Venezuela, the United States, and the Soviet Union. Because he was not an official UN delegate, Lemkin was not included on the committee, though he did sit in on, and contribute to, much of the subsequent deliberations. The Ad Hoc Committee met a total of 28 times before producing a new draft convention and commentary (UN Document E/794).

In regard to the three conceptual areas guiding our discussion, the listing of protected groups in the Ad Hoc Committee draft still included national, racial, religious, or political. The United States saw "linguistic" as an unnecessary inclusion "since it is not believed that genocide would be practiced upon them because of their linguistic as distinguished from their racial, national or religious, characteristics."[79] The Soviet Union and Poland questioned the inclusion of political groups, arguing that they lacked the stability of other groups, but a narrow vote of four to three dictated that political groups still would be included in this draft.

Second, the definition of genocide outlined by the Ad Hoc Committee was significantly diluted from the previous Secretariat draft. Physical and biological genocide were collapsed into one grouping with the acts constituting such genocide focused much more specifically on mortal destruction than some of the "life destruction" (for example, "deprivation of all means of livelihood") enumerated in the Secretariat draft. Cultural genocide, to which the United States was vehemently opposed, was retained. Presaging its removal in the final text, however, its definition was watered-down amid debate regarding the degree to which its inclusion might prevent many countries from ratifying the treaty.

Third, and finally, the principle of "universal enforcement," so clearly articulated in Lemkin's Madrid proposal as well as the Secretariat draft, was completely removed from the Ad Hoc Committee draft. Delegates feared its infringement on state sovereignty. National courts judging the acts of foreign governments could, it was argued, lead to "dangerous international tension."[80] In its place, Article VII stated that persons charged with genocide "shall be tried by competent tribunal of the State in the territory of which the act was committed." Although the same article still held out the promise of a "competent international tribunal," no plans for such a mechanism were discussed.

In late 1948, the convention on the crime of genocide entered the third, and final, stage of its drafting process. The Ad Hoc Committee draft now came before the Sixth Committee of the General Assembly. The Sixth Committee, responsible for legal matters, discussed and debated the draft from October 5 to November 9, 1948. During committee deliberations, Lemkin was seated behind the delegates, where, from time to time, he would pass notes to friendly representatives.[81] Eventually, the Sixth Committee agreed on a final draft resolution—built on compromise and negotiation—that was then submitted for consideration in the third session of the General Assembly.

Behind the scenes, undeterred by exclusion from the Ad Hoc Committee and relegation to the back rows of the Sixth Committee, Lemkin became a "one-man, one-globe, multilingual, single-issue lobbying machine" to ensure passage of the convention.[82] In July 1948, he had dropped everything to fly to Geneva to find "new friends" at the Economic and Social

Council to support the convention. He strategically surmised "that the delegates, away from home, were more lonely here than in New York and might have more time to listen to me."[83] He then moved on to Paris "learning the composition of the delegations and lining up strategic forces" in preparation for the General Assembly discussion of the convention.[84] While there, he cajoled "a number of friendly delegates" into streamlining the subcommittee procedure necessary for presentation of the convention to the General Assembly.[85]

Historian Jay Winter describes Lemkin as "a man of great conviction, but not great charm, he was an uncomfortable presence, someone not easily deflected. Speaking to him a second, third, or 33rd time could be tiresome or worse."[86] Benjamin Ferencz, chief prosecutor of the SS-Einsatzgruppen case at Nuremberg, recalled thinking that Lemkin was odd, maybe even "crazy."[87] Not above guilt-inducing hyperbole, Lemkin once wrote to the head of the Methodist women's council: "I know it is very hot in July and August for work . . . but let us not forget that the heat of this month is less unbearable to us than the heat in the ovens of Auschwitz and Dachau."[88] Various accounts refer to him as a pest, crank, or nudnik. Never one for small talk, this fits with A. M. Rosenthal's (columnist and executive editor at *The New York Times*) personal recollections of Lemkin walking ". . . the corridors of the UN. He stopped journalists, took junior delegates by the arm and hung on until they listened, at least a moment. To see an ambassador, he would plan and plot for weeks and sit for days in reception rooms." Rosenthal continued: "He [Lemkin] had no money, no office, no assistants. He had no UN status or papers, but the guards always let him pass . . . He would bluff a little sometimes about pulling political levers, but he had none."[89]

Because of his persistence, and despite the fact that he could certainly reach the bounds of pesky annoyance, Lemkin was able to rally a worldwide network of support for his cause. Whether viewed by his contemporaries as a "dreamer" or "fanatic," most would agree, as archivist Tanya Elder argues, "as a lobbyer, Lemkin was brilliant."[90] He used correspondence, petitions, articles, radio addresses, interviews, public lectures, and a broad range of coalitions to build support for the passage of the convention.

Due, in large part, to his tireless campaigning, the United Nations Convention on the Prevention and Punishment of the Crime of Genocide (commonly known as the Genocide Convention) was finally adopted at the Palais de Chaillot in Paris on December 9, 1948, one day before the end of the assembly. The final draft submitted by the Sixth Committee was adopted without alterations. Fifty-five delegates voted yes to the pact; none voted no. The Genocide Convention—UN Resolution 260

(III)—became the first human rights treaty adopted by the General Assembly of the UN. The following day would see the adoption by the UN of the nonbinding Universal Declaration of Human Rights, a milestone document in the history of human rights. Some see, arguably so, the passage of these two treaties—the Convention establishing international law and the Declaration encoding an aspirational set of normative universal principles—as the complementary core of modern international human rights law; two sides of one coin.[91]

An ill and destitute Lemkin managed to make the Paris Conference and was present when the treaty was adopted. Hours after the vote, Rosenthal recounts finding an exhausted Lemkin in a darkened Assembly Hall, "weeping as if his heart would break" and asking "please to be left in solitude."[92] Days later, Lemkin fell gravely ill and was hospitalized. For nearly 3 weeks, the doctors struggled with a diagnosis. Lemkin finally offered one himself: ". . . genociditis; exhaustion from the work on the Genocide Convention."[93]

The Genocide Convention includes 19 concise articles. Throughout, we can see fingerprints of Lemkin's influence, some traceable to his original 1933 Madrid proposal. We also see, however, some significant deviations from how Lemkin conceived of the crime of genocide and its punishment. Some were political compromises, necessary to ensure passage of the Convention. Others were rooted in intransigent notions of state sovereignty, race, and jurisdictional responsibilities that would prove divisive in committee deliberations.

The first two articles give the substance of the Convention. Article I noted that genocide can be "committed in time of peace or in time of war."[94] This was a significant deviation from the International Military Tribunal's initial confining of crimes against humanity to only those acts perpetrated after the outbreak of war. Although later international jurisprudence would clarify that crimes against humanity may also occur in peacetime, the 1948 Convention was groundbreaking in its decision that mass destruction of peoples need not be limited to armed conflict; war does not have to be present for genocide to occur. Peacetime atrocity was no longer beyond the reach of law.

Article II, however, is the central defining article of the Convention: "In the present Convention, genocide means any of the following acts committed with intent to destroy, in whole or in part, a national, ethnical, racial or religious group, as such: (a) killing members of the group, (b) causing serious bodily or mental harm to members of the group, (c) deliberately inflicting on the group conditions of life calculated to bring about its physical destruction in whole or in part, (d) imposing measures intended to prevent births within the group, or (e) forcibly transferring children of the group to another group."

Within Article II, we see two of the conceptual areas at play. First, Article II defines the protected groups as "national, ethnical, racial, or religious." In the Sixth Committee deliberations, Sweden had suggested adding "ethnical" to cover linguistic groups not connected to an existing state, a proposal passing by a one vote margin. Most noticeable, though, is the absence of "political" among the protected groups. The final report of the Sixth Committee, dated December 3, 1948, indicates that "the Committee [at its 75th meeting] decided to retain political groups, the vote being 29 in favour to 13 against, with 9 abstentions."[95] An asterisk, though, indicates that this decision was later reversed. Paragraph 21 of the same document indicates "a proposal was made by the representatives of Egypt, Iran and Uruguay to re-examine the question of excluding 'political groups' in article II of the Convention. Having heard a statement by the representative of the United States of America in favour of such exclusion . . . the Committee [at its 128th meeting], by a second vote of 22 to 6, with 12 abstentions, decided to exclude political groups from the groups protected by article II."[96]

Though the inclusion of political groups had survived for several sessions, it had been a matter of contention since the original Resolution 96 (I) in 1946. Supporters of its inclusion pointed out that future genocides would likely be committed mainly on political grounds and that the inclusion of political groups was consistent with the protection of religious groups—both were defined by beliefs in an idea. Many even argued that genocide, in its most serious form, was nearly always a political crime. If political groups were not included, some worried that perpetrators might hide behind the pretext of the political opinion of a racial or religious group to destroy it, without being liable to any international sanctions. It was commonly understood that political groups constituted an especially vulnerable population and there was no legally defensible principle that could justify their exclusion.

The proponents of protecting political groups under the Convention may have been equipped to win the battle with moral and logical force but they were unable to win the political war that ensued. The core of the opposition came from Eastern bloc countries led by the Soviet Union, which were joined by a number of Latin American states (Brazil, Peru, Venezuela, the Dominican Republic, and Uruguay) as well as Lebanon, Sweden, the Philippines, Egypt, Belgium, and Iran. These diverse voices argued for the exclusion of political groups on the grounds that such groups—mutable, imprecise, transient, unstable, and lacking in distinguishing characteristics—could not be objectively designated (under a mistaken assumption that national, ethnical, racial, or religious could be objectively designated). They maintained that membership in political groups was voluntary—unlike membership in national, ethnical, racial, or religious groups—and lacked permanency and consistency. (As we will see in Chapter 4, this is the distinction between achieved and ascribed social identity.) Although people can certainly change nationality and religion, such changes did not happen as frequently as people changing their political beliefs. In short, opponents held that political groups did not conform to the definition of genocide and would weaken the entire Convention.

Although not voiced publicly, legal scholar Beth Van Schaack also reminds us of the implicit reality that the Convention could not implicate member nations on the drafting committee. For instance, if political groups were included in the Convention, it could "inculpate Stalin's politically motivated purges of the *kulaks* (the petty bourgeois) during the forced collectivizations of agriculture in the late 1920s and early 1930s."[97] Clearly, many governments could have found themselves in a similar position—threatened with charges of genocide if political identity were to be included as a protected group in the definition.

The most significant objection, however, to the inclusion of political groups centered on the issue of state sovereignty. Opponents feared that the inclusion of political groups in the convention would expose nations to external intervention in their domestic concerns and political conflict within a country could become an international issue. In other words, including political groups in the convention would enter into the controversial issue of civil war and inhibit states that were attempting to suppress internal armed revolt. Countries such as Argentina, Brazil, the Dominican Republic, Iran, and South Africa joined the Soviet delegation and its allies in expressing concern that they could be accused of genocide if they fought against domestic political insurgencies.[98] Lemkin recounts the argument of Ambassador Gilberto Arnado of Brazil: "We in Latin America make revolutions from time to time, which involves the destruction of political opponents. Then we reconcile and live in peace. Later the group in power is thrown out in another revolution. Why should this be classified as the crime of genocide?"[99]

Ultimately, however, the exclusion of political groups from the listing of protected groups by the Sixth Committee would come down, ironically, to political compromise. The fear was simply too great that the passage of the Convention itself would be jeopardized by the inclusion of political groups. The United States reversed its previous insistence on the inclusion of political groups and its representative, Ernest Gross, gave voice to the reality behind this decision: "The United States delegation continued to think that its point of view was correct but, in a conciliatory spirit and in order to avoid the possibility that the application of the convention to political groups might prevent certain countries from acceding to it, he would support the proposal to delete from article II the provisions relating to political groups."[100] Most agreed with the need to produce an instrument that would be acceptable to a large number of Member States, and the inclusion of political groups was simply too contentious to risk. Even Lemkin, who had procedural doubts about the inclusion of political groups since the Secretariat draft, had reconciled himself to the reality that its inclusion would be an obstacle to the Convention. In his words: "I thought the destruction of political opponents should be treated as the crime of political homicide, not as genocide."[101]

Second, Article II enumerates the five acts of genocide: (1) killing members of the group, (2) causing serious bodily or mental harm to members of the group, (3) deliberately inflicting on the group conditions of life calculated to bring about its physical destruction in whole or in part, (4) imposing measures intended to prevent births within the group, or (5) forcibly transferring children of the group to another group. As Article II clearly explains, genocide means "any" of the listed acts, not "most" and certainly not "all" of the acts. An allegation of genocide is supported when any one of the five acts has been committed with the intent to destroy, in whole or in part, a national, ethnical, racial, or religious group, as such. The Sixth Committee struggled with whether to adopt a general flexible definition of genocide or explicitly enumerate specific acts of genocide. To say that genocide consists of any one act is to run the risk that other acts are omitted, or to lose the spirit of Lemkin's original conception of genocide as a "synchronized attack." Eventually, however, the principle of enumeration carried the day. The resulting list of acts was a significantly diluted version of the definition of genocide—including physical, biological, and cultural genocide—offered in the original Secretariat draft as written by the three experts and still appearing, in a reduced form, in the Ad Hoc Committee draft.

Although each of the acts of genocide in Article II was the subject of much definitional discussion and revision during the drafting process, the concept of "mental harm" had been particularly contentious. The words "or mental" had not appeared in the 1948 draft of the Ad Hoc Committee, despite China's insistence that such reference be included to cover the use of narcotic drugs as an instrument of genocide. The Chinese representative, Lin Mousheng, alleged that, during World War II, the Japanese "built a huge opium extraction plant" in the Manchurian city of Mukden and "intended to commit, and did commit, genocide by narcotics . . . the most sinister and monstrous conspiracy known in history."[102] Undeterred by their failure in the Ad Hoc Committee, China reintroduced a similar amendment during the Sixth Committee deliberations. Although that amendment was again defeated, a subsequent amendment proposed by India—adding "or mental" after the word "physical" (which would become "bodily" later in the drafting process)—was, curiously, narrowly adopted.[103] Though India's amendment did not include any particular reference to the use of drugs, the report of the Sixth Committee clearly indicates that the insertion of the words "or mental" encompasses "the desirability of including acts of genocide committed through the use of narcotics."[104]

In addition, the Sixth Committee had opted to exclude cultural genocide (an idea "very dear" to Lemkin) from the scope of the convention, though it did allow the compromise inclusion of forcible transfer of children as a punishable act.[105] This specific act was originally classified under the heading of cultural genocide in the 1947 Secretariat draft, before disappearing from the Ad Hoc Committee draft the following year. Ultimately, the Sixth Committee chose to support the inclusion of this act of genocide, from an amendment submitted by the representative of Greece, on the grounds "that the forced transfer of children had physical and biological effects since it imposed on young persons conditions of life likely to cause them serious harm or even death . . . The forced transfer of children could be as effective a means of destroying a human group as that of imposing measures intended to prevent births or inflicting conditions of life likely to cause death."[106] By forcibly placing children in another group, their original cultural identities are erased and replaced by new ones; in essence, this can be understood as cultural destruction, or acculturation by force.

Discussion around the exclusion of "cultural genocide" by name was spirited. Some thought the cultural essence of a group could be better protected through international human rights or minorities treaties. Others countered with the argument that cultural genocide was complementary to physical genocide; to not protect language, schools, books, shrines, places of worship, and historical monuments was to deny the reality that a group could be eliminated by the destruction of its culture. There was enough dissension that most could agree on one fundamental reality— retaining cultural genocide could pose a substantial risk to the passage of the convention. Unfortunately, Lemkin's key comparative insight—that there are many ways to destroy a group—was jettisoned for hope of a smooth passage of the resolution through the General Assembly.[107]

For the third conceptual issue, we turn to Article VI. Where Lemkin's 1933 proposal had advocated for a principle of universal "repression" or jurisdiction in which the crime of genocide could be prosecuted by any State, even in the absence of a territorial or personal link, the drafters of the Genocide Convention followed the Ad Hoc Committee draft in explicitly rejecting this principle and recognizing only territorial jurisdiction. As Article VI states: "Persons charged with genocide . . . shall be tried by a competent tribunal of the State in the territory of which the act was committed." As Van Schaack points out, choosing territorial over universal jurisdiction virtually guarantees impunity for perpetrators of genocide, because states will rarely prosecute their own.[108] Article VI went on to suggest that the crime of genocide may be tried by an "international penal tribunal as may have jurisdiction with respect to those Contracting Parties which shall have accepted its jurisdiction." This clause would eventually be fulfilled, nearly 50 years later, in the creation of ad hoc international tribunals to deal with genocides in the former Yugoslavia and Rwanda as well as the adoption of the Rome Statute of the International Criminal Court.

Though passed in 1948, the Genocide Convention would become operative in law only after a sufficient number of domestic ratifications (20) by Member States. Lemkin's work was far from done as he continued to lobby countries for ratification, often borrowing money to invite representatives to lunch. Meeting resistance from several major powers, he refocused his attention on small nations because they "need the protection of international law more than big nations."[109] Ethiopia was the first country to ratify the Convention on July 1, 1949. Australia followed on July 8, Norway on July 22, and Iceland on August 29. Lemkin also enlisted the support of religious leaders, foreign offices, and widely read newspapers and magazines in a broader campaign to mobilize popular support for ratification of the convention.

Finally, on October 16, 1950, the number of domestic ratifications surpassed what was needed for the Convention to come into effect. Article XIII of the Convention stipulated that the Convention "shall come into force on the ninetieth day following the date of deposit of the twentieth instrument of ratification." At that point—January 12, 1951—the Genocide Convention became codified in international law, binding on those nations that signed it. Just months later, the International Court of Justice issued an Advisory Opinion in which it asserted that the principles underlying the Convention are binding on all states, including those that have not ratified the Genocide Convention.[110] Samantha Power reminds us that the passage of the Genocide Convention enshrined, at least in principle, a new political reality—"states would no longer have the legal right to be left alone."[111] Political scientist Kathryn Sikkink goes further in viewing the Convention as the foundation for the development of a new norm—what she calls a "justice cascade"—that gave legitimacy and strength to the emerging notion that state officials, including heads of state, should be held criminally accountable for human rights violations.[112]

Following its passage, however, several major powers remained reluctant to ratify the Genocide Convention. The Soviet Union did so in 1954, but Britain only in 1970, and the United States not until 1988. Why? At the heart of the reluctance, as it had been for many countries since the initial resolution, was the issue of state sovereignty. As William Schabas points out, "states were being asked to accept an unprecedented encroachment on their sovereignty, namely, the existence of international obligations with respect to their treatment of civilians of their own nationality within their own borders."[113] Under the banner of state sovereignty, simply put, some states wanted to retain "the legal right to be left alone." The Soviet Union certainly did not want any investigation into Stalin's policies and practices any more than the United States wanted any investigation into Jim Crow laws and racial segregation. Britain and France certainly had no interest in anyone examining their historical human rights record in Kenya, Malaysia, Vietnam, and Algeria.

In all of this, however, most disturbing to Lemkin was the reluctance of his adopted country, the United States, to ratify the Convention. The United States was the first signatory on December 11, 1948. On June 16, 1949, President Truman had originally transmitted the Genocide Convention for the Senate's approval. He called on U.S. senators to outlaw the "world-shocking crime of genocide" because America had "long been a symbol of freedom and democratic progress to peoples."[114] Lemkin recognized the profound importance of U.S. ratification of the Convention. "Ratification by the United States is of particular importance," he wrote in 1951. "Without it, the Genocide Convention might well share the fate of the old League of Nations."[115]

Despite their signatory status and Truman's ringing endorsement—and Lemkin's relentless pursuit for Senate ratification of the Convention, with support from activist groups such as the American Jewish Committee and the U.S. Committee for a UN Genocide Convention—U.S. ratification would be frustrated at every turn. Some of the obstacles came from distracting fates of history, such as the outbreak of war in Korea in 1950 and the McCarthy hearings later that decade, which monopolized the attention of both policymakers and the public. Other obstacles came from the inherently vague nature of the Convention text itself, much of which will be discussed in Chapter 2. Still other obstacles were roused by the personal presence of Lemkin himself, which seemed to trigger antisemitic prejudice among some respondents. New Jersey Senator Alexander Smith, for instance, complained that the "biggest propagandist" for the Convention was "a man who comes from a foreign country and who speaks broken English." Although "sympathetic with the Jewish people," Smith argued that "they ought not to be the ones who are propagandizing [for the Convention] and they are."[116] The largest obstacle, however, would be state sovereignty and the desire of some U.S. legislators to protect "the legal right to be left alone."

For the United States, the conceptual issue of state sovereignty was problematized in the specific reality of racial segregation. Long-standing U.S. Representative Emanual Cellar (D-NY), for example, raised the question of whether a charge of genocide could be brought against a signatory country in the case of "a mob for a lynching, say, in Mississippi?" And, if so, would the United States agree to extradite the citizens involved for trial in another country? Cellar answered his own question: "The answer is yes. That is quite serious. That may involve yielding of some sovereignty."[117] Southern senators feared that the Convention was a back-door method of enacting federal antilynching legislation, or might even allow the UN to prosecute lynchers who had already been acquitted in U.S. courts. Although, as Samantha Power argued, "only a widely exaggerated reading" of the Convention, which was not retroactive, could have left southern lawmakers vulnerable to genocide charges, the fears remained real—and exploitable—nonetheless.[118]

These fears were amplified in 1951 with the publication by the Civil Rights Congress (CRC) of *We Charge Genocide: The Crime of Government Against the Negro People.*[119] The 238-page petition opens, following the title page, with an undated full-page photograph of the lynching of "two young Negro men" in Columbus, Mississippi—Dooley Morton and Bret Moore. The photograph is titled "The Face of Genocide." Two pages later, there is a reproduction of Articles II and III of the Genocide Convention. The petitioners—including notables such as W. E. B. Du Bois, William Patterson, and Paul Robeson—argued "that the oppressed Negro citizens of the United States, segregated, discriminated against and long the target of violence, suffer from genocide as the result of the consistent, conscious, unified policies of every branch of government."[120] The petition "scrupulously kept within the purview of the Convention on the Prevention and Punishment of the Crime of Genocide" with voluminous documentation of atrocities, beginning in 1945, tied specifically to Articles II and III of the Convention itself.[121] In the words of their closing summary: "Thus it was easy for your petitioners to offer abundant proof of the crime. It is everywhere in American life." The petition concludes by asking "that the General Assembly of the United Nations find and declare by resolution that the Government of the United States is guilty of the crime of Genocide against the Negro People of the United States and that it further demand that the government of the United States stop and prevent the crime of genocide."[122]

In December 1951, a delegation led by Robeson presented the petition to the UN Secretariat in New York while, at the same time, Patterson was presenting the petition to the UN General Assembly in Paris. In the end, given the strength of U.S. influence (particularly in the person of Eleanor Roosevelt, first chairperson of the UN Human Rights Commission, who dismissed the petition as "ridiculous"), the General Assembly of the UN never gave serious consideration to its adoption.[123] Despite that failure, *We Charge Genocide* was well received throughout Europe, adding to an increasing global awareness about the magnitude of racial problems in the United States.[124] It also found a receptive ear among pro-Soviet commentators as well as many blacks in America.[125] The reception among powerholders in the United States, however, was decidedly less enthusiastic, in part because of the well-known communist ties within the CRC. Critics dismissed the petition as mere Communist propaganda, suggesting that Americans who voiced such complaints were "disloyal."[126]

Similarly, perceiving that his Convention (dangerously close to becoming his alter ego) was irresponsibly misapplied by a fringe group, Lemkin hostilely accused Patterson and Robeson of being "un-American" elements serving a foreign power.[127] Later, in a June 14, 1953 op-ed piece for the *New York Times*, a still-irritated Lemkin argued that blacks, although they might experience discrimination, had not suffered the "essence of genocide—destruction, death, annihilation."[128] "To be unequal," Lemkin wrote," is not the same as to be dead."[129] In *We Charge Genocide*, Lemkin saw discrimination, not destruction. He went even further to make the dubious, and ill-founded, assertion that, if anything, blacks in the United States had conditions of increasing prosperity and progress.

Certainly, Lemkin's reaction to *We Charge Genocide* raises questions about his attitudes to black history and people. In his analysis of Lemkin's view of colonial rule in Africa, historian Dominik Schaller argues that "the way Lemkin has perceived Africans can only be described as racist."[130] Similarly, Dirk Moses writes of "Lemkin's status as a white male member of the European legal elite that condoned empire while criticizing its excesses."[131] Those depictions of his mindset, although perhaps contestable, may help us understand some of Lemkin's reaction to *We Charge*

Genocide. We also, though, should recognize that Lemkin saw discrimination and prejudice as individual, rather than group, problems. As such, in his mind, they were better addressed by the Universal Declaration of Human Rights than by the Genocide Convention. Perhaps most important, however, in understanding Lemkin's reaction to *We Charge Genocide* is his well-placed fear that allegations of genocide against the United States would be yet one more reason to delay, or even prohibit, American ratification of the Convention.

The racial charges of genocide against the United States, raised by the Civil Rights Congress in 1951, would reappear the following decade in debate surrounding U.S. involvement in Vietnam. In 1967, Jean-Paul Sartre, in his famous essay, "On Genocide," argued that U.S. actions in Vietnam were directly culpable in terms of Article II of the Genocide Convention.[132] For Sartre, genocidal intent was implicit in the facts of U.S. activities in Vietnam. Echoing the arguments in *We Charge Genocide*, Sartre even suggested that American policymakers tolerated atrocities against the Vietnamese because similar practices were tolerated against American blacks.[133] In late 1967, Bertrand Russell's International War Crimes Tribunal, of which Sartre was executive president, unanimously declared the United States guilty of the crime of genocide in Vietnam.

These reactions, on the heels of the Red Scare at home and in the midst of Cold War considerations abroad, effectively stopped Senate consideration of ratification of the Convention. Proisolationist arguments defending against any infringement on American sovereignty carried the day. Ultrarightest lobbying groups, such as the antisemitic Liberty Lobby and the conservative John Birch Society, fanned the flames against the Convention by characterizing it as a "vicious communist perversion." In its weekly tabloid, the *Spotlight*, the Liberty Lobby claimed that ratification of the Convention would allow missionaries to be tried before an international tribunal for genocide "on grounds that to convert cannibals in Africa to Christianity is to destroy a culture."[134]

Despite such widespread, and spectacularly misinformed, opposition, one man—Senator William Proxmire (D-WI)—remained committed to the passage of the Genocide Convention. On January 11, 1967, Proxmire declared that "the Senate's failure to act [to ratify the Convention] has become a national shame . . . I serve notice today that from now on I intend to speak day after day in this body to remind the Senate of our failure to act."[135] And speak day after day he did. On the Senate floor, Proxmire would give 3,211 speeches over a 19-year period urging the United States to ratify the Genocide Convention. Proxmire's speech-a-day approach to ratification (each speech had to be an original), although persistent, was not terribly effectual. Civilians died by the thousands in massacres in Nigeria, Bangladesh, Burundi, Cambodia, and elsewhere as Proxmire's daily soliloquies fell on deaf ears in a largely disinterested Senate chamber.

In April 1985, however, when President Reagan visited the Bitburg Military Cemetery in West Germany, a burial ground containing the graves of 49 Nazi Waffen SS officials, the resulting backlash would prove favorable for a renewal of the Senate discussion of the Genocide Convention. In 1984, Reagan had changed his preexisting position and decided to endorse (in a very passive sense) the Convention—joining the endorsements of every other president since Truman, with the exception of Dwight Eisenhower. Now, however, to quell the outrage of his poorly conceived visit to Bitburg (he infamously claimed that the German soldiers were "victims" of the Nazis "just as surely as the victims in the concentration camps"), Reagan had the political necessity to actively push for immediate ratification of the Convention. As recounted by Samantha Power, Harold Koh, a lawyer at the U.S. Department of Justice, said: "Bitburg wasn't *a* reason for the shift, it was the only reason."[136]

At long last, on February 19, 1986, the U.S. Senate voted 83 to 11 (six abstentions) in favor of making the United States the 98th nation to approve ratification of the Genocide Convention—38 years after it was approved by the UN General Assembly, 35 years after it officially entered into force, and 19 years after Proxmire began his speech-a-day activism. Senate Majority Leader Bob Dole (R-KS), claiming the high moral ground, said "We have waited long enough."[137] In truth, however, ratification did not come because the Senate had grown a conscience related to the Convention, rather it came because amends had to be made for Reagan's political misstep and ratification of the Convention was the most logical and accessible means to do so. Moreover, to protect U.S. state sovereignty, approval came only after agreement on a carefully worded set of "reservations, understandings, and declarations" that effectively rendered the ratification a symbolic act. The "sovereignty package" of attached disclaimers—two reservations, five understandings, and a declaration—allowed the United States to immunize itself from being charged with genocide by an international court. Under the doctrine of reciprocity, this also meant that the United States was effectively blocked from ever filing genocide charges in an international court against another perpetrator state. In essence, the Senate did not see ratification to the Convention as meaningfully binding in any significant way. As Senator Jesse Helms (R-NC), a leading framer of the sovereignty package that eviscerated the Convention, proudly crowed: "We might as well be voting on a simple resolution to condemn genocide—which every civilized person does."[138]

The final American legislation needed to implement the now-ratified convention was passed on January 25, 1988. However, it was not until October 1988 that the Senate finally passed the Genocide Convention Implementation Act, which was named the "Proxmire Act." On November 4, 1988, at a brief ceremony in a hangar at a rainy O'Hare Airport outside Chicago, President Ronald Reagan, crediting Lemkin for his seminal role, signed the act into law. Reagan, transparently seeking to regain political favor with Jews still angered by his blunder at Bitburg, said: "I am delighted to fulfill the promise made by Harry Truman to all the peoples of the world—and especially the Jewish people."[139] Proxmire, nearing the end of his Senate career, did not attend the signing, though the White House said he was invited. Genocide was now a punishable offense under U.S. federal law, though several countries lodged formal objections to many of the reservations included in the sovereignty package.

All told, the Genocide Convention stands as one of the most widely accepted treaties in international relations. In Lemkin's words, it is "a treaty for the people."[140] At present, 147 states have ratified or acceded to the Genocide Convention (once the treaty was closed for signature on January 12, 1951, states that did not sign the treaty can now only accede to it). The most recent accessions came from the State of Palestine on April 2, 2014, Malta on June 6, 2014, and Tajikistan on November 3, 2015. On December 11, 1948, the Dominican Republic signed the treaty but has yet to ratify it. Nearly 50 states are not yet parties to the Genocide Convention. On April 16, 2014, 20 years after the genocide in Rwanda, a unanimously adopted UN Security Council resolution called for universal ratification of the Genocide Convention by challenging "States that have not yet ratified or acceded to the Convention . . . to consider doing so as a matter of high priority."[141]

Lemkin was nominated for a Nobel Peace Prize repeatedly throughout the 1950s, though he never won. He did receive the Grand Cross of Cespedes from Cuba in 1950, the Stephen Wise Award of the American Jewish Congress in 1951, and the Cross of Merit of the Federal Republic of Germany in 1955. Despite this minor celebrity, however, Lemkin pretty well faded from public view after the ratification of the Genocide Convention in 1951. He was plagued by poor health, particularly high blood pressure, and lived an indigent life marked by piles of unsorted papers, poverty, hunger, and a few moth-eaten clothes. Lemkin "appears to have been one of Kafka's hunger artists, those moving, self-punishing creatures who cut themselves off from the world, preyed upon by a guilt they cannot name, making their misery into their life's work . . . His work on genocide finally became a trap from which he could not—and in the end did not wish to—escape."[142]

On August 28, 1959, after a heart attack at a bus stop on 42nd Street in New York City, Lemkin was taken to the nearest police station, where he died. He never lived to see a conviction for the crime to which he had given a name. Lemkin, who once described loneliness as "an essential condition of my life," passed away as he had lived for much of his life—alone.[143] The closing sentence in his *New York Times* obituary read succinctly: "He was a bachelor."[144] Having lost most of his family in the Holocaust and alienating many of his friends over the years with his "self-lacerating obsession," Lemkin's funeral would draw only seven people.[145] The celebration of his life did not even draw a minyan. Lemkin is buried in Mt. Hebron Cemetery in Queens, New York with a headstone that reads "The Father of the Genocide Convention."

Today, however, Lemkin is rightly recognized as one of the heroes in human rights history. In 2001, on the 50th anniversary of the Convention entering into force, Lemkin was honored by then-UN Secretary-General Kofi Annan as "an inspiring example of moral engagement."[146] Poland's Ministry of Foreign Affairs, under the leadership of Adam Rotfeld, named a conference room after him in 2005 and then mounted a commemorative plaque on the house in which Lemkin had lived in Warsaw.[147] Each year, T'ruah, The Rabbinic Call for Human Rights, grants a Raphael Lemkin Human Rights Award to preeminent leaders in the human rights field. Every other year, the Institute for the Study of Genocide grants the Lemkin Book Award for the best scholarly book in genocide studies. Several times a year, I develop the curriculum for, and teach in, the Raphael Lemkin Seminars for Genocide Prevention. Hosted by the Auschwitz Institute for Peace and Reconciliation, and held on the grounds of the Auschwitz-Birkenau State Museum in Poland, these seminars embody Lemkin's determination to build a worldwide network of government policymakers committed to the prevention of genocide.

Lemkin's story is one of an idea and a word. Due, in large part, to his single-minded activism, Churchill's "crime without a name" now has a name and that name is "genocide." Lemkin's legacy reminds us that words matter, names matter, and labels matter. We are also reminded, though, that naming a crime is not the same as eliminating it. As Lemkin once explained to a class of law students, the Convention was a "framework . . . a rallying point for thinking and acting. A starting point for a new conscience!"[148] And since its passage, it has stimulated much thinking—and controversy—about the word "genocide" and, unfortunately, far less acting about its reality and even less embodiment of a new conscience for humanity.

NOTES

1. Richard Rhodes, *Masters of Death: The SS-Einsatzgruppen and the Invention of the Holocaust* (New York, NY: Alfred A. Knopf, 2002), xi. Gas vans were also used for some of the killing operations by the Einsatzgruppen.
2. For additional details, see Richard Breitman, *Official Secrets* (New York, NY: Hill & Wang, 1998).
3. Winston Churchill, *Never Give In! The Best of Winston Churchill's Speeches* (New York, NY: Hyperion, 2003), 297–300. Also accessed July 15, 2013 at http://www.ibiblio.org/pha/timeline/410824awp.html.
4. For further reading about the activities of the Einsatzgruppen, I recommend Chapter 7 in Raul Hilberg's *The Destruction of the European Jews* (New York, NY: Holmes & Meier, 1985). An abridged version of the same work can be found in his one-volume student edition of the same name, also published by Holmes & Meier (1985). The *Historical Atlas of the Holocaust*, published by the United States Holocaust Memorial Museum (New York, NY: Macmillan, 1996), includes several helpful maps on the invasion of the Soviet Union and the murderous activities of the Einsatzgruppen (pp. 50–53). Martin Dean's *Collaboration in the Holocaust: Crimes of the Local Police in Belorussia and Ukraine, 1941–44* (New York, NY: St. Martin's Press, 2000) extends the discussion beyond the killing activities of the Einsatzgruppen to local collaborators who actively implemented Nazi genocide in Belorussia and Ukraine. Finally, Father Patrick Desbois' *The Holocaust by Bullets* (New York, NY: Palgrave Macmillan, 2008) offers a fascinating account of his race to identify the mass graves of victims killed by the Einsatzgruppen. The quote "no architecture of destruction" is taken from Paul Shapiro's introduction to that book (p. viii).
5. For those desiring a more detailed biographical account, I strongly recommend John Cooper's *Raphael Lemkin and the Struggle for the Genocide Convention* (New York, NY: Palgrave MacMillan, 2008) and William Korey's *An Epitaph for Raphael Lemkin* (New York, NY: Jacob Blaustein Institute for the Advancement of Human Rights, 2001). Lemkin's major archival papers are spread across three institutions in the United States—the Jacob Marcus Rader Center of the American Jewish Archives in Cincinnati, Ohio (donated 1965), the American Jewish Historical Society at the Center for Jewish History in New York City (donated 1975), and the 42nd Street Branch of the New York Public Library in New York City (donated 1982). There are at least three versions, one typed and two handwritten, of his incomplete and unpublished autobiography, *Totally Unofficial*, begun about 1951. The most complete copy was donated to the New York Public Library in August 1982. There, in the Manuscripts and Archives Division, *Totally Unofficial* can be found in Box 1, Folders 35–43 (Accession #83 M 39). Although I have worked often with those materials, I've chosen to reference selections from Lemkin's autobiography from Donna-Lee Frieze's authoritative *Totally Unofficial: The Autobiography of Raphael Lemkin* (New Haven, CT: Yale University Press, 2013). For the general reader, this is a much more accessible, and readable, source than the original papers and is the most current transcription of Lemkin's unpublished autobiography.
6. Frieze, *Totally Unofficial*, 3.
7. Ibid, 1.
8. A. Dirk Moses, "Genocide," *Australian Humanities Review* 55 (2013): 31.
9. Frieze, *Totally Unofficial*, 19.
10. Peter Balakian, *The Burning Tigris: The Armenian Genocide and America's Response* (New York, NY: Perennial, 2003), 345.

11. Frieze, *Totally Unofficial*, 20.
12. Samantha Power, *"A Problem From Hell:" America and the Age of Genocide* (New York, NY: Perennial, 2002), 17.
13. Adam Strom (ed.), *Totally Unofficial: Raphael Lemkin and the Genocide Convention* (Brookline, MA: Facing History and Ourselves, 2007), 3.
14. Frieze, *Totally Unofficial*, 20.
15. Ibid, 21.
16. Cooper, *Raphael Lemkin*, 21.
17. Strom, *Raphael Lemkin and the Genocide Convention*, 10.
18. Raphael Lemkin, "Acts Constituting a General (Transnational) Danger Considered as Offences Against the Law of Nations," Special Report presented to the 5th Conference for the Unification of Penal Law in Madrid (October 14–20, 1933), accessed August 1, 2013, http://www.preventgenocide.org/lemkin/madrid1933-english.htm.
19. Ibid.
20. Ibid.
21. Ibid.
22. Ibid.
23. Power, *A Problem from Hell*, 22.
24. Frieze, *Totally Unofficial*, 24.
25. Power, *A Problem from Hell*, 22.
26. Jean-Paul Sartre, "On Genocide," eds. Richard A. Falk, Gabriel Kolko, and Robert Jay Lifton, *Crimes of War* (New York, NY: Random House, 1971), 534.
27. Philip Spencer, *Genocide Since 1945* (New York, NY: Routledge, 2012), 17.
28. Quote on "the most important force" comes from Joshua S. Goldstein and Jon C. Pevehouse, *International Relations*, 9th ed. (New York, NY: Longman, 2011), 161; "ersatz religion" comes from Hugh Seton-Watson, *Nations and States: An Enquiry into the Origins of Nations and the Politics of Nationalism* (Boulder, CO: Westview Press, 1977), 465.
29. Walker Connor, "A Nation is a Nation, is an Ethnic Group, is a . . .," eds. John Hutchinson and Anthony D. Smith, *Nationalism* (New York, NY: Oxford University Press, 1994), 361.
30. Michael Ignatieff, *Blood and Belonging: Journeys into the New Nationalism* (New York, NY: The Noonday Press, 1993), 3.
31. Stuart Kaufman, *Modern Hatreds: The Symbolic Politics of Ethnic War* (Ithaca, NY: Cornell University Press, 2001), 25.
32. Andreas Wimmer, "States of War: How the Nation-State Made Modern Conflict," *Foreign Affairs*, accessed November 8, 2013 at http://www.foreignaffairs.com/articles/140245/andreas-wimmer/states-of-war?sp_mid=44308605&sp_rid=andhbGxlckBrZWVuZS5lZHUS1.
33. Omar Bartov, "Introduction," ed. Adam Strom, *Totally Unofficial: Raphael Lemkin and the Genocide Convention* (Boston, MA: Facing History and Ourselves, 2007), ix.
34. Richard W. Mansbach and Kirsten L. Taylor, *Introduction to Global Politics*, 2nd ed. (New York, NY: Routledge, 2012), 50.
35. Wimmer, "States of War."
36. Mark Levene, *Genocide in the Age of the Nation-State* (London, England: I. B. Tauris, 2005), 164.
37. Mark Mazower, "Violence and the State in the Twentieth Century," *American Historical Review* (October 2002): 1177.

38. A. Dirk Moses, "Toward a Theory of Critical Genocide Studies," *Online Encyclopedia of Mass Violence*, [online], published April 18, 2008, accessed July 8, 2014, http://www.massviolence.org/Toward-a-Theory-of-Critical-Genocide-Studies?decoupe_recherche=toward%20a%20theory%20of%20critical%20genocide%20studies&artpage=3#outil_sommaire_1.

39. Vamik Volkan, *Blood Lines: From Ethnic Pride to Ethnic Terrorism* (New York, NY: Farrar, Straus, and Giroux, 1997), 23.

40. Benedict Anderson, *Imagined Communities: Reflections on the Origin and Spread of Nationalism* (London, England: Verso, 1983), 6.

41. Alex Alvarez, *Governments, Citizens, and Genocide* (Bloomington, IN: Indiana University Press, 2001), 64.

42. Bartov, "Introduction," ix.

43. Ibid.

44. Martin Shaw, *What Is Genocide?* (Cambridge, England: Polity, 2007), 136.

45. See Richard Rubenstein's *The Cunning of History: The Holocaust and the American Future* (New York, NY: Harper & Row, 1978).

46. Bartov, "Introduction," x.

47. Nancy Scheper-Hughes, "Coming to Our Senses: Anthropology and Genocide," ed. Alex Hinton, *Annihilating Difference: The Anthropology of Genocide* (Berkeley, CA: University of California Press, 2002), 366.

48. Zygmunt Bauman, *Modernity and the Holocaust* (Ithaca, NY: Cornell University Press, 1989), 7.

49. Mark Levene, "Why Is the Twentieth Century the Century of Genocide?," *Journal of World History* 2 (2000).

50. Alvarez, *Governments, Citizens, and Genocide*, 67–68.

51. Charles S. Maier, "Consigning the Twentieth Century to History: Alternative Narratives for the Modern Era," *American Historical Review* 105 (2000): 812.

52. Cooper, *Raphael Lemkin*, 25.

53. Much of this timeline is drawn from Cooper's *Raphael Lemkin and the Struggle for the Genocide Convention*.

54. Frieze, *Totally Unofficial*, 115.

55. Quoted material in two sentences taken from Frieze, *Totally Unofficial*, 115–116.

56. Raphael Lemkin, *Axis Rule in Occupied Europe: Laws of Occupation, Analysis of Government, Proposals for Redress* (Washington, DC: Carnegie Endowment for International Peace, Division of International Law, 1944).

57. Lemkin, *Axis Rule*, 79.

58. Thomas M. Butcher, "A 'Synchronized Attack': On Raphael Lemkin's Holistic Conception of Genocide," *Journal of Genocide Research* 15 (2013): 253–271; see also A. Dirk Moses, "Lemkin, Culture, and the Concept of Genocide," eds. Donald Bloxham and A. Dirk Moses, *The Oxford Handbook of Genocide Studies* (New York, NY: Oxford University Press, 2010), 34.

59. Douglas Irvin-Erickson, "Genocide, the 'Family of Mind' and the Romantic Signature of Raphael Lemkin," *Journal of Genocide Research* 15 (2013): 273–296.

60. Stuart D. Stein, "Conceptions and Terms: Templates for the Analysis of Holocaust and Genocides," *Journal of Genocide Research* 7 (2005): 180.

61. John Q. Barrett, "Raphael Lemkin and 'Genocide' at Nuremberg, 1945–1946," eds. Christoph Safferling and Eckart Conze, *The Genocide Convention Sixty Years After Its Adoption* (The Hague, Netherlands: Asser Press, 2010), 39.

62. Frieze, *Totally Unofficial*, 118.

63. William A. Schabas, "The 'Odious Scourge': Evolving Interpretations of the Crime of Genocide," *Genocide Studies and Prevention* 1 (2006): 95.
64. Korey, *An Epitaph*, 25.
65. David L. Nersessian, "The Contours of Genocidal Intent: Troubling Jurisprudence from the International Criminal Tribunals," *Texas International Law Journal* 37 (2002).
66. New York Public Library, "Raphael Lemkin Papers, 1947–1959," Reel 2, Box 1, Folder 36, "Writings-Autobiography," "Chapters 1–4," p. 3.
67. Korey, *An Epitaph*, 26.
68. "Genocide," *Washington Post*, December 3, 1944, B4.
69. Frieze, *Totally Unofficial*, 129.
70. A video of Barnett's quote can be found in Fritz Mitchell's *Ghosts of Ole Miss* (ESPN Films, 2012).
71. Frieze, *Totally Unofficial*, 122.
72. UN Document A/C.6/SR.22, November 22, 1946.
73. Schabas, "The 'Odious Scourge': Evolving Interpretations of the Crime of Genocide," 96.
74. UN General Assembly, Fifty-Fifth Plenary Meeting, UN Document A/RES/96 (I), December 11, 1946, 188–189.
75. Howard Shneider, "Political Genocide in Latin America: The Need for Reconsidering the Current Internationally Accepted Definition of Genocide in Light of Spanish and Latin American Jurisprudence," *American University International Law Review* 25 (2010): 318.
76. The three principal drafts of the Convention are reproduced in their entirety in William A. Schabas, *Genocide in International Law: The Crime of Crimes*, 2nd ed. (Cambridge, England: Cambridge University Press, 2009), 655–671.
77. Quoted material is taken from the United Nations Economic and Social Council, "Draft Convention on the Crime of Genocide" (UN Document E/447), June 26, 1947, 47.
78. Ibid, 38.
79. Cited in Schabas, *Genocide in International Law*, 167–168.
80. Cooper, *Raphael Lemkin*, 124.
81. Ibid, 151.
82. Power, *A Problem from Hell*, 61.
83. Frieze, *Totally Unofficial*, 135.
84. Ibid, 151.
85. Ibid.
86. Jay Winter, "Prophet Without Honors," *The Chronicle of Higher Education* (June 3, 2013), accessed July 22, 2013 at http://chronicle.com/article/article-content/139515.
87. Hilary Earl, "Prosecuting Genocide before the Genocide Convention: Raphael Lemkin and the Nuremberg Trials, 1945–1949," *Journal of Genocide Research* 15 (2013): 323.
88. Ibid, 318.
89. A. M. Rosenthal, "On My Mind: A Man Called Lemkin," *New York Times*, October 18, 1988, A31, accessed July 22, 2013, http://www.nytimes.com/1988/10/18/opinion/on-my-mind-a-man-called-lemkin.html?pagewanted=print&src=pm.
90. Tanya Elder, "What You See Before Your Eyes: Documenting Raphael Lemkin's Life by Exploring His Archival Papers, 1900–1959," *Journal of Genocide Research* 7 (2005): 481.

91. Ana Filipa Vrdoljak, "Human Rights and Genocide: The Work of Lauterpacht and Lemkin in Modern International Law," *The European Journal of International Law* 20 (2010), 1163–1194.
92. Rosenthal, "On My Mind."
93. Frieze, *Totally Unofficial*, 179.
94. The complete text can be found at http://www.hrweb.org/legal/genocide.html, accessed January 23, 2011.
95. UN General Assembly, Report of the Sixth Committee, UN Document A/760, December 3, 1948, 2.
96. Ibid, 7.
97. Beth Van Schaack, "The Crime of Political Genocide: Repairing the Genocide Convention's Blind Spot," *The Yale Law Journal* 106 (1996): 2268.
98. Norman M. Naimark, *Stalin's Genocides* (Princeton, NJ: Princeton University Press, 2010), 22.
99. Frieze, *Totally Unofficial*, 161.
100. UN General Assembly, Sixth Committee Summary Records of Meetings, UN Document A/C.6/SR.128, November 29, 1948, 662.
101. Frieze, *Totally Unofficial*, 161.
102. UN Document E/794 (May 24, 1948), 15.
103. The chain of events during the deliberation is described in Stephen Gorove, "The Problem of 'Mental Harm' in the Genocide Convention," *Washington University Law Quarterly* (1951), 174–187.
104. UN Document A/760 (December 3, 1948), paragraph 10.
105. Frieze, *Totally Unofficial*, 172.
106. UN Document E/CN.4/Sub.2/416, July 4, 1978, paragraph 90.
107. In 1981, the United Nations Educational, Scientific, and Cultural Organization (UNESCO) would define ethnocide as meaning "…that an ethnic group is denied the right to enjoy, develop and transmit its own culture and its own language … We declare that ethnocide, that is, cultural genocide, is a violation of international law equivalent to genocide." See "UNESCO and the Struggle against Ethnocide: Declaration of San Jose" (December 1981), accessed August 28, 2014 at http://unesdoc.unesco.org/images/0004/000499/049951eo.pdf.
108. Van Schaack, "The Crime of Political Genocide," 2266.
109. Frieze, *Totally Unofficial*, 187.
110. Remarks titled "Enforcing the Genocide Convention," from a keynote speech given by the Hon. Judge Theodor Meron, Berlin, Germany (May 12, 2011).
111. Power, *"A Problem from Hell,"* 58.
112. Kathryn Sikkink, *The Justice Cascade: How Human Rights Prosecutions Are Changing World Politics* (New York, NY: Norton, 2011).
113. Schabas, "Evolving Interpretations of the Crime of Genocide," 102.
114. Cited in Power, *"A Problem from Hell,"* 64.
115. Korey, *An Epitaph*, 72.
116. Lawrence J. LeBlanc, *The United States and the Genocide Convention* (Durham, NC: Duke University Press, 1991), 20.
117. Elder, "What You See Before Your Eyes," 484.
118. Power, *"A Problem from Hell,"* 67.
119. Civil Rights Congress, *We Charge Genocide: The Crime of Government Against the Negro People* (New York, NY: Civil Rights Congress, 1951).
120. Civil Rights Congress, *We Charge Genocide*, xi.
121. Ibid, xii.

122. Ibid, 195, 196.

123. William Patterson, *The Man Who Cried Genocide* (New York, NY: International Publishers, 1971), 206.

124. See John Docker, "Raphael Lemkin, Creator of the Concept of Genocide: A World History Perspective," *Humanities Research* 16 (2010), accessed March 23, 2014 at http://press.anu.edu.au/apps/bookworm/view/Humanities+Research+Vol+ XVI.+No.+2.+2010/5271/docker.xhtml.

125. This receptive ear continued for decades and still lingers today. For instance, a 1979 "Themes in Twentieth Century American Culture" curriculum unit authored by the Yale-New Haven Teachers Institute included a chapter titled "The Negro Holocaust: Lynching and Race Riots in the United States, 1880–1950" (accessed October 5, 2014 at http://www.yale.edu/ynhti/curriculum/ units/1979/2/79.02.04.x.html). Even today, the petition still resonates. "We Charge Genocide" is the name of a grassroots, intergenerational effort to center the voices and experiences of the young people most targeted by police violence in Chicago, Illinois. The organization, whose title pays intentional homage to the petition, aims to confront the targeted repression, harassment, and brutality disproportionately faced by low-income people and young people of color.

126. Charles H. Martin, "Internationalizing 'The American Dilemma': The Civil Rights Congress and the 1951 Genocide Petition to the United Nations," *Journal of American Ethnic History* 16 (1997).

127. Patterson, *The Man Who Cried Genocide*, 191.

128. Raphael Lemkin, "Nature of Genocide," *New York Times*, June 14, 1953.

129. Cited in Elder, "What You See Before Your Eyes," 487.

130. Dominik Schaller, "Lemkin's View of Colonial Rule in Africa," *Journal of Genocide Research* 7 (2005): 536.

131. Moses, "Genocide," 36.

132. Jean-Paul Sartre, *On Genocide, and a Summary of the Evidence and the Judgments of the International War Crimes Tribunal* (Boston, MA: Beacon Press, 1968).

133. Ann Curthoys and John Docker, "Defining Genocide," ed. Dan Stone, *The Historiography of Genocide* (New York, NY: Palgrave Macmillan, 2010), 25.

134. Quoted material cited in Power, *"A Problem from Hell,"* 135.

135. Cited in Power, *"A Problem from Hell,"* 79.

136. Ibid, 163.

137. Karen Tumulty, "Senate Ratifies Treaty That Outlaws Genocide," *Los Angeles Times*, February 20, 1986.

138. Power, *"A Problem from Hell,"* 166.

139. Steven V. Roberts, "Reagan Signs Bill Ratifying U.N. Genocide Pact," *The New York Times* (November 5, 1988), accessed November 3, 2013 at http://www. nytimes.com/1988/11/05/opinion/reagan-signs-bill-ratifying-un-genocide-pact.html.

140. Raphael Lemkin, "Genocide as a Crime under International Law," *United Nations Bulletin* (January 15, 1948), 71.

141. UN S/RES/2150, "Threats to International Peace and Security," adopted April 16, 2014.

142. Michael Ignatieff, "The Unsung Hero Who Coined the Term 'Genocide'" (September 21, 2013) accessed November 14, 2013 at http://www.newrepublic. com//article/114424/raphael-lemkin-unsung-hero-who-coined-genocide.

143. Frieze, *Totally Unofficial*, 163.

144. "Raphael Lemkin, Genocide Foe, Dies," *The New York Times*, August 30, 1959.

145. Quoted phrase taken from Ignatieff, "The Unsung Hero."
146. United Nations Press Release SG/SM/7842 (June 13, 2001), accessed July 25, 2013 at http://www.un.org/News/Press/docs/2001/sgsm7842.doc.htm.
147. See http://www.ajc.org/site/apps/nlnet/content2.aspx?c=7oJILSPwFfJSG&b= 8479733&ct=1248210, accessed November 14, 2013.
148. Frieze, *Totally Unofficial*, 182.

CHAPTER 2

"By Their Rightful Name"

On April 6, 1994, on return from a regional peace summit in Dar es Salaam, the plane carrying Rwandan President Juvenal Habyarimana was shot down. Extremist members of Habyarimana's Hutu ruling party immediately blamed the assassination on a Tutsi-led paramilitary organization, the Rwandan Patriotic Front (RPF).[1] A clique of extremist Hutu leaders from the military high command seized power and used the pretext of that blame to implement a systematic plan of annihilation throughout Rwanda. In the capital city of Kigali, the killing of political opposition leaders—both Tutsis and moderate Hutus—began moments after the crash, on the basis of preestablished lists with instructions on how to find the victims. By noon the following day, the moderate political leadership of Rwanda was dead or in hiding.[2] The violence quickly spread from Kigali to the countryside, with thousands of Tutsi civilians being slaughtered in one village after another.

The gravity of the crisis was clear within days. As the death toll mounted, many were quick to use Lemkin's word—"genocide"—in describing the violence. On April 19, U.S.-based Human Rights Watch and other organizations approached the United Nations (UN) Security Council with reports from the field and made it clear that these acts constituted genocide. The Paris-based International Federation for Human Rights followed with a similar pronouncement on April 21. On April 23, a *New York Times* editorial began: "What looks very much like genocide has been taking place in Rwanda."[3] On April 27, Pope John Paul used his weekly general audience to "invite all leaders . . . to stop this genocide" in Rwanda.[4] On that same day, the Czechs and Argentines introduced a draft resolution to the UN Security Council that included the term.[5] Oxfam, clergy and missionaries on the ground in Rwanda, Doctors Without Borders, and the

International Committee of the Red Cross were providing reliable and cor-roborating evidence of the ethnic targeting of Tutsi that validated "geno-cide" as the appropriate description.

In the months before the genocide began, cables to the UN Department of Peacekeeping Operations from UN peacekeepers on the ground in Rwanda had warned of impending mass ethnic killings and the urgent need for reinforcements. UN Secretary-General Boutros Boutros-Ghali, in a response called "positively anemic . . . timid, indecisive, and deceitful" by one scholar, failed to inform the Security Council of these reports and ordered the peacekeepers to remain "impartial."[6] It would not be until the genocide was in its second month—with the greatest rate of murder hav-ing already occurred in the first 4 weeks—that Boutros-Ghali would begin using the word in reference to what was happening in Rwanda. On May 4, on ABC's *Nightline*, he finally used the word "genocide" in a public forum. In subsequent reports to the Security Council—the UN "enforcer" and the only principal organ whose resolutions are binding on member states—Boutros-Ghali, trying to affect a public persona of leadership, repeatedly stressed the need for responding to Rwanda.[7] On May 31, he reported to the Security Council that "there can be little doubt that it [Rwanda] consti-tutes genocide."[8] Again, on June 20, he delivered a perfunctory statement expressing "the need for an urgent and coordinated response by the inter-national community to the genocide which has engulfed that country."[9]

Responses from the UN Security Council—which has the authority to resolve international disputes through negotiation, sanctions, and even the use of force—were markedly equivocal.[10] Through April and May 1994, a series of UN Security Council resolutions strongly condemned "the very numerous killings of civilians" and recalled "that the killing of members of an ethnic group with the intention of destroying such a group, in whole or in part, constitutes a crime punishable under international law."[11] Despite its transparent reference in the phrase "a crime punish-able under international law," the word "genocide" appeared in none of the resolutions from the Security Council, each of which concluded with the ironically passive statement that the Security Council decided "to remain actively seized of the matter." There was a clear recognition that nam-ing the "matter" would carry with it an obligation—if not legal, at least moral—to confront the crime, and members of the Security Council were not prepared to take that step.[12]

For similar reasons, U.S. officials—who had used their consider-able power on the UN Security Council to obstruct any international response—evaded the use of the word "genocide." A recently declassi-fied May 26, 1994 e-mail to Donald Steinberg, who handled the Africa portfolio on President Clinton's National Security Council, cautioned that, although referring to the events in Rwanda as genocide would not create a legal obligation to stop it, "making such a determination will incrase [*sic*] political pressure to do something about it."[13] As another senior Administration official affirmed: "Genocide is a word that carries an enormous amount of responsibility."[14] David Rawson, the U.S. Ambassador to Rwanda at the time of the killings, agreed: "As a responsible Government, you don't just go around hollering 'genocide.'"[15]

As a result of such self-imposed political boundaries, officials in the U.S. State Department were authorized to state publicly only that "acts of genocide" were occurring in Rwanda; the use of the word "genocide" as descriptive of all killings in Rwanda was not authorized. (These hopelessly muddled directives led one frustrated journalist to ask the unanswerable: "How many acts of genocide does it take to make genocide?"[16]) It would not be until June 10 that U.S. Secretary of State Warren Christopher finally admitted publicly that the killing in Rwanda was genocide. During the entire 3 months of the genocide, the atrocities in Rwanda never warranted their own top-level meeting of policy advisers or the foreign policy team in the Clinton administration.

The center of Hutu extremism, Kigali, finally fell to the RPF on July 4, 1994. By July 19, the RPF was nearly in complete control of Rwanda and a unilateral ceasefire was declared. The genocide had ended. All told, at least 800,000 people were killed in just a hundred days in the spring and early summer of 1994 in Rwanda. Of these, the majority belonged to the Tutsi minority (indeed, it is almost impossible to find a Tutsi family that did not lose a member to the genocide), but more than 50,000 Hutus identified with opposition parties were also slaughtered. Charles Mironko estimates that "97% of child survivors . . . witnessed killing and death during the genocide," often the murder of their own parents and/or family members.[17] Rwanda stands as the most rapid, efficient, and intensive genocide in recorded history.

Nearly 3 months later, on October 1, 1994, an impartial Commission of Experts, established at the request of the UN Security Council, concluded that "Acts of genocide against the Tutsi group were perpetrated by Hutu elements in a concerted, planned, systematic and methodical way. These acts of mass extermination against the Tutsi group as such constitute genocide within the meaning of article II of the Convention on the Prevention and Punishment of the Crime of Genocide."[18] Their report, finally using the word "genocide," marked the first—and only—time, since the passage of the Genocide Convention in 1948, that the United Nations had officially identified an instance of genocide.

It would be nearly 4 years after the genocide, however, before President Clinton would acknowledge the killings in Rwanda as "genocide." On March 25, 1998, as part of an 11-day tour of Africa, Clinton had a 3-hour stop at the airport in Kigali. As his administration had maintained a political remoteness during the genocide, Clinton himself maintained a physical remoteness during his visit, venturing only as far as the tarmac at the Kigali airport— ostensibly because of security concerns. Clinton's remarks (often described as an "apology," though the word itself never appears in the published text of the speech) include nine references to "genocide," two of which are specific to Rwanda. In democratizing blame for the lack of response to the genocide, Clinton's carefully hedged acknowledgment cast a broad net: "The international community, together with nations in Africa, must bear its share of responsibility for this tragedy, as well. We did not act quickly enough after the killing began. We should not have allowed the refugee camps to become safe haven for the killers." In addition to those egregious inactions, Clinton invoked the noticeably absent power of Lemkin's word: "We did not immediately call these crimes by their rightful name: genocide."[19]

"By their rightful name." Genocide. The word that Lemkin coined, and the act for which he devoted his adult life to defining as an international crime, had certainly acquired a considerable weight in the half-century since its inception. It was a weight that international political leaders were unwilling to pick up for fear of being compelled to act. For those activists and politicians intent on responding to mass murder, it was a weight frequently swung as a cudgel of moral judgment or political one-upmanship. As Michael Ignatieff said: "Those who should use the word 'genocide' never let it slip their mouths, and those who do use the word 'genocide' banalize it into a validation of every kind of victimhood . . . What remains is not a moral universal which binds us all together, but a loose slogan which drives us apart."[20]

The name itself had become what Dirk Moses described as a "Janus-faced keyword," having multiple forms for multiple audiences.[21] Indeed, however much weight it had assumed, "genocide" had taken on an even greater amount of definitional controversy over the years—as a political, legal, empirical, moral, and analytical concept. "Genocide" quickly joined concepts such as democracy, justice, rule of law, citizenship, war, art, morality, nature, and science as what social theorist W. B. Gallie defined in 1956 as "essentially contested concepts." For Gallie, these are "concepts the proper use of which inevitably involves endless disputes about their proper uses on the part of their users."[22] In other words, essentially contested concepts are concepts that are understood, and used, inconsistently. Such conceptual blockages are not simply a result of confusion; rather, they are functional disagreements, often the cause of contentious contestation, that threaten the coherence of research in a field and its applications.[23] Gallie describes well the nature of these disputes: "Each party continues to maintain that the special functions which the term 'work of art' or 'democracy' or 'Christian doctrine' fulfils on *its* behalf or on *its* interpretation, is the correct or proper or primary, or the only important, function which the term in question can plainly be said to fulfil. Moreover, each party continues to defend its case with what it claims to be convincing arguments, evidence, and other forms of justification . . . although not resolvable by argument of any kind, [such apparently endless disputes] are nevertheless sustained by perfectly respectable arguments and evidence."[24]

As sociologist Christopher Powell points out, "genocide" is an essentially contested concept par excellence.[25] As an essentially contested concept, there has been ample debate—at times more contentious than productive—about the proper use, and meaning, of the word "genocide" since its inception. Among and between academics, lawyers, policy-makers, and activists, there are frequent accusations that the concept is being defined, or used, inappropriately by others. Underlying these substantive disputes is an assumption that there is "something" at the essence of genocide and the contest is to correctly determine what that "something" is.

Debates surrounding the essence of genocide have been entangled by cultural misappropriations of the word that further muddy our understanding of its "rightful name." The list of such ill-advised usages of the word, sometimes bordering on exploitive, is long, but here is a recent sampling:

- New York poet and spoken word artist Carlos Andres Gomez has a powerful 2007 piece titled "What's Genocide?" that includes AIDS, hepatitis B, and skin lightening cream as answers to the question.[26]
- In 2010, a *New York* magazine photograph of President Obama continuing the curious White House Thanksgiving tradition of granting a presidential pardon to a turkey carried the headline "President Obama Spares Two Turkeys From Annual Ritualistic Genocide."[27]
- In September 2013, Queen guitarist Brian May described the badger cull in Gloucestershire, UK as "genocide in the countryside."[28]
- The following month, *Washington Times* columnist Jeffrey Kuhner urged Christians to oppose the Affordable Care Act on the spectacularly misguided pretext that the law would fund abortions for members of

Congress and their staff, which he likened to "genocide masquerading as 'choice.'"[29]

- In November 2013, a San Jose, California city councilman reassured his constituency that an approved 3-month period of killing wild boars was not the same thing as "pig genocide."[30]
- A February 2015 statement from a Samoan fish exporter lamented a "marine genocide" being perpetrated by Chinese fishing boats in New Zealand waters.[31]
- In early March 2015, in naked pursuit of a manipulative political edge, Russian President Vladimir Putin said that Kiev's suspension of gas supplies to separatist parts of eastern Ukraine "smells of genocide."[32]
- Most recently, Kansas City Royal's baseball manager Ned Yost, referring to the delay of a spring training game in which a swarm of honey bees between home plate and first base had to be disposed of, disapprovingly said he had "never seen mass bee genocide like that."[33]

Why is a clear understanding of the word "genocide"—its "rightful name"—important? In a general sense, as philosopher Martin Buber reminds us, "power over the incubus is obtained by addressing it with its real name."[34] Vigilance has to be taken with the word so it does not become blurred, faded, meaningless, clichéd, or trite. By being used to describe everything, the verbal inflation of "genocide" comes to mean nothing. As columnist Frank Bruni points out, when nuance and perspective exit our language, they easily exit our conversation and our thinking as well. When everything is supposedly like everything else, nothing is distinctive.[35] For genocide scholar Helen Fein, we "work and act in a public arena in which the term 'genocide' [is] so debased by semantic stretch that it stirs suspicion. Virtually everything but genocide . . . is called genocide!"[36] Moreover, the word "genocide" has tremendous emotive power and, sometimes, as Jewish studies specialist Steven Katz argues, is "employed only for accusatorial and polemical rather than descriptive purposes . . . [and] is adopted by every persecuted group seeking to dramatize or expose its plight."[37] Indeed, the trivialization of "genocide," often used in the politics of victimhood as a convenient and shocking rhetorical substitute—or even metaphor—for other real sufferings, compromises its true meaning and is an insult to the past.

In a more specific sense, vigilance has to be taken with the word because of the different purposes it serves, and different implications it has, for different audiences. For *academics*, a clear understanding of the word "genocide" is important because it allows us to compare and contrast the complex social phenomenon of similar historical events that fall within the boundaries of that definitional classification. This is not to say that all academics agree on a consensual definition of "genocide"; indeed, one recent textbook lists 22 different definitions of "genocide" as developed by scholars in the field of genocide studies.[38] Fortunately, the intellectual stretching that comes from this definitional proliferation helps us parse out the essential defining characteristics of what may or may not constitute a case of genocide. For *lawyers and jurists*, "genocide" is a legal term, focused on the elements of legal culpability, seen as foundational for international human rights law. Here, the definition of genocide as a crime—used by courts of law, ad hoc tribunals, and the International Criminal Court—is more conservatively rooted in the parameters outlined in the Genocide Convention. In this way, the definition of genocide offered by the Convention has become a recognized part of customary international law. For *policymakers*, a clear understanding of the word "genocide" is important because it animates decision making in response to crisis. Do attacks on civilians constitute "genocide" or are they more accurately depicted as "ethnic cleansing," "long-standing tribal hatreds," "mass atrocities," or simply the excesses of "civil war?" How policymakers, both international and domestic, understand "genocide" within the structure of conflict directly impacts their response to it. Finally, for *global civil society*, "genocide" is an activist and mobilization term with implications for prevention and humanitarian intervention strategies. With those motives in mind, the word can be wielded by citizen-activists as a "call to action," often guilt induced, for a world that stands indifferent in the face of mass murder. For advocacy organizations reliant on donations to subsidize their cause, the word "genocide" as a slogan—even if controversial—has significant fund-raising implications.

It is also important to recognize that the rigid definitional framework of the Genocide Convention was a starting point rather than an ending. Over six decades of advances in international and domestic humanitarian law— as well as the fruit of academic, policy, and civil society discussions—have helped clarify many of the questions raised by the original conception of "genocide." As a result, there is more value to seeing the definition of genocide as dynamic and evolving, rather than static and inflexible.[39] Following the conceptual areas that framed our discussion of the drafting history of the Genocide Convention in Chapter 1, this chapter will explore those questions, and the responses that they generated, around three issues:

- First, while the drafters of the Genocide Convention, as we have seen, wrestled with the reasons to exclude political groups, what have been the implications of how *protected groups* are defined in the Convention? Why were the protections afforded by the convention constrained to only four such groups? Does such a constraint violate the fundamental principle of equality before the law? When is a group a group and what makes it a group? Can group membership be fluid and transient or must it be understood as stable and permanent? Who has the authority to define a protected group as such? Are the groups listed in the Convention the only groups to which it could or should be applied?

• Second, in the *acts defined as criminal*, what are defining characteristics of the acts of destruction? In what ways have recent international law and academic debate offered clarity regarding the acts understood as criminal? What does "intent" mean? How does intent differ from motive? How do we prove intent? What is the meaning of "in whole or in part?" Is the scale of "in part" determined quantitatively or qualitatively? How do "substantial" and "significant" differ as modifying adjectives for "in part?"

• Third, who holds *jurisdictional responsibility* for the crime of genocide? Is it limited to the territory in which the offence was committed? Or does jurisdiction depend on the nationality of the perpetrator and victim? Or should jurisdiction be considered more universally—meaning that any country could try any perpetrator, regardless of their nationality or of where the atrocities were committed?

The responses to all of these questions will help us bring some clarity to the "rightful name" of genocide. In so doing, we can then begin to determine the degree to which Lemkin's word has been successful in achieving what he hoped—protecting civilians from being "done to death."

PROTECTED GROUPS

A fundamental legal principle is equality before the law. That is, the law is the same for everyone; it should be applied in the same way to all. As Article 7 of the Universal Declaration of Human Rights states: "All are equal before the law and are entitled without any discrimination to equal protection of the law."[40] So, each of us, as individuals, is protected to the same degree by law. Because groups consist of individuals, we can extend the principle of equality before the law to groups. In theory, the group identity of a victim is not what determines whether she or he is a victim of murder, sexual harassment, or racial discrimination; those acts are criminal because of the acts themselves, they are not bound to the group identity of the victim. So, all groups are equally protected by law and that protection is particularly important for minority groups or groups that have less political or other power.

Certainly, as political scientist Scott Straus reminds us, group destruction was central to Lemkin's core vision of genocide.[41] His 1933 Madrid proposal, with its repeated use of the word "collectivity," revealed that Lemkin was thinking in the broadest possible terms about protected groups. Similarly, the 1946 text of UN Resolution 96(I) referred to "racial, religious, political and other groups"—implying a nonexhaustive and all-inclusive list of protected groups in which racial, religious, and political were merely examples of the types of groups meant to be protected. The 1947 Secretariat draft continued with "racial," "religious," and "political" groups, but replaced "other groups" with "national" and "linguistic" groups—implying an exhaustive and exclusive list of protected groups. "Linguistic" was considered redundant and deleted during Ad Hoc Committee deliberations in early 1948; however, in Sixth Committee deliberations later that same year, "ethnical" would be added to cover linguistic groups not connected to an existing state. During the same Sixth Committee deliberations, considerable debate swirled around the inclusion of "political" groups. Eventually, political compromise would lead to the exclusion of "political" groups from the final draft.

When the resolution came before the UN General Assembly in December 1948, the protected groups were narrowly restricted to four—national, ethnical, racial, or religious. Other groups—political, linguistic, ideological, economic, and social—had been actively considered and dismissed. Yet others—gender, cultural, disabled, age, and sexual orientation—were never considered. In omitting the "other groups" phrase from Resolution 96(I), the Convention does not even open the door for application to groups that may be seen as analogous to national, ethnical, racial, or religious groups. Only partly tongue-in-cheek, blogger Brian Kritz—referencing the 70,000 Australians who self-identify as belonging to the Jedi religion, believing in the Force and following the teachings of Yoda, Obi-Wan Kenobi, and Luke Skywalker—lampoons the haphazard nature of the Convention by pointing out that "members of a 'religion' based on a 1977 space opera [Star Wars] are protected under the law, while groups that are not 'national, ethnical, racial or religious' are left unprotected."[42] As genocide studies scholar Daniel Feierstein has argued, the narrow constriction of protected groups in the Genocide Convention constitutes a "violation of the elementary principle of equality before the law, protecting some groups and not others."[43] Indeed, the limitation of only four protected groups—leaving other groups beneath the law's protection—has been one of the most controversial aspects of the definition of genocide.

In 1978, a UN report, commissioned by the Sub-Commission on Prevention of Discrimination and Protection of Minorities of the UN Commission on Human Rights, referenced the issue of protected groups in the Genocide Convention. In that report, Special Rapporteur Nicodème Ruhashyankiko admitted that "defining the groups referred to in article II of the Convention seems to raise some problems, as does their limited number."[44] He offered an even-handed review of the definitional complexities raised in determining national, ethnic, racial, and religious group identities. In addressing "the problem of political groups," Ruhashyankiko echoed the conservative deliberations of the Sixth Committee three decades before with his "opinion that it would not be desirable to include political and other groups among the protected groups, in that a consequence of such inclusion would be to prevent some States from becoming parties to the new instruments."[45] Ruhashyankiko's report would be most remembered, however, for the political debate he ignited with his decision, at Turkey's insistence, to omit the Armenian genocide from his broad survey of historical cases of genocide.

Due, in part, to this controversy, a revised and updated report was later requested by the UN Economic and Social Council. Special Rapporteur Benjamin Whitaker, an activist lawyer from England, was given the "mandate to revise, as a whole, and update the study on the question of the prevention and punishment of the crime of genocide."[46] His report, submitted in July 1985, concluded that "the lack of clarity about which groups are, and are not, protected has made the Convention less effective and popularly understood than should be the case."[47] He progressively recommended that "the definition [of protected groups] should be extended to include a sexual group such as women, men, or homosexuals."[48] Although not specifically recommending the inclusion of political groups in the definition (but outlining an additional optional protocol as one possible solution to their inclusion), Whitaker does catalogue the reasons "a considerable number of commentators on the Convention" support the inclusion of political groups and cautioned that "most genocide has at least some political tinge . . . leaving political and other groups beyond the purported protection of the Convention offers a wide and dangerous loophole which permits any designated group to be exterminated, ostensibly under the excuse that this is for political reasons."[49]

As both the Ruhashyankiko and Whitaker reports demonstrate, in terms of how the four protected groups are defined, the Convention text itself offers no insight—apparently proceeding under the assumption that the meanings of national, ethnical, racial, and religious group identities are self-evident and stable. In truth, however, those meanings are no more self-evident than they are stable. Recent international case law, particularly of the ad hoc tribunals for Rwanda and the former Yugoslavia, has tried to offer some precision in regard to the meanings of the four protected group identities. For instance, the International Criminal Tribunal for Rwanda (ICTR) held "that a national group is defined as a collection of people who are perceived to share a legal bond based on common citizenship, coupled with reciprocity of rights and duties."[50] The tribunal went on to state: "An ethnic group is generally defined as a group whose members share a common language or culture. The conventional definition of racial group is based on the hereditary physical traits often identified with a geographical region, irrespective of linguistic, cultural, national or religious factors. The religious group is one whose members share the same religion, denomination or mode of worship."[51]

These definitions imply an "objective" standard of group identity that can be defined, with some certitude, by observable criteria. In practice, however, group categorization is not that simple. Group identities do not always have clear objective distinctions and often have significant overlap. They are variably perceived and have permeable boundaries.[52]

For instance, in many situations, national identity is less a matter of a legal bond with the state and more a matter of historical, cultural, religious, and linguistic connections. There may be people who are members of another state, or even stateless, yet still identify with the distinct communal connections that can underlie national identity. Defining ethnicity by those who share a common language or culture ignores that fact that different ethnic groups may, in fact, speak the same language and have essentially the same culture. Even the core elements of ethnicity—language and culture—are fluid and open to debate and reinterpretation. The hereditary physical traits mistakenly presumed to correspond to racial identity (which is, in fact, a highly socialized identity) may be all but wiped out due to high rates of intermarriage. Distinguishing, for instance, Hutu and Tutsi on the basis of hereditary physical traits had become so difficult, due to the high rate of intermarriage, that, in 1933, Belgian colonizers resorted to a nationally mandated system of ethnic identity cards. Finally, although the objective determination of religious identity seems the most straightforward, it is the least stable of the protected groups as, generally, people are free to join and leave religions as they wish. Moreover, religious identity is often fused with other identities. In the former Yugoslavia, for instance, ethnic and religious identity was so conflated that it only makes sense to speak of a merged "ethnoreligious identity"—Christian Orthodox Serbs, Roman Catholic Croats, and Muslim Bosniaks—when unpacking the conflict.

So, objective standards of national, ethnical, racial, and religious group identity are remarkably elusive and fraught with ambiguity. It is a matter of some clarity that the ICTR has held, as did the International Criminal Tribunal for the former Yugoslavia (ICTY), that these identities must be understood within their proper political, social, cultural, and historical context. Still, however, the reality that we each hold multiple identities, and that these identities can blend or intersect on many levels, has significant implications when the Convention applies to only four protected groups. Although we may be protected by one group membership we hold, we are likely left vulnerable by membership(s) in another unprotected group that we also hold. As Pieter Drost, a Dutch legal expert, argued shortly after the passage of the Convention: "A convention on genocide cannot effectively contribute to the protection of certain described minorities when it is limited to particular defined groups ... It serves no purpose to restrict international legal protection to some groups . . . because the protected members always belong at the same time to other unprotected groups."[53]

In light of these complexities, is there any value in even maintaining that protected groups objectively exist? Perhaps there is more value in holding that the perpetrators' definition of the victim group matters more than any "objective" standards, and even more than victims' perceptions of their own group membership. That is, if the groups subjectively exist in the minds and social context of the perpetrators, then they do, in fact, exist. If the perpetrators view the group as being national, ethnical, racial, or religious, then that view—regardless of its accuracy—outweighs any objective designation. As William Schabas, a leading authority on genocide in international law, notes: "Generally, it is the perpetrator of genocide who defines the individual victim's status as a member of a group protected by the Convention. The Nazis, for example, had detailed rules establishing, according to objective criteria, who was Jewish and who was not. It made no difference if the individual, perhaps a nonobservant Jew of mixed parentage, denied belonging to the group."[54]

In 1999, a Trial Chamber of the ICTR agreed, in part, with this more "subjective" socially constructed view in noting that an ethnic group could be "a group which distinguishes itself, as such (self identification); or, a group identified as such by others, including perpetrators of the crimes (identification by others)" and concluded that Tutsi were an ethnic group based on the existence of government-issued identity cards describing their ethnicity as such.[55] Later that same year, the ICTY maintained that "Although the objective determination of a religious group still remains possible, to attempt to define a national, ethnical or racial group today using objective and scientifically irreproachable criteria would be a perilous exercise whose result would not necessarily correspond to the perception of the persons concerned by such categorisation. Therefore, it is more appropriate to evaluate the status of a national, ethnical or racial group from *the point of view of those persons who wish to single that group out from the rest of the community* [italics mine]. The Trial Chamber consequently elects to evaluate membership in a national, ethnical or racial group using a subjective criterion."[56] In 2001, another Trial Chamber of the ICTR held that "if a victim was perceived by a perpetrator as belonging to a protected group, the victim could be considered by the Chamber as a member of the protected group, for the purposes of genocide."[57] Clearly, most of the judgments from the ad hoc tribunals do, on a case-by-case basis, treat the identification of protected groups as an essentially subjective matter.

Similarly, the International Commission of Inquiry on Darfur summarized the current state of international law as having "evolved from an objective to a subjective standard to take into account that collective identities and in particular ethnicity are, by their very nature social constructs, 'imagined' identities entirely dependent on variable and contingent perceptions, and not social facts, which are verifiable in the same manner as natural phenomena or physical facts."[58] Based on that reading, they concluded that the victimized Fur, Massalit, and Zaghawa tribes "subjectively make up a protected group" on the basis of the shared self-perception of two distinct groups—the tribes viewed as "African" and their opponents as "Arab"—even though both groups spoke the same language (Arabic) and embraced the same religion (Muslim).[59] So, as philosopher Larry May argues, it is sufficient for the group to "exist" when "both the perpetrators . . . *and* [italics in original] the victims . . . recognize the existence of a group that is being attacked."[60] As the Commission further pointed out, such subjective standards of group identity, publicly recognized, may eventually crystallize into very objective criterion in the minds of both groups involved—as well as in the eyes of international law. For the Commission, justification for the list of protected groups receiving a large and liberal interpretation is based on the principle "that the rules of genocide should be construed in such a manner as to give them their maximum legal effects."[61]

Over the years, legal scholars have come to agree with the courts on the complementary value of including a more subjective approach to defining group identity. For instance, in the first edition of his seminal volume on the topic, published in 2000, Schabas concluded "the subjective approach flounders because law cannot permit the crime to be defined by the offender alone. It is necessary, therefore, to determine some objective existence of the four groups."[62] With the publication of the second edition of that volume in 2009, however, Schabas had come around to a more approving view of the subjective approach: "In practice . . . the subjective approach seems to function effectively virtually all the time. Trying to find an objective basis for racist crimes suggest that the perpetrators act rationally, and this is more credit than they deserve."[63]

Academic debates over the definition of protected groups also have coalesced around the more subjective notion that it is the perpetrators' definition of the victim group that is central to its meaning. In these definitions of genocide, groups are social constructions born from the minds of the perpetrators. For Frank Chalk and Kurt Jonassohn, genocide is "a form of one-sided mass killing in which a state or other authority intends to destroy a group, *as that group and membership in it are defined by the perpetrator* [italics mine]."[64] Katz defines genocide as "the actualization of the intent, however successfully carried out, to murder in its totality any national, ethnic, racial, religious, political, social, gender or economic group, *as these groups are defined by the perpetrator* [italics mine], by whatever means."[65] For Mark Levene, "*it is the perpetrator, not the victim (or bystander) who defines the group*" [italics in original].[66] According to Straus, "Genocide is not carried out against a group bounded by essential internal properties. Rather, genocide is carried out against a group that the perpetrator *believes* [italics in original] has essential properties . . . however fictive such a belief may be."[67] Similarly, Jacques Semelin delineates the group as "the criteria by which it is identified being *determined by the perpetrator* [italics mine]."[68] Finally, Martin Shaw also argues against an objective, "real groups" criterion: "Genocide is an attempt to destroy a group of people, regardless of how far [much] groups *defined by perpetrators* [italics mine] correspond to 'real' groups, intersubjectively recognized by their members or objectively identifiable by observers."[69]

The openness of legal and academic discourse on defining group identity has been reflected in the reality that several national courts have gone beyond the bounds of the four protected groups in the Convention to implement domestic legislation reflecting a broader understanding of who is protected from genocide. In Bangladesh, Cambodia, Colombia, Costa Rica, Côte d'Ivoire, Ecuador, Ethiopia, Lithuania, Panama, Peru, Poland, and Slovenia, national legal systems have recognized genocide of political groups within their own domestic criminal codes.[70] Lithuania, Paraguay, and Peru also include "social groups" within their national legislation prohibiting genocide. At the broadest extreme, French legislation simply takes genocide to cover a nonexhaustive listing of any group, of whatever kind, whose identification is based on arbitrary criteria.[71] Similarly, the

Romanian penal code prohibits the destruction of a "collectivity," legislation under which a Romanian "extraordinary military court" (with little regard for due process) found Nicolae and Elena Ceausescu guilty of genocide in 1989.[72] In September 2013, Alexandru Visinescu, the former commander of a Communist-era prison in Romania, was charged with genocide by a Romanian national court, the first such charge since the Ceausescus. The next month, at the urging of the Institute for the Investigation of the Communist Crimes and the Memory of Romanian Exile, prosecutors also brought genocide charges against Ioan Ficior, former deputy commander of a Communist-era labor camp in Romania.

National legislation in these countries has sought to enlarge the scope of protected groups while remaining true to the object and purpose of the Convention. These courts see the four protected groups not as restrictive but as representative exemplars of the types of groups that the Convention was meant to embrace. In their view, no compelling substantive logic exists for limiting protected groups only to those listed in the Convention. Although these countries are certainly in the numerical minority, legal scholar Howard Shneider reminds us of an intriguing possibility of this emergent norm: "If enough countries pass legislation that includes political [and other] groups as a protected group, such state practice could eventually blossom into customary international law."[73] That is, national legislations—extensively buttressed by official government statements, diplomatic exchanges, opinions of national legal advisers, bilateral treaties, and decisions of national courts—could eventually establish widespread patterns of state behaviors or practices that come to be recognized as binding norms in international law.[74]

For years, academics in the field of genocide studies have followed a similar line of expansive thinking in regard to protected groups. Drost was the first to suggest that group membership be broadly understood as "human collectivity as such."[75] John Thompson and Gail Quets also emphasized the notion of a "social collectivity" as victims of genocide.[76] Helen Fein, one of the pioneers of genocide studies, speaks of "a collectivity" in defining group identity, as does Levene when he speaks of "an organic collectivity, or series of collectivities."[77] Similarly, Donald Bloxham defines genocide as the destruction of a "group's collective existence."[78] For Shaw, adopting "a generic definition, including all social groups, is the only coherent solution."[79] The notion of social groups is also central to Feierstein's analyses of genocidal social practices focusing on "the construction, destruction, and reorganization of social relations."[80]

The expansiveness of academic understandings of protected groups can be particularly seen in the terminological proliferation of "cides" running parallel to the concept of genocide. A sampling of these include "classicide" (destruction of social classes), "democide" (murder by government), "ecocide" (destruction of the natural environment and ecosystems), "eliticide" (destruction of the elite of a targeted group), "ethnocide" (meaning cultural genocide), "femicide/feminicide" (murder of females for being female), "fratricide" (killing of factional enemies within political movements), "gendercide" (destruction of male or female components of a group or of dissident sexual minorities), "Judeocide" (sometimes used in reference to the Nazi extermination of European Jews), "linguicide" (destruction and displacement of languages), "memoricide" (destruction of all traces of memory of a targeted group), "omnicide" ("death of all" by weapons of mass destruction), "poorcide" (genocide of the poor), "urbicide" (destruction of an urban environment, undermining the sustainability of its population), and "epistemocide" (eradication of a peoples' way of knowing and being).[81] To this list, Jacques Semelin adds "libricide" (destruction of libraries) and "culturicide" (destruction of cultures).[82] Australian historians Raymond Evans and Bill Thorpe also offer "indigenocide" to represent the supplanting of indigenous peoples by immigrants.[83] These terms not only reference a wide variety of destructions, but also include a sprawling view of protected groups not covered under the genocide convention.

Perhaps the parallel "cide" that has gained the most traction in the literature is "politicide." Political scientist Barbara Harff developed the concept of politicide as a lexical complement to the narrowness of protected groups as defined by the Convention. She distinguishes politicide from genocide as follows: "In genocides the victimized groups are defined primarily in terms of their communal characteristics. In politicides, by contrast, groups are defined primarily in terms of their political opposition to the regime and dominant group."[84] So, in politicides, victims are defined in regard to their political position (hierarchical or oppositional) rather than their membership in a national, ethnical, racial, or religious group. As an example of politicide, Harff argues that the Iraqi Kurds who were targeted for destruction in the *al Anfal* campaign of 1987 were targeted on the basis of their political support of certain opposition parties, rather than the ethnic identity of Kurd.[85] In her groundbreaking 2003 article on risk assessment, she enumerates 37 cases of genocides and politicides from 1955 to 2001, only five of which she identifies as genocide—the reminder are classified either as both genocide and politicide (seven cases) or as outright politicide (25 cases).[86]

Harff's concept of "politicide" reminds us, as we saw in Chapter 1, that political groups are an especially vulnerable population that are at a particular risk of being "done to death." From the communist atrocities of Stalin and Mao to the military dictatorships of Latin America, the Middle East, and Africa, the twentieth century was a particularly brutal period of political mass murder. Harff's research also testifies, though, to the difficulty in clearly differentiating "politicide" from "genocide." As many of her cases reveal, national, ethnical, racial, or religious victims of genocide are also often politically active and, therefore, are targeted on grounds of a political identity that overlaps other identities.

ACTS DEFINED AS CRIMINAL

As we have seen, for the acts defined as criminal, Article II of the Genocide Convention enumerates (a) killing members of the group, (b) causing serious bodily or mental harm to members of the group, (c) deliberately inflicting on the group conditions of life calculated to bring about its physical destruction in whole or in part, (d) imposing measures intended to prevent births within the group, or (e) forcibly transferring children of the group to another group.[87] As historian Ben Kiernan explains, the criminal acts (*actus reus*) referenced in Article II (a), (b), and (c) constitute lethal physical genocide; the acts referenced in Article II (d) and (e), preventing members of a group from reproducing, describe nonlethal biological genocide.[88] Genocide means "any" of the listed acts "committed with intent to destroy, in whole or in part" any of the four protected groups. Although, on the surface, the acts seem to consist exclusively of the commission of certain actions, it should be noted that genocide may be committed by "conscious acts of advertent omission" as well.[89]

The enumeration of criminal acts in Article II was certainly not without controversy. Drost, for instance, was struck by the limits of the acts defined as criminal: ". . . the five acts of genocide enumerated in Article II do not cover all possible ways and means of intentionally destroying a human group as such."[90] Others feared that the means of destruction were so exceedingly broad and open-ended that they could be used to apply to practices too mild to warrant interference in another state's domestic affairs. Fortunately, recent international case law, particularly of the ad hoc tribunals for Rwanda and the former Yugoslavia, coupled with substantive academic discourse in the field, offers some precision in regard to the three significant questions surrounding the (1) defining characteristics of the acts of destruction, (2) determination of "intent," and (3) meaning of "in whole or in part."

Defining Characteristics of Acts of Destruction. Lemkin's 1933 Madrid proposal included the dual crimes of "acts of barbarity" and "acts of vandalism" that would be declared "offences against the law of nations." Resolution 96(I) spoke more broadly of "a denial of the right of existence ... [resulting] in great losses to humanity in the form of cultural and other contributions." The 1947 Secretariat draft of the Convention, mirroring much of Lemkin's Madrid proposal, focused on physical, biological, and cultural acts of destruction. The following year, the Ad Hoc Committee draft collapsed physical and biological genocide into one grouping and, for the moment, retained cultural acts of destruction. The Sixth Committee draft, which would be incorporated in Article II of the final text of the Genocide Convention, opted for explicit enumeration of five specific acts of genocidal destruction defined as criminal (excluding cultural genocide) rather than a more general flexible definition of genocide. The defining characteristics of the five acts of destruction often suffer from the same lack of clarity as the protected groups. Some of the acts are rather straightforward, whereas others are more nuanced and complex.

The first criminal act in the Convention, (a) killing members of the group, whether through individual murders or group massacres, is the most explicit and obvious means of destruction. Even there, though, discrepancies have arisen. The ICTR, for instance, favored the French "meurtre" as more precise than the English ""killing" since "it is accepted that there is murder when death has been caused with the intention to do so" while "killing . . . could very well include both intentional and unintentional homicides."[91] Judges at the ICTY therefore chose to interpret "killing members of the group" in accordance with the definition of murder given in the Penal Code of Rwanda.

In contrast, (b) "causing serious bodily or mental harm to members of the group" is much less explicit and obvious. What constitutes "serious bodily or mental harm?" As early as 1961, the District Court of Jerusalem's judgment of Adolf Eichmann (the only significant judicial interpretation of the Genocide Convention for nearly five decades) gave some clarity in stating that Eichmann caused grave bodily and mental harm to millions of Jews "by the enslavement, starvation, deportation and persecution . . . and by their detention in ghettos, transit camps and concentration camps in conditions which were designed to cause their degradation, deprivation of their rights as human beings, and to suppress them and cause them inhumane suffering and torture."[92] Eichmann was specifically convicted of "crimes against the Jewish people" under Israeli national law, though a close reading of the judgment clearly indicates that this corresponds directly to the internationally recognized crime of genocide.

More recent advances in international law have included rape and sexual violence as "serious bodily or mental harm." In 1998, after an

indictment amended under pressure from nongovernmental organizations, the ICTR became the first international court to find an accused
person guilty of using rape to perpetrate the crime of genocide. The ICTR
held that rape and sexual violence "constitute genocide in the same way
as any other act as long as they were committed with the specific intent
to destroy, in whole or in part, a particular group, targeted as such."[93] This
judgment against the former *bourgmestre* (mayor) of Taba in Rwanda,
Jean-Paul Akayesu, concluded that he ordered Hutu to kill their Tutsi
neighbors and also ordered the rape and murder of Tutsi women in a cultural center under his control. During the trial, Tutsi women testified that
they had been subjected to repeated collective rape by Hutu paramilitaries, including assaults that Akayesu instigated. The court held that these
acts constituted acts of genocide: "Sexual violence was an integral part of
the process of destruction, specifically targeting Tutsi women and specifically contributing to their destruction and to the destruction of the Tutsi
group as a whole."[94]

Since the passage of the Convention, the understanding of "mental
harm," contentious throughout the drafting process, has remained controversial. The United States, in its Genocide Convention Implementation
Act of 1987, separated "mental harm" from "bodily injury," creating a sixth
criminal act, and defined the Convention's conception of mental harm as
anything causing "the permanent impairment of the mental faculties of
members of the group through drugs, torture, or similar techniques."[95]
Central to this understanding was the permanence of the harm done as
well as the recognition that the "harm be the result of some physical intru-
sion into the body."[96] So, for the United States—still intent on protecting
itself from allegations of genocide in regard to long-standing policies of
racial segregation and discrimination—the concept of mental harm, by
definition, excluded "psychological harm resulting from living conditions,
differential treatment by government authorities and the like."[97]

More recently, a 2005 judgment by a Trial Chamber of the ICTY found
that Bosnian men at Srebrenica who were paralyzed by "the fear of being
captured, and, at the moment of the separation, the sense of utter help-
lessness and extreme fear for their family and friends' safety as well as for
their own safety . . . who were separated, detained, abused and subsequently
killed suffered serious mental harm in that they knew what their fate was:
the last sight that many of the victims saw was killing fields full of bodies of
the Bosnian Muslim men brought to the execution site before them."[98] The
same Trial Chamber was further "convinced that the forced displacement
of women, children, and elderly people was itself a traumatic experience,
which . . . reaches the requisite level of causing serious mental harm."[99]

Some clarity regarding the elusive threshold for "serious" (having replaced "grievous" in the drafting process) had been established in the ICTY's 2001 judgment against Radislav Krstic, former Commander of the Drina Corps of the Bosnian Serb Army. Krstic was on trial for his leadership role at the genocide in Srebrenica in which over 8,000 Bosnian Muslim men and boys were systematically murdered and about 25,000 women, children, and elderly were forcibly transferred. In their judgment, "the Trial Chamber states that serious harm need not cause permanent and irremediable harm, but it must involve harm that goes beyond temporary unhappiness, embarrassment or humiliation. It must be harm that results in a grave and long-term disadvantage to a person's ability to lead a normal and constructive life . . . the Chamber holds that inhuman treatment, torture, rape, sexual abuse and deportation are among the acts which may cause serious bodily or mental injury . . . The Chamber is fully satisfied that the wounds and trauma suffered by those few individuals who managed to survive the mass executions do constitute serious bodily and mental harm."[100] Krstic became the first person to be convicted of genocide at the ICTY and was sentenced to 46 years in prison.[101]

The criminal act of (c) deliberately inflicting on the group conditions of life calculated to bring about its physical destruction captures more complex and longer-term methods of group destruction. As political scientist Ernesto Verdeja soberly points out, "the specific acts that constitute the imposition of destructive conditions are not defined in the convention because the framers realized that there are too many possible strategies that could qualify."[102] Nevertheless, the ICTR found that such acts could include "subjecting a group of people to a subsistence diet, systematic expulsion from homes and the reduction of essential medical services below minimum requirement."[103] In February 1999, Guatemala's Commission for Historical Clarification issued a report asserting that some of the state's counterinsurgency operations could be correctly deemed genocidal in intent. Included in that determination was the recognition that "whole villages were burnt, properties were destroyed and the collectively worked fields and harvests were also burnt, leaving the communities without food"—all of which, in the Commission's opinion, constituted the deliberate infliction of conditions of life calculated to bring about physical destruction in whole or in part.[104]

Similarly, although certainly a matter of continuing debate, many scholars have referenced the Ukrainian man-made famine of 1932–1933 (known in Ukraine as the "Holodomor" or "Death by Hunger"), in which three to five million kulak peasants perished, as another example of the deliberate infliction of destructive conditions of life. For Lemkin, speaking at a commemoration of the Ukrainian famine in New York in 1953, this was "a classic example of Soviet genocide."[105] As historian Norman Naimark concludes: "There is a great deal of evidence of government connivance [by Stalin's Soviet Union] in the circumstances that brought on the shortage of grain and bad harvests . . . and made it impossible for Ukrainians to find food for their survival . . . forced requisitioning removed the margin of sufficiency and sank the region into famine, desperation, and cannibalism."[106] In November 2006, the Ukrainian Parliament voted in favor of declaring the 1932–1933 famine an act of genocide perpetrated by Stalin's regime against the Ukrainian people.[107] In addition, the parliaments of Andorra, Argentina, Austria, Colombia, Ecuador, Estonia, Georgia, Hungary, Lithuania, Paraguay, Peru, Poland, Slovakia, and the United States, along with the senates of Australia and Canada, have recognized the famine as genocide against the Ukrainian people.

Given that there is no precise duration of time over which these destructive conditions of life need be imposed, legal scholar Sheri Rosenberg has suggested the phrase "genocide by attrition" to describe these indirect methods of destruction. Among them she includes "forced displacement, the denial of health and health care, the denial of food, and sexual violence."[108] Polish diplomat and jurist Manfred Lachs, noting how the Nazi authorities reduced the amount of food in occupied countries to 400 and even 250 calories a day, referred to this as "negative violence."[109] Such "conditions of life," even when resulting from omission, become, over time, "conditions of death," a slow process of annihilation of a targeted group. It is important to note that these conditions of life only must be "calculated" to bring about physical destruction in whole or in part. The result of the calculation—destructive or not—is immaterial to the charge itself. In those cases in which the calculation does lead to physical destruction, it is likely that the criminal charge will more properly be under (a) killing members of the group or (b) causing serious bodily or mental harm to members of the group.

The criminal act of (d) imposing measures intended to prevent births within the group, as Schabas points out, was animated by some of the postwar trials following the Holocaust.[110] For instance, the trial of Rudolf Hoess, former commandant of Auschwitz, included an indictment based, in part, on medical war crimes including castration, procedures intended to produce sterilization, and experiments causing premature termination of pregnancy. In the judgment offered by the Supreme National Tribunal of Poland, it was held that the medical experiments "were obviously devised at finding the most appropriate means with which to lower or destroy the reproductive power of the Jews, Poles, Czechs and other non-German nations . . . it seems obvious that they [the experiments] constituted the preparatory stage of one of the forms of the crime of genocide."[111] Hoess was found guilty of the alleged crimes and sentenced to death by hanging. The sentence was carried out on April 16, 1947, immediately adjacent to the crematorium of the former Auschwitz I concentration camp.

This criminal act was given substantial clarity, and breadth, by the ICTR in the Akayesu judgment. They held "that the measures intended to prevent births within the group, should be construed as sexual mutilation, the practice of sterilization, forced birth control, separation of the sexes and prohibition of marriages."[112] In patriarchal societies in which a child's social identity is determined by the identity of the father, the Chamber held that another example of a measure intended to prevent births within the group "is the case where, during rape, a woman of the said group is deliberately impregnated by a man of another group, with the intent to have her give birth to a child who will consequently not belong to its mother's group."[113] The Krstic Appeals Chamber also affirmed that the physical destruction of men in a patriarchal society, with the majority of the men killed officially listed as missing, leaves surviving spouses unable to remarry—thus effectively preventing births within the group. The judges concluded that such practice "had severe procreative implications for the Srebrenica Muslim community, potentially consigning the community to extinction . . . This is the type of physical destruction the Genocide Convention is designed to prevent."[114] Finally, the Akayesu Chamber held that measures intended to prevent births could also be mental, through threats or trauma that lead members of a group to choose not to procreate. In all of these examples, the policies and practices are clearly coercive; as Verdeja reminds us, "voluntary family planning and birth control programs are not genocidal, even if the state provides them."[115]

Lastly, Schabas points out that (e) forcibly transferring children of the group to another group as an act of genocide was added to the Convention as an enigmatic afterthought, given the drafters strong rejection of the concept of cultural genocide.[116] Clearly, however, forced transfer of children (commonly understood as anyone under the age of 18 years), when they do survive, is a destructive violation of identity. Original social identities are erased and replaced by new national, ethnical, racial, or religious identities. It is not simply the forced transfer that is at issue, but it is the forced transfer to another group that carries with it the imposition of a new group identity—including a new language, cultural practices, religious beliefs, and so on. Although the group members may remain physically alive after their forcible transfer, they are culturally destroyed via the overlay of a new group identity. In April 2015, citing the Convention definition of forcible transfer, the Global Justice Centre appealed to the

International Criminal Court to investigate the 2014 abduction of 276 Nigerian schoolgirls by the Islamist militant group Boko Haram as a possible case of genocide against the country's Christian community.[117] For Lemkin, the forcible removal of children from the group was the cruelest act of genocide.[118] The Rutaganda judgment by the ICTR further held that criminality went beyond the direct act of forcible transfer to also include "any acts of threats or trauma which would lead to the forcible transfer of children from one group to another group."[119] The forcible transfer of children is not only akin to Lemkin's original conception of cultural genocide, but also runs close to Martin Shaw's argument that group destruction is more appropriately seen "as involving a nexus between the destruction of collective ways of life and institutions and bodily and other harm to individuals."[120]

Forcible transfer of children as an act of genocide is often cited in settler colonial treatment of aboriginal populations. As precedent, Australia's "Stolen Generation" of aboriginal children forcibly transferred to nonindigenous institutions and families between the 1890s and 1970s was classified, by the Australian Human Rights and Equal Opportunities Commission, as a violation of article (e) of the Convention. Their 1997 report concluded that "the predominant aim of Indigenous child removals was the absorption or assimilation of the children into the wider, non-Indigenous community so that their unique cultural values and ethnic identities would disappear, giving way to models of Western culture . . . Removal of children with this objective in mind is genocidal."[121]

More recently, in October 2013, human rights activists in Canada sent a letter to James Anaya, UN special rapporteur on the rights of indigenous peoples, in which they claimed that several specific crimes against aboriginal people in Canada qualify as genocide. Among these crimes were forced involvement of malnourished aboriginal people in medical and nutrition experiments as well as the forcible removal, often violently, of about 150,000 aboriginal children from their homes for inclusion in government-funded, church-run residential schools from the 1870s until the 1990s. As genocide scholar David MacDonald asserts: "We know that tens of thousands of IRS [Indian residential schools] survivors had their lives shattered by seven generations of verbal, physical and sexual abuse. We know at least 4,100 kids died as a consequence of the system."[122] Outside of the residential school system, the authors of the letter also cited the forcible removal of aboriginal children for the purpose of adoption by white families.[123] Known as the "Sixties Scoop," estimates put the number of aboriginal children removed in Canada between the 1960s and the late-1980s at around 20,000.[124] In the view of Justice Murray Sinclair, head commissioner of the Truth and Reconciliation Commission of Canada: "The reality is that to take children away and to place them with another group in society for the purpose of racial indoctrination was— and is—an act of genocide and it occurs all around the world."[125] On June 2, 2015, the final report of Sinclair's commission, after 6 years of intensive research including 6,750 interviews, indeed concluded that Canada's residential schools amounted to "cultural genocide" of aboriginal people.[126]

Echoing Martin Luther King Jr.'s assertion that the United States "was born in genocide," scholars and activists also have applied article (e) to U.S. assimilationist policies and practices of forced transferral of Native Americans to residential boarding schools.[127] More than 100,000 Native Americans were forcibly transferred to such schools, designed to "kill the Indian, and save the man." There were still 60,000 Native children enrolled in boarding schools as their era was coming to a close in 1973.[128] In these schools, tribal identities were erased and "yielded a trauma of shame, fear, and anger that has passed from generation to generation fueling the alcohol and drug abuse and domestic violence that continues to plague Indian country."[129] Even though many more Native children were harmed in the United States than in Canada by boarding schools, statutes of limitations in the U.S. courts prohibit class action lawsuits against individuals or institutions related to the residential boarding schools. As will be discussed in Chapter 6, September 2000 brought an apology on behalf of the federal Bureau of Indian Affairs, but not the federal government as a whole. In December 2009 President Obama, in a private ceremony drawing scant media attention, signed a Congressionally approved "Apology to Native Peoples of the United States." Neither apology mentioned the word "genocide" or admitted any measure of liability.

In closing, we should note that Articles III and IV of the Genocide Convention provide some additional clarity regarding the acts understood as criminal. Article III, in addition to genocide, also prohibits other related, but separate, acts—including the conspiracy to commit genocide, direct and public incitement to commit genocide, attempts to commit genocide, and complicity in genocide. These four acts are not, strictly speaking, "genocide" and can be committed even if genocide itself never takes place. These acts can be understood in a preventive capacity—applying law even before the crime of genocide takes place. An ICTY Appeals Chambers broadened Article III even further by entering a conviction for "aiding and abetting" genocide against Radislav Krstic while another ICTY Appeals Chamber held that it is possible to commit genocide as part of a "joint criminal enterprise."[130] Although genocide is most often seen as a "crime of state," Article IV reminds us that "persons committing genocide or any of the other acts enumerated in Article III shall be punished, whether they are constitutionally responsible rulers, public officials or private individuals." So, acts constituting genocide need not be state planned or even have the active backing or complicity of a government. Article IV leaves clear room for the fact that genocide could be committed by nonstate actors (for example, terrorist organizations) or even private individuals.

Determination of "Intent." The material or objective element of the five criminal acts *(actus reus)* referenced in Article II is complemented by a mental or subjective element *(mens rea)*—captured in the deep complexity of the deceptively simple phrase "with intent." Certainly, for Lemkin, some conception of intent—purposeful action aimed at destruction—was central to the concept of genocide. His Madrid proposal spoke of the "goal . . . of extermination" and he used "knowingly" as a preface to the commission of various acts of destruction. Lemkin saw genocide as a "coordinated plan" with "objectives" and the ultimate "aim" of group destruction.[131]

As Schabas outlines, the drafting history of the Genocide Convention reflects Lemkin's substantive concern with the mental element of genocide.[132] Although Resolution 96(I) is too brief to dwell on issues of intent, Saudi Arabia's draft protocol from the previous month is replete with reference to words such as "intentional," "planned," "systematic," and "intent" in describing acts that constitute the crime of genocide.[133] The lead sentence of the preamble to the Secretariat draft proclaimed genocide as "the intentional" destruction of a group of human beings and later speaks of a "deliberate" act with "purpose."[134] Initially, the Ad Hoc Committee opted for the word "deliberate" rather than "intent," only later settling on the compromise phrase "deliberate acts committed with the intent to destroy" after a proposal from the United States.[135] In the Sixth Committee, after much debate over the issue of premeditation, the word "deliberate" was deleted—leaving us with the final Convention text of "acts committed with intent to destroy."[136] The type of intent required is not stated.

Similarly, most academic definitions also include "intent," or some variant of it, in their understanding of genocide. In his conceptual analysis, Straus reviews over a dozen of the prominent scholarly definitions of genocide and finds consistent reference to intent in words and phrases such as "deliberate," "explicit," "sustained purposeful action," "premeditated," "promotion and execution," "systematic," "actualization," and "intention."[137] Despite the prevalence, however, of some formulation of intentionality in how we define the mental element of genocide, its exact parameters remain elusive. What does "intent" mean? How does intent differ from motive? How do we prove intent?

First, the meaning of intent is central to criminal law, particularly as it sets it apart from other areas of legal liability that lie closer to inadvertent or negligent behavior. By including intent, Article II of the Convention makes clear that the acts defined as criminal must be committed with purpose. As Schabas points out, there are actually two distinct intents involved in Article II—the intent of the perpetrator to destroy the protected group in whole or in part as well as the intent of the underlying genocidal act to accomplish that destruction.[138] Similarly, Carla Del Ponte, former Chief Prosecutor of both the ICTY and the ICTR, has spoken of the specific intent to destroy the group as distinct and separate from the intent to act to carry out that destruction.[139]

The first attempt to codify the mental element of intent came from the 1998 Rome Statute of the International Criminal Court, which codified genocide and other serious international crimes. Article 30 of the Statute, falling under "General Principles of Criminal Law," understands the mental element as including both intent and knowledge. Intent is demonstrated when, in relation to conduct, a "person means to engage in the conduct" and, in relation to a consequence, a "person means to cause that consequence or is aware that it will occur in the ordinary course of events." Knowledge refers to "awareness that a circumstance exists or a consequence will occur in the ordinary course of events." [140] So, any of the five acts defined as criminal in the Genocide Convention must be committed with intent and knowledge that it will lead to destruction of the targeted group.

Much of recent international case law, though, has focused on intent rather than knowledge—likely because the word "intent" actually appears in the definition of the crime of genocide. To distinguish it from the broader notion of "general intent," courts often refer to the "special," "particular," "genocidal," or "specific intent" (*dolus specialis*) of genocide. General intent crimes require that the accused intended to do the criminal act, but not that the accused intended the precise harm or the precise result that occurred. Common assault is a general intent offense that does not require that the assailant intended the harm, only that the assailant meant to do the act that caused the harm. Specific intent crimes, on the other hand, require both the commission of the criminal act as well as a "special state of mind" designated by intent or purpose. Burglary, for example, is a specific intent offense that requires breaking and entering into someone's home with the purposeful and conscious intent to commit a crime.

The crime of genocide entails the specific intent to destroy, in whole or in part, a national, ethnical, racial, or religious group as such. A September 1998 ICTR decision held that "Special intent of a crime is the specific intention, required as a constitutive element of the crime, which demands that the perpetrator clearly seeks to produce the act charged."[141] Similarly, a 2001 ICTY appeals judgment found that "specific intent requires that the perpetrator, by one of the prohibited acts . . . seeks to achieve the destruction, in whole or in part, of a national, ethnical, racial, or religious group, as such."[142] Clearly, it is not enough to establish that unlawful killings of members of a protected group have occurred. Specific intent must also be established and that intent must specifically be to destroy the group in whole or in part. Where specific intent is not established, the act remains criminal (for example, a crime against humanity), but not as genocide. So, genocide must be "consciously desired, not simply negligently caused or recklessly risked."[143]

Though genocide is, by its nature, a collective crime, specific intent is a legal concept applicable to individuals, not groups. On one level, as Verdeja points out, this is perfectly appropriate and "allows us to avoid superficial and dangerous accusations, such as the charge that all Bosnian Serbs or Rwandan Hutus are guilty of genocide."[144] On another level, however, the focus on individual intent can misleadingly individualize what is an organized and collective endeavor. Verdeja continues: "By emphasizing individual intentionality, the current law treats genocide as reducible to individual intentions and downplays broader contextual elements."[145] In practice, then, the meaning of individual intent has to be understood within the more expansive scaffolding of genocidal plans or policies, however fluid they may be. So, individuals must have "either an intent to plan and initiate a collective enterprise [i.e., architects of genocide], or . . . an intent to participate in what one knows will be a collective enterprise" to destroy a group.[146]

Along these lines, legal scholar Kai Ambos has argued for a "differentiated interpretation" of individual specific intention that distinguishes according to the status and role of the perpetrator. For Ambos, the accepted legal understanding of individual specific intent should be upheld for top- and mid-level perpetrators, or "intellectual masterminds," who structure the organizational apparatus of genocide. For low-level perpetrators or "foot soldiers," however, he argues that mere knowledge of the genocidal context should suffice for prosecution. In his words: "As the low-level perpetrators were not involved in designing this plan but are, in a normative sense, only used as mere instruments to implement it, they need not possess the destructive special intent themselves but only know of its existence."[147] Although Ambos' characterization of the low-level perpetrators as "accessories," "instruments," "aiders," or "assistants" comes perilously close to minimizing their individual agency in perpetrating atrocities, he does challenge us to think in a more nuanced sense about the role of individual specific intention across the various actors (both state and nonstate) in the process of genocide.

Ambos' focus on a more lenient knowledge-based approach to intent (returning us to the definition of the mental element as outlined Article 30 of the 1998 Rome Statute of the International Criminal Court) concurs with an increasing number of scholars who see specific or special intent (*dolus specialis*) as too strict an interpretation of intent. As legal activist Katherine Goldsmith argues: "The use of *dolus specialis* as the intent required by the Genocide Convention completely goes beyond the original intent of the Convention's drafters . . . prevention and punishment of the crime of genocide is challenging enough. To include an intent requirement that is extremely difficult to prove after the fact, and which is a contested term in many civil law countries, renders the Genocide Convention both confusing and ineffective."[148] In practice, a broader, knowledge-based interpretation of intent has been generally favored by the ICTR in their argument that a perpetrator "is culpable because he knew or should have known that the act committed would destroy, in whole or in part, a group."[149] Supporters of such a knowledge-based approach argue that it would lead to an increased number of prosecutions and, arguably, would have a deterrent effect on future would-be perpetrators of genocide.

Second, it is important to distinguish "intent" from "motive" in understanding the mental element of genocide. Motive is the cause or reason or desire that prompts a person to act or fail to act. Intent, as we have seen, refers only to the state of mind with which the act is done or not done. Intent is what is aimed at; it is an expression of choice or agency or autonomy. Intent remains distinct from the motive for it; people may intend to commit the same crime, but for varying motives.

Indeed, motives—never explicitly mentioned in the Genocide Convention—are fundamentally irrelevant in ascertaining the mental element of "intent" that is central to the heart of genocide. Lemkin certainly was clear in his differentiation of intent from motive, even going so far as to argue that "the motivations on the side of the offenders are of no importance . . . [just as] the motives of a homicide are of no importance."[150] A 2001 ICTY Appeals Chamber affirmed "the necessity to distinguish specific intent from motive. The personal motive of the perpetrator of the crime of genocide may be, for example, to obtain personal economic benefits, or political advantage or some form of power."[151] They continued, though, to caution that "the existence of a personal motive does not preclude the perpetrator from also having the specific intent to commit genocide."[152]

The role of "motive" in the drafting of the Genocide Convention had been a matter of much debate. Although the Secretariat draft did not mention the term "motive," the Ad Hoc Committee draft opted to include the "motive of genocide" as one of four general elements included in the definition of genocide.[153] This became a significant, and rather lengthy, point of controversy during the Sixth Committee deliberations. In Lemkin's recollection, "the delegates seemed to get lost in an endless discussion of the motives for genocide."[154] Some believed that including an enumeration of motives for the crime of genocide was indispensable for precisely differentiating the new crime. In their view, not including motives would obscure the nature of the crime and lead to the scope of the Convention becoming too broad, prompting Iran's delegate to express his concern that "cases which were not in fact crimes of genocide might come to be considered as such."[155] Others countered that "in most countries, the penal code did not regard motive, but only intent and act, as constituent elements of a crime."[156] These voices saw an inclusion of motive as ambiguous, even dangerous, fearing that "motive" would unnecessarily narrow the crime by allowing alleged perpetrators "to claim that they had not acted under the impulse of one of the motives held to be necessary to prove genocide."[157]

Venezuela's delegate, Perez Perozo, attempting to find common ground, proposed the compromise phrase "as such" to "meet the views of those who wished to retain a statement of motives."[158] Although some expressed concern over the ambiguity of the phrase, several delegates favorably interpreted it as implicitly including the concept of motive in the definition, but without the explicitly restrictive limitation of enumerating the varieties of motive. After an extended back-and-forth debate over whether a similarly worded French proposal was an amendment to the Venezuelan amendment or an entirely new proposal in and of itself, the Venezuelan amendment was put to vote and narrowly adopted by 27 votes to 22, with two abstentions.[159]

As May points out, "it remains quite puzzling what the drafters of the Genocide Convention meant by adding the 'as such' words to the definition of genocide."[160] Records of the deliberations and close vote in the Sixth Committee attest to substantial confusion. Prior to the vote, the chairman was obliged to remind delegates that "the subject of the vote was the text of the amendment; its interpretation would rest with each Government when ratifying and applying the convention."[161] So, once passed, each country was left to conveniently give its own interpretation of "as such," not bound by the interpretation of the amendment's author. Even after the vote, however, the continuing debate was so intense that the chairman was harangued into confirming that he would include the statement of government-specific interpretation into the report of the meeting. Dissatisfaction still had not waned at the following meeting as one representative began by suggesting that a working group be established to "consider the problem raised by the adoption of the Venezuelan amendment," a suggestion that was eventually defeated by 30 votes to 15, with three abstentions.[162]

Since the passage of the Convention, the interpretation of "as such" has continued to be disputed by governments as well as by international jurisprudence and academia. Some interpretations adhere to Venezuela's original intent that the phrase connotes a suggestion of motive. Others point to the textual location of "as such," following the listing of protected groups, and suggest that the phrase is more accurately interpreted— grammatically and logically—as a reference to the extermination of members of a group simply because they belong to that group. The 1985 Whitaker report, for instance, interprets "as such" as stipulating that "in order to be characterized as genocide, crimes against a number of individuals must be directed at their collectivity or at them in their collective character or capacity."[163] International jurisprudence has followed a similar tack in insisting that "the intention must be to destroy the group 'as such', meaning as a separate and distinct entity."[164] Ultimately, however, the vagaries of the phrase have left us with indecisive and conflicting views on whether the words "as such" denote a motive element.

Regardless of how the Convention does, or does not, include implicit reference to motive, we must not diminish the explanatory and preventive importance of understanding motives for genocide. We cannot fully comprehend the crime without understanding the reasons why it came about. Although perpetrators must act intentionally to be held liable for genocide, their motives can be very diverse. Political scientist Benjamin Valentino, for instance, has outlined a typology identifying six specific motives that generate strong incentives for leaders to initiate mass killing as a rational strategy. These motives are classified under two broad categories of "dispossessive" mass killings that result from stripping people of their possessions, their homes, or their way of life (including communist, ethnic, and territorial motives) and "coercive" mass killings that use violence to coerce large numbers of civilians into submission (including counterguerrilla, terrorist, and imperialist motives).[165]

Third, and finally, given the legal centrality of intent, how do we prove it? This practical question of proof is particularly relevant because explicit manifestations of specific intent—dramatic courtroom confessions or the "smoking gun" documentation of written or verbal orders attesting to intent—are rare in the context of genocide trials. Here, we are helped, in part, by the Convention's focus on intent rather than motive. As May points out, "it is exceedingly hard to determine what motives are, but relatively easy often to read intentions off of actions."[166] Indeed, because intent is a state of mind, it can seldom be proved with direct evidence and ordinarily must be inferred from the facts of the case. As Schabas points out, "intent is a logical deduction that flows from evidence of the material acts."[167] So, the presence of intent in an accusation of genocide can be inferred from identifiable and systematic patterns of material actions that lead to the destruction of a group. As the Whitaker report suggests, "a court should be able to infer the necessary intent from sufficient evidence."[168] This view of inferring intent from direct evidence was affirmed by an ICTR Appeals Chamber that held: "By its nature, intent is not usually susceptible to direct proof. Only the accused himself has first-hand knowledge of his own mental state, and he is unlikely to testify to his own genocidal intent. Intent thus must usually be inferred."[169]

Indeed, inferring intent from conduct is widely accepted. Of course, there is a higher threshold for concluding that the intent is specifically genocidal, and not merely generally homicidal. At times, perpetrators may have directly betrayed genocidal intent through public speeches, in face-to-face or phone conversations, via written or radioed communications, by policy proposals, and so on. Most often, however, inference must be drawn more indirectly from "the general context, the perpetration of other culpable acts systematically directed against the same group, the scale of atrocities committed, the systematic targeting of victims on account of their membership in a particular group, or the repetition of destructive and discriminatory acts."[170] Contextual inferences might be drawn from the widespread use of euphemisms (for example, "clearing," "cleansing," "final solution," "liquidation," or "relocation"), off-the-record oral directives, segmented procedures of destruction, individual initiatives aimed at winning their superior's approval (for example, "working towards the Fuhrer"), or other general factors from which intent can be deduced. Courts in the Baltic region investigating crimes of the Stalinist regime have relied on precedents in international law to conclude that intent also can be deduced from the specifics of the crimes themselves— how many died, how organized the actions were, whether acts of arrest and deportation followed standard legal procedures of the time, the inclusion of hateful language and gratuitous brutality, and so on.[171] The ICTY has even held that the destruction of the cultural existence of a protected group (for example, the destruction of Muslim institutions and libraries) can be construed as indicators of genocidal intent.[172]

Moreover, proof of intent need not require extensive premeditation or the documented existence of a plan. In their judgment of Radislav Krstic, the ICTY said: "It is conceivable that, although the intention at the outset of an operation was not the destruction of a group, it may become the goal at some later point during the implementation of the operation."[173] They provide as an example an armed force that decides to destroy a protected group during a military operation whose initial, primary objective was totally unrelated to the fate of that particular group. The court went on to find that "the plan to ethnically cleanse the area of Srebrenica escalated to a far more insidious level that included killing all of the military-aged Bosnian Muslim men" just a day or two before the genocide began.[174] Similarly, a previous ICTY Appeals Chamber found that "the common plan or purpose may materialise extemporaneously and be inferred from the fact that a plurality of persons acts in unison to put into effect a joint criminal enterprise."[175] Courts also have affirmed that in the absence of a documented plan, a logical inference of proof that a plan exists can be drawn from the material acts of the crime itself. Another ICTY Appeals Chamber found that although "the existence of a plan or policy may facilitate proof of the crime . . . the existence of a plan or policy is not a legal ingredient of the crime" of genocide.[176]

Some scholars have gone beyond these court decisions and even argued that as intent is so difficult to prove, we should understand genocide simply as the causing of mass death to defenseless people. So, as Moses outlines, rather than merely seeing genocide as the intended action of a coherent agent (in particular, the state), a new generation of scholars is focusing on genocide as an impersonal structural process (including social forces in civil society) that does not necessarily require any intending agent.[177] Here scholars are opening room for larger, longer, and more complicated processes of imperialism and colonialism. In this more fluid and dynamic conception, explicit signs of intent to destroy may wax and wane as decades or even centuries of actors unfold. Although there is a possibility that moral agency is compromised when we drop intentionality as a defining characteristic of genocide, it is helpful to recognize the ways in which emergent social structures (such as colonization, settlement, and civilization) may lead to unintended consequences that look very much like genocide. As historian Tony Barta, in advancing his argument that Australia was a genocidal society, writes: "Genocide, strictly, cannot be a crime of unintended consequences . . . In real historical relationships, however, unintended consequences are legion, and it is from the consequences . . . that we have to deduce the real nature of the relationship."[178]

Ultimately, questions surrounding intent are important in the ways they impact determinations of genocide and our responses to events of mass atrocity. Certainly, the specific intent requirement has proven as problematic for preventive policymaking as it has for international law. For instance, the much-debated 2005 report of the International Commission of Inquiry on Darfur found that many of the acts defined as criminal by the Convention were, in fact, being perpetrated against Darfuris by Sudanese Government forces and militias under their control. When addressing issues of intent, however, the commission found a lack of genocidal intent behind these actions. In their conclusion, the commissioners wrote: "Generally speaking, the policy of attacking, killing and forcibly displacing members of some tribes does not evince a specific intent to annihilate, in whole or in part, a group distinguished on racial, ethnic, national or religious grounds. Rather, it would seem that those who planned and organized attacks on villages pursued the intent to drive the victims from their homes primarily for purposes of counter-insurgency warfare."[179] Despite also concluding that the determination of no genocidal intent "should not be taken as in any way detracting from or belittling the gravity of the crimes perpetrated in that region," the Commission's report, in reality, did detract from and belittle what was happening in Darfur.[180] Indeed, the conceptual ambiguities of defining "genocide," and, particularly, substantiating intent, created paralysis rather than consensus in responding to Darfur.[181]

For a commission whose investigation was prefatory to any judicial action, the assumption of a "singular, heavily value-laden original intention that informs all the actions of a perpetrator organization over a whole historical period" was simply too exacting a burden of proof to carry.[182] As activist Jerry Fowler points out, the "commission was not a court of law, nor was it adjudicating the fate of individual defendants."[183] Moreover, the unrealistic search for clear and explicit proof of intent consistently articulated by major decision makers in a genocidal regime ignores the reality that cascading radicalization of genocidal policy is the norm, not the exception. As historian Karl Schleunes has demonstrated for the Holocaust, genocide is rarely a premeditated "grand design" that leaders pursue from the outset.[184] Rather, genocidal policy incrementally evolves and adapts over time in the complex face of changing political, military, and social circumstances. In his work on ethnic cleansing, sociologist Michael Mann affirms that "it is rare to find evil geniuses plotting mass murder from the very beginning . . . murderous cleansing typically emerges as a kind of Plan C, developed only after the first two responses to a perceived ethnic threat fail."[185] So, although genocide is certainly perpetrated deliberately, the route to deliberation is usually complex, contingent, and circuitous. Given this reality, Verdeja advises policymakers—who must make decisions in real-time, as atrocities are ongoing—to "rather than apply [strict] legal expectations of genocidal intent . . . more usefully analyze perpetrators' capacity to inflict violence and their actual behavior and use this information to assess intentionality."[186]

Meaning of "In Whole or in Part." Even when the intent to destroy has been established, we are still left with the question of how much of the group has to be destroyed for the crime of genocide to have occurred. Is there a certain threshold of destruction that must be met? Can a single death, bodily injury, or forcible transfer of a child count as genocide? Or is the important question not one of quantity but rather one of intent?

In Lemkin's Madrid proposal, numbers seemed to matter less than the fact that the "attacks were carried out against an individual as a member of a collectivity . . . and undermine the fundamental basis of the social order."[187] The drafting history of the Genocide Convention reveals a clear recognition that the crime of genocide could have as its purpose the partial, not necessarily the whole, destruction of a group. Although the opening statement of Resolution 96(I) defined genocide as "a denial of the right of existence of entire human groups," a later paragraph of the same document spoke of groups having been destroyed "entirely or in part." Similarly, the Secretariat draft saw genocide as a "criminal act . . . with the purpose of destroying [groups of human beings] in whole or in part, or of preventing [their] preservation or development."[188] The Secretariat draft, in including "group massacres or individual executions" under the listed acts of destruction, also hinted that the quantitative threshold for "in part" might be rather low.[189] During Ad Hoc Committee deliberations, however, concern arose about the ambiguity of the phrase "in whole or in part" and a new text proposed by the United States eliminated the phrase in its entirety.[190] In the end, the final Ad Hoc Committee draft removed any reference to partial destruction by simply defining genocide as "acts committed with the intent to destroy a national, racial, religious or political group."[191]

During the Sixth Committee deliberation of the Convention, spurred by a Chinese proposal, Norway sought to restore language from the earlier drafts by submitting an amendment suggesting the words "in whole or in part" be inserted after the words "with intent to destroy" in Article II.[192] Although the Norwegian delegation did not want "to modify the sense of the second part of Article II," they did want to remind delegates "that it was not necessary to kill all the members of a group in order to commit genocide."[193] After extended discussion regarding this amendment, and three other proposed amendments related to Article II, the Norwegian amendment was adopted by 41 votes to 8, with two abstentions. As proposed, the final Convention text then read "genocide means any of the following acts committed with intent to destroy, in whole or in part."

Clearly, the phrase "in whole or in part" suffers from a lack of precision. "In whole" is clear, even if never realized. The extent of destruction is always bounded by the limits of territorial control and, even in territories under their control, perpetrators rarely achieve destruction "in whole," or in its totality. What, though, does "in part" mean? Is the scale of "in part" determined quantitatively or qualitatively? If the former, how many individuals constitute "in part?" Is such a threshold based on proportionate or absolute numbers? Or can "in part" refer to the more qualitative targeting of a specific part of the group (for example, the educated people, the leaders, male members)? As Straus points out, these are important questions from a preventive policymaking or activism perspective because "having a standard of total group destruction is self-defeating; concerned actors want to intervene before group destruction occurs."[194]

The "in part" question was actually raised during the Sixth Committee deliberations on Article II. In the same session in which the Norwegian amendment was passed, the French delegation "held that the crime of genocide existed as soon as an individual became the victim of acts of genocide. If a motive for the crime existed, genocide existed even if only a single individual were the victim."[195] The French delegation had even proposed an amendment to Article II, eventually withdrawn, that would extend the concept of genocide to cover cases in which a single individual was attacked as a member of a group. The U.S. delegation countered that "the concept of genocide should not be broadened to that extent" and other delegations agreed that the Convention should be restricted to cases of destructions of groups.[196] Indeed, the fact that the plural is used consistently in each of the listed acts of destruction in Article II strongly suggests that the framers of the Convention were certainly thinking of genocide as more than one victim—though "in part" still begged clarification.

Returning to the questions raised by the French delegation, the Ruhashyankiko report expressed "serious doubts as to the utility of a broad interpretation of the Convention" related to individual cases of murder.[197] In the Whitaker report, the Special Rapporteur suggested that "'in part' would seem to imply a reasonably significant number, relative to the total of the group as a whole, or else a significant section of a group such as its leadership." Still fearful of "too broad an interpretation," Whitaker offered that "considerations of both of proportionate scale and of total numbers are relevant."[198]

As Whitaker suggested, one way to think about "in part" is to do so *quantitatively* as absolute or proportionate total numbers of deaths. In his definition of mass killing, for instance, Valentino operationalizes "a massive number" as "at least fifty thousand intentional deaths over the course of five or fewer years."[199] Elsewhere, he and Jay Ulfelder use a measure of 1,000 civilian deaths to define mass killing.[200] In their evidence-based research on ending mass atrocities, Bridget Conley-Zilkic and Alex de Waal define "mass atrocities" as widespread and systematic violence that results in the deaths of 50,000 or more civilians within a 5-year period.[201] Political scientist Manus Midlarsky boundaries his cases of genocide to those described as "mass murder short of eradicating the entire group, but including a significant subset of that group in the killing." Midlarsky quantifies "significant subset" as "around 66–70%."[202]

Academics have variously included "substantial," "large part," "large scales," or "large portion" as quantitative measures in their working defini- tions of genocidal destruction.[203] Similarly, the U.S. Genocide Convention Implementation Act took a quantitative approach in describing the basic offense of genocide as including "the specific intent to destroy, in whole or in substantial part." The Act defined "substantial part" as meaning "a part of a group of such numerical significance that the destruction or loss of that part would cause the destruction of the group as a viable entity within the nation of which such a group is a part."[204] Likewise, the International Law Commission affirmed that "the crime of genocide by its very nature requires the intention to destroy at least a substantial part of a particular group."[205] Even then, it was clear that the answer to what constitutes "sub- stantial" would never be found in a rigid mathematical formula; rather it would come from judicial construction.[206]

The ICTY judgment against Goran Jelisic asserted that "it is widely acknowledged that the intention to destroy must target at least a *substan- tial* [italics in original] part of the group."[207] An ICTY appeals court agreed that "it is well established that ... the part must be a substantial part of that group" and that "the part targeted must be significant enough to have an impact on the group as a whole."[208] These standards are consistent with those adopted by the Trial Chambers of the ICTR. Although there is not a legal minimum percentage from which it is possible to infer that a "substantial" part of the group has been destroyed, courts have looked to the number of actual victims in proportion to the total number of people in the victim group. For example, an ICTY case against Dusko Sikirica held that 2–2.8% of Muslim victims in a municipality "would hardly qualify as a 'reasonably substantial' part of the Bosnian Muslim group in Prijedor ... this is not a case in which the intent to destroy a substantial number of Bosnian Muslims ... can properly be inferred."[209]

Such an approach is technically inconsistent with a literal reading of the Convention in which even a small number of victims could constitute the crime of genocide. In 1996, for instance, four gold miners in Brazil were convicted of genocide after the 1993 killing of 16 Yanomami Indians in the Venezuelan Amazon, a ruling upheld by Brazil's highest court in 2006.[210] Indeed, judgments of the Tribunals indicate that only one victim is required to meet the "members of the group" designation.[211] Because the Convention also criminalizes "attempt to commit genocide" in Article III, the crime of genocide—in theory—can even be committed with no victims at all. In practice, however, the number of victims—in terms of quantity or proportion—is necessarily relevant in assessing the perpetrator's intent. As Schabas points out, "The greater the number of actual victims, the more plausible becomes the deduction that the perpetrator intended to destroy the group, in whole or in part."[212]

Clearly, arbitrary quantitative measures of "in part," however defined, raise both ethical and practical issues. They can lead to a "hierarchy of horrible" in which one group's suffering, quantified only by numbers or proportions, becomes privileged over another group's sufferings. Six million deaths can become the unspoken standard by which all other genocides are measured. Quantitative understandings of "in part" also may be criticized for their insensitivity to targeted destruction based on status, role, or geography.

In response, many scholars have found that a more productive way to think about the meaning of "in part" is to do so *qualitatively*. Such an approach was prefaced by Whitaker's repeated use of the modifying adjective "significant" and has since been reiterated through subsequent qualitative interpretations of "in part" that have breathed judicial life into a deathly term.

One qualitative way of understanding "in part," for instance, would be as the selective destruction of significant social segments of a group. A UN-appointed Commission of Experts, tasked to examine violations of international law in the former Yugoslavia, made a contextual argument that "if essentially the total leadership of a group is targeted, it could also amount to genocide . . . Such leadership includes political and administrative leaders, religious leaders, academics and intellectuals, business leaders and others . . . [and] may be a strong indication of genocide regardless of the actual numbers killed."[213] The Sikirica court similarly held that "the intention to destroy in part may yet be established if there is evidence that the destruction is related to a significant section of the group, such as its leadership."[214] For the Jelisic court, "Genocidal intent . . . may also consist of the desired destruction of a more limited number of persons selected for the impact that their disappearance would have upon the survival of the group as such."[215]

Along these same lines, the ICTY judgment against Krstic focused on Srebrenica's adult males as a significant stratum of the social fabric of the

Muslim community. The court found that "the Bosnian Serb forces had to be aware of the catastrophic impact that the disappearance of two or three generations of men would have on the survival of a traditionally patriarchal society . . . The Chamber concludes that the intent to kill all the Bosnian Muslim men of military age in Srebrenica constitutes an intent to destroy *in part* [italics mine] the Bosnian Muslim group . . . and therefore must be qualified as genocide."[216]

Another qualitative way of understanding "in part" can come from examining genocidal intent that is limited to a targeted geographic zone—continent, country, region, city, town, village, or administrative municipality. Indeed, such a qualitative interpretation of "in part" has been widely accepted in international jurisprudence. At the International Court of Justice, for instance, Judge Elihu Lauterpacht argued that Serbs were guilty of genocide "clearly directed against an ethnical or religious group as such, and they intended to destroy that group, if not in whole certainly in part, to the extent necessary to ensure that the group no longer occupies the parts of Bosnia-Herzegovina coveted by the Serbs."[217] Likewise, in the Jelisic trial judgment, it was held that "genocide may be perpetrated in a limited geographic zone," region, or municipality.[218] The Krstic court held that ". . . the killing of all members of the part of a group located within a small geographical area, although resulting in a lesser number of victims, would qualify as genocide if carried out with the intent to destroy the part of the group as such located in this small geographical area."[219]

In conclusion, it seems clear that the textual location of "in whole or in part," coming immediately after "intent to destroy," firmly grounds the determination of "in part" in the intent of the perpetrator. As a result, Schabas reminds us, "the fundamental question is not how many victims were actually killed or injured, but rather how many victims the perpetrator intended to attack."[220] In other words, "in whole or in part" should be taken as referring to the intent of the perpetrator, not to the result. Indeed, a wealth of international case law has affirmed that "any act committed with the intent to destroy a part of a group, as such, constitutes an act of genocide within the meaning of the [Genocide] Convention."[221]

JURISDICTIONAL RESPONSIBILITY

Finally, for Lemkin, the issue of jurisdictional responsibility for the crime of genocide had been a priority since his original Madrid proposal. His suggestion of "universal repression"—meaning that any country could try a perpetrator, regardless of where the atrocities were committed—was a precursor to what is today called "universal jurisdiction." For Lemkin, universal repression meant that "a criminal cannot claim any right to asylum ... International law invokes the solidarity of the states in punishing such crimes, and makes the soil burn under the feet of such offenders."[222]

Although universal repression was among the objectives of those who proposed Resolution 96 (I), the final draft of the text does not include the principle by name and includes reference only to the "punishment of genocide [as] a matter of international concern" and recommends "international co-operation be organized between States with a view to facilitating the speedy prevention and punishment of the crime of genocide."[223] The following year, the Secretariat draft, under Article VII, specifically included the related notion of "universal enforcement," or the idea that contracting parties could "punish any offender . . . within any territory under their jurisdiction, irrespective of the nationality of the offender or of the place where the offence has been committed."[224]

During Ad Hoc Committee deliberations, however, any reference to universal repression or enforcement was completely removed. Summary notes indicated that those in favor of universal repression held that the national courts of a state that had committed genocide would certainly "not enforce repression of genocide"; that is, states would rarely prosecute themselves.[225] As genocide scholar Philip Spencer points out, even if there was a change in regime the chances of justice might be remote given that the new regime could include former members of the old regime. Alternatively, a radically new regime might implement victor's justice to exact revenge against an old regime.[226] In addition, as some of the delegates maintained, universal repression was consistent with international law related to trafficking in women and children, counterfeiting currency, and similar crimes of international concern. Other delegates of the Ad Hoc Committee, however, feared universal repression's infringement on state sovereignty, as well as its potential retaliatory political uses. "There is a danger," opponents suggested, "that the principle of universal repression might lead national courts to exercise a biased and arbitrary authority over foreigners."[227]

Following discussion, the principle of universal repression was rejected by four votes against two with one abstention. A subsequent proposal to reverse that decision was again rejected by four votes against two with one abstention. In the place of universal repression, Article VII of the final Ad Hoc Committee draft limited the jurisdictional terrain by urging that "persons charged with genocide . . . shall be tried by a competent tribunal of the State in the territory of which the act was committed or by a competent international tribunal."[228] The inherent understanding of this wording was that courts with territorial jurisdiction would take precedence, with a still-to-be-constituted international court acting only when the former had failed to act (known today as the principle of complementarity).

After fairly lengthy—and sometimes bitter—discussion, and consideration of several alternative amendments, the Sixth Committee followed the Ad Hoc Committee draft in explicitly rejecting universal repression in favor of territorial jurisdiction.[229] The Sixth Committee was particularly concerned with clarifying Article VII's brief mention of "a competent international tribunal." After deleting the phrase from consideration, a new drafting committee put forward an amended text. Becoming Article VI in the final text, the Sixth Committee draft—which would become the official text of the final Genocide Convention—read: "Persons charged with genocide . . . shall be tried by a competent tribunal of the State in the territory of which the act was committed, or by such international penal tribunals as may have jurisdiction with respect to those Contracting Parties which shall have accepted its jurisdiction." Although the text may be read as maintaining the principle of complementarity as understood in the Ad Hoc Committee draft, some states made clarifying declarations at ratification to ensure that they would not automatically be subject to the jurisdiction of any future international courts or tribunals.

In subsequent practice, however, the jurisdictional responsibility aspect of the Genocide Convention has undergone substantive expansion in customary international law. By customary international law, we are referring to a state's established pattern of general practices that are carried out from a subjective sense that the state is legally obligated to perform such actions; this is contrasted with state practices arising from contractual obligations imposed by formal written international treaties or laws. That is, customary international law emerges because nations feel compelled to behave in a certain way. In the 1961 case, for instance, of *Israel v. Eichmann*, the Israeli Supreme Court held that "[I]n the absence of an International Court, the international law is in need of the judicial and legislative authorities of every country, to give effect to its penal injunctions and to bring criminals to trial. The jurisdiction to try crimes under international law is universal."[230] Judicially, the court argued—directly contrary to Article VI of the Convention—that customary international law gave States "the universal *power* . . . to prosecute cases of this type . . . a power which is based on *customary* international law."[231] In essence, the court took the right of customary international law as overriding any legal limits of what they saw as the "compulsory minimum" obligation established by Article VI in the Convention. They viewed Eichmann as an enemy of the whole international community and his crimes as universally harmful; so, in the court's eyes, there was no compelling legal justification for his crimes to be restricted to the territorial jurisdiction of the state of which he was a citizen or in which the atrocities were perpetrated. Tellingly, countries that could have tried Eichmann under the principle of territorial jurisdiction did not protest Israel's precedent-setting exercise of universal jurisdiction.

The impact of the Eichmann trail on the issue of jurisdictional responsibility for genocide was such that by 1975, Israeli legal scholar Yoram Dinstein was able to summarize the current state of international criminal law as follows: "[T]he crime of genocide exists under both customary and conventional international law, and, whereas no universal jurisdiction pertains to it under conventional law . . . there is—and continues to be—a universal jurisdiction under customary law . . . jurisdiction existing on the strength of custom is wider than that accorded by the Convention."[232] Three years later, the Ruhashyankiko report even went beyond its usually conservative summative tone to recommend that "since no international criminal court has been established [as suggested by Article VI of the Convention], the question of universal punishment should be reconsidered . . . While recognizing the political implications of the application of the principle of universal punishment for the crime of genocide, the Special Rapporteur remains convinced that the adoption of this principle would help to make the 1948 Genocide Convention more effective."[233] Similarly, in arguing for an international criminal court, the 1985 Whitaker report bemoaned that "[I]n actual practice, mass murderers are protected by their own Governments . . . too often respect for State sovereignty, domestic jurisdiction and territorial integrity can, and does, take precedence over the wider human concern for protection against genocide."[234]

Although the world would continue to wait for some form of an international judicial body to deal with the crime of genocide, advisory and legal understandings of universal jurisdiction increasingly echoed the precedent set decades earlier by the Israeli Supreme Court. For instance, the 1994 UN Commission of Experts established to examine violations of international law in the former Yugoslavia asserted that "the only offenses committed in internal armed conflict for which universal jurisdiction exists are 'crimes against humanity' and genocide, which apply irrespective of the conflicts' classification."[235] Legal scholar Theodor Meron maintains that ". . . it is increasingly recognized by leading commentators that the crime of genocide (despite the absence of a provision on universal jurisdiction in the Genocide Convention) may also be cause for prosecution by any state . . . Once internal atrocities are recognized as international crimes and thus as matters of major international concern, the right of third states to prosecute violators must be accepted."[236] Amnesty International continues its appeal for all governments to enact and use legislation providing for universal jurisdiction. The International Law Commission has also endorsed universal jurisdiction for the crime of genocide. As Schabas summarizes: "Their [Israeli Supreme Court] audacious proclamation of a customary norm [for universal jurisdiction] has gone relatively unchallenged . . . Authority continues to grow in support of the proposition that, despite the terms of article VI, States may exercise universal jurisdiction over the crime of genocide."[237]

There are certainly numerous examples of national trials in which territorial jurisdiction was invoked to try perpetrators accused of the crime of genocide in the state in which the atrocities were committed (most notably in Rwanda). Since the landmark Eichmann trial, however, we have also seen several cases in which the customary right of universal jurisdiction has been exercised to try crimes regardless of the nationality of the perpetrator and victim or the location in which the crime occurred. According to Amnesty International, since the end of World War II, more than 15 countries have exercised universal jurisdiction in investigations or prosecutions of persons suspected of crimes under international law— including Australia, Austria, Belgium, Canada, Denmark, Finland, France, Germany, Netherlands, Norway, Senegal, Spain, the United Kingdom, and the United States. Others, such as Mexico, have extradited persons to other countries for prosecution based on the exercise of universal jurisdiction.[238] As just one recent example of the application of universal jurisdiction, in February 2014 a Paris court opened France's first trial of a suspect accused of complicity in the Rwandan genocide—a noteworthy break from the accusations that France had been harboring such perpetrators for the past 20 years. The trial was made possible by a 1996 national law that grants French courts universal jurisdiction for such exceptional crimes. The accused, Pascal Simbikangwa, was eventually found guilty of complicity in genocide and was sentenced to 25 years imprisonment.

Spain has been notably active in exercising the customary right of universal jurisdiction over the crime of genocide. In 1985, Spain passed an Organic Law that gave their national courts universal jurisdiction over certain egregious crimes regardless of the nationality of the victims and perpetrators—including the crime of genocide. Spain took, however, this principle of universal jurisdiction as more than simply an aspirational ideal and, in 1996, began actively investigating human rights cases arising from the human rights abuses in Argentina (1976–1983) and the Pinochet dictatorship in Chile (1973–1990). In 1998, Spanish magistrate Baltasar Garzon even attempted to extradite former Chilean dictator Augusto Pinochet from his house arrest in England on charges of genocide, terrorism, torture, and the various offenses that made up the crime of forced "disappearance" in Spain. Although the British government would eventually refuse to extradite Pinochet, Spain's attempt marked the first time that a former head of government had been arrested on the principle of universal jurisdiction.[239] In the words of the Center for Justice and Accountability, the Pinochet case "launched the modern concept of universal jurisdiction and opened the door to the exercise of universal jurisdiction over human rights crimes by national courts."[240]

Indeed, the following year, Guatemalan Nobel Peace Prize laureate Rigoberta Menchu and a group of Spanish and Guatemalan nongovernmental organizations walked through that open door and filed a suit in the Spanish National Court against eight senior Guatemalan government officials, including former dictator Rios Montt. The suit charged the defendants with terrorism, genocide, and systematic torture committed during the early 1980s. The case was initially dismissed by the Spanish National Court on the grounds that the plaintiffs had not adequately exhausted all available legal avenues in Guatemala (which, in reality, were virtually nonexistent). A subsequent appeal to the Spanish Supreme Court resulted in a finding of limited jurisdiction only for cases that showed a close tie to Spain. On September 26, 2005, however, Spain's highest court, the Constitutional Tribunal, overthrew the Supreme Court finding and affirmed that Spain was a country that observes the principles of universal jurisdiction for crimes of international concern. At present, the Spanish case against the senior Guatemalan officials is still in the pretrial investigation phase.[241]

In November 2013, a Spanish court indicted several former Chinese leaders on allegations of genocide, torture, and other crimes against humanity against the people of Tibet. After angry protests from China, economic and political interests led Spain's ruling Popular Party to adopt legal reforms drastically reducing the scope of their domestic universal jurisdiction law. As of March 2014, "no longer can Spanish criminal courts have jurisdiction over offences committed outside the Spanish territory irrespective of the perpetrator's or victims' nationality or any other link with Spain."[242] Although there is concern that the repeal of Spain's universal jurisdiction law would be a setback for human rights efforts worldwide, some of Spain's judges are not quite ready to shed their well-earned mantle as provocateurs of international criminal law. In April 2015, for instance, Spanish judge Pablo Ruz ruled that 11 Moroccan officials should stand trail on charges of genocide in connection with the former Spanish protectorate of Western Sahara from 1976 to 1991. Because many of the victims were considered Spanish citizens from that period, the judge's ruling is likely to stand—though the Spanish government has yet to decide whether it would seek the extradition of the suspects from Morocco.[243]

Despite Spain's recent retreat, however, the spirit of Lemkin's original principle of "universal repression," though not present in the final text of the Genocide Convention, has found renewed life in the development of customary international law. As Kenneth Roth, Executive Director of Human Rights Watch, has claimed: "It has come to the point where the main limit on national courts empowered to exercise universal jurisdiction is the availability of the defendant, not questions of ideology."[244] Indeed, as Schabas concludes: "Many of the norms in the Genocide Convention, including the definition itself, have remained essentially unchanged over the years. In one important respect, however, the Convention is woefully out of date . . . The Convention's failure to recognize universal jurisdiction is one of its historic defects, but one that is now resolved by the evolution of customary international law . . . The rejection of universal jurisdiction by the General Assembly that is reflected in article VI no longer corresponds to State practice . . . There is simply too much State practice and judicial authority to support a credible challenge to the principle of universal jurisdiction where genocide is concerned . . . Today, there can be little doubt that genocide is a crime subject to universal jurisdiction."[245]

During the drafting of the final text of the Genocide Convention in 1948, U.S. representative Ernest Gross stated that "Once those ratifications were secured, it might be possible, should occasion arise, to make certain improvements in the convention."[246] Gross' recommendation was instantiated in Article XVI of the Convention specifically allowing that "a request for the revision of the present Convention may be made at any time by any Contracting Party." Since its ratification in 1951, however, not one word of the Convention has been revised, or even revisited. In 1998, when the UN held a diplomatic conference in Rome to lay the groundwork for the establishment of an International Criminal Court, Cuba was the only voice to suggest a revision (namely the inclusion of social and political groupings and a reference to intentional conduct) to the Convention.[247] That lone voice was drowned out by a sea of "widespread support" agreeing, in the words of the representative from Greece, that "the definition of genocide [passed by the General Assembly fifty years earlier] posed no real problems."[248] So, the text of the Convention stands today exactly as it stood at the time of its ratification.

The Convention's definition of the crime of genocide was adopted, without significant change, in the statutes of the ad hoc criminal tribunals for the former Yugoslavia and Rwanda as well as the International Law Commission's Code of Crimes Against the Peace and Security of

Mankind and the Rome Statute of the International Criminal Court.[249] Despite its legal ubiquity, various activist groups and leaders continue to call for revision or outright replacement of the Convention—particularly in light of the fact that it has been invoked only one time by the UN and that was months after the genocide ended in Rwanda. Most recently, in 2012, the Institute for Cultural Diplomacy called for the creation of an independent committee within the United Nations to revisit and review the Convention, and in turn develop a specific proposal for a revision and amendment to the Convention.[250]

Despite these calls, however, today there is no substantive movement to consider revision of the Convention. Why is there such resistance to revisiting the Convention? From a cynical perspective, it could be argued that the Convention works just the way the Member States of the UN wish it to—it is both vague and narrow enough to ensure that it need never be invoked. In this sense, the Convention is not a "failure" but, rather, as it stands now, it is working quite well for its purposes—a consistent pattern of nonintervention when civilian populations are being "done to death." So, it is not broken, but it is ruthlessly effective.[251] Although portions of that perspective may be true, it is an incomplete truth without also recognizing that over six decades of evolution in international and domestic humanitarian law—complemented by input from academic, political, and civil society debate—has filled in many of the gaps and challenges of the Genocide Convention.

Still, we are right to question if our considerable efforts to find the essence of the essentially contested concept of "genocide" have reduced this "odious scourge" in any appreciable way. Even as early as 1985, Benjamin Whitaker lamented that ". . . although the Convention has been in force since 12 January 1951, any ascertainable effect of it is difficult to quantify, whereas all to [sic] much evidence continues to accumulate that acts of genocide are still being committed in various parts of the world."[252] It may even be argued that there have been more crimes of genocide committed since the passage of the Convention than before it. As Powell writes: "We should be struck by the fact that . . . the era in which genocide was made criminal for the first time is also the era in which it achieved effects of scale, efficiency, and frequency that stun the imagination."[253] As legal scholar Diane Orentlicher painfully reminds us, the Convention's "moral force is surely ironic," in light of its persistent failure to protect civilians from being "done to death" by genocide.[254] Indeed, today, our struggle is less with the substance of the Convention and the "rightful name" of genocide; rather, our struggle is more with finding the most effective ways to enforce the Convention's obligation to prevent, as well as to punish, genocide.

NOTES

1. Although, over the years, there has been considerable controversy surrounding the question of who, exactly, was responsible for shooting down the plane, the emerging consensus is that Hutu extremists opposed to negotiation with the RPF bore responsibility for the assassination. For instance, a 2012 report by experts appointed by the French Judges Marc Trevidic and Nathalie Poux concluded that the missile fire that brought down the Rwandan president's plane in 1994 and sparked the country's genocide came from a military camp controlled by his own ethnic group and not Tutsi rebels (see http://www.cnn.com/2012/01/11/world/africa/rwanda-president-plane/index.html, accessed July 7, 2014).

2. Romeo Dallaire, *Shake Hands with the Devil: The Failure of Humanity in Rwanda* (Toronto, Ontario, Canada: Random House, 2003), 232.

3. "Cold Choices in Rwanda," *The New York Times* (April 23, 1994), accessed August 27, 2013 at http://www.nytimes.com/1994/04/23/opinion/cold-choices-in-rwanda.html.

4. "Pope Deplores Genocide," *Chicago Tribune News* (April 27, 1994), accessed August 27, 2013 at http://articles.chicagotribune.com/1994-04-27/news/9404280028_1_weekly-general-audience-cor-unum-peace-conference.

5. Samantha Power, *"A Problem from Hell:" America and the Age of Genocide* (New York, NY: Perennial, 2002), 569 (n45).

6. Michael Barnett, *Eyewitness to a Genocide: The United Nations and Rwanda* (Ithaca, NY: Cornell University Press, 2002), 3.

7. Ibid, 133.

8. UN Document S/1994/640, May 31, 1994, 11.

9. UN Document S/1994/728, June 20, 1994, 1.

10. Ironically, Rwanda had become the newest nonpermanent member of the Security Council on January 1, 1994.

11. Quoted material taken from UN Document S/RES/918, May 17, 1994, 1–2.

12. In April 2014, during a commemoration of the 20th anniversary of the Rwandan genocide, former New Zealand ambassador Colin Keating, who was president of the UN Security Council in April 1994, issued a rare apology for the council's refusal to recognize that genocide was taking place in Rwanda and for doing nothing to stop it.

13. Clinton Presidential Records, National Security Council, e-mail from Alan Kreczko to Donald Steinberg, May 26, 1994, accessed July 7, 2014 at http://www.clintonlibrary.gov/assets/storage/Research%20-%20Digital%20Library/formerlywithheld/batch5/2006-0646-F.pdf.

14. Douglas Jehl, "Officials Told to Avoid Calling Rwanda Killings 'Genocide,'" *The New York Times* (June 10, 1994), accessed August 27, 2013 at http://www.nytimes.com/1994/06/10/world/officials-told-to-avoid-calling-rwanda-killings-genocide.html.

15. Ibid.

16. State Department briefing, Federal News Service, June 10, 1994. Also accessed August 27, 2013 at http://www.pbs.org/wgbh/pages/frontline/shows/evil/etc/slaughter.html.

17. Charles Mironko, *"Igitero*: Means and Motive in the Rwandan Genocide," *Journal of Genocide Research* 6 (2004), 58.

18. UN Document S/1994/1125, October 4, 1994, 2.

19. Accessed August 27, 2013 at http://millercenter.org/president/speeches/detail/ 4602. See also "Clinton's Painful Words of Sorry and Chagrin," *The New York Times* (March 26, 1998). Clinton would later describe his administration's inaction as one of the greatest regrets of his time in office. In 2013 he told an interviewer, "If we'd gone in sooner, I believe we could have saved at least a third of the lives that were lost . . . It had an enduring impact on me" (see Alissa J. Rubin and Maia de la Baume, "Claims of French Complicity in Rwanda's Genocide Rekindle Mutual Resentment," *The New York Times*, April 8, 2014).

20. The initial quote is from Michael Ignatieff, "Lemkin's Word" (February 26, 2001), accessed November 14, 2013 at http://www.newrepublic.com//article/politics/ lemkins-word; the second quote is from Michael Ignatieff, preface, in Simon Norfolk, *For Most of It I Have No Words* (London, England: Dewi Lewis, 1998).

21. A. Dirk Moses, "Genocide," *Australian Humanities Review* 55 (2013), 26.

22. W. B. Gallie first discussed "essentially contested concepts" at the March 21, 1956 Meeting of the Aristotelian Society at Bedford Square in London; the quoted material is taken from p. 169 of the proceedings. Christopher Powell offers an insightful analysis of Gallie's work in his "What Do Genocides Kill? A Relational Conception of Genocide," *Journal of Genocide Research* 9 (2007): 527–547.

23. The phrase "conceptual blockages" is taken from A. Dirk Moses, "Conceptual Blockages and Definitional Dilemmas in the 'Racial Century': Genocides of Indigenous Peoples and the Holocaust," *Patterns of Prejudice* 36 (2002).

24. The quoted material is taken from Gallie, pp. 168 and 169.

25. Christopher Powell, *Barbaric Civilization: A Critical Sociology of Genocide* (Montreal, Canada: McGill-Queen's University Press, 2011), 67.

26. The text of the piece can be found at http://www.rattle.com/poetry/2009/04/ whats-genocide-by-carlos-andres-gomez/, accessed September 1, 2013.

27. Accessed September 1, 2013 at http://nymag.com/daily/intelligencer/2010/11/ president_obama_spares_two_tur.html.

28. Accessed September 14, 2013 at http://www.thecourier.co.uk/news/uk/ brian-may-makes-badger-genocide-apology-1.130318.

29. Accessed October 17, 2013 at http://mediamatters.org/print/blog/2013/10/04/ wash-times-kuhner-smears-obamacare-as-facilitat/196278. Kuhner joins a long history of antiabortion campaigners who exploit the concept of genocide to get their message across more forcefully; one traveling antiabortion photomural exhibit, featuring graphic images of aborted fetuses, bills itself as the "Genocide Awareness Project."

30. Accessed November 8, 2013 at http://www.latimes.com/local/lanow/ la-me-ln-wild-boar-killings-pig-genocide-san-jose-20131106,0,120411. story#axzz2k3aAbvzx.

31. "Chinese Fishing Boats Accused of Engaging in 'Marine Genocide'" (February 11, 2015), accessed February 13, 2015 at http://www.undercurrentnews. com/2015/02/11/chinese-fishing-boats-accused-of-engaging-in-marine-genocide/.

32. Accessed March 3, 2015 at http://www.rferl.org/content/russia-ukraine-gas-putin-cuts-genocide/26869573.html.

33. Accessed March 20, 2015 at http://www.kansascity.com/sports/mlb/kansas-city-royals/article13086695.html.

34. Martin Buber, *I and Thou* (Edinburgh, Scotland: Clark, 1937), 58.

35. Accessed October 17, 2013 at http://www.nytimes.com/2013/10/08/opinion/ bruni-nazis-lynching-and-obamacare.html.

36. Helen Fein, "Genocide, Terror, Life Integrity, and War Crimes: The Case for Discrimination," in George Andreopoulos (ed.), *Genocide: Conceptual and Historical Dimensions* (Philadelphia, PA: University of Pennsylvania Press, 1994), 96.
37. Steven Katz, *The Holocaust in Historical Context: The Holocaust and Mass Death before the Modern Age*, Vol. 1 (New York, NY: Oxford University Press, 1994), 138.
38. Adam Jones, *Genocide: A Comprehensive Introduction*, 2nd ed. (New York, NY: Routledge, 2011), 16–20.
39. Jones (2011) refers to this as the "softer" position in the definitional debates within genocide scholarship.
40. Accessed September 6, 2013 at http://www.un.org/en/documents/udhr/.
41. Scott Straus, "Identifying Genocide and Related Forms of Mass Atrocity," Working Paper for the U.S. Holocaust Memorial Museum (October 7, 2011).
42. Brian Kritz, "Jedis and Genocide," *Ozy* (November 19, 2013), accessed January 8, 2014 at http://www.ozy.com/c-notes/the-jedi-religion-and-international-law/3543.article.
43. Daniel Feierstein, "The Concept of 'Genocidal Social Practices,'" in *New Directions in Genocide Research*, ed. Adam Jones (New York, NY: Routledge, 2012), 20.
44. UN Document E/CN.4/Sub.2/416, July 4, 1978, paragraph 58.
45. Ibid, paragraph 87; repeated in paragraph 622.
46. UN Document E/CN.4/Sub.2/1985/6, July 2, 1985, paragraph 1. Benjamin Whitaker passed away at the age of 79 years on June 9, 2014.
47. Ibid, paragraph 30.
48. Ibid.
49. Ibid, paragraphs 34 and 36, respectively.
50. *The Prosecutor versus Jean-Paul Akayesu*, Case No. ICTR-96-4-T, September 2, 1998, paragraph 512. Accessed September 6, 2013 at http://www.unictr.org/Portals/0/Case/English/Akayesu/judgement/akay001.pdf.
51. Ibid, paragraphs 513–515.
52. Martin Shaw, *What Is Genocide?* (Malden, MA: Polity, 2007), 99.
53. Pieter Drost, *The Crime of State, Vol. 2, Genocide* (Leyden, the Netherlands: A. W. Sijthoff, 1959), 122–123.
54. William A. Schabas, "The Law and Genocide," eds. Donald Bloxham and A. Dirk Moses, *The Oxford Handbook of Genocide Studies* (New York, NY: Oxford University Press, 2010), 133.
55. *The Prosecutor versus Clement Kayishema and Obed Ruzindana*, Case No. ICTR-95-1-T, May 21, 1999, paragraph 98. Accessed September 7, 2013 at http://www.unictr.org/Portals/0/Case%5CEnglish%5Ckayishema%5Cjudgement%5C990521_judgement.pdf.
56. *The Prosecutor versus Goran Jelisic*, Case No. IT-95-10-T, December 14, 1999, paragraph 70. Accessed September 7, 2013 at http://www.icty.org/x/cases/jelisic/tjug/en/jel-tj991214e.pdf.
57. *The Prosecutor versus Ignace Bagilishema*, Case No. ICTR-95-1A-T, June 7, 2001, paragraph 65. Accessed September 13, 2013 at http://www.ictrcaselaw.org/docs/doc22004.pdf.
58. *Report of the International Commission of Inquiry on Darfur to the Secretary-General*, UN Document S/2005/60, February 1, 2005, paragraph 499. Accessed September 13, 2013 at http://www.securitycouncilreport.org/atf/cf/%7B65BFCF9B-6D27-4E9C-8CD3-CF6E4FF96FF9%7D/WPS%20S%202005%2060.pdf.

59. *Report of the International Commission of Inquiry on Darfur to the Secretary-General*, paragraph 512.
60. Larry May, *Genocide: A Normative Account* (New York, NY: Cambridge University Press, 2010), 47.
61. *Report of the International Commission of Inquiry on Darfur to the Secretary-General*, paragraph 494.
62. William A. Schabas, *Genocide in International Law: The Crimes of Crimes* (Cambridge, England: Cambridge University Press, 2000), 110.
63. William A. Schabas, *Genocide in International Law: The Crime of Crimes*, 2nd ed. (Cambridge, England: Cambridge University Press, 2009), 128.
64. Frank Chalk and Kurt Jonassohn, *The History and Sociology of Genocide: Analyses and Case Studies* (New Haven, CT: Yale University Press, 1990), 23.
65. Steven Katz, *The Holocaust in Historical Context*, 131.
66. Mark Levene, *Genocide in the Age of the Nation State, Volume 1* (London, England: I. B. Tauris, 2005), 79.
67. Quoted in Levene, *Genocide in the Age of the Nation State*, 87.
68. Jacques Semelin, *Purify and Destroy: The Political Uses of Massacre and Genocide* (London, England: Hurst & Company, 2007); cited in Adam Jones, *Genocide: A Comprehensive Introduction*, 2nd ed. (New York, NY: Routledge, 2011), 20.
69. Shaw, *What Is Genocide?*, 103–104.
70. Schabas, *Genocide in International Law*, 161–162; also see note 117 in David Shea Bettwy, "The Genocide Convention and Unprotected Groups: Is the Scope of Protection Expanding Under Customary International Law?," *Notre Dame Journal of International & Comparative Law* 167 (2011): 184.
71. Schabas, "The Law and Genocide," 131.
72. For a description of the Romanian penal code, see http://preventgenocide.org/law/domestic/romania.htm (accessed September 22, 2013).
73. Howard Shneider, "Political Genocide in Latin America: The Need for Reconsidering the Current Internationally Accepted Definition of Genocide in Light of Spanish and Latin American Jurisprudence," *American University Law Review* 25 (2010): 352.
74. Wade Mansell, *Public International Law* (University of London, London, England: The External Programme, 2006), 43.
75. Drost, *The Crime of State*; also cited in Jones, *Genocide: A Comprehensive Introduction*, 16.
76. Cited in Jones, *Genocide: A Comprehensive Introduction*, 17.
77. Helen Fein, "Genocide: A Sociological Perspective," *Current Sociology* 38 (Spring 1990): 24; Levene, *Genocide in the Age of the Nation State*, 35.
78. Cited in Jones, *Genocide: A Comprehensive Introduction*, 20.
79. Shaw, *What Is Genocide?*, 99.
80. Daniel Feierstein, "The Concept of 'Genocidal Social Practices'," ed. Adam Jones, *New Directions in Genocide Research* (New York, NY: Routledge, 2012), 23.
81. Most "cides" in this list are taken from Jones, *Genocide: A Comprehensive Introduction*, 26–29. There is even a new global, grassroots campaign, "End Ecocide on Earth," to make the creation of environmental disasters a crime prosecutable by the International Criminal Court (see https://www.endecocide.org/en/).
82. Semelin, *Purify and Destroy*, 320.
83. Raymond Evans and Bill Thorpe, "The Massacres of Aboriginal History," *Overland* 163 (September, 2001): 36.

84. Barbara Harff, "Recognizing Genocides and Politicides," ed. Helen Fein, *Genocide Watch* (New Haven, CT: Yale University Press, 1992), 28. The term was first coined in Barbara Harff and T. R. Gurr, "Toward Empirical Theory of Genocides and Politicides: Identification and Measurement of Cases since 1945," *International Studies Quarterly* 37 (1988): 357–371.

85. Barbara Harff, "No Lessons Learned from the Holocaust? Assessing Risks of Genocide and Political Mass Murder since 1955," *American Political Science Review* 97 (2003): 58.

86. Ibid.

87. The complete text can be found at http://www.hrweb.org/legal/genocide.html, accessed January 23, 2011.

88. Ben Kiernan, *Blood and Soil: A World History of Genocide and Extermination from Sparta to Darfur* (New Haven, CT: Yale University Press, 2007), 13.

89. UN Document E/CN.4/Sub.2/1985/6, July 2, 1985, paragraph 40.

90. Drost (1959), 124.

91. *The Prosecutor versus Jean-Paul Akayesu*, Case No. ICTR-96-4-T, September 2, 1998, paragraph 500.

92. "Attorney General of the Government of Israel vs. Adolph Eichmann," District Court of Jerusalem, December 12, 1961, quoted in *The International Law Reports*, 36 (1968): 340; also cited in *The Prosecutor versus Jean-Paul Akayesu*, Case No. ICTR-96-4-T, September 2, 1998, paragraph 503.

93. *The Prosecutor versus Jean-Paul Akayesu*, Case No. ICTR-96-4-T, September 2, 1998, paragraph 731.

94. Ibid.

95. "Genocide Convention Implementation Act of 1987," 18 USC 1091, accessed November 3, 2013 at http://www.law.cornell.edu/uscode/text/18/1091.

96. Cited in Lawrence J. LeBlanc, *The United States and the Genocide Convention* (Durham, NC: Duke University Press, 1981), 106.

97. Ibid.

98. Judgment, *Prosecutor v. Vidoje Blagojevi and Dragan Jokic*, IT-02-60-T, January 17, 2005, paragraphs 647 and 649.

99. Ibid, paragraph 650.

100. Judgment, *Prosecutor v. Radislav Krstic*, UN-ICT Case No. IT-98-33-T, August 2, 2001, paragraphs 513 and 514.

101. On April 19, 2004, after an appeal court upheld a lesser charge for aiding and abetting genocide, the sentence was reduced to 35 years imprisonment. At present, Krstic is still serving his sentence at a prison in the United Kingdom.

102. Ernesto Verdeja, "Genocide: Debating Definitions," eds. Adam Lupel and Ernesto Verdeja, *Responding to Genocide: The Politics of International Action* (Boulder, CO: Rienner, 2013), 26.

103. *The Prosecutor versus Jean-Paul Akayesu*, Case No. ICTR-96-4-T, September 2, 1998, paragraph 506.

104. *Guatemala: Memory of Silence*, Report of the Commission for Historical Clarification: Conclusions and Recommendations (1999), paragraph 116.

105. See Roman Serbyn's "Lemkin on Genocide of Nations," *Journal of International Criminal Justice* 7 (2009): 123–130.

106. Norman M. Naimark, *Stalin's Genocides* (Princeton, NJ: Princeton University Press, 2010), 74–75. Naimark's estimate of 3–5 million deaths in the Ukraine (p. 70) is consistent with Nicolas Werth's figure of 3.5 to 3.8 million victims (p. 396 in Donald Bloxham and A. Dirk Moses, *The Oxford Handbook of Genocide*

Studies, 2010) as well as Timothy Snyder's figure of "no fewer than 3.3 million" (*Bloodlands*, 2010, p. 53). Estimates for famine-related deaths throughout the Soviet Union run as high as six to eight million. As Naimark concludes, however, "there is no consensus among historians about the numbers of victims" (p. 70).

107. Accessed November 12, 2013 at http://news.bbc.co.uk/2/hi/6193266.stm.

108. Sheri P. Rosenberg, "Genocide Is a Process, Not an Event," *Genocide Studies and Prevention*, 7 (2012): 20.

109. Cited in Schabas, *Genocide in International Law* (2nd ed), 177.

110. Ibid, 198.

111. The United Nations War Crimes Commission, *Law Reports of Trials of War Criminals* 7 (1948): 25–26. Accessed November 8, 2013 at http://www.loc.gov/rr/frd/Military_Law/pdf/Law-Reports_Vol-7.pdf.

112. *The Prosecutor versus Jean-Paul Akayesu*, Case No. ICTR-96-4-T, September 2, 1998, paragraph 507.

113. Ibid.

114. *Prosecutor v. Radislav Krstic*, Case No. IT-98-33-A, April 19, 2004, paragraphs 28 and 29.

115. Verdeja, "Genocide: Debating Definitions," 27.

116. Schabas, *Genocide in International Law* (2nd ed.), 201.

117. Peter Cluskey, "ICC Asked to Investigate Abduction by Boko Haram of 276 Nigerian Girls," *The Irish Times* (April 17, 2015), accessed April 20, 2015 at http://www.irishtimes.com/news/world/africa/icc-asked-to-investigate-abduction-by-boko-haram-of-276-nigerian-girls-1.2180056.

118. Donna-Lee Frieze, "New Approaches to Raphael Lemkin," *Journal of Genocide Research* 15 (2013): 248.

119. *The Prosecutor v. Georges Anderson Nderubumwe Rutaganda*, ICTR-96-3-T, paragraph 53.

120. Shaw, *What Is Genocide?*, 106.

121. "Bringing Them Home: Report of the National Inquiry into the Separation of Aboriginal and Torres Strait Islander Children from Their Families" (April 1997): 237. The full report is accessible at http://www.humanrights.gov.au/publications/bringing-them-home-report-1997. Also see Tony Barta's "Decent Disposal: Australian Historians and the Recovery of Genocide," ed. Dan Stone, *The Historiography of Genocide* (London, England: Palgrave Macmillan, 2010), 296–322. In a September 2014 interview, former Australian prime minister John Howard expressed his belief that the conclusion of the "Bringing Them Home" report alleging genocide was incorrect. Although accepting that there were "injustices," Howard, prime minister from 1996 until 2007, asserted: "I didn't believe genocide had taken place and I still don't." Accessed September 27, 2014 at http://www.thesundaily.my/news/1176354.

122. David MacDonald, "Genocide Is as Genocide Does," *Winnipeg Free Press*, September 25, 2014.

123. A copy of the letter was accessed November 8, 2013 at http://www.huffington-post.ca/bernie-farber/canada-genocide-first-nations_b_4122651.html. See also The Canadian Press, "At Least 3,000 Died in Residential Schools, Research Shows," accessed November 19, 2013 at http://www.cbc.ca/news/canada/at-least-3-000-died-in-residential-schools-research-shows-1.1310894.

124. See Suzanne Fournier and Ernie Crey, *Stolen from Our Embrace: The Abduction of First Nations Children and the Restoration of Aboriginal Communities* (Madeira Park, BC, Canada: Douglas & McIntyre, 1998).

125. Dawn Paley and Sandra Cuffe, "Genocide on Trial: Push for Justice in Guatemala Raises Questions about Canada's Residential Schools," *Canadian Dimension* (November/December, 2013), accessed January 3, 2014 at http://thetyee.ca/ News/2013/12/30/Genocide-Gautemala/. The September 2014 opening of the Canadian Museum for Human Rights revealed the extent of the degree to which Canada still grapples with its colonial past and the place of its indigenous communities. Although the museum includes a focused examination of five other genocides (the Ukrainian Holodomor, the Armenian genocide, the Holocaust, the Rwandan genocide, and the Srebrenica genocide in Bosnia), it does not recognize the experience of indigenous people in Canada as genocide. See https://humanrights.ca.

126. The Truth and Reconciliation Commission of Canada, "Honouring the Truth, Reconciling for the Future: Summary of the Final Report of the Truth and Reconciliation Commission of Canada" (2014), 1.

127. Martin Luther King, Jr., *Why We Can't Wait* (New York, NY: Penguin, 1963), 120.

128. Mary Annette Pember, "When Will U.S. Apologize for Boarding School Genocide?" (June 19, 2015), accessed June 22, 2015 at http://indiancountrytodaymedia network.com/2015/06/19/when-will-us-apologize-boarding-school-genocide-160797?page=0%2C2.

129. Bureau of Indian Affairs, U.S. Department of the Interior, "Gover Apologies for BIA's Misdeeds" (September 8, 2000), accessed November 8, 2013 at http:// www.bia.gov/idc/groups/public/documents/text/idc011935.pdf.

130. *Prosecutor v. Radislav Krstic*, Case No. IT-98-33-A (April 19, 2004), paragraphs 135–144; *Prosecutor v. Brdjanin*, Decision on Interlocutory Appeal, Case No. IT-99-36-A (March 19, 2004), disposition in paragraph 12.

131. Raphael Lemkin, *Axis Rule in Occupied Europe: Laws of Occupation, Analysis of Government, Proposals for Redress* (Washington, DC: Carnegie Endowment for International Peace, Division of International Law, 1944), 79.

132. See Schabas, *Genocide in International Law*, 257–260, for additional details.

133. UN Document A/C.6/86, November 26, 1946, Article I.

134. UN Document E/447, June 26, 1947.

135. UN Document E/794, May 24, 1948.

136. UN Document A/760, December 3, 1948.

137. Scott Straus, "Contested Meanings and Conflicting Imperatives: A Conceptual Analysis of Genocide," *Journal of Genocide Research* 3 (2001): 349–375.

138. Schabas, "The Law and Genocide," (2010), 138.

139. Keynote address delivered at the Seventh Biennial Meeting of the International Association of Genocide Scholars, Sarajevo, Bosnia-Herzegovina (July 10, 2007).

140. Rome Statue of the International Criminal Court, July 18, 1998, UN Document A/Conf.183/9, accessed January 14, 2014 at http://www.un.org/en/ga/search/ view_doc.asp?symbol=A/CONF.183/9. The Statute entered into force on July 1, 2002.

141. *The Prosecutor versus Jean-Paul Akayesu*, Case No. ICTR-96-4-T, September 2, 1998, paragraph 498.

142. *Prosecutor v. Goran Jelisic*, Case No. IT-95-10-A, July 5, 2001, paragraph 46.

143. Kiernan, *Blood and Soil*, 17. Ward Churchill has suggested degrees, or gradations, of genocidal intent that make room for "depraved indifference" as a form of genocide. See pp. 434–435 in his *A Little Matter of Genocide* (San Francisco, CA: City Lights Books, 1997).

144. Verdeja, "Genocide: Debating Definitions," 33.
145. Ibid.
146. May, *Genocide*, 121.
147. Kai Ambos, "Criminologically Explained Reality of Genocide, Structure of the Offence and the 'Intent to Destroy' Requirement," ed. Alette Smeulers,*Collective Violence and International Criminal Justice* (Antwerp, Belgium: Intersentia, 2010), 154.
148. Katherine Goldsmith, "The Issue of Intent in the Genocide Convention and Its Effect on the Prevention and Punishment of the Crime of Genocide: Toward a Knowledge-Based Approach," *Genocide Studies and Prevention* 5 (2010), quoted material taken from pp. 254 and 246.
149. *Prosecutor v. Jean-Paul Akayesu*, paragraph 520.
150. Cited in Douglas Irvin-Erickson, "Genocide, the 'Family of Mind' and the Romantic Signature of Raphael Lemkin," *Journal of Genocide Research* 15 (2013): 285–286.
151. *Prosecutor v. Goran Jelisic*, paragraph 49.
152. Ibid.
153. UN Document E/794, May 24, 1948, 14.
154. Donna-Lee Frieze (ed.), *Totally Unofficial: The Autobiography of Raphael Lemkin* (New Haven, CT: Yale University Press, 2013), 165.
155. UN Document A/C.6/SR.75, October 15, 1948, 119.
156. UN Document E/Cn.4/Sub.2/416, July 4, 1978, paragraph 104.
157. UN Document A/C.6/SR.76, October 16, 1948, 123.
158. Ibid, 124–125.
159. UN Document A/C.6/SR.77, October 18, 1948, 133.
160. May, *Genocide*, 144.
161. Ibid.
162. Quoted material taken from UN Document A/C.6/SR.78, October 19, 1948, 139.
163. UN Document E/CN.4/Sub.2/1985/6, July 2, 1985, paragraph 38.
164. Cited in *Prosecutor v. Radislav Krstic*, Case No. IT-98-33-T (August 2, 2001), paragraph 552.
165. See Chapter 3 in Benjamin A. Valentino, *Final Solutions: Mass Killing and Genocide in the 20th Century* (Ithaca, NY: Cornell University Press, 2004). One of the seminal works in the field, Frank Chalk and Kurt Jonassohn's *The History and Sociology of Genocide: Analyses and Case Studies* (New Haven, CT: Yale University Press, 1990) also offers a typology of genocide according to motive, noting that "in any actual case, more than one of these motives will be present" (p. 29).
166. May, *Genocide*, 140.
167. Schabas, *Genocide in International Law* (2nd ed.), 264.
168. UN Document E/CN.4/Sub.2/1985/6, July 2, 1985, paragraph 39.
169. *Sylvestre Gacumbitsi v. The Prosecutor*, Case No. ICTR-2001-64-A (July 7, 2006), paragraph 40.
170. *Prosecutor v. Goran Jelisic*, Case No. IT-95-10-A, July 5, 2001, paragraph 47.
171. Naimark, *Stalin's Genocides*, 25–26.
172. See Devrim Aydin, "The Interpretation of Genocidal Intent under the Genocide Convention and the Jurisprudence of International Courts," *The Journal of Criminal Law* (2014): 439.
173. *Prosecutor v. Radislav Krstic*, Case No. IT-98-33-T, August 2, 2001, paragraph 572.
174. Ibid, paragraph 619.

175. *Prosecutor v. Dusko Tadic*, Case No. IT-94-1-A, July 15, 1999, paragraph 227. This argument was also referenced in an ICTR Appeals Chamber rejection of an appellant's contention requiring proof of a prearranged common plan or operation (*The Prosecutor v. Clement Kayishema and Obed Ruzindana*, Case No. ICTR-95-1-A, June 1, 2001, paragraph 193).

176. *Prosecutor v. Goran Jelisic*, Case No. IT-95-10-A, July 5, 2001, paragraph 48.

177. A. Dirk Moses, "Conceptual Blockages and Definitional Dilemmas in the 'Racial Century': Genocides of Indigenous Peoples and the Holocaust," *Patterns of Prejudice*, 36 (2002).

178. Tony Barta, "Relations of Genocide: Land and Lives in the Colonization of Australia," eds. Isidor Wallimann and Michael N. Dobkowski, *Genocide and the Modern Age: Etiology and Case Studies of Mass Death* (Syracuse, NY: Syracuse University Press, 2000), 239.

179. *Report of the International Commission of Inquiry on Darfur to the Secretary-General* (January 25, 2005), paragraph 518. Additional details regarding intent can be found in paragraphs 513–517 and 519–521.

180. Ibid, paragraph 522.

181. See Scott Straus, "Darfur and the Genocide Debate," *Foreign Affairs* (January/February, 2005): 123–133.

182. Quoted material taken from Shaw, *What Is Genocide?*, 84.

183. Jerry Fowler, "A New Chapter of Irony: The Legal Implications of the Darfur Genocide Determination," *Genocide Studies and Prevention* 1 (2006): 35.

184. Karl A. Schleunes, *The Twisted Road to Auschwitz: Nazi Policy toward German Jews 1933–-1939* (Urbana, IL: University of Illinois Press, 1970).

185. Michael Mann, *The Dark Side of Democracy: Explaining Ethnic Cleansing* (New York, NY: Cambridge University Press, 2005), 8.

186. Verdeja, "Genocide: Debating Definitions," 34.

187. Raphael Lemkin, "Acts Constituting a General (Transnational) Danger Considered as Offences Against the Law of Nations," Special Report presented to the 5th Conference for the Unification of Penal Law in Madrid (October 14–20, 1933), accessed August 1, 2013, http://www.preventgenocide.org/lemkin/madrid1933-english.htm.

188. UN Document E/447, June 26, 1947, 5.

189. Ibid, 6.

190. UN Document E/AC.25/SR.12, April 23, 1948, 2.

191. UN Document E/794, May 24, 1948, 13.

192. UN Document A/C.6/228, October 12, 1948.

193. UN Document A/C.6/SR.73, October 13, 1948, 93.

194. Straus, "Identifying Genocide and Related Forms of Mass Atrocity," 15.

195. Ibid, 90–91.

196. Ibid, 92.

197. UN Document E/CN.4/Sub.2/416, July 4, 1978, 54.

198. UN Document E/CN.4/Sub.2/1985/6, July 2, 1985, 16.

199. Valentino, *Final Solutions*, 11–12.

200. Jay Ulfelder and Benjamin Valentino, "Assessing Risks of State-Sponsored Mass Killing," Political Instability Task Force (Washington, DC: 2008), accessed at http://papers.ssrn.com/sol3/papers.cfm?abstract_id=1703426 on July 11, 2014.

201. Bridget Conley-Zilkic and Alex de Waal, "Setting the Agenda for Evidence-Based Research on Ending Mass Atrocities," *Journal of Genocide Research* 16 (2014): 57.

202. Manus I. Midlarsky, *The Killing Trap: Genocide in the Twentieth Century* (Cambridge, England: Cambridge University Press, 2005), 10, 25.
203. See Israel W. Charny (ed.), *Encyclopedia of Genocide* (Vol. I) (Santa Barbara, CA: ABC-CLIO, 1999), 7 and Jones, *Genocide: A Comprehensive Introduction*, 16–20.
204. *Genocide Convention Implementation Act of 1987* (Public Law 100-606), November 4, 1988, section 1093 (8).
205. *Report of the International Law Commission on the Work of its Forty-Eighth Session* (May 6–July 26, 1996), accessed July 11, 2014 at http://legal.un.org/ilc/sessions/48/48sess.htm.
206. Also see LeBlanc, *The United States and the Genocide Convention*, Chapter 2.
207. *Prosecutor v. Goran Jelisic*, Case No. IT-95-10-T, December 14, 1999, text accessed July 10, 2014 at http://www.icty.org/x/file/Legal%20Library/jud_supplement/supp10-e/jelisic.htm.
208. *Prosecutor v. Radislav Krstic*, Case No. IT-98-33-A, April 19, 2004, paragraph 8.
209. *Prosecutor v. Dusko Sikirica, Damir Dosen, Dragan Kolundzija (Judgement on Defence Motions to Acquit)*, IT-95-8-T, International Criminal Tribunal for the former Yugoslavia (ICTY), 3 September 2001, quoted material taken form paragraphs 72 and 75, available at http://www.refworld.org/docid/414835554.html, accessed July 10, 2014.
210. See http://www.survivalinternational.org/news/1786, accessed August 8, 2014.
211. Schabas, *Genocide in International Law* (2nd ed.), 179.
212. Schabas, "The Law and Genocide," 136.
213. UN Document S/1994/674, May 27, 1994, paragraph 94.
214. *Prosecutor v. Dusko Sikirica*, paragraph 76.
215. *Prosecutor v. Goran Jelisic*, Case No. IT-95-10-T, December 14, 1999, paragraph 82.
216. *Prosecutor v. Radislav Krstic*, Case No. IT-98-33-T, August 2, 2001, paragraphs 584, 595, and 598.
217. Separate Opinion of Judge Lauterpacht, ICJ Reports (1993), 431–432. Accessed July 14, 2014 at http://www.icj-cij.org/docket/files/91/7323.pdf.
218. *Prosecutor v. Goran Jelisic*, Case No. IT-95-10-T, December 14, 1999, paragraph 83.
219. *Prosecutor v. Radislav Krstic*, Case No. IT-98-33-T, August 2, 2001, paragraph 590.
220. Schabas, "The Law and Genocide," 136.
221. *Prosecutor v. Radislav Krstic*, Case No. IT-98-33-T, August 2, 2001, paragraph 584.
222. Raphael Lemkin, "Genocide as a Crime under International Law," *United Nations Bulletin* (January 15, 1948): 70.
223. UN General Assembly, Fifty-Fifth Plenary Meeting, UN Document A/RES/96 (I), December 11, 1946, 189.
224. United Nations Economic and Social Council, "Draft Convention on the Crime of Genocide" (UN Document E/447), June 26, 1947, 38.
225. United Nations Economic and Social Council, "Report of the Committee and Draft Convention Drawn Up by the Committee" (UN Document E/794), May 24, 1948, 32.
226. Philip Spencer, *Genocide Since 1945* (London, England: Routledge, 2012), 18.
227. United Nations Economic and Social Council, "Report of the Committee and Draft Convention Drawn Up by the Committee" (UN Document E/794), May 24, 1948, 32.
228. Ibid, 29.

229. A detailed summary of the supporting and opposing arguments for "universal punishment" can be found in paragraphs 190–211 of the Ruhashyankiko report (UN Document E/CN.4/Sub.2/416, July 4, 1978).

230. *Attorney General v. Adolf Eichmann*, Criminal Case 40/61, paragraph 12. Accessed July 28, 2014 at http://www.nizkor.org/ftp.cgi/people/e/eichmann. adolf/transcripts/ftp.cgi?people/e/eichmann.adolf/transcripts/Judgment/ Judgment-002.

231. Cited in Yoram Dinstein, "International Criminal Law," *Israel Yearbook on Human Rights* 5 (1975): 62.

232. Ibid.

233. UN Document E/CN.4/Sub.2/416, July 4, 1978, paragraph 211; repeated in paragraph 627.

234. UN Document E/CN.4/Sub.2.1985/6, July 2, 1985, paragraph 76.

235. UN Document S/1994/674, May 27, 1994, paragraph 42.

236. Theodor Meron, "International Criminalization of Internal Atrocities," *The American Journal of International Law* 89 (July 1995): 569, 576.

237. Schabas, *Genocide in International Law*, 429.

238. Accessed July 16, 2014 at http://www.amnesty.org/en/international-justice/ issues/universal-jurisdiction.

239. After his return to Chile in March 2000, the Chilean Supreme Court withdrew his senatorial immunity and Pinochet was indicted at the request of Judge Juan Guzman. Charges were dismissed in 2002 on the grounds of Pinochet's declining mental state, but further charges were brought after a court reversed the ruling of dementia in 2004 and deemed Pinochet fit to stand trial. Pinochet died in December 2006 without having been convicted of any of the crimes for which he was accused.

240. Accessed July 16, 20114 at http://www.cja.org/article.php?id=342.

241. National prosecution of Rios Montt in Guatemalan courts is set to recommence in January 2015. Montt's trial marks the first time a former head of state was tried for genocide in his home country.

242. Rosa Ana Alija Fernandez, "The 2014 Reform of Universal Jurisdiction in Spain: From All to Nothing," *Zeitschrift fur International Strafrechtsdogmatik* (2014), 726, accessed April 11, 2015 at http://www.zis-online.com/dat/artikel/ 2014_13_883.pdf.

243. Carlotta Gall, "Spanish Judge Accuses Moroccan Former Officials of Genocide in Western Sahara," *The New York Times* (April 10, 2015), accessed April 11, 2015 at http://www.nytimes.com/2015/04/11/world/europe/spanish- judge-accuses-moroccan-former-officials-of-genocide-in-western-sahara. html?emc=edit_tnt_20150411&nlid=67962175&tntemail0=y&_r=0.

244. Kenneth Roth, "The Case for Universal Jurisdiction," *Foreign Affairs* (September/ October, 2001), accessed July 16, 2014 at http://www.foreignaffairs.com/arti- cles/57245/kenneth-roth/the-case-for-universal-jurisdiction.

245. Schabas, *Genocide in International Law*, 435, 647–648.

246. UN General Assembly, Sixth Committee Summary Records of Meetings, UN Document A/C.6/SR.128, November 29, 1948, 662.

247. Quoted material from Schabas, "The Law and Genocide," 130.

248. UN Document A/Conf.183/C.1/SR.3, June 17, 1998, 146, 149, 151.

249. William A. Schabas, "The 'Odious' Scourge': Evolving Interpretations of the Crime of Genocide," *Genocide Studies and Prevention* 1 (2006): 97.

250. Accessed September 1, 2013 at http://www.culturaldiplomacy.org/gphr/index. php?en_initiatives_the-un-genocide-convention.

251. Samantha Power has made this same argument regarding U.S. policy in her *"A Problem from Hell:" America and the Age of Genocide* (New York, NY: Perennial, 2002), xxi.

252. UN Document E/CN.4/Sub.2.1985/6 (July 2, 1985), paragraph 71.

253. Powell, *A Critical Sociology of Genocide*, 72.

254. Diane F. Orentlicher, "Genocide," eds. Roy Gutman and David Rieff, *Crimes of War* (New York, NY: W. W. Norton, 1999), 153.

CHAPTER 3

"By Our Words and Actions"

Pol Pot, born Saloth Sar in 1925, was one of a core of Cambodian student radicals, educated in Paris, who developed "a syncretic ideology, a toxic mix of anti-colonial, nationalist, racist, Stalinist, and Maoist ideas."[1] Inspired by his early membership in the French Communist Party, Pol Pot wanted to return Cambodians to the nostalgic grandeur of their past through a revolutionary agrarian plan that would harken back to the glories of the Angkor Empire of the twelfth to the fourteenth centuries. Central to this creation of a fully communist society was a Khmer nationalism built on ridding the diverse and multiethnic Cambodia of those deemed not "borisot" (pure). The impure included the educated, those "tainted" by anything foreign, and a wide range of "heredity enemies," especially the Vietnamese and other ethnic and religious minorities (persons of Chinese, Thai, Lao, or Kola ancestry as well as the Cham Muslim).

By 1962, Pol Pot had become leader of the Cambodian Communist Party and begun to wage a guerrilla war, leading an armed resistance movement known as the Khmer Rouge (Red Khmers or Cambodians), against the Cambodian government. Despite their high aspirations, the Khmer Rouge appeared to have marginal prospects of revolutionary success. Pol Pot himself described the Khmer Rouge as "fewer than five thousand poorly armed guerrillas . . . scattered across the Cambodian landscape, uncertain about their strategy, tactics, loyalty, and leaders."[2] That would begin to change, however, when the first U.S. ground troops were sent to neighboring Vietnam in March 1965. By 1970, the Vietnam War had spilled into the Cambodian countryside and extensive U.S. bombing campaigns, with massive civilian casualties, "drove an enraged populace into the arms of an insurgency [the Khmer Rouge] that had enjoyed relatively little support until the bombing began, setting in motion . . . the rapid rise of the Khmer Rouge."[3] By

1973, when the United States finally had withdrawn its last troops from Vietnam, General Lon Nol's U.S.-backed Cambodian government—now bereft of American military aid—was incapacitated by corruption, incompetence, and economic and military instability. On April 17, 1975, Pol Pot's Khmer Rouge communist party, enjoying a surge of popular support, overthrew what remained of the weakened military regime of Lon Nol. Pol Pot, "Brother Number One," installed himself as Prime Minister of Cambodia, proclaiming the new state of Democratic Kampuchea (DK).

Immediately after their seizure of power, the Khmer Rouge executed a ruthless evacuation of the two million inhabitants ("new people") of the capital, Phnom Penh. Thousands died of exhaustion and starvation. In the next weeks, the rest of the nation's cities were evacuated in a "forced rustification," with hospitals emptied, schools closed, factories deserted, money and wages abolished, monasteries cleared, and libraries scattered. There was a clear policy of "urbicide" to do away with cities as symbols of group identity, modernity, and mixed physical, social, and cultural spaces.[4]

The Khmer Rouge cut Cambodia off from the world. The new independent Khmer state was to be "uninfluenced by the West or the trappings of wealth and privilege."[5] Foreign and minority languages were banned and neighboring countries were attacked to regain ancient "lost territory." Free speech and free travel, even between villages, were eliminated. Cambodia's Theravada Buddhist religion—to which roughly 90% of the nation's population claimed adherence—was banned as reactionary. Following the lead of Maoist China, farming was completely collectivized with peasants forced into unpaid collective labor. The DK constitution abolished private property and failed to guarantee any human rights protections. In the 4 years of the Khmer Rouge reign, no Cambodian was free. "There were no political, civil, or human rights. To avoid being targeted, people did not wear glasses; no one dared speak French; and reading a novel was considered a capital offense."[6] There were no practicing lawyers, doctors, teachers, engineers, or scientists since it was presumed that any peasant could pick up the "simple" truths of these professions through experience.

In this prison camp state of eight million inmates, Ben Kiernan, founder of the Cambodian Genocide Program at Yale University, conservatively estimates that 1.7 million people (21–24% of the total population) were worked, starved, or beaten to death from 1975 to 1979.[7] Historian Robert Cribb maintains that the death toll was a little over two million.[8]

On January 7, 1979, Phnom Penh fell to the Vietnamese who installed a puppet regime—the People's Republic of Kampuchea—consisting largely of Cambodian communists who had deserted Pol Pot in 1977–1978. Pol Pot was forced to flee to the hill country bordering Thailand. There, the Khmer

Rouge set up guerrilla bases and, in a reconfigured coalition, continued to be recognized as the legal representative of Cambodia to the United Nations (UN) for another 15 years. No country in the world was willing to file a case against them in any international courts. Finally, in 1994, the Cambodian government outlawed the Khmer Rouge and urged civilians and guerrillas to defect. By 1997, the Khmer Rouge had splintered and Pol Pot's last loyalists had fled. Pol Pot was captured by other Khmer Rouge, given a perfunctory show trial, and placed under house arrest. On April 15, 1998, Pol Pot, at 70 years of age, was reputed to have died from undisclosed medical difficulties and his body was reportedly burned in the presence of Thai officials.

The international push for a tribunal to bring perpetrators of the Cambodian genocide to justice did not begin until after the fall of the Soviet Union.[9] Eventually, on May 13, 2003, after years of negotiation, the UN General Assembly approved an Agreement with the Royal Government of Cambodia to establish an ad hoc national court, with international participation, to try surviving Khmer Rouge leaders for genocide. On October 4, 2004, after a yearlong political stalemate in Phnom Penh, the joint tribunal—officially called the Extraordinary Chambers in the Courts of Cambodia (ECCC) for the Prosecution of Crimes Committed during the Period of Democratic Kampuchea—was ratified by lawmakers in the Cambodian National Assembly.

Nearly three decades after the fall of the Khmer Rouge, the court became fully operational in June 2007. Since its inception, the court has struggled with the long-term effects of government obstruction and non-cooperation. Several top Cambodian officials, including Prime Minister Hun Sen, were once themselves members of the Khmer Rouge and have a vested interest in constraining the circle of accountability encompassing the atrocities. As a result, the sum total of the court's work to date, at the cost of over $220 million, has been the trials of five persons in two cases.[10]

In July 2010, Kaing Guek Eav (alias Duch)—the former Chairman of the Khmer Rouge S-21 Security Center in Phnom Penh, accused of overseeing the deaths of approximately 15,000 people—was sentenced to 35 years in prison for crimes against humanity (later raised to a life sentence by the Supreme Court Chamber). Proceedings against Ieng Sary, Pol Pot's brother-in-law and Foreign Affairs Minister, were terminated following his death in March 2013 and those against his wife, Ieng Thirith (Minister of Social Affairs), have been stayed since November 2011 as she was found unfit to stand trial due to dementia. Most recently, on August 7, 2014, the court found the remaining two defendants—Nuon Chea, the regime's chief ideologist, and Khieu Samphan, its Head of State—guilty of crimes against humanity and sentenced them to life imprisonment.

In an upcoming second phase of the segmented trial for Nuon Chea and Khieu Samphan, the ECCC will address the charge of genocide, but only in relation to two Cambodian minorities—the Vietnamese and the Cham Muslim populations.[11] It is estimated that about 20,000 ethnic Vietnamese and 90,000 Cham Muslims (a minority ethnoreligious group) were killed by Pol Pot's regime.[12] Although the members of these two groups died in greater proportions (for instance, 36% of Cambodia's Cham population perished under the Khmer Rouge), the largest absolute numbers of victims came from the ethnic Khmer Cambodian majority— a group accounting for over 1.3 million of the total deaths from 1975 to 1979.[13] Sometimes referred to as an "autogenocide," the largest victim group—the Khmer—was also the group to which the perpetrators belonged. Unable to get its judicial mind around that challenge, the court has decided that the Khmer—who make up 90% of the Cambodian population today—will be left out of consideration for the genocide charge. In the words of a spokesperson for the court, Lars Olsen: "It is impossible to say it was an intent to destroy the Khmers. The perpetrators were of the same nationalities as the victims."[14] This was affirmed by Marcel Lemonde, one of the ECCC's international investigating judges: ". . . to establish that a genocide occurred, a group [national, ethnical, racial or religious] needs to have been identified, and that group cannot be the quasi entirety of the population—otherwise the notion [of genocide] no longer makes sense."[15]

Although Khmer survivors of Pol Pot's regime felt vindicated by the guilty verdicts and life sentences of Nuon Chea and Khieu Samphan on the charges of crimes against humanity, they also felt betrayed by the court's decision not to include Khmer victims in the subsequent genocide charge. Autogenocide—in this case Khmers killing other Khmers—is not excluded by the Genocide Convention. Moreover, echoing the contention from Chapter 2 that it is the perpetrators' definition of the victim group that is central to its meaning, it is clear that ethnic Khmer were reimagined as different sorts of social identities by the Khmer Rouge. This restructuring of Cambodia's national community allowed the Khmer Rouge to strategically manufacture the boundaries, and differences, of the Khmer victim group. The court's curious decision, however, to exclude this reality from the second phase of the trial stands as a revictimization of the Khmer survivors of the Cambodian genocide. One Khmer woman, now living in exile, said that Khmer were denied their "right to the precise term for what was done to us . . . [it was as though] history had not been understood." Another called the decision "an insult."[16]

As the Khmer throughout Cambodia faced their own deaths and the deaths of those they loved, the semantics of whether they were victims of "genocide" were irrelevant. Their indescribable suffering under Pol Pot's regime remains more potent than any term we could devise to describe it. In the insult of judicial offenses felt by many Khmer survivors and victims' families, however, we see a not-so-subtle hierarchy of suffering in which genocide stands as the marquee crime—taking higher billing over the supposedly lesser violations of war crimes, crimes against humanity, or ethnic cleansing.

In retrospect, this hierarchy was instantiated with the origins of the word "genocide." In a 1948 piece in the *United Nations Bulletin*, Lemkin wrote: "Indeed, genocide must be treated as the most heinous of all crimes. It is the crime of crimes."[17] The Whitaker report described genocide as "the ultimate crime and the gravest violation of human rights."[18] Since then, numerous legal tribunals—from the International Criminal Tribunal for the former Yugoslavia (ICTY) to the International Criminal Tribunal for Rwanda (ICTR) to the International Law Commission—have invoked the phrase "crime of crimes" in reference to the crime of genocide. Even William Schabas' landmark *Genocide in International Law* volume carries the subtitle *The Crime of Crimes*, clearly placing genocide at the apex of the pyramid of international crimes.[19] This distinctive ignominy suggests that the crime of genocide is more egregious, and carries more gravity, than that of war crimes, crimes against humanity, or ethnic cleansing. An ICTY Appeals Chamber, for instance, stated that "the crime of genocide is singled out for special condemnation and opprobrium . . . This is a crime against all humankind."[20]

In a strict legal sense, however, there is no hierarchy of international crimes and the word "genocide" says nothing about the scale of the crime. As an ICTR Appeals Chamber noted, "there is no hierarchy of crimes under the Statute, and . . . all of the crimes specified therein are 'serious violations of international humanitarian law', capable of attracting the same sentence."[21] Schabas agrees that "there are almost no distinctions to be made in terms of the legal consequences that flow from characterizing a crime as 'genocide', or 'crimes against humanity', or 'war crimes.'"[22] Similarly, the International Commission of Inquiry on Darfur wrote: "[G]enocide is not necessarily the most serious international crime. Depending upon the circumstances, such international offences as crimes against humanity or large scale war crimes may be no less serious and heinous than genocide."[23]

In practice, though, there is a hierarchy in which genocide is, in fact, singled out for "special condemnation and opprobrium" by the courts. Plea agreements, wary of the stringent evidentiary requirements for proof of intent and targeted destruction that must be satisfied to convict on the charge of genocide, generally opt for increased chances of success for conviction of crimes against humanity or war crimes. As Patricia Wald, a former judge on the ICTY, relates, ". . . in the prosecutor's world, genocide can and is used as a bargaining chip because of its super-stigma; it can be negotiated down to crimes against humanity in exchange for a guilty plea and the accuseds' help in prosecuting others . . . [T]he charge of a crime against humanity . . . can indeed leave room for bargaining down to a war crime if a plea appears likely."[24] Similarly, a review of sentencing decisions of the tribunals reveals that, generally, convictions for genocide result in the longest terms. So, it does appear, in practice, that although all international crimes are serious, one—genocide—is more serious than the others. The notion of genocide as the "crime of crimes" is also reinforced in popular media as well as in diplomatic and policymaking circles.

We must be diligent, though, against the development of a hierarchy of mass violence in which genocide trumps, and marginalizes, all other forms of large-scale destruction. Psychologist David Moshman suggests three reasons for caution in designating a hierarchy of mass violence: (1) there is substantial ambiguity, as we have seen, about what qualifies as genocide, (2) actual human rights catastrophes do not confine themselves conveniently to any one conceptual category; rather they often spill across an overlapping range of conceptual categories, and (3) there are individual and criminal fates arguably worse than death (for example, slavery and torture) that leave the abstract notion of genocide as the ultimate measure of criminal evil open to question.[25] In his 2004 testimony on Darfur before the U.S. Senate Foreign Relations Committee, then-U.S. Secretary of State Colin Powell also spoke of the danger that a hierarchy of mass violence can pose to effective response: ". . . let us not be too preoccupied with this [genocide] designation. These people are in desperate need and we must help them. Call it a civil war; call it ethnic cleansing; call it genocide; call it 'none of the above.' The reality is the same. There are people in Darfur who desperately need the help of the international community."[26] Moreover, as Gareth Evans points out, there is danger that a hierarchy of mass violence can actually become counterproductive in such a way that were genocide not to be proven in a given case, "lesser" charges of war crimes or crimes against humanity could be triumphantly claimed as vindication by the accused—as evidenced by the Sudanese government's elated reaction after the 2005 UN report finding no evidence of their genocidal intent, but clear and compelling evidence of their commission of major war crimes and crimes against humanity.[27]

In short, there is considerable risk in letting genocide become the "sacred" or "absolute evil" against which all other serious violations of international humanitarian law are somehow seen as "less than."[28] As a result, academics, lawyers and jurists, policymakers, and global civil society increasingly are coming to see value in understanding genocide in the broader context of an umbrella conceptual framework of mass atrocities that also includes war crimes, crimes against humanity, and—in subsumed form—ethnic cleansing. These categories of mass atrocity are not mutually exclusive. They certainly contain some overlap, as evidenced by the fact that defendants at international tribunals are often indicted on the same criminal acts for two, or even all three, of the legal categories of genocide, war crimes, or crimes against humanity. Indeed, with few exceptions, Schabas notes that nearly every atrocity committed in Bosnia and Herzegovina was characterized as both a war crime and a crime against humanity by the courts.[29] These categories are also, though, individually distinguishable in some important conceptual, and practical, features.

War crimes, according to legal scholar Steven Ratner, have been a concept in international law for many centuries. Tracing limitations on the conduct of armed conflict back to the Chinese warrior Sun Tzu (sixth century BCE) through the Hindu code of Manu (200 CE) and on through Roman and European law, Ratner writes that the "first true trial for war crimes is generally considered to be that of Peter von Hagenbach, who was tried in 1474 in Austria and sentenced to death for wartime atrocities."[30] The Hague Conventions of 1899 and 1907 officially regulated categories of combatants and noncombatants as well as the types of weapons deemed legitimate for warfare. Article 6(b) of the 1945 London Charter of the International Military Tribunal at Nuremberg defined war crimes as "violations of the laws or customs of war," including, but not limited to, "murder, ill-treatment or deportation to slave labour or for any other purpose of civilian population of or in occupied territory, murder or ill-treatment of prisoners of war or persons on the seas, killing of hostages, plunder of public or private property, wanton destruction of cities, towns or villages, or devastation not justified by military necessity."[31] Subsequently, each of the four 1949 Geneva Conventions (on wounded and sick on land, wounded and sick at sea, prisoners of war, and civilians) included its own list of "grave breaches" of rules of war and the 1977 Additional Protocols to the Geneva Conventions clarified and expanded that list. Building on this corpus of work, the most recent catalogue of war crimes appeared in the 1998 Rome Statue of the International Criminal Court (ICC).[32]

War crimes are serious violations of a body of law known as international humanitarian law or the law of armed conflict. Some war crimes are prohibited by treaty and others by customary law; some are prohibited in international conflicts alone, some in internal conflicts alone, and some in all conflicts.[33] In terms of individual criminal responsibility, war crimes can be committed by military personnel against enemy military personnel or civilians, but also by civilians against enemy military personnel or other civilians. There is no statutory limitation for war crimes. Although there is no comprehensive and complete list of war crimes, Joseph Stefanelli of the ICTR suggests that war crimes include crimes committed against (1) protected persons, including noncombatants or those no longer taking part in the conflict (for example, the injured or prisoners of war), (2) enemy combatants or civilians using prohibited *methods* (for example, directly targeting civilians or militarizing a civilian location), (3) enemy combatants or civilians using prohibited *means* (for example, chemical or biological agents), and (4) specially protected persons and objects (for example, medical personnel, hospitals and medical transports, and humanitarian relief workers or agencies).[34] In short, war crimes include a range of prohibited behaviors that occur in the context of armed conflict.

The distinguishing definitional context is that war crimes cover atrocities committed only during armed conflict. So, war crimes must be perpetrated in the context of warfare, either between two states (an international armed conflict) or between two forces in a civil war (or other internal armed conflict). It is not necessary that a state of war per se be recognized by either side. Armed conflict is the contextual key for war crimes. If there is no armed conflict, there cannot be a war crime. In a sense, "war crimes" are really more aptly understood as "armed conflict crimes." Riots or isolated, sporadic acts of violence, although they may lead to criminal behavior, will not evidence—by definition—war crimes.

War crimes differ from genocide in three important respects. First, war crimes need not evidence any intent to destroy a group in whole or in part. Second, the protective reach of war crimes is expansive and not simply limited to national, ethnical, racial, or religious groups. Third, although genocide is a crime that can be "committed in time of peace or in time of war," war crimes are contextually limited only to times of armed conflict.[35]

Although the legal distinctions between war crimes and genocide may be somewhat clear, their exact conceptual and explanatory linkages—that is, the questions of how and why war connects to genocide—remain debatable. We recognize that war is bounded by rules of armed conflict between two organized groups of combatants whereas genocide, conversely, refers to nonlegal, large-scale attacks on civilian populations. Empirically, we also recognize that although most wars do not lead to genocide, genocide "does occur mostly in war and is often related to the strategic war aims of the state."[36] Indeed, under the cover of international wars between states, we have seen the Armenian genocide, the Holocaust, the Kurdish genocide in Iraq, and genocide in the former Yugoslavia. During civil wars within countries, we have seen genocides in Rwanda and Darfur. Warfare related to settler colonialism has also been conducive to genocide, as we have seen in the destruction of the Herero and Nama in German Southwest Africa and of native populations in Australia and North America. As revealed by the Cambodian case, even the resolution of war can be a prompt for genocide. On those few occasions when genocide occurs in times of peace, even then it is typically within a "war-like political environment" in which militarized regimes seek to destroy their alleged enemies (for example, Stalin-era USSR, Mao-era China, and Indonesia).[37] Finally, genocide can sometimes even play a role in provoking new political conflict and war, as in the case of the Congo civil war (also involving neighboring countries) that traced its roots directly to the Rwandan genocide.[38]

Even though war and genocide may sometimes coexist, it remains contestable whether they are two points on the same related continuum or two distinct varieties of destruction. On the one hand, Martin Shaw sees genocide as an extreme form of the general category of war, intimately related but fundamentally distinguishable by the construction of civilian groups as enemies.[39] On the other hand, some view war and genocide as mutually exclusive "unlike phenomena . . . that have little in common except that they produce large numbers of casualties."[40] Still others, vying for a compromise position, seek to maintain a conceptual distinction between war and genocide while exploring the range of connections and the extent to which causality (direct or indirect) can be determined among them.[41] For instance, genocide scholars Eric Markusen and David Kopf argue that "one connection on which there is considerable consensus is that war in general, and total war in particular, create psychological, social, and political conditions conducive to genocidal killing."[42] In their view, war, in preparation and implementation, reflects a collective mindset and climate best described as a "genocidal mentality."[43] Similarly, political scientist Adam Jones argues that war accustoms a society to a climate of violence, increases fear and hatred in a society, eases genocidal logistics, provides a smokescreen for genocide, fuels in-group solidarity and out-group enmity, magnifies humanitarian crisis, and stokes grievances and a desire for revenge.[44]

At the least, however, most agree that war is the major enabling context—if not a catalyst—of genocide throughout history. Since 1945, 67% of episodes of mass killing occurred within a context of armed conflict. Since the late Cold War, between 1980 and 2010, that figure rose to 85%.[45] Clearly, the violence of war is multidirectional and one of those directions can be genocidal. As historian Paul Bartrop has argued: ". . . there can be no doubt that war contains within it the potential for a genocidal regime to realise its aims, and probably more easily than in the absence of war."[46] Joseph Goebbels, head of the Ministry for Public Enlightenment and Propaganda in Nazi Germany, understood horribly well the facilitative relationship between war and genocide. In a March 27, 1942 diary entry, Goebbels wrote: "It is a battle of life and death between the Aryan race and the Jewish bacillus . . . Here, as in other matters, the Fuhrer is the steadfast champion and spokesman of a radical solution, which this situation demands and which therefore appears to be unavoidable. Thank God that now, during wartime, we have a whole series of opportunities that would be closed off to us in peacetime. Hence, we need to use them."[47]

Crimes against humanity is a more recent twentieth-century concept, originating in the 1907 Hague Convention preamble. When the phrase was used by the Allies in 1915 to describe what we know today as the Armenian genocide, it had no recognized legal definition. In 1945, however, the London Charter of the International Military Tribunal at Nuremberg codified crimes against humanity in Article 6(c) as "Murder, extermination, enslavement, deportation, and other inhumane acts committed against any civilian population, before or during the war; or persecutions on political, racial or religious grounds in execution of or in connection with any crime within the jurisdiction of the Tribunal, whether or not in violation of the domestic law of the country where perpetrated."[48] As defined at Nuremberg, the concept of crimes against humanity was created to prosecute atrocities committed within the borders of Germany against German civilians.

The Allies were worried, however, about the breadth of the extent to which this new concept could be applied. In the woefully understated words of Justice Robert Jackson, "We [the US] have some regrettable circumstances at times in our own country in which minorities are unfairly treated."[49] The British, French, and Russians shared similar concerns. So, the Tribunal decided to limit the scope of crimes against humanity to wartime. Registering no conviction for any criminal act committed prior to Germany's invasion of Poland on September 1, 1939, the court confirmed that crimes against humanity could not—by definition—be committed in peacetime.[50]

As we have seen in Chapter 1, the limited scope of crimes against humanity established at the initial Nuremberg trial was frustrating for many involved in the drafting of the Genocide Convention. As Schabas points out, vulnerable emerging states were particularly desirous of

international criminalization of atrocities in peacetime for their own protection.[51] Over time, this desire would be met. In addition to gaining some
measure of protective satisfaction in the passage of the Convention, other
advances in humanitarian law would also broaden the scope of crimes
against humanity—including extending the crimes to peacetime. To date,
there has been no specialized international convention on crimes against
humanity; however, there was, as Schabas notes, a "dramatic enlargement
of the ambit of crimes against humanity during the 1990s."[52] Most notably, crimes against humanity would be included in the statutes of the ICTY
and ICTR and case law from both tribunals would clarify and enlarge the
scope of the crime under international human rights law.

The most recent step in this evolving process was the codification—and
further expansion—of crimes against humanity in the Rome Statute of
the ICC as acts "committed as part of a widespread or systematic attack
directed against any civilian population."[53] The criminal acts listed in
Article 7 of the statute include murder, extermination, enslavement,
deportation or forcible transfer, imprisonment, torture, rape and other
forms of sexual violence, persecution, enforced disappearance, apartheid,
and a catch-all category of other inhumane acts that cause great suffering or serious injury. These acts must be part of a widespread (a matter of
scale) *or* systematic (a matter of organization) attack—disjunctive rather
than conjunctive––either rather than both. There is no statutory limitation for crimes against humanity. Article 7 contains no reference to armed
conflict as a contextual requirement of crimes against humanity.

Crimes against humanity are particularly odious because they constitute an egregious attack on human dignity; that is, the act injures not just
the victim, but tears at the fabric of what it means to be human. Hannah
Arendt captured this sense of an offense against all humanity in her description of the Holocaust as "a crime against humanity perpetrated upon the
body of the Jewish people."[54] Crimes against humanity can be perpetrated,
in time of war or time of peace, by individuals acting in a state capacity
(for example, military commanders and soldiers, police officers) or by private individuals, not in isolation but with knowledge that their acts are
part of a widespread or systematic attack. The primary victims protected
by international laws against these crimes include all civilian populations
(a government's own citizens or those of another state), though increasing protections for military personnel are also being included under the
continuing legal evolution of crimes against humanity in customary law.[55]

As Wald notes, "crimes against humanity is a big tent set up on ground
that overlaps both war crimes and genocide."[56] Crimes against humanity
differ from the crime of genocide because they do not require intent to

destroy a group in whole or in part. Rather, crimes against humanity must target only a given group (much broader in reach than the limited protected groups of the Convention) and be widespread or systematic. In addition, the criminal acts included under crimes against humanity are also much broader than the five acts of destruction criminalized for genocide. In relation to war crimes, crimes against humanity are distinct because they are not limited to times of armed conflict; rather, crimes against humanity, like genocide, are now understood to occur in times of peace or in times of war. Although crimes against humanity have some additional proof burdens over war crimes, they are not particularly onerous.[57]

Finally, while having no formal legal definition, *ethnic cleansing* is often included as a distinct, autonomous category of mass atrocity. Although the act of forcible removal and transfer of a people is as old as antiquity, the origins of the term "ethnic cleansing" are recent, even if exactly unclear. One scholar suggests it was used immediately after World War II by Poles and Czechs intending to cleanse their countries of Germans and Ukrainians.[58] Another scholar argues that the term was first used in 1981 by the minority Serbs in Kosovo, alleging that Kosovar Albanians sought to drive them from their ancient homeland.[59] Yet another traces it to the late 1980s when Russian journalists used the term to describe the forced displacement of Christian Armenians from Azerbaijan.[60] Regardless of its exact origin, in May 1992, the Bosnian War would bring the term to the forefront of our international vocabulary for political violence—albeit, in an ironic reversal, as a reference to Serb attempts to drive Muslims out of self-perceived Serb territory in northern and eastern Bosnia.[61] As Shaw points out, the contemporary meaning of ethnic cleansing originated as a euphemistic perpetrators' term that camouflaged "the destructive character of the removal of groups from territories where they lived."[62]

Journalists, politicians, and nongovernmental international organizations quickly seized on the term as intuitively descriptive—even the defining characteristic—of the violence that was occurring throughout former Yugoslavia. By 1993, noted *New York Times* columnist William Safire would coronate ethnic cleansing as "[T]his generation's entry in the mass-murder category." He went on to assert that ethnic cleansing "has become a major coinage, now used without quotation marks or handled without the tongs of so-called."[63] Indeed, by 1994, the UN General Assembly no longer bracketed the term in quotation marks.[64] In academic circles it soon became common to use the term in reference to a wide variety of geographic expulsions in the nineteenth and twentieth centuries.[65]

Despite its widespread popularity, and near ubiquity in recent discourse surrounding mass violence, the conceptual definition of ethnic cleansing remains elusive. A 1993 UN report to the Security Council, acknowledging that the term was relatively new, defined ethnic cleansing as "rendering an area ethnically homogenous by using force or intimidation to remove persons of given groups from the area," a definition also accepted by the International Court of Justice.[66] Sociologist Andrew Bell-Fialkoff defined ethnic cleansing as "the expulsion of an 'undesirable' population from a given territory due to religious or ethnic discrimination, political, strategic or ideological considerations, or a combination of these."[67] The 2000 Stockholm Accords on Ethnic Cleansing saw ethnic cleansing as "the systematic annihilation or forced removal of the members of an ethnic, racial or religious group from a community or communities in order to change the ethnic, racial or religious composition of a given region."[68] Similarly, for legal scholar Drazen Petrovic, ethnic cleansing "is a well-defined policy of a particular group of persons to systematically eliminate another group from a given territory on the basis of religious, ethnic or national origin."[69] Gareth Evans defines ethnic cleansing even more broadly to include "outright killing, expulsion, acts of terror designed to encourage flight, and rape when perpetrated either as another form of terrorism or as a deliberate attempt to change the ethnic composition of the group in question."[70] For historian Norman Naimark, ethnic cleansing is "a profoundly modern experience" characterized by the removal of "a people and often all traces of them from a concrete territory. The goal [of the perpetrators] . . . [is] to seize control of the territory they had formerly inhabited."[71] Finally, for historian Benjamin Lieberman, the definition of ethnic cleansing is "closely related to geography . . . [referring] to removal of a group from a particular area. It is a means for forced remaking of human landscape."[72]

Even if we could find consensus on a conceptual definition of ethnic cleansing—likely focused around forced removal or displacement of a civilian population—its relation to the other mass atrocity categories of genocide, war crimes, and crimes against humanity remains contested. As just one example, Larry May has argued that "sometimes the acts of ethnic cleansing should count as satisfying the *actus reus* element of the crime of genocide . . . [that is] the acts of ethnic cleansing and genocide are often the same acts."[73] Schabas, in contrast, maintains that there is a fundamental difference between the acts of genocide and ethnic cleansing. He writes: "While the material acts performed to commit the crimes may often resemble each other, they have two quite different specific intents. One [ethnic cleansing] is intended to displace a population, the other [genocide] to destroy it."[74] A 2007 judgment of the International Court of

Justice added little clarity as it asserted that ethnic cleansing "can only be a form of genocide within the meaning of the Convention . . . However, this does not mean that acts described as 'ethnic cleansing' may never constitute genocide."[75] Similarly, although Naimark contends that "ethnic cleansing and genocide are two different activities, and the differences between them are important," even he admits that "both literally and figuratively, ethnic cleansing bleeds into genocide"—particularly when, as often happens, forced removal of a population leads to a group's destruction.[76]

UN deliberations have further muddled the issue. For instance, a 1992 UN General Assembly resolution sloppily described the "abhorrent policy" of ethnic cleansing as "a form of genocide"—a reference reaffirmed in a number of subsequent UN resolutions.[77] Ethnic cleansing was later included in the landmark UN 2005 World Summit Outcome document—along with genocide, war crimes, and crimes against humanity—as one of the international offenses from which each individual state, and the international community, has the responsibility to protect civilian populations.[78] Even today, the UN Office of the Special Adviser on the Prevention of Genocide follows suit by including "alerting relevant actors to the risk of genocide, war crimes, ethnic cleansing and crimes against humanity" as part of their mission statement.[79]

For all of its popular appeal, however one defines or categorizes ethnic cleansing, the term offers more heat than light. For academics, ethnic cleansing is a distinction without a difference. No conceptual singularity is attached to the term that usefully distinguishes it from genocide, war crimes, or crimes against humanity. For lawyers and jurists, ethnic cleansing remains a nebulous blanket term that can cover a host of criminal offenses related to forced removal or displacement of civilian populations—all of which are already codified under other legally recognized mass atrocity crimes. For instance, Article 7 of the Rome Statute outlining crimes against humanity includes as one of its listed acts (d) deportation or forcible transfer of population and understands this to mean "forced displacement of the persons concerned by expulsion or other coercive acts from the area in which they are lawfully present."[80] As an example from case law, an ICTY Trial Chamber found that the forcible displacement of women, children, and elderly people from Srebrenica amounted to the crime of genocide because it reached a "requisite level of causing serious mental harm"—even in the absence of intent for physical extermination.[81] Finally, in a tragic reversal of intention, ethnic cleansing often works, for policymakers and global civil society, as a catchy emotive phrase—without legal standing—that can actually end up excusing the international community from complying with duties laid down by international law for the recognized crimes of genocide, war crimes, and crimes against humanity.[82]

Just as we have been careful with parsing the word "genocide," we must be careful with distinguishing it from, and relating it to, other forms of mass violence. I see genocide as one form of large-scale and deliberate violence directed at civilian populations. I do not see it as the "apex of the pyramid," the "crime of crimes," or even the general framework under which all other forms of mass atrocity should be placed. Rather, I see genocide as one of three criminal categories of mass atrocity—joining war crimes and crimes against humanity under that conceptual umbrella framework. Each of these categories—distinguishable from each other in important respects and overlapping in others—is a serious violation of international humanitarian law and each is subject to universal jurisdiction.

David Scheffer, former U.S. ambassador at large for war crimes issues, has long advocated the use of the shorthand term "atrocity crimes" to cover any combination of genocide, war crimes, or crimes against humanity. In addition to being more easily understood by the public, such an adaptable term—with no legal threshold to satisfy and not triggering any legal ramifications—can avoid, in his opinion, the "dangerously divisive political game" that most often leads to stalemate and inaction in the face of large-scale violence.[83] For Scheffer, "public officials, military officers, the media, and academics [should] be free to describe genocide, crimes against humanity (including the emerging crime of ethnic cleansing), and serious war crimes as atrocity crimes meriting timely and effective responses in political, military, and judicial terms."[84] By using "atrocity crimes" as a collective description, we can then concentrate on what needs to be done to end the violence rather than engage in protracted debate about how to categorically define the violence. It should then be left, he argues, to academics, lawyers, and jurists to work out which terminological label—genocide, war crimes, or crimes against humanity—is most appropriate for a given case. Scheffer's sensible proposal of consolidation of these crimes under one unifying term has been affirmed in the general decisions of the ad hoc tribunals as well as the spirit underlying the work of the International Law Commission, the Rome Statute of the International Criminal Court, and even the United Nations itself with its now customary use of "atrocity crimes" as the favored phraseology to pair with "genocide."[85] Similarly, the Stanley Foundation, a private nongovernmental organization, recently convened its inaugural meeting of the Global Action Against Mass Atrocity Crimes initiative.

For some, however, "atrocity *crimes*" still leaves a disabling "impression that specific legal criteria must be met before taking preventive or protective action."[86] In lieu of that potentially limiting read of the term, we increasingly see the use of the more general term "mass atrocities." An explicitly nonlegal term, "mass atrocities" opens the world's eyes more broadly to cases of civilian persecution and suffering. What it sacrifices in clarity and specificity, it more than makes up for in its coherence and simplicity. In my work with academics, policymakers, and global civil society, I have seen the breadth of this term widely embraced, as reflected in President Obama's creation of the Atrocities Prevention Board; our Auschwitz Institute for Peace and Reconcilation's launching of the Latin American Network for Genocide and Mass Atrocity Prevention; and the Budapest Centre's Task Force on the EU Prevention of Mass Atrocities. As a shorthand descriptor, "mass atrocities"—referring to civilians being done to death by any of the criminal acts of genocide, war crimes, or crimes against humanity—recognizes that prevention of those atrocities, and protection of civilians from those atrocities, need not wait until specific legal criteria for those crimes are met.

We must remember, however, that the terminology employed to describe large-scale destruction is only one facet of its prevention. As legal scholar Martha Minow has argued in response to Scheffer's proposal, "the problems . . . will not be cured by new words . . . renaming legal categories will do little to address underlying problems of leadership and will . . . new names will not undo the reluctance of individuals, nationals, and international organizations to respond to mass violence."[87] Fortunately, the new words and new names have been supplemented by a new international norm meant to overcome the world's demonstrated reluctance to engage in the prevention of civilians being done to death.

In September 2000, the International Commission on Intervention and State Sovereignty (ICISS), a global commission of 12 members co-chaired by the Honorable Gareth Evans from Australia and His Excellency Mohamed Shanoun from Algeria, was established by the Government of Canada in response to the challenge posed by then-UN Secretary General Kofi Annan to rethink states' obligation in the face of genocide—a challenge spurred by the international community's failure to prevent and respond in a timely manner to genocides in Rwanda in 1994 and Srebrenica in 1995. At stake in the discussion, as it was nearly 80 years earlier for Lemkin, was the very concept of state sovereignty. Should the international community supersede state sovereignty when civilian lives are at risk? Or is state sovereignty, as recognized by Article 2(7) of the UN Charter, an unconditional and unassailable right?

In 2001, ICISS issued its final report titled *The Responsibility to Protect*.[88] The ICISS report—the culmination of 12 months of intensive research, worldwide consultations, and deliberation—offered a new conceptualization of state sovereignty that focused on the responsibility of states toward their populations and toward all populations at risk of genocide and other mass atrocities. This concept, known as the responsibility to protect and commonly referred to as R2P, moved state sovereignty from an unconditional right to a conditional privilege, from absolute to contingent, and from *sovereignty as control* to *sovereignty as responsibility*.[89] In the words of journalist Richard Just, "the essence of the responsibility to protect is an insistence that the fate of people matters more than the sovereignty of governments."[90]

R2P also changed the calculus of the role of the international community when a state fails or refuses to protect populations under its care. Specifically, the ICISS report held: "Where a population is suffering serious harm, as a result of internal war, insurgency, repression or state failure, and the state in question is unwilling or unable to halt or avert it, the principle of non-intervention yields to the responsibility to project."[91] Quite simply, R2P offered a "standard for how governments should treat their own people and how the world community should respond when national commitments are not kept."[92]

This new international norm embraced three specific responsibilities:

- *The responsibility to prevent*—to address both the root causes and direct causes of internal conflict and other human-made crises putting populations at risk.
- *The responsibility to react*—to respond to situations of compelling human need with appropriate measures, which may include coercive measures such as sanctions and international prosecution, and, in extreme cases, military intervention.
- *The responsibility to rebuild*—to provide, particularly after a military intervention, full assistance with recovery, reconstruction, and reconciliation, addressing the causes of the harm the intervention was designed to halt or avert so as to prevent relapse into further violence.

Although its concepts are firmly grounded in established norms of international law, R2P is not itself law nor does it carry any legal obligations for governments. Rather, it is an emerged norm, a tool of moral suasion, and a political commitment that, rather than creating new law, confirms and crystallizes existing legal obligations.[93] As international security expert Alex Bellamy says: "When states committed to the RtoP concept . . . they were effectively acknowledging the legal obligations that they already had and committing themselves to ensuring that this existing law be upheld everywhere, all the time."[94]

The U.S.-led invasion of Iraq in 2003, premised in part on the specious grounds of civilian protection, left a rocky soil on which the seed of R2P was to develop. Despite that unfortunate timing, coming just 2 years after the release of the ICISS report, the concept of R2P has garnered a wealth of international support in its short lifetime. There has been widespread appreciation for moving from the language of "right" to "responsibility" in discussing state sovereignty, just as there has been for moving from the language of "intervention" to "protection" in discussing the role of the international community. R2P has been hailed as an innovative doctrine and, according to historian Martin Gilbert, is "the most significant adjustment to national sovereignty in 360 years."[95] A leading academic press has a book series on R2P and there is a journal, the *Global Responsibility to Protect (GR2P)*, devoted exclusively to the concept. There is a global network of R2P Focal Points—facilitated by the governments of Denmark, Ghana, Australia, and Costa Rica—that convenes annually to strategize on how best to encourage the promotion of R2P at the national level. International civil society organizations—such as the International Coalition for the Responsibility to Protect, the Global Centre for R2P, the Asia-Pacific Centre for R2P, and the Canadian Centre for the Responsibility to Protect—have emerged as tireless advocates for the principle.

Most significantly, R2P was unanimously adopted by more than 150 heads of state and government meeting at the UN General Assembly World Summit in September 2005 in New York—the largest-ever gathering of world leaders. The outcome document from that summit affirmed that "each individual State has the responsibility to protect its populations from genocide, war crimes, ethnic cleansing and crimes against humanity." Moreover, the document continued, "the international community, through the United Nations, also has the responsibility . . . to help to protect populations" from those same mass atrocities.[96] The following year, a unanimously adopted UN Security Council resolution reaffirmed the principle of the responsibility to protect.[97] Since then, the Security Council has referred to R2P in 23 resolutions and six Security Council presidential statements, with the first link of R2P to a particular conflict coming in an August 2006 resolution on Darfur. In 2008, the UN Secretary-General appointed a Special Adviser on the Responsibility to Protect.[98] Beginning in 2009, the Secretary-General has issued an ongoing series of annual thematic reports on the operationalization of R2P. Following each of the reports, the General Assembly then meets in an informal dialogue with Member States, UN officials, and civil society organizations to discuss the report and how best to implement the R2P norm—with an overwhelming number of Member States from all regions of the world, often led by the

Global South, reaffirming their support for the norm each year. At the most recent dialogue in September 2015, global consensus again prevailed with only a few countries—Belarus, Cuba, India, Russia, Sudan, Syria, and Venezuela—voicing self-serving oppositional positions that civilian protection responsibilities belonged only to the state and not the international community.

The original ICISS report—including the responsibilities to prevent, react, and rebuild—was the germinal idea that gave birth to the concept of R2P. The subsequent UN translation of R2P, as articulated in the 2005 World Summit Outcome Document, moved it from a concept to a doctrine. It is that doctrine of R2P, clarified by subsequent and ongoing UN deliberations, to which states have actually agreed. This evolved, and evolving, understanding of R2P continues to inform policymaking for state and international actors in regard to the protection of populations.

In his initial annual report in 2009, Secretary-General Ban Ki-moon issued a policy explanation of what R2P is and a comprehensive strategy for its implementation.[99] Ban Ki-moon translated R2P as having three pillars, nonsequential (that is, there is no set sequence as to which pillar should be used when) and with no one pillar being more important than the others:[100]

- *Pillar I* affirms that States carry the primary responsibility for the protection of their populations (whether nationals or not) from genocide, war crimes, crimes against humanity, and ethnic cleansing.

In an ideal world, States would fulfill this primary responsibility of protection or, if unable, seek outside assistance to do so. Given the reality of the less-than-ideal world in which we live, however, the other two pillars of the UN conceptualization address the international community's concurrent responsibilities as good global citizens:

- *Pillar II* says that the international community (including the UN, regional organizations, governments, and civil society) has a commitment to assist States in acquiring the capacity to fulfill their primary responsibility of protecting their population from mass atrocities. This is especially crucial when States are confronting powerful armed rebel or terrorist groups committing atrocities against their population.
- *Pillar III* follows with the commitment that, when a state is manifestly failing to protect its population from mass atrocities, or may even be perpetrating the atrocities themselves, then the international community has the responsibility to take timely and decisive action to prevent and halt genocide, war crimes, crimes against humanity, and ethnic cleansing.

Although not identical to the three ICISS responsibilities, we can certainly see the notions of prevent, react, and rebuild embedded in the UN's translation of R2P. Pillars I and II are clearly grounded in a preventive tone—either the State assuming its preventive obligations (I) or the international community assisting the state in fulfilling its preventive obligations (II). Pillar III is conceptually equivalent with the "responsibility to react," though it replaces the "unwilling or unable" phrase with "manifestly failing" in describing the threshold for intervention. Although recognizing its importance in preventing the recurrence of violence, ICISS's concept of the "responsibility to rebuild" was not included in the UN interpretation of R2P. This was primarily because participants at the World Summit believed rebuilding would be better addressed through the work of the Peacebuilding Commission. Established in December 2005, the Peacebuilding Commission's central focus is supporting peace efforts and recovery in postconflict countries—perfectly resonant with ICISS's original notion of the "responsibility to rebuild."[101]

It is Pillar III of the UN conceptualization that—given its implications for intrusive and coercive measures without state consent or even against a state's will—has drawn an inordinate amount of attention. For some, R2P is a political weapon, a pretext for regime change—wrapped in the noble trappings of "humanitarianism"—that can be strategically used by global powers to self-servingly dictate the political, social, cultural, economic, and religious directions of fragile states. In their eyes, R2P is the new face of colonialism, humanitarian imperialism, and proxy war. They see R2P as synonymous with unwarranted military intervention and perhaps better understood as R2I—the right to intervene—or, even, R2K—the right to kill.[102] A May 2014 report by the Global Policy Forum saw "military action as the core of the [R2P] doctrine" and argued that, in practice, the whole R2P doctrine is skewed "towards the extreme option of coercive intervention."[103] Other critics even suggest that R2P can inadvertently increase civilian casualties, at least in the short term, by inciting opposition groups to intentionally provoke government repression in order to call on the world's protection through intervention.[104]

These critical voices, although disproportionately loud relative to their dwindling numbers, are important cautionary reminders of how R2P could be exploitatively used and, in that regard, remind us of our necessary diligence to ensure that the principle is not compromised by those bent on using it for less noble geopolitical purposes. They also remind us of the compelling need to establish transparent decision-making criteria and principles that guide the UN Security Council in authorizing the collective use of force. That said, however, I do think these criticisms are off-base in three regards.

First, the reality does not dovetail with the concerns of R2P being a limitless license for the unwarranted use of military intervention.[105] It is important to understand that nothing about R2P permits action outside the UN Charter. So, any decision for the use of coercive force will come through the UN Security Council. To date, the only examples of coercive intervention being authorized by the UN Security Council under the context of R2P are the 2011 cases of Libya and Côte d'Ivoire. Although not often referenced by the U.S. government directly, and certainly relatively unfamiliar to the U.S. public, the earmarks of R2P are on much of recent U.S. foreign policy. In August 2014, for instance, President Obama justified yet another U.S. military intervention in Iraq on the basis of "a mandate to help" and the upholding of "international norms"—obliquely invoking the spirit of the responsibility to protect.[106] Even with those inclusions, however, the list of coercive interventions justified, at least indirectly, by the principle of R2P, remains very short. Unfortunately, though, the reductionist notion of R2P as synonymous with military intervention has hindered a fuller commitment to its more nuanced interpretation and implementation. As policy researchers Kees Homan and Marianne Ducasse-Rogier point out: "The association of R2P with military intervention led to a growing reluctance [after 2011] on the part of many states (including China and Russia) to implement—or even refer to—the principle as such."[107] As a result, the UN Security Council has, to date, failed to pass a meaningful resolution for responding to nearly 5 years of ongoing mass atrocities in Syria, in which an estimated 250,000 people have been killed along with widespread sexual violence amid massive displacement of civilian populations.

Second, part of the restraint on limitless license comes from the political and intellectual evolution surrounding the original ICISS suggestion that R2P can be activated in cases of "overwhelming natural or environmental catastrophes, where the state concerned is either unwilling or unable to cope, or call for assistance."[108] Recognizing that such a canvas was far too broad, the 2005 World Summit Outcome Document specifically narrowed the application of R2P to that subset of cases in which at-risk populations are suffering from war crimes, crimes against humanity, genocide, and ethnic cleansing. Although R2P applies everywhere and all the time for those four mass atrocities, it is not meant to apply to other large-scale human suffering and protection issues (for instance, natural disasters, climate change, nuclear weapons, poverty, or disease). As Michael Barnett and Thomas Weiss point out, ". . . the responsibility to protect is . . . not about the protection of everyone from everything."[109] This understanding has been reaffirmed numerous times since 2005 and, today, R2P is universally understood to be limited to these four categories of mass atrocity. These clear boundaries are an additional brake on the notion of limitless license of unwarranted military intervention.

Third, viewing R2P as being synonymous with military intervention shortchanges the myriad ways in which the international community can take action in regard to mass atrocities. The protection of civilians is not a dichotomous choice between putting boots on the ground or doing nothing. In the span of response options, R2P understands military intervention to be the last tool at the bottom of a very deep toolbox—a "desperately serious, extraordinary, and exceptional" last resort considered only after all other measures have failed.[110] Even when used, such intrusive and coercive intervention is done only with the idea of laying the foundation for a state to reassume its protection obligations. In this regard, R2P is not about regime change through military intervention; rather, it is about changing the behavior of regimes that are unwilling or unable to protect their populations. We must recognize that taking action in the face of mass atrocities includes, as we will see in Chapter 5, a broad range of political, economic, legal, and other options that fall far short of active military intervention. In fact, the more coercive a measure is, the less likely it is to be employed.

In short, R2P is not a reactive responsibility waiting to be triggered by horrific events. Whether it is the three responsibilities of the ICISS report or the three pillars of the UN conceptualization, the key is to understand them as mutually supportive and reinforcing rather than myopically allowing one piece—"eleventh hour" reacting—to predominate our field of vision. Indeed, although certainly less high-profile than UN Security Council authorizations for intervention based on R2P, the underlying principles of R2P have been invoked in a range of recent international preventive responses to potential crisis situations (for instance, political elections in fragile states) as well as reactive and rebuilding crisis situations. When understood holistically (and accurately), R2P opens our eyes to this broad spectrum of underutilized "soft power" measures of civilian protection that are less intrusive and coercive. Seen in this light, we recognize that most of the work of R2P can, and should, be done outside of UN Security Council authorizations for collective action—by international and regional organizations, neighbors, states, private companies and businesses, and global civil society. Ultimately, the success of R2P is not measured in how quickly the world responds to a crisis situation, but, rather, in whether we have fewer crises to which to respond.

In "a blink of an eye in the history of ideas," R2P has moved from an emerging norm to an emerged norm—meaning a stable, widely held belief about what is appropriate behavior.[111] R2P has become a matter of habit and institutionalized internalization that has cascaded through most international, regional, and national actors. As a norm, R2P expresses a commonly shared, and broadly institutionalized, set of values, preferences, and, ultimately, behaviors that guide states' domestic and foreign policy. In the words of international relations scholars Martha Finnemore and Kathryn Sikkink, "norms by definition embody a quality of 'oughtness' and shared moral assessment, norms prompt justifications for action and leave an extensive trail of communication among actors that we can study."[112] R2P is a normative statement of "oughtness" about our collective responsibility for the protection of civilians from being done to death.

R2P today has a taken-for-granted quality and is no longer a matter of broad debate or contentious attempts to renegotiate the principle.[113] It has emerged as a very fit idea, sharpened by the evolutionary pressures of extensive political and intellectual scrutiny. It is now part of our international vocabulary in any discussions related to mass atrocities. R2P gives us a political and conceptual framework for "never again." It is a reinforcing friend of sovereignty, rather than an undermining enemy. As Adama Dieng, UN Special Adviser on the Prevention of Genocide, has said: ". . . the responsibility to protect is a principle that seeks to strengthen the sovereignty of states, not weaken it. History has shown that building societies resilient to atrocity crimes reinforces State sovereignty and increases prospects for peace and stability."[114]

By 2011, UN Secretary-General Ban Ki-moon could say, ". . . it is a sign of progress that our debates are now about how, not whether, to implement the responsibility to protect. No Government questions the principle."[115] Indeed, the lingering questions about R2P are with how, where, when, and by whom it should be implemented. Even then, however, we should bear in mind that ". . . the greatest danger is not that governments will intervene improperly to stop atrocities but that they will not act at all."[116]

In a 2012 address at a Stanley Foundation conference, Ban Ki-moon summarized the current state, and future hope, of R2P: "In 2011, history took a turn for the better. The Responsibility to Protect came of age; the principle was tested as never before. The results were uneven, but at the end of the day, tens of thousands of lives were saved. We gave hope to people long oppressed. In Libya, Côte d'Ivoire, South Sudan, Yemen and Syria, by our words and actions, we demonstrated that human protection is a defining purpose of the United Nations in the twenty-first century . . . Together, let us work, with optimism and determination, to make the Responsibility to Protect a living reality for the peoples of the world."[117]

As prioritized in the original ICISS report, "prevention is the single most important dimension of the responsibility to protect."[118] This conception of R2P as a doctrine of prevention—a responsibility to prevent—has been repeatedly affirmed by the UN Secretary General and in the annual informal dialogues with Member States, UN officials, and global civil society organizations. Why is genocide prevention so important? In short, genocide prevention reduces four types of costs—human, instability, economic, and diplomatic. Genocide prevention is primarily focused on reducing human costs through the protection and preservation of human life and security. In addition, however, genocide prevention reduces instability costs by contributing to national peace and stability in fragile countries, as well as promoting regional and international peace and stability. Prevention's importance also reduces economic costs as prevention is much less costly than intervening to stop genocide or rebuilding in the aftermath of a mass destruction that has destroyed the development trajectory of a state or region. Finally, genocide prevention reduces diplomatic costs as it reinforces state sovereignty by limiting the more intrusive and invasive forms of response, from other States or international actors, that may be required to halt genocide.[119]

Part II of this book reflects and affirms this understanding by focusing on the preventive measures—our words and actions—that can be applied to protect civilians from being done to death. This continuum of strategies includes preventing genocide from ever taking place, preventing further atrocities once genocide has begun, and preventing future atrocities once a society has begun to rebuild after genocide. Central is the notion that prevention does not end when the violence begins; rather prevention of genocide is a multilayered approach running throughout the preconflict, midconflict, and postconflict cycle. As Evans argues: "'Prevention' language can reasonably be applied at *all* stages of the conflict cycle."[120]

Let us contextualize this continuum of prevention strategies in an analogy.[121] Imagine you are standing beside a river and see someone caught in the current and struggling for their life. You jump in and manage to pull the victim ashore. Just as you catch your breath, however, another person in distress comes downstream . . . followed by another and another and another. Rather than remaining downstream and exhausting your-self on the rescue of individuals already in distress, you travel upstream to find the source of the problem. You may discover a hole in a bridge or per-haps the lack of a protective fence on a cliff. You have changed, though, the calculus of what prevention means—rather than expending your resources and energy on rescuing people in crisis, you can now try to stop the crisis at its source. Saving victims in crisis and fixing the source of the crisis are both forms of prevention—as is helping victims the moment they fall into the river rather than waiting until they have been swept downstream—each simply occurs at different stages of the process of prevention. Clearly, focusing prevention efforts on the source of the crisis, before it happens, is more efficient and less costly than managing the consequences of the crisis once it has occurred. You may not stop all of the people from falling into the river, at least not right away, but—by addressing the root cause—you have decreased the risk and there will be far fewer people to rescue downstream.

This analogy is uncomfortably close to the real-life tragedy of thousands of bodies, as many as one hundred an hour, washing down the Kagera River into Lake Victoria in Uganda—the second largest body of fresh water in the world—at the height of the Rwandan genocide. Except, in that case, the bodies had already lost their struggle for life. At that point, addressing the root cause of the problem upstream fell secondary to the severe down-stream consequences in Uganda. A May 21, 1994 news report cited "the difficulty of fighting off the wild animals and dogs feeding on the bodies" as well as the "acute health hazard" caused by the decaying corpses wash-ing ashore in southern Uganda or onto islands in Lake Victoria.[122] Villagers in the region were warned to boil drinking water and to cook all fish thor-oughly in order to prevent epidemics of cholera and other diseases.

Following a population-based health model in which the aim is the prevention of the disease of genocide and other mass atrocities, Part II of this book is structured around three stages in a continuum of prevention strategies—primary, secondary, and tertiary. Primary prevention (Chapter 4) is upstream prevention—fixing the hole in the bridge or constructing a protective barrier to prevent people from falling into the river. Upstream prevention is the "before" analysis of the longer-term governance, histori-cal, economic, and societal factors that leave a country at risk for genocide and other mass atrocities and the inoculation avenues open to mitigating those risk factors. Secondary prevention (Chapter 5) is midstream preven-tion—the rescue of victims just as they hit the water but before they are swept further downstream. Midstream prevention "during" the crisis cap-tures the immediate, real-time relief efforts—political, economic, legal, and military—that are direct crisis management tactics to slow, limit, or halt the mass violence. Finally, tertiary prevention (Chapter 6) is downstream prevention—the hopeful resuscitation of victims who were swept away because upstream or midstream prevention failed. Downstream prevention refers to the "after" efforts to foster resiliency by dealing with the acute long-term consequences of mass violence through pursuits of justice, truth, and memory to help stabilize, heal, and rehabilitate a postgenocide society. The strategies available to us for upstream prevention are far more numerous, and much less costly, than the available strategies for midstream prevention once genocide has broken out or, even more so, for downstream prevention for rebuilding after the genocide is over.

Although choosing—for narrative purposes—to consider these stages of prevention in three discrete chapters, I do not mean to create an artificial distinction between them, boundary them in mutually exclusive boxes, nor suggest an overly simplistic sequential approach to the protection of populations. Mass atrocities are often more cyclical than linear.[123] So upstream, midstream, and downstream prevention efforts work in an interconnected and synergistic, rather than isolated, fashion. I also do not mean to imply a strict temporal process; most conflicts are an intricate tangle of preconflict, midconflict, and postconflict at any one time. As a result, the defining element of an upstream preventive approach, for example, is not "when" it takes place but rather that it seeks to address the underlying causes of conflict. "In theory, interventions to prevent conflict upstream can be undertaken at any point during the conflict cycle, even at the same time as measures to address the symptoms of conflict are also being carried out."[124] In short, these stages of prevention, and the measures involved in each, are complexly linked and state responsibility, buttressed by international assistance for capacity building, is threaded throughout all three stages of the continuum.

In his concluding chapter to *The Drowned and the Saved*, his last completed work, Auschwitz survivor Primo Levi reminds us of the importance of genocide prevention. Written more than 40 years after the end of the Holocaust, Levi writes: "It happened, therefore it can happen again: this is the core of what we have to say. It can happen, and it can happen everywhere." This quote is featured in the lobby of the information center at the Memorial to the Murdered Jews of Europe in Berlin, Germany. Left out, however, is the next sentence: "I do not intend to nor can I say that it will happen."[125] Although Levi was likely hedging his bets against the repetition of something so unthinkable—even as he admits in 1986 that "precursory signs loom before us" in several corners of the world—I believe he is also challenging us to recognize that even though genocide can happen again, it does not have to happen again. Genocide is not pre-ordained, despite its persistent occurrence, as an inevitable reality of the human experience.

Over a quarter of a century later, in 2014, Adama Dieng echoed Levi's concern, as well as his hope: "We must accept that there is no part of the world that can consider itself immune from the risk of genocide and all regions and all States must build resistance to these crimes . . . We owe to them [the millions of men and women who have lost their lives to genocide] and to ourselves and future generations to realize a world free of genocide. We are still far from that, but we aim to make it happen."[126] Although Levi and Dieng are separated by a vast crevasse of time, culture, and distance, together they push us to acknowledge our collective responsibility for doing what we can to prevent genocide from happening again.

NOTES

1. Philip Spencer, *Genocide Since 1945* (New York, NY: Routledge, 2012), 67.
2. Taylor Owen and Ben Kiernan, "Bombs Over Cambodia," *The Walrus* (October, 2006): 63.
3. Ibid, 67.
4. See Adam Jones, *Genocide: A Comprehensive Introduction*, 2nd ed. (New York, NY: Routledge, 2011), 291–292.
5. Wendy Lambourne, "Justice After Genocide: Impunity and the Extraordinary Chambers in the Courts of Cambodia," *Genocide Studies and Prevention* 8 (Spring 2014): 30.
6. George Chigas and Dmitri Mosyakov, "Literacy and Education under the Khmer Rouge." Accessed September 4, 2014 at http://www.yale.edu/cgp/literacyandeducation.html.
7. Ben Kiernan, *Blood and Soil: A World History of Genocide and Extermination from Sparta to Darfur* (New Haven, CT: Yale University Press, 2007), 547.
8. Robert Cribbs, "Political Genocides in Postcolonial Asia," eds. Donald Bloxham and A. Dirk Moses, *The Oxford Handbook of Genocide Studies* (New York, NY: Oxford University Press, 2010), 462–463.
9. Kosal Path and Elena Lesley-Rozen, "Introduction," *Genocide Studies and Prevention* 8 (Spring 2014): 3.
10. In March 2015, three additional former Khmer Rouge leaders—Im Chaem, Meas Muth, and Ao An—were charged with criminal conduct during the regime's reign, including crimes against humanity.
11. As the regime's two most senior surviving members, the defendants' advanced age and poor health mean that it is highly unlikely the case will reach a final judgment, not expected until mid-2019.
12. Kiernan, *Blood and Soil*, 549.
13. See footnote 179 in Randle C. DeFalco, "Cases 003 and 004 at the Khmer Rouge Tribunal: The Definition of 'Most Responsible' Individuals According to International Criminal Law," *Genocide Studies and Prevention* 8 (Spring 2014): 65.

See also Ben Kiernan, "The Cambodian Genocide, 1975–1979," eds. Samuel Totten and William S. Parsons, *Centuries of Genocide: Essays and Eyewitness Accounts*, 4th ed. (New York, NY: Routledge, 2013), 326.

14. Accessed September 9, 2014 at http://humanrightsdoctorate.blogspot.com/2009/12/genocide-and-cambodia.html.

15. Quote taken from Stephanie Giry, "The Genocide That Wasn't," *The New York Review of Books Blog*, accessed September 4, 2014 at http://www.nybooks.com/blogs/nyr-blog/2014/aug/25/khmer-rouge-genocide-wasnt/?insrc=hpss.

16. Ibid.

17. Raphael Lemkin, "Genocide as a Crime under International Law," *United Nations Bulletin* (January 15, 1948): 70.

18. UN Document E/CN.4/Sub.2/1985, July 2, 1985, paragraph 14.

19. William A. Schabas, *Genocide in International Law: The Crime of Crimes*, 2nd ed. (Cambridge, England: Cambridge University Press). See p. 11, footnote 32 for a summary of trial statements referencing genocide as the "crime of crimes."

20. *Prosecutor v. Radislav Krstic*, Case No. IT-98-33-A (April 19, 2004), paragraph 36.

21. *Prosecutor v. Clement Kayishema and Obed Ruzindana*, Case No. ICTR-95-1-A (June 1, 2001), paragraph 367.

22. William A. Schabas, "Semantics or Substance? David Scheffer's Welcome Proposal to Strengthen Criminal Accountability for Atrocities," *Genocide Studies and Prevention* 2 (2007): 34–35.

23. *Report of the International Commission of Inquiry on Darfur to the Secretary-General* (January 25, 2005), paragraph 522.

24. Patricia M. Wald, "Genocide and Crimes Against Humanity," *Washington University Global Studies Law Review* 6 (2007): 627, 631–632.

25. David Moshman, "Conceptual Constraints on Thinking about Genocide," *Journal of Genocide Research* 3 (2001): 443.

26. Secretary Colin L. Powell, "Testimony Before the Senate Foreign Relations Committee" (September 9, 2004), accessed August 1, 2014 at http://2001-2009.state.gov/secretary/former/powell/remarks/36042.htm.

27. Gareth Evans, *Responsibility to Protect: Ending Mass Atrocity Crimes Once and For All* (Washington, DC: Brookings Institution, 2008), 13.

28. The phrase "sacred evil" comes from Jeffrey C. Alexander's essay in *Remembering the Holocaust: A Debate* (New York, NY: Oxford University Press, 2009).

29. Schabas, "Semantics or Substance?," 31.

30. Steven R. Ratner, "Categories of War Crimes," eds. Roy Gutman, David Rieff, and Anthony Dworkin, *Crimes of War: What the Public Should Know* (New York, NY: W. W. Norton, 2007), 420.

31. Nuremberg Trial Proceedings Vol. 1, Charter of the International Military Tribunal, August 8, 1945, accessed July 29, 2014 at http://avalon.law.yale.edu/imt/imtconst.asp#art6.

32. Rome Statute of the International Criminal Court, November 10, 1998, Article 8. Accessed July 28, 2014 at http://legal.un.org/icc/statute/romefra.htm.

33. See W. J. Fenrick, "Crimes in Combat: The Relationship Between Crimes Against Humanity and War Crimes," Guest Lecture Series of the Office of the Prosecutor (March 5, 2004): 2.

34. Joseph Stefanelli, "War Crimes: Legal Frameworks and Lessons for Prevention," paper presented at a conference sponsored by the Auschwitz Institute for Peace and Reconciliation (Arusha, Tanzania), March 19, 2014.

35. Quoted material taken from Article I of the Genocide Convention.

36. Scott Straus, "Identifying Genocide and Related Forms of Mass Atrocity," Working Paper for the US Holocaust Memorial Museum (October 7, 2011): 17.
37. For discussions of the examples listed in this paragraph, see Patrick Wolfe, "Settler Colonialism and the Elimination of the Native," *Journal of Genocide Research* 8 (2006); Peter B. Owens, Yang Su, and David A. Snow, "Social Scientific Inquiry Into Genocide and Mass Killing: From Unitary Outcome to Complex Processes," *Annual Review of Sociology* (2013): 72; and Paul Bartrop, "The Relationship Between War and Genocide in the Twentieth Century: A Consideration," *Journal of Genocide Research* 4 (2002): 519–532.
38. Lydia Polgreen, "After Clashes, Fear of War on Congo's Edge," *The New York Times* (December 13, 2007).
39. Martin Shaw, *What Is Genocide?* (Cambridge, England: Polity Press, 2007), 111.
40. Kurt Jonassohn, "What Is Genocide?," ed. Helen Fein, *Genocide Watch* (New Haven, CT: Yale University Press, 1992), 22.
41. For a summary, see Scott Straus, "Political Science and Genocide," eds. Donald Bloxham and A. Dirk Moses, *The Oxford Handbook of Genocide Studies* (New York, NY: Oxford University Press, 2010), 176–178.
42. Eric Markusen and David Kopf, *The Holocaust and Strategic Bombing: Genocide and Total War in the Twentieth Century* (Boulder, CO: Westview Press, 1995), 243. The ways in which war serves as a catalyst for genocide are outlined on pp. 64–65 of this book.
43. Ibid, 62.
44. Adam Jones, *Genocide: A Comprehensive Introduction*, 2nd ed. (New York, NY: Routledge, 2011), 81–85.
45. Alex J. Bellamy, "Mass Atrocities and Armed Conflict: Links, Distinctions, and Implications for the Responsibility to Prevent," The Stanley Foundation (2011): 2.
46. Bartrop, "The Relationship Between War and Genocide," 530.
47. Quoted in Jeffrey Herf, *The Jewish Enemy: Nazi Propaganda During World War II and the Holocaust* (Cambridge, MA: Harvard University Press, 2006), 149.
48. Nuremberg Trial Proceedings Vol. 1, Charter of the International Military Tribunal, August 8, 1945, accessed July 29, 2014 at http://avalon.law.yale.edu/imt/imtconst.asp#art6.
49. Cited in Schabas, "Semantics or Substance?," 33.
50. See William A. Schabas, "Evolving Interpretations of the Crime of Genocide," *Genocide Studies and Prevention* 1 (Fall, 2006): 94–95.
51. Ibid, 96.
52. William A. Schabas, "Convention for the Prevention and Punishment of the Crime of Genocide," (2008): 3. Accessed August 1, 2014 at http://legal.un.org/avl/pdf/ha/cppcg/cppcg_e.pdf. Also note that *The Crimes Against Humanity Initiative* continues to advocate for a comprehensive international convention on the prevention and punishment of crimes against humanity (http://law.wustl.edu/harris/crimesagainsthumanity).
53. Rome Statute of the International Criminal Court, November 10, 1998, Article 7. Accessed July 28, 2014 at http://legal.un.org/icc/statute/romefra.htm.
54. Cited in Wald, "Genocide and Crimes Against Humanity," 624.
55. Stefanelli, "War Crimes."
56. Wald, "Genocide and Crimes Against Humanity," 625.
57. Ibid, 629.
58. Schabas, *Genocide in International Law*, 221.

59. Drazen Petrovic, "Ethnic Cleansing––An Attempt at Methodology," *European Journal of International Law* (1994): 343.

60. Gary Clayton Anderson, *Ethnic Cleansing and the Indian: The Crime That Should Haunt America* (Norman, OK: University of Oklahoma Press, 2014), 7.

61. Laura Silber and Allan Little, *Yugoslovia: Death of a Nation* (New York, NY: Penguin, 1996), 244.

62. Martin Shaw, *What Is Genocide?* (Cambridge, England: Polity Press, 2007), 49.

63. William Safire, "On Language: Ethnic Cleansing," *The New York Times* (March 14, 1993).

64. Schabas, *Genocide in International Law*, 224.

65. Historian Norman Naimark's well-received book on political violence in twentieth-century Europe (*Fires of Hatred*) carried the term ethnic cleansing in its subtitle. More recently, historian Gary Clayton Anderson's book carries the term in its lead title—*Ethnic Cleansing and the Indian: The Crime that Should Haunt America*.

66. UN Document S/25275 (February 10, 1993), paragraph 55.

67. Andrew Bell-Fialkoff, "A Brief History of Ethnic Cleansing," *Foreign Affairs* (Summer 1993), accessed July 30, 2014 at http://www.foreignaffairs.com/articles/48961/andrew-bell-fialkoff/a-brief-history-of-ethnic-cleansing.

68. Derek Davis, "Confronting Ethnic Cleansing in the Twenty-first Century," *Journal of Church and State* 42 (2000): 693.

69. Petrovic, "Ethnic Cleansing," 351.

70. Evans, *Responsibility to Protect*, 13.

71. Norman M. Naimark, *Fires of Hatred: Ethnic Cleansing in Twentieth-Century Europe* (Cambridge, MA: Harvard University Press, 2001), 3.

72. Benjamin Lieberman, "'Ethnic Cleansing' versus Genocide?," eds. Donald Bloxham and A. Dirk Moses, *The Oxford Handbook of Genocide Studies* (New York, NY: Oxford University Press, 2010), 44.

73. Larry May, *Genocide: A Normative Account* (New York, NY: Cambridge University Press, 2010), 105–106.

74. Schabas, *Genocide in International Law*, 234.

75. International Court of Justice, *Summary of the Judgment of 26 February 2007*, 8. Accessed July 31, 2014 at http://www.icj-cij.org/docket/index.php?p1=3&p2=3&case=91&code=bhy&p3=5.

76. Naimark, *Fires of Hatred*, 3–4.

77. UN Document A/RES/47/121 (December 18, 1992).

78. UN Document A/60/L.1, September 15, 2005, paragraph 139.

79. See their webpage at http://www.un.org/en/preventgenocide/adviser, accessed July 31, 2014.

80. Rome Statute of the International Criminal Court, November 10, 1998, Article 7. Accessed July 28, 2014 at http://legal.un.org/icc/statute/romefra.htm.

81. *Prosecutor v. Vidoje Blagojevic and Dragan Jockic*, Case No. IT-02-60-T (January 17, 2005), paragraph 650.

82. Petrovic, "Ethnic Cleansing," 359.

83. David Scheffer, "Defuse the Lexicon of Slaughter," *The New York Times* (February 23, 2012), accessed August 1, 2014 at http://www.nytimes.com/2012/02/24/opinion/defuse-the-lexicon-of-slaughter.html?_r=0.

84. David Scheffer, "Genocide and Atrocity Crimes," *Genocide Studies and Prevention* 1 (2006): 237.

85. See Sevane Garibian, "A Commentary on David Scheffer's Concepts of Genocide and Atrocity Crimes," *Genocide Studies and Prevention* 2 (2007): 43–50.

86. USAID, "Field Guide: Helping Prevent Mass Atrocities," (2015), 4.

87. Martha Minow, "Naming Horror: Legal and Political Words for Mass Atrocities," *Genocide Studies and Prevention* 2 (2007): 37–38.

88. International Commission on Intervention and State Sovereignty, *The Responsibility to Protect* (Ottawa, Canada: International Development Research Centre, 2001).

89. The RtoP abbreviation is also often used, particularly, by the UN, simply because R2P does not translate meaningfully into other languages. Italicized material (in original) comes from ICISS, *The Responsibility to Protect*, 13. The notion of "sovereignty as responsibility" was originally laid out by Francis M. Deng et al., *Sovereignty as Responsibility: Conflict Management in Africa* (Washington, DC: The Brookings Institution, 1996). See also Roberta Cohen and Francis M. Deng, *Masses in Flight: The Global Crisis of Internal Displacement* (Washington, DC: The Brookings Institution, 1998).

90. Richard Just, "We Can't Just Do Nothing," *New Republic* (August 27, 2009), accessed August 17, 2014 at http://www.newrepublic.com/article/books-and-arts/we-cant-just-do-nothing.

91. ICISS, *The Responsibility to Protect*, xi.

92. Madeleine K. Albright and Richard S. Williamson, "The United States and R2P: From Words to Action," 2013, 14.

93. See Sheri P. Rosenberg, "Responsibility to Protect: A Framework for Prevention," *Global Responsibility to Protect* 1 (2009): 442–477.

94. Alex J. Bellamy, *The Responsibility to Protect: Towards a "Living Reality"* (UNA-UK, April 2013), 6.

95. Martin Gilbert, "The Terrible 20th Century," *Globe and Mail* (Toronto), January 31, 2007. Also cited in Gareth Evans, "The Responsibility to Protect in Action," *Courier* 74 (Spring 2012): 5.

96. Quoted material comes from paragraphs 138 and 139, respectively, of the 2005 World Summit Outcome Document. See UN Document A/RES/60/1 (October 24, 2005).

97. UN S/Res/1674 (April 28, 2006).

98. The initial appointee was Dr. Edward Luck (2008–2012) and his successor, appointed in July 2013, is Dr. Jennifer Welsh.

99. See UN Document A/63/677 (January 12, 2009).

100. Perhaps reinforcing the nonsequential nature of the three pillars, the UN Secretary-General's annual reports tackled Pillar III in 2012 (UN Document A/66/874), Pillar I in 2013 (UN Document A/67/929), and Pillar II in 2014 (UN Document A/68/947).

101. At present, countries currently on the Peacebuilding Commission's agenda include Burundi, Sierra Leone, Guinea, Guinea-Bissau, Liberia, and the Central African Republic.

102. The R2I moniker came from Miguel d'Escoto Brockmann, a Nicaraguan diplomat at the UN. See "An Idea Whose Time Has Come—and Gone," *The Economist* (July 23, 2009), accessed August 14, 2014 at http://www.economist.com/node/14087788. For the R2K reference, see Finian Cunningham, "'Responsibility to Kill' (R2K): Washington Gives Green Light to Toxic Terror in Bahrain," accessed August 14, 2014 at http://www.globalresearch.ca/responsibility-to-kill-r2k-washington-gives-green-light-to-toxic-terror-in-bahrain/29064.

103. Lou Pingeot and Wolfgang Obenland, *In Whose Name? A Critical View on the Responsibility to Protect* (Bonn, Germany: Global Policy Forum, 2014), 33–34.

104. See Diana Johnstone, "R2P and 'Genocide Prevention': The Good Intentions That Pave the Road to War," accessed August 14, 2014 at http://www.counter-punch.org/2013/02/01/the-good-intentions-that-pave-the-road-to-war and Alan J. Kuperman, "The Moral Hazard of Humanitarian Intervention: Lessons from the Balkans," *International Studies Quarterly* 52 (2008): 49–80.

105. I have borrowed the phrase "limitless license" from Albright and Williamson, "The United States and R2P," 7.

106. The full text of President Obama's speech was accessed August 19, 2014 at http://www.whitehouse.gov/the-press-office/2014/08/07/statement-president.

107. Kees Homan and Marianne Ducasse-Rogier, "Who's Afraid of the Responsibility to Protect?," *Clingendael Policy Brief* (December 2012): 1.

108. ICISS, *The Responsibility to Protect*, 33.

109. Michael Barnett and Thomas G. Weiss, *Humanitarianism Contested: Where Angels Fear to Tread* (New York, NY: Routledge, 2011), 83.

110. Gareth Evans, *The Responsibility to Protect: Ending Mass Atrocity Crimes Once and For All* (Washington, DC: The Brookings Institution, 2008), 59.

111. The "a blink of an eye" quote comes from Evans, *The Responsibility to Protect*, 31; the meaning of a norm is taken from David J. Simon, "Building State Capacity to Prevent Atrocity Crimes: Implementing Pillars One and Two of the R2P Framework," *Policy Analysis Brief* (September 2012): 6.

112. Martha Finnemore and Kathryn Sikkink, "International Norm Dynamics and Political Change," *International Organization* 52 (1998): 892.

113. This is what Finnemore and Sikkink describe as norm internalization. Also see Kathryn Sikkink's *The Justice Cascade: How Human Rights Prosecutions Are Changing World Politics* (New York, NY: W. W. Norton, 2011).

114. Comments accessed August 18, 2014 at http://venitism.blogspot.com/2014/08/prevention-of-genocide.html.

115. See UN SG/SM/13838 (September 23, 2011), accessed August 13, 2014 at http://www.un.org/News/Press/docs/2011/sgsm13838.doc.htm.

116. See "The Responsibility to Protect: A New Norm for Preventing and Halting Mass Atrocities," at http://www.responsibilitytoprotect.org.

117. Secretary-General Ban Ki-moon, "Address to Stanley Foundation Conference on the Responsibility to Protect" (January 18, 2012), accessed August 18, 2014 at http://www.un.org/sg/statements/?nid=5813.

118. ICISS, *The Responsibility to Protect*, xi.

119. These reasons are taken from United Nations, "Framework of Analysis for Atrocity Crimes: A Tool for Prevention," (2014), 2.

120. Gareth Evans, *The Responsibility to Protect: Ending Mass Atrocity Crimes Once and For All* (Washington, DC: Brookings Institution Press, 2008), 281.

121. This analogy is compiled from examples given at http://www.ucdenver.edu/academics/colleges/PublicHealth/research/ResearchProjects/piper/PREVENT/education/Documents/Outline1.pdf and http://www.iwh.on.ca/wrmb/primary-secondary-and-tertiary-prevention (both accessed February 10, 2015).

122. Donatella Lorch, "Thousands of Rwanda Dead Wash Down to Lake Victoria," accessed February 12, 2015 at http://partners.nytimes.com/library/world/africa/052194rwanda-genocide.html.

123. USAID, "Field Guide: Helping Prevent Mass Atrocities," (2015), 26.

124. Saferworld, "Upstream Conflict Prevention: Addressing the Root Causes of Conflict" (September, 2012), 2.

125. Quoted material is taken from Primo Levi, *The Drowned and the Saved* (New York, NY: Vintage International, 1988), 199.

126. Quoted material is taken from UN News Centre, http://www.un.org/apps/news/story.asp?NewsID=49556 (December 9, 2014), accessed December 14, 2014.

PART II

A Continuum of Prevention Strategies

CHAPTER 4

Upstream Prevention Strategies

Avoiding "A Path to Hell"

On March 20, 1993, in the midst of the atrocities that were ripping apart the seams of the former Yugoslavia, the mainly Muslim wartime government of Bosnia and Herzegovina instituted legal proceedings against what was then known as the Federal Republic of Yugoslavia (which after 2003 became known as Serbia and Montenegro and, later, simply as Serbia after the secession of Montenegro in June 2006). Following a provision laid out in Article IX of the Genocide Convention, the suit was filed with the International Court of Justice (ICJ) at The Hague in the Netherlands. The ICJ (also known as the World Court) is the principal judicial organ of the United Nations (UN) and hears only those cases involving states, not individuals. The suit alleged past and continuing violations of the Genocide Convention based on crimes committed by Serbia against the people and State of Bosnia and Herzegovina. These alleged crimes included killing, murdering, wounding, raping, robbing, torturing, kidnapping, illegally detaining, and exterminating the citizens of Bosnia and Herzegovina. The suit, in addition to requesting that Serbia cease and desist immediately from these breaches of international law, sought unspecified reparations for damages to person and property.

Serbia would neither cease nor desist until the end of the war and the signing of the Dayton Peace Agreement on December 14, 1995. In the years following, counterclaims and divisions within the newly established national government of Bosnia–Herzegovina (which included Serbian representatives) delayed the hearing of the case. Finally, nearly 13 years after the initial filing, oral arguments in the case began on February 27, 2006. In the opening statements, Bosnia's representative to the court, Sakib Softic, said: "We are here because the Belgrade [Serbia] authorities have taken the non-Serbs of Bosnia [Muslims and Croats] on a path to hell, a path littered with dead bodies, broken families . . . and lost futures."[1]

A year later, on February 26, 2007, the 15-judge panel of the ICJ issued a controversial judgment in which it declared Srebrenica "genocide" but decided that the remaining abuses of the 1992–1995 war did not evidence the intent required to meet the legal definition of genocide (it is important to note that the court's jurisdictional authority did not include ruling on Serbia's alleged responsibility for war crimes or crimes against humanity). In William Schabas' words, the court treated ". . . the [Srebrenica] massacre as an isolated and ultimately idiosyncratic event within a broader conflict whose essence was not fundamentally genocidal."[2] In a divisive compromise judgment, the court found that Serbia itself was not directly responsible or even complicit in the Srebrenica genocide, based on the lack of requisite specific intent and the specious belief that the state did not have effective control over its proxy Bosnian Serb forces at Srebrenica. The court did hold Serbia responsible, however, for violating the legal duty to *prevent* genocide as well as *punish* those responsible for the perpetration of genocide at Srebrenica (including the failure to turn over indictees to the International Criminal Tribunal for the former Yugoslavia, or ICTY). Because, however, the court believed there was no certainty that Serbia could have succeeded in preventing the genocide, no reparations for damages were assessed.

This landmark judgment, against a state rather than individuals, left Serbia as the first nation to have been found in legal violation of the UN Genocide Convention since its adoption in 1948. The ruling—registered before the ICTY had convicted any individual of committing genocide— affirmed state, not simply individual, responsibility for international crimes, including the crime of genocide. More notably, the ICJ judgment indicated that there is a legal, not solely ethical, duty of the State to prevent genocide occurring outside its own territory. That is, a State's obligation to prevent genocide is not restricted to its own borders; preventing genocide—acting within the boundaries specified by international law and the UN Charter—also is an obligatory State action for genocide committed outside its borders. As Schabas argues, "[T]he court's approach to the duty to prevent genocide dovetails neatly with . . . a 'responsibility to protect,' and it provides further support for the entrenchment of this doctrine within customary international law."[3]

The ICJ's findings draw our attention back to Article I of the Genocide Convention. This opening article affirms that genocide is a crime under international law that contracting parties (that is, states) agree to undertake to "prevent and to punish." Article I is not merely a pretentious preamble to the other 18 articles in the Convention. Rather, as the ICJ held, "Article I, in particular its undertaking to prevent, creates obligations distinct from those which appear in the subsequent Articles."[4] The dual obligations to prevent and to punish, although certainly distinct, are just as certainly interrelated—effective prevention should eliminate the need for punishment, just as effective punishment should serve as a deterrent preventive practice. As the court held, however, the State's obligation to prevent genocide is "normative and compelling" and cannot be "merged in the duty to punish, nor can it be regarded as simply a component of that duty."[5] The court continues: "The obligation to prevent the commission of the crime of genocide is imposed by the Genocide Convention on any State party which, in a given situation, has it in its power to contribute to restraining in any degree the commission of genocide."[6]

On a very specific level, the ICJ judgment was about Serbia's default on its obligation in the face of the serious risk of genocide at Srebrenica. More broadly, however, the ICJ judgment speaks of a shared international obligation of States to prevent genocide. As Judge Elihu Lauterpacht wrote in the ICJ's ruling on preliminary measures, ". . . the duty to 'prevent genocide' is a duty that rests upon all parties and is a duty owed by each party to every other."[7] So, although this obligation may vary greatly from State to State (depending on geography, political strength and stability, and so on), there is a collective international duty to use all available means to prevent genocide.

Although the ICJ judgment focused specifically on this legal duty in the face of a serious risk of genocide, academics, policymakers, and global civil society have drawn the circle much more broadly—focusing on primary preventive strategies that come long before a serious risk of genocide has emerged. Prevention begins with an understanding of how genocide happens and why. Only then, once we have traced the etiology of the disease, can we begin to find ways to prevent it from ever taking place. This is upstream prevention, focusing on the underlying causes of genocide, with an aim toward understanding the ways in which a society can be inoculated against the risk of its occurrence.

The fact that both war (a high-intensity violent conflict) and genocide have multiple roots and at least some of those roots are intertwined has deep implications for the prevention of genocide.[8] As discussed in

Chapter 3, war does not always lead to genocide and genocide does not always occur in the context of war. Peacetime atrocities, as pointed out by Alex Bellamy, can occur in the context of state-directed suppression, communal violence, or postwar retribution.[9] Such peacetime atrocities have been seen in nineteenth-century Russian pogroms, China's Cultural Revolution, and the persecution of Uzbeks in Kyrgyzstan.[10] This reality— that genocide can happen in times of peace—means that strategies for genocide prevention cannot always be made equivalent to those for violent conflict prevention. That is, strategies for genocide prevention must be sensitive to a possibility of peacetime occurrence that, by definition, is not relevant for strategies of violent conflict prevention.

In genocide prevention, the measures used and those targeted by a particular strategy, as well as the objectives and type of engagement, may be narrower than the measures deemed suitable for violent conflict prevention. Where a violent conflict prevention strategy might consider the use of amnesty for perpetrators, for instance, such a strategy for genocide prevention would compromise criminal accountability in an unacceptable way.[11] In yet other ways, genocide prevention strategies may be broader, including, for example, physical protection for vulnerable groups, a tool rarely associated with violent conflict prevention.[12] In some cases, the exact same prevention tools might have decidedly different targets or objectives when tailored to the context of genocide or violent conflict prevention. In genocide prevention, for example, sanctions may be used coercively to target specific actors we are seeking to dissuade from committing atrocities. In the case of violent conflict prevention, the same tool could be directed cooperatively at several actors we are seeking to bring together in a consensual peace agreement.[13]

In many ways, though, the preventive implications for violent conflict and genocide are markedly interconnected; many of the actions taken to prevent the former will necessarily reduce the occurrence of the latter. Just as the number of drowning incidents is likely to increase as more people head to the water on a hot day, the number of genocidal conflicts will increase as more violent conflicts emerge globally. So, understanding the general sources of violent conflict, and how they may be mitigated, will go a long way toward helping us at least indirectly prevent, or reduce the number of, genocides. As Bellamy argues, "there can be no meaningful and effective agenda for the prevention of genocide and mass atrocities that does not incorporate the prevention of armed conflict and the measures commonly associated with it."[14] In short, the prevention of violent conflict should be a core element of any genocide prevention strategy.

This significant logical overlap between violent conflict prevention and genocide prevention is particularly evident in the subject of this chapter—upstream prevention strategies that aim to mitigate the risk of mass violence in a given society. Such upstream strategies, whether seen through a violent conflict prevention or genocide prevention lens, offer very similar, even generic, preventive measures for the two forms of violence. These measures aim to nourish the roots of a stable and sustainable peace by creating structures proactively responsive to the underlying sources of violent or genocidal conflict. Given that 1.5 billion people currently live in countries under the threat of large-scale organized violence, it is a matter of desperate life-and-death urgency that we unpack these root sources with an eye toward prevention of such atrocities.[15] To that end, this chapter will (1) examine the role of social identity as a source of violent or genocidal conflict and (2) assess the underlying structural factors that put states at risk for such conflict.

SOCIAL IDENTITY AS A SOURCE OF VIOLENT OR GENOCIDAL CONFLICT

What are the sources of violent conflict? Among these can be a scarcity of, and competition for, vital natural resources (agricultural land, forests, water, food, energy, minerals, metals, oil, and so on) and inequities in the allocation of such resources. In September 2014, for instance, the U.S. National Intelligence Strategy cited water shortages, as well as fierce competition for food and energy, as posing global security threats—at the same level of concern as the proliferation of weapons of mass destruction, terrorism, and cyberattacks on critical infrastructure.[16] The fact that wars are disproportionately concentrated in the world's poorest countries also suggests poverty and economic depression as potent sources of violent conflict, as well as debilitating consequences of such conflict (an average of 30 years of economic growth is lost through a civil war and the country's international trade takes on average 20 years to recover).[17] State-sponsored abuses of human rights can lead to oppositional responses that trigger even greater levels of violent internal conflict. Other sources of violent conflict include political and social inequalities, state crises, fragile political systems transitioning from dictatorships to democracies, territorial disputes, and a history of grievances and provocations between groups.[18]

Perhaps, however, the most increasingly potent sources of the divisions and violent conflict that rattle our contemporary world—and intersecting with many of the sources listed above—are issues of identity. As journalist

Fareed Zakaria has observed: "The questions that fill people with emotion are 'Who are we?' and, more ominously, 'Who are we not?'"[19] At the turn of the twenty-first century, international relations scholar Mary Kaldor argued that identity, along with globalization, would be the key concepts for understanding the new conflicts of the post-Cold War era.[20] Indeed, a review of armed conflicts from around the world in 2013 cited identity as a main cause of conflict in 21 of the 35 reported cases.[21] At present, nationalist parties—many with xenophobic tendencies—are enjoying a resurgence of political power across the globe. Ethnic and racial tensions continue to deface the landscape of community after community. A January 2014 Pew Research Center report found that the share of countries with a high level of social hostilities involving religious identities had reached a 6-year peak—increasing in every major region of the world except the Americas.[22] Today, there is widespread agreement that it is identity groups, and organizations claiming to represent such groups, that are at the core of contemporary violent conflicts.[23]

So, what do we mean by identity and why does it play such a significant role in intergroup conflict? On one level, we can think of identity as a personal construct; the self-conceptualizations that define us in relation to, or in comparison with, other individuals. When asked who we are, this level of personal identity—"I-identity"—focuses on characteristics that are relatively unique to how we define ourselves as an individual. On another level, however, identity is a social construct; it is a conceptualization of the self that derives from membership in an emotionally significant social category or group to which we perceive ourselves as belonging. On this level, when asked who we are, we focus on social identities—"we-identity"—tied to memberships in groups that are important to us at that particular moment in our lives.[24] Our social identities allow groups to enter into our sense of who we are. These personal and social identities subsumed under our self-concept are inherently and reciprocally related; the former is built on our perceived individual uniqueness and the latter on our shared group sameness.[25] Different contexts prime different constructs of our identities; personal identity may be salient in one context and we may readily shift to social identity in another context.

For social identities, the ambiguous nature of how groups are defined means that the issue is less one of objective group membership and more one of a subjective psychological sense of symbolic attachment to a specific social identity. In defining the specific attachment characteristics of ethnic or national group identity, social psychologist Herbert Kelman speaks of "... its enduring characteristics and basic values, its strengths and weaknesses, its hopes and fears, its reputation and conditions of

existence, its institutions and traditions, its past history, current purposes, and future prospects."[26] Social identities include groups or categories based on race, socioeconomic status or social class, religion, gender,
sex, age, sexual orientation, ethnicity, nationality, ability/disability, language, and so on. These social identity markers are a preexisting part of
the structured societies into which we are born. Over the course of our
lives, our social identities become central to the integrity of who we are
and also, when applied to others, help us make sense of a very complex
social world. In this sense, groups are more than simply a collection of
individuals; rather groups are rich avenues of understanding who we, and
others, are.

Some of these social identities are ascribed, written on us at birth.
Such social identities—race, sex, ethnicity, and so on—are seen as relatively impermeable and fixed. Other social identities are achieved, earned,
or chosen throughout the course of our lives. Such social identities—
socioeconomic status, religion, nationality, and so on—are seen as more
plastic and transient. A far greater number of modern social identities
are subject to choice than in the past. Moreover, many social identities
have a fluid, permeable nature to their boundaries and straddle both the
ascribed and achieved categories. In Northern Ireland, for instance, religious identity, which some across the world may see as achieved, is really
better understood as ascribed—you are the religion into which you are
born. In some caste-like societies, you can be born into a profession or
craft, an ascribed identity that modern societies would more commonly
see as achieved. A family's socioeconomic status could be achieved, but
would be an ascribed identity for its children.

Some social identities—whether ascribed or achieved—give us power
and privilege in some environments, and others leave us feeling vulnerable
and unsafe in other environments. At certain times and in certain places,
some social identities are subordinated to a broader superordinate social
identity. During spells of patriotic fervor, for instance, the larger national
identity of "American" may be more operative for how an individual
answers who they are than the embedded hyphenated identity of African-
American, Asian-American, Latino-American, Native American, and
so on. Conversely, the disintegration of the former Yugoslavia following
the death of Marshal Tito in 1980 saw a devolution from a superordinate
social identity of "Yugoslavian" to the triggering of a host of subordinate
ethnic identities (with strong nationalist overtones) of Serbian, Croatian,
Slovenian, and so on. Finally, some social identities simply indicate an affiliate relationship; not necessarily one in which we actively contribute to the
performance of the group. For instance, fans of a national football team

during the World Cup find that affiliate social identity very emotionally significant and tie a large part of their self-esteem to the successes, and failures, of the team with which they have aligned themselves—their triumphs become our triumphs and their shame our shame.

The activation of our various social identities is context dependent—influenced by where we are at, who we are with, and what we are doing in our daily lives. In addition to being contextual, social identity is dynamic and changeable. It is "multitiered and quite malleable under certain circumstances."[27] At any given moment, the social identity relevant to us at that point in time is about what we have in common with a group—"us" and "we"—rather than what is unique about us as a person. From a social identity perspective, our uniqueness is drawn from the fact that our various social identities are multiple and overlapping; they are interwoven threads that answer the complex question of who we are. We can be Chilean, a woman, a politician, an activist, wealthy, and gay all at the same time. Our social identity is not a zero-sum game in which holding one negates holding any others. That is, we can hold one social identity without detracting from, or giving up on, other social identities that—in different circumstances and settings—may be more important to us. The salience of our identification with a particular social identity even varies over time—where religion may have been the defining social identity marker at one point in my life, it may not have been at another point.

In itself, group-based social identity is not problematic. It can be a healthy source of social understanding; it gives us a sense of who we, and others, are based on group memberships. We should recognize, though, that who we are is very strongly tied to who we are not; it is easier to be Hutu if there is someone else to be Tutsi. So, social identity can become dangerous when it begins to draw evaluative and emotional boundaries between those in my group and those not (the "other"). Social psychologists refer to these groups as "in-groups" (us) and "out-groups" (them). The in-group is any group to which we belong or with which we identify. In-groups can range from small, face-to-face groupings of family and friends to larger social identities such as race, ethnicity, gender, or religion. Out-groups are any groups to which we do not belong or with which we do not identify. Assigning people to in-groups and out-groups—that is, social categorization—has important consequences for how social identity can become a source of violent or genocidal conflict.

On one level, the power of social identity leads us to perceive other in-group members as more similar to us than out-group members. We solidify this perception, known as the *assumed similarity effect*, by exaggerating the similarities within our own group. Even in laboratory experiments, when we have been arbitrarily assigned to a nominal group, we assume other in-group members are similar to us on a surprisingly wide range of thoughts, feelings, and behaviors. We complement this in-group similarity with a corresponding belief that all members of the out-group are alike as well. This *out-group homogeneity effect* leads us to believe that if we know something about one out-group member, we know something about all of them; they are all interchangeable. This overgeneralization can even extend to perceptual recognition; research has found, for instance, that people of other races are perceived to look more alike than members of our own race.[28] We then amplify our assumed similarity of in-group members and homogeneity of out-group members by drawing ever starker lines between "us" and "them." We draw these lines by exaggerating the differences between our group and the out-group. This exaggeration of differentness, termed the *accentuation effect*, leaves us biased toward information that enhances the differences between groups and less attentive to information about similarities between members of different groups.

To this point, all our discussion of social identity has done is reveal our tendencies as cognitive misers—we think in-group members are similar to us and out-group members are all alike, and we overestimate the differences between "us" and "them." These seem like fairly innocuous cognitive biases that are, at worst, depersonalizing—both for the ways in which we forfeit our uniqueness in favor of the assumed similarity of our in-group as well as for the ways in which we exaggerate the perceived sameness of out-group members. Unfortunately, however, as social psychologist Gordon Allport argued in his 1954 classic *The Nature of Prejudice*, there is a psychological primacy to the survival value of in-groups—"We live in them, by them, and, sometimes, for them"—that leaves such biases seldom affectively neutral.[29] Indeed, experience and research have demonstrated that we generally like people we think are similar to us and dislike those we perceive as different. That is, the mere act of dividing people into groups inevitably sets up a bias in favor of the in-group and against the out-group. The bias has been defined broadly as ". . . an unfair evaluative, emotional, cognitive, or behavioral response toward another group in ways that devaluate or disadvantage the other group and its members either directly or indirectly by valuing or privileging members of one's own group."[30] Such in-group favoritism, labeled the *in-group bias*, has been demonstrated across a wide range of groups, ages, contexts, and tasks.[31]

Why is the in-group bias so prevalent in intergroup relations? The search for a theoretical understanding to this question began in the mind of Henri Tajfel, a Polish Jew studying at the Sorbonne, in Paris, at the outset of World War II. After volunteering to serve in the French Army, he was captured by the Germans and became a prisoner of war. During that time, Tajfel was struck by the ways in which simple social categorization—for example, being a French Jew as opposed to a Polish Jew—had direct life and death consequences. Tajfel saw firsthand how social identities fundamentally changed the ways people saw and related to others. After his release, and his discovery that his entire family had been killed during the Holocaust, Tajfel focused his professional career as a social psychologist "on a life-long quest to understand what happens psychologically when people categorize themselves and others into groups."[32]

Tajfel, joined by his colleague, John Turner, believed that the major underlying psychological motive for in-group bias was the need to improve self-esteem. In their social identity theory, we enhance our self-esteem by allowing the in-group to become an extension of ourselves.[33] To maximize this avenue to develop (or borrow) positive self-esteem, however, we must see our group as not only distinct but superior to other groups. We can do this by boosting the status of the group to which we belong, as well as by denigrating and discriminating against the groups to which we do not belong. That is, since we derive part of our self-esteem from the groups with which we identify, we are motivated to perceive ". . . the in-group and the out-group on dimensions that lead the in-group to be judged positively and the out-group to be judged negatively."[34] This evolved competitive dynamic, although not inherently conflictual, may certainly lead to discriminatory intergroup behavior—even in the absence of a realistic conflict of interests, previously existing hostility, or social interaction between groups. In summarizing a robust research program of experiments on intergroup relations, Tajfel and Turner state: "The basic and highly reliable finding is that the trivial, ad hoc intergroup categorization leads to in-group favoritism and discrimination against the out-group."[35]

It is in-group bias—particularly when based on group membership perceived as impermeable and fixed—that helps us understand why social identity matters as a source of violent or genocidal conflict. To be sure, discrimination *for* in-groups and discrimination *against* out-groups are not necessarily and inevitably two sides of the same coin. However rarely, it is possible to have an in-group preference for those that we acknowledge to be "us" without the reciprocal presence of hostile thoughts, feelings, or behaviors toward out-groups of "them." Even in these exceptional instances, however, in-group favoritism is anything but benign over the long term. As social psychologist Marilynn Brewer summarizes: "The very factors that make in-group attachment and allegiance important to individuals also provide a fertile ground for antagonism and distrust of those outside the in-group boundaries. The need to justify in-group values in the form of moral superiority to others, sensitivity to threat, the anticipation of interdependence under conditions of distrust, social comparison processes, and power politics all conspire to connect in-group identification and loyalty to disdain and overt hostility toward out-groups."[36] As she points out, these factors are likely to be especially powerful in highly segmented, hierarchically organized societies—exactly the types of societies that often give birth to large-scale organized violence.

Jolle Demmers, co-founder of the Centre for Conflict Studies at Utrecht University in the Netherlands, also speaks of the escalatory process of identity group dynamics that can lead to violent conflict—particularly during times of crisis. She focuses on the ways in which group comparison—which lies at the heart of social identity theory—can lead to group competition and, ultimately, to group hostility. As she writes: "The more alike people are, the more relevant they will perceive the other for the purpose of identity comparison and the more acute their possible inter-group competition."[37] So, minor differences—perhaps unimportant in themselves—become mobilizing major differences through group comparison. Group identity competition shifts the nature of relations ". . . from *inter-personal* (interaction between people is determined by their personal relationships and their respective individual characteristics) to *inter-group* (the behaviour of individuals towards each other is determined by their membership of different groups."[38] As social identity theory predicts, the escalation of group competition to group hostility, although not inevitable, is possible when in-group members fear, realistically or not, that what makes them distinct and superior is under threat from out-group members.

Moreover, as social psychologists Sonia Roccas and Andrey Elster point out, there is a "conflict-enhancing feedback loop" between social identity and intergroup conflict. In a tragically symbiotic relationship, the effects of social identity on conflict are reciprocated by the effects of conflict on social identity. Conflict can increase the salience of social identity in such a way as to intensify the sense of commitment and loyalty to the in-group, as well as antagonism toward the out-group. As Roccas and Elster write: ". . . intergroup conflict is likely to lead to a simplified social identity, which in turn might lead to less tolerance and to intensification of conflict. . . Simple identities increase conflict, and conflict simplifies identities."[39] So, the instantiation of social identities can be more than simply a cause of violent or genocidal conflict, it can also be a consequence of such conflict. That is, social identity can be reified—"turned into something hard, unchangeable, and absolute"— by violent or genocidal conflict.[40] Slavenka Drakulic, a Croatian journalist, spoke of this transformation as the war neared her town of Zagreb in January 1992. Comparing her contextually imposed new national social identity to an ill-fitting shirt, she wrote: "You may feel the sleeves are too short, the collar too tight. You might not like the colour, and the cloth might itch. But there is no escape; there is nothing else to wear . . . So right now, in the new state of Croatia, no one is allowed not to be a Croat."[41]

Several scholars have privileged the role of identity as a source of genocidal conflict. For feminist philosopher Claudia Card, for instance, the harm of genocide is best understood in the destruction of social identity. She writes: "It [genocide] targets people on the basis of who they are rather than on the basis of what they have done, what they might do, even what they are capable of doing."[42] Although those latter factors—what a target group has done, what they might do, or what they might be capable of doing—are often used as justifications for their extermination, it is who they are— their social identity—that is the real target for extermination. She continues: "The very idea of selecting victims by social group identity suggests that it is not just the physical life of victims that is targeted but the social vitality behind that identity."[43] Similarly, in her concept of "identicide," peace practitioner Sarah Jane Meharg focuses on "the destruction of any or all of the particular qualities that make up, not necessarily the actual elimination of people, but rather, the places which they have constructed over time and in which they habitually live, and their customary and routinised social practices."[44] In her view, the intentional annihilation of social identity is a precursor framework to the actual physical extermination of a people.

Likewise, Christopher Powell speaks of a "collective social identity" that is victimized by the violent destruction of genocide. In other words, social identity is what genocide kills. For Powell, genocide is *"an identity-difference relation of violent obliteration* [italics in original] . . . that involves a fundamental qualitative transformation, from a relation that assigns the Other an inferior or denigrated position in the wider figuration to which both persecutor and persecuted belong, to one that works to deny them any position at all."[45] Political scientist Maureen Hiebert also speaks of a collective social identity of victims that is manipulated or "reconstructed" by perpetrators in such a way that victims are viewed as a threatening internal enemy through the mere fact of their continued physical existence.[46] In these ways, for both Powell and Hiebert, social identity can become a genocidal imperative used to forge in-group solidarity and undermine the normal inhibitions against the destruction of an out-group. Our cause is sacred; theirs is evil. We are the victims; they are the victimizers. It is rarely *our* enemy or *an* enemy, but *the* enemy—a usage of the definite article that hints of something eternal and immutable, abstract and evil.

The influential role of social identity in genocidal conflict is affirmed by the UN Office of the Special Adviser on the Prevention of Genocide: "While conflict has many causes, genocidal conflict is identity-based. Genocide and related atrocities tend to occur in societies with diverse national, racial, ethnic or religious groups that are locked in identity-related conflicts. It is not simply differences in identity, whether real or perceived, that generate conflict, but the implication of those differences in terms of access to power and wealth, services and resources, employment, development opportunities, citizenship and the enjoyment of fundamental rights and freedoms."[47] Obviously, identity-related genocidal conflicts go far beyond the four protected social identities (national, ethnic, racial, and religious) of the Genocide Convention. Any of the myriad ways people can define themselves as a social group offers an opportunity for privileging identity that, in a violent environment, can become a destructive source for genocidal conflict. As peace scholar Jay Rothman argues, identity becomes "conflictual when two identities are negatively interdependent, in a zero-sum or threatening relationship. When my being me depends on you not being you, or when your being you threatens my being me."[48]

In sum, social identity is *a* source, but far from *the* only source, of violent or genocidal conflict. It does remind us, however, that not all conflict is reducible simply to competition for vital natural resources, political power, economic gains, territorial expansion, or historical memory. Rather violent or genocidal conflict—particularly in a world in which no country is perfectly homogeneous—can also be about competition between social identities seeking to maintain, restore, or claim a favored identity status. Although not all social identity conflicts end in genocide, social identity matters deeply in understanding the etiology of how people are done to death in genocidal conflict. And it matters particularly in its intersection with a range of underlying structural factors that put states at risk for such conflict.

RISK FACTORS FOR VIOLENT OR GENOCIDAL CONFLICT

To prevent violent or genocidal conflict, we must understand the forces behind it. Indeed, upstream preventive strategies are intimately tied to an accurate understanding of the underlying risk factors that place a society at peril for violent or genocidal conflict. Understanding why, where, and when violent or genocidal conflict will erupt is crucial as a basis for preventive action by academics, lawyers, policymakers, global civil society, and, even, the potential victim group. Such information, allowing us to identify potential crisis situations, is the basis of *early warning systems*. As researcher

Alexander Austin points out, early warning systems are not new mechanisms. They have been in existence since the 1950s, primarily used by military strategic intelligence to predict attacks but also used by international altruistic organizations to forecast humanitarian and natural disasters such as earthquakes, drought, food shortages, and famine.[49] More recently, however, early warning systems have been developed for forecasting a range of violent conflict situations, including genocidal conflict.

An early warning system is an upstream preventive process that allows us to respond to potentially violent conflict before it becomes deadly. Early warning begins with an assessment of risk factors—the longer-term and slower moving structures, measures, society-wide conditions, and processes that put states at risk for violent or genocidal conflict. Such factors—often embedded with social identity issues—include how authority in a country is exercised, how a history of conflict is interpreted, economic conditions, and social fragmentation. A global scan to collect verifiable data based on these background risk factors then allows us to generate ongoing "watch lists" of fragile countries—or situations of concern—that can be monitored for further signs of instability before a crisis fully develops. Rather than thinking of these underlying risk factors in causal terms, they are best understood as probabilistic predictions, not infallible, that maximize our forecasting power for violent or genocidal conflict. That is, risk factors increase the risk or susceptibility to genocide, but do not equate to its inevitable occurrence. As a rough analogy, a person may have several of the major risk factors for cardiovascular disease (for example, age, sex, heredity, smoking, blood cholesterol, physical inactivity, and so on) without necessarily ever succumbing to a stroke—though certainly, from a probability standpoint, the more risk factors you have, the greater your chance of developing some form of coronary heart disease.

As Austin has outlined, some early warning systems for violent conflict are heavily quantitative, relying on systematic empirical data collection or the use of other preexisting large data banks (often from previous conflicts). Examples of data sources used in quantitative early warning systems include the University of Maryland's Minorities at Risk Project that tracks 284 politically active ethnic groups throughout the world from 1945 to the present and the University of Michigan's Conflict and Peace Data Bank of daily international and domestic events or interactions. In this same quantitative vein, Thomas Chadefaux recently used a 60 million page database of newspaper articles over the last century to develop a weekly risk index that was able to predict the onset of war within the next few months with up to 85% confidence.[50] Other systems are more qualitative, relying on field-based reports or special envoys that often privilege civil society and the "eyes and ears" of local sources on the ground more than government or open source data reporting. Examples of qualitative early warning systems, often used in lobbying of policymakers, are reflected in the advocacy work of Human Rights Watch, Amnesty International, and the International Crisis Group. Still others blend quantitative and qualitative approaches, often in a networking capacity to bridge the divide between nongovernmental and governmental sectors. The best known example of this blended network approach is the London-based Forum on Early Warning and Early Response.[51]

This diversity of methodologies, coupled with competing and even contradictory views of what constitutes a risk factor, has led to the proliferation of several dozen models of early warning systems—developed and used by national governments, militaries and intelligence services, international and regional organizations, academics, nongovernmental organizations, civil society, think tanks, and private enterprises throughout the world. Some of these ever-evolving models focus on early warning for the onset of political instability, state fragility, civil unrest, or general violent conflict and others focus more particularly on the atrocity crimes of genocide, war crimes, and crimes against humanity. Due to a lack of comparable data, most (certainly not all) of the models focus on the more common reality of state-led mass killing rather than relatively rarer mass killings perpetrated by nonstate actors (however, even where nonstate actors are perpetrators, they usually do so with the complicity of the state or in a "failed state" situation in which the rule of law has disintegrated).[52] The models are built on a wide range of risk factors and even a greater number of corresponding objective indicators to help determine the degree to which any risk factor is present in a given situation. Illustrating the complexity involved in risk assessment, a 2008 report from the Center for Strategic and International Studies, surveying only 30 such models, found more than 800 indicators of risk used by those models alone.[53] Similarly, in my consulting work with the Economic Community of West African States, I have seen how their alert and response structure for early warning (ECOWARN) has evolved to rely on 66 indicators—ranging from declining student attendance in schools or an outbreak of crop disease to the abuse of power or misuse of public resources by a chieftaincy or traditional institution.

An exhaustive, encyclopedic review of current early warning systems for violent or genocidal conflict is beyond the scope of this book. Instead, we will look at a digest of the most commonly cited risk factors from the most widely utilized early warning systems, with a particular focus on those factors especially relevant for assessing countries' risks for onsets of mass violence, some cases of which could evolve into genocide.[54] The actors behind these risk factors can be the state, proxies of the state, or nonstate parties from which the state has failed to protect its population.[55] This approach rests on the belief that violence—whether manifested in violent conflict or genocide—has the same underlying structural conditions, leading to similar preventive implications. As developmental economist Frances Stewart argues in her analysis of civil war, "policies that are likely to prevent civil war also are likely to reduce the risk of genocide."[56]

Lists of risk factors are constantly evolving, but this summary, mined from a wide range of multidisciplinary research, combines the strengths of various systems to give us a comprehensive and empirically supported list of 20 risk factors that helps us understand the preconditions for a violent or genocidal society. For ease of illustration, I have grouped these risk factors into four broad categories—*governance, conflict history, economic conditions*, and *social fragmentation*. We should note, however, that many of these risk factors are cross-cutting and intersecting issues, not easily confined to one discrete category. The erosive effects of state and public sector corruption, for instance, have deep and interrelated governance, economic, and social impacts. Moreover, as we have discussed, no one of these risk factors should be taken as causal or, even, predominant in their contributing importance; rather, they should be contextually understood—in conjunction with the presence of other risk factors—as somehow associated with increasing the probability of violent or genocidal conflict (Box 4.1).

Governance

Governance refers, broadly, to the ways in which authority in a country is exercised. How are governments selected, monitored, and replaced? What is the capacity of the government to develop and implement sound policies? To what degree do the citizens respect the state and the institutions that govern them?[57] Nearly all early warning systems include various traits of governance as risk factors for violent or genocidal conflict. Here are five specific risk factors related to governance.

Regime Type. Autocracy and democracy define opposite ends of a theoretical governance scale. Autocracies—including absolutist monarchies, authoritarian, dictatorial, or military regimes—are repressive one-party states with an absence of effective contestation for political

Box 4.1

CATEGORIES OF RISK FACTORS FOR VIOLENT OR GENOCIDAL CONFLICT

GOVERNANCE

Regime Type
State Legitimacy Deficit
Weakness of State Structures
Identity-Based Polar Factionalism
Systematic State-Led Discrimination

CONFLICT HISTORY

History of Identity-Related Tension
Prior Genocides or Politicides
Past Cultural Trauma
Legacy of Vengeance or Group Grievance
Record of Serious Violations of International Human Rights
and Laws

ECONOMIC CONDITIONS

Low Level of Economic Development
Economic Discrimination
Lack of Macroeconomic Stability
Economic Deterioration
Growth of Informal Economies and Black Markets

SOCIAL FRAGMENTATION

Identity-Based Social Divisions
Demographic Pressures
Unequal Access to Basic Goods and Services
Gender Inequalities
Political Instability

leadership and sharp restrictions on citizens' participation in the political process. Democracies have open and competitive elections with well-institutionalized political participation. Between these two ends of the governance scale lies "anocracy"—governments that are "neither fully democratic nor fully autocratic but, rather, combine an incoherent mix of democratic and autocratic traits and practices."[58] Anocracies "raise expectations for political participation but are not able to accommodate them."[59] Anocracies often appear in the transition from autocracy to greater democracy or, conversely, when emerging democratic institutions are undermined and a state becomes susceptible to "autocratic backsliding." What is the relationship of these three regime types to the risk of violent conflict or genocide?

Although there are certainly historical incidents of genocide being carried out by governments with some semblance of democratic institutions (namely, the American, Australian, and Canadian destruction of indigenous populations), Barbara Harff's seminal work on risk assessment found that the probability of mass murder was highest under autocratic regimes.[60] In her ongoing annual risk assessments, fully institutionalized autocracies have remained one of the consistent risk factors influencing new onsets of genocide. The notion that authoritarian regimes have a greater likelihood of engaging in genocide than democratic governments is borne out by that fact that between 1955 and 2008, 18 genocides occurred in autocracies and only two in democracies (Sudan in 1956 and Pakistan in 1973). During that same time period, 20 genocides occurred in anocracies.[61] Restricting his analysis to 10 cases of genocide onset during civil conflicts, political scientist Nicolas Rost found that "four occurred in countries that were authoritarian in the previous year, and six in anocracies."[62] Consistent with these findings, other research has shown that, over the past 50 years, anocracies are 10 times more likely to experience intrastate conflict than democracies and two times more likely than autocracies.[63]

Other findings suggest a rough "inverted U" relationship between regime type and risk of violent conflict or genocide. In other words, full democracies and full autocracies are fairly stable and low risk; it is anocratic mixed or partial regimes, particularly those in transition, that are most volatilely unstable and high risk. As political scientist Ian Bremmer argues, "for a country that is 'stable because it's closed' to become a country that is 'stable because it's open,' it must go through a transitional period of dangerous instability."[64] Empirically, sociologist Jack Goldstone and colleagues found that partial autocracies and partial democracies (that is, anocracies) had "markedly higher relative odds of future instability than full democracies or full autocracies."[65] Most particularly, they found that the relative odds of future instability for partial democracies with factionalism (that is, a pattern of sharply polarized and uncompromising competition between political blocs) were over 30 times greater than for full autocracies. Benjamin Goldsmith, chief investigator of the Atrocity Forecasting Project at the University of Sydney, led a research team in using an out-of-sample approach to forecasting the onset of genocide that included data for all states in the world during a given year rather than just in-sample data from states already experiencing instability. The second stage of their model, focusing on the annual likelihood of genocide onset, found that mixed regimes were a potent risk factor in forecasting the onset of genocide.[66] This is particularly concerning given the fact that from 1989 to 2013 the number of anocracies in the world increased from 30 to 53.[67]

So, although the path to democracy is a stony one, diverse research does suggest that states with a lower degree of democratization—particularly anocratic states—are at greater risk for the onset of violent conflict or genocide. Why? Generally, it stems from the fact that states with a lower degree of democratization have fewer institutional constraints on executive power and state security, effectively leaving power holders unaccountable for their decision-making policies and behaviors. As Harff argues: "Democratic and quasi-democratic regimes have institutional checks on executive power that constrain elites from carrying out deadly attacks on citizens . . . the democratic norms of most contemporary societies favor the protection of minority rights and the inclusion of political opponents."[68] In regimes with a lower degree of democratization, the institutional constraints on power holders are compromised by the lack of an independent and impartial judiciary, media, or police. National civil society, as well as international civil society, is muzzled and there is limited cooperation between the regime and international and regional human rights mechanisms.[69] Restrictions on freedom of speech, expression, association, or assembly for the country's citizens lead to a loss of political space and voice for opposition.

States with a lower degree of democratization also tend to have no professional military that is answerable to legitimate civilian control. State security forces, loyal to the regime and often led by friends and kin of the elite, operate with impunity and few constraints—creating a "state within a state," "no-go zones," or an elite "army within an army." These forces often have a disproportionate influence on the government; in turn, they often receive disproportionate government expenditures in their favor. State-sponsored or state-supported private militias or irregular forces may develop that terrorize political opponents or those civilians seen as supportive of the opposition.[70] For example, in the Darfur region of Sudan (whose government is characterized by Harff as a partial autocracy), government-sponsored *Janjaweed* militias were responsible for most of the atrocities in the state's counterinsurgency campaign against alleged rebel bases and their sympathizers.

State Legitimacy Deficit. To what degree is the state perceived by its citizens to be a legitimate actor representative of the people as a whole? Is there respect for the constitution, the national authorities, and representatives of the government? How transparent and accountable are state institutions and processes? Are there strong oversight mechanisms for the state? Is the state perceived to be criminal? Does the state have the confidence of its people? These are questions of state legitimacy and any perceived deficit in that legitimacy can leave a governance system at risk.

Endemic levels of corruption—entrusted public power exercised for private gain—are particularly damaging to state legitimacy. Corruption implies that the state has been "captured" by elites and private or corporate interests.[71] Corruption, both internal and transnational, leads to a jungle of personal empires.[72] The integrity of people in positions of authority cannot be assumed and, as a result, the state's legitimacy is called into question. Each year, the independent nongovernmental organization Transparency International issues a "Corruption Perceptions Index" scoring countries on a scale from 0 (highly corrupt) to 100 (very clean). Their most recent analysis of 175 countries found that more than two-thirds of countries scored below 50 on this measure of the perceived level of public sector corruption—from children denied an education to elections decided by money not votes to counterfeit medication to public procurement contracts—leading the organization to declare corruption a global threat.[73] In situations in which corruption is skewed along identity lines, it serves as a fuel for identity-based conflict.[74] In terms of state legitimacy, corruption is a corrosive agent that erodes public trust in governance.

State legitimacy can also be negatively impacted by constitutional changes to prolong the stay of those already in power. In Uganda, for instance, former guerrilla fighter Yoweri Museveni has served as President since 1986. He stood for, and won, open elections in 1996 and 2001. He was seen as exemplifying a new generation of African leadership, a stable antithesis of the heavy-handed "big men" who so often dominated politics on the continent. After the 2001 elections, however, political allies of Museveni campaigned to loosen the two-term constitutional limits on the presidency, allowing him to stand for, and win, election again in 2006 and for a fourth time, in an election disputed by both the European Union and the opposition, in 2011. In a bid to discourage others with presidential ambitions, Uganda's ruling party passed a 2014 resolution urging Museveni to run for reelection in 2016. Currently, political allies of Museveni continue to pursue a "life presidency project" as they are seeking to remove the constitutional age limit of 75 years on the presidency to allow Museveni to stand for election yet again in 2021 (though some believe Museveni, who says he does not know the exact date he was born, will already have passed the constitutional age limit by 2016).[75] This unwillingness to follow constitutional norms and the reluctance to cede power—partnered with increasingly high levels of state corruption—have led many in Uganda to question the legitimacy of the state in which they live, some even daring to suggest that it has become a one-party dictatorship. Neighboring Rwanda is facing some of the same governance dynamics in their run-up to 2017 presidential elections with the recent implementation of constitutional changes to term limits that would effectively allow President Paul Kagame to stay in power until 2034. Similar political machinations will play out in the Democratic Republic of Congo, the Republic of the Congo, and Benin over the coming years.

For states that have a legitimacy deficit, we often see the manifestation in rallies, peaceful demonstrations, mass protests against state authority or policies, uprisings, or even riots. As researchers Monty Marshall and Benjamin Cole write: "Mass protest should not be viewed as an exercise in democracy, but, rather, as a signal that the political process, whether democratic or autocratic, is failing to adequately recognize the levels of discontent and dissent and properly address an important and valued issue in public policy."[76] The mass mobilizations central to the Civil Rights Movement in the United States, for instance, were clear and compelling reflections of discontent that signaled widespread perceptions of a state delegitimized by *de facto* and *de jure* racial segregation, discrimination, and exclusion. Similarly, following Museveni's disputed election to a fourth term in 2011, thousands of Ugandans expressed their concerns with the legitimacy of the state—its electoral process, corruption, and economic policies—by engaging in peaceful "walk-to-work" protest demonstrations. Deadly crackdowns by government security forces only added to the perceived state legitimacy deficit. The October 2014 ouster of Burkina Faso's Blaise Compaore followed national protests over a controversial parliamentary vote to change the constitution that would have extended his 27 years in power. In that particular case, civilians' protest over a perceived state legitimacy deficit led to a relatively peaceful political transition during which the country's constitution, though temporarily suspended, ultimately would be respected. Most recently, in late April 2015, violent clashes in Burundi were triggered by President Pierre Nkurunziza's bid for a constitutionally prohibited third term in office. Opponents fear that Nkurunziza's political ploy to sidestep constitutional limits could threaten a 2005 peace deal that ended the country's 12-year civil war in which more than 350,000 people were killed.[77]

Weakness of State Structures. To what degree can the state provide basic public services and answer people's needs? How effective are state structures—hospitals, schools, police departments, courts systems, sanitation, public transportation, and so on? Does the state enforce contracts and property rights? To what degree does the state follow the rule of law?

Can the state protect its citizens or do crime and violence threaten to overrun the state? All of these indicate the relative strength or weakness of state structures and, as state structures weaken, the risk of violent or genocidal conflict increases. As peacekeeping trainers Kwesi Aning and Frank Okyere point out: "When states are weak, regime security takes priority over all other responsibilities, including the responsibility to protect the population."[78]

The quality of provision of basic public services, in both rural and urban areas, can be measured through several quantitative benchmarks of services, goods, and infrastructure—housing costs; education enrollment and literacy rates (including gender differences); fuel supply; access to medicine, number of clinics and hospitals, and number of physicians; potable water; safe roads; adequate sanitation; amount of airports and railroads for sustainable development.[79] Corruption negatively impacts the provision of many of these basic services as corrupt politicians and public sector officials invest resources in projects that offer personal enrichment or public recognition rather than less spectacular investments in infrastructure projects such as schools, hospitals, and roads that would benefit entire communities.[80] A state too weak, or corrupt, to provide an acceptable quality of such basic public services tears at the social fabric of a society. Particularly problematic are situations in which basic public services are restricted to the power holders and those elites, or kin, with whom they wish to share such resources. As the African Development Bank Group concluded: "The central driver of fragility is weak state institutions. All other factors associated with fragility are in themselves linked to weak state institutions as a driving force."[81]

The degree to which the state follows the rule of law is another clear indicator of the relative strength or weakness of its state structures. Although often used, the "rule of law" is a difficult term to define. For the UN, the rule of law is understood as ". . . a principle of governance in which all persons, institutions and entities, public and private, including the State itself, are accountable to laws that are publicly promulgated, equally enforced and independently adjudicated, and which are consistent with international human rights norms and standards. It requires, as well, measures to ensure adherence to the principles of supremacy of law, equality before the law, accountability to the law, fairness in the application of the law, separation of powers, participation in decision-making, legal certainty, avoidance of arbitrariness and procedural and legal transparency."[82] States in which the rule of law is compromised often have rising numbers of political arrests, illegal detentions, voter intimidation, torture, and forced relocation or exile—all of which involve denial of due process consistent with international norms and practices. Unlawful state violence may become the norm, with security forces participating in illegal activities (road blocks, extortion, kidnappings, and so on) and criminal networks (drugs, natural resources, weapons smuggling, human trafficking, and so on).[83]

A final measure of the relative strength or weakness of state structures is the degree to which the state can protect its own civilian population from atrocity crimes. Does the state, for instance, have a legal framework for civilian protection—including ratification and domestication of relevant international human rights and humanitarian law treaties? Does it have the resources, training, and independent institutions to enforce such frameworks? When such frameworks or institutions are inadequate or simply do not exist, ". . . populations are left vulnerable to those who may take advantage of the limitations of the dysfunction of State machinery, or to those that may opt for violence to respond to real or perceived threats."[84] Civilian populations can often be caught in an unforgiving vise between a weak state structure and nonstate parties—rival militias, guerilla forces, opposition groups, armed insurgents, or private armies—agitating for extreme solutions to that weakness. The ongoing war between government and opposition forces in Syria, for instance, has killed more than 250,000 civilians and left millions more as refugees or internally displaced persons. Instability can even come from third parties outside of the state— neighboring states or international coalitions—seeking to take advantage of weak state structures to engage in the internal affairs of the state.

Identity-Based Polar Factionalism. As discussed previously, there is widespread agreement that social identity groups, and organizations claiming to represent such groups, lie at the core of many contemporary violent and genocidal conflicts. Elites and state institutions fragmented among identity lines—racial, ethnic, religious, class, clan, or tribe—often lead to a high level of political contentiousness and identity-based factionalism. Marshall and Cole define factionalism as "polities with parochial or ethnic-based political factions that regularly compete for political influence in order to promote particularist agendas and favor group members to the detriment of common, secular, or cross-cutting agendas."[85] Such factionalism can become so sharply oppositional and uncompromising that it segues into a volatile polar factionalism between identity-based political groups and the governing elites. It then becomes a winner-take-all approach to politics with "the transference of potentially negotiable material interests to emotively-charged and ultimately non-negotiable symbolic issues."[86] As Marshall and Cole conclude: "Polar factionalism tends to radicalize both anti-state and state factions and lead the political process toward greater levels of confrontation and greater depths of intransigence, placing it at the gateway to political instability and regime change."[87]

For years, Harff has focused on the identity-based nature of a ruling elite and its impact on risks of genocide and politicide. Her initial 2003 assessment found "risks of geno-/politicide were two and a half times more likely in countries where the political elite was based mainly or entirely on an ethnic minority."[88] This risk was considerably amplified when such elites also advocated an exclusionary ideology. Her most recent 2013 assessment refines the issue by distinguishing between an elite simply representing a minority and a situation in which the elite are also "politically contentious."[89] Goldstone et al. have offered additional recent empirical support for the belief that "a polarized politics of exclusive identities or ideologies, in conjunction with partially democratic institutions" are the most exceptionally unstable type of regime.[90] Similarly, Marshall and Cole's summary of their research found "that countries with [polar] factionalism are twice as fragile on average as those without factionalism."[91]

Identity-based polar factionalism is fueled by exclusionary and harmful ideologies, often nationalistic in intent and propagated by extremist rhetoric in politics, education, hate radio, and media. These ideologies— rooted in the "us" and "them" binaries of the in-group bias—are based on the supremacy of a certain identity or on extremist versions of identity.[92] They also often include themes of communal irredentism or communal solidarity.[93] For instance, Slobodan Milosevic's call to unite all Serbs into one state—a "Greater Serbia"—was based on the grounds of an extremist nationalist ideology rooted in Serbian identity. As journalist Ed Vulliamy states: "On this land [a Greater Serbia], wherever lived a Serb, Serbs and only Serbs were to live, with others removed by death or deportation."[94] In Rwanda, the theme of communal solidarity and identity-based exclusion were broadcast on the airwaves of RTLM radio. A nominally private radio station receiving support from the government-controlled Radio Rwanda, RTLM began broadcasting on July 8, 1993 and quickly established itself as part of a campaign to promote extremist Hutu ideology. During the 1994 genocide, one particular broadcast was repeated several times over: "*The inyenzi* [a Kinyarwanda word meaning 'cockroach'] have always been Tutsi. We will exterminate them. One can identify them because they are of one race. You can identify them by their height and their small nose. When you see that small nose, break it."[95] As Mark Lattimer summarizes: "Where the ruling elite has an ideology informed by ethnic or religious nationalism, minorities may find themselves defined outside the concept of the 'nation' or the 'people.'"[96]

Clearly, legitimate and effective governance is compromised by the rise of identity-based polar factionalism and the political exploitation of such differences. The military and judicial systems become more polarized and less representative of the population. Equal access to political activity and participative decision making becomes more restricted. There is limited freedom of political expression, especially for those proposing compromise. Resource accumulation and distribution are unfairly distributed on the basis of identity. Cross-identity respect dissolves in the face of social fragmentation. The legitimacy of the state is called into question as non-representative of the citizenry and there may be frequent breakdowns in government with a high turnover of political elites.[97] Such factionalism "is often accompanied by confrontational mass mobilizations, as occurred in Venezuela in the early 2000s and Thailand prior to the 2006 military coup, and by the intimidation or manipulation of electoral competition."[98]

Systematic State-Led Discrimination. Finally, systematic state-led discrimination against a minority group—including removal of civil liberties, restricting educational access, arbitrary detention or imprisonment, torture as state policy, large-scale illegal round-ups of civilians, the revocation of the right to citizenship, expropriation or destruction of property (including cultural religious and sacred sites)—is a governance risk factor that weighs heavily as a concern for the protection of civilians. For some, such systematic discrimination represents the foundational cornerstones of risk that can escalate into genocide.[99] Indeed, the empirical support for systemic state-led discrimination as a potent risk factor is robust. Looking specifically at the onset of genocide, for example, the Atrocity Forecasting Project found that "states that systematically discriminate and repress minority groups are more likely to use genocide when faced with armed threats from within."[100] Similarly, using the Minorities at Risk indicators for political or economic discrimination, Harff found that state-led discrimination—state policies and practices deliberately restricting the political and/or economic rights of specific minority groups—was a significant influence on the onset of genocide and politicide.[101] Using the same data set but focusing more broadly on the onset of civil wars, Goldstone et al. affirmed that "countries with high levels of state-led discrimination against at least one minority group . . . faced roughly triple the relative odds of future civil war onsets than those without such discriminations."[102]

Systematic state-led discrimination is an example of what the UN refers to as an "enabling circumstance or preparatory action." In other words, these are "events or measures, whether gradual or sudden, which provide an environment conducive to the commission of atrocity crimes, or which suggest a trajectory towards their perpetration."[103] One of the pioneers in the field of genocide studies, Gregory Stanton, agrees that such discrimination is one of the early stages of the process of genocide, often paving the way for the organization of, and preparation for, mass murder.[104] Certainly, systematic state-led discrimination is a clear signal of a lack of respect for fundamental human rights and a dark portend of what may escalate with the onset of state instability. Rost suggests that increases in the level of violations of the most basic human rights during periods of instability substantially increases the risk of future genocide.[105] "Put simply," as summarized by the Atrocity Forecasting Project, "states that institutionalize abuse of their populations are more likely to abuse them on a large scale during periods of instability."[106] The Darfuri population in western Sudan, for example, was victimized by systematic state-led discrimination for years prior to the onset of genocide in 2003. When the Sudanese government initiated its counterinsurgency campaign in the Darfur region, the well-instantiated institutionalized abuse of the Darfuri population was an easy stepping stone from which the perpetrators could launch genocidal violence. Similarly, the Indonesian genocide, although primarily an anticommunist purge after a failed coup in 1965, also targeted Chinese Indonesians who, for years, had been the communal victims of anti-Chinese discrimination.

Implications for Upstream Prevention. Knowing the destabilizing risk factors associated with governance helps us understand the ways in which governance systems can be structured upstream to reduce the risk of violent conflict or genocide:

- First, although "some nations have well-functioning governments without the presence of effective democratic institutions," and current events remind us that democratization is not a guaranteed one-way ticket to stability, research clearly indicates that full democracies—whose definition can, admittedly, be elusive—are significantly less at risk for violent conflict or genocide.[107] At the very least, political institutions should elevate inclusion, representativeness, power-sharing, and cross-identity group coalition building over winter-take-all majority rule.[108] From a prevention standpoint, diffusion of power and institutional constraints on executive power and state security—including an independent, impartial, and inclusive judiciary, media, police, and military—are important democratic safeguards against the onset of violent conflict and genocide. An engaged, active, and resilient civil society—a vital interface of accountability between the people and the government—can also be a factor of restraint, particularly when plugged into international networks.[109]

- Second, governance systems can be structured to increase the legitimacy with which the state is viewed by its people, as well as by the international community. "Legitimacy strengthens capacity because the state can rely mainly on non-coercive authority."[110] Building citizens' robust acceptance of the state's "right to rule" means addressing issues related to process legitimacy (observance of agreed or customary rules of procedure) as well as output legitimacy (perceptions about state performance and the provision of services).[111] In practice, attending to those two sources of legitimacy includes removing public sector corruption (including the provision of appropriate remuneration for public officials to disincentivize engaging in corruption), following written constitutional policies and norms, and increasing the level of transparency and accountability for state institutions and processes. Many of these activities fall under the umbrella of security sector reform (SSR), referring to efforts "aimed at improving a country's capacity to deliver justice and security in a transparent, accountable, and professional manner."[112] Although SSR is typically thought of as a peacebuilding tool in postconflict settings, it can also be understood as a preventive upstream structural reform effort—particularly when initiated as part of a larger democratic reform plan meant to reinstill trust in the legitimacy of the state.

- Third, state structures can be developed and administered so as to ensure fair and equitable provision of basic public services. The rule of law should be central to state functioning and compliant with international norms and practices. The state should also develop a legal framework for civilian protection, including the ratification and domestication of relevant international human rights and humanitarian law treaties as well as the creation of national committees dedicated to the prevention of genocide and mass atrocities. These frameworks for civilian protection can be complemented by the professionalization of security sector and judicial personnel in training and education.

- Fourth, the political elite of governance systems can be inclusive and representative of the multiplicity and plurality of overlapping identities in its population—racial, ethnic, religious, class, clan, or tribe. Although political mobilization along identity lines is not inherently violence provoking, it should be managed in constructive ways that reduce susceptibility to identity-based polar factionalism and ensure equal access to political activity and participative decision making at all levels of the political structure. The state should be defined with no reference to a dominant social identity. As political scientist Kal Holsti argues, a common characteristic of politically stable countries "is an inclusive political system and political parties that transcend ethnic and language groups and that focus instead on policy differences."[113]

- Finally, respect for fundamental human rights can be institutionalized throughout all segments of a society. The state should be intentional about nondiscriminatory policies and practices protecting all minority groups within its territory, particularly during periods of political instability. In February 2015, the UN High Commissioner for Human Rights, Zeid Ra'ad Al Hussein, outlined his vision for universal implementation of this respect for fundamental human rights: "Before every child on this planet turns nine, I believe he or she should acquire a foundational understanding of human rights, and that these concepts should grow in depth and scope as he or she develops. The underlying values of the curriculum would be virtually identical in every school, deriving from the Universal—and universally accepted—Declaration of Human Rights. In this way, from Catholic parochial schools to the most secular public institutions, and indeed Islamic madrassahs, children could learn— even in kindergarten—and experience the fundamental human rights values of equality, justice and respect."[114]

Conflict History

To return to our cardiovascular disease analogy, some of the risk factors— age, sex, and heredity—are nonmodifiable. Whether part of your genetic heritage or simply part of the process of getting old, these risk factors are the organic burden we carry. Although these particular risk factors are nonmodifiable, there are a host of other modifiable risk factors—smoking, blood cholesterol, and physical inactivity—that can help moderate the risk saddled on us by the nonmodifiable factors. So, while recognizing our nonmodifiable history, we do not have to be an unremitting slave to it; we can understand that history in the context of other modifiable factors. Similarly, conflict history in a state or region is a nonmodifiable risk factor for the onset of future genocide—if it happened, it cannot be unhappened. What can be modified, however, are the ways in which that history is remembered, taught, processed, and understood. As novelist Jonathan Safran Foer argues, memory is not simply "a second-order means of interpreting events."[115] Rather, as we will discuss in more detail in Chapter 6, memory is an active sense that can both accentuate the power of conflict history as a risk factor in genocide as well as diminish it. With that in mind, here are five specific risk factors related to conflict history and the ways in which it is remembered in a postconflict society.

History of Identity-Related Tension. Histories of governance, economic, and social fragmentation often go hand-in-hand with histories of identity-related tension and legacies of past conflict from those tensions. For social psychologist Ervin Staub, a history of identity-related tension serves as a risk factor because it leads to "ideologies of antagonism" that are "the outcome of a long history of hostility and mutual violence. Such ideologies are worldviews in which another group is perceived as an implacable enemy, bent on one's destruction. The welfare of one's own group is best served by the other's demise."[116] These ideologies, steeped in a history of identity-related tensions, can be a significant risk factor even if only a segment of a population holds the ideology. In Staub's view, ideologies of antagonism "seemed to have roles in the start or maintenance of violence in the former Yugoslavia, between Israelis and Palestinians, and in Rwanda."[117]

Today, by almost any measure, Africa is the most conflict-ridden continent in the world.[118] Although there are many underlying factors—historical and contemporary—contributing to that reality, a significant influence has been histories of identity-related tension born from the ravages of colonialism. Eons of stable social identities were reconfigured by colonizers bent on divide-and-rule politics. Convinced of their nation's right to rule the world, European colonizers, as journalist Andrew Rice writes, yoked "dozens of disparate societies and cultures into one fictive agglomeration" throughout their realms of conquest in Africa.[119] In many places, colonial manipulation created arbitrary "tribes" and social identities. The reification of these artificial social identities often resulted in long histories of intergroup conflict and the eventual development of the type of ideologies of antagonism described by Staub.

Perhaps nowhere was this dynamic more aptly illustrated than in Rwanda. Precolonial Rwanda was one of the most centralized and rigidly stratified societies in the Great Lakes region. In this vertically structured society, Hutu peasant farmers—making up about 85% of the total population—were, for all practical purposes, on the lowest rung of the political, economic, and social ladders. Power, status, and wealth were generally in the hands of the Tutsi—a cattle-owning minority accounting for a bit less than 15% of the population. The two social identities were understood as fluid indicators of social status, class, or caste—the more cattle you owned, the more wealth, prestige, and power you could claim. As Scott Straus points out, these social identities were not fixed: "After acquiring enough cattle, a Hutu could become Tutsi."[120] Indeed, some Hutu bought cattle and worked their way into the aristocracy and some ill-fated Tutsi became poor peasant farmers. For most of their precolonial history, the two groups coexisted peacefully.

With the arrival, however, of colonial occupiers in the late nineteenth century, the meanings of Hutu and Tutsi would be transformed. Most notably, Belgium—Rwanda's colonial ruler after World War I—would reshape and mythologize the class descriptors of Hutu and Tutsi as immutable ethnic identities. Not only were the meanings of the categories themselves changed, but also how those categories related to the allocation of power. Reflecting the European obsession with pseudoscientific race theories, the Belgians were devoted to the idea of a racialized Tutsi superiority and imposed a system of apartheid on Rwanda in which Hutus were denied all privileges. In the mid-twentieth century, under international pressure to prepare Rwanda for independence, Belgium switched sides and instituted political reforms that led to the overthrow of the Tutsi monarchy and the securing of power by a *de facto* republican regime under Hutu rule. By the time Belgium withdrew from Rwanda in 1962, the country had become a mirror image of its prior self—a Hutu-dominated republic with the Tutsi minority effectively excluded from participating in the political life of the country.

This polarization of Hutus and Tutsis, a construction of colonial occupation, led to a deadly escalation in identity-related tension with regional implications. During the political upheaval of 1959–1962, an estimated 200,000 Tutsi fled widespread anti-Tutsi violence in Rwanda, with the majority finding asylum in neighboring Uganda, Burundi, and Zaire (present-day Democratic Republic of Congo). From 1963 to 1964, attacks by Tutsi exiles from Burundi led to retaliatory massacres of Tutsi civilians in Rwanda. In 1972, a failed Hutu insurgency against a Tutsi ethnocracy in Burundi led to the killing of 2,000 to 3,000 Tutsi civilians and the reprisal slaughter of 100,000 to 200,000 Hutu civilians. The following year, with their fears and insecurities stoked by the massacres in Burundi, there was a return to violence in Rwanda with a series of purges of Tutsis to create "ethnic proportionality."[121] In 1990, another failed invasion of Rwanda by Tutsi exiles ("refugee-warriors"), this time from Uganda, only added to the escalating history of identity-related tension in the region. The onset of genocide in Rwanda on April 7, 1994—culminating in the most rapid and efficient genocide in the twentieth century—was the final act in a tragedy decades in the making. Although its origins are multitude, the Rwandan genocide was, at the very least, an indirect descendent of the ideologies of antagonism generated from a colonial legacy of identity-related tension and conflict.

Prior Genocides or Politicides. In terms of risk factors, a particularly notable indicator related to conflict history comes from whether the country in question has experienced a genocide or politicide in its prior history.

Specifically, countries with past experiences of genocide are at a substantially higher risk of experiencing future cases of genocide. This risk factor appeared in Harff's original 2003 assessments and has remained throughout. As she writes: "The risks of new episodes (of genocide or politicide) were more than three times greater when state failures occurred in countries that had prior geno-/politicides."[122] Similarly, the Atrocity Forecasting Project found years since a previous genocide or politicide to be one of the six most potent predictive factors for the onset of genocide. In their list of states at a high risk of genocide, there was a cluster of states at the top with a comparatively short time interval since their last genocide.[123] Rost's forecasting models also found that a history of genocide increases the predictive power for future genocides.[124]

To date, nine countries have been wracked by more than one genocide since 1946: the Democratic Republic of the Congo, Burundi, Rwanda, Angola, Sudan, Iraq, China, Pakistan, and Indonesia.[125] Although these countries vary in current states of political (in)stability, each of them appear as at-risk on at least one (often several) published watch lists. Why is a prior genocide or politicide so potent a risk factor? Certainly, there appears to be a habituation factor at play. As Helen Fein, another of the doyens of genocide studies, has pointed out, perpetrators of genocide are often "repeat offenders" who have become habituated to mass atrocity as a strategic response to challenges to state security.[126] Social anthropologist Alex de Waal, in describing Sudan's record of serial genocide against the south Sudanese and the Darfur region, speaks of these preexisting patterns of state behavior as "genocide by force of habit."[127] Because genocide is never "successful" in the sense of wiping out the entirety of a targeted group, there is also the existence of "repeat threats" from surviving members of targeted groups in many postgenocide societies.

Recently, however, the magnitude of risk posed by a prior genocide has become a matter of debate. A 2011 report, for instance, by political scientist Chad Hazlett reevaluated Harff's original 2003 model and found that prior genocides were not predictively significant in forecasting genocides over the course of a given political instability event.[128] Even Harff's most recent 2013 assessment, although still including past genocides or politicides as one of her "strongly statistically significant" risk factors, includes the following curiously contradictory footnote: "Past genocides seem for some reason to inoculate states from resorting to it again, according to the new analyses. This finding will be the subject of follow-up analyses."[129] Looking more broadly at the risk factor of ethnic war in the previous 15 years, Goldstone and colleagues found that particular variable had no statistical significance in forecasting political instability.[130] Risk engineers Nassim Nicholas Taleb and Gregory Treverton go a step further and argue that past shocks to a society may even prove to be a stabilizing influence. Although not directly addressing past genocides as one of those shocks, their unique notion of "no stability without volatility" is grounded in research suggesting that "states that have experienced a worst-case scenario in the recent past (say, around the previous two decades) and recovered from it are likely to be more stable than those that haven't."[131]

Past Cultural Trauma. Histories of identity-related tension, some of which even include genocidal violence, leave their indelible mark in the legacies of trauma. As political scientist Jens Meierhenrich points out, we can think of two trauma types when studying the impacts of genocide.[132] *Psychological trauma*, at an individual level, stems from the stereotyping, prejudice, discrimination, dehumanization, persecution, and attempted extermination of a victim targeted by a genocidal process. For some, such traumatic events may trigger normal, transitory, adaptive responses of the mind and body that dissipate when the event is over, allowing them to return to a normal level of functioning. For others, however, the effects of traumatic events are so serious and persistent as to lead to a pathological reaction—the widely cited diagnostic category of Posttraumatic Stress Disorder (PTSD). People who have PTSD suffer from symptoms of reexperiencing (e.g., flashbacks or recurrent dreams related to the event), avoidance (e.g., staying away from distressing reminders of the event), negative cognitions and mood (e.g., persistent negative emotional state or markedly diminished interest in significant activities), and alterations in arousal (e.g., irritable behavior, exaggerated startle response, sleep disturbances).[133] Work by Stanford's Research Group on Collective Trauma and Healing suggests that traumatic stress can even damage an individual's DNA and DNA repair mechanisms, leading to an increased risk for numerous diseases.[134] Although the clinical presentation of PTSD varies, the "disorder may be especially severe or long-lasting when the stressor is interpersonal and intentional."[135] As philosopher Susan Brison describes in her gripping personal narrative of trauma: "When the trauma is of human origin and is intentionally inflicted . . . it not only shatters one's fundamental assumptions about the world and one's safety in it, but it also severs the sustaining connection between the self and the rest of humanity. Victims of human-inflicted trauma are reduced to mere objects by their tormenters: their subjectivity is rendered useless and viewed as worthless."[136]

As a point of fact, the highest rates of PTSD (ranging from one-third to more than one-half of those exposed) are found among survivors of "rape, military combat and captivity, and ethnically and politically motivated internment and genocide."[137] As just one of many published examples, a 2009 study found that two-thirds of children and adolescents who survived the Rwandan genocide still suffered from PTSD symptoms a year later.[138] More recently, a 2013 study of survivors and former prisoners accused of participation in the Rwandan genocide found considerable rates of PTSD and substantial depressive and anxiety symptoms in both populations.[139] Research on the intergenerational transmission between mothers who survived the Khmer Rouge regime in Cambodia and their daughters found that parental PTSD symptoms were predictive of their children's anxiety level.[140] Other research on the intergenerational impacts of such a high trauma load suggests that this relationship is not simply mediated by family dynamics but may be embedded in a physical transmission or "embodied history" of the trauma itself.[141] Clearly, diagnosing and treating the silent wounds of psychological trauma experienced at an individual level must be a priority in rebuilding a postgenocide society, particularly if we hope to reduce the intergenerational transmission of such trauma.

In considering risk factors related to conflict history, however, of more relevance is a second type of trauma—*cultural trauma*. The concept of cultural trauma is meant to capture the collective manifestations of what a society has experienced in genocide. At the psychological level, trauma comes from individuals directly experiencing the pain of genocide and is embedded in the structure of personality.[142] At the cultural level, however, trauma comes from the entering of suffering into the core of the social group's sense of its own identity. Cultural trauma becomes crystallized and embedded in the structure of society.[143] As sociologist Jeffrey Alexander writes: "Cultural trauma occurs when members of a collectivity feel they have been subjected to a horrendous event that leaves indelible marks upon their group consciousness, marking their memories forever and changing their future identity in fundamental and irrevocable ways."[144]

Cultural trauma is socially constructed. So, rather than trauma emerging from the traumatic events themselves, trauma comes from the social reconstruction of those events. As Alexander writes: "Events are not inherently traumatic. Trauma is a socially mediated attribution . . . Events are one thing, representations of these events quite another."[145] Cultural trauma is historically made, not born.[146] Because cultural trauma is socially constructed, people do not have to live through the traumatic event itself to be victimized by it. In June 2014, I was visiting Sanski Most, Bosnia-Herzegovina at the time of their worst floods in over 120 years. It was Bosnia's largest humanitarian disaster since the war in the 1990s and many of the town residents, most of whom were survivors of mass atrocities committed during the war, lost everything—for the second time in two decades. I was struck, though, by how teenagers in the community, not alive at the time of the war, had the same sense of revictimization as their elders—the cultural trauma in the region ran so deep that this first loss in their young lives felt like the second. Sometimes, cultural trauma is even constructed on imagined events that can "be as traumatizing as events that have actually occurred."[147] As a social construction, past cultural trauma can lead to a redefinition of collective social identity that becomes reified in memorials, museums, school textbooks, rituals, performances, commemorations, sacred routines, and popular culture.

As a risk factor, past cultural trauma is impactful in two ways. First, past cultural trauma can hand down unhealed psychological and social wounds that leave a postgenocide society acutely vulnerable to future outbreaks of genocide or mass atrocity. Feelings of loss, displacement, injustice, and a possible desire for revenge can motivate or incentivize individuals or groups to resort to large-scale violence as a way to achieve "justice" or respond to real or perceived threats.[148] For Staub, past victimization can leave a deep mistrust of other people that, coupled with fear, makes "it difficult to resolve new conflict or to respond to a new threat in a manner commensurate with the actual threat. Believing that they need to defend themselves, members of the group may strike out in the face of new conflict or threat, even when forceful self-defense is not necessary."[149] The influence of unresolved past cultural trauma can even come into play for perpetrator groups that continue to blame the victims for their own victimization and, as a result, may engage in new episodes of violence. Second, the reconstruction of past cultural trauma can intersect with a reconstruction of social identities in some destructive ways. Social identities can become disrupted, reconfigured, and hierarchically reorganized to redistribute power and privilege in a postgenocide society by dividing rather than uniting. As sociologist Arthur Neal summarizes in his work on national trauma and collective memory: "All collective traumas have some bearing on national identity. While in some cases national trauma results in enhancing a sense of unity within a society, there are other cases in which collective traumas have fragmenting effects."[150]

Legacy of Vengeance or Group Grievance. Building on histories of identity-related tension, some of which may have been genocidal, as well as past cultural trauma, it is common for there to be a legacy of vengeance or group grievance pervading a postconflict society.[151] The politicization of these legacies is particularly notable as a risk factor. Such legacies leave a society with deep cleavages, even putting some societies at risk for violent retribution by vigilantes, militias, and extremists who are motivated by these legacies of vengeance or group grievance. At times, diaspora communities prove to be a major actor in the sustaining and animating—through memory, funds, and supplies—of such legacies.

Legacies of vengeance built on injustices of the past can go back centuries. As just one example, Serb national mythology was built on a legacy of vengeance dating back to the 1389 martyrdom of Prince Lazar. Lazar's death, representing the death of the Serb nation, was the beginning of five centuries of humiliating rule by the Ottoman Turks—a traumatic event resonating through generations of Serb "victims." In this ahistorical passion play, with Lazar as an explicit Christ figure, Slavic Muslims were reimagined as Christ killers. It would not be until they were purged from the Serbian people that the nation of Serbia could be resurrected again.[152] This legacy of—even call to—vengeance was enshrined as a key piece of Serb nationalist tradition and genocidal ideology during the violent collapse of Yugoslavia.

Group grievances are born in the painful legacies of groups that have been denied autonomy, self-determination, or political independence; subjected to institutionalized persecution, repression, oppression, or political exclusion; and victimized by nationalist political rhetoric or scapegoating.[153] Such experiences leave aggrieved groups feeling as the "other," outside of the nation, voiceless and powerless in the face of their imposed marginalization. Of particular import for group grievances is an absence of dispute resolution or transitional justice mechanisms—either through legislative frameworks, judicial systems, or community-based structures—to which aggrieved groups can turn for recourse. When there are no mechanisms for peaceful conciliation of different group interests, group grievances are left to fester as truth, reparation, reconciliation, and reintegration are held hostage. In the absence of such avenues of justice, perpetrators' actions are, and may continue to be, committed with impunity.

Often, legacies of group grievances are exacerbated by celebrations of historical events recalling victories of one group over another. In Northern Ireland, for instance, the "marching season" between Easter Monday and the end of August each year sees tens of thousands of Protestants taking to the streets to march in nearly 3,000 parades.[154] These celebrations of Protestant triumphalism mark the victory of Protestant King William of Orange over Catholic King James II at the Battle of the Boyne in 1690. The height of the marching season culminates in the annual Orange Order's Twelfth of July marches, often routing through Catholic districts in 19 main parades held across Northern Ireland. These sectarian interfaces are flashpoints for conflict and the parades routinely see hundreds of protestors or marchers charged in riot-related disorders. In 2013–2014 alone, the Police Service of Northern Ireland spent an estimated $76 million on policing controversial marches and street protests.[155]

Record of Serious Violations of International Human Rights and Laws. A final risk factor related to conflict history is a cross-cutting issue throughout the previous four risk factors in this category—a record of serious violations of international human rights and laws. On December 10, 1948, the day following the passage of the UN Genocide Convention, the UN adopted the nonbinding Universal Declaration of Human Rights (UDHR), a milestone document in the history of human rights. The UDHR, for the first time in human history, spelled out the basic civil, political, economic, social, and cultural rights that all human beings should enjoy— the right to life, liberty, and security of person; equality before the law; no subjection to torture, arbitrary arrest, detention, or exile; the rights to freedom of movements, thought, conscience, religion, and nationality; and so on.[156] These are the inherent entitlements that belong to every person simply as a consequence of being human.[157]

Since the passage of the UDHR, and its elaboration in the 1966 International Human Rights Covenants, a body of international human rights law has developed to legally ensure the respect, protection, and fulfillment of those universal human rights. International human rights law applies at all times, in peace and in war. That body of law is complemented by a body of international humanitarian law (also known as the law of war or the law of armed conflict) that specifically seeks to regulate and limit the use of violence in armed conflict. A society with a record of serious violations of these internationally recognized human rights and laws, established by treaty or custom, suggests an at-risk society practiced on the compromise of the protection of its civilians. Arguing that respect for human rights places self-imposed restraints on the behavior of a state, political scientists David Sobek, M. Rodwan Abouharb, and Christopher Ingram investigated pairs of all states from 1980 to 2001 and found that a lack of respect for human rights increased the probability of conflict between states.[158] Other research has found that countries with recent human rights abuses have a more than twofold increase in the risk of civil war in the subsequent year than countries with a strong history of respect for human rights.[159]

For the UN, a record of these types of serious violations is a particularly potent risk factor in its framework of analysis for atrocity crimes: "Atrocity crimes in general and genocide in particular are preceded by less widespread or systematic serious violations of international human rights and humanitarian law. These are typically violations of civil and political rights, but they may include also severe restrictions to economic, social and cultural rights, often linked to patterns of discrimination or exclusion of protected groups, populations or individuals."[160] The UN's 2013 launching of a new "Rights Up Front" initiative further emphasized severe human rights violations as an early warning sign of atrocities.[161] As we have previously seen, escalations in the level of violations of the most basic human rights during periods of instability substantially increases the risk of future genocide.[162] Although an escalation in these violations is a clear indicator of imminent conflict, a historical record of a pattern of misconduct in these areas also serves notice of a society at risk.

Implications for Upstream Prevention. Recognizing the risk factors inherent in the conflict history of a given society helps us understand the ways in which the burden of that nonmodifiable history can be moderated by how a society chooses to carry it:

• First, although histories of identity-related tension can reify social identities in ways that perpetuate risk, we also recognize that social identities are fluid and changeable. Social identities can be reconfigured in ways to reduce, rather than exacerbate, the historical tensions, and resulting ideologies of antagonism, behind them. In Rwanda, for example, there has been a conscious choice to focus on the superordinate identity of "Rwandan" rather than the subordinate identities of "Tutsi" and "Hutu." In so doing, the country is attempting to inclusively redefine social identities, without amputating ethnic heritage, in such a way as to diminish the considerable risk left by the history of identity-related tension in the region.

• Second, we can encourage ways in which the remembrance, teaching, processing, and understanding of prior genocides might actually work to inoculate states from resorting to such violence again. As Taleb and Treverton suggest, there may be a "virtue of volatility" in which the shock of genocide could be educational to a state, causing it "to experience posttraumatic growth."[163] Countries that survive a prior genocide may find a strength that could not be discovered elsewhere—an antifragility culled from the chaos of disorder. Such discovery requires deep wells of commitment to justice, truth, and memory, but is far better than simply resigning a country's fate to "high risk" because it will not, or cannot, unpack the ways in which its prior genocide can be transformative rather than perpetually divisive.

• Third, past cultural trauma, as a social reconstruction, can be repackaged as a unifying rather than dividing influence within society. As Alexander argues, "however tortuous the trauma process, it allows collectivities to define new forms of moral responsibility and to redirect the course of political action."[164] Social solidarities can be extended rather than bounded. Moreover, as policy analysts at The World Bank

have argued, "investing in mental wellbeing among post-conflict populations contributes to strengthening social capital . . . [and the] ability
to form relations of trust, cooperation and mobilization for collective
action."[165] Central to these pursuits, as Meierhenrich reminds us, is the
recognition that treatment of past cultural trauma—whatever form it
takes—must be sensitive to promoting trauma recovery rather than
trauma renewal.[166]

- Fourth, societies can have in place functioning, open, and transparent
  dispute resolution or transitional justice mechanisms to address legacies of vengeance or group grievance. Victims should have free expression to advocate for the redress of their grievances, whether through
  individual criminal accountability, reparation, truth-seeking, or reconciliation processes. At the community level, women—often viewed
  as more neutral and less threatening or politicized—can play a unique
  role in these processes.[167] Comprehensive reform measures in the security and judicial sectors, complemented by a strong civil society presence, may be necessary to ensure the safe practice of this voice and
  advocacy.[168]

- Finally, the proactive duty to protect all human rights, without discrimination, and implement related laws lies first and foremost with
  states. This includes the translation of human rights treaties and the
  enactment of them in national legislation, training judicial and security
  sector personnel in human rights and laws, the dissemination of human
  rights texts and information, and engagement with regional and international organizations to promote and protect human rights.[169] In addition, community-based human rights institutions can be engaged as a
  natural and necessary complement to national human rights institutions. Of particular importance is the specific protection of minority,
  women, and children's rights.

Economic Conditions

As we have seen, the risk factor categories of governance and conflict history are built on the longer-term and slower moving structures, measures,
society-wide conditions, and processes that put states at risk for violent or
genocidal conflict. In this sense, they are a collection of lagging indicators,
often fixed snapshots of times past rather than a dynamic moving picture
of times present. This is particularly true for risk factors in the category of
economic conditions. Many of these factors are based on glimpses of economic data that are collected, collated, and translated at a given moment

in time. So, the fluid real-time economic realities of a present-day state may diverge, sometimes drastically, from these static data points.

Perhaps because of these temporal issues of data collection and accessibility, Goldstone et al. encourage "scholars in this field to redirect their attention from the economic to the institutional foundations of political instability."[170] Although I certainly agree that the quantitative support for economic risk factors is not as robust as that for many of the other risk factors we have, and will, examine, I think it premature to redirect our attention without a consideration of how economic conditions might interact with governance, conflict history, and social fragmentation to place a society at risk for violent or genocidal conflict. Economic data reflect helpful longer-term and slower moving trends of economic development, stability, and deterioration— potentially important indicators of the economic resilience of a society and its degree of susceptibility to risk of violent or genocidal conflict. Here are five specific risk factors related to economic conditions.

Low Level of Economic Development. Although violent or genocidal conflict does not occur only in poor countries, a low level of economic development is a robust risk factor in the prediction of many kinds of mass violence. As the African Development Bank Group argues: "There is substantial evidence of a correlation between low levels of economic development and state fragility . . . Low levels of economic production, characterized by particularly low levels of agricultural productivity and little investment in manufacturing, are root causes of fragility . . . Those affected become disenfranchised, especially young people who become cannon fodder for uprisings."[171]

Why is there a strong correlational relationship between low levels of economic development and violent or genocidal conflict? Some research suggests this relationship stems from the low opportunity cost to individuals who engage in mass violence.[172] That is, people in a poverty-ridden society stand to lose very little—and possibly gain very much—by taking advantage of the opportunity to engage in mass violence. Ruling elites can manipulate the perceived economic incentives of perpetrating genocide by blaming the victim group for society's poor economic condition or by legitimizing the looting of victims' assets to incentivize and reward compliance.[173] In my work with perpetrators in Rwanda, for instance, it was clear that Hutu extremists convinced *genocidaires* that Tutsi were responsible for Rwanda's economic difficulty and that the looting of their property— houses, radios, sheet metal roofing—was legitimate compensation for the suffering Tutsis had caused Hutus throughout the region. This does not mean to imply that poorer people are more likely to participate in killing; indeed, Straus found that "violence did not start in the poorest areas of the country" during the Rwandan genocide and that perpetrators were "not *comparatively* [italics mine] poor . . . or underemployed."[174] Rather, it simply means to point out the ways in which power holders in a society with a low level of economic development can manipulate the perceived opportunity costs to encourage the perpetration of mass atrocities.

Other scholars focus more on the relationship between poverty and state weakness. For example, using the variable of gross domestic product (GDP) per capita (that is, GDP divided by the number of people in a country), Rost found strong predictive power from this economic measure for the onset of genocide one year out. In his theoretical explanation for this finding, Rost asserts that "a low level of economic development indicates a weak state, which may resort to indiscriminate violence when confronted with threat as the government does not have enough resources at its disposal to accommodate political opposition or to repress opposition so comprehensively that it does not pose a threat."[175] An inability to accommodate or repress opposition means that such opposition—unless exterminated—may rise and succeed.[176]

In a cold calculus, the late economist Gerald Scully even suggested that genocide obeys the law of demand. Using real GDP per capita as his economic variable, Scully theorized that where per capita income is low, life is viewed by authorities as cheap and expendable. Conversely, where per capita income is higher, killing the population is more costly. Considering the marginal benefit in this context as continued rule or privilege (or even the "pleasure" obtained from inflicting terror), and the marginal cost as the incremental national output lost from the killing, Scully suggests that a ruling group will choose to practice genocide as long as the marginal benefit exceeds the marginal cost. Producing—killing—becomes bad "business" when the cost in terms of lost gross national product exceeds the benefit in continued rule or privilege. Using a regression in logarithmic form on a sample of 31 nations that had killed 10,000 or more of their citizens, Scully found "an inverse relationship between the amount of state-sponsored killing of the domestic population and the price of the people being killed [based on real GDP per capita income]."[177] He goes on to argue that the slowdown in murder rates in the 34-year period after Stalin (1954–1987), as well as the post-Mao era (1977–1987), may be due to the "economic fact that the population [became] more productive (valuable)" in producing economic growth.[178]

Economic Discrimination. Low levels of economic development are seldom distributed evenly across a population. Uneven economic development, particularly when group-based, can be a potent risk factor. Scholars often refer to such group-based economic discrimination—defined as differential "access to desirable economic goods, conditions, or positions"—as a form of horizontal inequality (inequality between and among groups as compared to vertical inequality between individuals or households).[179] Economic discrimination manifests not only in large economic gaps related to income levels, but also in impoverishment of justice, education, employment opportunities, job training, and housing for minority groups.[180] These variances can be particularly notable along urban and rural lines, with many economic amenities isolated to the capital city of a state. Institutionalized systems of patronage and nepotism also may restrict fair access to employment and a range of economic opportunities.[181]

When this inequality—real or perceived—is group-based, deep group grievances, sometimes resulting in the rise of communal nationalism or violence, can result. Deprived groups can resort to violence to redress the inequality or privileged groups can mobilize with violence to preserve their privilege. As peace researcher Jonas Claes writes: "Horizontal inequalities serve as a risk factor that may increase the likelihood of mass violence, particularly when embedded in local narrative or manipulated by the political elite. Actual or perceived horizontal inequalities allow conflict entrepreneurs to mobilize ethnic, religious, political, or geographical community members around a subjective motive and justify extreme violence against an identity-based or political group."[182]

Research consistently reveals that the probability of conflict is higher in areas with greater economic discrimination.[183] Specific quantitative studies on the relationship between economic discrimination and the onset of genocide, however, are limited. What exists, though, does suggest a strong correlational relationship. For Rost, "economic discrimination against the ethnic group from which members of armed groups that oppose the government in the civil conflict are recruited (and that the armed group often claims to represent) is a useful sign of the risk of genocide."[184] Although not a causal factor, he certainly sees economic discrimination as part of the process that may lead to genocide—as seen in the economic expropriation Nazi Germany inflicted on Jews in their territorial control early in the process of the Final Solution. Economists Charles Anderton and John Carter also found a large and significantly predictive relationship between economic discrimination against a minority group and the onset of genocide.[185] Using a different measure of income inequality, the Gini index, research by public policy scholar Marie Besancon, while finding that "economic inequality profoundly impacts revolutions, with an eightfold increase in predicted likelihood of conflict if a country is three times more unequal," only found a slight correlation of greater income inequality with greater genocide occurrence and severity.[186]

Lack of Macroeconomic Stability. Macroeconomics refers to the broad economic factors that affect an entire nation or the nation's economy (as opposed to microeconomics in which the focus is on factors that affect decisions made by companies and individuals). These broad economic factors at the heart of macroeconomics include consumer price inflation, changes in unemployment, national income, rate of growth, gross domestic product, currency stability, and price levels.[187] Countries with negative trends in these broad factors have a lack of macroeconomic stability and are particularly vulnerable to adverse internal and external shocks to their economic system.

As Taleb and Treverton point out, an absence of economic diversity is of particular concern for macroeconomic stability. "For a state to be safe," they argue, "the loss of a single source of income should not dramatically damage its overall economic condition."[188] Although specialization certainly brings gains in efficiency, it can also leave a vulnerability to unforeseen events. This lack of economic diversification is made "worse when large state-sponsored or state-friendly enterprises dominate the economy; these tend to not only reduce competitiveness but also compound the downside risks of drops in demands for a particular commodity or product by responding only slowly and awkwardly to marker signals."[189] For example, fuel export-dependent countries—such as Iraq, Yemen, Libya, Syria, Palestinian territories, Mali, and Egypt—have limited financial buffers that leave them more vulnerable to a decline in oil price.[190]

Related to economic diversification, Harff's analyses have long suggested trade openness as a highly sensitive predictor of genocide risk. The underlying notion is that a lack of economic interdependence with the global economy may signal an international isolation that leaves a country at greater risk for macroeconomic instability. Echoing her previous work, a 2012 risk assessment analysis by Harff found that risks were highest in countries with the lowest trade openness scores (measured as the total value of exports plus imports as a percentage of GDP).[191] Her follow-up 2013 assessment, however, found that trade openness was no longer statistically significant—at least not in that particular analysis.[192] Likewise, Rost found that a variable measuring the amount of trade did not improve risk assessments in his analysis.[193] As Anderton points out, future research to clarify the role of trade openness in genocide risk needs to consider broader empirical measures of trade as well as a wider range of trade and conflict issues.[194]

Economic Deterioration. Economic deterioration, whether chronic or acute, often stems from a lack of macroeconomic stability. As the Fund for Peace argues, a "sharp decline with high inflation and low GDP" is a key economic pressure indicator for state collapse. This economic deterioration is often progressive but can manifest in sudden drops in commodity prices, trade revenue, and foreign investment or in the collapse, hyperinflation, or devaluation of the national currency.[195] The Russian currency, for instance, went down by well over half since Vladimir Putin's decision to invade Ukraine.[196] As Adam Jones points out, a severe economic crisis throws the material base of people's lives into question, "may undermine the legitimacy and administrative capacity of state authorities . . . and may encourage rebellious, revolutionary, and secessionist movements."[197] In response, ruling authorities may respond with mass violence as a means of maintaining power.

For Staub, deteriorating economic conditions are more significant than poverty in explaining the onset of mass violence. So, the issue is less an absolute measure of income or wealth, but more the unexpected deterioration in an accustomed level of either. He maintains that it was the economic deterioration in Rwanda—when the price of its primary exports, tin and coffee, greatly declined in world markets—that was, in combination with other difficult life conditions, a direct influence on the genocide. Staub writes: ". . . economic deterioration frustrates both material needs and the psychological needs of whole groups of people for security, effectiveness, and identity. People worry that they will be unable to take care of themselves and their families."[198]

The relationship of a state to international economic actors also has implications for economic deterioration. An overreliance on international aid, unregulated foreign investment, and low levels of foreign direct investment can be a fragile economic stool on which to stand. As Atanas Gotchev, former director of the Bulgarian Early Warning System, points out, "a high debt burden and mounting trade deficit limit the opportunities for social investment, which fuels social turmoil."[199] A large foreign debt burden, coupled with a drastic depletion of foreign exchange reserves, can lead to significant state instability. Argentina has defaulted on its sovereign debt 10 times, most recently in 2014, and has experienced a significant economic deterioration as a result. For Taleb and Treverton, "debt is perhaps the single most critical source of fragility . . . Debt issued by a state itself is perhaps the most vicious type of debt, because it doesn't turn into equity; instead, it becomes a permanent burden. Countries cannot easily go bankrupt—which, ironically, is the main reason people lend to them, believing that their investments are safe."[200]

Growth of Informal Economies and Black Markets. Finally, the growth of informal economies and, particularly, illegal black markets can have a significant impact on the level of risk for violent or genocidal conflict within a given society. Variously referred to as "hidden economies," "underground economies," "ingenuity economies," or "shadow economies," these informal economies provide goods and services that are paid for in cash and not regulated by traditional government, labor regulations, trade agreements, or tax structures. Informal economies provide workers with a chance to liberate their entrepreneurial spirit, unregulated by bureaucracy and unburdened by taxes. They can also be a financial coping mechanism, particularly during times of economic crisis. It has been argued that the total value of informal economies (close to $10 trillion) is second only to the US GDP of $14 trillion.[201] "In 2009, the OECD [Organisation for Economic Co-operation and Development] concluded that half the world's workers (almost 1.8 billion people) were employed in the shadow economy. By 2020, the OECD predicts the shadow economy will employ two-thirds of the world's workers."[202]

Although many informal economies operate legally, there is a darker side of these economies—the subset of illegal black markets—that particularly places a society at increased risk of violent or genocidal conflict. Of significant concern are black markets developed around the drug trade, human trafficking, trading networks in minerals, and weapons smuggling. Profits from these black markets often finance major criminal networks as well as nonstate armed challenges to state power.[203] In Guinea-Bissau, for instance, illegal profits received by the political elite from the drug trade led to a series of destabilizing events.[204] Particularly notable as a risk factor for violent or genocidal conflict is the illegal trafficking of assault weapons and ammunition (often intersecting with the drug trade). Such trafficking, for instance, from the United States to Mexico and elsewhere in the Americas has supplied national and transnational criminal networks with the arms to destabilize societies and states throughout the region. According to the Council on Foreign Relations, "the gun-related homicide rate in Latin America exceeded the global average in 2010 by more than 30%. The World Bank estimates that crime and violence cost Central America nearly 8% of its GDP when accounting for the costs of law enforcement, security, and health care."[205] Clearly, the destabilizing influence of illegal black markets, particularly in arms trafficking, challenges the normal functioning of governance and the rule of law. Security expert R. T. Naylor summarizes the impact of arms trafficking on violent conflict: "Weapons are easily available to all who have the ability to pay, and the global explosion of illicit activity has put the means of payment within the grasp of a remarkably diverse set of insurgent groups, paramilitary forces, militant religious sets and unabashed bandit gangs."[206]

Implications for Upstream Prevention. Although still an emerging area of research, it seems clear that the linkage between economic risk factors and violent or genocidal conflict is self-reinforcing; the former serves as a driver for the latter and the latter destroys the accumulated physical, social, and human capital that are essential to improving economic development, inclusiveness, stability, and resiliency in a postconflict society.[207] So, examining the risk factors associated with economic conditions helps us understand the ways in which upstream economic initiatives might mitigate the risk of violent or genocidal conflict in a given society:

- First, societies can focus on sustainable economic development and growth that increase the opportunity costs for individuals who may choose to engage in mass violence—that is, people are secure enough economically that they have more to lose by engaging in mass violence than they have to gain. Moreover, when civilians in a society have high value in terms of their contribution to the gross national product, then would-be perpetrators may be dissuaded from committing atrocities because the marginal cost exceeds the marginal benefit of such violence. The development of civilians with "high value" to the gross national product necessitates broad and inclusive investments in jobs, training, and education—the dividends of peace.

- Second, the promotion of horizontal equality is crucial to the reduction of economic discrimination. As Claes asserts: "Horizontal equality strategies include a broad range of political, economic, and social policy measures to increase actual and perceived equity in the distribution of assets, income, and opportunity between groups."[208] Economic discrimination can be addressed with a range of policy measures that includes previously marginalized groups—among them, redistribution mechanisms, fiscal reform, employment programs, antidiscriminatory initiatives, women's economic empowerment, and safety net programs. As political scientist David Simon argues: "Strong and independent institutions governing economic management . . . [should make] more transparent the process by which resources are received and distributed by the government."[209] Many of these policies go hand-in-hand with overall economic development and growth. Indeed, "redistributing slices of the economic pie . . . is more palatable for privileged groups if the economic pie itself is growing."[210]

- Third, macroeconomic stability can be encouraged by policies and practices of economic diversification—in terms of sources of income, commodities produced, and increased representation of independent (as opposed to state-sponsored or state-friendly) domestic enterprises in the upper tiers of economic leadership. Macroeconomic stability— built on internal economic integration within the state (for example, developing economic infrastructure and fiscal capacity)—can also be complemented by economic interdependence with the global economy, including state participation in trade agreements, multilateral treaties, and international trade. The supporting of community economic development and local ownership further stabilizes a country's macroeconomic situation. In short, "every step taken towards reducing poverty and achieving broad-based economic growth is a step toward conflict prevention."[211]

- Fourth, states can be sensitive to signs of, and remedies for, deteriorating economic conditions. Economic development and diversification are important long-term antidotes, but states should also be prepared to take immediate relief action (e.g., tax cuts, social pensions, unemployment insurance, job creation, relief or social welfare plans, and microcredit) to slow or halt economic deterioration where possible. "Priority needs to be given to labor-intensive public and community works, increased agricultural productivity and domestic private sector development."[212] When foreign debt burdens are shackling economic development, multilateral debt restructuring processes may be necessary to avoid a return to a crippling economic deterioration that could leave a country in chaos.

- Finally, the risk posed by illegal black markets—whether in drugs, human trafficking, or weapons smuggling—can be countered by state ratification of international treaties (for instance, the Inter-American Convention Against the Illicit Manufacturing of and Trafficking in Firearms, Ammunition, Explosives, and Other Related Materials) to criminalize such operations. Some legal markets—such as minerals and arms—could be incorporated more cleanly into the formal economy. In the case of arms, for instance, the policies of incorporation could be complemented by national practices (such as requiring universal background checks or using trace data to police illicit firearms) to disarm criminal elements of illegal weapons.

Social Fragmentation

Negative trends among risk factors in the categories of governance, conflict history, and economic conditions shackle a society in the bonds of fragility. This can lead to, as well as be the result of, an increased susceptibility to social disharmony and isolation. This state of disconnect between the larger society and the groupings of some members of that society is known as fragmentation. Although fragmentation can manifest itself along economic, institutional, or geographic lines, this final category focuses on risk factors related specifically to social fragmentation. Social fragmentation can be defined "as a process in modern society by which different groups form parallel structures within society, which have little or no consistent interaction between them over the full spectrum of the social experience."[213] In the World Bank's view, "social fragmentation can permeate society, erupting, for example, as domestic violence in the household, rising crime and violence in the community, and massive corruption and civil conflict at the state level."[214] Where social cohesion can unite a people and strengthen a society, social fragmentation splinters a people, reduces the resiliency of a society, and places it at increased risk for violent or genocidal conflict. Here are five specific risk factors related to social fragmentation.

Identity-Based Social Divisions. Identity-based social divisions—particularly when intertwined with differential access to power, wealth, status, and resources—are a considerable source of risk. As we have seen in our discussion of the in-group bias, social identity matters deeply as a source of intergroup conflict. Social identity can be manipulated by power holders to create or deepen societal divisions and advance their own partisan interests. Individuals prioritize divisive subordinate identities rather than being closely connected to the unifying superordinate identity of the state or nation. Unstable environments are particularly lethal brews for fostering intergroup tension among identity lines. In this vein, the targeted victim group is perceived as an existential threat, or, in the words of Australian scholar Rhiannon Neilsen, a "toxification" considered collectively and fundamentally lethal to the perpetrator group.[215] The reality of this threat is less important than its perception in the mind of the dominant group. Moreover, the degree of existential threat perceived to be posed by the enemy increases as the power-holding capacities of the dominant group decrease.

As Stanton has described, the rise of identity-based social divisions can be conceptualized in the stages of an escalatory process that begins with classification ("us and them") and continues through symbolization (giving names and symbols to the classification) and on to discrimination (a dominant group denies rights of the powerless). The fourth stage in his process is dehumanization, or the denying of one group's humanity by the other group.[216] In this stage, identity-based social divisions are fueled by polarizing speech promoting hatred or inciting violence against a particular group. Such hate speech is especially potent when tolerated or encouraged by the state. Although there is no universally accepted definition of hate speech, certain parameters have evolved that prove helpful in distinguishing hate speech from freedom of expression. For the Council of Europe, for instance, hate speech covers all forms of expression that "spread, incite, promote or justify racial hatred, xenophobia, anti-Semitism or other forms of hatred based on intolerance, including: intolerance expressed by aggressive nationalism and ethnocentrism, discrimination and hostility against minorities, migrants and people of immigrant origin."[217] Hate speech can be propagated through mass media, public political speech, websites, graffiti, digital social networks, SMS blasts, and even rumor and gossip.[218] Although hate speech by itself does not directly cause violence, it can—in the context of other social and political factors—be used to incite discrimination, hostility, or violence against a particular group.

Perhaps the clearest current example of the role of hate speech and incitement in fostering identity-based social divisions comes from Burma (renamed Myanmar by the military government in 1989). Over the past 4 years in Burma, there have been repeated episodes of anti-Muslim violence fired by hate speech in the form of rumors, misinformation, and inflammatory accusations spread through a wide array of social media. As Nay Phone Latt, a Burmese blogger and activist, has said: "In Myanmar today, even if we are not shooting each other with guns, we are shooting each other with words."[219] In July 2014, for instance, violence broke out after a Buddhist woman was paid to make false rape claims against two Muslim brothers in Mandalay. Dehumanizing hate speech and incitement have been central strategies in the exclusionary platform of the ultranationalist 969 movement, led by Burmese Buddhist monk Ashin Wirathu. In a 2013 interview, Wirathu said: "Muslims are like the African carp. They breed quickly and they are very violent and they eat their own kind. Even though they are minorities here, we are suffering under the burden they bring us."[220] In January 2015, he called the UN special envoy to Burma, Yanghee Lee, a "bitch" and a "whore"—comments that, in the view of UN human rights chief Zeid Ra'ad Al Hussein, amounted to "incitement to hatred."[221] Wirathu's long and well-disseminated (he has more than 37,000 followers on Facebook) trail of incendiary rhetoric and slanderous images has fostered a cavernous divide based on social identity and led to a rapidly worsening situation for Muslims in Burma.

Demographically, the degree of homogeneity or heterogeneity of social identity in a given society can provide a glimpse into the identity-based social divisions underlying social fragmentation. It is tempting to jump to an assertion that the more diverse a country is, the more disharmonious and socially fragmented it is. Europe, for instance, has been criticized for allowing "excessive immigration without demanding enough integration—a mismatch that has eroded social cohesion, undermined national identities, and degraded public trust."[222] Although there are certainly competing and conflicting interests that may come with diversity, research does not support the notion that more diverse countries are also inherently more conflict prone. The majority of diverse societies are at peace. Indeed, a World Bank policy research report found that "substantial ethnic and religious diversity significantly reduces the risk of civil war . . . Controlling for other characteristics, a society is safer if it is composed of many such groups than if everyone has the same ethnicity and religion . . . Although ethnically diverse societies are commonly seen as fragmented, ethnicity provides an effective basis for social networks. Such societies might therefore be less atomistic than homogenous societies."[223] This finding is complemented by the UN's assertion that the risk posed by social identity is "not the existence of diversity within the population of a country, nor is it those differences per se that cause conflict between groups. Instead, it is a discrimination based on such differences, and persistent patterns of it, that establish divisions within society which serve both as a material cause and a perceived justification of group violence."[224]

Nondiverse societies—marked by an ethnic dominance in which the largest ethnic group in a multiethnic society constitutes between 45% and 90% of the population—have a risk of rebellion that is about 50% higher than societies without such identity dominance. This characteristic of ethnic dominance, often wielded for exclusionary political and social purposes, appears in about half of developing societies. Just as identity dominance can be a risk factor, however, so too can identity polarization with two relatively large groups of approximately the same size. "A completely polarized society, divided into two equal groups, has a risk of civil war around six times higher than a homogenous society."[225]

Manipulating identity to sow, or exacerbate, social divisions slows a state from building resiliency or overcoming fragility. The undermining impact of identity-based social divisions reduces incentives for trust, cooperation, dialogue, and long-term social exposure. As consultant Seth Kaplan argues: "Society becomes obsessed by the conflict between identity groups, not with generating wealth or increasing national prestige."[226] The results of such an obsession include a diversion of resources from promoting sustainable development and growth to simply managing the disabling impasse caused by intergroup tension. This can have life and death consequences in some societies. In sub-Saharan Africa, for instance, the least ethnically divided societies are able to spend five times more per capita than the most divided societies on HIV prevention and treatment programs.[227]

Demographic Pressures. Social fragmentation can be escalated with demographic pressures that can be particularly taxing for already fragile societies. Some demographic pressures stem from population issues such

as voluntary group resettlement patterns that may lead to border disputes, ownership or occupancy of land controversies, contested access to
transportation outlets, or disputed control of religious or historical sites.
Demographic pressures may also come from a "high population density relative to food supply, access to safe water, and other life-sustaining resources"
or divergent rates of population grown among competing social identity
groups. At times, infrastructure development and industrial projects may,
while benefitting the state in general, have very particular stressor impacts
(for example, environmental hazards or agricultural failure) on a specific
demographic population (typically, indigenous peoples).[228]

An oft-cited demographic pressure comes from skewed population dis-
tributions, most notably a "youth bulge." When a country has achieved
success in reducing infant mortality, but its mothers still have a high fertility rate, then a disproportionate share of the population ends up being
composed of children and young adults. According to former World Bank
Chief Economist Justin Yifu Lin, this youth bulge (variously defined as a
high proportion of 15 to 24 or 29 year olds relative to the adult population) is about 7 percentage points higher in less developed countries. It is
especially prevalent in Africa and fragile states. In a decade, it is expected
that Africa's youth bulge will account for 28% of its population. In fragile states, almost 75% of the population is under 30 years of age. As Lin
points out, this youth bulge can be a demographic dividend if there are
enough opportunities for full employment in productive activities.[229]
When such opportunities, however, are not available, low opportunity cost
means that large cohorts of unemployed disaffected youth—particularly
young males—offer a ready and cheap supply of rebel or terrorist labor,
increasing the risk of armed conflict. In 2007, for instance, there were 67
countries with youth bulges, of which 60 were experiencing some form of
social unrest or violence.[230]

A range of studies offers empirical support for the correlation between
countries prone to civil conflicts and those with burgeoning youth populations. Demographers Richard Cincotta and Elizabeth Leahy suggest a "60-
percent-under-30" benchmark for risks of civil conflict, based on their
findings that nearly a quarter of all states with more than 60% of their
population under 30 years of age had at least one incident of civil conflict
in the following decade—compared to just a 7% rate for countries with less
than 60% of their population under 30 years of age.[231] Similarly, a 2012
expert paper commissioned by the UN found that the presence of youth
bulges increased the risk of conflict outbreak significantly in the half century from 1950 to 2000. "For every percentage point increase in the youth
population (relative to the adult population)," the report concluded, "the

risk of conflict increases by more than 4 per cent. When youth make up more than 35 per cent of the adult population, which they do in many developing countries, the risk of armed conflict would be 150 per cent higher than in countries with an age structure similar to most developed countries."[232] Although declining fertility rates in many countries will dissipate the influence of youth bulges in the coming years, continuing high fertility rates in the Middle East, Africa, and parts of Asia—with many countries in those regions expected to triple in population by 2100—will remain as a significant demographic pressure for the foreseeable future.[233]

Still other demographic pressures are sparked by crisis situations, often exacerbating already-stressed societies. Repression, violence, even catastrophic natural disasters, can lead to a massive displacement of population across, or within, a state's borders. Refugees leaving or entering a country, or internally displaced persons (IDPs) within their own country, can activate tectonic shifts in demographic pressures that increase a state's or region's vulnerability to instability and conflict. Minority Rights Group International considers massive movement of refugees and IDPs as one of its 10 key conflict risk indicators.[234] Perhaps nowhere are the destabilizing effects of massive movement of refugees and IDPs as apparent as in Syria. At present, since the outbreak of civil war in March 2011, over 4 million Syrians have fled to neighboring Turkey, Lebanon, Jordan, Egypt, and Iraq with another 6.6 million Syrians internally displaced and trapped within their own country.[235] The state and regional repercussions of this forced displacement—about 1 family displaced every 60 seconds—have been enormous and stand as the worst humanitarian crisis in the world.

Even when there are plans for the relocation and settlement of refugees and IDPs, issues of safety, security, and civilian protection still come into play. Too often, refugee camps become sites of violence—rife with torture and rape, sometimes even perpetrated by camp workers and officials entrusted with the protection of refugees. Moreover, emblematic of the maxim that "no good deed goes unpunished," political scientist Edward Luttwak even has suggested that refugee camps with "a higher standard of living" can become "desirable homes" that prevent integration, inhibit emigration, and keep resentments aflame. Although acknowledging that the conditions in refugee camps are abysmal by Western standards, Luttwak argues that they often exceed what is locally available to nonrefugees, thus perpetuating a permanent refugee population that has no good reason to repatriate or move elsewhere. As he illustrates with the case of refugee camps along the Democratic Republic of Congo's (DRC) border with Rwanda, these camps "sustain a Hutu nation that would otherwise have been dispersed, making the consolidation of Rwanda impossible and providing a base for radicals to launch more Tutsi-killing raids across the border."[236] Though written in 1999, Luttwak's analysis still resonates today in the ongoing instability in eastern DRC caused by the Democratic Forces for the Liberation of Rwanda (FDLR)—rebels born from the flight of Hutu extremists to eastern Congo after the 1994 Rwandan genocide who now claim to protect the more than 129,000 Hutu refugees still remaining in the region.

These large-scale demographic pressures can lead to a range of destabilizing consequences including disease epidemics (even pandemics), environmental degradation, malnutrition and starvation, drought, and land and resource competition—any of which can bring about a severe humanitarian crisis. In a brutal cycle, this emergence of a humanitarian crisis can exacerbate state or regional fragility, resulting in an increased risk of violent conflict or genocide.

Unequal Access to Basic Goods and Services. As we have seen, the intersection of social identities and inequalities is a volatile one. Horizontal inequalities, or inequalities that coincide with identity-based social divisions, can be strong drivers of conflict. Whether economic, social, political, or cultural, inequalities between and among social identity groups can leave one group feeling discriminated against and the other enjoying privileges that it fears to lose.[237] Particularly relevant to social fragmentation are horizontal social inequalities—issues of group-based unequal access to basic goods and services, including "health, education, water, sanitation, communications and infrastructure."[238] Having equal access to such basic goods and services is a common social expectation. For fragmented societies, however, this is an expectation often unmet as the ability to access these basic goods and services varies "within and across different social groups and geographic locations; rural communities and women and girls . . . are particularly vulnerable to being underserved."[239]

In fragile states, the normative assumption of equal access to health services hinges on a realistic capacity to deliver such services to the population. Where that capacity is limited, equality of access will be severely compromised. Researchers often use infant mortality rates (the number of infants dying before reaching 1 year of age, per 1,000 live births in a given year) as "a good surrogate for a wide range of indicators of material standard of living and quality of life."[240] Although certainly tapping into both economic development and social welfare policies, perhaps what infant mortality rates are most indicative of is the capacity of a state to deliver core health services to its population. In this sense, countries with high infant mortality rates signal a general weakness of state and institutional structures. When understood as such a proxy measure, a wide variety of research indicates that high infant mortality "is a powerful predictor of civil wars, ethnic wars, adverse regime changes and genocide."[241] Goldstone et al., for instance, found "the odds of future instability in countries at the 75th percentile in global infant mortality levels were nearly seven times higher than in countries at the 25th percentile."[242]

Although the general relationship between high infant mortality rates and conflict is robust, specific research on the relationship between group-based differences in infant mortality rates and conflict is scarce. Consistent with what the general research suggests, however, economist Luca Mancini did find a positive correlation between horizontal inequality in child mortality rates and the occurrence of deadly ethnocommunal violence in Indonesia.[243] In Mancini's words: "Group differences in child mortality rates often reflect inequalities in other socio-economic dimensions such as levels of education, family income/wealth, and housing conditions."[244] He concludes with a specific connection to risk: "Horizontal inequality in child mortality is a very visible type of inequality which can be used instrumentally by ethnic elites to mobilize co-ethnics."[245]

Access to education is another basic service that can be negatively impacted by horizontal social inequalities. For example, political scientist Gudrun Ostby hypothesized that the higher the level of horizontal social inequality in a country—operationalized as differential access to educational opportunities—the higher the risk of civil conflict. Indeed, she found that for countries "with low levels of horizontal social inequality (5th percentile), the probability of onset of civil conflict is any given year is 1.75%." When horizontal social inequality between groups increases from the 5th to the 95th percentile, however, "the probability of conflict more than doubles, to 3.7%."[246] This is consistent with research suggesting that large cohorts of poorly educated youth, often reflecting horizontal social inequalities in educational access, increase the risk of conflict in societies.[247]

Finally, providing equal access to basic services is predicated on fair service delivery. Unfortunately, however, horizontal inequalities can even extend to delivery of those basic infrastructure services. A December 2007 report by the Forum for Civic Initiatives and Saferworld, for instance, found that electricity provision was a driver of conflict in Kosovo. Although some areas of Northern Kosovo continued to receive good electricity provision from Belgrade, other areas throughout Kosovo were experiencing scheduled and unscheduled power cuts. This uneven distribution of electricity—a basic social service—throughout Kosovo, coupled with difficulties paying the bills, caused resentment and frustration that was "often directed against other communities rather than the Kosovo Energy Corporation."[248]

Gender Inequalities. The relationship between gender inequalities and conflict often focuses on how the consequences of conflict affect women and men differently. In a significant way, however, we can also understand gender—and its correspondent inequalities in gender-defined rights—as a driver of conflict. A 2013 Oxfam report describes several examples of gender inequalities fueling conflict: "In South Sudan, for example, high bride price fuels cattle raiding and conflict between tribal groups; in Gaza, patriarchal values create a sense that leadership is about self-interest rather than protecting the community; in Afghanistan, women may be 'given' or 'taken' to settle community disputes and conflicts."[249] In some cases, gender inequalities may also drive conflict by leading women and girls to become combatants. A 2010 Saferworld survey in Nepal, for instance, found that nearly 20% of Maoist female combatants cited the desire to challenge gender inequality and promote the empowerment of women as their main reason for joining the rebellion—with another 25% having joined in response to sexual abuse and rape by opposing state security forces.[250]

There is an increasingly widespread recognition among researchers of the role gender inequalities play as a risk factor in violent conflict. In one of the seminal studies, political scientist Mary Caprioli found that domestic gender inequality was correlated with a state's greater use of violent military solutions to resolve international disputes.[251] Looking more specifically at intrastate rather than international conflict, Erik Melander, deputy director of the Uppsala Conflict Data program in Sweden, also found that gender inequality was significantly predictive of higher levels of intrastate armed conflict (that is, civil war).[252] A 2009 OECD policy paper included unequal gender relations among its list of key structural risk factors for armed violence.[253] Two years later, the Institute for Economics and Peace found a strong correlation between three separate measures of gender equality (in public, at work, and in private) and a general measure of state peacefulness (the Global Peace Index, or GPI). For each of the measures, as gender equality decreased, a country's ranking on the GPI decreased (particularly on the index's internal peace measure).[254] Focusing specifically on gender inequalities in family law and practice (including marriage, divorce, custody, inheritance, and other intimate family issues), international security expert Valerie Hudson and her colleagues discovered that levels of state peacefulness decreased as the level of inequities in family law and practice increased.[255]

In addition, gender inequalities have been shown to be a cross-cutting issue intersecting other risk factors for violent and genocide conflict. For example, economist Daniel Kaufmann, in a study of 80 countries, found that corruption increased as women's social and economic rights decreased.[256]

Political scientist Steven Fish, in looking at the connection between Islam and regime type, argues that the most significant driver of the low degree of democratization in Muslim societies is the subordination of women and girls. As he concludes: "The station of women, more than other factors that predominate in Western thinking about religious systems and politics, links Islam and the democratic deficit."[257] There are a range of other studies confirming strong cross-national linkages between the treatment of women and a wide array of economic and health variables.[258]

Finally, one of the clear indicators of gender inequalities being deeply embedded within society is a lack of physical security for women—often manifest in gender-based violence. "There is considerable evidence that gender inequality—in the form of social economic, legal and political inequalities—is a root cause of violence against women."[259] Indeed, social epidemiologist Lori Heise found that the most consistent predictor of the use of violence by men against women and girls is the discriminatory attitudes and norms toward women and girls that underlie gender inequalities.[260] Hudson et al. examined the level of physical security of women in a society—including the prevalence of domestic violence, rape, martial rape, and murder of women—in relationship to levels of peacefulness. They found that it is the physical security of women (even more so than levels of democracy, wealth, or prevalence of Islamic culture) that is most predictive of "which states would be the least peaceful or of the most concern to the international community or have the worst relations with their neighbors."[261] In short, there is a strong correlation between levels of gender-based violence and conflict. As a 2013 joint consultation report by the UN and Saferworld summarized: "There is emerging evidence that a high prevalence of violence against women within societies may be a structural cause or enabling factor for armed conflict and instability at the national level."[262]

Political Instability. Social fragmentation is exacerbated in the face of political instability. Political instability intersects many of the risk factors already discussed in the general category of governance. The governance category was concerned with the ways in which a state's structure and authority are exercised and how that might relate to the risk of violent conflict or genocide. The risk factors in that category were fairly static elements that alert us to *where* violent conflict or genocide might be more likely. Our discussion of political instability, however, looks more closely at internal or external threats to a state's authority or legitimacy that can intensify social fragmentation. The fluid risk factors associated with political instability—what political scientist Matthew Krain has term "openings in the political opportunity structure"—are a bridge from where to *when* violent conflict or genocide might be most likely.[263]

Political instability is a key indicator of risk in a wide range of assessment models. Goldsmith et al., for instance, include political instability as one of their six most powerful predictors for determining at-risk states for genocide and politicide. They argue there is no instance of the onset of genocide (or politicide) in which the state in question is not also experiencing another form of serious political instability in the same year.[264] Similarly, Harff maintains that major instances of political instability preceded almost all historical cases of genocide or politicide.[265] Both of these studies based their operationalization of political instability on data from the Political Instability Task Force (PITF), a U.S. government-sponsored research project formerly known as the State Failure Task Force. The PITF understood that political instability included four distinct types of state failure events: revolutionary wars, ethnic wars, adverse (nondemocratic) regime changes, and instances of genocide and politicide. Although the risk associated with prior genocides or politicides has already been discussed in the conflict history category, this section will complement and extend the PITF definition by looking at the impact of political instability on social fragmentation through four lens: adverse regime changes, threats of armed conflict (internal, regional, or international), neighboring state conflicts, and a high proportion of the population under arms.

Adverse regime changes, particularly "autocratic backsliding," may lead to a scaled collapse of democratic institutions, a failure of central state authority, and territorial disintegration. Adverse regime changes, particularly when abrupt, are accompanied by a wide range of state actions that can exacerbate political instability. For instance, in the midst of these changes, it is not uncommon to see imposition of curfews, politically motivated arrests, and defection from peace agreements. These repressive actions, in turn, raise questions about state legitimacy and can prompt civil and labor unrest, perhaps even antistate terrorism. In counterresponse, the state may become even more repressive and a brutal cycle begins that breeds an environment conducive to the commission of mass atrocity.[266] Indeed, research has found that a change in the type of regime of a country in the previous 3 years—particularly a movement toward authoritarianism—was an especially important time-variant factor in year-on-year forecasting for the onset of genocide or politicide.[267]

Political instability is also heightened in the face of threats of internal, regional, or international armed conflict. Nationalist or radical opposition movements can feed a political instability that raises the threat of various forms of internal armed conflict (for example, a domestic insurgency or outright civil war) related to self-determination or autonomy. As we saw in Chapter 3, the threat of a major regional or international armed conflict can create preparatory psychological, social, and political conditions best described as a "genocidal mentality." Rost summarizes the genocide risk posed by war: "International and domestic war are linked to a higher risk of genocide, either because of the threat they pose to a country's government or because the government can use the conflict as a cover for genocide."[268] Although threats of armed conflict exacerbate political instability, their actualization leads to "periods characterized by a high incidence of violence, insecurity and the permissibility of acts that would not otherwise be acceptable. In addition, the capacity of States to inflict harm is usually at its peak during periods of conflict."[269]

Given the permeability of many national borders, neighboring state conflicts—or living in "a conflict-ridden neighborhood"— can also heighten levels of political instability within a given country. This is particularly true when a country is dependent on unstable neighbors for vital assets (for example, access to the sea or water) or when insurgent groups are using neighboring countries as a platform for operations and weapons storage.[270] A number of studies have shown that neighborhood conflict is a significant predictor of political instability. For instance, Goldstone et al. discovered that countries with four or more neighbors experiencing armed conflict were far more likely to have future onsets of instability.[271] Similarly, Goldsmith et al. also found that the number of neighboring states with internal conflict produced the best forecasting performance for the onset of political instability.[272] As the African Development Bank Group points out, the "risk [of living in a conflict-ridden neighborhood] is particularly high in cases of ethnic conflicts where similar ethnic groups span across borders of neighboring countries . . . Several factors explain the extent to which bad neighborhood fuels conflicts on the continent: The spill-over effect as a result of proximity; the existence and ease with which roving mercenaries move from one conflict to another; the proliferation of weapons in one conflict fueling others as a result of the porous borders in Africa and the interest of states in fueling conflict by supplying arms and providing havens for fighters."[273]

Finally, political instability increases as the proportion of a population under arms—legally or illegally—increases. The Atrocity Forecasting Project suggests that an increase in the proportion of a population in the regular military (what they call the "human defence burden")— particularly in interaction with fewer institutional constraints on executive power—is one of the most powerful predictors for genocide onset.[274] This finding confirms previous research demonstrating that the probability of genocide increases as the size and strength of government security forces increase—though only in states in which the executive leaders face few constraints upon their decision making.[275] The risk posed by a population under arms also goes beyond the military and security sector. There can be a more general "weapons effect" that comes from a growing illicit arms trade, increase in arms flow, stockpiling of weapons, and an expansion of private defense firms, irregular fighters, and security forces on the streets. An enhanced accessibility to weapons is particularly noticeable in Africa, home to 100 million of the estimated 600 million small arms and light weapons currently circulating in the world.[276] This societal escalation in armed capacity (even, as in the case of machetes in Rwanda, a proliferation in nonconventional weapons that can be used to inflict harm) can, in conjunction with other risk factors, be an important enabling factor for violent or genocidal conflict.[277]

Implications for Upstream Prevention. Social fragmentation is a threat to social cohesion—that is, the "behaviour and attitudes within a community that reflects a propensity of community members to cooperate."[278] The promotion of intergroup social cohesion (cooperating across social identity group lines) is particularly relevant for reducing the likelihood of violent or genocidal conflict. Kaplan lays out the far-ranging implications of strong social cohesion: "Countries whose citizens share common ideas about who they are and how they should work together are far more likely to enjoy the state legitimacy and good governance necessary to spur and sustain economic and political development."[279] Recognizing the deep intrinsic and instrumental value in the promotion of social cohesion, here are several implications for upstream genocide prevention:

- First, states have a responsibility to constructively manage diverse social identities in ways that lead to a more inclusive superordinate social identity of "us" rather than the more divisive subordinate social identities that leave antagonistic clusters of "thems." In addressing a future for the new Middle East, for example, international studies scholar Ahmed Souaiaia pleads for a reconstruction of ". . . national identities that are more inclusive and more egalitarian in terms of rights and dignity."[280] In a pluralistic society, this civic nationalism is accomplished not by mere superficial contact but by deep engagement and appreciation of the "other" through cross-cutting relations in education, sports, religion, cultural programs, and physical integration in housing, schools, and work.[281] As Staub argues, "deep engagement between people belonging to different groups . . . especially in the framework of cooperation in joint projects in the service of shared goals . . . can lead to experiencing the humanity of the other."[282] Côte d'Ivoire's national football team, for instance, comes from both sides of the country's North/South divide but has stepped forward as an example of a unified national institution and has initiated peacebuilding and development initiatives throughout the troubled country. Of particular importance in mitigating the risk posed by identity-based social divisions is fostering an awareness of, and education about, countering hate speech. The new technologies that have allowed the proliferation of hate speech via social media can also be used to create real-time "nowcasting" (as opposed to forecasting) platforms to help identity and monitor such rhetoric, build counternarratives to hate speech, fact-check media stories, reject violence, and promote positive relations among various groups. In 2013, for instance, Sisi ni Amani of Kenya disseminated peace messaging via SMS programming to prevent and deescalate tensions and violence surrounding the upcoming elections, resulting in a largely peaceful and legitimate election.[283]

- Second, demographic pressures can be countered by resource development and equitable distribution, family planning measures and education, disease control, and sustainable environmental policies. Societies experiencing a youth bulge can transform the associated risks into a demographic dividend with job training and employment, constructive political participation, conflict resolution and community dialogue, and education and tolerance training.[284] Peace researcher Henrik Urdal also suggests that an investment in secondary education experience lowers the conflict rate in countries with large youth male bulges.[285] Human-made crisis situations or natural disasters leading to a massive displacement of the civilian population require cooperative stabilization efforts by the office of the UN High Commissioner for Refugees (UNHCR), domestic and international nongovernmental organizations, and host governments.[286] When these efforts include the establishment of refugee camps, such camps should not become a semipermanent substitute for—or even a deterrent to—a durable solution allowing for the safe return or resettlement of a refugee population.[287]

- Third, state and civilian authorities can redress horizontal social inequalities by providing equal access to basic goods and services across all social identity groups. It is more than the provision of goods and service at play; it is fair access to them among different social identity groups that should be a key priority. Indeed, the International Dialogue's "New Deal for Engaging in Fragile States" includes "accountable and fair service delivery" as one of its five peacebuilding and statebuilding goals.[288] The normative assumption of equal access to health, education, water, sanitation, communications, and infrastructure should be realized across policy and practice, particularly in a fragile or developing state.

- Fourth, women can be recognized not only as victims of conflict, but as a corrective to it. An October 2000 UN Security Council Resolution (UNSCR 1325) affirmed "the important role of women in the prevention and resolution of conflicts and in peace-building" and stressed "the importance of their equal participation and full involvement in all efforts for the maintenance and promotion of peace and security, and the need to increase their role in decision-making with regard to conflict prevention and resolution."[289] Six years later, speaking on his last International Women's Day as UN Secretary-General, Kofi Annan reaffirmed "that no policy [referring to the empowerment of women and girls] is more important in preventing conflict, or in achieving reconciliation after a conflict has ended."[290] As a postgenocide society, for example, Rwanda has taken seriously the contributions that women's skills and experiences can bring to public policy discussions. Gender rights are now enshrined in Rwanda's constitution and a remarkable 64% of Rwanda's parliamentarians are women, the highest proportion of any parliament in the world and the only one with a female majority.[291] Similarly, Guatemalan women are playing a key role as agents of change in their country's ongoing peacebuilding process. States should remain diligent about increasing participation by women in decision making and dialogue, including adopting national action plans on UNSCR 1325. As Oxfam summarizes: "'Gender' is not the optional extra which we simply can't manage in fragile contexts, because we have more urgent things to do. Tackling gender inequality *must* be heart and centre of fragility programming, to both secure women's rights *and* promote peace and stability in such contexts."[292]

- Finally, in terms of upstream prevention strategies to protect against political instability, the risk of adverse regime changes can be decreased with well-established democratic institutions and the presence of an independent and impartial judiciary, media, and police as well as a robust national civil society. In this regard, local nonstate actors, including traditional and religious leaders, may "provide a critical buffer against atrocity risk relative to the state."[293] Threats of internal, regional, or international armed conflict can be mitigated by stable governance and economic conditions, as well as cooperation with international and regional human rights laws and treaties. The destabilizing impact of neighboring state conflicts can be decreased in the presence of functioning and respected regional conflict resolution mechanisms. Lastly, the size and strength of government security forces can be moderated by strong institutional constraints on the use of force, just as a societal escalation in armed capacity can be curbed by nondiscriminatory gun control laws and the policing of illicit arms trade.

CONCLUSIONS

The risk factors cited in this chapter focus less on causation and more on the correlative and predictive value they hold for an increased likelihood of violent or genocidal conflict. As the Atrocity Forecasting Project summarized: ". . . [our] intention is to maximize forecasting power, rather than to assess causal relationships. As such, the predictors . . . should not be understood as factors necessarily *causing* genocide onset. Rather, they are better understood as risk indicators *somehow* associated with an increased likelihood of genocide. An appropriate analogy might be to symptoms of medical conditions. High blood pressure is associated with a higher risk of heart disease, and it is also a cause. But chest pain too is a predictor of heart trouble, although it is not a cause."[294]

Staying with the cardiovascular disease analogy, you will not necessarily develop coronary heart disease if you have a particular risk factor. No one risk factor exists in a vacuum. Indeed, "all other things being equal" is not an applicable phrase for understanding the intricacies of how risk factors interrelate. Each individual case is a unique and complex outcome of multicausal, multidimensional, and mutually reinforcing interactions of deeply enmeshed risk factors. There certainly are many cases in which a significant number of risk factors exist but in which cardiovascular disease does not occur. But the more risk factors you have, the greater the likelihood that you will develop cardiovascular disease, unless you take action to modify those risk factors that can be modified.

Similarly, not all—or even most—of these 20 risk factors need to be present to determine a significant risk of violent or genocidal conflict occurring. Although violent or genocidal conflict rarely takes place in the absence of these risk factors, there will be some negative cases in which many of the risk factors are present but such conflict does not occur (for instance, in Côte d'Ivoire). But the more risk factors for violent or genocidal conflict that are present, the greater the risk that accelerating factors may escalate a crisis situation or that a triggering event could actually lead to the onset of mass violence. So, although the singular effects of any one risk factor may be relatively small, their cumulative impact can be deadly in breaking the back of a society.

Genocide prevention is not what makes headlines, but it is what prevents the worst of headlines from being made. Like genocide itself, upstream prevention is a process, not an event. It is a long-term strategy of building underlying structures of societal and state durability related to governance, the interpretation of conflict history, economic conditions, and social cohesion. Upstream genocide prevention is built on sustained efforts to increase the capacity and resilience of societies to inoculate themselves against the risk of mass atrocity. These are long-sighted measures—often underappreciated or even unrecognized because they have led to a nonevent—intended to minimize the necessity for mid-stream crisis management or reactive measures (which are the subject of Chapter 5).

The examples of upstream prevention strategies we have discussed for each category of risk factors are universal, that is, they can—and should—be applied broadly for a population regardless of their current state of risk. Although many developed states think of genocide prevention as a foreign policy issue, it should also be recognized as a domestic concern as no state is immune to the risk of genocide. Upstream strategies for genocide prevention can also be selectively applied to populations that have been identified in some ways as being at a heightened risk for genocide.

Multilateral regional organizations oblige member states to surrender a measure of state sovereignty for the sake of collective goals. For example, the Association of Southeast Asian Nations (ASEAN) has demonstrated a constructive capacity to partner with existing institutions, mechanisms, and relevant government actors of the 10 countries within their organization to promote genocide prevention. For their most durable and sustainable effectiveness, however, it is important that upstream strategies for genocide prevention come from within a society rather than being imposed from without. Localized community-based initiatives that are highly responsive to the unique internal dynamics of the society are crucial in building a state's resilience, reducing its susceptibility to genocide, and, ultimately, reinforcing a state's sovereignty. In addition, increased "emphasis should be placed on building the capacity of nonstate actors, including traditional and religious institutions, to identify and monitor risk factors preceding mass atrocity crimes."[295]

The work of my colleagues at the Auschwitz Institute for Peace and Reconciliation (AIPR), for instance, has intersected with the birth of national mechanisms for the prevention of genocide and other atrocity crimes in Mexico, the United States, Uganda, Kenya, Tanzania, Central African Republic, Democratic Republic of the Congo, Argentina, and Paraguay. As just one example from this list, Tanzania's National Committee for the Prevention and Punishment of the Crime of Genocide, War Crimes, Crimes Against Humanity and All Forms of Discrimination (TNC), established in February 2012, was the first of its kind in the Great Lakes Region, site of some of Africa's most intractable and violent conflicts.

Housed within Tanzania's Ministry of Constitutional and Legal Affairs, this committee includes a broad-based national membership drawn from government, civil society, and faith-based organizations. In addition to several AIPR-led training seminars to build the capacity of the committee, the group has developed collaborative ties with a range of other international partners, including the UN's Office of the Special Adviser on the Prevention of Genocide and the Swiss Agency for Development and Cooperation. Since its inception, the TNC has had a remarkable impact throughout Tanzania, leading Peace Forum workshops, bringing diverse religious leaders together to brainstorm strategies for the promotion of social cohesion, establishing Joint Peace Committees in regions throughout the country, and conducting periodic risk assessments of conflict-prone areas in Tanzania and its neighboring countries.

At the conclusion of our most recent training seminar in March 2014, a note from a member of the TNC captured well the importance of genocide prevention and it is appropriate that her voice conclude this chapter: "To those who were attending such training for the first time it was an eye opener. It is one thing to hear or read in the media but the subject of genocide acquires quite a different meaning once one is acquainted with its meaning and receives practical examples of where it has happened. It moves from being a concept to becoming a reality; a horrible crime which every human being worth the name needs to prevent in his or her own capacity. This training has proved that each and everyone has a role to play, and that he is as much a possible victim like any other if deliberate and stern measures are not used to prevent. Equally important is the fact that mass atrocity crimes are planned, and so, prevention should also be strategically planned right from the grassroots where things happen, involving all stakeholders. That makes prevention work a responsibility for all, from national, regional and international levels."[296]

NOTES

1. Associated France Press, "Bosnia Accuses Serbia of Genocide 'Hell'" (February 27, 2006).
2. William A. Schabas, "Genocide and the International Court of Justice: Finally, a Duty to Prevent the Crime of Crimes," *Genocide Studies and Prevention* 2 (2007): 112.
3. Schabas, "Genocide and the International Court of Justice," 102.
4. See "Application of the Convention on the Prevention and Punishment of the Crime of Genocide: Summary of the Judgment of 26 February 2007," accessed September 2, 2014 at http://www.icj-cij.org/docket/files/91/13687.pdf.

5. Judgment in "Case Concerning the Application of the Convention on the Prevention and Punishment of the Crime of Genocide," International Court of Justice (February 26, 2007), paragraph 427.

6. Ibid, paragraph 461.

7. Cited in William A. Schabas, *Genocide in International Law: The Crime of Crimes* (2nd ed.) (Cambridge, England: Cambridge University Press, 2009), 527.

8. Though the boundaries are contested, wars are typically defined as resulting in over 1,000 battle-deaths (including civilians as well as combatants) in a year. See, for instance, *Mini-Atlas of Human Security* (Brighton, England: Myriad Editions, 2008), 10 and Stephen L. Quackenbush, *International Conflict: Logic and Evidence* (Thousand Oaks, CA: CQ Press, 2015), 32.

9. Alex Bellamy, "Mass Atrocities and Armed Conflict: Links, Distinctions, and Implications for the Responsibility to Prevent" (The Stanley Foundation, February 2011), 3.

10. Rachel Gerber, "Preventing Genocide: More than War," *Courier* 70 (2011): 4.

11. Claudia Diaz, personal communication, February 9, 2015.

12. USAID, "Field Guide: Helping Prevent Mass Atrocities," (2015): 8.

13. See Bellamy, "Mass Atrocities and Armed Conflict," 6.

14. Ibid, 2.

15. Dan Smith, *The Penguin State of the World Atlas*, 9th ed. (Brighton, England: Myriad Editions, 2012), 66.

16. Shane Harris, "Water Wars," accessed September 19, 2014 at http://www.foreignpolicy.com/articles/2014/09/18/water_wars_climate_change_intelligence_strategy?utm_source=Sailthru&utm_medium=email&utm_term=Flashpoints&utm_campaign=2014_FlashPoints%2009%2F18RS.

17. Dan Smith, *The Penguin State of the World Atlas*, 66. For an extensive review of conflict economics, see Charles H. Anderton, "A Research Agenda for the Economic Study of Genocide: Signposts from the Field of Conflict Economics," *Journal of Genocide Research* 16 (2014): 113–138.

18. For a broad review, see Frances Stewart, "The Causes of Civil War and Genocide: A Comparison," eds. Adam Lupel and Ernesto Verdeja, *Responding to Genocide: The Politics of International Action* (Boulder, CO: Lynne Rienner, 2013), 47–83.

19. Accessed September 19, 2014 at http://fareedzakaria.com/2014/07/06/identity-not-ideology-is-moving-the-world/.

20. Mary Kaldor, *New and Old Wars: Organized Violence in a Global Era* (Stanford, CA: Stanford University Press, 1998). The book was released in a third edition in 2012.

21. Institute for Economics and Peace, "Five Key Questions Answered on the Link between Peace & Religion" (October, 2014): 6. Available for download at http://www.economicsandpeace.org.

22. Pew Research Center, "Religious Hostilities Reach Six-Year High" (January 2014).

23. See Jolle Demmers, *Theories of Violent Conflict: An Introduction* (New York: Routledge, 2012), 9.

24. "I-identity" and "we-identity" are taken from the work of German sociologist Norbert Elias (1897–1990). See his *What Is Sociology?* (New York, NY: Columbia University Press, 1978) and *The Civilizing Process: State Formation and Civilization* (Oxford, England: Basil Blackwell, 1982).

25. Demmers, *Theories of Violent Conflict*, 20. See also Jeffrey R. Seul, "'Ours Is the Way of God': Religion, Identity, and Intergroup Conflict," *Journal of Peace Research* 36 (1999): 554.

26. Herbert C. Kelman, "The Place of Ethnic Identity in the Development of Personal Identity: A Challenge for the Jewish Family," ed. Peter Y. Medding, *Studies in Contemporary Jewry: Coping with Life and Death: Jewish Families in the Twentieth Century* (New York, NY: Oxford University Press, 1999), 16.

27. I. William Zartman and Mark Anstey, "The Problem," eds. I. William Zartman, Mark Anstey, and Paul Meerts, *The Slippery Slope to Genocide: Reducing Identity Conflicts and Preventing Mass Murder* (New York, NY: Oxford University Press, 2012), 6.

28. The research literature on what is known as "cross-race recognition deficit" is robust. See, for instance, Siri Carpenter, "Why Do 'They All Look Alike'?" *American Psychological Association Monitor on Psychology* 31 (December 2000): 44 and Daniel B. Wright, Catherine E. Boyd, and Colin G. Tredoux, "Inter-racial Contact and the Own-race Bias for Face Recognition in South Africa and England," *Applied Cognitive Psychology* 17 (2003): 365–373.

29. Gordon W. Allport, *The Nature of Prejudice* (Boston, MA: The Beacon Press, 1954), 42.

30. John F. Dovidio and Samuel L. Gaertner, "Intergroup Bias," eds. Susan T. Fiske, Daniel T. Gilbert, and Gardner Lindzey, *Handbook of Social Psychology*, 5th ed., Vol. 2 (Hoboken, NJ: John Wiley & Sons, 2010), 1084.

31. See James Waller, *Becoming Evil: How Ordinary People Commit Genocide and Mass Killing*, 2nd ed. (New York, NY: Oxford University Press, 2007), 173–179.

32. Alexa Ispas, *Psychology and Politics: A Social Identity Perspective* (New York, NY: Psychology Press, 2013), vii.

33. Henri Tajfel and John C. Turner, "The Social Identity Theory of Intergroup Behavior," eds. Stephen Worchel and William G. Austin, *Psychology of Intergroup Relations*, 2nd ed. (Chicago, IL: Nelson-Hall, 1986), 7–24.

34. Jan E. Stets and Peter J. Burke, "Identity Theory and Social Identity Theory," *Social Psychology Quarterly* 63 (2000): 225.

35. Tajfel and Turner, "The Social Identity Theory of Intergroup Behavior," 14.

36. Marilynn B. Brewer, "The Psychology of Prejudice: Ingroup Love or Outgroup Hate?" *Journal of Social Issues* 55 (1999): 442.

37. Demmers, *Theories of Violent Conflict*, 42.

38. Ibid, 43.

39. Sonia Roccas and Andrew Elster, "Group Identities," ed. Linda R. Tropp, *The Oxford Handbook of Intergroup Conflict* (New York, NY: Oxford University Press, 2012), 115, 116.

40. Demmers, *Theories of Violent Conflict*, 27.

41. Cited in Demmers, *Theories of Violent Conflict*, 27; original quote may be found in Slavenka Drakulic, *The Balkan Express: Fragments from the Other Side of the War* (New York, NY: W. W. Norton, 1993), 52.

42. Claudia Card, "Genocide and Social Death," *Hypatia* 18 (2003): 72.

43. Ibid, 76.

44. Sarah Jane Meharg, "Identicide: Precursor to Genocide," Working Paper 05 for Center for Security and Defence Studies at Carleton University (November, 2006), 1.

45. Christopher Powell, "What Do Genocides Kill? A Relational Conception of Genocide," *Journal of Genocide Research* 9 (2007): 542–543.

46. Maureen Hiebert, "The Three 'Switches' of Identity Construction in Genocide: The Nazi Final Solution and the Cambodian Killing Fields," *Genocide Studies and Prevention* 3 (2008): 6.

47. Accessed September 8, 2014 at http://www.un.org/en/preventgenocide/adviser/genocide_prevention.shtml and "Prevention of Genocide" (August 17, 2014), accessed August 18, 2014 at http://venitism.blogspot.com/2014/08/prevention-of-genocide.html.

48. Jay Rothman, "The Insides of Identity and Intragroup Conflict," in Zartman et al., *The Slippery Slope to Genocide*, 156.

49. Alexander Austin, "Early Warning and The Field: A Cargo Cult Science?" eds. Alex Austin, Martina Fischer, and Norbert Ropers, *Transforming Ethnopolitical Conflict: The Berghof Handbook* (Wiesbaden, Germany: Springer Fachmedien Wiesbaden, 2004), 129–150.

50. Thomas Chadefaux, "Early Warning Signals for War in the News," *Journal of Peace Research* (2014): 5–18.

51. Unless otherwise cited, the examples in this paragraph are taken from Austin, "Early Warning and The Field: A Cargo Cult Science?" eds. Austin, Fischer, and Ropers, *Transforming Ethnopolitical Conflict*.

52. See Minority Rights Group International, *Peoples under Threat* (2014), 6. Accessed December 22, 2014 at http://www.minorityrights.org/download.php@id=1353.

53. Frederick Barton and Karin von Hippel, "Early Warning? A Review of Conflict Prediction Models and Systems" (Washington, DC: Center for Strategic & International Studies, 2008).

54. Among others, the primary early warning systems reviewed in this research include Gregory Stanton's "Ten Stages of Genocide" (2013, http://genocide-watch.net/genocide-2/8-stages-of-genocide); Barbara Harff's ongoing models of risk assessment (see her most recent "Risks of New Onsets of Genocide and Politicide in 2013," http://www.gpanet.org/content/risks-new-onsets-genocide-and-politicide-2013); the Minority Rights Group International's "Peoples under Threat" (2014, http://www.minorityrights.org/12369/peoples-under-threat/peoples-under-threat-2014.html); the University of Sydney's "Atrocity Forecasting Project" (http://sydney.edu.au/arts/research/atrocity_forecasting/); the Fund for Peace's "CAST: Conflict Assessment Framework" (2014, http://library.fundforpeace.org/library/cfsir1418-castmanual2014-english-03a.pdf); the "Early Warning Project," a joint initiative of the U.S. Holocaust Memorial Museum and the Dickey Center for International Understanding at Dartmouth College (http://www.earlywarningproject.com); the Sentinel Project's "Risk Factor List" (https://thesentinelproject.org/what-we-do/early-warning-system/risk-factors-list/); the World Bank's "Worldwide Governance Indicators" (http://info.worldbank.org/governance/wgi); the European Commission's "Checklist for Root Causes of Conflict" (http://www.eplo.org/assets/files/3.%20Resources/EU%20Documents/European%20Commission_ Programming%20Fiche_ Conflict_Prevention.pdf); ECOWAS' "Early Warning and Response Network" (http://www.ecowarn.org); the Forum on Early Warning and Early Response-Africa (http://www.fewer-international.org/pages/africa); the International Crisis Group's "CrisisWatch" (http://www.crisisgroup.org/en/publication-type/crisiswatch); the Jacob Blaustein Institute for the Advancement of Human Rights' *Compilation of Risk Factors and Legal Norms for the Prevention of Genocide* (New York, NY: The Jacob Blaustein Institute for the Advancement of Human Rights, 2011); and the United Nations' "Framework of Analysis for Atrocity Crimes" (2014, http://www.un.org/en/preventgenocide/adviser/pdf/frame-work%20of%20analysis%20for%20atrocity%20crimes_en.pdf). All websites listed in this note were accessed January 15, 2015.

55. Jacob Blaustein Institute for the Advancement of Human Rights, *Compilation of Risk Factors and Legal Norms for the Prevention of Genocide*, xii.
56. Frances Stewart, "The Causes of Civil War and Genocide: A Comparison," eds. Lupel and Verdeja, *Responding to Genocide*.
57. These defining features of governance are taken from the "Worldwide Governance Indicators" project, accessed January 16, 2015 at http://info.worldbank.org/governance/wgi.
58. Monty G. Marshall and Benjamin R. Cole, *Global Report 2014: Conflict, Governance, and State Fragility* (Vienna, VA: Center for Systemic Peace, 2014), 21.
59. Nicolas Rost, "Will it Happen Again? On the Possibility of Forecasting the Risk of Genocide," *Journal of Genocide Research* 15 (2013): 49.
60. Barbara Harff, "No Lessons Learned from the Holocaust? Assessing Risks of Genocide and Political Mass Murder since 1955," *American Political Science Review* 97 (2003).
61. Rost, "Will it Happen Again?," 49.
62. Ibid, 56.
63. Maarten Gehem, Philipp Marten, Matthijs Maas, and Menno Schellekens, *Balancing on the Brink: Vulnerability of States in the Middle East and North Africa* (The Hague Centre for Strategic Studies, 2014), 12.
64. Ian Bremmer, *The J Curve: A New Way to Understand Why Nations Rise and Fall* (New York, NY: Simon & Schuster, 2006), 5.
65. Jack A. Goldstone, Robert H. Bates, David L. Epstein, Ted Robert Gurr, Michael B. Lustik, Monty G. Marshall, Jay Ulfelder, and Mark Woodward, "A Global Model for Forecasting Political Instability," *American Journal of Political Science* 54 (2010): 197.
66. Benjamin E. Goldsmith, Charles R. Butcher, Dimitri Semenovich, and Arcot Sowmya, "Forecasting the Onset of Genocide and Politicide: Annual Out-of-Sample Forecasts on a Global Dataset, 1988–2003," *Journal of Peace Research* 50 (2013): 437–452.
67. See http://www.systemicpeace.org/polity/polity4.htm, accessed February 23, 2015.
68. Harff, "No Lessons Learned," 63.
69. United Nations, "Framework of Analysis," 15.
70. See Fund for Peace, "CAST: Conflict Assessment Framework," 14.
71. World Bank, "Worldwide Governance Indicators."
72. See the Organisation for Economic Co-operation and Development's "Foreign Bribery Report" of 2014, accessed January 26, 2015 at http://www.oecd.org/corruption/launch-foreign-bribery-report.htm/.
73. See http://www.transparency.org, accessed January 17, 2015.
74. I. William Zartman, *Preventing Identity Conflicts Leading to Genocide and Mass Killings* (New York, NY: International Peace Institute, 2010), 12.
75. See http://www.monitor.co.ug/News/National/Museveni-unfit-to-stand-in-2016---UYD/-/688334/2457248/-/2qd60j/-/index.html, accessed January 17, 2015.
76. Marshall and Cole, *Global Report 2014*, 21.
77. "Burundi: Deadly Protests Erupt After President Seeks Third Term" (April 26, 2015), accessed April 27, 2015 at http://www.redpepper.co.ug/burundi-deadly-protests-erupt-after-president-seeks-third-term/.
78. Kwesi Aning and Frank Okyere, "Responsibility to Prevent in Africa: Leveraging Institutional Capacity to Mitigate Atrocity Risk," *Policy Analysis Brief* (The Stanley Foundation, January 2015): 3.
79. See Fund for Peace, "CAST: Conflict Assessment Framework," 12.

80. See http://www.transparency.org/whoweare/organisation/faqs_on_corruption/9/#costsOfCorruption, accessed January 17, 2015.
81. African Development Bank Group, "Drivers and Dynamics of Fragility in Africa," *Africa Economic Brief* 4 (2013): 3.
82. United Nations Security Council, Document S/2004/616 (August 23, 2004), 4.
83. European Commission, "Checklist for Root Causes of Conflict."
84. United Nations, "Framework of Analysis," 12.
85. Marshall and Cole, *Global Report 2014*, 5.
86. Ibid.
87. Ibid.
88. Harff, "No Lessons Learned from the Holocaust?," 67.
89. See http://www.gpanet.org/content/risks-new-onsets-genocide-and-politicide-2013#_edn2, accessed January 22, 2015.
90. Goldstone et al., "A Global Model," 198.
91. Marshall and Cole, *Global Report 2014*, 6.
92. United Nations, "Framework of Analysis," 13.
93. Fund for Peace, "CAST: Conflict Assessment Framework," 15.
94. Ed Vulliamy, *The War is Dead, Long Live the War* (London, England: Vintage Books, 2012), xxvi.
95. Linda Melvern, *Conspiracy to Murder: The Rwanda Genocide* (London, England: Verso, 2006), 210.
96. Mark Lattimer, *State of the World's Minorities 2006* (Minority Rights Group International, December 2005), 9.
97. These indicators are taken from Fund for Peace, "CAST: Conflict Assessment Framework," 15. The Minority Rights Group International's annual "Peoples under Threat" reports also include the rise of factionalized elites as one of its 10 risk indicators.
98. Goldstone et al., "A Global Model," 196.
99. See Jacob Blaustein Institute for the Advancement of Human Rights, *Compilation of Risk Factors and Legal Norms for the Prevention of Genocide.*
100. Charles R. Butcher, Benjamin E. Goldsmith, Dimitri Semenovich, and Arcot Sowmya, "Understanding and Forecasting Political Instability and Genocide for Early Warning" (2012): 20. Accessed January 22, 2015 at http://sydney.edu.au/arts/research/atrocity_forecasting/publications.
101. Harff, "Detection: The History and Politics of Early Warning," 96.
102. Goldstone et al., "A Global Model," 197.
103. United Nations, "Framework of Analysis," 16.
104. Stanton, "Ten Stages of Genocide."
105. Rost, "Will It Happen Again?," 57.
106. Butcher et al., "Understanding and Forecasting Political Instability," 20.
107. Quoted material taken from the Institute for Economics & Peace, "Structures of Peace: Identifying What Leads to Peaceful Societies" (2011): 9.
108. David J. Simon, "Building State Capacity to Prevent Atrocity Crimes: Implementing Pillars One and Two of the R2P Framework," *Policy Analysis Brief* (The Stanley Foundation, September 2012): 3.
109. Scott Straus, "Retreating from the Brink: Theorizing Mass Violence and the Dynamics of Restraint," *Perspectives on Politics* 10 (2012): 343–362.
110. OECD, *Supporting Statebuilding in Situations of Conflict and Fragility: Policy Guidance* (OECD Publishing, 2011), 37.
111. Ibid, 37–38.

112. Jonas Claes, "Atrocity Prevention at the State Level," *Peace Brief* 144 (2013): 2.

113. Cited in Adam Jones, *Genocide: A Comprehensive Introduction*, 2nd ed. (New York, NY: Routledge, 2011), 570.

114. Accessed February 8, 2015 at http://www.ushmm.org/confront-genocide/ speakers-and-events/all-speakers-and-events/can-atrocities-be-prevented/ un-high-commissioner-for-human-rights-address.

115. Jonathan Safran Foer, *Everything is Illuminated* (New York, NY: Harper Perennial, 2002), 198.

116. Ervin Staub, "The Psychology of bystanders, Perpetrators, and Heroic Helpers," eds. Leonard S. Newman and Ralph Erber, *Understanding Genocide: The Social Psychology of the Holocaust* (New York, NY: Oxford University Press, 2002), 30.

117. Ibid.

118. See, for instance, the Heidelberg Institute for International Conflict Research's "Conflict Barometer 2013," accessed January 25, 2015 at http://www.hiik.de/en/ konfliktbarometer/.

119. Andrew Rice, *The Teeth May Smile but the Heart Does Not Forget: Murder and Memory in Uganda* (New York, NY: Picador, 2009), 8.

120. Scott Straus, *The Order of Genocide: Race, Power, and War in Rwanda* (Ithaca, NY: Cornell University Press, 2006), 20.

121. Ibid, 190.

122. Harff, "No Lessons Learned from the Holocaust?," 66.

123. Butcher et al., "Understanding and Forecasting Political Instability," 15.

124. Rost, "Forecasting the Risk of Genocide," 50.

125. Ibid.

126. Helen Fein, "Accounting for Genocide after 1945: Theories and Some Findings," *International Journal on Minority and Group Rights* 1 (1993): 79–106.

127. Alex de Waal and Gregory H. Stanton, "Should President Omar al-Bashir of Sudan Be Charged and Arrested by the International Criminal Court? An Exchange of Views," *Genocide Studies and Prevention* 4 (2009), quote found on pp. 334 and 339.

128. Chad Hazlett, "New Lessons Learned? Improving Genocide and Politicide Forecasting" (2011), accessed February 1, 2015 at http://www.ushmm.org/m/ pdfs/20111102-hazlett-early-_warning-lessons-learned.pdf.

129. Harff, "Risks of New Onsets of Genocide and Politicide in 2013," accessed February 1, 2015 at http://www.gpanet.org/content/risks-new-onsets-genocide-and-politicide-2013. Preliminary review of her 2015 assessment suggests that the risk factor of past genocides has a substantial *inhibiting* effect that, however, wears off over time. After 40 years it becomes a positive risk factor.

130. Goldstone et al., "A Global Model," 207.

131. Nassim Nicholas Taleb and Gregory F. Treverton, "The Calm Before the Storm," *Foreign Affairs* (January/February 2015), accessed February 1, 2015 at http:// www.foreignaffairs.com/articles/142494/nassim-nicholas-taleb-and-gregory-f-treverton/the-calm-before-the-storm.

132. Jens Meierhenrich, "The Trauma of Genocide," *Journal of Genocide Research* 9 (2007): 549–573.

133. See American Psychiatric Association, *Diagnostic and Statistical Manual of Mental Disorders*, 5th ed. (Washington, DC: American Psychiatric Publishing, 2013), 271–272.

134. Summaries of the group's research can be found at https://traumaandhealing. stanford.edu, accessed February 5, 2015.

135. American Psychiatric Association, *Diagnostic and Statistical Manual of Mental Disorders*, 5th ed., 275.
136. Susan J. Brison, *Aftermath: Violence and the Remaking of a Self* (Princeton, NJ: Princeton University Press, 2002), 40.
137. American Psychiatric Association, *Diagnostic and Statistical Manual of Mental Disorders*, 5th ed., 276.
138. Roger Dobson, "Post-Traumatic Stress Disorder Common Among Child Survivors of Rwandan Genocide," *British Medical Journal* 338 (2009): 564.
139. Heide Rieder and Thomas Elbert, "Rwanda—Lasting Imprints of a Genocide: Trauma, Mental Health and Psychosocial Conditions in Survivors, Former Prisoners and Their Children," *Conflict and Health* 7 (2013).
140. See, for instance, Nigel P. Field, Sophear Muong, and Vannavuth Sochanvimean, "Parental Styles in the Intergenerational Transmission of Trauma Stemming from the Khmer Rouge Regime in Cambodia," *American Journal of Orthopsychiatry* 83 (2013): 483–494.
141. Judith Shulevitz, "The Science of Suffering" (November 16, 2014), accessed February 7, 2015 at http://www.newrepublic.com/article/120144/trauma-genetic-scientists-say-parents-are-passing-ptsd-kids.
142. Neil J. Smelser, "Psychological Trauma and Cultural Trauma," eds. Jeffrey C. Alexander, Ron Eyerman, Bernhard Giesen, Neil J. Smelser, and Pitor Sztompka, *Cultural Trauma and Collective Identity* (Berkeley, CA: University of California Press, 2004), 41.
143. Meierhenrich, "The Trauma of Genocide," 554.
144. Jeffrey C. Alexander, "Toward a Theory of Cultural Trauma," in Alexander et al., *Cultural Trauma and Collective Identity*, 1.
145. Ibid, 8, 10.
146. Smelser, "Psychological Trauma and Cultural Trauma," 37.
147. Alexander, "Toward a Theory of Cultural Trauma," 8.
148. United Nations, "Framework of Analysis," 13.
149. Ervin Staub, *Overcoming Evil: Genocide, Violent Conflict, and Terrorism* (New York, NY: Oxford University Press, 2011), 218–219.
150. Arthur G. Neal, *National Trauma & Collective Memory: Major Events in the American Century* (Armonk, NY: M. E. Sharpe, 1998), 31.
151. See Minority Rights Group International, "Peoples under Threat 2014."
152. See Michael A. Sells, *The Bridge Betrayed: Religion and Genocide in Bosnia* (Berkeley, CA: University of California Press, 1998).
153. Fund for Peace, "CAST: Conflict Assessment Framework," 7.
154. Jonathan Tonge, *Northern Ireland: Conflict and Change*, 2nd ed. (London, England: Prentice Hall, 1998), 92.
155. Henry McDonald, "Orange Order March in Belfast Begins Peacefully," accessed February 8, 2015 at http://www.theguardian.com/uk-news/2014/jul/12/orange-order-march-belfast-northern-ireland.
156. 440 different translations of the UDHR can be found at http://www.ohchr.org/EN/UDHR/Pages/Introduction.aspx, accessed February 8, 2015.
157. See International Committee of the Red Cross, "International Humanitarian Law and International Human Rights Law: Similarities and Differences" (January, 2003).
158. David Sobek, M. Rodwan Abouharb, and Christopher G. Ingram, "The Human Rights Peace: How the Respect for Human Rights at Home Leads to Peace Abroad," *The Journal of Politics* 68, (2006): 519–529.

159. The World Bank, *World Development Report 2011: Conflict, Security, and Development* (Washington, DC: The World Bank, 2011), 82.
160. United Nations, "Framework of Analysis," 11.
161. See https://www.un.org/apps/news/story.asp?NewsID=46778&Cr=human+ri ghts&Cr1=, accessed March 1, 2015.
162. Rost, "Will it Happen Again?," 57.
163. Taleb and Treverton, "The Calm Before the Storm."
164. Alexander, "Toward a Theory of Cultural Trauma," 27.
165. Florence Baingana, Ian Bannon, and Rachel Thomas, *Mental Health and Conflict: Conceptual Framework and Approaches* (Washington, DC: World Bank, 2005), 10.
166. Meierhenrich, "The Trauma of Genocide," 563.
167. See USAID, "Women & Conflict," accessed February 13, 2015 at http://pdf. usaid.gov/pdf_docs/pnadj133.pdf.
168. United Nations, "Framework of Analysis," 11.
169. International Committee of the Red Cross, "International Humanitarian Law and International Human Rights Law: Similarities and Differences" (January, 2003).
170. Goldstone et al, "A Global Model for Forecasting Political Instability," 205.
171. African Development Bank Group, "Drivers and Dynamics," 4.
172. Tor Georg Jakobsen, Indra De Soysa, and Jo Jakobsen, "Why Do Poor Countries Suffer Costly Conflict? Unpacking Per Capita Income and the Onset of Civil War," *Conflict Management and Peace Science* 30 (2013): 140–160.
173. Charles H. Anderton and John R. Carter, "On Risk Factors for Genocide: A Theoretical and Empirical Inquiry," unpublished paper (2011), 10.
174. Straus, *The Order of Genocide*, 127.
175. Rost, "Forecasting the Risk of Genocide," 50.
176. Anderton, "A Research Agenda for the Economic Study of Genocide," 123.
177. Gerald W. Scully, "Democide and Genocide as Rent-Seeking Activities," *Public Choice* 93 (1997): 81.
178. Ibid, 82.
179. Quoted material taken from Ted Robert Gurr, *Peoples versus States: Minorities at Risk in the New Century* (Washington, DC: United States Institute of Peace, 2000), 109, 111; Anderton, "A Research Agenda for the Economic Study of Genocide," 124.
180. Fund for Peace, "CAST: Conflict Assessment Framework Manual," 9.
181. Henk-Jan Brinkman, Larry Attree, and Sasa Hezir, "Addressing Horizontal Inequalities as Drivers of Conflict in the Post-2015 Development Agenda" (2013): 10–11.
182. Jonas Claes, "Atrocity Prevention at the State Level," *Peace Brief* 144 (Washington, DC: United States Institute of Peace, 2013), 3.
183. See, for instance, Gudrun Ostby, "Inequalities, the Political Environment and Civil Conflict: Evidence from 55 Developing Countries," ed. Frances Stewart, *Horizontal Inequalities and Conflict: Understanding Group Violence in Multiethnic Societies* (Basingstoke, England: Palgrave Macmillan, 2008).
184. Rost, "Forecasting the Risk of Genocide," 57.
185. Anderton and Carter, "On Risk Factors for Genocide."
186. Marie L. Besancon, "Relative Resources: Inequality in Ethnic Wars, Revolutions, and Genocides," *Journal of Peace Research* 42 (2005): 393–415.

187. Definitions and list of factors taken from http://www.investopedia.com/terms/m/macroeconomics.asp, accessed February 15, 2015.
188. Taleb and Treverton, "The Calm Before the Storm."
189. Ibid.
190. See The Hague Centre for Strategic Studies, Strategic Monitor 2014: Four Strategic Challenges, accessed February 15, 2015 at http://www.hcss.nl/reports/strategic-monitor-2014-four-strategic-challenges/144/.
191. Barbara Harff, "Assessing Risks of Genocide and Politicide: A Global Watch List for 2012," accessed February 15, 2015 at http://www.gpanet.org/webfm_send/120.
192. Harff, "Risks of New Onsets of Genocide and Politicide in 2013."
193. Rost, "Forecasting the Risk of Genocide," 67.
194. Anderton, "A Research Agenda for the Economic Study of Genocide," 125.
195. Fund for Peace, "CAST: Conflict Assessment Framework," 10.
196. Allister Heath, "Russia's Economic Crisis Could Easily End in Yet Another Sovereign Default," accessed February 15, 2015 at http://www.telegraph.co.uk/finance/economics/11297915/Russias-economic-crisis-could-easily-end-in-yet-another-sovereign-default.html.
197. Jones, *Genocide* (2nd ed.), 569.
198. Staub, *Overcoming Evil*, 116.
199. Atanas Gotchev, "The Bulgarian Early Warning System: Implementation, Outcomes and Significance for Policy-Making," in *Thinking the Unthinkable: From Thought to Policy* (Bratislava, Slovakia: United Nations Development Programme, 2003), 191.
200. Taleb and Treverton, "The Calm Before the Storm."
201. Robert Neuwirth, *Stealth of Nations: The Global Rise of the Informal Economy* (New York, NY: Anchor, 2012).
202. Quote taken from http://freakonomics.com/2011/11/01/the-black-market-is-the-second-largest-economy-in-the-world/, accessed February 15, 2015.
203. James Putzel, "Regional and Global Drivers of Conflict: Consequences for Fragile States and Regions," paper presented at the World Bank Headline Seminar on the Regional and Global Dimensions of Conflict and Peace Building, Addis Ababa (October 2009).
204. Claes, "Atrocity Prevention at the State Level," 3.
205. Council on Foreign Relations, "A Strategy to Reduce Gun Trafficking and Violence in the Americas," accessed February 15, 2015 at http://www.cfr.org/arms-industries-and-trade/strategy-reduce-gun-trafficking-violence-americas/p31155.
206. R. T. Naylor, "The Rise of the Modern Arms Black Market and the Fall of Supply-Side Control," ed. Virginia Gamba, *Society Under Siege: Crime, Violence and Illegal Weapons* (Pretoria, South Africa: Institute for Security Studies, 1997), 46–47.
207. Namsuk Kim and Pedro Conceicao, "The Economic Crisis, Violent Conflict, and Human Development," *International Journal of Peace Studies* 15 (2010): 29–43.
208. Claes, "Atrocity Prevention at the State Level," 3.
209. Simon, "Building State Capacity to Prevent Atrocity Crimes," 4.
210. Bellamy, "Mass Atrocities and Armed Conflict," 6.
211. International Commission on Intervention and State Sovereignty, *The Responsibility to Protect* (Ottawa, Canada: International Development Research Centre, 2001), 22.
212. African Development Bank Group, "Drivers and Dynamics," 10.

213. Eric Sean Williams, "The End of Society? Defining and Tracing the Development of Fragmentation through the Modern and into the Post-Modern Era" (2010): 47. Accessed February 20, 2015 at http://aladinrc.wrlc.org/bitstream/handle/1961/9237/Williams_cua_0043A_10094display.pdf?sequence=1.

214. World Bank, "Social Fragmentation," 175, accessed February 20, 2015 at http://siteresources.worldbank.org/INTPOVERTY/Resources/335642-1124115102975/1555199-1124115187705/ch6.pdf/.

215. Rhiannon Neilsen, "Toxification as a More Indicative Early Warning Sign for Genocide," paper presented at the biennial meeting of the International Association of Genocide Scholars (Winnipeg, Canada), July 19, 2014.

216. Stanton, "Ten Stages of Genocide."

217. Council of Europe, Recommendation No. R (97) 20 (October 1997), 107.

218. Jones, *Genocide* (2nd ed.), 570.

219. Accessed February 20, 2015 at http://www.usip.org/publications/2015/02/18/wielding-technology-combat-dangerous-speech-in-myanmar.

220. Tin Aung Kyaw, "Buddhist Monk Wirathu Leads Violent National Campaign against Myanmar's Muslims," accessed February 20, 2015 at http://www.globalpost.com/dispatches/globalpost-blogs/groundtruth-burma/buddhist-monk-wirathu-969-muslims-myanmar.

221. Accessed February 20, 2015 at http://www.bbc.com/news/world-asia-30928744.

222. Kenan Malik, "The Failure of Multiculturalism: Community Versus Society in Europe," Foreign Affairs (March/April 2015), accessed April 22, 2015 at http://www.foreignaffairs.com/articles/143048/kenan-malik/the-failure-of-multiculturalism?cid=nlc-foreign_affairs_this_week-022615-the_failure_of_multiculturalis_5-022615&sp_mid=48114338&sp_rid=andhbGxlckBrZWVuZS5lZHUS1.

223. Paul Collier, V. L. Elliott, Haard Hegre, Anke Hoeffler, Marta Reynal-Querol, and Nicholas Sambanis, *Breaking the Conflict Trap: Civil War and Development Policy* (Washington, DC: The World Bank, 2003), 57.

224. UN "Framework of Analysis for Atrocity Crimes," 18.

225. Collier et al., *Breaking the Conflict Trap*, 58.

226. Seth Kaplan, "Identity in Fragile States: Social Cohesion and State Building," *Development* 52 (2009): 469.

227. Ibid, 467.

228. Examples in this paragraph, as well as quoted material, come from Fund for Peace, "CAST: Conflict Assessment Framework Manual," 5.

229. Justin Yifu Lin, "Youth Bulge: A Demographic Dividend or a Demographic Bomb in Developing Countries?" (January 5, 2012), accessed February 20, 2015 at http://blogs.worldbank.org/developmenttalk/youth-bulge-a-demographic-dividend-or-a-demographic-bomb-in-developing-countries.

230. Katherine Carter, "Is Youth Bulge a 'Magic Indicator' for the Failed States Index?" (2013), accessed February 20, 2015 at http://www.newsecuritybeat.org/2013/10/youth-bulge-magic-indicator-failed-states-index/.

231. Richard P. Cincotta and Elizabeth Leahy, "Population Age Structure and Its Relation to Civil Conflict: A Graphic Metric," *Environmental Change and Security Program* 12 (2006–2007): 55–58.

232. Henrik Urdal, "A Clash of Generations? Youth Bulges and Political Violence," Expert Paper No. 2102/1 (New York, NY: United Nations, 2012), 7.

233. Demographic projection taken from Carter, "Is Youth Bulge a 'Magic Indicator' for the Failed States Index?"

234. Minority Rights Group International, "Peoples under Threat."
235. Accessed February 20, 2015 at http://www.internal-displacement.org/middle-east-and-north-africa/syria/ and http://data.unhcr.org/syrianrefugees/regional.php.
236. Edward N. Luttwak, "Give War a Chance," *Foreign Affairs* (July/August 1999): 43.
237. Kofi Annan, "Peace and Development—One Struggle, Two Fronts" (October 19, 1999), accessed February 21, 2015 at http://reliefweb.int/report/afghanistan/united-nations-secretary-general-kofi-annan-address-world-bank-staff-peace-.
238. OECD, *Supporting Statebuilding in Situations of Conflict and Fragility: Policy Guidance* (DAC Guidelines and Reference Series, 2011), 34.
239. Ibid.
240. Harff, "No Lessons Learned from the Holocaust?," 64.
241. Butcher et al., "Understanding and Forecasting Political Instability and Genocide," 6. Also see J. Joseph Hewitt, Jonathan Wilkenfeld, Ted Robert Gurr, and Birger Heldt (eds.), *Peace and Conflict 2012* (College Park, MD: Center for International Development and Conflict Management, 2012).
242. Goldstone et al., "A Global Model for Forecasting Political Instability," 197.
243. Luca Mancini, "Horizontal Inequality and Communal Violence: Evidence from Indonesian Districts," CRISE Working Paper No. 22 (November 2005).
244. Ibid, 25.
245. Ibid, 30.
246. Quoted material from Gudrun Ostby, "Polarization, Horizontal Inequalities and Violent Civil Conflict," *Journal of Peace Research* 45 (2008): 155.
247. See Urdal, "A Clash of Generations?"
248. Forum for Civic Initiatives and Saferworld, "Kosovo at the Crossroads: Perceptions of Conflict, Access to Justice and Opportunities for Peace in Kosovo" (December 2007), iii. Accessed February 21, 2015 at http://saferworld.org.uk/resources/view-resource/296-kosovo-at-the-crossroads.
249. Oxfam, "Governance and Fragility" (2013), accessed February 21, 2015 at http://policy-practice.oxfam.org.uk/publications/governance-and-fragility-what-we-know-about-effective-governance-programming-in-306683.
250. Saferworld, "Common Ground? Gendered Assessment of the Needs and Concerns of Maoist Army Combatants for Rehabilitation and Integration" (November 2010), accessed February 22, 2015 at http://www.saferworld.org.uk/resources/view-resource/502-common-ground.
251. Mary Caprioli, "Gendered Conflict," *Journal of Peace Research* 37 (2000): 51–68.
252. Erik Melander, "Gender Inequality and Intrastate Armed Conflict," *International Studies Quarterly* 49 (2005): 695–714.
253. OECD, "Armed Violence Reduction: Enabling Development" (2009), 33. Accessed February 21, 2015 at http://www.poa-iss.org/kit/2009_OECD-DAC_Guidlines.pdf.
254. Institute for Economics and Peace, "Structures of Peace" (2011), accessed February 21, 2015 at http://economicsandpeace.org/wp-content/uploads/2011/09/Structures-of-Peace.pdf.
255. Valerie M. Hudson, Bonnie Ballif-Spanvill, Mary Caprioli, and Chad F. Emmett, *Sex & World Peace* (New York, NY: Columbia University Press, 2012).
256. Daniel Kaufmann, "Challenges in the Next Stage of Corruption," in *New Perspectives in Combating Corruption* (Washington, DC: Transparency International and World Bank, 1998).

257. M. Steven Fish, "Islam and Authoritarianism," *World Politics* 55 (2002): 37.
258. See Valerie M. Hudson, Mary Caprioli Bonnie Ballif-Spanvill, Rose McDermott, and Chad F. Emmett, "The Heart of the Matter: The Security of Women and the Security of States," *International Security* 33 (2008/2009): 27.
259. Henk-Jan Brinkman, Larry Attree, and Sasa Hezir, "Addressing Horizontal Inequalities as Drivers of Conflict in the Post-2015 Development Agenda" (2013): 13. Accessed February 22, 2015 at http://www.saferworld.org.uk/ resources/view-resource/725-addressing-horizontal-inequalities-as-drivers-of-conflict-in-the-post-2015-development-agenda.
260. Lori L. Heise, "What Works to Prevent Partner Violence: An Evidence Overview" (September 2012), Expert Paper prepared for UN Women, accessed February 22, 2015 at http://www.saferworld.org.uk/resources/view-resource/ 725-addressing-horizontal-inequalities-as-drivers-of-conflict-in-the-post-2015-development-agenda. http://www.unwomen.org/~/media/headquar-ters/attachments/sections/csw/57/egm/egm-paper-lori-heisse%20pdf.pdf.
261. Hudson et al., "The Heart of the Matter," 41.
262. Brinkman et al., 14.
263. See Matthew Krain, "State-Sponsored Mass Murder: The Onset and Severity of Genocides and Politicides," *The Journal of Conflict Resolution* 41 (1997): 331–360.
264. Goldsmith et al., "Forecasting the Onset of Genocide and Politicide," 439.
265. Harff, "Assessing Risks of Genocide and Politicide: A Global Watch List for 2012."
266. UN, "Framework of Analysis for Atrocity Crimes," 10.
267. Goldsmith et al., "Forecasting the Onset of Genocide and Politicide."
268. Rost, "Will It Happen Again?," 49.
269. UN, "Framework of Analysis for Atrocity Crimes," 10.
270. "European Commission Check-list for Root Causes of Conflict," accessed February 24, 2015 at http://www.eplo.org/assets/files/3.%20Resources/ EU%20Documents/European_Commission_European_Commission_ Checklist_Root_Causes_of_Conflict.pdf.
271. Goldstone et al., "A Global Model for Forecasting Political Instability," 197. As they point out, of the 160 countries with populations greater than 500,000 in 2003 nearly half (77) had four or more bordering countries.
272. Goldsmith et al., "Forecasting the Onset of Genocide and Politicide," 440.
273. African Development Bank Group, "Drivers and Dynamics of Fragility in Africa," 5.
274. Butcher et al., "Understanding and Forecasting Political Instability and Genocide for Early Warning."
275. Michael Colaresi and Sabine C. Carey, "To Kill or to Protect: Security Forces, Domestic Institutions, and Genocide," *The Journal of Conflict Resolution* 52 (2008): 39–67.
276. African Development Bank Group, "Drivers and Dynamics of Fragility in Africa," 5.
277. UN, "Framework of Analysis for Atrocity Crimes," 16.
278. Elisabeth King, Cyrus Samii, and Birte Snilstveit, "Interventions to Promote Social Cohesion in Sub-Saharan Africa," *Journal of Development Effectiveness* 2 (2010): 337.
279. Kaplan, "Identity in Fragile States," 466.

280. Accessed October 2, 2014 at https://www.opendemocracy.net/arab-awakening/ahmed-e-souaiaia/ending-religious-and-ethnic-states-will-help-prevent-genocidal-impul.
281. Pauline H. Baker, "Getting Along: Managing Diversity for Atrocity Prevention in Socially Divided Societies," *Policy Analysis Brief* (Stanley Foundation, September 2012).
282. Staub, *Overcoming Evil*, 330, 341.
283. See http://www.sisiniamani.org, accessed February 28, 2015. For additional examples, see U.S. Agency for International Development, *Preventing Atrocities: Five Key Primers* (2014), accessed February 28, 2015 at https://freedomhouse.org/report/special-reports/preventing-atrocities-five-key-primers#.VPHZFZOo6os.
284. See U.S. Agency for International Development, *Youth & Conflict: A Toolkit for Intervention* (2005), accessed February 28, 2015 at http://pdf.usaid.gov/pdf_docs/pnadb336.pdf.
285. Urdal, "A Clash of Generations?"
286. Fund for Peace, "CAST: Conflict Assessment Framework Manual," 6.
287. See Mac McClelland, "How to Build a Perfect Refugee Camp," *The New York Times Magazine* (February 13, 2014).
288. See http://www.pbsbdialogue.org/, accessed February 28, 2015.
289. UN S/Res/1325 (October 31, 2000).
290. Accessed February 28, 2015 at http://www.un.org/press/en/2006/sgsm10370.doc.htm.
291. Accessed February 28, 2015 at http://www.theguardian.com/global-development/2014/apr/07/rwanda-women-empowered-impoverished.
292. Accessed February 28, 2015 at http://policy-practice.oxfam.org.uk/blog/2014/03/gender-inequality-as-a-driver-of-conflict.
293. Aning and Okyere, "Responsibility to Prevent in Africa," 6.
294. Charles R. Butcher, Benjamin E. Goldsmith, Dimitri Semenovic, and Arcot Sowmya, "Political Instability and Genocide in the Asia-Pacific: Risks and Forecasts" (2012), 14. Accessed December 22, 2014 at http://sydney.edu.au/arts/research/atrocity_forecasting/publications.
295. Aning and Okyere, "Responsibility to Prevent in Africa," 1.
296. Note from training of Tanzania National Committee for the Prevention of Genocide (March 19–21, 2014).

CHAPTER 5

Midstream Prevention Strategies

"Sometimes We Must Interfere"

For the first half of the twentieth-century, Sudan—Africa's largest country—existed under joint British–Egyptian administration. The colonial powers ruled an Arab Muslim North and an African Christian and animist South as though they were two distinct entities, with the North receiving substantially more support for technological, economic, and political development. Even hiring policies reflected the bias: "The colonial administration in Khartoum was filled with Oxford and Cambridge graduates, while a less refined corps of military men, widely mocked as the 'bog barons,' was dispatched to the south."[1] Over time, a strong sense of Arab-Muslim nationalism grew in the relatively well-developed Northern region, while the unequal distribution of power and wealth left a cascading sense of neglect and alienation among the Southern region's remote, marginalized, and less-developed indigenous tribes. When independence finally came for Sudan in 1956, these identity-based religious, ethnic, economic, and regional divisions were well entrenched. Unresolved tensions between the Khartoum government in the North and tribal leaders in the South (many of whom would splinter multiple times into competing rebel groups) would lead to two rounds of protracted and brutal civil wars, the first from 1962 to 1972 and the second from 1983 to 2005, costing the lives of over 2 million civilians and causing massive internal displacement of millions more.[2]

Finally, in 2005, a North/South Comprehensive Peace Agreement brought an end to the second civil war, along with the promise of a south Sudanese referendum on independence in 6 years. Although the peace was fragile and sporadic fighting continued to destabilize the region, leaders eventually reached a deal on terms for the proposed referendum of independence for the South. On January 9, 2011, nearly 99% of ballots cast by some 3.6 million South Sudanese voted for full independence from Sudan. Six months later, on July 9, 2011, the international community celebrated the Republic of South Sudan's arrival as the world's newest sovereign nation. As foreign policy expert Ty McCormick pointed out, "the new nation faced long odds. At independence, it had virtually no civil institutions, about 120 doctors for a population of roughly 9 million, and a total of 35 miles of paved roads spanning a territory the size of France. It was also landlocked, ethnically diverse, and entirely dependent on oil revenue. In other words, it faced every major challenge identified by social scientists as a predictor of state failure."[3] Although billions of dollars in development aid from international donors helped address some of those challenges, the seemingly insurmountable issue has, yet again, been one based in identity.

South Sudan, whose capital is in Juba, is a multiethnic society with more than 60 different ethnic communities. Political leaders—many of whom are former rebels who fought against one another—have politicized ethnicity, using ethnic patronage to build their power bases. In July 2013, sensing the ambition of strong political rivals, President Salva Kiir, an ethnic Dinka (the largest ethnic group in South Sudan), dismissed his entire cabinet, including the vice president, Dr. Riek Machar, an ethnic Neur (the second largest ethnic group in South Sudan). On the night of December 15, 2013, this tribal-infused political power struggle erupted into widespread ethnic fighting between an army faction loyal to embattled President Kiir and rebels loyal to former vice president Machar. Ethnic differences in South Sudan quickly became "the vehicle of mobilization and the source of massacres, human rights violations and hatred."[4] Navi Pillay, the former UN high commissioner for human rights, observed: "There is palpable fear among civilians of both Dinka and Neur backgrounds that they will be killed on the basis of their ethnicity."[5] Similarly, Daniel Bekele, Africa director at Human Rights Watch, concluded: "Appalling crimes have been committed [by both government and rebel forces] against civilians for no other reason than their ethnicity."[6]

At present, tens of thousand of people are estimated to have been killed in interethnic Dinka–Neur fighting throughout the country, with accounts of ethnically motivated atrocities, including widespread sexual violence, by both sides. Although the UN Security Council has issued a statement of "strong condemnation," it has stopped short of implementing sanctions to prohibit the warring factions from buying more weapons, arguing that such sanctions might unfairly tip the balance in favor of the rebel forces. In early 2016, however, the Security Council did suggest that rival leaders Kiir and Machar should have their financial assets frozen and be barred from traveling outside the country.[7] To date, nearly 2 million South Sudanese civilians have been driven from their homes, with about 500,000 of those fleeing to neighboring countries. With farmers missing their planting seasons, the threat of famine looms and an estimated 7 million people are at risk of hunger and disease, with more than 2 million of those regarded as "food-insecure"—not far from famine status.[8] Widespread and systematic looting of humanitarian warehouses only adds to the deprivations. At least eight ceasefire or peace agreements have broken down (most within hours), with recent talks in Addis Ababa, Ethiopia stalling in early March 2015. With both sides blaming each other for the failure to arrive at a settlement, female peace activists in South Sudan have desperately suggested that all women "deny their husbands conjugal rights until they ensure that peace returns."[9] In the bleak words of John Khamis, a 38-year-old man who has spent much of his nation's existence sheltered in a camp on a United Nations (UN) base: "There is no more country. I don't know how the fighting stops now."[10]

The crisis in South Sudan is not a hypothetical case study nor is it a bygone event shrouded in the mists of history. It is a real-time tragedy of suffering in a country birthed by war but nurtured in a spirit of considerable international hope and optimism that a stable nation could be built in this fragmented region. I have worked directly as a trainer with several members of South Sudan's Human Rights Commission as well as its fledgling National Committee for the Prevention of Genocide, War Crimes, Crimes Against Humanity and all Forms of Discrimination. I have seen firsthand the commitment of South Sudanese academics, lawyers, policymakers, and civil society members to transforming the aspirational dream of a new nation into the hardscrabble on-the-ground reality of building institutions and structures that allow for the realization of that dream. So, it is particularly painful to see that work, and that hope and optimism, dashed by those intent on division and identity politics. As a result, the region and the world must now turn its attention from the building of a nation to the protection of one—developing preventive strategies to slow, limit, or stop the continuation or escalation of violence against civilians in South Sudan.

In 1986, during his acceptance speech for the Nobel Prize for Peace, noted Holocaust survivor Elie Wiesel said: "Sometimes we must interfere. When human lives are endangered, when human dignity is in jeopardy, national borders and sensitivities become irrelevant. Whenever men or women are persecuted because of their race, religion, or political views, that place must—at that moment—become the center of the universe."[11] At present, South Sudan is just one of several places that must—at this moment—become the center of the universe in which we must interfere to stop civilians from being done to death.

To return to the river analogy introduced in Chapter 3—and that forms the scaffolding of Chapters 4, 5, and 6—the preventive strategies most relevant for the ongoing violence in South Sudan are secondary midstream responses. The primary upstream preventive strategies—the longer-term processes of building underlying structures of societal and state durability related to good governance, fair interpretation and transmission of conflict history, resilient economic conditions, and inclusive social cohesion—have seemingly failed, or, at the very least, have not been given time to take seed in a country planted less than 5 years ago. As a result, South Sudan has fallen into the river of crisis and is in imminent need of rescue before it is swept further downstream into genocide. Our midstream preventive strategies are immediate, real-time direct crisis management tactics to slow, limit, or stop the mass violence.

The current crisis in South Sudan raises many prevention questions that form the framework of this chapter. First, what are the factors that accelerate and trigger an at-risk country's descent into crisis? Second, why does substantial early warning, based on extensive risk assessment and an awareness of the relevant accelerators and triggers, so seldom translate into an equally substantial early response? Finally, what are the political, economic, legal, and military response tools at our disposal for midstream preventive strategies?

ACCELERANTS AND TRIGGERS

As Nicolas Rost points out: "Genocide is an extremely rare event and predicting or assessing the risk of rare events is difficult."[12] That said, the forecasting models we surveyed in Chapter 4 do a very solid job of assessing the risk of onset for violent or genocidal conflict, with most having predictive accuracy rates in the range of 80–90%. So, although there is still much work to be done on refining the core tools of risk assessment models, we have a good handle on the crucial quantitative and qualitative information we need to do a global scan and generate ongoing "watch lists" of at-risk countries. Identifying the contextual preconditions that leave a state vulnerable to violent, even genocidal, conflict should then focus the international community's attention on situation monitoring for the most pressing cases of concern.

To return to an analogy used in the preface to this book, risk assessment helps us identify countries in which the "wood is stacked" for risk of violent or genocidal conflict. To understand, though, the "matches" that may be struck to set that wood afire requires an analysis of accelerating factors that lead to a rapid escalation of crisis and the triggering factors that spark the onset of conflict itself. Accelerants and triggers help us understand the transformation of possibilities into probabilities. The distinction between accelerants and triggers is captured well by Bulgarian scholar Atanas Gotchev. He describes accelerating factors as "identifiable and monitorable . . . linked to the broader background conditions of a specific tension or crisis situation . . . in the absence of background preconditions [that is, risk factors], accelerators are not accelerators, they are simply events." Gotchev continues: "Triggers may be distinguished from accelerators as single events (for instance, assassination of a political leader), which in the presence of background conditions and accelerators precipitate the transformation of the final stage of a tension situation into a crisis . . . typically [triggers] are not known in advance . . . and it is very difficult to precisely specify them far in advance of an actual crisis."[13]

We can think of accelerants as "changes in the strategic situation that increase incentives or feasibility for perpetrators or enablers to mobilize people or resources for atrocities."[14] The changes in the strategic situation, internal to the state, which could serve as accelerants are numerous. Following the four-category framework of risk factors we laid out in Chapter 4, some accelerants are related to issues of governance—regime transitions (particularly if unconstitutional), major government or legal reforms, state imposition of restrictions on the press and social media, gradual isolationism and withdrawal from the international community, release of political prisoners, purging security forces of minority groups, or marginalization of political moderates. Postconflict peace stabilization programs that are poorly designed or implemented, and have a biased depiction of conflict history, can also accelerate intergroup tension in an at-risk state. Economically, accelerants can come from overdependence on foreign aid or peacekeeping missions, a marked increase in unemployment, or the looming prospect of international sanctions. Finally, accelerants can be found in threats to social cohesion—such as the presence of foreign enablers, failed ceasefires or peace agreements, restrictions on freedom of assembly or movement of a target group, an increase in arrests or the disappearance of members of a target group, the mobilization of an armed group or groups, rising discrimination, forced separation or displacement of groups, an upsurge in hate speech and the organization of hate groups, the large-scale purchase or import of small arms, or actual outbreaks of limited violence (what Alex Bellamy calls "trial massacres") against a targeted group.[15]

At other times, as developmental studies expert James Putzel argues, accelerants may come from changes in the strategic situation that are external to the state, particularly impactful when the state is at risk of violent or genocidal conflict. These "negative externalities that can exacerbate conflict in fragile states" include external military intervention into the territory of a state; nonstate armed groups operating across borders and the movement of refugees; the impact of externally imposed structural reforms; illicit trade in drugs, arms, and minerals; an international financial crisis; and climate change.[16] Also relevant as an external accelerant would be increasing regional destabilization associated with living in a conflict-ridden neighborhood.

Accelerants, whether internal or external to the state in question, build on preexisting risk conditions to open "windows of atrocity risk" in which unforeseen triggers can instigate the perpetration of mass atrocities.[17] An at-risk society with accelerants is like a stack of dry wood doused in gasoline; the outbreak of a fire is likely and unavoidable unless preventive measures are taken. Arson investigators use the term "flashover" to describe the point at which radiant heat causes a fire in a room to become a room on fire.[18] Similarly, triggering factors are those flashover points at which a society at risk for genocide becomes a society caught in the lethal grip of genocide. Triggers are the discrete precipitating events, or chain of events, that can push an at-risk state over the brink; they are the "intervening variables between the existence of conditions necessary for the occurrence of conflict and the outbreak of conflicts."[19] Triggers are the dynamic, real-time stressors that can make the outbreak of violent or genocidal conflict likely or imminent.

The range of triggers is broad and diverse and triggers are often difficult to predict or identify in advance. Moreover, whether an event becomes a trigger for violent or genocidal conflict is extremely context dependent. For Barbara Harff, triggers include "natural disasters that provide opportunities to rebel groups to increase antigovernment actions; assassinations of key leaders; expulsion and evacuation of foreigners; and terrorist attacks."[20] Benjamin Goldsmith et al. offer empirical evidence that "whether at least one (successful or unsuccessful) political assassination took place in a given year" had significant predictive power for the onset of genocide or politicide.[21] Other triggers include coups, sudden deployment of security forces, acts perceived as treacherous by a targeted group, contested succession or secession, social media attacks, battlefield victories, closure or liquidation of large employers, environmental crises, epidemics, acts of incitement, the taking of a census, or the actual onset of armed conflict. The UN's "Framework of Analysis" even embeds triggering factors as one of its eight common risk factors for atrocity crimes, including among its indicators "measures taken by the international community perceived as threatening to a State's sovereignty" as well as "discovery of natural resources or launching of exploitation projects that have a serious impact on the livelihoods and sustainability of groups or civilian populations."[22]

Other potential triggers are more easily predictable and identifiable in advance. In our cardiovascular disease analogy, the well-known heart attack triggers are exertion, exposure to cold, emotion, and eating—any of which might precipitate a stroke, more likely in someone with preexisting risk factors. Sensitivity to the triggers, particularly in the context of the underlying preexisting risk factors, can give us the lead time to modify lifestyle choices as well as avoid what might lead to a heart crisis. Similarly, foreseeable triggers for violent or genocidal conflict can include "deadlines for significant policy action, legal judgments, and anniversaries of highly traumatic and disputed historical events."[23] Particularly notable as foreseeable triggering factors are elections in deeply divided, fragile, or conflict-prone societies. Although it may be difficult to precisely anticipate how contentious or contested the elections will be, poorly planned elections in at-risk societies are a notable harbinger of violent or genocidal conflict. A database of sub-Saharan Africa's national elections from 1990 to 2008, for instance, revealed that some form of violence accompanied 58% of elections, with the majority of violence occurring before election day.[24] Charles Butcher et al. demonstrated that elections are among a set of time-sensitive variables that, taken collectively, significantly enhance the precision of forecasting the onset of genocide or politicide.[25] Indeed, the prevention of electoral violence as a triggering factor—understood as a process rather than an event—has become "a well-established multibillion dollar industry that sends peacebuilding practitioners across the globe."[26]

In sum, once we have identified countries as at-risk for violent or genocidal conflict, understanding the role of accelerants and triggers allows us to obtain a better idea of which countries are more likely to experience the onset of violence at a certain moment in time. As Gotchev describes: "Risk assessment provides the context, while early warning is an interpretation that the outbreak of conflict in a given high-risk situation is likely and unavoidable if appropriate policy measures are not taken in time."[27] Sensitivity to the accelerating or triggering events—the environmental stressors—that could lead to the onset of violent or genocidal conflict gives us an advocacy tool to provide relevant actors with significantly more lead time to take preventive action before conflicts actually erupt.

There remains, however, a final bridge to cross between having the information at hand and translating that information into preventive action. No matter how accurate our risk assessment tools, nor how clearly we have identified accelerants and triggers, civilians will continue to be done to death unless we can transform substantial early warning into an equally substantial early response.

EARLY WARNING–EARLY RESPONSE GAP

The necessity of early warning is affirmed by the 2008 Albright and Cohen report: "Effective early warning does not guarantee successful prevention, but if warning is absent, slow, inaccurate, or indistinguishable from the 'noise' of regular reporting, failure is virtually guaranteed."[28] Early warning, based on extensive risk assessment and an awareness of the relevant accelerators and triggers, is necessary for the prevention of genocide because it alerts us to the threat of new or renewed conflict in plenty of time for preventive action. Early warning gives us time to decide what to do and then to prepare to do it. By itself, however, early warning is not sufficient. Early warning matters only if we can summon the will to translate it into early response. Indeed, our problems in preventing genocide are less about a lack of early warning and more about a lack of early action. Bridging the gap between early warning and early response is crucial to preventing genocide; we cannot assume that simply having adequate information will elicit an adequate response.

Where early warning systems allow us to identity the risks of developing crisis situations, early response systems lay out the actions needed to avoid the escalation of those crisis situations. Indeed, the promise of early warning is that it will prompt an early preventive response. Even the most perfect early warning system, however, will be of little use if there is no desire—based on the sanctity of state sovereignty or the lack of clarity about what form of action to take—to act on the information. As Adama Dieng has said: "Today we have to move beyond early warning to early action. We have to strengthen the capacity of our institutions to respond in a timely and effective way to potential conflicts and to the threat of grave and massive human rights violations. Even the best system of early warning will be less helpful unless States are able and willing to take action when the warning is received."[29]

In 1997, international relations expert Alexander George and political scientist Jane Holl first identified the "warning-response" gap in a Carnegie Commission report on preventing deadly conflict. "If events such as in Bosnia, Kuwait, and Rwanda," they asked, "are known (and increasingly knowable, given the rapidly contracting nature of global interactions), why are they not prevented?"[30] Rather than a lack of timely or accurate early warning, George and Holl posited a systematic warning–response gap as the key factor in understanding policy delay or paralysis in the face of deadly conflict. They cited six reasons, related to decision makers' information processing, for this warning–response gap:

- the relatively low stakes perceived to be at risk for a given state's vital national interests;
- the uncertainty and interpretive ambiguity of knowing which trouble spots are likely to explode and when;
- the lack of theories and models to assess and predict the significance of early warning indicators;
- the dread of "false triggers," or a "cry wolf" phenomenon, that may register preventive actions as premature or unnecessary;
- the impracticality of responding with preventive actions given the large number of low-level crises and the ever-growing limitation of resources; and
- the fear of a "slippery slope" engagement in a potentially intractable problem.[31]

Similarly, the Albright and Cohen report admits: "Warnings always entail a degree of uncertainty, and human beings naturally resist paying certain costs today, even if small, to protect against uncertain future costs; this is true of bureaucracies all the more so. Add to this the incentives for political leaders to focus on short-term costs and benefits, and the tendency for bureaucracies to resist risky action, and it should not surprise us that it is difficult to generate support for preventive action."[32] Indeed, with such a list of compelling barriers to preventive action, the surprise is not that we have a warning–response gap; rather, the surprise is that the gap between warning and response is *ever* bridged.

For many, this warning–response gap can best be bridged by making sure that "early warning is not simply the sharing of information about an impending crisis, let alone the wail of a siren announcing the imminence of such a crisis. Early warning goes beyond the collection and sharing of information to include both analysis of that information *and* the formulation of appropriate strategic choices given the analysis."[33] That is, the impact of early warning can be heightened by also offering appropriate response strategies to the at-risk situation, rather than simply warning that an at-risk situation is getting worse. As Swedish political scientist

Annika Bjorkdahl suggests, political will and capability can be strengthened by presenting "decision makers with a clear policy alternative which identifies the tools and strategies relevant to the main objective of the preventive effort."[34] So, in essence, bridging the warning–response gap, rather than being thought of as "where there is a will, there is a way," might be best framed as "where there is a way, there is a will."[35]

As political scientist Christoph Meyer et al. emphasize, however, just adding policy or action recommendations to early warning does not close the warning–response gap, even when early warning is regionalized or localized "by directly involving those who will have to carry the brunt of the consequences should a conflict escalate."[36] It can be more helpful, they argue, to approach early warning as a nuanced and graduated persuasive process—rather than an informational, educational, or alerting activity with a simple binary outcome of action or no action. Drawing on an extensive body of social scientific literature, they distinguish between five distinct stages of persuasion—reception, attention, acceptance, prioritization, and the decision to mobilize. When applied to early warning, warning can fail to elicit response—for various reasons—at each stage. For instance, even if a decision maker has received an early warning, attended to it, and accepted its veracity, the decision maker may still be unconvinced that the pending crisis is a greater priority than other current or future crises pressing for attention. So, in this case, low prioritization of the early warning becomes a barrier to preventive response. Recasting the warning–response problem as a special case of persuasive discourse can go a long way toward understanding how early warning is best communicated at each stage of the communication process. In so doing, we increase our gap-bridging chances "to raise a given recipient's awareness about a potential threat to a valued good or interest to enhance her ability to take preventive or mitigating action."[37]

Crucial to this persuasive process is the collective mobilization of political will. The oft-stated notion that "nations don't have friends, nations have interests" reminds us of the importance of prioritizing how responding to genocide is in our best interests. Unfortunately, baser political and strategic interests too often override moral and humanitarian concerns. As Meyer et al. argue, the calculus underlying political will "is not 'do we care about x,' but 'how much do we care about x in comparison to y and z.'"[38] Often, what states care most about is the well-being of their own citizens rather than the protection of civilians from genocide in other countries. Noted Argentine legal activist Juan Mendez states: "I have no doubt that the greatest contributing factor to humankind's inability to protect vulnerable populations from slaughter is the absence of political will to act on the part of leaders that do have the solution at their disposal."[39] In reality, though, the issue is not an absence of political will; rather, the issue is political will misplaced and the subsequent need for a reshaping of how we interpret "national interests." As the International Commission on Intervention and State Sovereignty (ICISS) report argued, "these days, good international citizenship is a matter of national self-interest. With the world as close and interdependent as it now is, and with crises in 'faraway countries of which we know little' as capable as they now are of generating major problems elsewhere (with refugee outflows, health pandemics, terrorism, narcotics trafficking, organized crime and the like), it is strongly arguable that it is in every country's interest to contribute cooperatively to the resolution of such problems, quite apart from the humanitarian imperative to do so."[40]

In addition to the content and packaging of the early warning message, as well as the collective mobilization of political will, efforts to bridge the warning–response gap must also take into account the logistical mechanics of how a decision to activate a preventive response comes about. These logistical mechanics are particularly notable, and especially paralyzing, in UN decision-making processes related to preventive response. The Security Council is the UN's enforcer, "the only UN principal organ whose resolutions are binding on member states."[41] The Security Council—more powerful than the General Assembly and far more powerful than the office of the Secretary-General—has as its primary responsibility the maintenance of international peace and security (Article 24).[42] The Security Council confers the stamp of legitimacy for preventive response. It is to the Security Council that requests for preventive response in the face of mass atrocity—ranging from economic sanctions to the establishment of peacekeeping missions to military action to the creation of tribunals—come. It is also, unfortunately, in the Security Council where too many of these requests for preventive response die.

The UN Security Council consists of 15 members, five of whom are permanent and 10 of whom are elected on proportional geographic bases by the General Assembly to 2-year terms. The Permanent Five (P5) members include China, France, the Russian Federation, the United Kingdom, and the United States. The P5 hold absolute veto power, initially conferred in 1945, over any proposed resolution. "When a P5 member votes no on a resolution, that kills it, even if the other fourteen council members vote yes."[43] This veto power can be used to reject any resolution that threatens a P5 member's strategic interests. Although the P5's use of vetoes in the Security Council is relatively rare, it is too often used in the face of requests for preventive response to stop civilians from being done to death. Since the end of the Cold War, for instance, "the United States has vetoed 14 draft resolutions, most of them involving the Israeli-Palestinian conflict; Russia has vetoed 11 concerning its allies, like the government of Syria."[44] Most recently, on four occasions since 2011, Russia and China have exercised their veto power "to protect the government and armed groups in Syria from resolutions designed to confront crimes against humanity and war crimes."[45] As the ICISS report lamented, "it is unconscionable that one veto can override the rest of humanity on matters of grave humanitarian concern."[46]

The warning–response gap inherent in the outmoded mechanics of the UN Security Council—particularly in cases of mass atrocities—is a notable contributor to what Simon Adams, Executive Director of the Global Center for the Responsibility to Protect, has described as "an enormous reservoir of cynicism and pessimism . . . regarding the ability of the United Nations—a creaking twentieth-century organization—to confront and overcome twenty-first century problems."[47] Recognizing the influential role played by the Security Council, proposals for reform have come from many quarters, even from among the P5 members themselves. France and the United Kingdom (both of whom last resorted to the veto in 1989), for example, support the idea of P5 members voluntarily limiting veto power "when a clear majority [of the Security Council] supports proposed action to mitigate the risk of a mass-atrocity crime"—a sensible proposal ignored, to date, by China, Russia, and the United States.[48]

Others argue for a radical structural overhaul of the Security Council to more accurately reflect the geopolitical realities of the twenty-first century. "Since the council was created in 1945, more than a hundred nations have come into existence, former pariah states like Japan, Germany, and South Africa have rejoined the world community, and many developing nations have become economic and trade dynamos."[49] Such realities beg for an enlargement of the Security Council (last done in 1965 with an increase in the number of nonpermanent members from 6 to 10), perhaps even including an increase in the number of permanent members—though such a move would undoubtedly complicate, to an even greater degree, power politics on the Council and perhaps even lead to slower responses.

Other proposals suggest that the issue of majority—currently requiring the consent of nine of the 15 members (assuming one of the P5 members does not exercise veto power)—be complemented by a rule of supermajority (perhaps 12 members) that could override a P5 veto. In late 1993, even the General Assembly of the UN established an Open-Ended Working Group on the Question of Equitable Representation On and Increase in the Membership of the Security Council and Other Matters Related to the

Security Council. Despite the ambition of its name, its been widely dubbed the "never-ending working group" and has yet to advance any substantive proposals.[50]

In spite of the urging of UN Secretary-General Ban Ki-moon for member states to restructure the Security Council, no reform proposals have been put to a vote as the oligarchy of P5 members is unwilling to compromise its privileged power. Although, as political scientist Thomas Weiss argues, "every solution raises as many problems as it solves," the absence of any action on such proposals leaves the fundamental credibility of the Security Council, and even the United Nations itself, at stake.[51] Indeed, "a Council of fifteen members that does not fully embrace the expanding influence of Asia, Latin America and Africa and that relies on postwar definitions of influence will continue to face sharp criticism."[52] As Laurent Fabius, France's minister of foreign affairs, argued in his call for self-restraint on the use of vetoes in the Syrian tragedy: "A United Nations stalemate that lasts for two years, entailing dramatic human consequences, cannot be accepted by the global conscience . . . For all those who expect the United Nations to shoulder its responsibilities in order to protect populations, this situation is reprehensible."[53]

Indeed, even the most perfect of early warning systems is tragically impotent if the gap to early response cannot be bridged. In January 2015, speaking at the commemoration of the 70th anniversary of the liberation of Auschwitz-Birkenau, UN Deputy-Secretary-General Jan Eliasson, an honest critic of his organization's own limitations, affirmed the significance of closing the gap between early warning and early response: "It is important that we examine why we continue to fail to prevent mass atrocities, despite lessons learned, despite knowledge of causes and drivers and despite our assurances of 'never again' . . . Genocide can only happen when we ignore the warning signs—and are unwilling to take action."[54]

PREVENTIVE RESPONSE TOOLS
INTERRUPTING GENOCIDE

Bridging the warning–response gap is easier said than done. As Alex Bellamy points out: "International society's default response to genocide is to stand aside and hope that the blood-letting comes to an end incidentally. This is despite the emergence of a clear moral, political—and some would say legal—responsibility to take timely and decisive action to put an end to genocide."[55] Clearly, the marshaling of political will is a key piece in bridging the warning–response gap—particularly reliant, as we have discussed previously, on the reception, attention, acceptance, and prioritization of a prevailing interest in responding to genocide. In addition, however, once we have reached the point of deciding to mobilize a preventive response, we must decide what form that response will take. Whether it is academics, lawyers, policymakers, or global civil society, wanting to do something does not translate into doing something unless we have a clear understanding of the response tools at our disposal. To that end, we must be aware of the wide range of preventive response tools on which we can draw to slow, limit, or stop the continuation or escalation of genocide. In addition, we must understand how such tools are best applied and the level—and limits—of their potential effectiveness. Bridging the warning–response gap involves not just a persuasive discourse that can amass and focus political will but also knowledge of, and familiarity with, the breadth of preventive response tools available in our toolbox for interrupting genocide.

The metaphor of a toolbox of preventive response tools implies much more than "fixing" something through external (particularly military) intervention; indeed, if the only tool you have is a hammer, every problem has to look like a nail. Rather, the toolbox includes a wealth of diverse and creative tools that can strategically build, create, imagine, and bring to life a blueprint of a society in which civilians are protected from being done to death. These tools can be understood as levers to help slow, limit, or stop genocidal conflict that is imminent or ongoing. As Archimedes said: "Give me a place to stand and with a lever I will move the whole world."[56] The prevention toolbox encompasses a range of levers that provide a place to stand in order to, if properly applied, move a portion of the world away from genocide.

The type of leverage required to effect change can be thought of along a spectrum of influence that runs from cooperative to coercive. This spectrum of influence is more about how a preventive response tool is used than about what the tool itself is. That is, the same preventive response tool may be used cooperatively or coercively, as incentive or as punishment.

At one end of this spectrum, preventive response tools can be used to encourage change through rewards for cooperation and progress. "The three principal sets of rewards are: (a) those that respond to economic needs, (b) those that respond to political needs for legitimacy and recognition, and (c) those that respond to needs for assurances and security guarantees."[57] When used cooperatively, preventive response tools involve interest-based positive incentives for change that lead to a jointly determined (rather than unilaterally imposed) outcome in which actors are reliant on mutual gains for maintenance. Such incentives "have to be credible and attractive enough to have an impact and be offered at the appropriate time during negotiations or mediation. There is a risk that they will be seen as offering too much to individuals or governments that have violated human rights."[58] Despite that risk, the cooperative use of preventive response tools offers a carrot that can be more appealing, and likely less costly, than a stick. As policy studies scholar David Cortright suggests, the cooperative use of response tools "foster cooperation and goodwill . . . hope, reassurance and attraction . . . 'an impression of sympathy and concern.'"[59]

At the other end of the spectrum, preventive response tools can attempt to outright force change through coercive threats and punishments against noncooperation. When used coercively, response tools are power-based negotiations built on restrictive or punitive pressure for the actors to change their behavior or risk negative consequences. Such coercive strategies may be costly, increase the possibility of backlash, and require force for maintenance. Again, on the coercive use of response tools, Cortright suggests that "[they] create hostility and separation. Threats tend to generate reactions of fear, anxiety, and resistance . . . [they] send a message of 'indifference or active hostility.'"[60] Despite those psychological realities, however, coercive strategies may also be our best preventive bet for protecting civilians at a given moment in a given case of genocide. When used effectively, lower-order nonintrusive coercive strategies can eliminate the need to resort to the most intrusive higher-order coercive measure—nonconsensual military intervention.

Often, preventive response tools—whether used cooperatively as the "carrot" or coercively as the "stick"—have a basis of conditionality linked to their application. "If you do *x* (or stop doing *x*), then we will do *y*" or "we will (continue to) provide *x*, unless you start doing *y*—in which case we will take *x* away." As peace researchers Aaron Griffiths and Catherine Barnes point out, however, conditionality is only "successful if the value of the benefit exceeds the costs of compliance with attached conditions or expectations."[61] Overall, the most effective mix of coercive and cooperative inducements for preventive response tools is very situation specific and dependent on "the geographical location, political character, and economic profile of the target country" and the motivations of its relevant actors. [62] As a result, the selection and application of preventive response tools will vary from case to case; there is no general blueprint and they do not necessarily need to be used in a graduated progression.[63] Moreover, preventive response tools work best as part of a flexible interdependent strategy with underlying principles, rather than as a pick-and-choose application of isolated tools in a haphazard trial-and-error approach. That is, the response tools themselves are not policy, but, rather, they are instruments of policy. Finally, although preventive response tools are typically targeted at perpetrators of genocide (whether state or nonstate actors), they can also be applied as levers of behavioral change or opportunity for a range of other actors—including decision makers, victims, bystanders, and third-party enablers.[64]

It is also crucial to recognize that the degree of choice we have in selecting a preventive response tool is directly correlated with the timing of our anticipated response. As the path to genocide intensifies, the range of preventive response tools in the toolbox decreases. That is, we have the greatest range of preventive response tools, particularly those used in a cooperative manner, in at-risk situations in which the descent into violent or genocidal conflict is only still on the horizon. Once, however, a country is exposed to accelerants that open "windows of atrocity risk," the range of available preventive response tools decreases significantly. Even in the depths of genocide, though, we still have a surprising range of preventive response tools at our disposal—falling far short of the last resort of non-consensual coercive military intervention.

Ultimately, the purpose of response tools—couched in a principle of "do no harm"—is to prevent civilians from being done to death by slowing, limiting, or stopping the continuation or escalation of genocide. Such midstream prevention can be accomplished by mitigating the conditions that facilitate genocide; exposing, isolating, and punishing perpetrators and their enablers; establishing the resolve, credibility, and capability of the international community to respond; protecting potential victims and target groups; diminishing perpetrator motivation or capability to commit genocide; and convincing bystanders and negative actors it is not in their best interests to support perpetrators or an offending regime.[65] Although several of the response tools to be discussed seem to be most easily deployed by lawyers or policymakers, academics and global civil society play a crucial role as catalysts for the international community and states to assume their preventive responsibilities in the face of genocide. That is, although all of us may not be in a position to make decisions about the implementation of these response tools, each of us is in a position to exercise our voice regarding the necessity of their implementation—and that voice is considerably strengthened when backed by knowledge regarding the diversity, limits, and effectiveness of the preventive response tools available in the face of genocide (Box 5.1). We will examine the various research- and practice-informed levers in our toolbox in the four preventive response compartments of political, economic, legal, and military response tools.[66]

Box 5.1

COMPARTMENTS OF PREVENTIVE RESPONSE TOOLS

POLITICAL PREVENTIVE RESPONSE TOOLS

Coooperative

- Diplomatic Legitimization and Recognition Benefits
- Resources for Enabling Dialogue
- Political and Field Missions
- Support for Human Rights Promotion, Monitoring, and Documentation

Coercive

- Threat or Application of Political or Diplomatic Sanctions
- Condemnation
- Sporting or Cultural Boycotts
- Proscription of Individuals and Organizations

ECONOMIC PREVENTIVE RESPONSE TOOLS

Cooperative

- Lifting of Existing Sanctions or Embargoes
- Debt Relief or Increased Aid
- New Funding or Investment
- Trade Incentives

Coercive

- Targeted Financial Sanctions
- Trade Embargoes
- Freezing or Seizing of Monetary Assets
- Divestment or Aid Conditionality

LEGAL PREVENTIVE RESPONSE TOOLS

Cooperative

- Monitors to Observe Compliance with Human Rights Standards and Law
- Offers of Amnesty or Immunity
- Domestic Support of Dispute Resolution Mechanisms
- References to Existing International Law or Norms

Coercive

- Action by UN Organs
- Human Rights Investigations
- Threats of Referral or Actual Referral for Criminal Prosecution
- Exercise of Universal Jurisdiction

MILITARY PREVENTIVE RESPONSE TOOLS

Cooperative

- Military Aid or Training
- Confidence and Security-Building Measures
- Security Guarantees for the Protection of Civilians
- Consensual Preventive Deployment

Coercive

- Restricted Arms, Movements, and Communications
- Heightened Military Presence in the Region
- Credible Threat of Military Force
- Use of Military Force for Nonconsensual Coercive Intervention

---

Political Preventive Response Tools

Political preventive response tools include a range of particularly potent cooperative and coercive measures to influence perpetrators as well as decision makers, victims, bystanders, and third-party enablers. Their use is based on the assumption that "the choice to engage in atrocities is a policy choice, one with clear goals."[67] If, indeed, genocidal violence is instrumental, then there is a range of political preventive response tools that can be applied to challenge an offending regime's behavior by signaling a shift in the global sensitivity from permissive to prohibitive. Such response tools can slow, limit, or stop genocide by affecting the calculus of genocide and encouraging change through rewards for cooperation and progress.

One array of interest-based positive incentives incorporates *diplomatic legitimization and recognition benefits* to shape the behavior of an offending regime. The cooperative use of diplomatic legitimization and recognition benefits is based in "a foreign policy strategy which depends to a significant degree on positive incentives to achieve its objectives."[68] At its best, such a strategy makes clear the rewards available for positive behavior change to a perpetrating regime even as it makes clear the adverse consequences of not changing that behavior. Interest-based positive incentives can include offers of diplomatic recognition, normalization of relations, official state visits and receiving of representatives, public praise, favored diplomatic status, upgrading the diplomatic presence in that state, or access to membership in coveted international organizations. In 2012, for instance, the United States assigned an ambassador to Myanmar (for the first time since 1990) to reward that long-isolated government for the release of hundreds of political prisoners as well as other demo-cratic reforms. In exchange, Myanmar reassigned a full ambassador to Washington. As another example, membership in the European Union (EU) has been a powerful incentive for foreign policy change in countries seeking admittance. Serbia's attempts to achieve candidate status to the EU, for instance, eventually facilitated the capture and arrest of Ratko Mladic and also led to improving (albeit still tenuous) diplomatic relations with neighboring Kosovo. At present, Serbia has formally begun accession negotiations for EU membership. Even the behavior of nonstate actors can be modified with measures of engagement, legitimization, and recogni-tion. As Griffiths and Barnes illustrate: ". . . when former US President Clinton allowed representatives of Sinn Fein (widely viewed as linked to the Irish Republican Army) to visit Washington, [it opened] new channels for pro-agreement Irish Americans to exercise influence with them."[69]

Another collection of political preventive measures can involve the cooperative provision of *resources for enabling dialogue* between perpetra-tors and target victim groups. These can include support for mechanisms of mediation, problem-solving workshops, structured dialogue, and other backing for existing or planned domestic conflict resolution processes. The promotion of music, art, films, and theater also "can emphasize the humanity of victims, the cruelty of perpetrators, and the apathy of bystanders . . . [calling] attention to [mass atrocity] situations in ways that may resonate strongly with different audiences."[70] Dialogue through informal negotiations "that do not have a lot of scrutiny may be useful to scope out a potential framework that can be achieved with more formal or higher level proceedings."[71] Support and technical assistance from inter-national and regional organizations can also be extended, when parties are willing, to back more formal or higher level negotiations. Also included in these measures are financial and technical support for the develop-ment of domestic early-warning response systems, the training of public officials, and political party building. In addition, as Gareth Evans points out, a range of nongovernmental organizations—including the Carter Center, the Community of Sant'Egidio, and the Geneva-based Centre for Humanitarian Dialogue—has also played significant international roles in enabling dialogue for cooperation and progress in conflict settings.[72]

Of particular import as a political preventive response tool is the coop-erative use of *political and field missions*. Political missions are defined as "multilateral teams of primarily civilian experts that rely largely on political persuasion to find a nonviolent way out of crises."[73] Political mis-sions, generally deployed by international or regional organizations, can include forming "groups of friends" among regional or UN membership, ambassadors on the ground, or the use of eminent persons or envoys as intermediaries for third party mediation (such as the good offices of the UN Secretary-General or the head of a regional organization). Celebrities are often recruited as prominent persons in the deployment of political missions. Many UN humanitarian agencies employ a range of celebrities— from singers to athletes to actors and actresses to supermodels—as Goodwill Ambassadors who, as in the case of Oscar-winning actor Forest Whitaker's work in Uganda and South Sudan, promote peacebuilding at the local level in areas of conflict. The purpose of such political missions is the application of preventive diplomacy, meaning "action to prevent disputes from arising between parties, to prevent existing disputes from escalating into conflict and to limit the spread of the latter when they occur."[74] Central to the application of preventive diplomacy is the development of consensus- and coalition-building efforts that incentivize, through norms and partner building, the cessation of hostilities. The process of such preventive diplomacy can come through unofficial dialogue (often called Track 2 diplomacy), confidential negotiations, summits, or even a more formal binding arbitration from a national or international court (for instance, the International Court of Justice).

Field missions can include fact-finding missions and data collection, observer and monitoring missions, and commissions of inquiry. Commissions of Inquiry (COIs) are particularly invaluable types of field mission that provide "a means to gather objective and up-to-date information and . . . recommendations."[75] Recent COIs include the UN Security Council's COI for Central African Republic, the Human Rights Council's COIs for Gaza, Syria, Democratic Republic of Korea, Eritrea, and Libya, and the African Union's COI for South Sudan, as well as investigation reports to the UN Human Rights council on Sri Lanka and Ukraine.[76] Such public missions, often including interviews with refugees in neighboring countries, are particularly effective when conducted multilaterally with other countries, regional organizations, or the UN. Field missions also can be used preventively in reinforcing election reform, support, and monitoring. The efficacy of field missions in these electoral areas was seen in Kenya in early 2008. Following a violently contested December 2007 presidential election, escalating conflict was defused by an African Union-mandated mediation panel that established, among other things, formal commissions to review electoral law and practice in Kenya. Not only did this field mission help deescalate a growing crisis situation, but it also led to a river of international support to develop conflict prevention and resolution mechanisms in the run-up to the 2013 presidential election—an election received as largely peaceful and legitimate.[77] In sum, "while not all abusers can be stopped or deterred, an international presence in the form of field missions can reduce perpetrators' 'political space' and thus can have a positive impact."[78]

A final set of political preventive response tools used cooperatively includes *support for human rights promotion, monitoring, and documentation.* This set of tools can involve normative, material, and financial support for promoting human rights with regional actors and states. The UN's "Human Rights up Front" initiative, for example, was launched in late 2013 as a response tool to "ensure the UN system takes early and effective action, as mandated by the Charter and UN resolutions, to prevent or respond to large-scale violations of human rights or international humanitarian law."[79] At the beginning of the crisis in South Sudan, this initiative provided the rationale for the decision of the UN Mission to open its doors to protect some 75,000 South Sudanese civilians fleeing the onset of the mass violence. In addition, this set of tools can include training in technical expertise for monitoring and documentation. Most often, the sources of independent human rights documentation are frontline indigenous human rights organizations and lawyers that then report the information to external organizations. Although such information may be used in an eventual legal investigation, human rights documentation can be used as a preventive tool to change the calculation of perpetrators by negating any sense of impunity or invisibility for their crimes. It can also lead to other useful policy action to slow, limit, or stop the continuation or escalation of genocide.[80] "Local human rights defenders, equipped with mobile communications technologies, can serve as a vital dispersed network throughout a country to document atrocity crimes and report that information to both national and international actors" in order to "deliver justice and a renewed sense of social inclusion, for victims, and serve as an early warning network of renewed instability."[81]

Central to the preventive success of many cooperative political response strategies is the consent of the host government, a rarity when the government is the primary actor responsible for the atrocities being addressed in a given area. So, when cooperative political response tools have failed to prevent the continuation or escalation of genocide, there are a variety of coercive preventive response measures that may be considered.

Particularly common is the *threat or application of political or diplomatic sanctions.* Political or diplomatic sanctions entail "severing formal diplomatic ties with a country or significantly downgrading ties from the normal level of diplomatic activity for foreign policy purposes."[82] The intent of such coercive measures, relatively low cost to implement, is to change the calculus of perpetrator behavior and to make the continuation or escalation of atrocities too costly for an offending regime. Such measures can include recalling or expelling diplomats, the withdrawal of a political mission or embassy, restrictions on diplomatic representation, downgrading diplomatic relations, or suspension or expulsion from international organizations. Although some of these measures are taken in times of crisis when countries are worried about the safety of their diplomatic personnel, they can also be used as power-based preventive responses, even if largely symbolic, to increase restrictive or punitive pressure for the target country to change its offending behaviors. In May 2012, for instance, the U.S. State department—3 months after closing its embassy in Damascus—expelled Syria's top diplomat in response to a massacre in the Syrian town of Houla. Similar expulsions of Syrian ambassadors were done in Australia, Great Britain, Canada, France, Germany, Italy, and Spain.[83] Other forms of diplomatic sanction can be subtler than absolute recall, expulsion, or withdrawal. For instance, even when a country chooses to maintain a diplomatic presence in a state on the verge of genocidal conflict, diplomats "can limit their activities in a matter that undermines the legitimacy of potential perpetrators."[84] As another example, at their annual summit in January 2007, the African Union opted for a form of diplomatic sanction in their refusal to give their rotating chair to Sudanese President Omar al-Bashir—a punitive response to the ongoing genocide in Sudan.[85]

Another common coercive political preventive response tactic is unilateral or multilateral *condemnation*. Often referred to as "naming and shaming," such condemnation in international forums can publicly call regimes to account for noncooperation with human rights standards and agreements. Unilateral condemnation can come from a state or an international human rights organization. At the state level, condemnation of a regime can be done with direct reference to a regime's perpetration of atrocities or even more indirectly through political acknowledgment and support of opposition groups. International human rights organizations produce extensive naming and shaming background reports on states that use political terror. Recent research has shown that these types of reports actually have a negative effect on the likelihood and magnitude of government killing.[86] Multilateral condemnation can come from a nonbinding resolution of the UN General Assembly or resolutions of other UN bodies (for example, the Human Rights Council). The UN Special Advisers on the Prevention of Genocide and the Responsibility to Protect frequently issue statements of "concern" or "alarm" drawing attention to crisis situations. Particularly notable, however, are activities of the UN Security Council. These "can include briefings and consultations, and may result in any of several options including a consensus Press Statement, a statement by the President of the Security Council (which also requires consensus) and/or a series of progressively stronger and legally binding resolutions."[87]

Mass protests by global civil society also can work as an effective complement, or catalyst, to multilateral naming and shaming approaches. By drawing international attention to a perpetrator regime, such protests can be a coercive lever for political preventive responses to genocide. Perhaps most notable in this regard was the development of the Save Darfur Coalition (SDC). Founded in 2004 in response to the crisis in Darfur, the SDC grew into an alliance of more than 190 faith-based, advocacy, and human rights organizations. Their mission to raise public awareness and mobilize a massive response to the atrocities in Darfur was advanced through local, national, and international rallies and events that applied pressure on political leaders to end the genocide in Darfur. Controversy remains over the effectiveness of the Darfur lobby. Mahmood Mamdani, the most vocal critic, contends that however well-intentioned the movement was, its driving imperative was "to act before seeking to understand."[88] Such neglect and ignorance of the context in Sudan, he argues, led to dangerous misunderstandings of the conflict and misguided notions of the best forms of preventive response. Mamdani's specific critiques about the Darfur lobby notwithstanding, it is clear that the public pressure generated by mass protests by global civil society has the potential to leverage influence for responding to genocide. As legal scholars Rebecca Hamilton and Chad Hazlett predict, "the [Save Darfur] movement's ultimate contribution will be measured less in terms of its impact on the people of Darfur, and more in terms of the foundation it has established and precedents it has set for responding to subsequent twenty-first century atrocities."[89]

Although, as Evans points out, "naming shames only those familiar with that emotion," condemnation can internationalize issues by building, at its best, a public coalition of opposition to a perpetrator regime.[90] In this sense, the spotlighting of bad behavior does not rely on a feeling of shame to reform perpetrators' abuses; rather, the spotlighting draws the attention of international actors capable of inflicting tangible costs (politically, economically, legally, or militarily) if the atrocities are not stopped. Indeed, empirical research by political scientist Jacqueline H. R. DeMeritt confirmed that "by calling attention to abusive states, human rights NGOs and the United Nations can reduce both the likelihood and severity of state-sponsored murder."[91] In such a situation, perpetrators may be more receptive to diplomatic overtures suggesting face-saving ways to change their behavior.

Yet another political preventive response tool to coercively slow, limit, or stop genocide is the implementation of *sporting or cultural boycotts*. This can include the boycotting of events held in perpetrating countries or the exclusion of representatives from a perpetrating country in international events. Sporting or cultural boycotts can be important preventive response tools of isolation from international society as well as condemnation of an offending regime. Movements to boycott the Berlin Olympics of 1936, for instance, surfaced early in Great Britain, France, Sweden, Czechoslovakia, the Netherlands, and the United States. Boycott supporters expressed concern that participation in the Games would be an explicit endorsement of Hitler's policies and practices. In the end, however, appeasement ruled the day as antiboycott advocates argued that participating in the Games "would help to tie Germany into the community of nations" rather than turn them "more belligerent."[92] As author Daniel James Brown states, the demise of the boycott movement "was a victory for Adolf Hitler, who was rapidly learning just how ready the world was to be deceived."[93]

Conversely, the sporting and cultural boycotts of South Africa in the 1960s generated punitive pressure that led to incremental changes in domestic apartheid policy. In 1968, for instance, the UN General Assembly requested all States and organizations "to suspend cultural, educational, sporting and other exchanges with the racist regime and with organizations or institutions in South Africa which practice apartheid."[94] Eventually, in concert with a range of other coercive policy tools, the sporting and cultural boycotts—reaffirmed in several subsequent UN resolutions and supported by antiapartheid groups around the globe—were credited with a large role in the dismantling of apartheid in South Africa.[95]

A final set of political preventive response tools that can be used coercively involves the *proscription of individuals and organizations*. These measures can include travel bans on targeted persons that limit the capacity of alleged or would-be perpetrators to raise funds for their destructive activities. Travel bans further disrupt the ability of individuals and organizations to maintain international ties. For example, in response to the ongoing crisis in South Sudan, a March 3, 2015 UN Security Council resolution imposed a travel ban requiring all Member States to "take the necessary measures to prevent the entry into or transit through their territories of any individuals" or entities obstructing reconciliation or peace processes, undermining the political process, or abusing human rights in South Sudan.[96] Such bans can also be extended to family members and supporters. As Evans summarizes, "visa bans for major international retail and entertainment destinations have been known to cause serious pain to a number of serially offending national leaders. And even more painful, interestingly, appear to be bans on entry to attend school or university."[97]

In conclusion, the deployment of each of these political preventive response tools varies along a spectrum of diplomatic engagement. The cooperative provision of legitimization and recognition benefits, resources for enabling dialogue, political and field missions, and support for human rights promotion, monitoring, and documentation all rely on varying degrees of diplomatic engagement with a perpetrating regime. To the degree they work, they work because external actors remain diplomatically engaged with the regime whose behavior they wish to modify. The more coercive measures of threat or application of political or diplomatic sanctions, condemnation, sporting or cultural boycotts, and proscription of individuals and organizations involve graduating degrees of diplomatic disengagement from the perpetrating regime. The deterrent effect of these measures is presumed to be in the symbolic or very tangible isolation they impose on individuals and organizations committing atrocities. Which end of the diplomatic spectrum—engaged or disengaged—is the most effectual political tack to take when seeking to slow, limit, or stop genocide is best determined on a case-by-case basis.

On the one hand, we should be wary about assuming that increased diplomatic engagement, or a "diplomatic surge," is an intuitively reasonable and faultless preventive response tool—particularly when used in isolation from other response tools. Recent empirical research by political scientist Matthew Krain found that diplomatic engagement "may actually enhance the legitimacy of the regime with important domestic constituents, or even reinforce their image of themselves as actors behaving legitimately . . . increased diplomatic engagement with a perpetrator might signal the international community's willingness to tolerate the atrocities without further international action to stop them."[98] Krain even found that encouraging new or deeper diplomatic engagement in the context of neutral interventions (for instance, the on-ground presence of peacekeepers or monitors) may signal to perpetrators "a desire to avoid confrontation on the part of the international community" and even lead to a sense of permissiveness than can escalate the killing.[99]

On the other hand, although diplomatic disengagement can send a strong message, it also shifts the spotlight away from a perpetrating regime and erodes the political and diplomatic options to positively influence an offending country's behaviors. Indeed, Krain found that diplomatic sanctions do not raise the costs of genocide to the perpetrators but "merely reduce the flow of information without credibly signaling intent or commitment . . . [and] neither impede nor divide perpetrators and may actually increase cohesion given the perception of hostility from abroad."[100] Moreover, diplomatic disengagement "makes it harder . . . to gather intelligence about target actions or sanction effectiveness, communicate . . . desired outcomes and maintain influence overall in the target state . . . It also makes it harder to assess target state vulnerabilities, tailor appropriate sanctions policies to the situation and 'gauge the target's reaction to sanctions and assess their impact' . . . when diplomacy representation is downgraded or eliminated, negotiation is made more difficult."[101] These limits of diplomatic disengagement are affirmed by the ongoing crisis in Syria, in which atrocities continue unabated despite the diplomatic isolation of the Assad regime—one of several coercive measures that seem to have only heightened the regime's intransigence.

Economic Preventive Response Tools

Economic preventive response tools include an array of incentivizing cooperative and penalizing coercive measures to influence perpetrators as well as decision makers, victims, bystanders, and third-party enablers. With both the cooperative and coercive use of economic preventive tools, care must be taken that the implementation of response strategies mitigates rather than exacerbates conflict. In addition, both cooperative and coercive uses of economic measures must be understood to be different from regular developmental and humanitarian assistance programs in that they are used specifically as preventive response tools.[102]

Although it may seem poor form to offer rewards for perpetrators to stop behaving in bad ways, cooperative economic measures offer very potent interest-based positive incentives for behavior change. As Evans points out: "Although sometimes less popular with critical domestic audiences, who would often prefer to bludgeon perceived bad guys into submission than reward their actual or potential wrongdoing with taxpayer-funded handouts, incentives have the great attraction for policymakers that they actually tend to work—albeit probably best with some sticks in reserve as well."[103]

In some cases, the cooperative incentive-based tools used can include the alleviation of previously implemented coercive punishment-based tools. For instance, the *lifting of existing sanctions or embargoes* can be a cooperative inducement to reward a perpetrator regime for the cessation of mass killing. Such a reward, however, is much easier said than granted. As Griffiths and Barnes point out, "lifting sanctions can be complicated. Sometimes those targeted with sanctions do not believe that they will be lifted even if they comply (as happened at certain points in Iraq and Sudan) . . . Often there is little reason for the parties to change tack, as they are already paying the price of isolation."[104] Indeed, for as much as the international community has focused on imposing sanctions and embargoes, it has given far less thought to how they might best be lifted. As Peter Feaver (political scientist) and Eric Lorber (attorney) assert, if we prove "incapable of ending sanctions after its demands are met, the targeted state will have little incentive to favorably adjust its activities."[105] In their specific analysis of the United States, they suggest three main obstacles to easing the effect of sanctions in exchange for good behavior: (1) domestic policies related to the interplay of Congress and presidential executive orders, (2) coordination problems with different countries and international organizations, and (3) the private sector's understandable reluctance to engage with formerly sanctioned countries and companies. Attending to these types of obstacles, both domestically and internationally, can go a long way toward assuring future offending regimes that the lifting of existing sanctions or embargoes offers real incentive for compliance with international expectations of responsible behavior. Central to this, as will be discussed later in this section, is a more deliberate designing of sanctions that not only specifically target the intended actor but also can be more easily lifted if the target actor changes its behavior.

Offers of *debt relief or increased aid* could also change the behavior of an offending regime. In cases in which a country's "foreign debt is contributing to increased likelihood of conflict, it may be appropriate to arrange reduction, deferral, or cancellation of its debt payments."[106] Such debt relief, as well as increased foreign aid, also can be considered for neighboring countries in need of help to address the refugee and spillover effects from living in a bad neighborhood. Because of the conflict in neighboring Syria, for instance, Lebanon was host to 1,185,241 registered Syrian refugees as of April 2015. The UN High Commissioner for Refugees (UNHCR) has appealed for a staggering $1,973,915,104 as its total funding requirement for 2015 to deal with this humanitarian crisis.[107] Offers of increased aid may be particularly enticing in cases in which significant humanitarian assistance is needed and the offending regime is unable, or unwilling, to bear the entire humanitarian cost. Such assistance is especially powerful coming just at the onset of crisis as it may potentially ameliorate some of the drivers of conflict.[108]

Promises of *new funding or investment* also could incentivize an offending regime. Among these measures might be an exchange rate adjustment. "An exchange rate adjustment is a procedure adopted to eliminate the valuation effects arising from movements in exchange rates from data expressed in a common currency (generally the US dollar)."[109] A positive exchange rate adjustment can increase a country's purchasing power and economic strength. An international coalition can also incentivize cooperation by offering advocacy on the target country's behalf to the International Monetary Fund (IMF) or World Bank. These two entities can be important sources of new funds or investments to stabilize a fragile society. Investments by foreign corporations are particularly impactful in generating economic growth and providing development, employment, and wealth.[110]

Finally, there is a range of *trade incentives* that can be used as cooperative preventive response tools. Among these inducements for more favorable trade terms are tariff reductions, favorable taxation treatments, direct purchases, favored status, subsidies to exports or imports, providing export or import licenses, guaranteeing investments, sponsoring membership in a regional economic organization, or offering access to technology. Technological access can be particularly helpful as a cooperative preventive response tool if paired with initiatives of what crisis response practitioner Patrick Meier has termed "digital humanitarianism."[111] It took 38 years for radio to reach 50 million people worldwide, 13 years for television to reach that same number, but only 4 years for the Internet to reach 50 million people worldwide.[112] Certainly, access to the Internet has reshaped how we think about and interact with our world. As then-U.S. Secretary of State Hillary Clinton emphasized in a 2010 policy speech: "The spread of information networks is forming a new nervous system for our planet . . . Now, in many respects, information has never been so free. There are more ways to spread more ideas to more people than at any moment in history. And even in authoritarian countries, information networks are helping people discover new facts and making governments more accountable."[113] In this sense, the offer of technological access as a trade incentive, particularly to a country with a struggling infrastructure, can both reward good behavior as well as potentially serve as a preventive response tool for any future bad behavior.

Perhaps because of the ethical quandary involved in rewarding "bad people" for "good behavior," and the real-life consequence that those same "bad people" begin to demand even more rewards for "good behavior," it seems more common to see economic preventive response tools used coercively through threats and punishments against noncooperation.[114] Such measures—broadly understood in literature and practice as economic sanctions—attempt to raise the economic costs of perpetrating genocide beyond a bearable threshold for the perpetrators. Although individual countries or coalitions of countries can impose economic sanctions, they have binding force on the entire international community only when authorized by the UN Security Council under Chapter VII of the UN Charter.[115] "The use of mandatory sanctions is intended to apply pressure on a State or entity to comply with the objectives set by the Security Council without resorting to the use of force."[116] Research suggests that economic sanctions can force perpetrators to reduce the duration of ongoing atrocities, though not their severity.[117] More generally, however, such "sanctions, especially those originating in civil society, may have a 'socializing' effect. They send the message that if particular behaviour persists then the target may be excluded from its chosen 'reference group' (such as the 'West' or the 'international community')."[118]

Most notable among economic preventive measures used coercively are threats, or implementation, of *targeted financial sanctions.* "Targeted or 'smart' sanctions aim to minimize the harmful effects on civilian populations" by focusing on the pressure points of the specific regime, organization, or individual to be sanctioned.[119] Preventive response tools included in this category can be "investment bans (blocking investment by private and state-owned companies in the target country) . . . and visa bans against private companies that commit or facilitate gross human rights violations through the provision of information technology to monitor, track or target people for killing, torture or other grave abuses."[120] The denial of access to overseas financial markets, as well as to designated private banks and investors through which target countries access the global financial system, could be particularly detrimental. Such coercive financial measures also can involve denying, limiting, or suspending credits, aids, and loans available to the offending regime, its agencies, and those domestic economic actors who deal with international financial institutions and markets.[121]

The threat of such financial sanctions can often be more effective than their actual imposition. In 1999, for instance, "the mere threat to withhold loans and aid to Indonesia . . . badly shook Indonesia's currency and helped spur Jakarta to rein in the military in East Timor."[122] Even when carefully specified, however, targeted financial sanctions are not precision tools and their impact can vary considerably, often in unforeseen directions. As Feaver and Lorber point out, financial sanctions may advance political objectives at first but later stand in their way.[123] If not designed carefully, such sanctions may have a greater negative impact on civilians than they do on the elite to which they were targeted. Indeed, the elite are typically able to insulate themselves from any direct damage caused by financial sanctions and, sometimes, even benefit from such sanctions.

Similarly, comprehensive or selective *trade embargoes* could isolate an offending regime economically to such an extent that it could be crippling.

Such embargoes could involve the freezing or dissolution of trade agreements as well as limits placed on a country's or regime's income-generating activities (such as oil, diamonds, timber, or drugs) by restricting the trade of specific goods and commodities that provide power resources and revenues.[124] Profits from these commodity-specific activities "may be very directly related to the conflict in question, often constituting either the principal motivation for it, the means to start or sustain it, or both."[125] Such concern led, for instance, to the development of the Kimberley Process—an international program that aims to prevent the flow of conflict diamonds while helping to protect legitimate trade in rough diamonds.[126] As another example, a trade embargo on the sales of technology (computers, cell phones, satellite communications, informational technology) that could support the commission of genocide can help mitigate violence. Even a ban on "luxury goods" for specific entities and individuals on a designated list can be considered. For example, an October 2006 list of UN sanctions against North Korea, targeted at Kim Jong-il's well-known taste for expensive imported delicacies and goods, dictated that "Member States shall prevent the direct or indirect, new supply, sale, or transfer to the DPRK of luxury goods."[127] A partial or complete ban of trade or commerce can be a power-based tool to impose restrictive and punitive pressure on an abusive regime. Such embargoes could also be imposed against other countries that are supporting the target country.[128]

Freezing or seizing of monetary assets is another economic preventive response tool that can be used coercively to force behavioral change. These coercive measures can target the foreign assets of a country, rebel movement, or terrorist organization. More specifically, they can impose asset restrictions on targeted persons or even the outright seizure of their assets. When imposed multilaterally, the freezing or seizing of international accounts held by an offending country's government, businesses, or individuals can restrict access by perpetrators, their families and associates, or those persons designated as key supporters or enablers.[129] "Monetary assets can be held for the duration of the crisis and subsequently released or transferred to another legitimate custodian. In some cases it may be appropriate to use these assets as compensation for surviving victims."[130]

The freezing of assets played a considerable role in the international community's response to the regime of Muammar el-Qaddafi in Libya. In 2011, the United States and the European Union imposed a bilateral asset freeze on Qaddafi. This was followed by a multilateral UN Security Council resolution that added an arms embargo, travel bans, and targeted economic sanctions to the asset freeze. In the first week of sanctions, $36 billion in Libyan funds were locked down—denying Qaddafi "the funds to import heavy weapons, to hire foot solder mercenaries, or to contract with elite commando units."[131] According to sanctions scholar George Lopez, "the combination of UN, EU and US targeted sanctions played a considerable role in degrading both the regime's firepower and its support among Libyan elites."[132] Following Qaddafi's death, the unfreezing of assets slowly thawed, though there remains "no worldwide legal framework or treaty setting procedures for tracing, recovering and repatriating assets misappropriated or abused by deposed regimes."[133]

Threats, or implementation, of *divestment or aid conditionality* can also harm a regime's economic viability as well as have a suasive influence on outside countries or parties that provide support to the offending country. The withdrawal of investment, particularly when coupled with the retraction of IMF or World Bank support, can be a significant power-based tactic to apply punitive pressure on a regime to stop the continuation or escalation of genocide. For instance, the U.S. Sudan Accountability and Divestment Act of 2007 (SADA) granted state and local governments the authority to divest assets in companies that conduct business in Sudan and prohibited U.S. Government contracts with such companies. Seeking to maximize the impact on the Sudanese government while minimizing the impact on its civilians, SADA specifically targeted four key economic sectors in Sudan: power production, mineral extraction, oil-related activities, and production of military equipment.[134] Although Sudan's continued economic relationship with its major trading partner, China, limited the overall impact of these divestment strategies, such strategies were not entirely without effect. Within 3 years of the passage of SADA, for example, a total of about $3.5 billion in assets was diverted or frozen from 67 operating companies conducting business in Sudan.[135] In addition to its financial impact, divestment strategies can also help shape public discourse and moral awareness about a perpetrating regime's atrocities. Ultimately, such divestment strategies may be most effective when situated within larger movements of corporate social responsibility and socially responsible investing.

Likewise, when offending regimes are heavily dependent on aid, the implementation of aid conditionality could prove costly. Aid conditionality "means targeting development assistance so as to achieve particular policy responses from the recipient—for example, the holding of proper elections or the cessation of some more direct human rights abuse."[136] Aid even can be redirected to economic support of victim groups and their partners. Such conditionality is not without controversy. As Evans points out, it is particularly "contentious whether the denial of aid to people suffering under a recalcitrant regime is ever likely to do more good than harm."[137] As a result of this uncertainty, and with a desire to avoid strategies that may further harm civilians already under duress, coercive preference usually goes to the implementation of targeted financial sanctions, trade embargoes, the freezing or seizing of specific monetary assets, or divestment.

In conclusion, although the use of economic sanctions continues to increase, their actual effectiveness still remains a matter of scholarly debate. As political scientist Taehee Whang summarizes, "the conventional [scholarly] wisdom is that sanctions rarely work as a measure of coercion . . . [there is a] widespread knowledge of sanctions failures in an instrumental sense."[138] When we expand the focus beyond the most difficult and protracted conflicts, however, the success rate of economic sanctions is more pronounced. A recent analysis of 888 cases of economic sanctions imposed from 1971 to 2000, for example, found that "30% of those with known final outcomes ended with partial or total concessions from the target and another 25% ended with negotiations."[139]

Beyond their instrumental effectiveness, some also argue for a symbolic value of sanctions that justifies their use; a "prudent middle path between intervening militarily and standing idly by."[140] In 1967, for instance, noted Norwegian peace scholar Johan Galtung wrote: "If economic sanctions do not make a receiving nation comply, they may nevertheless serve functions that are useful in the eyes of the sending nation(s) . . . When military action is impossible for one reason or another, and when doing nothing is seen as tantamount to complicity, then something has to be done to express morality, something that at least serves as a clear signal to everyone that what the receiving nation has done is disapproved of. If the sanctions do not serve instrumental purposes, they can at least have *expressive* functions."[141] Domestically, the symbolic power of sanctions, as Whang demonstrated, can be used politically as "a low-cost way of displaying strong leadership during international conflicts."[142] Indeed, using data on U.S. presidential approval ratings from 1948 to 1999, Whang found a marked increase in the popularity of U.S. presidents (a "domestic audience benefit") from simply the initiation of sanctions—regardless of their eventual effectiveness. Globally, the symbolic function of sanctions lies in the signaling of normative values to international audiences.

To complement their symbolic value, attending to several factors can enhance the instrumental effectiveness of economic sanctions to generate at least partial compliance:

- First, the aims of the sanction "need to be clear, consistent and well-articulated so that they are fully understood by the target."[143] Central to that communication is a precise delineation of the persons or entities targeted as well as the conditions to be met for lifting the sanctions. Used in this way, sanctions can "provide a framework for new bargaining opportunity between target and imposers."[144]

- Second, sanctions should be implemented with enough specific scope to ensure that sufficient costs, without being excessively punitive, are imposed on the target from the outset rather than gradually escalated. Perpetrators are unlikely to be deterred by the typical first steps of minor or symbolic measures. Taking time to make sanctions "bite" is not acceptable in cases of genocide where such time is measured in the mounting loss of human lives.

- Third, the impact of sanctions is maximized when implemented with broad-based international cooperation that boosts the legitimacy of the sanctions. Sanctions are "owned" by the international community and the global broad-based support of sanctions helps ensure the political will necessary to implement them. In addition, multilateral cooperation also can minimize, at least normatively, the circumvention of sanctions by countries interested in continuing to cooperate with a sanctioned regime.

- Finally, the use of sanctions should be seen as a specific tool, not an overall strategy. When sanctions become the policy rather than a tool of policy, they are more likely to fail. So, sanctions should be coupled with other diverse response tools to most effectively slow, limit, or stop genocide.[145] In the view of UN Secretary-General Ban Ki-moon: "There is ample evidence that sanctions have enormous potential to contribute to the maintenance of international peace and security when used not as an end in themselves but in support of a holistic conflict resolution approach that includes prevention, mediation, peacekeeping, and peacebuilding."[146]

Legal Preventive Response Tools

Legal measures underlie the enforcement, or at least its threat, of several of the political and economic preventive response tools we have outlined. There are also, however, an impressive catalog of specific legal response tools that can be used preventively, in cooperative or coercive ways, to interrupt genocide. To appreciate their preventive breadth, it is necessary to move our conceptualization of legal tools beyond their application in long-term upstream approaches (such as the promotion of rule of law and human rights) and downstream retributive justice (such as trials of alleged perpetrators). Rather, we must reconceptualize legal tools as midstream preventive responses to encourage, or force, real-time change through slowing, limiting, or stopping an ongoing genocide.

Although it is perhaps easiest to think of legal response options as coercive measures, there is an array of cooperative legal response tools that can be used preventively. For instance, the deployment of *monitors to observe compliance with human rights standards and laws* can be a cooperative tool to incentivize conformity with international expectations regarding the protection of civilians. Such monitoring can encourage transparency and "in addition to scrutinizing the actions of perpetrators . . . can illuminate the role of negative actors who give them the necessary support."[147] Moreover, these types of deployments can "help reassure communities or groups feeling themselves at risk"—though it is important that such reassurance not translate into an overconfidence that emboldens opposition groups for retaliatory violence.[148] An international team of compliance monitors can even aid in the preventive development of an atrocity-reporting system, increased intelligence gathering and sharing, and the countering of hate speech and media.[149]

Perhaps a more controversial tool, *offers of amnesty or immunity* can be extended as a cooperative incentive to perpetrators who are willing to stop their commission of atrocities or as a way to secure their testimony against higher-level perpetrators or decision makers. "Amnesty and immunity are protections granted to individuals or groups of people that guarantee that they will not be brought to justice for crimes that they may have committed."[150] There is no established formal or customary prohibition on the offer of amnesties for international crimes. Although amnesty is typically a retroactive act of "forgetting" the criminal behavior, conditional offers of extending such exoneration could be used as midstream preventive tools in exchange for the cessation of genocidal acts. As the 2013 *Belfast Guidelines on Amnesty and Accountability* outline, at different stages, amnesties can facilitate positive objectives of "encouraging combatants to surrender and disarm; persuading authoritarian rulers to hand over power; building trust between warring factions; facilitating peace agreements; releasing political prisoners; encouraging exiles to return; providing an incentive to offenders to participate in truth recovery or reconciliation programmes."[151] The framers of those guidelines assert that the legitimate use of amnesties is bounded to those cases that "require individual offenders to engage with measures to ensure truth, accountability and reparations."[152] In their view, amnesties offered unconditionally are illegitimate and "have the effect of preventing investigations and ensuring impunity for persons responsible for serious crimes."[153]

In comparison, immunity is a protection granted by the position held by the person in question. Functional immunity protects certain senior officials from prosecution in other countries for acts committed within the context of their official duties; personal immunity protects certain senior officials from all lawsuits while they are in office.[154] It is now generally recognized that neither form of immunity protects state actors from prosecution in international courts for the most serious international crimes (including genocide). For example, both Slobodan Milosevic and Omar al-Bashir have been indicted by international criminal courts while they were sitting heads of state. Still, however, reassurances that such immunity (whether functional or absolute) will be honored in exchange for cooperation and progress toward a peaceful resolution may be a powerful incentive to change behavior or access information about crimes that may not otherwise come to light.

As Evans writes: "As much as it may shock the conscience to contemplate not pursuing prosecutions when major perpetrators of atrocity crimes are involved, this [offers of amnesty or immunity] can be helpful in certain circumstances in ending conflict, and in saving as a result a great many more lives."[155] He continues, though, to point out that such offers are suitable only in the most exceptional of cases. As he argues: "Justice serves too many public policy goals to ever be lightly traded away."[156] Similarly, a U.S. policy planning handbook concludes that "while these measures [offers of amnesty or immunity] may provide some short-term advantages, they may be detrimental to longer-term efforts to seek justice and reconciliation, and may be a bad precedent for would-be perpetrators elsewhere."[157]

The international community can also offer to aid a country in *domestic support of dispute resolution mechanisms*. Establishing, or reinforcing, domestic options for interrupting genocide generally does not have to start from scratch. "Every society has a range of informal and formal, traditional and more modern dispute resolution mechanisms . . . the challenge for international interveners is to work as best as possible to build on what's there while trying to nurture domestic support for constructive, progressive, and meaningful reforms."[158] In some contexts, it requires a particular sensitivity to support specific local mechanisms in a spirit true to broader international human rights principles. In addition, the strongest preventive application of these cooperative measures goes beyond the customary justice sector boundaries of formal judiciary, courts, and legal profession. Rather, it also includes nonstate and informal actors such as councils of chiefs and other traditional leaders, oversight organizations (including ombudsmen's offices and human rights commissions), and civil society organizations (including legal assistance and advocacy organizations as well as human rights groups).[159]

Finally, cooperative pressure can be exerted through *references to existing international law or norms* prohibiting genocide and encouraging the responsibility of a sovereign state to protect civilians within its borders. Such references—often heard in speeches of senior policymakers or global leaders—are simply pointed reminders of the laws and norms that prohibit criminal conduct against civilians; they are not themselves threats of referral, or actual referral, for criminal prosecution. There is a deep catalogue of existing international law (such as the Geneva Conventions and their Additional Protocols; the Convention against Torture and other Cruel, Inhuman or Degrading Treatment or Punishment; and the International Convention for the Protection of All Persons from Enforced Disappearance) or norms (such as the responsibility to protect and the responsibilities of transnational corporations with regard to human rights) that provides referential bases to apply cooperative pressure for an offending regime to change its behavior. As we have seen, the Genocide Convention, although focusing much attention on the punishment of genocide, also contains clear reference to a preventive dimension— including as punishable, in Article 3, acts of conspiracy to commit genocide, direct and public incitement to commit genocide, and attempts to commit genocide. As legal scholar William Schabas points out, each of these punishable acts is "aimed at future violations" and clearly implies the use of international law in a preventive capacity.[160]

The boundary between cooperative and coercive use of legal preventive response tools can be rather difficult to discern at times. The carrot can quickly become the stick in the face of rapidly growing risks and the first indicators of genocide. In such cases, legal preventive response tools can be used coercively to slow, limit, or stop genocide through punishments and threats against noncooperation.

One coercive use of legal preventive response tools to force change in the behaviors of an offending regime or perpetrators involves appeals for *action by UN organs*. Article 8 of the Genocide Convention urges "any contracting party [to] call upon the competent organs of the United Nations to take such action under the Charter of the United Nations as they consider appropriate for the prevention and suppression of acts of genocide or any of the other acts enumerated in Article 3."[161] Although calls for such action certainly crossover as a type of political preventive response tool, they can also be used coercively as the initiation for a range of legal preventive response tools. The "competent organs" described in Article 8 of the Genocide Convention are delineated in Article 7 of the Charter of the United Nations and include the Secretariat, Security Council, General Assembly, International Court of Justice, Economic and Social Council, and the Trusteeship Council (which, as of November 1, 1994, suspended operations with the granting of independence to Palau). Of these so-called "principal organs," each has the capacity to play a preventive role in the face of genocide. As Schabas describes, for instance, "the Security Council, the General Assembly, the Secretariat and the Economic and Social Council all took action in Rwanda, either in their own right or through their subsidiary bodies."[162]

Although, in the case of Rwanda, preventive responses by UN organs failed to stop the killing, it also stands true that these same organs have helped create a large body of international law outlining and protecting human rights. "Most member states have signed and ratified some eighty treaties (also called conventions or covenants) that cover particular aspects of human rights."[163] These treaties, including the Genocide Convention (the first human rights treaty adopted by the General Assembly of the UN), offer legal preventive response tools that can be referenced, and put into play, by the actions of UN organs. Complementing the work of the principal organs, the UN Committee on the Elimination of Racial Discrimination (CERD)—a committee of independent experts composing one of 10 human rights treaty bodies that monitor implementation of the core international human rights treaties—has taken a special interest in genocide prevention in recent years. In 2005, CERD adopted a Declaration on the Prevention of Genocide in which it noted "that the international community has a further responsibility to act, inter alia with force if necessary as a last resort, in collective response to threats of genocide and other massive violations of human rights when a State fails to protect its citizens."[164]

Perhaps, however, the most significant preventive action taken by UN organs has been the establishment of a Special Adviser on the Prevention of Genocide. Inaugurated with the appointment of Juan Mendez in July 2004, the office of the Special Adviser "acts as a catalyst to raise awareness of the causes and dynamics of genocide, to alert relevant actors where there is a risk of genocide, and to advocate and mobilize for appropriate action."[165] Although the Special Adviser's office cannot make a determination on whether genocide in a given context has occurred, it is charged with the collection of information necessary to act in a timely fashion as a mechanism of early warning to the Secretary-General and, through that office, to the Security Council, on actions to prevent or halt genocide. In 2007, the complementary work of a Special Adviser on the Responsibility to Protect was merged to form a joint office with the work and activities of the Special Adviser on the Prevention of Genocide.[166] To date, the success of the office as a preventive response tool has been more pronounced in its upstream national and regional training programs than it has as a midstream early warning mechanism to the Secretary-General and the Security Council. Mendez, replaced in 2007 by Francis Deng, has been particularly vocal about the preventive obstacles imposed by the Special Adviser's lack of direct access to the Security Council.[167] As it continues to evolve, however, the Special Adviser's office can, and should, emerge as a significant UN organ for the prevention of genocide.

Human rights investigations can also be initiated to interrupt genocide. Such investigations may be a natural coercive consequence when the cooperative presence of international human rights monitors and observers fails to slow, limit, or stop ongoing atrocities. Human rights documentation, during an atrocity, can have a preventive impact by placing punitive pressure on perpetrators whose crimes are being investigated. Documentation by local investigators is particularly important. "Local investigators have the ability to blend in and work 'under the radar', speak the local dialect, and can travel to areas which might be off limits to international observers, such as the United Nations or African Union."[168] The power of local documentation was revealed dramatically in July 2014 with the release of over 55,000 photographs documenting an estimated 11,000 individuals killed and tortured by the Syrian regime of President Bashar al Assad. The source of that documentation, a former Syrian military police forensic photographer, is unique given that he was employed by the regime perpetrating the atrocities. Communication and advocacy plans, along with security precautions for local monitors, are especially vital in ensuring that the information documented can be used to force a change in the behavior of the offending regime or perpetrators. In addition, international support for the investigation of mass atrocities, including the forensic examination of atrocity crimes scenes, may also mitigate the continuation or escalation of genocidal violence.[169]

Such documentation, central to human rights investigations, can also be collected from far above ground level. The Satellite Sentinel Project, for instance, uses cutting edge satellite imagery and data analysis to document human rights crimes as they develop and unfold in Sudan and South Sudan.[170] Similarly, the Sentinel Project (an unrelated Canada-based organization) is using unmanned aerial vehicles (UAVs or drones) in the Tana Delta region of eastern Kenya for preventive purposes. "If we determine that violence is imminent we can use our networks to alert authorities, warn those in danger, and even provide safety guidance based on our observations from the sky. In the event that violence is already taking place, we can implement the same measures to mitigate risk to residents while working to document the events by gathering aerial evidence of the perpetrators which cannot be collected safely from the ground."[171] The midstream preventive implications of such technology lies in the restrictive and punitive power it generates as perpetrators know that the world is, literally, a witness to their atrocities.

Another coercive measure to place pressure on an offending regime or individuals is *threats of referral or actual referral for criminal prosecution*. For cases involving states, Article 9 of the Genocide Convention cites the preventive responsibilities of the International Court of Justice as the organ to which states can take alleged breaches of the Convention. To date, 14 such cases have appeared before the court (including the case of *Bosnia and Herzegovina v. Serbia and Montenegro*, as described at the beginning of Chapter 4). For cases involving individuals, these measures can include domestic indictments against individuals, though often the state in question is unwilling or unable to perform this judicial responsibility. Criminal indictments against individuals can also come from specialist international courts—such as the UN Security Council-mandated International Criminal Tribunal for the former Yugoslavia (established in 1993), the International Criminal Tribunal for Rwanda (1994), and the Special Tribunal for Lebanon (2009). In some cases, specialist courts may have more of a hybrid construction, involving both international and national features and most often grafted onto a local judicial system—such as the Serious Crimes Panels in the District Court of Dili in East Timor (2000), the "Regulation 64" Panels in the Courts of Kosovo (2000), the Special Court for Sierra Leone (2002), the War Crimes Chamber in the State Court of Bosnia-Herzegovina (2005), and the Extraordinary Chambers in the Courts of Cambodia (2006). Although the practical limitations of such specialist courts will be discussed in Chapter 6, their fundamental preventive limitation is that they are ad hoc courts most often created, or only becoming functional, after the conflict has ended. So, from a preventive standpoint, it is only the specter of referral to such courts that has the potential to force change in the behavior an offending regime or individual perpetrators.

Partially in response to this reality, the International Criminal Court (ICC) was established in 1998 as a permanent, treaty-based court "to help end impunity for the perpetrators of the most serious crimes of concern to the international community."[172] Preventively, threats of referral, or actual referral, for criminal prosecution before the ICC, a standing court, should leave would-be perpetrators far more conscious of their vulnerability to prosecution. Sudanese President Omar al-Bashir's indictments for war crimes, genocide, and crimes against humanity, for example, were the first time the ICC directly charged a sitting head of state and were envisioned as a coercive lever to force change in his regime's behavior. Unfortunately, however, the lack of cooperation from Sudan, coupled with an absence of coercive pressure from the Security Council to take "necessary measures" to enforce compliance, left Bashir and other Sudanese officials charged by the ICC free to continue their commission of mass atrocities with impunity. In December 2014, in the face of such noncooperation, the ICC decided to suspend their criminal investigations of atrocities in Darfur (though the indictments remain in place). Although this complete negation of the ICC's authority flies in the face of the supposed deterrent nature of referral, idealists still express hope that the preventive significance of the ICC "is not limited to its ability to prosecute perpetrators of mass atrocity but also its ability to act as a deterrent to future gross violations of human rights. This is because of the real rather than imagined possibility of prosecution even when the government of a state is unable or unwilling to pursue justice for victims of mass atrocities."[173]

Finally, the evolution of customary international law provides for the *exercise of universal jurisdiction* over the crime of genocide. As discussed in Chapter 2, the exercise of universal jurisdiction means that any country can try a perpetrator of genocide, regardless of where the atrocities were committed. Although not provided for under conventional law in the Genocide Convention, universal jurisdiction has become an accepted part of customary international law and has been exercised by several countries, particularly in the European Union and North America. In 2001 for instance, a Belgian court exercised the right of universal jurisdiction in sentencing two Rwandan nuns (both of whom had fled to Belgium after the end of the genocide) to prison for their role in the Rwandan genocide. "It was the first time Belgium had used a law passed seven years ago, allowing its courts to hear cases of alleged human rights violations even if they were committed abroad."[174] Although Belgium's exercise of universal jurisdiction is restricted to cases in which an alleged perpetrator is on Belgian territory, other countries—most notably, Spain—have a very aggressive record in exercising the customary right of universal jurisdiction over alleged perpetrators not residing in their territory. As such, the coercive exercise of universal jurisdiction over the crime of genocide can have powerful preventive implications as a legal response tool. The notion that perpetrators may not find a safe haven simply by leaving the country, during or after the period in which their crimes were perpetrated, can be a significant pressure point in forcing a change in their behavior. Although there is concern that the recent repeal of Spain's universal jurisdiction law is a setback for the exercise of universal jurisdiction worldwide, genocide still remains a crime subject to universal jurisdiction and its exercise has the potential to be an important deterrent tool to apply restrictive or punitive pressure on an offending regime or perpetrators.

In conclusion, when used coercively, each of these legal preventive response tools assumes a deterrent effect of legal accountability. That is, change can be forged through the threat of punishment. As Evans points out, the establishment of specialist tribunals to deal with crimes committed in specific conflicts, the establishment of the ICC, and the more common exercise of universal jurisdiction should have coalesced to concentrate "the minds of potential perpetrators on the risks they run of international retribution."[175] Unfortunately, however, the limited scope of criminal convictions in the specialist tribunals, coupled with the even more limited scope of cases currently under investigation or trial by the ICC, leaves a correspondingly limited deterrent effect for perpetrators. As Evans writes, "... not enough convictions [either by the specialist courts or the ICC] have yet accumulated to give potential perpetrators any real sense that impunity for mass atrocity crimes really is a thing of the past."[176] Even if that sense of future punishment can be established, however, it still may not have the expected impact on perpetrators whose conception of time and accountability is bounded to the murderous urgency of the present. Moreover, as discussed previously, the exercise of universal jurisdiction currently seems in retreat. The future suggests that it likely will be exercised even less often than in 2008 when Evans lamented: "Not many countries—only around a dozen—of those that have legislated to allow their courts to apply universal jurisdiction, have shown much inclination to do so."[177] As a result, the degree to which the deterrent of legal accountability serves a preventive function for would-be perpetrators remains uncertain.

Military Preventive Response Tools

To this point, we have seen the rich and diverse array of tools, whether used cooperatively or coercively, that can be employed as midstream measures to interrupt genocide. The final compartment of preventive response tools relates to military responses. Clearly, the military can play a supportive role in many of the cooperative and coercive political, economic, and legal preventive measures previously discussed. Moreover, the specter of military response—whether implemented cooperatively or coercively—often gives teeth to the other preventive categories. Too often, however, military preventive response tools—particularly the most extreme tool of nonconsensual coercive intervention—are used in isolation as the only seemingly viable alternative to slowing, limiting, or stopping genocide. To be most effective, any application of military response tools should embed them as a coordinated element of an integrated and diverse strategy. Military measures should not be considered the exclusive or ultimate tool in responding to genocide. Nor should they been seen as "an all-or-nothing choice between taking no military action and launching a major intervention."[178]

Among the wide range of cooperative response tools that can be brought to bear to mitigate the continuation or escalation of genocidal violence are offers of *military aid or training*. Although such offers can be controversial, when used as a tool of cooperative diplomacy they can be powerful incentives for perpetrators to stop their destructive behavior. In situations in which such incentives are already offered, "their expansion may be an additional motivation."[179] Military aid and training constitute a type of security sector reform aiming to ensure that "armed forces, police, and intelligence services are competent and democratized."[180] Although generally seen as an upstream or downstream preventive measure, offers of such support also can incentivize changes in real-time behavior by an offending regime, particularly one caught in the grip of crisis while transitioning from a military to civilian-controlled government. In such situations, military aid can be given in the form of credits to buy weapons or equipment from the donor country or countries. Training to professionalize military forces may be especially enticing for countries attempting to strengthen weak state structures and correct a perceived state legitimacy deficit. In some cases, military aid and training can even be provided to indigenous opposition groups in an attempt to help them slow, limit, or stop genocide.

Although offers of such aid can encourage positive change in perpetrator behavior during a crisis situation, care must be taken that it does not come at the expense of humanitarian and development assistance—and particularly that it does not backfire in the near term or long term and lead to more civilian casualties. In January 2013, for instance, U.S. General Carter Ham acknowledged that too much U.S. military training for officers from the Malian army focused on tactics, strategy, and technical matters rather than "values, ethics, and a military ethos."[181] So, the delivery of military aid and training to Mali (one of 134 countries that received such assistance from the United States in 2012), originally meant to provide stability in the face of rapidly growing risks, has turned into aid and training for an army now accused of massacring scores of civilians in rebel-held territory. As policy analyst John Norris has argued, although "there are many examples of successful US military training programs," there are also "lots of headline cases that have gone badly wrong over the years—from training Indonesian troops that carried out atrocities in East Timor to the billions poured into the Egyptian military to the scores of tainted graduates from the School of the Americas that ran riot in Central America during the 1980s."[182]

Confidence and security-building measures (CSBMs) function to make the conduct of states and opposition groups more calculable and predictable, so that they can have certain expectations with regard to each other's behaviors. Although they can be used to build trust as an upstream or downstream preventive measure, CSBMs may also be used as midstream preventive tools to address or resolve escalating crises. Used cooperatively, these forms of military preventive response tools can be deployed to "lessen tensions by increasing transparency of capabilities and intentions, allaying anxieties or suspicions and improving predictability for the parties involved, clarifying intentions about military force and political activities."[183] In 2000, for instance, the Organization of American States initiated a series of CSBMs between Belize and Guatemala that included agreements on military and police patrols as well as contacts between defense ministries of the two countries.[184] Whether initiated by individual governments, nonstate actors, or regional or international third party actors, reciprocal information exchanges between conflicting parties (particularly on the physical disposition of military, paramilitary, or police forces) can reduce high levels of mistrust and decrease the fear of genocidal violence.[185] Such exchanges can be accompanied by agreements regarding demobilization, disarmament, and force restructuring. Moreover, the intelligence gathered from these exchanges, subject to independent verification, may be used to provide target victims with information and practical help to evade the perpetrators of violence.[186]

Security guarantees for the protection of civilians, often in the form of safe havens or evacuation, could also incentivize an offending regime by giving them an option to concentrate or relocate a target group in a protected area. A "safe haven" refers to the defensive protection of civilians in a fixed location. "A safe haven is a specific and limited form of security guarantee, often but not exclusively intended to provide for the safe delivery of humanitarian aid, but in all cases demanding a genuine commitment to protect civilians with force if necessary."[187] Unfortunately, as the world saw in Srebrenica, the "genuine commitment" of a "security guarantee" can prove very disingenuous when safe havens are actually threatened. The assault on Srebrenica, a small town tucked away in a steep-sloped valley in eastern Bosnia–Herzegovina, has come to symbolize the brutality of the Bosnian war. There, for 3 years, nearly 40,000 refugees, mostly Muslim, sought safe haven from Bosnian Serb forces bent on their destruction. Tragically, "it was never disarmed nor was it ever really protected—a betrayal of both of the key designations that 'safe haven' was supposed to indicate."[188] In July 1995, during the waning days of the war and despite the presence of UN troops, Serb forces advanced into Srebrenica where they separated Muslim women, children, and the elderly from military-aged men. Over the course of the next several days, the Serb forces captured and executed 8,372 unarmed Muslim men and boys (some as young as 10 years of age) on football fields, in gymnasiums, and in abandoned factories and warehouses.[189] It was the worst atrocity committed on European soil since World War II and illustrated the vital preventive lesson that "an internationally mandated safe haven is only as good as the capacity to protect it."[190]

Finally, *consensual preventive deployment* can be used cooperatively to constrain hostilities. "At the request of a government or with its consent, peacekeepers (both civilian and military personnel) can be called upon to reduce suffering and limit or control violence."[191] Although traditional peacekeeping missions are more generally seen as downstream measures that support or enforce a political settlement or ceasefire that already has been reached, consensual preventive deployment is a midstream defensive military mission with the primary purpose of protecting civilians in situations of rapidly growing risks or the first indicators of genocide. Organized by multilateral international and regional organizations, consensual preventive deployment is a proactive deterrent to keep a volatile situation from escalating into acute, even genocidal, violence. Some examples include UN preventive deployment in Macedonia (1992–1999), the British-led peace support operation in Sierra Leone (2000), the UN Mission in the DRC (1999–2008), and the UN operation in Burundi (2004–2006). "The deterrent utility of this kind of deployment . . . lies not in the numbers on the ground but in the demonstration of high-level international interest and concern in the situation: it puts all the parties under close international scrutiny, and there is at least an implication of willingness to take further action if there is any resort to violence."[192]

Unfortunately, the request or consent of governments for deployment of third party troops is relatively rare. For potential troop-contributing nations, issues of financial cost and difficulties of justifying such involvement to domestic constituencies can also be problematic. Moreover, even when used, the operational risks of consensual preventive deployment can "cause an unintended escalation as the perceived window of opportunity closes in the eyes of the perpetrator. Intended victims may feel themselves protected by the force, and empowered to undertake their own retribution."[193] Reflecting the inherent limits of consensual preventive deployment, preliminary research has found that whether their deterrent effect is presumed to be in the role of witness or as an impartial intervener, such deployments "have no statistically significant effect on the severity of genocide."[194]

Cooperative strategies in the use of military preventive response tools hold great promise. Often, they can even be used to reward cooperation and progress by being reinstalled after a period of suspension (for instance, the resumption of military aid or training after positive change in an offending regime's behavior). By the time genocide is triggered, however, perpetrators may be particularly resistant—because of the scale of resources and commitment they have already invested in the process of destruction—to any form (military or otherwise) of cooperative preventive response strategies.[195] So, generally, greater deterrent weight comes either from positive incentives being used coercively (for instance, the withdrawal of military aid or training programs) or the outright implementation of coercive measures to force change through threats and punishments against noncooperation.

Restricted arms, movements, and communications can disrupt the means and capabilities of the destructive capacity of perpetrators. Arms embargoes can be applied by individual states, coalitions of states, or regional or subregional organizations, but are best known as a familiar response tool of the UN Security Council (UNSC). Although some UNSC arms embargoes are voluntary, UN Member States are legally obliged to enforce those declared as mandatory.[196] Most recently, on April 14, 2015, for instance, the UNSC passed a mandatory arms embargo against Houthi rebel militia and fighters in Yemen.[197] At present, repeated calls for the UNSC to pass a mandatory arms embargo on South Sudan have yet to be heeded. The EU does, however, have a long-standing arms embargo on Sudan that was amended in July 2011 to also include the newly independent state of South Sudan (though the supply of nonlethal military equipment and related assistance to support security sector reform was exempted from the arms embargo). When used as a tool in a larger, coherent policy package, research on UN arms embargoes imposed from 1990 to 2006 revealed a positive impact on the target's behavior in 25% of those cases.[198] Ultimately, however, the legal and administrative framework to ensure maximum effectiveness of arms embargoes is very difficult to implement, leading some to conclude that "although frequently employed, arms embargoes have been the least effective form of sanction."[199]

Embedded in restricting the movements of perpetrators is the opportunity to create "different modalities of coercive protection of civilians . . . where victims can seek refuge and humanitarian aid can be delivered, the creation of humanitarian corridors and the protection of aid convoys and aid workers or other international personnel working to protect local populations at risk."[200] The area control necessary to create such buffers between victims and perpetrators—as well as leave corridors open for international humanitarian assistance—likely will require coercive strategies to restrict or contain the movements of perpetrators.

Finally, restricted communications can be used coercively to "dissuade mass atrocities, foment mutual distrust within the perpetrators' ranks, weaken their morale, and reduce popular support for the regime and actions related to mass atrocities."[201] Such efforts can include the prevention of incitement (such as jamming radio or television transmissions from the ground in-country, a neighboring country, or from the air) as well as the countering of hate media with leaflet drops and electronic countermeasures. In Rwanda, for instance, much has been written about the preventive potential lost when the U.S. administration decided not to jam transmissions from RTLM, an extremist hate radio station that, in the words of Lt. General Romeo Dallaire, force commander of the UN mission to Rwanda, "was a direct instrument in promoting genocide."[202]

As the coercive use of military tools escalates, a *heightened military presence in the region* can be a strong deterrent threat for a perpetrator regime. At times, the mere threat of such a presence—through headquarters activation or mission assignment, increased alert status, and deployment preparations—may send a strong enough message to perpetrators to mitigate the continuation or escalation of genocide.[203] At other times, actual troop deployment to the region—offshore or in a neighboring country—may be necessary to make the deterrent threat credible. In this case, "military resources are deployed without an actual intervention on the territory of the targeted state, and accordingly the question of consent does not arise."[204] Such nonterritorial shows of posturing and force (for example, port visits by naval vessels and the conducting of military exercises) can help prevent a conflict from spreading regionally as well as serving as a highly visible means of international scrutiny. In addition, these measures "would familiarize forces with the area of operation [and] permit additional intelligence gathering" as well as providing a rapid response capacity should the crisis escalate quickly.[205] Unfortunately, a heightened military presence in the region may also lead perpetrators to "accelerate their conduct of atrocities because they may perceive a window of opportunity that is closing."[206] So, care must be taken that the heightened military presence in the region be used constructively to defuse the crisis situation rather than escalate it.

Building on a heightened military presence in the region, the *credible threat of military force* can be a strong deterrent for a perpetrator regime. Five multinational organizations have authority to pose such a credible threat to slow, limit, or stop genocide—the North Atlantic Treaty Organization (NATO), European Union (EU), Economic Community of West African States (ECOWAS), African Union (AU), and the UN. Particularly interruptive would be a credible threat of military force based on regional or international rapid deployment capability. The 28 member countries of NATO, for instance, have plans for a Very High Readiness Joint Task Force (VJTF) "that will be able to deploy within a few days to respond to challenges that arise."[207] Conceived of as a "spearhead force" within NATO's long-standing multinational response force, plans are to have the VJTF operationally capable by 2016.

The 28 member countries of the EU have already developed standing Battle Groups, small rapid reaction forces to give Europe the means to quickly intervene in any developing global security crisis. Operationalized in 2007, the Battle Groups—looking to complement but not challenge NATO's response force—are combat-trained units of 1,500 personnel, two of whom are on standby for a 6-month period and are deployable within 10 days after an EU decision and could be sustainable for 30 days. Larger member states contribute their own Battle Groups whereas smaller member states create joint Battle Groups (for example, the Nordic Battle Group composed of seven participating countries). At present, despite its high level of political support throughout Europe, not one decision to deploy an EU Battle Group has been adopted. The closest it came was in late 2013 when plans were drawn up to send an EU Battle Group into the rapidly escalating crisis in the Central African Republic. Unfortunately, however, the only fully operational Battle Group on standby at the time was Britain and London's reaction to the idea was so hostile that the deployment plans were immediately dropped.[208] As a result of the lack of credibility and effectiveness of the Battle Groups, in March 2015, Jean-Claude Juncker, the president of the European commission, advocated for a standing army to help the EU "design a common foreign and security policy."[209] Immediately rejected by the United Kingdom, it is very unlikely that the proposal will gain any serious traction among the majority of EU member states.

Although, as discussed in Chapter 4, the 15 member countries of ECOWAS have focused more attention on the establishment of an early warning system (ECOWARN) than on the establishment of rapid deployment capability, the 54 member states of the AU have proposed the development of a multinational African Standby Force (ASF) within each of Africa's five subregions. Article 4(h) of the 2000 Constitutive Act of the AU grants "the right of the Union to intervene in a Member State pursuant to a decision of the Assembly in respect of grave circumstances, namely: war crimes, genocide and crimes against humanity."[210] To advance that right, the ASF would include military, police, and civilian personnel on standby in their countries of origin and ready for rapid deployment in situations of growing risks and escalating crisis in Africa. The ASF is part of a broader African Peace and Security Architecture plan that, as one critic suggests, "is only taken seriously by those who make their living from it."[211] Indeed, African heads of state seem to have little interest in delegating power to the AU and "national-level efforts to both stall and undermine the ASF soon robbed it of its momentum."[212] In addition, although the proposed multidisciplinary nature of the ASF (military, police, and civilian personnel) was promising, the military seems to have an increasingly dominant role in shaping its development. In October 2015, twice-deferred plans to hold a field training exercise for the ASF finally began with an aim to make the 25,000-strong force ready for deployment by January 2016.[213]

Internationally, some have argued for the creation of a United Nations Emergency Peace Service (UNEPS) to serve as a permanent standing UN service (around 15,000–18,000 military, civilian police, judicial experts, and relief professionals) to complement other actors in protecting civilians at imminent risk of mass atrocities.[214] This civil society-led proposal stems from the fact that the UN is notorious for late deployments of peacekeepers, along with underresourcing of both troops and supplies. In April 2014, for example, the UN responded to the crisis in the Central African Republic by establishing the Multidimensional Integrated Stabilization Mission in the Central African Republic (MINUSCA) with a mandate to protect civilians from threats of violence. Ten months later, the deployment of peacekeepers had still not reached full strength; only 8,500 of the force's potential 11,800 were deployed. Full deployment was not expected until April 2015—a full year after the UN gave the green light—leaving MINUSCA severely compromised in its ability to fulfill their mandate. This is not an isolated incident. Recent research revealed that of 15 UN missions authorized within the past 15 years, the average time from formal authorization to initial deployment was 46 days. In nine of those 15 missions, "less than 15% of the authorized force was deployed within the first 90 days and, on average, full deployment was not achieved until nearly 13 months later."[215] In the face of genocide, such bureaucratic lags––waiting for Member States to contribute troops of their own national armies to work under the Blue Helmet of the UN, securing resources and supplies for deployment, coordinating chains of command structure— are measured in the loss of thousands of lives. As former UN Secretary-General Kofi Annan said, the UN is "the only fire brigade in the world that has to wait for the fire to break out before it can acquire a fire engine."[216]

In the eyes of Australian peace researcher Annie Herro, having a specialized service on permanent standby would give us "the ability to respond immediately to (immanent) crises, operating with a 'first-in, first-out' deployment philosophy, and would have a maximum deployment of six months. It would thus close the gap between the UNSC resolution sanctioning an operation and action. Having UNEPS readily available might also assist in obtaining UNSC authorization for the use of force and reduce unilateral interventions."[217] To date, despite the sensibility of the proposal, and its considerable merits, the 193 Member States of the UN have yet to embrace it. There is concern, particularly in the Global South, that the UNEPS would become a tool of interest of powerful states and be used to violate the sovereignty of less powerful states for purposes other than the protection of civilians. As one representative admitted, too many Member States are not comfortable giving the UN "an independent force that they fear may be used against them."[218]

The on-ground preventive impact of such regional and international forces is impossible to ascertain as, in practice, most really exist only on paper to this point. Ultimately, however, the threat of military force is credible only if such a force exists. Even if, and when, the force exists, any deterrent effect can only come from the member states' actual willingness to agree to put their troops in harm's way in the face of genocidal violence. As we have seen in our brief review of NATO's VJTF, the EU Battle Groups, the AU's African Standby Force, and the proposed UN Emergency Peace Service, member states of such organizations are hesitant to do so unless there is a compelling reason of national interests. So, the degree of credibility we can assign to the threat of military force from these organizations, even when such force exists and is operational, remains debatable.

Finally, the most costly use of a military preventive response tool is the *use of military force for nonconsensual coercive intervention.* Nonconsensual coercive measures to protect civilians by militarily defeating the perpetrators can range from unconventional warfare (for example, military intervention to "organize resistance forces to undermine a complicit government, give potential victims the means to defend themselves, or divert the adversary's focus from other areas") to precision targeting (for example, "strikes and raids . . . conducted against key military or government targets") to a full military intervention via an air campaign or deployment of ground troops.[219] Obviously, as the graduated responses increase in severity, so do the corresponding risks of unintended escalation, lethal collateral damage, military losses on the part of the intervening forces, increased intransigence of the perpetrators or offending regime, or mission creep.[220]

The use of military force for nonconsensual coercive intervention poses significant costs. To the civilians it is meant to protect, military intervention can inflame hostilities and put them at greater risk by further destabilizing the state in which they reside. To a perpetrator regime it is meant to defeat, military intervention can rouse sympathy among bystander nations and lead perpetrators to blame the victims for the costs they are now suffering. To an international order predicated on state sovereignty, military intervention can undermine that "last defense against the rules of an unequal world" and raise the abusive threat of powerful states meddling in the affairs of those less powerful.[221] To the intervening forces, military intervention can lead to massive expense, equipment loss, and casualties—often in a country or region with no readily apparent national interests. Benjamin Valentino, for instance, estimates that the United States spent between $280,000 and $700,000 for each Somali life it spared during a military intervention in the early 1990s. As he summarizes, "military intervention is a particularly expensive way to save lives."[222]

Given these considerable costs, some have questioned whether the use of military force for nonconsensual coercive intervention should even be in the toolbox. Bridget Conley-Zilkic, for instance, has likened its presence to the plot device known as "Chekhov's gun." In warning against extraneous detail in storytelling, Chekhov is reputed to have advised: "If you say in the first chapter that there is a rifle hanging on a wall, in the second or third chapter it absolutely must go off."[223] For Zilkic, having the coercive tool of military intervention in the toolbox, or "hanging on the wall," foreshadows its use over less harmful preventive response tools in the toolbox. In her view, we must demilitarize the imagination of atrocities prevention by recognizing the wide variety of preventive response tools that, if applied successfully, make it absolutely unnecessary to resort to coercive military actions.[224]

For better or worse, however, the use of military force is the bite behind the bark of the other preventive response tools and, as such, will always be "hanging on the wall." This is why it is acutely necessary to clearly define the parameters that justify and legitimize the use of such force. The foundational principle of nonintervention is "the norm from which any departure has to be justified" and the coercive use of military force is a clear departure in need of equally clear justification.[225] A common ground, transparent understanding of these parameters is crucial because "the chances for successful intervention rise if military operations are seen as legitimate by the international community and local populations . . . Military measures in response to mass atrocities are controversial and will lack international support if they are seen as a smokescreen for narrow national self-interests."[226] Central to defining the parameters for the use of lawful and legitimate military force as a preventive response tool in the face of genocide are three questions—when to intervene, how to intervene, and who should intervene?[227]

When to Intervene? In terms of when to intervene, one just cause consideration comes from "situations where large scale loss of civilian life or ethnic cleansing is threatened or taking place."[228] Similarly, for the Danish Institute of International Affairs, the level of violations that triggers a military intervention should involve "extreme cases of gross and massive violations of human rights or international humanitarian law."[229] As discussed in Chapter 3, these extreme cases have been given definitional life in the legal conceptual framework of mass atrocities that includes genocide, war crimes, crimes against humanity, and—in subsumed form—ethnic cleansing. Although some insist that actual violations of these laws must be occurring to trigger intervention, others argue for intervention to prevent likely or imminent violations. The ICISS report, for example, suggests "military action can be legitimate as an anticipatory measure in response to clear evidence of likely large-scale killing. Without this possibility of anticipatory action, the international community would be placed in the morally untenable position of being required to wait until genocide begins, before being able to take action to stop it."[230]

Another consideration related to the timing of intervention is that of last resort. "The responsibility to react—with military coercion—can only be justified when the responsibility to prevent has been fully discharged."[231] The use of military force for nonconsensual coercive intervention is the exceptional and extraordinary preventive tool of last resort; it is used only when all other preventive response tools have been tried and have failed to slow, limit, or stop the continuation or escalation of genocide. For some, however, rapidly escalating situations of crisis often means that there may not be time for all other preventive response tools to be tried. Even when circumstances dictate that all other preventive response tools cannot be exhausted, they must still be carefully considered and "there must be at least reasonable grounds for believing that . . . if the measure had been attempted it would not have succeeded."[232]

A final consideration related to the timing of intervention relates to the chances of success for slowing, limiting, or stopping genocide. Although dependent on how success is defined, the timing of an intervention must be weighed on the reasonable prospects of how likely it is to protect civilians from being done to death, particularly in comparison to the consequences of inaction. "Military action can only be justified if it stands a reasonable chance of success, that is, halting or averting the atrocities or suffering that triggered the intervention in the first place."[233] Even if military intervention is successful in stopping genocide in its immediate tracks, longer-term issues remain. As human rights advocate Holly Burkhalter asks: "Does the intervention preserve or revert to a status quo that is grossly abusive? Are perpetrators left in positions of authority? Will civilians remain at risk once international forces depart?"[234] Military action is particularly difficult to justify if it raises the possibility of triggering a larger regional, or even global, conflict.

How to Intervene? How should the use of military force for nonconsensual coercive intervention be carried out as to ensure maximum effectiveness in slowing, limiting, or stopping genocide? In terms of how to intervene, central is the notion of right intention or proper purpose based on the humanitarian concern of protecting civilians from being done to death. Though absolute purity of motive is unreasonable to ask, "the primary purpose of the intervention must be to halt or avert human suffering."[235] Although other events—the overthrow of a regime, the alteration of borders, the occupation of territory—may coincide with the mandate of protection in some cases, they are not legitimate objectives to justify military intervention. Determining right intention or proper purpose can be inferred from collective or multilateral rather than unilateral intervention, ensuring the intervention is supported by the people for whose benefit the intervention is intended, and the extent to which other countries in the region are supportive of the intervention.[236]

Given right intention, the doctrine of proportionality requires that the military intervention not threaten greater destruction of human life than the action it is opposing. How do we ensure that the intervention does more good than harm? As Valentino cautions, "using force to save lives usually involves taking lives, including innocent ones."[237] Although it is certainly true that the results of military intervention are impossible to predict in advance, it is just as true that the deadly results of inaction— particularly in response to a regime that has proved resistant to other preventive response tools—are relatively easy to predict. Some confidence regarding proportionality can be gained from ensuring that "the scale, duration and intensity of the planned military intervention should be the minimum necessary to secure the humanitarian objective in question."[238] Embedded in the use of proportional military responses is a respect for, and adherence to, international humanitarian law standards as well as a commitment to "never use weapons that are incapable of distinguishing between civilian and military targets."[239]

Proportionately need not require a disproportionate number of troops. As security analyst Anna Bacikowska has argued, "a fairly small number of forces, if deployed swiftly with the support of appropriate capabilities, could have a significant impact in a short period of time."[240] Dallaire, for instance, has long held that a mere 4,000 trained troops, entrusted with a mandate allowing the use of force to protect civilians, could have stopped the Rwandan genocide in its tracks.[241] (Unfortunately, when the genocide began, Dallaire had only 2,600 troops—of whom 350 were military observers—later reduced to a rump force of 450 soldiers at the height of the killings.[242])After the Rwandan genocide, an international panel of senior military leaders affirmed that "a reinforced brigade of 5,000 troops, operating under a robust mandate, could have subdued the killers and returned some semblance of order to the country."[243] Other cases of imminent risk have confirmed that the deployment of a fairly small number of forces can significantly mitigate escalating violence. Six years after the Rwandan genocide, for instance, fewer than 800 British combat soldiers helped save Sierra Leone's capital, Freetown, from being captured by a brutal rebel army. Similarly, in 2013, "a French force of only 4,500 personnel broke al-Qaeda's grip on northern Mali."[244]

The operational dimensions of how to intervene to protect civilians in the face of genocide and mass atrocity present challenges different from traditional warfighting and traditional peacekeeping operations. In 2010, the civil-society initiated Mass Atrocity Response Operations (MARO) Project sought to address this problem by developing a planning handbook for how military forces might respond in the face of mass killings of civilians. The Project, recognizing the unique operational and moral challenges confronted by military forces in atrocity settings around the globe, "developed operational concepts, a tailored planning guide, tabletop exercises, and other tools for military institutions and political actors . . . to halt mass atrocity" as part of a broader integrated strategy.[245] In terms of the most potent form of military intervention in slowing, limiting, or stopping the killing during ongoing instances of genocide, Krain's empirical study of genocides or politicides from 1955 to 1997 weighed several alternative hypotheses regarding the potential effects of intervention. As opposed to impartial interventions or those that simply signal world interest by the presence of a witness, he found that "the most effective way for the international community to intervene militarily to reduce the severity of an ongoing genocide or politicide is to directly challenge the perpetrator . . . by opposing, restraining, or disarming perpetrators and/or removing them from power."[246]

Who Should Intervene? Finally, the question of who should authorize and implement intervention is pivotal to defining the parameters for justifiable and legitimate use of military force as a preventive response tool. Article 42 of Chapter VII in the UN Charter confers on the Security Council the right to "take such action by air, sea or land forces as may be necessary to maintain or restore international peace and security."[247] For the framers of the ICISS report, though acknowledging the limitations of the Security Council, there is "absolutely no doubt that there is no better or more appropriate body than the Security Council to deal with military intervention issues for human protection purposes. It is the Security Council which should be making the hard decisions in the hard cases about overriding state sovereignty . . . Collective intervention blessed by the UN is regarded as legitimate because it is duly authorized by a representative international body; unilateral intervention is seen as illegitimate because self-interested."[248] Even when some unilateral interventions have been seen as acceptable in hindsight (India into East Pakistan in 1971, Tanzania into Uganda in 1978, and Vietnam into Cambodia in 1979), most agree "actions beyond self-defense or those authorized by the UN Security Council are generally considered illegitimate and/or illegal."[249]

What should the response be, however, when the Security Council fails to act? In 1999, for instance, UN Secretary-General Kofi Annan challenged states to consider how they would have reacted if a coalition of states had been prepared to act in defense of the Tutsi civilians during the 1994 genocide—but did not, or could not, receive prompt Security Council authorization. "Should such a coalition have stood aside," he asked, "and allowed the horror to unfold?"[250] In response, the ICISS report suggests that in the presence of Security Council inaction, right authority could come from an "emergency special session" of the UN General Assembly or, less ideally, from regional organizations (particularly those composed of neighboring countries), subregional organizations, ad hoc coalitions, or individual states. In 1999, for instance, the NATO intervention in Kosovo occurred without Security Council authorization. Although, in the absence of such approval, the NATO invasion may not have been legal, an independent international commission recognized it as legitimate. "The Commission considered that the intervention was justified because all diplomatic avenues had been exhausted and because the intervention had the effect of liberating the majority population of Kosovo from a long period of oppression under Serbian rule."[251]

Although military intervention authorized by the UN for the protection of civilians may be the ideal, "the most common form of military intervention that ends atrocities is an interested one, that is, one undertaken for more traditionally articulated national security reasons."[252] In addition to the pre-UN mobilization of allied forces in World War II against Nazism, more recent examples of interest-based military interventions include the Vietnamese invasion of Cambodia to purge the Khmer Rouge, India's intervention in Bangladesh to stop the cleansing of Hindus by the West Pakistan government, and the Rwandan Patriotic Front's defeat of Hutu extremists in Rwanda.[253] As the ICISS report cautions, however, "there is a risk . . . that such interventions, without the discipline and constraints of UN authorization, will not be conducted for the right reasons or with the right commitment to the necessary precautionary principles."[254]

CONCLUSIONS

In conclusion, the mistaken belief that short of full-scale coercive military intervention, little or nothing can be done to respond to an ongoing genocide is a failure of preventive creativity.[255] Although we are aware of the tools in the preventive toolbox, we still need to articulate better principles for how they are used. "Future work should emphasize the interactions between the various tools that slow or stop the killing, so as to better understand how best to deploy 'all the means at our disposal.'"[256] As public affairs specialist Alan Kuperman warns, a poorly conceived and poorly implemented response to genocide can create a "moral hazard" that increases the very human suffering that it intends to alleviate.[257] Certainly, used in isolation, any one of the preventive response tools is unlikely to slow, limit, or stop genocidal violence. Employed, though, in conjunction with other tools, and as part of larger overall framework conditioned on the principle of "do no harm," the strategic application of several of these preventive response tools can go a long way toward mitigating genocide and protecting civilians.

Midstream prevention is an attempt to slow, limit, or stop the continuation or escalation of genocidal violence. Understanding the factors that accelerate and trigger an at-risk country's descent into crisis are important steps in understanding how a society at risk of genocide becomes a society trapped in the deadly grip of genocide. Bridging the gap between substantial early warning and an equally substantial early response involves knowledge about the use, and effectiveness of, preventive response tools (political, economic, legal, and military) that can be applied as levers of change at the sign of rapidly growing risks and first indicators, or at the onset of genocide itself. The use of these midstream tools is an admission that measures of upstream prevention have failed, at least for the time being, in the country of concern. If the deep and rich toolbox of midstream preventive measures, however, fails to mitigate genocidal violence—either because we do not choose to use them or we use them ineffectually—how do genocides end? How does the killing stop if we have not been able to interrupt genocide?

As seminal work by Conley-Zilkic and Alex de Waal suggests, although there are notable cases in which genocide ends because perpetrators have been militarily defeated, the most common ending to mass atrocities is that the killers simply decide they have "killed enough."[258] In these cases, perpetrators remain in power and decide to stop killing for a variety of reasons—including the rise of moderates, the ascent of an indigenous resistance movement, or the dissemination of damning information to influential actors outside the regime. Most often, however, the killing ends simply because the perpetrators have sufficiently brought the target group within their control. In effect, the perpetrators have succeeded; their goals have been accomplished. The killing has served its strategic purpose and is no longer needed as policy.

For Valentino, ". . . mass killing is most accurately viewed as an instrumental policy—a brutal strategy designed to accomplish leaders' most important ideological or political objectives and counter what they see as their most dangerous threats."[259] This recognition of genocide as a rational tool of policy—rather than an emotional acting out of age-old hatreds—underscores the need for a research- and practice-informed understanding of effective midstream prevention. If we choose to let genocide run its course, we know where that course will end—thousands, hundreds of thousands, or even millions of civilians done to death. To stop genocide in its tracks, genocide must come to cost more to the perpetrators than the benefits they are receiving from using it; the policy tool of genocide must become unsustainable. If academics, lawyers, policymakers, and global civil society can mobilize the collective will to make that happen—through cooperative or coercive use of political, economic, legal, and military measures—then the offending regime may be pulled, or pushed, to resorting to less lethal policy tools.

As of early-February 2016, the violence in South Sudan continued to escalate with reports of widespread killings, rape and other forms of sexual violence, abductions of women and children, forced cannibalism, and the burning and destruction of towns and villages. An African Union report, dated January 29, 2016, said: "There is limited consolidation of peace, a worrying economic decline and violence ongoing. The economy is in particularly dire straits, with foreign reserves rapidly diminishing, growing inflation and rapid depreciation of the national currency."[260] Civilians are still being done to death in South Sudan as the dreams of a new nation remain mired in the nightmare of violent, even genocidal, conflict. Simon Deng, a former child slave in Sudan and now a human rights activist, mourns: "There is a

Rwanda genocide taking place . . . in Southern Sudan. And we're not even following it . . . Shame on us if [we] don't listen and don't pay attention."[261] On May 28, 2015, yet another joint UN statement admonished: "It is the collective responsibility of the international community to take decisive steps to end the protracted suffering of the South Sudanese people."[262] This collective responsibility—whether advocated by academics, lawyers, policymakers, or global civil society—has yet to be engaged. In the crying need for decisive steps, we have only yet to see indecisive passivity. All the upstream preventive work of nation building and risk assessment lies fallow in the yawning gap between early warning and substantive response. In the face of such destruction, the world still wrings its hands. Not because we do not know what to do; as shown in this chapter, the range of tools in our preventive toolbox that can be used to mitigate the continuation or escalation of genocidal violence is well known. Rather than a lack of knowledge, it is yet another occasion of a lack of collective will to apply that knowledge. If we continue to choose not to effectively employ response tools to slow, limit, or stop South Sudan's genocide in midstream, we will be left downstream to pick up the flotsam of yet another society overwhelmed by the flood of genocide.

When the killing in South Sudan ends—either because the world has chosen, in Wiesel's words, "to interfere" by employing a strategic framework of preventive response tools or, more likely, simply because the killing has accomplished its strategic purpose for the perpetrators—our preventive attention will turn from responding to genocide to rebuilding in its aftermath. For that, Chapter 6 examines the downstream preventive strategies built on justice, truth, and memory to resolve the sources of genocidal conflict and lead to a lasting and sustainable peace.

NOTES

1. Ty McCormick, "Unmade in the USA: The Inside Story of a Foreign-Policy Failure," accessed March 29, 2015 at http://foreignpolicy.com/2015/02/25/unmade-in-the-usa-south-sudan-bush-obama/.
2. Additional background material on the conflict in Sudan can be found at http://www.insightonconflict.org/conflicts/sudan/conflict-profile/, accessed March 29, 2015.
3. Ty McCormick, "Unmade in the USA."
4. Princeton N. Lyman, "The Conflict in South Sudan: The Political Context," testimony prepared for the U.S. Senate Foreign Relations Committee (January 9, 2014). Accessed January 21, 2014 at http://www.usip.org/publications/the-conflict-in-south-sudan-the-political-context.

5. Colum Lynch, "How the U.S. Triumph in South Sudan Came Undone," *FP Report* (December 26, 2013), accessed January 7, 2014 at http://www.foreignpolicy. com/articles/2013/12/24/how_the_us_triumph_in_south_sudan_came_ undone?utm_source=Sailthru&utm_medium=email&utm_term=Flashpoints%20 Complete%2010%2F7&utm_campaign=Flashpoints%2012-27-13.

6. Human Rights Watch, "South Sudan: Ethnic Targeting, Widespread Killings" (January 16, 2014), accessed January 21, 2014 at http://www.hrw.org/news/ 2014/01/16/south-sudan-ethnic-targeting-widespread-killings.

7. Rick Gladstone, "More South Sudanese Seek Shelter at U.N. Bases," *The New York Times* (April 8, 2015): A10 and Colum Lynch, "U.N. Panel Calls for Sanctions on South Sudan's Warring Leaders," accessed February 6, 2016 at http://foreignpolicy.com/ 2016/01/25/u-n-panel-calls-for-sanctions-on-south-sudans-warring-leaders/.

8. Gladstone, "More South Sudanese Seek Shelter at U.N. Bases."

9. Accessed March 29, 2015 at http://www.bbc.com/news/blogs-news-from-elsewhere-29754506.

10. Marc Santora, "Crisis Spreads in South Sudan as War Rages," *The New York Times* (June 23, 2015: A1.

11. Accessed April 17, 2015 at http://www.nobelprize.org/nobel_prizes/peace/lau-reates/1986/wiesel-acceptance_en.html.

12. Nicolas Rost, "Will It Happen Again? On the Possibility of Forecasting the Risk of Genocide," *Journal of Genocide Research* 15 (2013): 59.

13. Atanas Gotchev, "The Bulgarian Early Warning System: Implementation, Outcomes and Significance for Policy-Making," in *Thinking the Unthinkable: From Thought to Policy* (Bratislava, Slovakia: United Nations Development Programme, 2003), 186–187.

14. U.S. Department of State's Bureau of Conflict and Stabilization Operations and USAID's Center of Excellence on Democracy, Human Rights and Governance, "Atrocity Assessment Framework: Supplemental Guide to Conflict Assessment Frameworks" (2015, working draft, unclassified), 7.

15. Alex Bellamy, "Mass Atrocities and Armed Conflict: Links, Distinctions, and Implications for the Responsibility to Prevent," *The Stanley Foundation Policy Analysis Brief* (February, 2011): 13.

16. James Putzel, "Regional and Global Drivers of Conflict: Consequences for Fragile States and Regions," paper prepared for the World Bank Headline Seminar on the Regional and Global Dimensions of Conflict and Peace Building, Addis Ababa, October 10–12, 2009, 1.

17. The "windows of atrocity risk" phrase comes from U.S. Department of State and USAID, "Atrocity Assessment Framework," 7.

18. David Grann, *The Devil & Sherlock Holmes: Tales of Murder, Madness, and Obsession* (New York, NY: Vintage Books, 2011), 84.

19. African Development Bank Group, "Drivers and Dynamics of Fragility in Africa," *Africa Economic Brief* (2013): 3.

20. Barbara Harff, "Detection: The History and Politics of Early Warning," eds. Adam Lupel and Ernesto Verdeja, *Responding to Genocide: The Politics of International Action* (Boulder, CO: Lynne Rienner, 2013), 104.

21. Benjamin E. Goldsmith, Charles R. Butcher, Dimitri Semenovich, and Arcot Sowmya, "Forecasting the Onset of Genocide and Politicide: Annual Out-of-Sample Forecasts on a Global Dataset, 1988–2003," *Journal of Peace Research* 50 (2013): 440.

22. United Nations' "Framework of Analysis for Atrocity Crimes" (2014, http://www.un.org/en/preventgenocide/adviser/pdf/framework%20of%20analysis%20for%20atrocity%20crimes_en.pdf), 17, accessed April 17, 2015.

23. Madeleine K. Albright and William S. Cohen, *Preventing Genocide: A Blueprint for U.S. Policymakers* (US Holocaust Memorial Museum, the American Academy of Diplomacy, and the Endowment of the United States Institute of Peace, 2008), 37.

24. Scott Straus and Charlie Taylor, "Democratization and Electoral Violence in Sub-Saharan Africa, 1990–2008," ed. Dorina A Bekoe, *Voting in Fear: Electoral Violence in Sub-Saharan Africa* (Washington, DC: United States Institute of Peace, 2012).

25. Charles R. Butcher, Benjamin E. Goldsmith, Dimitri Semenovich, and Arcot Sowmya, "Understanding and Forecasting Political Instability and Genocide for Early Warning" (2012), 17. Accessed January 22, 2015 at http://sydney.edu.au/arts/research/atrocity_forecasting/publications.

26. Jonas Claes, "On the Prevention of Election Violence," *United States Institute of Peace Insights* (Winter, 2015): 1.

27. Gotchev, "The Bulgarian Early Warning System," 185.

28. Albright and Cohen, *Preventing Genocide*, 17.

29. UN News Centre, "UN Marks 65th Anniversary of Landmark Treat on Preventing, Punishing Genocide," accessed April 4, 2015 at http://www.un.org/apps/news/story.asp?NewsID=46692#.VSAHq_nF-So.

30. Alexander L. George and Jane E. Holl, "The Warning-Response Problem and Missed Opportunities in Preventive Diplomacy," *A Report to the Carnegie Commission on Preventing Deadly Conflict*, accessed April 4, 2015 at http://carnegie.org/fileadmin/Media/Publications/PDF/The%20Warning-Response%20Problem%20and%20Missed%20Opportunities%20in%20Preventive%20Diplomacy.pdf, 4.

31. Ibid, 9–10.

32. Albright and Cohen, *Preventing Genocide*, 22.

33. Howard Adelman, "Difficulties in Early Warning: Networking and Conflict Management," ed. Klaas van Walraven, *Early Warning and Conflict Prevention: Limitations and Possibilities* (Leiden, Netherlands: Nijhoff Law Specials, 1998), 57.

34. Annika Bjorkdahl, "Developing a Toolbox for Conflict Prevention," in Stockholm International Peace Research Institute, *Preventing Violent Conflict: The Search for Political Will, Strategies and Effective Tools* (Stockholm, Sweden: Stockholm International Peace Research Institute, 2000), 17.

35. John N. Clarke, "Early Warning Analysis for Humanitarian Preparedness and Conflict Prevention," *Journal of Humanitarian Assistance* (2004): 10, accessed April 4, 2015 at www.jha.ac/articles/a146.pdf.

36. Christoph O. Meyer, Florian Otto, John Brante, and Chiara de Franco, "Recasting the Warning-Response Problem: Persuasion and Preventive Policy," *International Studies Review* 12 (2010): 560.

37. Ibid, 567.

38. Ibid, 561.

39. Project for a UN Emergency Peace Service (UNEPS), *Standing for Change in Peacekeeping Operations* (New York, NY: Global Action to Prevent War, 2009), 44.

40. Report of the International Commission on Intervention and State Sovereignty (ICISS), *The Responsibility to Protect* (Ottawa, Canada: International Development Research Centre, 2001), 36.

41. Linda Fasulo, *An Insider's Guide to the UN*, 2nd ed. (New Haven, CT: Yale University Press, 2009), 38.
42. David M. Malone, "Security Council," in Thomas G. Weiss and Sam Daws, *The Oxford Handbook on the United Nations* (New York, NY: Oxford University Press, 2007), 117.
43. Fasulo, *An Insider's Guide to the UN*, 41.
44. Somini Sengupta, "Why the U.N. Can't Solve the World's Problems," *The New York Times* (July 27, 2014), SR5.
45. Simon Adams, "The Responsibility Not to Veto," Global Centre for the Responsibility to Protect (January 21, 2015): 2.
46. ICISS, *The Responsibility to Protect*, 51.
47. Adams, "The Responsibility Not to Veto," 4.
48. Quoted material taken from Gareth Evans, "Limiting the Security Council Veto" (February 4, 2015), accessed April 16, 2015 at http://www.project-syndicate. org/commentary/security-council-veto-limit-by-gareth-evans-2015-02.
49. Fasulo, *An Insiders Guide to the UN*, 56.
50. Edward C. Luck, "Principal Organs," in Weiss and Daws, *The Oxford Handbook on the United Nations*, 661.
51. The quoted material is from Thomas G. Weiss, "Politics, the UN, and Halting Mass Atrocities," eds. Lupel and Verdeja, *Responding to Genocide*, 227.
52. Project for a UN Emergency Peace Service (UNEPS), *Standing for Change in Peacekeeping Operations*, 30.
53. Laurent Fabius, "A Call for Self-Restraint at the U.N.," *The New York Times* (October 4, 2013), accessed April 16, 2015 at http://www.nytimes.com/2013/ 10/04/opinion/a-call-for-self-restraint-at-the-un.html.
54. Remarks taken from http://www.un.org/sg/dsg/statements/index.asp?nid=593, accessed April 16, 2015.
55. Alex J. Bellamy, "Military Intervention," eds. Donald Bloxham and A. Dirk Moses, *The Oxford Handbook of Genocide Studies* (New York, NY: Oxford University Press, 2010), 615.
56. Accessed April 21, 2015 at http://math.nyu.edu/~crorres/Archimedes/Lever/ LeverQuotes.html.
57. Aaron Griffiths and Catherine Barnes, "Incentives and Sanctions in Peace Processes," accessed April 21, 2015 at http://www.c-r.org/accord-article/incentives-and-sanctions-peace-processes, 11. I am indebted to my colleague, Hank Knight, for suggesting the concept of a lever as a preventive tool.
58. Budapest Centre for the International Prevention of Genocide and Mass Atrocities, *The EU and the Prevention of Mass Atrocities: An Assessment of Strengths and Weaknesses* (European Union, 2013), 55.
59. David Cortright, "Positive Inducements in International Statecraft," Fraser Forum (June 2000), accessed May 3, 2015 at http://oldfraser.lexi.net/publica-tions/forum/2000/06/section_05.html.
60. Ibid.
61. Griffiths and Barnes, "Incentives and Sanctions in Peace Processes," 9.
62. Albright and Cohen, *Preventing Genocide*, 57.
63. *Mass Atrocity Prevention and Response Options (MAPRO): A Policy Planning Handbook* (Carlisle, PA: U.S. Army Peacekeeping and Stability Operations Institute, 2012), 103.
64. Albright and Cohen, *Preventing Genocide*, 66.
65. Taken from *MAPRO*, 82.

66. The literature on preventive response tools is fairly bounded and tends toward repetition more than exposition of effective application. Box 5.1 is adapted from several primary sources and is augmented with additional materials as noted in the text. The primary source materials include Albright and Cohen, *Preventing Genocide*; Griffiths and Barnes, "Incentives and Sanctions in Peace Processes"; Alex Bellamy, "Mass Atrocities and Armed Conflict"; Gareth Evans, *The Responsibility to Protect*; ICISS, *The Responsibility to Protect; Mass Atrocity Prevention and Response Options (MAPRO)*; Budapest Centre, *The EU and the Prevention of Mass Atrocities*; West African Civil Society Institute, *Responsibility to Protect: Training Toolkit for Civil Society Actors and Multidimensional Peace Support Personnel in West Africa* (Accra, Ghana: WACSI, 2013); and International Coalition for the Responsibility to Protect, *A Toolkit on the Responsibility to Protect*, accessed May 1, 2015 at http://responsibility-toprotect.org/ICRtoP%20Toolkit%20on%20the%20Responsibility%20to%20Protect%20high%20res.pdf.

67. Matthew Krain, "The Effects of Diplomatic Sanctions and Engagement in the Severity of Ongoing Genocides or Politicides," *Journal of Genocide Research* 16 (2014): 27.

68. Richard N. Haass and Meghan O'Sullivan, "Terms of Engagement: Alternatives to Punitive Policies," *Survival* 42 (2000): 114.

69. Griffiths and Barnes, "Incentives and Sanctions in Peace Processes," 12.

70. *MAPRO*, 99–100.

71. Ibid, 86.

72. Evans, *The Responsibility to Protect*, 108.

73. Jonas Claes, "Atrocity Prevention through Persuasion and Deterrence: Political Missions and Preventive Deployments," *United States Institute of Peace Brief* 128 (2012): 1.

74. WACSI, *Responsibility to Protect*, 29.

75. Navi Pillay, "Stopping Mass Atrocities and Promoting Human Rights: My Work as the UN High Commissioner for Human Rights," lecture delivered as the Fourth Annual Gareth Evans Lecture on October 29, 2014 at the CUNY Graduate Center in New York City.

76. Ibid.

77. A 2014 report by the US Institute of Peace, however, did suggest that Kenyans perceived the electoral experience as one of "tense calm" or "unstable peace." Report was accessed May 2, 2015 at http://www.usip.org/publications/elections-and-violent-conflict-in-kenya-making-prevention-stick.

78. *The EU and the Prevention of Mass Atrocities*, 54.

79. Quoted material taken from http://www.un.org/sg/rightsupfront/, accessed May 1, 2015.

80. USAID, "Field Guide: Helping Prevent Mass Atrocities" (2015): 25.

81. USAID, "Preventing Atrocities: Five Key Primers" (September 2014): 14–15.

82. Isabelle MacGregor and Devin C. Bowles, "Looking Upstream: Increasing Options to Prevent Genocide," ed. Colin Tatz, *Genocide Perspectives IV: Essays on Holocaust and Genocide* (Sydney, Australia: The Australian Institute for Holocaust & Genocide Studies, 2012), 445.

83. Joshua E. Keating, "So, How Do You Expel an Ambassador, Anyway?," accessed May 2, 2015 at http://foreignpolicy.com/2012/05/29/so-how-do-you-expel-an-ambassador-anyway/.

84. *MAPRO*, 93.

85. BBC News, "African Snub to Sudan Over Darfur," accessed May 1, 2015 at http://news.bbc.co.uk/2/hi/africa/6310025.stm.
86. Jacqueline H. R. DeMeritt, "International Organizations and Government Killing: Does Naming and Shaming Save Lives?," International Interactions 38 (2012): 611.
87. MAPRO, 90.
88. Mahmood Mamdani, Saviors and Survivors: Darfur, Politics, and the War on Terror (New York, NY: Three Rivers Press, 2010), 3.
89. Rebecca Hamilton and Chad Hazlett, "'Not On Our Watch:' The Emergence of the American Movement for Darfur," ed. Alex de Waal, War in Darfur and the Search for Peace (Cambridge, MA: Harvard University Press, 2007), 366.
90. Evans, The Responsibility to Protect, 111.
91. DeMeritt, "International Organizations and Government Killing," 597.
92. Guy Walters, Berlin Games: How the Nazis Stole the Olympic Dream (New York, NY: William Morrow, 2006), 59.
93. Daniel James Brown, The Boys in the Boat: Nine Americans and Their Epic Quest for Gold at the 1936 Berlin Olympics (New York, NY: Penguin, 2013), 225.
94. Cited at http://www.un.org/en/events/mandeladay/apartheid.shtml, accessed May 2, 2015.
95. Enuga S. Reddy, "The United Nations and the Struggle for Liberation in South Africa," South Africa Democracy Education Trust (ed.), The Road to Democracy in South Africa, Vol. 3 (Pretoria, South Africa: Unisa Press, 2008), 41–139.
96. UN Security Council Resolution 2206 (March 3, 2015). Also see summary at http://pcr.uu.se/research/smartsanctions/.
97. Evans, The Responsibility to Protect, 112.
98. Krain, "The Effects of Diplomatic Sanctions," 28–29.
99. Ibid, 44.
100. Ibid, 25, 28.
101. Ibid, 30–31.
102. ICISS, The Responsibility to Protect, 24.
103. Evans, The Responsibility to Protect, 94.
104. Griffiths and Barnes, "Incentives and Sanctions in Peace Processes," 11.
105. Peter D. Feaver and Eric Lorber, "Penalty Box: How Sanctions Trap Policymakers," Foreign Affairs (June 6, 2014).
106. MAPRO, 116.
107. Accessed May 4, 2015 at http://data.unhcr.org/syrianrefugees/country.php?id=122#.
108. MAPRO, 119–120.
109. OECD "Glossary of Statistical Terms," definition accessed May 2, 2015 at https://stats.oecd.org/glossary/detail.asp?ID=876.
110. MAPRO, 118–119.
111. Patrick Meier, Digital Humanitarians: How Big Data Is Changing the Face of Humanitarian Response (New York, NY: CRC Press, 2015).
112. Accessed May 4, 2015 at http://visual.ly/reaching-50-million-users.
113. Hillary Clinton, "Remarks on Internet Freedom" (January 21, 2010). Accessed May 4, 2015 at http://www.state.gov/secretary/20092013clinton/rm/2010/01/135519.htm.
114. The phrase "rewarding 'bad people' for 'good behavior'" comes from Albright and Cohen, Preventing Genocide, 69.
115. A complete list of UN Sanctions can be found at http://pcr.uu.se/research/smartsanctions/spits_sanctions_list/.

116. UN Security Council Sanctions Committees, accessed May 4, 2015 at http://www.un.org/sc/committees/.
117. Krain, "The Effects of Diplomatic Sanctions," 27.
118. Griffiths and Barnes, "Incentives and Sanctions in Peace Processes," 11.
119. Ibid.
120. *The EU and the Prevention of Mass Atrocities*, 54–55.
121. George A. Lopez, "Tools, Tasks and Tough Thinking: Sanctions and R2P," policy brief written for the Global Centre for the Responsibility to Protect (October 3, 2013), 2.
122. Albright and Cohen, *Preventing Genocide*, 70.
123. Feaver and Lorber, "Penalty Box: How Sanctions Trap Policymakers."
124. Lopez, "Tools, Tasks and Tough Thinking," 2.
125. Evans, *The Responsibility to Protect*, 114.
126. See http://www.kimberleyprocess.com/en, accessed May 4, 2015.
127. UN Security Council Resolution 1718, accessed May 4, 2015 at http://www.un.org/sc/committees/1718/.
128. *MAPRO*, 119.
129. Lopez, "Tools, Tasks and Tough Thinking," 2.
130. *MAPRO*, 118.
131. Lopez, "Tools, Tasks and Tough Thinking," 1.
132. Ibid.
133. Leon Watson, "What Will Happen to Gaddafi's Billions?," accessed May 4, 2015 at http://www.dailymail.co.uk/news/article-2051912/Gaddafis-death-Governments-hand-dead-Libyan-tyrants-frozen-assets.html.
134. Rachel Doane, "Human Rights Situation in Darfur Prompts Trend in Divestment from Sudan," accessed May 4, 2015 at http://www.internationaljusticeproject.com/human-rights-situation-in-darfur-prompts-trend-in-divestment-from-sudan/.
135. US Government Accountability Office, "Sudan Divestment." GAO-10-742 (2010), 5.
136. Evans, *The Responsibility to Protect*, 93.
137. Ibid.
138. Taehee Whang, "Playing to the Home Crowd? Symbolic Use of Economic Sanctions in the United States," *International Studies Quarterly* 55 (2011): 787, 788.
139. Cited in Peter Wallensteen, Erik Melander, and Frida Moller, "The International Community Response," eds. I. William Zartman, Mark Anstey, and Paul Meerts, *The Slippery Slope to Genocide: Reducing Identity Conflicts and Preventing Mass Murder* (New York, NY: Oxford University Press, 2012), 291.
140. Feaver and Lorber, "Penalty Box: How Sanctions Trap Policymakers."
141. Johan Galtung, "On the Effects of International Economic Sanctions: With Examples from the Case of Rhodesia," *World Politics* 19 (1967): 412.
142. Whang, "Playing to the Home Crowd?," 787.
143. Lopez, "Tools, Tasks and Tough Thinking," 2.
144. Ibid.
145. This four points are a compilation of research from Lopez, "Tools, Tasks and Tough Thinking," Albright and Cohen, *Preventing Genocide*, 70, *The EU and the Prevention of Mass Atrocities*, 55, and "Making Targeted Sanctions Effective: Guidelines for the Implementation of UN Policy Options" (Uppsala, Sweden: Department of Peace and Conflict Research, Uppsala, University, 2003).
146. Fasulo, *An Insider's Guide to the UN*, 46.
147. *MAPRO*, 100.

148. ICISS, *The Responsibility to Protect*, 24.
149. *MAPRO*, 100–101.
150. Accessed May 8, 2015 at http://www.trial-ch.org/en/resources/international-law/amnesty-and-immunity.html.
151. Transitional Justice Institute, *The Belfast Guidelines on Amnesty and Accountability* (Belfast, Northern Ireland: University of Ulster, 2013), 9.
152. Ibid, 10.
153. Ibid, 9.
154. Accessed May 8, 2015 at http://www.trial-ch.org/en/resources/international-law/amnesty-and-immunity.html.
155. Evans, *The Responsibility to Protect*, 118.
156. Ibid, 118–119.
157. *MAPRO*, 92.
158. USAID, "Preventing Atrocities: Five Key Primers" (September 2014): 31.
159. Ibid, 29.
160. William A. Schabas, *Genocide in International Law: The Crime of Crimes*, 2nd ed. (Cambridge, England: Cambridge University Press, 2009), 520.
161. The complete text of the Genocide Convention can be found at http://www.hrweb.org/legal/genocide.html, accessed January 23, 2011.
162. Schabas, *Genocide in International Law*, 540.
163. Fasulo, *An Insider's Guide to the UN*, 139–140.
164. Committee on the Elimination of Racial Discrimination, "Declaration on the Prevention of Genocide," CERD/C/66/1 (October 17, 2005).
165. Accessed May 8, 2015 at http://www.un.org/en/preventgenocide/adviser/.
166. At present, Mr. Adama Dieng is the current Special Adviser on the Prevention of Genocide and Dr. Jennifer Welsh is the Special Adviser on the Responsibility to Protect.
167. Juan Mendez, panel presentation delivered at the conference titled "Deconstructing Prevention: The Theory, Policy, and Practice of Mass Atrocity Prevention," Benjamin N. Cardozo School of Law (New York, NY), February 26, 2013.
168. USAID, "Preventing Atrocities: Five Key Primers" (September 2014): 15.
169. *MAPRO*, 91.
170. Accessed May 8, 2015 at http://www.satsentinel.org/documenting-the-crisis.
171. Adrian Gregorich, "Drones for Peace and Protection," accessed May 9, 2015 at https://thesentinelproject.org/2015/04/17/drones-for-peace-and-protection/.
172. Accessed May 9, 2015 at http://www.icc-cpi.int/en_menus/icc/about%20the%20court/Pages/about%20the%20court.aspx.
173. WACSI, *Responsibility to Protect*, 29.
174. BBC News, "Nuns Jailed for Genocide Role" (June 8, 2001), accessed May 9, 2015 at http://news.bbc.co.uk/2/hi/europe/1376692.stm.
175. Evans, *The Responsibility to Protect*, 99.
176. Evans, *The Responsibility to Protect*, 100.
177. Ibid.
178. Albright and Cohen, *Preventing Genocide*, 73.
179. *MAPRO*, 104.
180. Evans, *The Responsibility to Protect*, 101.
181. Quote taken form http://www.bbc.com/news/world-africa-21195371, accessed May 17, 2015.
182. John Norris, "Is America Training Too Many Foreign Armies?" (January 28, 2013), accessed May 13, 2015 at http://foreignpolicy.com/2013/01/28/is-america-training-too-many-foreign-armies/.

183. Accessed May 17, 2015 at http://extranet.creativeworldwide.com/CAIIStaff/ Dashboard_GIROAdminCAIIStaff/Dashboard_CAIIAdminDatabase/ resources/ghai/toolbox5.htm.
184. Simon J. A. Mason and Matthias Siegfried, "Confidence Building Measures (CBMs) in Peace Processes," in *Managing Peace Processes: Process Related Questions* (African Union and the Centre for Humanitarian Dialogue, 2013), 61.
185. Evans, *The Responsibility to Protect*, 101.
186. *The EU and the Prevention of Mass Atrocities*, 69.
187. Evans, *The Responsibility to Protect*, 125.
188. Bridget Conley-Zilkic and Alex de Waal, "Setting the Agenda for Evidence-Based Research on Ending Mass Atrocities," *Journal of Genocide Research* 16 (2014): 71.
189. See Scott Anderson, "Life in the Valley of Death," *The New York Times Magazine* (June 1, 2014), accessed August 8, 2014 at http://www.nytimes.com/interactive/2014/05/29/magazine/srebrenica-life-in-the-valley-of-death.html?_r=0.
190. Evans, *The Responsibility to Protect*, 125.
191. WACSI, *Responsibility to Protect*, 29.
192. Evans, *The Responsibility to Protect*, 103.
193. Claes, "Atrocity Prevention through Persuasion and Deterrence," 4.
194. Matthew Krain, "International Intervention and the Severity of Genocides and Politicides," *International Studies Quarterly* (2005) 49: 378.
195. Griffiths and Barnes, "Incentives and Sanctions in Peace Processes," 10.
196. See http://www.sipri.org/databases/embargoes for an arms embargoes database, accessed May 13, 2015.
197. UN Security Council Resolution 2216 (April 14, 2015), S/Res/2216.
198. Damien Fruchart, Paul Holtom, Siemon T. Wezeman, Daniel Strandow, and Peter Wallensteen, *United Nations Arms Embargoes: Their Impact on Arms Flows and Target Behaviour* (SIPRI and Uppsala University: SPITS, Department of Peace and Conflict Research, 2007).
199. David Cortright, George A. Lopez, and Linda Gerber-Stellingwerf, "Sanctions," in Weiss and Daws, *The Oxford Handbook on the United Nations*, 359.
200. *The EU and the Prevention of Mass Atrocities*, 73.
201. *MAPRO*, 109.
202. Romeo Dallaire, *Shake Hands with the Devil: The Failure of Humanity in Rwanda* (London, England: Arrow Books, 2003), 375. Also see Jamie Frederic Metzl, "Rwandan Genocide and the International Law of Radio Jamming," *The American Journal of International Law* 91 (1997): 628–651.
203. *MAPRO*, 107–108.
204. ICISS, *The Responsibility to Protect*, 58.
205. Quoted material taken from *MAPRO*, 106.
206. Sarah Sewall, Dwight Raymond, and Sally Chin, *Mass Atrocity Response Operations: A Military Planning Handbook* (Cambridge, MA: Harvard College, 2010), 68.
207. Accessed May 14, 2015 at http://www.nato.int/cps/en/natolive/topics_49755.htm.
208. Judy Dempsey, "The Depressing Saga of Europe's Battle Groups" (December 19, 2013), accessed May 11, 2015 at http://carnegieeurope.eu/strategiceurope/ ?fa=53975.
209. Andrew Sparrow, "Jean-Claude Juncker Calls for EU Army," *The Guardian* (March 8, 2015), accessed May 11, 2015 at http://www.theguardian.com/world/2015/mar/ 08/jean-claude-juncker-calls-for-eu-army-european-commission-military.

210. Accessed May 11, 2015 at http://www.au.int/en/about/constitutive_act.
211. Olaf Bachmann, "The African Peace and Security Architecture (APSA)––a Design withoutBuilders"(July21,2014),accessedMay11,2014athttp://isnblog.ethz.ch/government/the-african-peace-and-security-architecture-a-design-without-builders.
212. Ibid.
213. Accessed February 6, 2016 at http://www.bbc.com/news/world-africa-34570755.
214. See, for instance, UNEPS, *Standing for Change in Peacekeeping Operations* (New York, NY: Global Action to Prevent War, 2009).
215. Kavitha Suthanthiraraj, *United Nations Peacekeeping Missions: Enhancing Capacity for Rapid and Effective Troop Deployment* (New York, NY: Global Action to Prevent War, 2008), cited in UNEPS, *Standing for Change in Peacekeeping Operations*, 19.
216. Accessed May 12, 2015 at http://www.un.org/en/peacekeeping/issues/military.shtml.
217. Annie Herro, "UN Emergency Peace Service and R2P," accessed May 12, 2015 at http://www.auschwitzinstitute.org/blog/2015/01/27/un-emergency-peace-service-and-the-responsibility-to-protect/. See also Annie Herro, *UN Emergency Peace Service and the Responsibility to Protect* (New York, NY: Routledge, 2015).
218. Cited in Herro, "UN Emergency Peace Service and R2P."
219. Quoted material taken from *MAPRO*, 113.
220. Sewall et al., *Mass Atrocity Response Operations*, 68–69.
221. Quote is from Algerian President Abdelaziz Bouteflika, cited in Barbara Crossette, "U.N. Chief Wants Faster Action to Halt Civil Wars and Killings," *The New York Times* (September 21, 1999): A12.
222. Benjamin A. Valentino, "The True Costs of Humanitarian Intervention: The Hard Truth About a Noble Notion," *Foreign Affairs* (November/December 2011): 66.
223. Accessed May 19, 2015 at https://www.writingclasses.com/WritersResources/AskTheWriterDetail.php?ID=327.
224. Bridget Conley-Zilkic, annual Zeta Chi Rho lecture delivered at Keene State College (September 29, 2014).
225. ICISS, *The Responsibility to Protect*, 31.
226. *The EU and the Prevention of Mass Atrocities*, 70, 71.
227. Mary Locke and Jason Ladnier, "Criteria for Military Intervention in Internal Wars: The Debate," *Fund for Peace Reports* 2 (December 2001).
228. ICISS, *The Responsibility to Protect*, 34.
229. Cited in Locke and Ladnier, "Criteria for Military Intervention in Internal Wars," 3.
230. Evans, *The Responsibility to Protect*, 142.
231. ICISS, *The Responsibility to Protect*, 36.
232. ICISS, *The Responsibility to Protect*, 36.
233. ICISS, *The Responsibility to Protect*, 37.
234. Holly Burkhalter, "Memorandum to the President: Secretary of State," in Council on Foreign Relations, *Humanitarian Intervention: Crafting a Workable Doctrine* (Washington, DC: Council on Foreign Relations, 2000), 25.
235. ICISS, *The Responsibility to Protect*, 35.
236. Evans, *The Responsibility to Protect*, 143.
237. Valentino, "The True Costs of Humanitarian Intervention," 66.
238. ICISS, *The Responsibility to Protect*, 37.
239. Cited in Locke and Ladnier, "Criteria for Military Intervention in Internal Wars," 5.

240. Anna Barcikowska, "EU Battlegroups––Ready to Go?,", *European Union Institute for Security Studies* (November 2013): 4.

241. See Linda Melvern, *Conspiracy to Murder: The Rwanda Genocide* (London, England: Verso, 2004), 232–235.

242. See http://www.ushmm.org/confront-genocide/speakers-and-events/all-speakers-and-events/a-good-man-in-hell-general-romeo-dallaire-and-the-rwanda-genocide, accessed May 18, 2015.

243. Col. Scott R. Feil, "Could 5,000 Peacekeepers Have Saved 500,000 Rwandans?: Early Intervention Reconsidered," *ISD Reports* 3 (April, 1997): 2–3. For a contrasting opinion, see Alan J. Kuperman, "Rwanda in Retrospect," *Foreign Affairs* (January/February 2000): 94–118.

244. David Blair, "To Prevent Another Rwanda, All It Takes Is a Few Well-Trained Troops" (April 3, 2014), accessed May 18, 2015 at http://www.telegraph.co.uk/news/worldnews/africaandindianocean/rwanda/10742690/To-prevent-another-Rwanda-all-it-takes-is-a-few-well-trained-troops.html.

245. Sewall et al., *Mass Atrocity Response Operations*, 5–6.

246. Krain, "International Intervention and the Severity of Genocides and Politicides," 383, 363.

247. Accessed May 18, 2015 at http://www.un.org/en/documents/charter/chapter7.shtml.

248. ICISS, *The Responsibility to Protect*, 48, 49.

249. Cited examples come from Locke and Ladnier, "Criteria for Military Intervention in Internal Wars," 5; quoted material is from Albright and Cohen, *Preventing Genocide*, 75.

250. United Nations, "Secretary-General Presents His Annual Report to the UN General Assembly" (September 20, 1999), SG/SM/7136.

251. Schabas, *Genocide in International Law*, 531.

252. Conley-Zilkic and de Waal, "Evidence-Based Research on Ending Mass Atrocities," 70.

253. Ibid.

254. ICISS, *The Responsibility to Protect*, 55.

255. Albright and Cohen, *Preventing Genocide*, 56.

256. Krain, "The Effects of Diplomatic Sanctions," 47.

257. See Alan J. Kuperman, "The Moral Hazard of Humanitarian Intervention: Lessons from the Balkans," *International Studies Quarterly* 52 (2008): 49–80.

258. Conley-Zilkic and de Waal, "Evidence-Based Research on Ending Mass Atrocities," 60.

259. Benjamin A. Valentino, *Final Solutions: Mass Killing and Genocide in the 20th Century* (Ithaca, NY: Cornell University Press, 2004), 3.

260. Jeffrey Gettleman, "African Union Says Crisis in South Sudan is Worsening," The New York Times (February 1, 2016), accessed February 6, 2016 at http://www.nytimes.com/2016/02/02/world/africa/african-union-issues-biting-report-on-crisis-in-south-sudan.html?emc=edit_tnt_20160202&nlid=67962175&tntemail0=y.

261. Accessed May 31, 2015 at http://www.washingtonexaminer.com/former-slave-on-hunger-strike-outside-the-white-house-obama-is-doing-nothing-to-stop-genocide-in-south-sudan/article/2564922.

262. Accessed May 31, 2015 at http://www.unwomen.org/en/news/stories/2015/5/joint-statement-on-attacks-in-south-sudan.

CHAPTER 6

Downstream Prevention
Strategies

"This Is for Those Who Want Us to Forget"

On March 24, 1976, following years of an increasingly radicalized political climate, a military junta ousted the Argentine constitutional government of President Isabel Peron.[1] Argentina became the latest in a series
of Latin American countries to become a pawn in the ideological struggle
between the United States and the Soviets, a proxy battle in a Cold War that
respected no territorial boundaries. The United States feared a geopolitical "domino effect" in which, if one Latin American country fell to Soviet
expansionism, others would fall as well. Seeking to curb this possibility,
and recognizing that military alliances were easier to build than political
alliances, the United States aligned itself with a regional ideology—known
as the National Security Doctrine—that sought to repress internal threats
of subversion. In this pursuit, "the 'enemy' was not only revolutionary
movements but any populist, religious, or indigenous movements with
progressive ideas aimed at bringing about social change."[2] To gain a foot-
hold on the frontlines of the war against communism, the United States
supported, and sometimes even covertly brought to power, strategically
important military regimes throughout Latin America.

Upon seizing power in Argentina, the military regime, with key economic
and military assistance from the United States, immediately targeted guerrilla opponents characterized as subversive left-wing terrorists—among
them, members of trade and student unions, communists and socialists,
journalists, psychologists, sociologists, pacifists, artists, and political and

religious dissidents. "Victims were abducted as they stepped off buses, as they walked home from work or school, or in midnight raids of private residences and of the safe houses where members of guerrilla groups or of banned trade and student organizations lived in hiding."[3]

Although many scholars refer to the reign of the military regime as the "Dirty War," to do so is to unduly legitimate the regime's contention that it was, in fact, fighting a war. In reality, the regime wielded a systematic and massive exercise of state terrorism to reconfigure Argentine society. The regime's Process of National Reorganization institutionalized terror at every level of daily life with the aim "to define and create 'authentic Argentines.'"[4] They were, in the words of Argentine genocide studies scholar Daniel Feierstein, seeking "to reshape social relationships by means of terror and death . . . to substantially alter the life of the whole" through the partial destruction and transformation of Argentine society.[5] For the regime, there had to be a social surgery to "remove the evil" from every part of society and make way for the new order to be installed in Argentina.[6] General Iberico Saint Jean, military governor of Buenos Aires, stated it clearly: "First we'll kill all the subversives; then we'll kill all the collaborators; then the sympathizers; then those who remain indifferent; and finally, we'll kill the undecided."[7]

Throughout the country, the military regime developed over 500 clandestine detention centers (CDCs) for the torture of political opponents. There was not a single Argentine city that did not have a CDC nearby.[8] To be *chupado* ("sucked up") by a CDC was the first step in the kidnapping–torturing–disappearing methodology of the military regime.[9] The psychological and physical torture at the CDCs was notably sadistic and cruel. For instance, Daniel Eduardo Fernandez, a 19-year-old boy detained in the Club Atletico CDC, recalls a device called "the rectoscope" that "consisted of inserting a tube into the victim's anus, or into a woman's vagina, then letting a rat into the tube. The rodent would try to get out by gnawing at the victim's internal organs."[10]

One of the largest CDCs was the Naval School of Mechanics (*Escuela de Mecanica de la Armada*, or ESMA as abbreviated in Spanish) in Buenos Aires. Located in the urban core of Argentina's largest city, about 5,000 people were tortured and killed at ESMA, many of them drugged with a sedative and taken out on "flights of death" over the River Plate and thrown alive into the river or Atlantic Ocean—sanctioned by the Argentine Catholic church hierarchy as "a Christian form of death."[11]

With the humiliating loss of the Malvinas/Falklands War in June 1982, and mounting political opposition at home, a democratically elected civilian government replaced the last military dictatorship in Argentina on

December 10, 1983. Over the nearly 8 years of the military regime, an estimated 30,000 people, mostly young Argentines, had been disappeared—
los desaparecidos. Because few of the remains of the disappeared have been
found and identified, some Argentines opt to have their own ashes put
in the River Plate since they see it as a collective grave and a symbolic
reunion with the disappeared. Not all of those kidnapped and detained
for torture were disappeared. There were some 10,000 political prisoners
and around 300,000 exiles, afraid of being done to death by their own
government were they to stay in country.[12] On December 19, 2012, the
Federal Criminal Tribunal of the city of La Plata, province of Buenos Aires,
held that the military regime unequivocally sought the extermination of
a national group and, as a result, the Argentine experience from 1976 to
1983 could be framed, without qualification, as the international crime of
genocide (Article 2, sections a, b, c, and e).

The legacies and reverberations of this societal destruction became a divisive identity issue inherited, literally, by the next generation of Argentines.
Some of the CDCs included clandestine maternity units in which pregnant
prisoners were kept alive until they had given birth. From these units,
about 500 children of the disappeared were taken at birth and placed in
homes of the military regime (sometimes to the very people who killed
their parents) or persons close to the regime. To locate these illegally appropriated children, the Grandmothers of Plaza de Mayo (*Abuelas de Plaza de
Mayo*) was founded on October 22, 1977. Their stated mission is "to locate
all the children who were kidnapped and disappeared by political repression and restore them to their legitimate families, and to make sure such
a terrible violation of the human rights of children does not happen ever
again, demanding punishment for all those responsible."[13] So rather than
a search for missing persons, it is a search for missing identity. In March
1980, the Abuelas achieved the restitution of their first grandchild. In 1993,
the National Commission for the Right to Identity (*Comision Nacional por el
Derecho a la Identidad*, or CONADI) began to coordinate a national data bank
with the genetic maps of all the families with disappeared children, with a
similar aim of giving the living disappeared their identity back. Since then,
another 112 of the 500 kidnapped children have been found.

Estela de Carlotto, a former teacher and school principal, is current
President of the Abuelas. Carlotto's daughter, Laura, a young history student and political activist, was 2 months pregnant when she was arrested
by the military regime in November 1977. Kept alive and held in captivity
at the La Cacha CDC, several witnesses reported that Laura gave birth on
June 26, 1978 while handcuffed. Only with her newborn son for less than
5 hours before he was given for adoption to two farm workers the regime

trusted to raise him according to "Western and Christian" values, Laura was murdered 2 months later.[14] Mourning the loss of her daughter, but determined to find her kidnapped grandson, Carlotto joined the Abuelas and became its most recognizable face, earning the United Nations Prize in the Field of Human Rights in 2003. During the life of her work, she celebrated the discovery of each illegally appropriated child as if it was her own. With each celebration, her heart hoped to be one child closer to finding her own grandchild, but, at the age of 83, even Carlotto's determined optimism began to fade. Then, on August 5, 2014, in one of the year's biggest news stories in Argentina, the hoped for finally happened—the 114th kidnapped child to be found was her long-sought grandson. At the press conference announcing the discovery of her grandson, Carlotto said: "This is for those who want us to forget, who want us to turn the page, as if nothing had happened. We have to keep looking for those who are still missing because other grandmothers want to feel what I am feeling today. Because I did not want to die without hugging him. And now I will be able to hug him."[15]

Today, academics, lawyers, policymakers, and civil society in Argentina continue to challenge those who want to forget. ESMA, the most notorious of the CDCs, has been rebranded as a "Space for Memory and the Promotion and Defense of Human Rights." In front of ESMA's main building, facing bustling Del Libertador Avenue, stands a monument of three pillars. A similar monument welcomes visitors to every memorialized CDC in Argentina. On each of the three pillars is inscribed one of three words—Justicia, Verdad, Memoria: Justice, Truth, Memory.

Justice, truth, and memory lie at the heart of tertiary downstream prevention strategies. The primary upstream preventive strategies have failed and the secondary midstream strategies have, in the best case, been deployed to stop the genocide or, in the worst case, been kept on the sidelines or proven ineffectual. In either case, however, there remains a society torn apart by genocide that has to be repaired and rebuilt—perhaps even transformed—so as to prevent the deadly cycle of violence from beginning again. Although the primary responsibility for such downstream prevention lies with the State, there is most often a critical need—particularly in the destructive wake following the use of military force for nonconsensual coercive intervention—for international assistance in building the capacity for downstream prevention.

To return to the river analogy introduced in Chapter 3, the hole in the bridge was not repaired and we chose not to, or could not, rescue the victims just as they hit the water. So, we are now left with the hopeful resuscitation of victims who were swept away in the rapids, along with the rebuilding of the bridge so that the crisis does not happen again. This analogy contextualizes the three different stages of the cyclical process of prevention—preventing genocide from ever taking place (Chapter 4), preventing further atrocities once genocide has begun (Chapter 5), and preventing future atrocities once a society has begun to rebuild after genocide (Chapter 6). In this regard, the ending of genocide and mass atrocity is transitional; it is really the immediate beginning of the next phase of prevention. The stream of downstream prevention, at its best, has confluence with the stream of upstream prevention to become one powerful preventive river of postgenocide recovery. As Gareth Evans argues: "Postconflict peacebuilding is not the end of the process of conflict resolution; it has to be the beginning of a new process of conflict prevention, with the focus again on structural prevention, tackling the longer-term, root causes of the violence in question."[16] Only by seeing prevention in this cyclical, integrated way can we hope to decrease the future likelihood of genocide.

Attempts to stabilize, heal, and rehabilitate a postgenocide society fall under the general conceptual framework of "transitional justice." Transitional justice refers to "judicial and non-judicial measures that have been implemented ... to redress the legacies of massive human rights abuses."[17] It involves dealing with, rather than ignoring through some form of collective forced amnesia, the legacy of mass atrocity. This multidisciplinary field emerged in the late 1980s and early 1990s in response to demands by human rights activists in postauthoritarian Latin America and postcommunist Eastern Europe for justice and accountability for former abusive regimes. The 1986 publication of *Transitions from Authoritarian Rule*, a major four-volume work focused on Latin America and Eastern Europe, is commonly cited as the boundary-defining text of the new field of transitional justice.[18]

The emerging field of transitional justice was given an important grounding in international law with a 1988 decision of the Inter-American Court of Human Rights. The case of *Velasquez Rodriguez v. Honduras* addressed targeted forced disappearance practices by the Honduran government during the early 1980s. In September 1981, Rodriguez, a graduate student and teacher involved in political activities considered dangerous to national security by the Honduran state, was kidnapped in broad daylight in the parking lot of a movie theater in downtown Tegucigalpa, detained, interrogated, and tortured. Over the following 3 years, about 150 additional Hondurans disappeared in a similar manner. Rodriquez was never seen again and the Court found "a reasonable presumption that he had been killed."[19] In its landmark decision, the court held the government of Honduras liable for the disappearance of Rodriquez, as well as three other victims represented in the case, and ordered the government to pay reparations to the families of the victims. The court also prescribed the international legal obligations of states to take reasonable steps to prevent human rights violations, conduct a serious investigation when such violations occur, and impose suitable sanctions on those found responsible for the violations.

Although not a unique form of justice per se, transitional justice is unique in its specific application to a society attempting to come to terms with a legacy of authoritarianism, civil war, massive human rights violations, or violent, even genocidal, conflict. "It is not a type of justice, but rather a *context* of justice for societies undergoing transformation."[20] Transitional justice does not always immediately coincide with the political transition from an abusive government to a more tolerant one. Indeed, it may be some time before a society has the strength and freedom to unpack its violent past. In Argentina, for instance, the pursuit of transitional justice was not linear, but rather was erratic with a 17-year period of impunity and amnesty (1986–2003) sandwiched between initial attempts to bring perpetrators to justice and the reopening of trials. As another example, in July 2013, the Ugandan government enacted a National Transitional Justice Policy to deal with "a post-independence [since 1962] political history marred by conquest, repression and bloodshed" in which it is estimated that over 300,000 people were killed.[21] Regardless of when it comes, however, transitional justice—even if offering too little—can never come too late.

Transitional justice does not happen quickly. Rebuilding after genocide is a particularly slow process and takes considerable time. In a society trying to recover from genocide, everything is a priority for a state that often has a limited capacity to respond to even the most urgent of priorities. As a result of such postconflict realities, research by Mthuli Ncube and Basil Jones of the African Development Bank Group has found that "a country's transition from a state of fragility to one of resilience involves a long process that may take 20 to 40 years."[22] Similarly, the 2011 *World Development Report* examining institutional transformations in fragile states found that "it took the 20 fastest-moving countries an average of 17 years to get the military out of politics, 20 years to achieve functioning bureaucratic quality, and 27 years to bring corruption under reasonable control."[23] Throughout this process, which often takes at least a generation, the fragility of a rebuilding state leaves it particularly vulnerable to the onset of renewed violent conflict or mass atrocity.

Nor does transitional justice come easily. To deal with the past is to open a wound that may be more comfortably, at least in the short term, left ignored. Long term, however, to let the wound fester is to invite the recurrence of another, perhaps even more grievous, conflict-laden future. As Goran Simic, an expert in the field of transitional justice, argues in his analysis of postgenocide Bosnia: "Dealing with the past will not be easy, but it is essential. Dealing with our own past by bringing closure and offering justice for all, perpetrators and victims, is the only right way. This path will not remove crimes from history. It will not repair souls that have been torn apart. But it will offer them the option to move on, and future generations will be able to live without the baggage of what went before."[24]

At its best, transitional justice gives force to human rights norms that were systematically and egregiously violated. Central to transitional justice, and illustrative of the cyclical and integrated nature of genocide prevention, are institutional reforms, particularly those relating to assurances of physical security. As international policy scholar Roland Paris has argued, "without a reasonable assurance of physical security for the bulk of the population, there is little hope of achieving progress on institution-building, intercommunal reconciliation, reconstruction and development."[25] In practice, the pursuit of physical security means impunity must become accountability, exclusion must become inclusion, and distrust must become legitimacy.[26] To accomplish these transitional objectives, and to ensure that human rights are defended and mass atrocities prevented, state protection capacity must be built. For security analyst Sean McFate, there are three linked programs that states, with assistance from the international community, can use to build such protection capacity. First, justice sector reform (JSR) promotes the rule of law by drafting new rights-based constitutions and dispensing justice with greater accountability, transparency, accessibility, and efficiency. Second, disarmament, demobilization, and reintegration (DDR) disbands those groups—militias, terrorists, gangs, insurgents, armed political factions, and other nonstatutory forces—that challenge the rule of law and attempts to transfer them safely back into civil society. Finally, McFate argues, security sector reform (SSR) is necessary to professionalize all levels of the security sector, to develop moral and competent oversight bodies, institutions, and security forces that become defenders against human rights abuses rather than perpetrators of them.[27] Cycling back to Chapter 4, each of these activities—JSR, DDR, and SSR—intersects with the longer-term preventive processes of building underlying structures of societal and state durability related to good governance, fair interpretation and transmission of conflict history, resilient economic conditions, and inclusive social cohesion.

Indeed, the infrastructures for building a sustainable peace through transitional justice are myriad. International, national, local, or "traditional" measures of transitional justice can include judicial mechanisms of accountability such as criminal prosecutions as well as nonjudicial mechanisms of fostering civic trust such as reparation and compensations programs, truth commissions, memorialization and commemoration, national dialogue, vetting and lustration, gender justice, and trauma healing. The Transitional Justice Data Base Project includes a global database of over 1,000 mechanisms (trials, truth commissions, amnesties, reparations, and lustration policies) used from 1970 to 2007.[28]

This chapter will specifically focus on the roles played by mechanisms of justice, truth, and memory. Entire books could be, and have been, written on each of these transitional justice tools and how they enable a postconflict society to move from a divided past to a shared future. With that in mind, this chapter will only be able to scratch the introductory surface of the depth involved in understanding how justice, truth, and memory can rebuild a society drowning in the aftermath of genocidal violence and fulfill the preventive imperative of ensuring that "never again" becomes a legitimate and attainable goal for a postgenocide society.

JUSTICE

In the transitional justice framework, the concept of justice is seen as having two arms. *Retributive justice*, grounded in the rule of law, is perpetrator focused and is based on the conviction that perpetrators should suffer for crimes they have committed and inflicted on others. Such justice focuses on prosecution and punishment and "attempts to distance itself from vengeance by emphasizing the importance of proportionality and procedural and substantive requirements that constrain the actions of the court and provide protections for the accused."[29] *Restorative justice*, conversely, is more victim focused and suggests that perpetrators—rather than simply being prosecuted and punished—should work to repair the harm they have inflicted on others. Such justice focuses on issues of reparation and mediation in the relationships between victim, perpetrator, and their community. These two arms of justice should not be seen as mutually exclusive or competitors in a zero-sum game. Rather, they are complementary or parallel arms of justice that, when used in tandem, can be important preventive steps in reconstructing the self and society after genocide.

Retributive Justice. The use of retributive justice to hold World War I aggressors accountable for their atrocities was relatively unsuccessful. "The defeated nations were unwilling to confront their crimes, and the victors had little interest in committing the necessary resources and attention required to ensure that the trials were successful."[30] Following

World War II, however, it became clear that justice, in some form, was due the perpetrators. For Soviet leader Joseph Stalin and British Prime Minister Winston Churchill, justice would best be served by "summarily executing a few thousand top Nazi officials by firing squad."[31] Eventually, however, the Allies agreed on establishing an international (actually, multinational) judicial process to prosecute alleged perpetrators of wartime atrocities. The cornerstone of this process was the International Military Tribunal at Nuremberg (1945–1946). Charged with prosecuting crimes against peace, war crimes, and crimes against humanity, the tribunal indicted 22 senior German political and military leaders. When the trial ended, three defendants were acquitted, 12 were sentenced to death by hanging, and seven received prison terms ranging from 10 years to life. While the Nuremberg tribunal would be the first and last joint Allied prosecution of Nazi criminals, it was paralleled by the lesser-known International Military Tribunal for the Far East. Commonly known as the Tokyo War Crimes Trials (1946–1948), this international tribunal worked within a criminal jurisdiction similar to Nuremberg. The Tokyo tribunal presided over the prosecution of nine senior Japanese political leaders and 18 military leaders, each of whom was found guilty and sentenced to punishments ranging from 7 years imprisonment to death.

Together, the Nuremberg and Tokyo international tribunals contributed immensely to the emerging development of international criminal law related to mass atrocity. As legal scholar Martha Minow writes: "The World War II war crimes trials represent the possibility of legal responses [to mass atrocity], rather than responses grounded in sheer power politics or military aggression."[32] Although certainly subject to critique, not the least of which is the lack of any apparent deterrent effect, these two multinational tribunals were the first "successful" modern international prosecution of major war criminals and are the point of origin in which many of our subsequent mechanisms of retributive justice took root. Although a few states had a strong enough independent judiciary to attempt domestic prosecutions for large-scale human rights violations, there would be a significant gap in time between the Nuremberg and Tokyo tribunals and the next attempt to prosecute crimes of mass atrocity in international settings. It would be nearly five decades before the United Nations (UN) established the next ad hoc international criminal tribunals—the International Criminal Tribunal for the Former Yugoslavia (ICTY, established in 1993) and the International Criminal Tribunal for Rwanda (ICTR, established in 1994).

The ICTY and ICTR were structured very similarly, shared the same appellate chamber, and, until August 2003, even shared the same chief prosecutor. As we have seen in previous chapters, both tribunals have made incredibly substantial contributions to the expansion of international criminal law related to genocide and mass atrocity. Their legal opinions have enunciated many of the norms, and fleshed out many of the weaknesses, inherent in the Genocide Convention and its implementation. In addition to "the broad-based furthering of the development and application of international criminal law," the works of the tribunals also "have encouraged the growth of domestic war crimes legislation and prosecutions."[33]

For Minow, however, such international tribunals can be critiqued on three fronts. First, is the notion of retroactivity or the concern that defendants face "charges under norms that had not been previously announced or broadcast, in a forum using procedures that also had not existed previously."[34] That is, is it just to punish offenders for an act understood as legal at the time it was committed? Although the risks of retroactivity apply most clearly to the Nuremberg and Tokyo tribunals, where the legal "norms guiding the prosecution were not explicitly or specifically in place at the time of the offenses," both the ICTY and ICTR have been asked to "resolve questions that have never before been answered in international settings, and some that have never been dealt with in any legal setting."[35] As Minow points out, the blazing of these new legal trails—for example, the legal characterization of rape, intent, duress, ethnic cleansing, and command responsibility—has a dubious retroactive consequence "of applying norms to people who did not know at the time of the conduct in question the content of the norms by which they could be judged."[36]

Minow's second criticism relates to politicization of international tribunals that can undermine "the ideals of impartiality and universal norms."[37] As Minow points out, "political alignments of powerful nations remain crucial to any international tribunal's existence, funding, and management."[38] Moreover, politicization can also rear its head during the actual judicial process in cases in which the trial becomes political theater, a "show trial" of asymmetrical domination, rather than an exercise in justice and the rule of law. Such politicization of international tribunals is often referred to as "victor's justice" and was raised for both the Nuremberg and Tokyo tribunals. For example, Chief Justice Harlan Stone, then a member of the U.S. Supreme Court, privately labeled the Nuremberg trial as a "high class lynching party."[39] More recently, a report by the International Crisis Group found "the victims of the crimes of the RPF [the victorious Rwandan Patriotic Front] denounce it [the ICTR] as an instrument of the Kigali regime, seeing the ICTR as a symbol of victor's justice" since it has handed out no indictments for members of the RPF for crimes allegedly committed during the 1994 genocide.[40] Such illegitimate expressions of judicial power can be devastating to the credibility and legitimacy of international trials.

Finally, Minow's third criticism of international tribunals is one of selectivity. "Only a small portion of those who could be charged with violations became the target of prosecutions for actions ... the actual set of individuals who face prosecution is likely to reflect factors far removed from considered judgments about who deserves prosecution and punishment."[41] Factors underlying selectivity can include the difficulty of locating those who "elude arrest and prosecution by escaping, or dying, or concealing their identities, their conduct, or the evidence implicating them ... [or those who] avoid arrest because their national or political party or ethnic group remains enough of a victor or ruling power" as well as simply inadequate resources (too few courtrooms, lawyers, witnesses, forensic experts, and so on) for judicial prosecution.[42] These patterns of selectivity, bordering on a perception of arbitrary justice, help partially explain the limited number of indictments over the course of the more than two decades existence of the ICTR and ICTY. The ICTR has indicated a grand total of 93 individuals, only a tiny fraction of those responsible for the atrocities in Rwanda. Although the relative track record of the ICTY is a bit better, with 161 indictments, Serb nationalists have used the selectivity of those brought forward for prosecution at The Hague (94 of whom are Serb) to propagandize them into a martyr status in their homeland. Milosevic further used the ICTY as a high-profile platform to affirm this alleged selectivity by arguing that he, and all Serbians, was being unjustly singled out as responsible for the wars.

To Minow's criticisms regarding retroactivity, politicization, and selectivity, can be added the reality that off-site international tribunals "create a chasm between the court and local populations, a brand of justice that smacks of imperialism and is not anchored in local culture."[43] The ICTY, based in The Hague, Netherlands, and the ICTR, located in Arusha, Tanzania, both have struggled with public outreach to its native constituencies. As one example, in the words of human rights investigator Ivana Nizich, "the people of the former Yugoslavia view the ICTY as an amorphous body in the Hague that was created by the international community to ameliorate its own guilt. They do not believe that the Tribunal is there to provide justice to them; it is 'someone else's' tribunal."[44] Similarly, the ICTR, where the accused are detained in sanitary conditions, well-fed, and well-clothed, seems worlds away culturally from the destitute reality of many survivors in Rwanda who are irreparably scarred and wounded (physically and psychologically) and live each day in hopes of finding sustenance to live another. With little public education or publicity surrounding the ICTR's work, the common sentiment of Rwandans is captured in one survivor's statement: "What is the Arusha tribunal? Come on, it is useless!"[45]

Finally, ad hoc international tribunals have a history of staggering runaway costs and repeated delays of completion dates. At their height, the ICTY and ICTR had more than 2,000 employment posts and a combined annual budget exceeding a quarter of a billion dollars—a figure consuming almost 10% of the total UN budget. The outlandish expense of the tribunals has prompted some critics to question how those funds might have been better used in the pursuit of postgenocide rebuilding. "The ICTR diverted enormous resources that could have been used to rebuild parts of Rwanda's shattered judiciary," including rebuilding local courthouses, improving jails, endowing a law school with appropriate facilities, and training a generation of Rwandan lawyers.[46] Research in 2003 by criminologist George Yacoubian found that that "it is . . . twenty times more expensive to prosecute (but not incarcerate) a genocidal perpetrator in the ICTR, and ten times more expensive in the ICTY, than it is to convict *and* execute a murderer in the United States . . . $45.5 million per genocidal conviction [in the ICTR] . . . $22.5 million per conviction [in the ICTY]."[47] In addition to this meager return on investment, closure dates for the time-limited tribunals have been continually revised, with the most recent forecasted closure of the ICTY in 2017—7 years later than its anticipated completion date. The ICTR's formal closure on December 31, 2015, was 5 years later than anticipated. As legal scholar Stuart Ford argues, however, these criticisms of cost and length must be considered in the context of the incredible complexity of the criminal trials considered by the tribunals. His quantitative analysis reveals that when this unparalleled complexity is accounted for, the ICTY actually has been more efficient than cases of comparable gravity and complexity tried in domestic courts.[48]

In the face of such substantive criticisms, it is tempting to look to national trials in domestic courts for postgenocide retributive justice. We have seen such attempts taken up, with varying degrees of success, in the domestic courts of Poland, Bangladesh, Rwanda, Romania, Cambodia, Ethiopia, states of the former Yugoslavia, Iraq, and some Latin American states. Too often, however, domestic courts, particularly those recently torn apart by genocidal violence, lack sufficient resources and expertise to undertake the complex task of prosecuting genocide. The ICTY and ICTR were established precisely because devastated domestic judicial mechanisms in the former Yugoslavia and Rwanda could no longer fulfill their roles. After the genocide in Rwanda, for instance, there were only 10 lawyers left in a country with jails bulging with 130,000 alleged perpetrators and a caseload that would take judges 110 years to clear.[49] This is testament to the fact that genocide overwhelms justice. That is, it is hard to envision any postgenocide society that would have the functional domestic judicial mechanisms to bring retributive justice in any immediate sense. Moreover, domestic courts may also be even greater prey to high levels of corruption, ethnic bias, and politicization.

In Argentina, for instance, bold domestic prosecutions of the military regime began early but parliamentary and military opposition led to a "Full Stop" law in 1986 that mandated the end of all investigations and prosecutions of those accused of political violence during the dictatorship. This was followed in 1987 by a "Due Obedience" law that exempted violators from punishment if they had acted within the scope of obeying orders from superiors. These two laws effectively halted retributive justice in Argentina until being declared unconstitutional in 2003. More recently, in June 2015, Francisco Palomo, the lawyer who represented former Guatemalan military leader Efrain Rios Montt against genocide charges, was shot dead as preparations for Montt's retrial in a national court were under way. Although the motive is still under investigation, it seems clear that Palomo's murder is tied to the politicization of Montt's trial in the Guatemalan domestic courts.

Given these real limitations of national trials, in recent years we have seen the development of specialist courts with a mixed or hybrid construction. These courts involve both international and national judicial features and are most often grafted onto a local judicial system. "Hybrid courts are candidates for contexts where there is little domestic institutional capacity to prosecute major crimes, including legal, forensic, and technical expertise for fair prosecutions."[50] As introduced in Chapter 5, examples of such courts include the Serious Crimes Panels in the District Court of Dili in East Timor (established in 2000), the "Regulation 64" Panels in the Courts of Kosovo (2000), the Special Court for Sierra Leone (2002), the War Crimes Chamber in the State Court of Bosnia-Herzegovina (2005), and the Extraordinary Chambers in the Courts of Cambodia (2006). This increasing global reliance on hybrid courts speaks of the empowering value of local ownership and participation in retributive justice mechanisms. The linguistic, cultural, logistical, and physical accessibility of hybrid courts can be a vital piece of social repair in a postgenocide society as well as a key component in rebuilding the capacity and credibility of the local legal system.

As just one example, the War Crimes Chamber in the State Court of Bosnia–Herzegovina, based in Sarajevo, is fully integrated into the domestic legal system of Bosnia–Herzegovina. With its first proceedings beginning on March 9, 2005, the Chamber handles cases transferred to it by the ICTY as well cases brought to it at the national or local level. The Chamber's verdicts are handed down in accordance with the domestic laws of Bosnia–Herzegovina, trials are conducted in one of the national languages, and convicted persons serve their sentences in domestic prisons. The majority of key staff positions related to the work of the Chamber are held by Bosnian nationals. Although international judges and prosecutors do work in the Chamber, it is planned that the international presence will phase out over time and eventually disappear completely, leaving a fully domestic State Court. In the meantime, as I have witnessed in personal visits to the Court, the international judges and prosecutors continue to build local state capacity with training sessions for national staff on international humanitarian law, human rights, mass atrocity investigations, media awareness initiatives, and public outreach. By May 2012, the Court had "concluded an impressive 79 cases against 108 accused . . . with a further 68 cases ongoing."[51]

Though hybrid courts, by borrowing on some of the strengths and credibility of international courts, can certainly counter some of the limitations of national courts, they are not without their limits. Legal scholar Ethel Higonnet, for instance, argues that "one of the hybrid model's worst flaws is that instead of incorporating the best of the international and local judicial systems, it may reflect the worst of both."[52] Even when hybrid courts are physically located in the country of concern, for instance, "the transplant of foreign modes of law, with its wigs and gowns, and imposing high-security courtrooms separate international law from local populations."[53] Attempts to implement quality public outreach activities to make the legal process more palatable to domestic constituencies, however, carry their own risk. As Higonnet warns: "The further hybrids deviate from an international tribunal prototype, the more they risk being manipulated by ethnic, military, or political factions."[54] Although it is indeed true that issues such as witness protection, staff intimidation, corruption, and politicization may be as threatening to hybrid courts as they are to domestic courts, the international presence—however defined and carried out– in hybrid courts does lend some counteracting measure of legitimacy, resources, experience, technical knowledge, and *gravitas* to the courts.

Finally, the most recent mechanism of retributive justice came with the establishment of the International Criminal Court (ICC). Formed by the Rome Statue of the International Criminal Court on July 17, 1998, and entering into force on July 1, 2002, the ICC is a permanent, standing international tribunal with near universal jurisdiction to prosecute individuals (not groups or States) accused of war crimes, crimes against humanity, and genocide (and, beginning in 2017, crimes of aggression). The Court is the manifestation of a long-held aspiration—traceable to the mid-nineteenth century—for a permanent, standing international tribunal. Seated at The Hague, the ICC is an independent international organization, not part of the UN system (though it does borrow much of its basic structure from the ICTY and ICTR). The Court operates on the principle of complementarity, meaning that it serves as a backup institution that prosecutes cases only when national criminal justice systems are unwilling or unable to carry out such prosecutions. Cases come before the court in one of three ways: (1) States Parties to the Statute (123 at present) refer situations to the Court, (2) the UN Security Council can request that the Court launch an investigation into a situation of concern (irrespective of the nationality of the accused or the location of the crime), or (3) the Court's prosecutor may initiate investigations on the basis of information received from reliable sources about crimes involving nationals of a State Party or of a State that has accepted the jurisdiction of the ICC.

At present, 23 individual cases in nine situations have been brought before the ICC. Four States Parties to the Rome Statute—Uganda, the Democratic Republic of the Congo, the Central African Republic (two separate situations), and Mali—have referred situations occurring on their territories to the Court. In addition, the UN Security Council has requested that the Court launch investigations into Sudan (for the situation in Darfur) and Libya—both non-States Parties. Finally, the Court's prosecutor has initiated investigations into Kenya and Côte d'Ivoire. Across all of these cases, the court has publicly issued warrants for 36 people but won only two convictions.

Even though it is the most heavily represented region among the Court's membership, and the Court is conducting preliminary examinations in a number of countries across several continents, each of the countries currently in open cases before the ICC is African, as are all of the current indictees.[55] As a result, relations between Africa and the ICC are severely strained as the Court is perceived to be a neocolonist tool to further repress Africa. "African governments argue that the ICC is practicing a form of 'selective justice' and that it is avoiding diplomatically, economically, financially and politically strong countries, such as the United States, the United Kingdom, Russia and China, because these countries can threaten the ICC's existence."[56] In February, 2014, triggered by the UN Security Council's rejection of their demand for the ICC to suspend the trial of Kenyan president Uhuru Kenyatta, the African Union urged its members to "speak with one voice" against international criminal proceedings targeting sitting presidents.[57] Later that year, ICC prosecutors withdrew charges against Kenyatta based on a lack of cooperation that left insufficient evidence for criminal prosecution. Although vociferous proposals for African nations to withdraw from the ICC have now subsided, the Kenyatta decision still portends ill for the Court's immediate, and future, relevance in Africa and elsewhere.

The work of the ICC is particularly compromised because it does not have its own police force and must rely on State cooperation for the arrest and transfer of suspects—cooperation that is very difficult to ensure in many cases. On March 4, 2009, for instance, Sudanese President Omar Hassan al-Bashir was indicted on five counts of crimes against humanity and two counts of war crimes; he was additionally indicted on three counts of genocide on July 12, 2010. Since Bashir's original indictment, a series of ICC member states failed to arrest him when he visited—including Kenya, Qatar, Ethiopia, Saudi Arabia, Chad, Malawi, Congo, and Egypt. Most recently, in June 2015, a South African human rights organization filed court action to prevent Bashir from leaving an African Union summit meeting in Johannesburg. In response, South Africa's ruling African National Congress said the ICC was "no longer useful for the purposes for which it was intended," allowing Bashir to scurry away from South Africa on his presidential jet just hours before the Pretoria High Court ruled that the government was legally required to arrest him.[58] The South African government is now in contempt of its own courts. Such lack of political will, coupled with the limited resources of the prosecutor's office and the lack of support from the UN Security Council, left ICC prosecutor Fatou Bensouda with little option other than to formally suspend investigations in Darfur, although the indictments against Bashir will remain in place.

The long-term viability and legitimacy of the Court are not helped by the lack of engagement from powerful countries that have neither signed nor ratified the Rome Statute, officially refusing to submit to the Court's authority—including the United States, China, India, Pakistan, Indonesia, Turkey, Egypt, Sudan, Iran, Israel, and Russia. Barring a referral from the UN Security Council—exceptionally unlikely since three of these countries enjoy veto power as permanent members of that council and the rest have a powerful veto member patron on the council—these countries effectively have insulated themselves from the court's jurisdiction. This suggests that international justice unfairly applies only to "the most powerful individuals of the world's middle powers and poor countries, but not to the lowest-ranking soldiers of the United States, Russia, or China."[59] With this pronounced lack of support from these potentially influential global partners, and so few prosecutions to its name, the credibility of the ICC must be built on showing "the world that it can be a successful permanent institution in international law with clear standards and goals, as well [as] successful indictments, prosecutions and convictions of heinous war criminals in different parts of the world."[60]

In conclusion, as Ernesto Verdeja points out, retributive justice holds violators individually responsible for their actions, helps curtail demands for vengeance, generates a public authoritative record of crimes and evidence, and, in theory, can serve as a deterrent to would-be future perpetrators of genocide and mass atrocity.[61] Similarly, Kathryn Sikkink describes the "justice cascade" of a "dramatic new trend in world politics toward holding individual state officials, including heads of state, criminally accountable for human rights violations."[62] Sikkink's empirical research on Latin America suggests that the impact of such trials actually improves protection for human rights. As she summarizes: "Transitional countries in which human rights prosecutions have taken place are less repressive than countries without prosecutions . . . In addition, countries surrounded by more neighbors with transitional prosecutions are less repressive, which may suggest a deterrence impact of prosecutions across borders."[63]

As Verdeja also points out, however, trials as mechanisms of retributive justice can be criticized for "their cost, their adversarial structure, their lack of resonance with victims and the broader public, and—for international tribunals—their remoteness from the communities that suffered."[64] Most disconcerting is the way in which trials oversimplify distinctions between perpetrators and victims. "The complexity," Verdeja writes, "of collaboration, bystander responsibility, and broader political and social-psychological dynamics are discarded in favor of legally neat distinctions between violator and victim."[65] As a result, the individualized nature of trials—excluding collaborators, bystanders, and other interested states—undermines their collective preventive impact.[66]

To be sure, we must be careful to avoid blurring responsibility lines to the degree that, at some point, we walk too close to the dangerous explanatory line of blaming victims for their own victimization. It may also be that, although it is very difficult to show that bystanders are legally guilty, retributive justice can go a long way toward discussing openly the "false moral innocence" of bystanders.[67] Nonetheless, Verdeja is correct in reminding us that the backward-looking and reductive nature of retributive justice (for instance, prosecuting only a handful of perpetrators) sometimes can distort, rather than clarify, history and, without intention, end up taking us away from the moral scrutiny necessary to repair and rebuild a postgenocide society. From a downstream preventive standpoint, the meager number of criminal indictments and convictions for genocide severely compromises any presumed deterrent effects of retributive justice. There also is serious question about the degree to which retributive justice can aid or "heal" victims of genocide or reconcile a postgenocide society. As transitional justice expert Brandon Hamber summarizes the global state of the field, contrary to Sikkink's regional conclusions, "there is limited empirical data to suggest that trials . . . deter future war crimes, gross human rights violations, or genocide, or that trials improve intergroup relations."[68]

Certainly, none of this is to say that retributive justice has no role to play as a preventive downstream measure. Impunity for perpetration of genocide is unacceptable. The obscenity that a person stands a better chance of being tried and judged for killing one human being than for killing one hundred thousand cannot be allowed to stand.[69] As Minow points out, "to find the trial process wanting against the aspiration of truly dealing with the complex past is not to find it worthless as a response to atrocity."[70] Sikkink similarly reminds us that "justice—like democracy—is one of those powerful concepts that in practice always falls short of our ideals."[71] Although judgments against aspirations and ideals are always found lacking, retributive justice can be seen as one piece—necessary but certainly far from sufficient—of the complex, holistic preventive process in repairing and rebuilding a postgenocide society.

Restorative Justice. The dynamic and evolving field of restorative justice reaches beyond prosecution and punishment to focus on repairing the social harm caused by mass atrocity. It is a recognition of the "need for justice mechanisms for victims, not just offenders."[72] As Minow summarizes: "Restorative justice emphasizes the humanity of both offenders and victims. It seeks repair of social connections and peace rather than retribution against offenders. Building connections and enhancing communication between perpetrators and those they victimized, and forging ties across the community, takes precedence over punishment or law enforcement."[73] Central to the theory of restorative justice are cooperative processes that allow all willing stakeholders (victims, perpetrators, and bystanders) to meet (in-person or through letter, video, or a third party) and take steps toward the transformation of people, relationships, and communities.[74] For Verdeja, restorative justice "frames political violence not only as the violation of the law or an individual's legal rights, but as a social phenomenon that undermines community well-being."[75] Retributive justice is not shelved in favor of restorative justice; rather, prosecution and punishment are subordinated to the comprehensive restoration of just and meaningful social relations. We will briefly examine the role of reparations (material, symbolic, and psychosocial) as mechanisms of restorative justice as well as some tradition-based community models of restorative justice.

The right of reparation is "a principle of law that has existed for centuries, referring to the obligation of a wrongdoing party to redress the damage caused to the injured party."[76] Lemkin clearly considered this right for victims of genocide as reflected in the fact that the subtitle for his *Axis Rule in Occupied Europe* included "proposals for redress." Article XIII of the Secretariat draft on the convention of the crime of genocide, of which Lemkin was a co-author, provided for reparations to victims of genocide by asserting that "the State shall grant to the survivors of the human group that is a victim of genocide redress of a nature and in an amount to be determined by the United Nations."[77] The explanatory comments for the Secretariat draft defended reparations on grounds "that populations are to a certain extent answerable for crimes committed by their governments which they have condoned or which they have simply allowed their governments to commit."[78] The draft went on to define the parameters of "the obligation to make reparations to victims of genocide" as including compensation or pensions, restitution of seized property, special benefits to survivors (such as houses and scholarships), and, collectively (very Lemkin-esque), "reconstitution of the moral, artistic and cultural inherence of the group (including reconstruction of monuments, libraries, universities, churches, etc.)."[79]

Although this specific provision did not make it into the final draft of the Genocide Convention, the general principle of the right of reparation is now firmly established in international law. In 2005, the UN General Assembly adopted the *Basic Principles and Guidelines on the Right to a Remedy and Reparation for Victims of Gross Violations of International Human Rights and Serious Violations of International Humanitarian Law.*[80] Applicable to victims of genocide, the *Basic Principles and Guidelines* are based on existing international obligations and include 27 articles affirming States' obligations, the status and the rights of victims (individually or collectively, both direct and indirect), and the broad range of material and symbolic means to grant reparation to victims—including restitution, compensation, rehabilitation, satisfaction, and guarantees of non-repetition. The following year, Article 24 of the International Convention for the Protection of all Persons from Enforced Disappearances further elaborated victims' right of reparation.[81]

A wide range of jurisprudence in international, regional, and domestic courts has acknowledged, affirmed, and provided for victims' right to reparation. The Rome Statute creating the ICC, for instance, also created a Trust Fund for Victims to implement Court-ordered reparations as well as assist in setting up innovative projects to meet victims' physical, material, or psychological needs. Since 2008, the Trust Fund has provided support to over 110,000 victims of crimes under the jurisdiction of the Court through integrated physical and psychological rehabilitation and/or material support at both the individual and community levels.[82] In theory, if seldom in practice, both the ICTY and ICTR also allow victims to bring requests to a national court or other competent body to obtain compensation for crimes within their mandates. African, European, and Inter-American regional courts also have provisions for reparations, as do an increasing number of domestic judicial and human rights mechanisms.

Material reparations can be offered either in terms of financial compensation for economically assessable damage or the restitution of seized or stolen land, art, ancestral remains, sacred objects, and so on. As social psychologists Aarti Iyer and Craig Blatz point out, material reparations raise difficult questions: "How much is a lost life worth? How does one determine the monetary value of denied human rights, or lack of access to education, or property confiscated generations ago? Is there a statute of limitations on when reparations are no longer feasible?"[83] Despite the complexity, or even near impossibility, of answering these questions, material reparations can be used to address economic vulnerability and at least partially repair the social harm caused by genocide or mass atrocity.

Most often, perpetrators have no capacity to pay for the material damages they have imposed on victims. So, it remains for the state, often in partnership with the international community, to build capacity for such reparations at the collective and individual level. Shortly after World War II, for instance, West Germany paid Israel about DM 3 billion for crimes associated with the Holocaust.[84] Other collective material reparations to benefit all members of a victim group can include educational scholarships, affirmative action, and social assistance programs. On an individual level, Canada has offered cash payments of $10,000 to former residents of residential schools and the Australian province of Tasmania offered between $5,000 and $20,000 to aboriginal victims of the "stolen generation."[85] The Chilean government continues to pay lifetime pensions of about $260 per month to survivors of human rights violations committed by the Pinochet regime; relatives of those killed receive more than three times that amount.[86] As of November 2012, Germany's postwar reparations program had paid more than $89 billion in individual compensation payments since 1952, mostly to Jewish victims, and continues to meet regularly to revise and expand the guidelines for qualification.[87] Colombia's comprehensive "Justice and Peace Law" of 2005, the largest national effort at redress in the world, provides reparations to victims of the continuing armed conflict "to alleviate their suffering, compensate their social, moral and material losses, and restitute their citizen rights."[88] Finally, as the ICTR ground to a close, Rwandan officials continued to work with the Tribunal to establish some form of compensation mechanism, either individually or as a collective, for genocide survivors (though some reparation cases have been filed under *gacaca* courts).[89]

Restitution of lost, stolen, or destroyed property can be a legal morass, especially when involving transnational issues, that can take years to resolve. The Conference on Jewish Material Claims Against Germany and the World Jewish Restitution Organization have been particularly effective in initiating and supporting wide-ranging efforts toward the restitution of Jewish-owned art, Judaica, and other cultural property lost and plundered during the Holocaust. Less successful over the years have been campaigns to restore native lands stolen by colonizing groups; these involve actions that, if successful, would lead to a global redistribution of resources. As Elazar Barkan, a leading scholar on restitution issues, has written in regard to this negotiating of historical injustices between unequal parties: "The state determines the 'price'—in the form of restitution to the indigenous peoples—it is willing to pay for its new identity according to a calculus that is anything but rational or driven by market mechanisms. In most cases the indigenous peoples can at most plead the moral component but are made to accept offers they cannot refuse."[90]

Most recently, with the approach of its centennial commemoration, restitution attempts for property lost or stolen during the Armenian genocide have drawn international headlines. In December 2014, an Armenian-American, Zuart Sudjian, filed suit against Turkey to regain control of her family property lost during the Armenian genocide. Today, this land houses the Diyarbakir Airport and is worth tens of millions of dollars. Sudjian's suit was followed in May 2015 with a branch of the Armenian Apostolic Church filing a similar claim to regain religious property lost during the Armenian genocide. If Turkey's Constitutional Court rejects hearing the case, the claimants have declared that they will take the case to the European Court of Human Rights in Strasbourg, France. Even the U.S. Air Base at Injirlik is located on land owned by several Armenian families who filed a 2010 lawsuit (still pending) in U.S. Federal Court against the Turkish government. Such suits have led to "Armenians all around the world now asking what happened to our families' property, their homes" and a positive ruling (rather unlikely) in any of these cases, at the domestic or international level, would open a flood of similar restitution lawsuits from Armenians worldwide.[91]

Symbolic reparations "can be accorded in a number of different ways, including public acts of atonement and official apologies, creating public spaces to pay homage to victims, and establishing museums, monuments, and days of remembrance to preserve collective memory."[92] Such forms of reparation allow for psychological and social, rather than material, amends. As will be discussed later in this chapter, the mechanism of public commemoration, especially joint commemorations between victim and perpetrator groups, can be particularly healing as symbolic reparation. "When a past injustice is memorialized, it is, in a real sense, institutionalized. By establishing national and regional monuments to solemnize and memorialize . . . commemoration of past injustices would serve as a present commitment to reparative steps to redress past injustices and their current effects."[93] Such reparative attempts to symbolize past injustices, and include them in future historical narratives, likely coincide with some form of material reparations to ensure the financial commitment necessary for public commemoration and maintenance in collective memory.

Perhaps the most commonly studied, and even more commonly utilized, mechanism of symbolic reparations is apology. "Apology refers not to the transfer of material items or resources . . . but to an admission of wrongdoing, a recognition of its effects, and, in some cases, an acceptance of responsibility for those effects and an obligation to its victims."[94] As sociologist Nicholas Tavuchis describes, "to apologize is to declare voluntarily that one has *no* excuse, defense, justification, or explanation for an action (or inaction)."[95] In some cases, apology comes after bilateral negotiations between the victim and perpetrator group (often prompted after extensive lobbying by the victim group); in other cases, the perpetrator group makes a unilateral decision to offer an apology to the victim group.[96]

On the positive side, an apology, when done properly with full, unqualified acceptance of responsibility by the perpetrator, can carry with it an attitude of reconciliation. An apology is a forthright public acknowledgment of illegitimate or undeserved harm. It affirms the validity of the victims' narrative history and, as a form of restorative justice, restores that history to the global narrative.[97] "Official apologies can correct a public record, afford public acknowledgement of a violation, assign responsibility, and reassert the moral baseline to define violations of basic norms."[98] Nationalist identity, perhaps built on a denial of victims' suffering, can be reconfigured by a sincere, contrite, and remorseful apology. As Barkan writes: "Often, by validating and showing respect for the victims' memory and identity, the very recognition of past injustices constitutes the core of restitution. It is a recognition that transforms the trauma of victimization into a process of mourning and allows for rebuilding."[99] An apology is a change in posture, a public confession of guilt and vulnerability, a profound break with the past, paving a road to intergroup reconciliation in a postgenocide society. It is an act of communication that reminds all parties of human rights norms because the perpetrator has admitted to violating them.[100] At its best, an apology is a pledge to a new future, a clear commitment to change that guarantees nonrepetition of the atrocities. As human rights scholar Damien Short argues in his analysis of Australian reconciliation: "Through official acts of remembrance, such as apologies, national governments can influence the way society remembers the past, which in turn has implications for present and future public policy."[101]

On the other hand, an apology, particularly when done poorly, may be seen as an empty gesture of performative guilt that does more for allaying the conscience of the perpetrator group, or assuaging public outrage, than it does for healing the wounds of the victim group. As Barkan asks, "unless accompanied by material compensation or restitution, does not the apology merely whitewash the justice?"[102] When unaccompanied by material reparations, apology can be perceived as superficial, insincere, or meaningless.[103] Apologies that are incomplete, or qualified by a "but" that boundaries a limited responsibility in fear that the victim group may demand costly reparations, can do more to reinforce intergroup hostility than heal it. "In Rwanda sometimes confession and apology, in front of communities, with perpetrators showing little emotion and seeming to speak in an arrogant manner, create pain and anger in survivors."[104] Apologies that require acceptance on the part of victims, rather than granting them the power to choose to "accept, refuse, or ignore the apology," can be a form of revictimization.[105] Apologies that do not include clear plans to modify policies and practices in regard to the victim group can be seen as purely symbolic and desultory gestures, manipulative political attempts to wipe the slate clean as if the violations never occurred.

Particularly problematic are cases "when an offer of apology comes from persons who have no ability actually to accept or assume responsibility, or who have only remote connections with either the wrongdoers or the victims."[106] Such apology by proxy is often seen in official government statements of contrition over genocide or mass atrocity. As one example, in September 2000, on the occasion of the 175th anniversary of the establishment of the federal Bureau of Indian Affairs (BIA), Kevin Gover, head of the BIA and a member of the Pawnee Nation of Oklahoma (and now director of the Smithsonian Institution's National Museum of the American Indian), formally apologized for the agency's "legacy of racism and inhumanity" that included massacres, relocations, and the destruction of Indian languages and cultures. With tears in his eyes, Gover apologized on behalf of the BIA, but not the federal government as a whole. "This agency participated in the ethnic cleansing that befell the Western tribes," he said. "This agency set out to destroy all things Indian . . . the legacy of these misdeeds haunts us . . . it must be acknowledged that the deliberate spread of disease, the decimation of the mighty bison herds, the use of the poison alcohol to destroy mind and body, and the cowardly killing of women and children made for tragedy on a scale so ghastly that it cannot be dismissed as merely the inevitable consequence of the clash of competing ways of life."[107]

To that time, Gover was the highest-ranking U.S. official ever to make such a statement regarding the treatment of American Indians. His speech was widely reported nationally as well as internationally. Gover's emotional remarks hit many of the keynotes of a good apology—"let us begin by expressing our profound sorrow for what this agency has done in the past . . . these wrongs must be acknowledged if the healing is to begin . . . by accepting this legacy, we accept also the moral responsibility of putting things right." Many of the 300 tribal leaders, BIA employees, and federal officials in attendance wept openly and Gover received a standing ovation at the end of his remarks. The formal apology opened the door, at least a crack, for a transformation of a national identity mired in—yet willfully ignorant of—its subterranean history of genocidal crimes against indigenous peoples. For Susan Masten, chairwoman of California's Yurok tribe, "it was a very heroic and historic moment."[108] Testifying to the speech's poignancy, psychiatrist Aaron Lazare, in his work On Apology, wrote: "I find the apologies from [Abraham] Lincoln and Gover to be heart-wrenching, the most difficult of all those I describe in this book to read without tears . . . Accepting these responsibilities is part of what we mean when we speak of having a national identity."[109]

As legal scholar Christopher Buck points out, however, Gover's speech "was met with more cynicism than praise," some calling it "like a peace pipe without real peace."[110] Other critics believed Gover was the wrong person to accept or assume responsibility for the historical injustices perpetrated against Native Americans. As Eugene Johnson (Siletz) said: "Kevin Gover is Indian. An apology coming from him is like having a black official in the U.S. government apologize to the black populace for slavery, Rosewood, the KKK, etc. It's like having a Jew apologize to the Jewish populace for Nazi atrocities enacted during WWII. His apology is truly offensive to me."[111] Even Gover later admitted: "It's too bad, in a way, that it could not be said to the Indians by the non-Indian (federal) leadership, because there's a great deal of irony for an Indian apologizing to other Indians for what the non-Indians did to them."[112] Recognizing that the Clinton administration did not oppose Gover's speech, but neither did they endorse it, Lloyd Totralita, the governor of New Mexico's Acoma Pueblo tribe, stated: "If we could get an apology from the whole government, that would be better."[113] (Such an apology finally came on December 19, 2009 with the Congressional passage, and presidential signing, of the "Apology to Native Peoples of the United States," stealthily camouflaged in just over one page of a 67-page unrelated defense spending bill and admitting no liability.[114]) Other critics found Gover's apology too watery in its refusal to call the crime by its rightful name. Though alluding to the legacy of genocide with eight poignant references to "never again" in his speech (in fact, Gover's speech has come to be known as the "Never Again" speech), Jim Craven (Blackfoot) pointed out that "Gover has explicitly stipulated to every single type of act mentioned in Article II of the UN Convention on Genocide as constituting genocide while refusing to use that word."[115]

As the above example illustrates, in the aftermath of genocide, an apology—however well-intentioned or well-constructed—is inevitably inadequate. Even Gover noted: "It does not matter to me that the apology did not resonate throughout Indian Country. No apology could."[116] That said, however, Iyer and Blatz do present research- and practice-informed suggestions for engineering an optimal apology. In short, "the more thorough [apologies] are in their content, the more effective they are at promoting peaceful feelings."[117] Specifically: "Apologies should then include as may sincerity statements as is appropriate, and should carefully consider the specific needs and concerns of the various parties involved. To the extent that it is possible, apologies should also be formally endorsed by the group or government representatives. Lastly, apologies should be delivered to as many of the original victims of the harm-doing as possible."[118] Although admitting that apologies—even when optimally constructed and presented—may not necessarily promote forgiveness, Iyer and Blatz do suggest that they promote "some kinds of peaceful feelings" that can produce a limited positive effect on intergroup relations.[119]

Finally, *psychosocial reparations* can focus on repairing broken individual lives as well as repairing the social fabric of broken communities. For human rights scholars Laurel Fletcher and Harvey Weinstein, such reparations are important in the social reconstruction that must follow the social breakdown of genocide.[120] Although sharing some intersections with material and symbolic reparations, psychosocial reparations— broadly defined as repairing our psychological interaction with the social environment in which we live—are an important complement for a more inclusive restorative justice.

On an individual level, psychosocial reparations are rehabilitative and, as defined in Article 21 of the *Basic Principles and Guidelines*, can include therapeutic services and healthcare, as well as legal and social services. The state-proposed *Transitional Justice Strategy for Bosnia and Herzegovina*, for example, includes three measures of psychosocial reparation for individuals: "(1) psychosocial support to victims and people in need through creating a sustainable referral system and strengthening existing institutions mandated to provide services of this kind, as well as amendment of relevant laws and practices, (2) employment of victims and disabled people for the purpose of achieving their economic independence and self-sufficiency, and (3) creating programs for psychological strengthening and re-socialization of victims and disabled people through their inclusion in various social, cultural and sport activities."[121] In Rwanda, by 1997, trauma counseling and psychoeducational work with child survivors were trying to repair the individual brokenness left in the wake of the genocide.[122] Today, the Rwandan government annually commits 6% of state revenues toward the Fund for the Support of Genocide Survivors (FARG), an organization primarily focused on education, healthcare, housing, and socioeconomic welfare (including the promotion of skills development for income-generating projects) for survivors.[123]

On the collective level, psychosocial reparations "may include group therapies, micro-enterprise development as well as conflict resolution programs. Cultural initiatives may include support for the arts, rebuilding libraries and other cultural monuments and memorializing community losses. Redevelopment efforts frequently focus on restoring health and social services. Economic renewal requires at a minimum the restoration of the physical infrastructure and perhaps wholesale economic restructuring."[124] Social psychologist Ervin Staub, for instance, offers group therapy in Rwanda for survivors, perpetrators, and bystanders that includes "experiential components, specifically having people write, or draw, or just think about their experiences during the genocide and then share these experiences with each other, with participants also trained in empathic responding to others' stories . . . [as well as] learning about the effects of trauma . . . [and] examining paths to healing."[125] Similar group reconciliation projects are ongoing in South Africa, Cambodia, and Sierra Leone.[126] In psychosocial reparations at the collective level, community-generated responses representing their aspirations for social repair should be privileged. Often, these responses demand the redistribution of resources to enhance the livelihood of victims. "Truth commissions in Peru, Guatemala, and El Salvador," for example, "called for significant investments in public education, housing, employment, and economic development in indigenous areas most affected by the violence."[127]

Despite its status as a growing moral trend, there is very little research examining what makes for successful reparations in a postgenocide society. And reparations—whether material, symbolic, or psychosocial—will always engender controversy, perhaps even to a degree that destabilizes a postgenocide society more than stabilizes it. Perpetrators, and bystanders, may believe that amends have been made and the memory of the offense can be closed. Survivors may believe that "reparations of any sort do not provide an adequate moral response to their suffering. They may see it as a kind of 'blood money' or attempt by the state to wash its hands of future responsibility."[128] Reparations also can threaten social cohesion, especially, as in the case with Rwanda, when the recipient group has a perceived history of already enjoying unique privileges.[129] "Reparations payments alone generally do not satisfy victims' needs for broader acknowledgement of what happened, and in some cases only raise more demands for full investigations."[130] In short, reparations can never repair. As Minow cautions: "Restitution of stolen art, bank accounts, or ancestral bones may return the physical objects but not the world in which they were taken."[131]

On the other hand, an absence of reparations can equate to an absence of acknowledgment that makes it difficult for a postgenocide society to move from a divided past to a shared future. The pursuit of reparations—particularly as part of a broader, comprehensive initiative of retributive and restorative justice—gives voice to survivors and may offer them a renewed sense of dignity, recognition, and belongingness that can help a postgenocide society move from intergroup conflict to intergroup peace. As Iyer and Blatz remind us, "at least for the victim group, the only alternative more controversial than a specific reparation proposal is not to even try to compensate the harm."[132]

In addition to reparations, there is a range of *tradition-based community models* of restorative justice that aim to repair and rebuild a post-conflict society. There is a growing recognition that such models "may deal with intergroup and communal conflict more effectively than standard Western culpability models."[133] Examples of such tradition-based community models of restorative justice can be found in Mozambique, Timor-Leste, Uganda, Guatemala, Sierra Leone, Liberia, Nigeria, Burundi, Somalia, Rwanda, and the Democratic Republic of Congo (DRC). The DRC, for instance, has utilized Baraza peace courts for community-led conflict resolution and restorative justice. "Baraza" is a Swahili word meaning "gathering." First established in 2010, nine Barazas operate in rural villages through South Kivu and are made up of community members democratically elected. Women are intentionally integrated into the work of the Barazas, sometimes even to the extent of creating an all-female court as a safe space to hear women's allegations of marital rape and sexual violence. Decisions of the Barazas, typically achieved in 2–3 weeks, can include restorative measures of private or public apology, work in community development projects, or monetary compensation. Preliminary evaluation data suggest that the Barazas, having resolved over 1,500 cases at present, may be significantly more effective in successfully resolving conflicts and reducing violence than national justice mechanisms in the DRC.[134]

The best-known, and most controversial, example of a tradition-based community model of restorative justice, however, is the *gacaca* courts of Rwanda. Resurrecting a long-defunct traditional system of conflict resolution for minor civil disputes, *gacaca* was repurposed by the Rwandan government to rebuild "the social fabric which had been completely destroyed, a task that was practically impossible to carry out using the classical system of justice."[135] *Gacaca*, an African solution to an African problem, was grounded in the power of community—justice from and within the population—run by local community members trained (in a very limited sense) as judges, encouraging the active participation of local community members, and aiming to reconcile local communities by dispensing justice in the very location in which the crimes had occurred. Often meeting outdoors in a marketplace or in an open green space (*gacaca* is a Kinyarwandan word referring to a type of grass that grew in Rwanda), the courts provided gripping scenes of victims encountering, and confronting, perpetrators. Perpetrators were required to request forgiveness for their actions as well as confess and express remorse.

Operating from pilot cases in June 2002 to the courts' official closure in June 2012, the government of Rwanda claims that *gacaca* tried close to two million people with about 65% of those found guilty, with many sentences commuted to community service.[136] Although the numbers are likely outlandish, in the government's narrative, *gacaca* helped to heal the wounds of the past by bringing local, grassroots truth, justice, and reconciliation. As Larry May states: "The decentralized trials of the *gacaca* have been credited with helping the communities repair themselves, by bringing community and perpetrator together."[137] From the perspective of many human rights groups, however, any supposed benefit of restorative justice came at the cost of compromises in the rights of those accused before the courts. Critics claimed that the mechanics of *gacaca* fell well short of international legal standards, particularly the minimum fair trail rights. In a particularly critical report, Human Rights Watch alleged "apparent miscarriages of justice, the use of *gacaca* to settle personal and political scores, corruption, and procedural irregularities."[138]

In truth, depicting any of these tradition-based community models as restorative rather than retributive is a false dichotomy. As the Rwanda example illustrated, these models include elements of both restorative and retributive justice. On one hand, *gacaca* had clear elements of restorative justice in its focus on encounters between victims and offenders. On the other hand, *gacaca* had clear elements of retributive justice "in that proceedings are held and judges pass sentence."[139] As May stated: "The *gacaca* process in Rwanda has attempted to provide a modicum of retribution for the victims and their families."[140] Whatever their mix of restorative and retributive justice, as Hamber summarizes, such models "are increasingly being recognized as a critical component of addressing intergroup relations within the transitional justice field either through operating on their own or in conjunction with other practices including prosecutions and trials."[141]

In conclusion, by the mid to late 1990s, restorative justice "emerged as the victor among many competitors in the 'new justice' race. Inclusive, capacious, and aspirational, restorative justice seemed to offer something for everyone."[142] In terms of genocide prevention, restorative justice aims to make whole a postgenocide society. In that, it may be attempting the impossible, particularly if used in isolation from other measures of transitional justice. When used along with with such measures, however, restorative justice is a vital piece of the preventive process in repairing and rebuilding a postgenocide society.

TRUTH

In his introduction to the Chilean Truth and Reconciliation Commission's Report, Jose Zalaquett says: "Although the truth cannot really in itself dispense justice, it does put an end to many a continued injustice—it does not bring the dead back to life, but it brings them out from silence."[143] Indeed, threaded throughout the pursuit of both retributive and restorative justice as downstream preventive measures is the corresponding pursuit of truth—not as an alternative, but as a necessary adjunct. Truth even may be understood as the foundation of both forms of justice. It could further be argued that truth may be its own form of justice. As Richard Goldstone, the first prosecutor of the ICTY, said, "the public and official exposure of the truth is itself a form of justice."[144]

Postgenocide societies often have parallel narratives or even contentious, competing "truths." In Bosnia and Herzegovina, for example, children learn history through the "radically different and incompatible" perspectives of their own ethnic community—Bosniak, Serbian, or Croatian.[145] On a more conceptual level, political scientist Phil Clark speaks of *gacaca*'s pursuit of three types of truth—historical and legal truths, emotional and psychological truths, and collective and restorative truths.[146] The existence of multiple truths, historically or conceptually, does not devalue the currency attached to truth as a downstream preventive measure. A 2005 UN Human Rights Resolution, tellingly titled "Right to the Truth," affirmed "the importance of respecting and ensuring the right to the truth ... the right of victims ... to know the truth regarding [gross human rights] violations, including the identity of the perpetrators and the causes, facts and circumstances in which such violations took place ... so as to contribute to ending impunity."[147] Such resolutions remind us how important the collective pursuit of truth is in the preventive process of repairing and rebuilding a postgenocide society. We will examine that pursuit through three lenses—truth commissions, solving the fate of missing persons, and education reform.

Truth Commissions. Truth-seeking initiatives can include freedom of information legislation as well as declassification of archives and secret police files. Increasingly, however, the most commonly utilized mechanism is the establishment of a truth commission. In 2001, Priscilla Hayner, co-founder of the International Center for Transitional Justice, gave us the first comprehensive scholarly work on truth commissions. In a second edition published 10 years later, Hayner outlined five defining characteristics of a truth commission: "A truth commission (1) is focused on past, rather than ongoing, events; (2) investigates a pattern of events that took place over a period of time; (3) engages directly and broadly with the affected population, gathering information on their experiences; (4) is a temporary body with the aim of concluding with a defining report; and (5) is officially authorized or empowered by the state under review."[148] In short, truth commissions are commonly understood as "official, nonjudicial bodies of a limited duration established to determine the facts, causes, and consequences of past human rights violations."[149]

As nonjudicial bodies, truth commissions cannot hold individuals criminally liable for their actions and rarely have subpoena powers.[150] The structure of truth commissions is diverse, as are their investigative methods, and their mandates are very specific to the particular needs of the society within which they are created. "Generally, the recommendations of a commission push for reforms within the government and other social structures that perpetuated abuse. Recommendations may also advocate for reparation to victims, propose memorialization efforts and reconciliation plans, and implicate the bodies or groups most responsible for any abuses committed. In some cases individual perpetrators may be named."[151]

Within the parameters outlined by Hayner, we can identify over 50 substantive bodies of inquiry that fit the definition, even if not using the actual name, of a truth commission since Uganda, under the Idi Amin regime, organized the first one in 1974.[152] Indeed, "the theory and practice of truth commissions have gained so much credibility in recent decades than an emerging international 'right to truth' is now widely recognized."[153] As a matter of fact, on March 24, 2011, the world observed the first International Day for the Right to the Truth Concerning Gross Human Rights Violations and for the Dignity of Victims (the specific date was chosen in recognition of the human rights work of Archbishop Oscar Romero of El Salvador who was assassinated on March 24, 1980).

In Hayner's view, the five strongest truth commissions were South Africa's Truth and Reconciliation Commission (1995–2002), Guatemala's Commission for Historical Clarification (1997–1999), Peru's Truth and Reconciliation Commission (2001–2003), Timor-Leste's Commission for Reception, Truth and Reconciliation (2002–2005), and Morocco's Equity and Reconciliation Commission (2004–2006). The first widely known truth commission, however, was Argentina's National Commission on the Disappearance of Persons (generally referred to by its Spanish acronym, CONADEP). CONADEP was a special commission created by presidential decree on December 15, 1983, less than 1 week after President Raul Alfonsin had taken office. Modeled on civil society commissions set up by the U.S. Congress to deal with specific issues, CONADEP was a special commission of "notables" that included "prestigious public figures from the spheres of journalism, law, culture, science, and religion."[154] Chaired by Ernesto Sabato, one of Argentina's leading novelists, the commission was composed of 13 commissioners and five secretaries. CONADEP's initial mandate was, over a period of 6 months, "to receive reports of disappearances (after which it would immediately refer them to the courts), inquire into the fate of the disappeared, locate abducted children, report to the courts any attempt to conceal or destroy evidence and, lastly, issue a final report."[155] The work of the commission was to be "the result of a shared effort by the constitutional government and the majority of Argentine human rights organizations."[156] By the time that work was completed, even without cooperation from the armed forces and restricted by mandate to looking only at a portion of the human rights abuses that took place under the military regime, the Commission could boast of "collecting several thousand statements and testimonies [over 7,000], verifying or establishing the existence of hundreds of secret detention centres, and compiling over 50,00 pages of documentation."[157]

The commission's final report, *Nunca Mas* ("Never Again"), was submitted to President Alfonsin on September 20, 1984. The report made no judgments of individual responsibility, it was simply, in the words of legal scholar Ronald Dworkin, a story with "two themes: ultimate brutality and absolute caprice."[158] It made the atrocities committed by the military regime a public truth and proved their material existence as soon as possible after the fall of the regime. A new collective memory was created (or at least historical revisionism was reduced) and no one in Argentine society could any longer claim complete ignorance. Published in a shorter, book-length version, *Nunca Mas* "was an immediate best-seller: 40,000 copies were sold on the first day of its release, 150,000 copies in the first eight weeks. It has now been reprinted well over twenty times, and by 2007 had sold more than 500,000 copies, standing as one of Argentina's best-selling books ever."[159] In Argentina, "the social impact of the *Nunca Mas* report . . . created a truth and an ethical demand. The humanitarian narrative emphasized in the report presented the disappeared as human beings whose rights had been trampled on."[160] Outside Argentina, the work of the commission and the publication of *Nunca Mas* (even down to adopting its title) became a model for truth commissions in the democratization process throughout Latin America as well as globally (including South Africa).

As politician Roberto Canas of El Salvador suggests, "Unless a society exposes itself to the truth it can harbour no possibility of reconciliation, reunification and trust."[161] Such exposure, however, is difficult and controversial. "Truth commissions . . . are given a mammoth, almost impossible task with usually insufficient time and resources to complete it; they must struggle with rampant lies and denials to uncover still-dangerous truths that many in power may resist."[162] As a result, some suggest that truth commissions are better seen as historical events—perhaps even morality plays—rather than historical sources.[163]

Moreover, our general assumptions about the positive consequences of truth-telling may need to be checked. In 2004, for instance, political scientist David Mendeloff famously debunked eight common claims of truth-telling advocates (including both criminal investigations and prosecutions as well as less punitive historical fact-finding and truth commissions)—that truth-telling leads to (1) social healing and reconciliation, (2) justice, (3) an authoritative historical record, (4) public human rights education, (5) the promotion of institutional reform, (6) democracy, and (7) the preemption and (8) deterrence of future atrocities. Similarly, peace researcher Karen Brouneus challenged the notion that truth-telling leads to individual healing. Surveying 1,200 *gacaca* witnesses, she found that they suffered from higher levels of depression and posttraumatic stress disorder (PTSD) than did nonwitnesses, even when controlling for cumulative trauma exposure. Brouneus concluded that "This study proposes that the protracted engagement in the past that truth and reconciliation processes inherently involve may lead to a cyclic rumination of past trauma instead of a successful emotional processing of the past."[164]

Cautious skeptics of truth-telling and truth commissions abound. For Mendeloff, "truth-telling advocates claim far more about the power of truth-telling than logic or evidence dictates. This is not to say that truth-telling has no role to play in preventing the resumption of violent conflict in post-war societies, only that proponents likely overstate its importance."[165] Similarly, for Hamber, "much of what it is thought truth commissions can do at the intergroup level is based on assumption, individual case examples, and limited empirical evidence. Truth commissions are often imbued with a magical power by those who advocate for them most strongly."[166] Michael Ignatieff writes that "The past is an argument and the function of truth commissions, like the function of honest historians, is simply to purify the argument, to narrow the range of permissible lies" rather than provide an absolute truth.[167] Finally, for anthropologist Erin Daly: "The problem is that the truth neither *is* nor *does* all that we expect of it. It is not as monolithic, objective or verifiable as we would like it to be, and it cannot necessarily accomplish the ambitious goals we assign it."[168]

Each of these cautious skepticisms is intellectually responsible, but should not be taken as arguments against having truth commissions in the aftermath of genocide. Rather, they should be taken as calls for recognizing both the limits of truth commissions (particularly when used in isolation from other transitional justice mechanisms) as well as the need for continuing comparative empirical research on their specific impact. As Minow suggested in 1998, and as still rings true today, the reparative societal benefits of truth commissions are "a line of future inquiry rather than a current conclusion."[169] We can at least hypothesize, however, that truth commissions may be one piece of the reparative puzzle as "the wounds begin to heal with the telling of the story and the national acknowledgment of its authenticity."[170] Indeed, one recent study, repeating our familiar refrain of a holistic approach to transitional justice, found that truth commissions "alone have a negative impact on [improving human rights and democracy], but contribute positively when combined with trials and amnesty."[171] Such findings hint at the reality of what truth commissions can offer in interaction with other transitional justice mechanisms—they can establish narrative records of fact and public accountability; protect, acknowledge, and empower victims and survivors; and inform policy, promote change in groups and institutions, and contribute to social and political transformation in a postgenocide society.[172] As Minow summarizes: "The commission can help set a tone and create public rituals to build a bridge from a terror-filled past to a collective, constructive future."[173]

In building that bridge, truth commissions complement rather than contradict the work of retributive justice. The availability of truth commissions should not be used as an excuse to waive retributive justice. Nor should truth commissions be seen as second-best alternatives to retributive justice for perpetrators. As Verdeja argues: "This old debate between justice and truth has been superseded . . . and now it is more common to see commissions and trials operating together in a variety of ways."[174] As a complementary mechanism to retributive justice, "truth commissions have . . . helped redress the inherent individualist bias of human rights laws and instruments, bringing social processes and consequences to the fore."[175] As shown in Sierra Leone, "courts and Truth Commissions can work together [even simultaneously] toward the same goals of transitional justice . . . [though] it is better that they work in parallel, rather than attempting to formalize and develop a relationship between them."[176] Similarly, in Argentina, prejudicial evidence produced by CONADEP was subsequently used as a key resource in the prosecution of human rights abuses committed by the military junta.

It is right that Hayner has the last word in reminding us of the tremendous promise of truth commissions: "[Truth commissions] can reveal a global truth of the broad patterns of events, and demonstrate without question the atrocities that took place and what forces were responsible. If it is careful and creative, it can also go far beyond simply outlining the facts of abuse, and contribute to a much broader understanding of how people and the country as a whole were affected, and what factors contributed to the violence. This cannot be the whole truth—that is impossible to provide in one report. But it can hope to represent a broad—and specific— truth that will be accepted across society."[177]

Solving the Fate of Missing Persons. The weight imposed on survivors regarding the fate of missing persons, particularly family members, is staggering. A family member of a victim of human rights abuses under the Pinochet regime in Chile lamented: "Until recently we were expecting to find him alive. Today we are looking for his bones. This will never end . . . this long nightmare, from which I don't know any more if I can awake because I forgot normal life . . . I need to know what happened to him . . . Every time I eat good food, I ask myself if he is not hungry."[178] Thousands of similar bones lie buried throughout postatrocity societies around the world, leaving thousands upon thousands of family members living the seemingly interminable nightmare, sliding back and forth between despair and hope, of not knowing what happened to their loved ones or even where they remains are to be found.

The right of families to know the fate of their missing relatives is codified in Articles 32 and 33 of the Protocol Additional to the Geneva Conventions, as well as in the International Convention for the Protection of all Persons from Enforced Disappearance (Article 24), the Universal Declaration on Human Rights (Article 3), and the International Covenant on Civil and Political Rights (Article 23).[179] Legal rulings by the European Court of Human Rights and a wide array of domestic legislation have upheld these obligations. Building on these normative and legal prec-edents, the case of postgenocide Bosnia and Herzegovina (BiH) offers one example in which this right has been drawn upon as an aspirational foun-dation of transitional justice.

At the end of the hostilities in 1995, an estimated 35,000 people in the territory of the former Yugoslavia were unaccounted for. In response, in October 2004, the Bosnian parliament passed the Law on Missing Persons, establishing "the principles for improving the tracing process, the definition of a missing person, the method of managing the central records, realization of social and other rights of family members of miss-ing persons, and other issues related to tracing missing persons from/in Bosnia and Herzegovina."[180] Central to the law was Article 3 (The right to know): "Families of missing persons have the right to know the fate of their missing family members and relatives, their place of (temporary) residence, or if dead, the circumstances and cause of death and location of burial, if such location is known, and to receive the mortal remains."[181]

The Law on Missing Persons, drafted in advisement with the International Committee of the Red Cross and the International Commission on Missing Persons, was the first national legislation of its kind in the world and it was hoped that it would be a template for other countries tasked with the burden of solving the fate of missing persons, either from human-made or natural disasters. At present, however, major parts of the Law have yet to be put into practice. In December 2014, Kathryne Bomberger, direc-tor of the International Commission on Missing Persons, stated: "Bosnia needs to implement the Law on Missing Persons—especially in forming a centralised database of missing persons and creating a fund for support to families, so they could achieve some financial rights."[182] Bosnia's chief prosecutor, Goran Salihovic, agreed and viewed the creation of a fund to assist victims' families as "the most important issue."[183]

Partly in recognition of these deficiencies, BiH's state-proposed *Transitional Justice Strategy*, the final draft of which was completed in March 2013, included solving the fate of missing persons as the first stra-tegic objective in its truth-telling platform.[184] The Strategy agreed that "the slow pace of the process of finding the missing persons" was due, in part, to the lack of implementation of the Law of Missing Persons.[185] Specific concerns were raised regarding the insufficient implementation of two particular articles—registration of the death of a missing person (Article 27) and the establishment of a fund to enable families of missing persons to receive monthly benefits (Article 15). Poor implementation of both articles leave it exceptionally difficult for families of missing persons to exercise rights guaranteed under the Law. The *Strategy* also noted "the lack of professional and technical capacities necessary for the full func-tioning of the Missing Persons Institute and insufficient capacities of the institutions engaged in locating individual and mass graves and carrying out exhumations."[186] From a criminal standpoint, the families of miss-ing persons were particularly troubled over the state's failure to recognize enforced disappearance as an independent criminal act. Unfortunately, although replete with proposed solutions, the *Transitional Justice Strategy* lies dormant in the BiH Parliament, still awaiting action on its adoption.

Despite the limitations of the Law on Missing Persons, and the glacial pace of parliamentary review of the *Transitional Justice Strategy*, non-governmental organizations have taken strong steps toward solving the fate of missing persons from the 1992–1995 war. Article 7 of the Law on Missing Persons called for the establishment of a central state institution to deal with the issue of missing persons. That central institution was the Missing Persons Institute (MPI) of Bosnia and Herzegovina. Launched on August 30, 2005 as a state-level institution, MPI is charged with "pro-viding for a sustainable domestic mechanism to locate missing persons regardless of their ethnic, religious or national affiliation, or their role in past hostilities. MPI also ensures that mass gravesites are protected, documented and properly excavated, and that relatives of the missing and others are able to participate in the institution's work."[187]

In this work, MPI benefits from the assistance of its co-founding part-ner, the International Commission on Missing Persons (ICMP). Created at the initiative of U.S. President Bill Clinton in 1996, ICMP is an intergov-ernmental organization that "has been active in some 40 countries that have faced large numbers of missing persons as a result of natural and man-made disasters, wars, widespread human rights abuses, organized crime and other causes."[188] As I have witnessed firsthand in BiH, ICMP helped develop the country's institutional capacity to address the issue of missing persons in a nondiscriminatory manner and provided invaluable technical assistance in locating, recovering, and identifying missing per-sons. ICMP is particularly known for its expertise in running the world's leading high-throughput DNA identity testing system, matching DNA from bones found in mass graves to DNA profiles of living relatives.

Today, Bosnia's MPI continues its work in the midst of persistent needs to be strengthened and supported. Despite their limitations, however, the remains of approximately 70% of persons reported missing in BiH as a consequence of the war have been found and identified. On July 11, 2015, on the twentieth commemoration of the Srebrenica genocide, MPI announced that 115 recently exhumed and identified victims would be buried. All things considered, "no other post-conflict country has achieved such a high rate of resolving cases of missing persons."[189] Still, however, BiH has 52 associations of families of missing persons and thousands of families who have "forgot normal life" as they remain waiting for their loved ones to be found and identified.[190]

Empirical research on the efficacy of resolving the fate of missing persons as a downstream preventive measure for genocide is absent. In the reaction of Estela de Carlotto, however, we see the fulfillment that comes when a life lived in postponement is reunited with some aspect of a missing loved one—the knowledge of their fate, the return of their remains, or, in her case, the discovery of their offspring. It is a turning of the page, a long sought acknowledgment of truth, one step in the lengthy reparative journey of downstream prevention in a postgenocide society. Recognizing a trend observed in many countries around the world since 1981, the UN General Assembly adopted August 30 as the International Day of the Victims of Enforced Disappearance, to be observed beginning in 2011. The day of commemoration is yet another affirmation of the fundamental right of families to know the truth regarding the fate of missing relatives.

Education Reform. As discussed in Chapter 2, as early as 1953, Lemkin referred to the Ukrainian man-made famine of 1932–1933 as genocide. Over the years, an increasing number of international scholars, as well as parliaments and senates around the world, have come to share Lemkin's view. Since its independence from the Soviet Union in 1991, Ukrainian students were taught, with some circumspection, the historical truth of the famine as genocide. Then, in November 2006, the Ukrainian Parliament formally declared the famine an act of genocide perpetrated by Stalin's regime against the Ukrainian people and the "Holodomor" became embedded in official national consciousness. Today, however, teachers in southeastern Ukraine, under orders from the newly installed separatist government, have thrown away their existing Ukrainian history textbooks and are using a new curriculum that has recast the history of the famine. In this new curriculum, called "Fatherland History," students "are getting the sanitized version, in which the famine was an unavoidable tragedy that befell the entire Soviet Union."[191] The word "genocide" is no longer used to describe the Ukrainian famine.

Aside from the control of territory during a conflict, nothing is fought over as much as the control of history after a conflict. Education is on the frontlines of that battle and its reform can constitute a key downstream preventive measure. As Karen Murphy, International Director for Facing History and Ourselves, has said: "In authoritarian and divided societies with identity-based conflicts, education has quite often been used as an instrument of inequality and division and as a medium for spreading myths and misinformation, as occurred in Rwanda. Yet, we are slow to apply the same kind of rigorous reforms to this section that we would do for the judiciary, military and police."[192] Certainly, the right to truth that underlies truth commissions and solving the fate of missing persons is equally applicable to education reform.

Education is foundational to human development but its preventive reach goes even further. Comprehensive education reform in postgenocide societies has direct ties to the longer-term preventive processes of building underlying structures of societal and state durability related to good governance, resilient economic conditions, and inclusive social cohesion. "Through its impact on economic growth, education helps catalyze transitions to democracy and helps preserve robust democratic governance. Education also helps improve outcomes ... Because of these important links to other powerful drivers of development, educational investments should be understood as dynamic and transformational levers of change."[193] Similarly, Clara Ramirez-Barat, my colleague and Director of the Educational Policies Program at the Auschwitz Institute for Peace and Reconciliation, argues: "Working with younger generations on TJ [transitional justice] measures is fundamental to building democratic societies. At a pivotal moment in the political history of a country, the direct involvement of children and youth in TJ processes can contribute to building children and youth's knowledge of human rights as well as their capacity for active citizenship."[194]

Education reform is most relevant, though, as a preventive measure associated with a fair interpretation and transmission of conflict history—particularly in postconflict settings where, often, children and youth comprise more than half of the affected population.[195] Indeed, comprehensive education reform—through textbooks, curriculum, and school trips—has been a key transitional justice mechanism in many postatrocity societies, including Germany, Chile, Guatemala, Kenya, Peru, Sierra Leone, and Argentina.

As one example, by 2002, coverage of the genocide perpetrated by Pol Pot's regime had disappeared from junior and senior high school textbooks in Cambodia. In response, and recognizing the need for comprehensive education reform as a downstream preventive measure, the Genocide Education Project of the Documentation Center of Cambodia (DC-Cam) was launched in 2004. A civil society-led initiative, the project was developed to assist the Cambodian Ministry of Education in educating schoolchildren about the history of the Cambodian genocide. In 2007, DC-Cam released a textbook, *A History of Democratic Kampuchea*, the first book of its kind written by a Cambodian, to national high schools and other private schools around Cambodia. Today, an estimated one million high school students in 1,321 schools have received the book. A corresponding *Teacher's Guidebook* was first released in 2009 with an updated version released in 2014. DC-Cam has also led training for nearly 4,000 Cambodian high school teachers as well as university instructors, police, and, national army officers.[196] Testifying to the impact of these comprehensive educational reforms, questions about the Khmer Rouge regime were included in the country's history graduation examination in 2009.[197]

Currently, the need for comprehensive education reform is a particular focus, and a grave concern, in BiH. As political scientist Jelena Subotic points out, "public education [in BiH has] been used to entrench mutually incompatible versions of the past and contribute to a renewed cycle of mistrust, untruth, and injustice."[198] In Bosnia, history has developed an ethnicity of its own as Bosniak, Serbian, and Croatian students use three very different sets of history textbooks. "Hence, children in Sarajevo, Banja Luka, and Mostar, for example, learn radically different and incompatible accounts about the causes of the war in Bosnia between 1992 and 1995."[199] In Bosnian education, truth is dangerously plural. Instead of serving a preventive function, the multiplicity of truth actually serves to increase ethnic division and politicization of memory. As Subotic concludes: "The problem with history education in the Western Balkans, then, is that this region's histories are multiple, contradictory, and mutually exclusive. Far from being a tool for social cohesion and healing, they continue to be instruments of political othering, alienation, and further injustice."[200]

Efforts for comprehensive education reform in BiH, mostly driven by international actors, have been difficult to initiate and maintain. As Subotic argues, the curricular ethnicization of education is compounded by larger patterns of ethnic segregation that result in the physical separation of Bosniak, Serbian, and Croatian students. U.S.AID's "Education for a Just Society," the latest in a long line of international efforts, aims to address these dual problems by developing curricular materials to be used in integrated educational settings to promote peace and reconciliation in BiH. The 3-year project, with an end date of July 2016, targets schools in 18 BiH communities, involving more than 1,800 students and 270 teachers, policymakers, and educational professionals. Teachers and trainers will develop model lesson plans that promote justice, diversity, and social cohesion. Students will prepare community and national events to share their visions for a peaceful future.[201]

Although the near- and long-term results of this project have yet to be measured, it is clear that transitioning from conflict to stability is a multigenerational task. As Murphy points out, however, it is also "a multi-generational opportunity, possibly the only sector with this kind of reach." She continues: "Adult teachers and department of education representatives are themselves citizens who may have been actors during the conflict as well as witnesses and victims. They often need to wrestle with the violent past and its legacies, and the myths and misinformation in which they are perhaps invested, before they teach and discuss these things with students . . . a new generation of citizens."[202] Education reform that creates a credible truth about past atrocities provides a reparative chance for a postgenocide society to move from a divided past to a shared future. In so doing, it can be a vital piece in helping heal a society torn apart by genocide and preventing the deadly cycle of violence from beginning again.

MEMORY

Luis Bunuel (1900–1983) was a Spanish film director and the father of surrealist cinema. He opened his 1982 autobiography with a remembrance of the last 10 years of his mother's life, when she was gradually losing her memory. Reflecting on his similar, and increasing, lapses of memory as he aged, Buneul writes: "You have to begin to lose your memory, if only in bits and pieces, to realize that memory is what makes our lives. Life without memory is no life at all, just as an intelligence without the possibility of expression is not really an intelligence. Our memory is our coherence, our reason, our feeling, even our action. Without it, we are nothing."[203]

Bunuel's reflections on the role of memory in individual life can also be applied to the role of memory in collective life, particularly in the life of collectives after genocide and mass atrocity. In 2003, for instance, on the thirtieth anniversary of Pinochet's coup, Chilean president Ricardo Lagos challenged his country to continue to face their violent past. Twelve years after the conclusion of Chile's National Commission on Truth and Reconciliation, Lagos announced the formation of a second truth commission specific to a group of victims largely left out of the first Commission's purview—former prisoners illegally detained and tortured for politically motivated reasons during the period of military rule. Lagos told his fellow Chileans that they had to, again, collectively confront this traumatic past because "without yesterday there is no tomorrow."[204]

Lagos' words—"without yesterday there is no tomorrow"—are a collective restatement of Bunuel's comments on individual memory—"without it, we are nothing." Both are eloquent reminders that downstream prevention is not just about what happened during an episode of genocide and mass atrocity (justice and truth) but also about how we remember it (memory). As Zeid Ra'ad Al Hussein, former permanent Representative of Jordan to the United Nations and now UN High Commissioner for Human Rights, wrote regarding the intersection of justice, truth, and memory in the search for a sustainable peace: "The truth must claim its rightful place, not just in courts of law, but also in the settlement of armed conflicts. And yet the truth can only claim its place if it is properly determined, understood and agreed upon by the former warring sides."[205]

Memory is the active past that helps give shape and meaning to our social identities. To be sure, a postatrocity society can have too much memory. Such tyranny of memory can nurture persistent beliefs of victimization and injustice. These are destructive seeds that can be sown for future atrocities, "vulnerable to any misguided individual with charisma and leadership skills able to exploit and abuse lingering historical grievances for political ends in a way that revives historical hatreds to create new challenges to international peace and security."[206] In her reflections on Communism, for instance, Croatian writer Slavenka Drakulic wrote: "I came to the conclusion that we did not have 'too much history,' as it is often said about this part of the world. Rather we had too much memory and too many myths. And, in my life experience, this is a dangerous combination that has often resulted in ideology and manipulation leading to conflict and terrible suffering."[207]

To be equally sure, however, a postatrocity society can also leave itself at risk of future atrocity by having too little memory. Forgetting is not an acceptable response to atrocity. Forced amnesia, however secure it appears on the surface, leaves a deep societal insecurity. Wounds left untended, and unacknowledged, can prove crippling with time. The push and pull of memory remain potent, even when spoken only in whispers. An unresolved historical narrative, resulting in conflicting and competing collective memories, can be an erosive undercurrent leading to social fragmentation, particularly in a postatrocity society.

Recognizing that memory cannot be subordinated to justice and truth, but, rather, is a complement to them, we will examine the role of memory in transitional justice through three questions—what is collective memory, how does memorialization sustain collective memory, and how does memorialization promote transitional justice?

What Is Collective Memory? As historian Dan Stone writes: "Genocide is bound up with memory, on an individual level of trauma and on a collective level in terms of the creation of stereotypes, prejudice, and post-genocide politics."[208] Intuitively, memory resonates with us as an individual phenomenon—"part of the development of the self or personality."[209] As collective memory studies scholars Jeffrey Olick, Verad Vinitzky-Seroussi, and Daniel Levy ask: "What could be more individual than remembering, which we seem to do in the solitary world of our own heads as much as in conversation with others?"[210] As Stone points out, though, there is a collective phenomenon of memory that also is crucial in addressing the perpetration, and I will argue, the prevention, of genocide: "The perpetration of genocide requires the mobilization of collective memories, as does the commemoration of it ... collective memories of past suffering are almost always brought to bear on current crises, lending them cultural meaning—the weight of dead ancestors weighing on the minds of the living—and imbuing them with added ferocity. Memory fuels genocide."[211]

So, what are we talking about when we talk about "collective memory"? Contemporary use of the term traces back to the work of French sociologist Maurice Halbwachs (1877–1945), a protégé of Emile Durkheim. In 1925, Halbwachs published *Social Frameworks of Memory* in which he laid out his initial views on memory as a social construction defined by shifting social frames. As he famously wrote in a posthumous essay published after his death in a Nazi concentration camp: "It is in society that people normally acquire their memories. It is also in society that they recall, recognize, and localize their memories."[212] So, in order to have memories, we must exist in a social setting.[213] That is, all memory—even individual memory—is essentially a social process. As sociologist Ron Eyerman summarizes: ". . . memory is always group memory, both because the individual is derivative of some collectivity, family, and community, and also because a group is solidified and becomes aware of itself through continuous reflection upon and recreation of a distinctive, shared memory."[214] Similarly, political scientist Ziya Meral writes: "What is *remembered* is not simply *the past* as it was. This *past* is not simply remembered by the individual as an independent act, but by partaking in the collective, which provides the individual with an account and a mental template and this, in return, shapes the individual memory."[215]

Collective memory is the shared past, framed in the present, binding social group members together and connecting successive generations with one another. In essence, collective memory "is not simply synonymous with the way in which the past is represented in the present; it is itself constitutive of the present. Meaning and identity go hand in hand."[216] The past gets its meaning through its link to the present. There is a "past present" in each of us. It is a negotiated outcome, a cognitive map, of interaction between multiple social identities—national, racial, ethnic, political, gender, religious, professional, familial, class, and so on.

Collective memory is not organic in the sense that it is a "group mind" passed on through genetic transmission. Rather, "collective memories originate from shared communications about the meaning of the past that are anchored in the life-worlds of individuals who partake in the communal life of the respective."[217] In other, and hopefully clearer, words, collective memory entails the construction and transmission of stories, artifacts, food and drink, symbols, traditions, images, and music—the cultural birthright that we inherit as a member of a social identity group. Collective memory also includes the traumas, both suffered and perpetrated, of a social identity group. In this sense of "soul wounds" or "blood memories," collective memory transmits the staggering loss of an assumptive world that grounded, secured, stabilized, and oriented people—a past fragmented by "a dramatic loss of identity and meaning, a tear in the social fabric."[218] As Eyerman states: "Collective memory specifies the temporal parameters of past and future, where we came from and where we are going, and also why we are here now."[219]

Collective memory is a selective embodiment of pasts and their meanings. "Out of many possible pasts, some are lost, while others are the subjects of careful strategies of maintenance and reproduction."[220] That is, the collective memory of a constant past is not preserved with objective facticity, but is subjectively reconstructed in the variable social context of the needs of the present. This social context not only defines what is remembered but also what is forgotten; there are some "unknown knowns" that we repress because they are too painful to know through admission. As a result, the significance of collective memory lies in its constructed meaning, not in its historical accuracy. As historian Pierre Nora writes: "Memory is life, borne by living societies founded in its name. It remains in permanent evolution, open to the dialectic of remembering and forgetting, unconscious of its successive deformations, vulnerable to manipulation and appropriation, susceptible to being long dormant and periodically revived."[221]

As a social construction, "collective memories often become embroiled in ... disputes as they are strategically manipulated by social actors to alter the balance of power between groups."[222] Memory makers—government, religion, education, and media—compete to construct collective memory by establishing the social frames that will accommodate only those memories that suit their agenda. This is a "meaning struggle" for power rather than truth; it is a mobilization to control a binary master narrative—simplistically identifying victims and perpetrators—that fits a group's subjective interests rather than an objective account of historical processes. As George Orwell famously wrote about the dangers of totalitarian society in his novel 1984: "Who controls the past controls the future: who controls the present controls the past."[223] In this sense, memory makers use collective memory the way a drunk uses a lamppost—for support rather than illumination. As historian Michael Kammen asserts: ". . . societies in fact reconstruct their pasts rather than faithfully record them, and that they do so with the needs of contemporary culture clearly in mind—manipulating the past in order to mold the present."[224] In such cases, collectives live by memory rather than truth and such "memory is never shaped in a vacuum" and its motives "are never pure."[225]

In Rwanda, for example, government and social institutions control much of the collective memory—in the minds of some critics, a clear manipulation of the past in order to mold the present. Transitional justice scholar Katherine Conway, for instance, writes of contemporary Rwanda: "Limits to memory include restrictions on the freedom of speech, a focus on minimizing ethnic identity, methods of memorialization, and control over the versions of memory that are taught in schools, celebrated during the month of April, and discussed in public spaces."[226] As she points out, such restrictions not only limit memory but also serve to limit the debate about the past. For Conway, a "healthy memory environment" allows for a right to truth in order to understand history, a space for contestation of differing interpretations of memory, the recognition of memory as both a public and private phenomenon, and an acknowledgment that memory is intrinsic to the formation of community and identity. Such a "healthy memory environment," recognizing the impossibility of many different people sharing a common mind, embraces strategies that can "shift a population towards deeper understanding, and potentially reconciliation, in both private and public spheres" of memory.[227] Similarly, in historian Peter Novick's work on the Holocaust and collective memory, he argues: "If there are lessons to be extracted from encountering the past, that encounter has to be with the past in all its messiness; they're not likely to come from an encounter with a past that's been shaped and shaded so that inspiring lessons will emerge."[228]

A recent example of the literal embodiment of collective memory becoming embroiled in power-based disputes was seen in Visegrad, BiH. Before the war, about two-thirds of the eastern Bosnian town's 21,000 residents were Muslim. In 1992, Serb paramilitaries entered Visegrad and massacred Muslims throughout the town and surrounding villages. Hundreds were killed on the well-known sixteenth-century Mehmed Pasa Sokolovic Bridge over the Drina River—visible from almost every balcony and window in Visegrad—and their bodies dumped into the river. The river now is considered to be the biggest mass grave in BiH. Others were detained in houses and burnt alive. The ICTY concluded that Visegrad was subjected to "one of the most comprehensive and ruthless campaigns of ethnic cleansing in the Bosnian conflict."[229] All told, some 3,000 Bosniaks were murdered in the Visegrad municipality from 1992 to 1995. Today, Visegrad, located in the Serb-dominated entity of Republika Srpska, has an estimated population of about 12,000 people, with 1,500 of them Bosniaks. On May 26, 2012, in Visegrad's Starziste Muslim cemetery, a stone monument to 60 Bosniak victims of the war was erected reading: "To all killed and missing Bosniaks, children, women and men, victims of genocide in Visegrad."

The monument—a stark statement of the continuing struggle over collective memory—immediately drew protests from the Serb residents of Visegrad. In a published statement, the Ministry of Labour and Veterans of Republika Srpska said: "Inaccurate statements and unfounded claims about the armed conflict in the 1990s, from which inappropriate conclusions may be drawn concerning the victims of one ethnic group, leads to the suspicion that individuals are putting out such statements for malicious reasons. Such acts can have unwanted consequences for all the citizens of Bosnia and Herzegovina."[230] Criticizing the selective use of memory, the mayor of Visigrad, Slavisa Miskovic, agreed the word "genocide was offensive to local people because there is no proof of verdict about genocide in Visegrad."[231] After much back-and-forth, on January 23, 2014, Bosnian Serb civil authorities, accompanied by 150 police in riot gear and turning up an hour earlier than announced to avoid protests, used a grinder to physically erase the word "genocide" from the monument. Not to be deterred, a group of Bosniak war widows surreptitiously restored the word in lipstick, only for it to be covered over in municipal white paint a few days later.

Collective memory does not always have to be divisive; it also can be used as an influential mechanism of transitional justice to promote a sense of community and social cohesion. This was affirmed in a January 17, 2014 concept note for a UN Security Council briefing on the theme "War, its lessons and the search for a permanent peace." The concept note was annexed as a letter to the UN Secretary-General from the Jordanian Presidency. The note pointed out that "most of what the United Nations has achieved in maintaining international peace and security has been mainly physical" (for example, mediation between political opponents, security sector reform, and economic development).[232] "What the United Nations has not understood well enough," the note continued, "is how it can help forge a deeper reconciliation among ex-combatants and their peoples based on an agreed or shared narrative, a shared memory, of a troubled past. This is especially relevant to sectarian, or ethnic, conflicts, as well as wars driven by extreme nationalism or ideologies."[233] To redress this, and recognizing that preserving documents of State is an evidentiary prerequisite for any shared narrative, or collective memory, the note proposes that the Security Council consider mandating "a small United Nations historical advisory team" to help a postatrocity state set up a functional national archive or national historical commission.[234]

How Does Memorialization Sustain Collective Memory? As sociologist Victor Roudometof points out, "there is a multitude of ways through which collective memory is standardized and reproduced. These include: national holidays, public lectures, articles in the popular press, documentaries, pictures, statues, and other media of a bewildering variety."[235] Most notably, perhaps, collective memory is given breath and made real in memorialization efforts. Such efforts "include museums and memorials that preserve public memory of victims and raise moral consciousness about past abuse, in order to build a bulwark against its recurrence."[236] The ties of such efforts to embodied collective memory are clear: "While collective memory is constructed, in part, by members of a society who actually lived through an event, it is also constructed by subsequent generations who represent the past vicariously through books, films, memorials, museums, and so forth."[237] That is, the collective memory of historical events is intimately tied to, and influenced by, the collective representations produced and reproduced by social groups that lived through the events as well as subsequent generations for whom it is not the experience itself that is traumatic but rather the reproduction of it.

Memorialization is the embodied scar of collective memory—how memory is perpetuated. As a tool of collective memory, memorialization certainly can be used as a weapon of identity politics wielded to divide and bludgeon rather than unify and heal. To memorialize past atrocity is to highlight the scar of a divided past. Rather than a deformation, though, that scar can be thought of as a "good scar." For women's studies scholar Sara Ahmed, a "good scar" is not one that is invisible; rather "A good scar is one that sticks out, a lumpy sign on the skin. It's not that the wound is exposed or that the skin is bleeding. But the scar is a sign of the injury: a good scar allows healing, it even covers over, *but the covering always exposes the injury, reminding us of how it shapes the body.* Our bodies have been shaped by their injuries; scars are traces of those injuries that persist in the healing or stitching of the present. This kind of good scar reminds us that recovering from injustice cannot be about covering over the injuries."[238] We will look at these "good scars" through four forms of memorialization efforts or "memory practices"—spontaneous, traditional, sites and public space, and performative.

Spontaneous memorials are an initial response to traumatic death—car accidents, murders, fires, terrorist attacks, the untimely death of a celebrity, or even the timely, yet still traumatic, loss of a well-known figure. Spontaneous roadside memorials to commemorate victims of car and bike accidents are found throughout the American Southwest and Latin America, as well as in many European countries. We have seen spontaneous memorials emerge at sites of school shootings (for example, Columbine High School in Littleton, Colorado in 1999 and Sandy Hook Elementary School in Newtown, Connecticut in 2012). In June 2014, a racially motivated mass shooting at the Emanuel African Methodist Episcopal Church in Charleston, South Carolina was being spontaneously memorialized with bouquets of flowers, balloons, and teddy bears on the church steps. The tragic death by fire of 194 young people at a Buenos Aires disco in 2004 triggered a range of spontaneous memorials and national protests. The terrorist attacks of 9/11 in the United States left indelible visible expressions of spontaneous grief in nearby Union Square Park. When Great Britain's Lady Diana, Princess of Wales, died in a car accident in 1997, the world collectively grieved with spontaneous memorials, the most notable of which were mountains of flowers and mementoes left at the entrance to Kensington Palace. Similarly, Pope John Paul II's death in 2005, although not unexpected, ignited massive spontaneous memorials in an incredible outpouring of emotion and loss around the world.

Spontaneous memorials, temporarily transforming public space into sacred space, are often the first step in the grieving process; they are an urgent attempt to comprehend the incomprehensible. They are "a private individualized act of mourning . . . open for public display."[239] Spontaneous memorials are unofficial and undirected, not sanctioned by any institution. Stirred by social media, they typically start within hours of the death, generally at the site of the death or a place associated with the deceased, and often involve a mounting accumulation of individual mementos that create a shrine to the deceased. In this perpetual process of change, some of these mementos are traditional (crosses, flowers, and national flags) where others are more idiosyncratic and convey a private, personal meaning (coins, unopened cans of beer, and personal letters). "Nobody, whether church, government or media, tells grievers how to construct these shrines or what objects should be placed there."[240] Spontaneous memorials are inclusive remembrances—sites of pilgrimage—in which anyone, those who may or may not have known the deceased, can participate at any time. Moreover, spontaneous memorials have no expected ritual behavior. "Mourners have been known to weep, pray, curse, gawk, and even videotape at the scene; some express emotions that are taboo at more traditional memorials, especially anger and guilt."[241]

In Rwanda, for instance, the 100-day frenzy of killing left a "traumascape" with dozens of massacre sites of traumatic death.[242] Some were public spaces, such as schools, that now became sacred spaces; others were sacred spaces, such as churches and mission compounds, that now became desacralized spaces. In each of them, however, lay thousands of Tutsi and moderate Hutu who had been slaughtered by Hutu extremists. To some degree, to think about what these sites should mean and how they should be managed seemed trivial compared to the other pressing needs of rebuilding the postgenocide Rwandan society. So, as an initial step in a collective, national grieving process, Rwanda decided to leave the massacre sites intact; the shattered bones and skulls, blood-stained clothing, and personal effects of the victims were left as they had fallen. When I first visited three of these sites—churches at Nyamata, Nyarabuye, and Ntarama—I could easily see skulls cleaved by machete or riddled by bullet holes or large baseball-sized holes caused by the blunt force trauma of a club or *masu* (a club studded with nails). Blood-stained walls looked down on forearm bones with defensive machete wounds, littered among limbs that had been hacked off. Clothes, machetes, identity cards, hymnals, and glasses were scattered throughout the "raw and macabre" sites.[243] Forensic anthropologist Clea Koff describes her visit to the church at Ntarama in 1996: "I saw backless pews just like those in Kibuye church, but these were draped with the mummified and decomposing remains of *a lot* of people, their clothes both sticking to them and falling off, and everything sort of melting down onto the floor between the benches. It was difficult to see where the bodies ended and the floor began. It was difficult to see the floor at all."[244]

This initial decision to leave the massacre sites as found, in effect, to create a spontaneous memorial, was not, as rhetoric scholar Sara Guyer explains, a result of a lack of sufficient resources, a national tradition of mourning, or unworked-through grief and trauma.[245] Rather, I would argue, the spontaneity of the memorialization was in its admission that the living could not yet figure out how to bury the dead. The sight of the bodies—the actual gruesome visibility, the literal disembodiment of a people—was the only immediate way for Rwandan society to begin to comprehend the incomprehensible and to express the inexpressible individual and collective grief. Unfortunately, although the sites display actual remains, they do not commemorate individuals. "A pile of unrelated bones or a shelf with rows of carefully arranged skulls does not commemorate a person."[246] As a result, for Stone, the remains provoke "the shock and horror that are appropriate responses to genocide, but their anonymity means that they also recapitulate the logic of genocide: the reduction of individual human beings to representatives of a (perpetrator-defined) group."[247] Moreover, as Guyer points out, the overwhelming reality of the remains, including the stench, actually "resist comprehension and meaning—not least because they accost the senses of those who visit them."[248]

More than simply a cathartic expression of individual and collective grief, however, spontaneous memorials also "may include a political-social message about the cause of death, implications of the death, or both."[249] In this way, spontaneous memorials can become focal points for protest and expression of discontent. "Through their [citizens'] actions, they also send out messages asking for action: 'this should not have happened,' 'somebody has to take responsibility,' or simply 'a different world is possible.'"[250] Similarly, for folklorist Jack Santino, spontaneous memorials "reflect and comment on public and social issues. The Malice Green site in Detroit, where an African American man was killed while in policy custody, is a comment on police brutality. Roadside crosses reflect road conditions and drunk driving issues. September 11 shrines reflect on terrorism or political violence. In Northern Ireland, they reflect and implicitly comment on paramilitary violence by forcing recognition of the havoc it wrecks on ordinary people ... By translating social issues and political actions into personal terms, the shrines are themselves political statements."[251] In short, the visual reality of spontaneous memorials, an embodiment of the voice of the people, offers a compelling challenge to power-holders and perpetrators: "Now: defend your actions, your politics, in light of that."[252]

To return to Rwanda, after 21 years, the spontaneous memorials of 1994 have now morphed into fixed, permanent, more traditional memorials. Visually, they have evolved as the Rwandan government attempts to appease both those in favor of continuing to display the human remains to compellingly present "a specter of past violence as a permanent future possibility" and those who believe it is disrespectful to the victims and their families to leave the dead on display rather than bury them. Their major evolution, though, has been in their clear and consistent use as political statements—not only by victimized citizens but also by a government fearful of denial and intent on using the memorials "as an instrument of repression."[253] For Africanist Filip Reyntjens, the wielding of memorials in this way is one of the means by which the Rwandan genocide has become "a source of legitimacy astutely exploited to escape condemnation, not unlike the way in which the Holocaust is used to deflect criticism of Israel's policies and actions towards the Palestinians."[254] Moreover, from a social standpoint, these memorials, rather than promoting cohesion and reconciliation, may well entrench social cleavages and lead to divisive social fragmentation. For Guyer, "it may be rather that the bones continue to prevent mourning from taking place. In some sense, these memorials can be understood as much a *cause* of Rwanda's enduring trauma—the awkward correlation of an open tomb and the memory of violence—as an *effect*."[255]

Spontaneous memorials are, by their nature, impermanent. They eventually will be removed or simply succumb to the effects of time—flowers will wither, notes will blow away, mementos will be archived. In their place, particularly in postatrocity societies, often come *traditional memorials*. Traditional memorials have a formal process of creation and, as we have seen in the Visegrad example, most clearly represent the struggle to control the interpretation of history. As thanatologist Jon Reid writes: "These memorials—usually years in the planning process, including design competitions, scale models, and fund-raising efforts—commemorate those who died in battle and those who were great leaders. Groundbreaking ceremonies draw public attention to what is under construction, and formal unveiling ceremonies once again emphasize the significance of the subject of the memorialization. These memorials are often constructed many years following the event, such as a war or the death of the historical figure. These events and memorials are public and specifically designed to commemorate something or someone specific. Usually, the significance and purpose for the memorial are clear."[256]

Traditional memorials to genocide and mass atrocity can be found in every postatrocity society as well as in the transplanted communities of diaspora victims and their descendants. On April 24, 2015, for instance, the world's newest traditional memorial to the Armenian genocide opened in Pasadena, California in the United States. Unveiled in the week before the one hundredth commemoration of the Armenian genocide, the memorial is a carved-stone basin of water straddled by a 16-foot-tall metal tripod of three columns leaning into one another. The tripod represents similarly shaped gallows from which Armenian leaders were hanged during the genocide. Twelve pomegranate trees flank the memorial, representing each of the "lost provinces" of Armenia. From the top of the tripod, a drop of water falls every 21 seconds. Over the course of a year, 1.5 million drops of water—one teardrop for each of the genocide victims—will drop into a basin adorned with the ancient Armenian symbol for eternity. Design committee chairman William Paparian, former mayor of Pasadena, described the memorial as "emotionally compelling" and expressed his hope that the "memorial will inspire a similar emotional connection in those who encounter it, for generations to come."[257] Although the significance and purpose of this traditional memorial is clear, it also remains open enough to subjective interpretation to create an affective environment, more about feeling than thinking, that "transforms the visitors themselves into part of the work and that should provoke in them sensations and emotions of an immediate manner."[258]

Given the difficulty of accessing some sites of traditional memorials, we are seeing a rise in the creation of virtual genocide memorials. *Through the Glass Darkly*, for instance, is an interactive website—replete with photos, maps, and testimonies—devoted to genocide memorials in Rwanda.[259] Another website allows visitors to take an interactive three-dimensional tour of the Armenian Genocide Museum-Institute in Yerevan, Armenia.[260] As blogger Erin Kirkpatrick argues, although certainly imposing a physical and psychological distance that decreases the impact of the actual sites, virtual memorials such as these "can broaden our awareness by reaching out to an audience that may otherwise not be able to access these sites in person—either for financial or political reasons. As well, they provide an additional resource for educating the public and provide individuals with a space to grieve in private."[261]

Finally, there are some traditional memorials that actually serve as "countermonuments." Coined as a term by Holocaust memory studies scholar James Young, countermonuments are "brazen, painfully self-conscious memorial spaces conceived to challenge the very premise of their being."[262] The classic example of a countermonument is Jochen Gerz and Esther Shalev-Gerz's vanishing *Monument Against Fascism* in Hamburg-Harburg, Germany. Not wanting "an enormous pedestal with something on it presuming to tell people what they ought to think," the Gerzes unveiled a uniquely interactive 40-foot-high, 3-foot-square pillar in a pedestrian shopping mall in the gritty commercial city of Harburg in 1986.[263] The pillar "was made of hollow aluminum plated with a thin layer of soft, dark lead. A steel-pointed stylus with which to score the soft lead was attached at each corner by a length of cable" and a temporary inscription near the pillar's base encouraged visitors to sign their names on the pillar in recognition that "it is only we ourselves who can rise up against injustice."[264] As 5-foot sections were covered with signatures, the monument was lowered into the ground. Between its opening on October 10, 1986 and its disappearance on November 10, 1993, the monument collected 70,000 signatures (and more than a little graffiti) and was lowered into the ground eight times. Today, "nothing is left but the top surface of the monument, now covered with a burial stone inscribed to 'Harburg's Monument Against Fascism.'"[265] As performance studies scholar Kerry Whigham points out, such countermonuments resist the monumentality and permanence of traditional memorials. They transmit the burden of memory to the visitor rather than contain the memory in the monument.[266]

Site and public space memorials attempt to connect us to a moment in history by serving as a literal, or symbolic, reminder of past atrocities. The use of sites as memorials can be found in former Nazi death and concentration camps of the Holocaust, throughout the killing fields and detention centers of Cambodia, at the Door of No Return in Senegal's Goree Island, at the Villa Grimaldi interrogation and torture center in Santiago, Chile, on a gable wall in Derry, Northern Ireland reading "You Are Now Entering Free Derry," and in the former battery factory of the Srebrenica-Potocari Memorial Center where Serb soldiers, in the headquarters of the Dutch UN battalion, separated men and boys from families for execution. Public space memorials may be formally designated (for instance, parks and open spaces) and "set outside of the framework of daily life as places for remembrance and commemoration of a bloody past" or informally created through the use of graffiti, murals, street art, or social media.[267] However configured, site and public space memorials are places in which "community is represented and where acts of civil integration and promotion take place."[268]

In Argentina, as we have already discussed, the site of ESMA was converted from a place of torture and death into a space for memory and human rights. In 1998, Argentine President Carlos Menem moved the Navy out of ESMA and proposed to demolish the buildings as a monument to national unity. Public outcry was so great that the Argentine courts annulled the demolition. On March 24, 2004—Argentina's Day of Remembrance for Truth and Justice marking the anniversary of the last military coup—the Federal Government and the Government of the City of Buenos Aires, with active involvement of human rights organizations, finally signed an agreement establishing the campus' restitution to the City and the Navy's formal eviction. Four years later, ESMA, a 42-acre and 34-building complex, was declared a National Historic Landmark and opened as Latin America's largest human rights museum—a living museum housing cultural centers, human rights activist groups, and the National Memory Archive. Recently, however, transfer of ESMA from the City back to the national state has raised questions regarding the political use (or abuse) of the site of memory—exacerbated in 2014 with the opening of the Malvinas Museum on the grounds of ESMA. Although Argentine president Cristina Fernández de Kirchner insists the museum is not to commemorate a war but to document the history of a plunder, others see its placement at ESMA as blatant exploitation of a site of memory for political propaganda.

A fascinating complement to the power of place at ESMA is the nearby Park of Memory (*Parque de la Memoria*) in Buenos Aires. Evocatively situated in public space on the shores of the Rio de la Plata, the river described in the Park's guidebook as "a mute witness to the destiny of many of the victims," the Park of Memory was conceived in 1997 by human rights organizations as "a memory park that would include a monument bearing the names of the disappeared and assassinated in addition to a group of commemorative sculptures."[269] Today, spanning 35 acres in a landfill zone, the empty hill of the Park of Memory is sliced by the jagged steles of the Monument to the Victims of State Terrorism, engraved with the names of the people (still under revision and elaboration) who disappeared or were assassinated by forces of State terrorism between 1969 and 1983. On the monument, "all the names of the loved ones that the dictatorship sought to erase, can be found."[270] The monument is complemented by nine sculptures of contemporary art throughout the Park—including one, "Reconstruction of the portrait of Pablo Miguez," installed in the waters of Rio de la Plata. In addition, the Park includes an information center with a database on the victims and a meeting space dedicated to cultural and artistic activities. The preventive hopes of the Park of Memory are clear: "Current and future generations who visit it will come face to face with the memory of the horrors committed, with a heightened consciousness of the need to keep watch so that these deeds can NEVER AGAIN be repeated."[271]

Finally, *performative memorials* refer to activities of remembrance and commemoration. For performance studies scholar Diana Taylor, such memorials enact "embodied memory: performances, gestures, orality, movement, dance, singing—in short, all those acts usually thought of as ephemeral, nonreproducible knowledge."[272] Often, performative memorials become "transferential spaces" in which "people might have an experience of events through which they did not live" but by which they "might gain access to processual, sensuously immersed knowledge."[273] In other words, performative memorials can make the traumas become "imaginable, thinkable, and speakable to us."[274] From a downstream preventive standpoint, civil society can, and often does, use performative memorials as a catalyst for states to assume their transitional justice responsibilities after atrocity.

In Peru, for instance, some 69,280 people, the majority from Quechua-speaking indigenous communities, were forcibly disappeared during an internal armed conflict between the government and subversive groups (most notably, the Mao-inspired Shining Path) from 1980 to 2000. Beginning in November 2009, Peruvian women from urban and rural areas, in collaboration with indigenous human rights organizations, developed the Scarf of Hope (*Chalina de la Esperanza*) as a performative memorial for the disappeared. In this piece of memory, knitted panels of different colors, some with the name of the missing person and the date and place of their disappearance, were pieced together, with many of the panels left blank. The scarf becomes, in Taylor's words, an "archival memory" that "works across distance, over time and space."[275] As a performative memorial, though, the scarf also enacts memory in the presence of its makers and its viewers. The "one-kilometer long scarf created in knitting sessions (known as knit-athons) in public spaces brought visibility to those absent and gave participants the opportunity to demand truth and justice."[276]

The development of a performative memorial to bring visibility to those absent also can be seen in the global drive to commemorate May 31 as annual White Armband Day. In Prijedor, BiH, on May 31, 1992, Bosnian Serb authorities ordered the non-Serb population to mark their homes with white flags or sheets. In addition, they were ordered to place a white armband around their sleeves before leaving their homes. During the 1992–1995 war, over 3,000 civilians, mostly Muslim, were killed in the municipality of Prijedor. Tens of thousands more were detained in concentration camps. In 2012, ahead of the twentieth anniversary of the white armband decree, Prijedor activists used social media to inaugurate White Armband Day as a performative memorial to combat genocide denial and promote victims' rights to remembrance and dignity. The movement quickly caught on and, today, hundreds of thousands of people across the globe commemorate May 31 with the performative memorial of wearing white armbands or placing a white sheet on their window.

Likely the most notable performative memorial, however, is to be found in the work of Argentina's Mothers of the Plaza de Mayo (*Madres de Plaza de Mayo*). On the Thursday afternoon of April 30, 1977, a year following the military coup, a small group of mothers of the disappeared met at the Plaza de Mayo square in the city center of Buenos Aires. Plaza de Mayo, situated in the heart of Argentina's political and financial center, stands in front of Casa Rosada, or Pink House, the president's residence and the heart of the military government. Most of the mothers who met there were housewives; few worked outside the home. Some had not finished primary school and others could not read or write. They were of diverse geographic origins, with many coming from small towns outside Buenos Aires, and from varied economic and social classes. What they shared, however, was living the nightmare of a missing relative. When they met at the Plaza that April afternoon, their intention was to ask President Videla about the whereabouts of their missing children. Military authorities, who had forbidden public gatherings of more than three people, approached the women and demanded that they circulate rather than assemble. "In response," Hebe de Bonafini recalls, "we started grabbing each other in pairs, arm to arm, and started walking in circles around the square. There was nothing illegal about that."[277]

The following Thursday, the mothers reappeared to march around the square. Every week, the number of mothers grew as the number of disappeared also grew. To identify each other, the women began wearing a white headscarf, made of their children's diapers. Over time, the headscarves were embroidered with the names and dates of the wearers' disappeared children. Some carried photos of their missing children around their neck; others pasted their photos on huge placards. All used their presence at the Plaza to negate the state-sponsored erasure of their loved one. This trauma-driven performative memorial was not, however, without its costs. Some of the mothers were arrested, tortured, and even killed. To stay ahead of the police, they sometimes met in different places on different days to hold their demonstrations. Through it all, though, the movement continued and began to transform Argentine society. "Plazas in cities, towns, and villages are key places where women met, shared feelings, developed friendships, designed strategies for future mobilization, and rendered the network visible to the general public."[278] Still today, every Thursday at 3:30 p.m., the Madres meet at the Plaza de Mayo to march. Although their numbers are dwindling, their Thursday marches, of which I have participated in several, remain an inclusive performative memorial in the continuing struggle for human rights in Argentina, Latin America, and worldwide.

In Argentina, the spiritual home of male machismo, it was the Mothers of Plaza de Mayo who took the lead in the first public protest against military rule. Over the years, the Madres have been internationally recognized for their human rights activism, even immortalized in song by U2's *Mothers of the Disappeared*. They have served as an inspirational example of how women can mobilize in the face of human rights abuses and mass atrocity. As a result, other mother-formed human rights movements took place in Chile, Brazil, Uruguay, Guatemala, Honduras, and Sri Lanka. The Madres also demonstrate the commanding power of a performative countermonument. As Susana Torre writes: "The purpose of these demonstrations is to prevent national closure on the episode ... In their literal embodiment of lived memory, they continue to oppose, symbolically and politically, the very idea of memorialization ... the Mother's presence on the square is a perpetual reminder of unfinished justice."[279]

How Does Memorialization Promote Transitional Justice? As James Young argues, memorialization attempts to propagate an "illusion of common memory."[280] In so doing, however, such efforts, by design or not, "may relieve viewers of their memory burden," allowing us to sidestep actual engagement with the issues.[281] As he writes: "In this age of mass memory production and consumption, in fact, there seems to be an inverse

proportion between the memorialization of the past and its contempla-
tion and study. For once we assign monumental form to memory, we have
to some degree divested ourselves of the obligation to remember."[282] In
essence, memorialization may not memorialize events so much as it bur-
ies them beneath national myth and political propaganda. From a preventive standpoint, Meral also cautions that "we cannot assume or expect
that mere remembrance will deter future atrocities, and far from acting as
a deterrent, remembering can be, and has been, the cause of new ones."[283]
Indeed, the pervasive use of memorialization in BiH, for instance, is so
politicized and biased that it has actually increased ethnoreligious divisions since the cessation of hostilities.[284] Similarly, Mendelof claims that
"there is no inherently logical reason why collective forgetting of painful,
divisive episodes from the past might not be more conductive to harmony
and cooperation than truth-telling."[285]

These cautions are well-noted and remind us that memorialization
poorly used can be societally destructive, particularly in a postatrocity setting. That said, however, there are good uses of memorialization that, in
conjunction with justice and truth, can serve vitally important downstream
preventive functions in a postatrocity society. Memorialization can evoke
strong personal connections to the events they memorialize. In so doing,
they can help people come to terms with the divided past and, perhaps,
make the transition to a shared future easier. As Hayner writes: "One must
confront the legacy of past horrors or there will be no foundation on which
to build a new society. Bury your sins, and they will reemerge later. Stuff
skeletons in the closet, and they will fall back out of the closet at the most
inauspicious times. Try to quiet the ghosts of the past, and they will haunt
you forever—at the risk of opening society to cycles of violence, anger, pain,
and revenge."[286] By compelling individuals to confront their collective past
and think about their role in society, memorialization can form an important preventive step for the future. As memory studies scholar Roger Simon
argues: "Public practices of remembrance are always about the future."[287]

Moreover, I think it a logical, empirical, and moral stretch to argue that
collective forgetting is an acceptable response to genocide and atrocity.
Collective forgetting favors the perpetrators, not the victims; in a very real
sense, collective forgetting is a retraumatization of the victims. The pursuit of transitional justice and the prevention of genocide is threatened, not
aided, by collective forgetting. As historian Tzvetan Tordorov argues, "the
choice we have is not between remembering and forgetting; because forgetting can't be done by an act of will, it is not something we can choose
to do. The choice is between different ways of remembering."[288] As Meral
admits: "No matter how effective the state seeks to impose 'forgetting,' or no

matter how much we 'wish' that such things did not happen, mass atrocities leave powerful traces. And no matter how much the larger society 'moves on,' different groups, primarily the survivors and their families will possess countermemories."[289] These countermemories, or divided narratives, are a direct threat to the rebuilding of a postatrocity society. Memorialization can be one of the ways to develop a more inclusive shared narrative. In the former Yugoslavia, for instance, Subotic encourages states in the region to "create national days of memory for victims of atrocities their own troops have committed, and set up museums or other types of memorial sites to remember victims and survivors." As she points out, such "memorialization efforts are important in their own right, but they are [also] a necessary component of a comprehensive post-conflict justice framework."[290]

Ramirez-Barat suggests six specific ways in which memorialization can promote transitional justice.[291] First, memorialization promotes the preservation and recovery of memory (both physical and symbolic). As such, memorialization is a preventive stand against the denial of atrocity, which Gregory Stanton has identified as among the surest indicators of further atrocities.[292] Second, memorialization can provide recognition to victims, both as individuals who have been harmed as well as citizens of a community whose rights have been violated. In this way, memorialization functions as a form of symbolic reparation. Third, memorialization can contribute to acknowledging and raising awareness about past abuses. "In this sense, they [memorials] look inward at national histories to identify and publicly repudiate the harm inflicted upon fellow nationals, and they try to understand horrible acts committed by people who often were entrusted with roles of leadership that were supposed to include the obligation to protect and govern."[293] Fourth, memorialization can promote public debate and deliberation. As we have seen in our discussion of performative memorials, such activities can be the catalyst for states to assume their transitional justice responsibilities after atrocity. Fifth, memorialization can promote the recovery of truth and the pursuit of justice. *Memoria Abierta* in Argentina, for example, works to ensure that all records of what happened during the last military dictatorship and its consequences are accessible and serve the purposes of research and education of future generations.[294] Sixth, and finally, memorialization promotes prevention, or "guarantees of non-recurrence," by engaging the general public—and particularly the youth—in a productive dialogue about a repressive past. In this way, memorialization can establish links between what occurred in the past and what needs to occur in the present and future to encourage broader preventive values of democracy, peace, human rights, civic engagement, and critical thinking.

Justice, truth, and memory can be important mechanisms of helping a society reconcile itself with its past. How necessary is it, though,
for groups that were at the heart of the conflict to reconcile with each
other? To answer that question, we must first understand the varieties
of meaning inherent in the abstract term "reconciliation." In itself, intergroup reconciliation is not a simple concept. Some see it as process, some
as outcome, and some as both. For public affairs scholar David Crocker,
"there are at least three meanings of reconciliation, ranging from 'thinner'
to 'thicker' conceptions." At the thinnest level, reconciliation is simply
peaceful coexistence, meaning "no more than that former enemies comply with the law instead of killing each other." Although certainly prefer-
able to genocide, we would hope that postatrocity societies could aim for
a bit more in terms of establishing and maintaining a mutually respect-
ful relationship between groups. Crocker describes this second conception of reconciliation: "While they may continue to disagree and even
be adversaries, former enemies must not only live together nonviolently
but respect each other as fellow citizens as well." Finally, for Crocker,
the thickest concept of reconciliation, likely taking generations, is "as a
shared comprehensive vision, mutual healing and restoration, or mutual
forgiveness."[295] Similarly, for South African activist Desmond Tutu, this
thickest conception of reconciliation "is a way to transform individuals
and the whole society. It is a way to look at perpetrators of human rights
abuses and see brothers and sisters. A way to look at the victim in oneself
and see a survivor."[296]

More recently, closely paralleling Crocker, social psychologist Arie
Nadler has suggested that some clarity can be achieved with thinking of intergroup reconciliation along three dimensions of change—
sociocultural, relational, and identity-related. Sociocultural reconciliation
is "predicated on societal changes in the direction of greater intergroup
equality." Such transformations of power relationships and structural
inequalities between the haves and the have-nots can be an important
step in restoring, or creating, intergroup harmony. Relational reconciliation is built on "relations of trust and positive perceptions of 'the other.'"
Such reconciliation is achieved by "repeated positive, friendly, equal, and
cooperative encounters between adversarial groups." Finally, identity-
related reconciliation is "predicated on the removal of conflict-related
threats to the collective identities of each of the parties." This diffusion of
identity-related threats "requires a social exchange whereby perpetrators
provide genuine apologies in exchange for victim's forgiveness."[297]

From a preventive standpoint, these various conceptions of reconciliation may be seen as points along a continuum of social repair. The cessation

of hostilities is the minimal form of reconciliation that must be in place for the mechanisms of justice, truth, and memory to be accessed. Over time, these transitional justice mechanisms, particularly when requiring a culture of encounter and intergroup cooperation, may lead to a deeper level of reconciliation in which there is a collective "working through" of the past. At this level, reconciliation is understood as the facing and the processing of the past, rather than its forgetting and erasure. It is putting the past in its place rather than drawing a line in the sand and pretending it never happened. Instead of closing a chapter, this conception of reconciliation is about opening a new chapter through the collective pursuit of justice, truth, and memory. In a sense, it is less reconciliation between two groups and more a reconciliation with a collective past. Both of these forms of reconciliation are reasonable expectations for postgenocide societies.

The pursuit of the deepest level of reconciliation, however, is the most aspirational and also the most context dependent. In Argentina, for instance, transitional justice has proceeded without any nod to "mutual healing and restoration" or "forgiveness" given that perpetrators feel no remorse for what they have done. In the Argentine context, the pursuit of justice, truth, and memory—along with the eventual passing of the generation of perpetrators—is what will allow society to put the past in its place. As Argentine journalist Horacio Verbitsky said of reconciliation in the Argentine experience: "That word makes no sense here. The political discourse of reconciliation is profoundly immoral, because it denies the reality of what people have experienced. It isn't reasonable to expect someone to reconcile after what happened here."[298]

Similarly, the word makes little literal sense for indigenous victims of genocide. Reconciliation implies the reestablishment of a conciliatory state—a state that they assert never existed with colonizers. In the indigenous context, to "reconcile" with a group with which you were never "conciled" to begin with is a futile pursuit.

On the other end of the contextual spectrum, Rwanda is steeped in an evangelical Christian tradition for which reconciliation—within oneself, between groups, and with God—is a fundamental worldview concept. More broadly, "the notion of reconciliation has been part of African systems of dispute resolution for centuries."[299] In the Rwandan context, as I have witnessed in the living room of a survivor speaking to the perpetrator who killed her family, forgiveness as a necessary condition for reconciliation is prescribed and expected, regardless of the victim's readiness to do so. Indeed, the social pressures on survivors to forgive the sins committed against them are such that, to an outsider, it comes across as almost morally objectionable.

In short, however defined, some form of intergroup reconciliation—at the very least, the cessation of killing and the establishment of peaceful coexistence—is necessary to begin a lengthy, likely generational, process of deep and fundamental societal transformation that inoculates that society against future genocidal violence. And central to that process are the mechanisms of justice, truth, and memory.

Verbitsky, a prominent Argentine journalist best known for reporting the confessions of Francisco Scilingo, a retired naval officer who admitted to throwing live prisoners out of airplanes and into the sea on the so-called "flights of death," said: "People always ask, 'Why reopen wounds that have closed?' Because they were badly closed. First you have to cure the infection, or they will reopen themselves."[300] Societal wounds that reopen after genocide leave a society at considerable risk. This is why, from a downstream prevention standpoint, it is vital to focus on social repair—"closing the wounds"—after genocide.

As we have seen, justice, truth, and memory can be important mechanisms of social repair in a postgenocide society. They are paths that cleave a trail to societal reconstruction. Although States carry the primary responsibility for such repair, the international community (including international and regional organizations, neighbors, states, private companies and businesses, and civil society) has a responsibility to assist States in building the capacity to carry out that repair. It is also important to note that no one transitional justice mechanism can address the myriad problems facing a postgenocide society. "The large number of victims, inadequate legal systems, and traumatized societies require countries to adopt multiple transitional justice mechanisms."[301] No single mechanism of transitional justice—be it rooted in justice, truth, or memory—is as impactful on its own as when combined with the others.

NOTES

1. For a detailed analysis of military dictatorships in Argentina throughout the twentieth century, see Mara Soledad Catoggio, "The Last Military Dictatorship in Argentina (1976–1983): The Mechanism of State Terrorism," *Online Encyclopedia of Mass Violence* (2010).
2. Daniel Feierstein, "National Security Doctrine in Latin America," eds. Donald Bloxham and A. Dirk Moses, *The Oxford Handbook of Genocide Studies* (New York, NY: Oxford University Press, 2010), 492.
3. Francisco Goldman, "Children of the Dirty War," *The New Yorker* (March 19, 2012): 56.

4. Goldman, "Children of the Dirty War," 57.
5. Daniel Feierstein, "Political Violence in Argentina and its Genocidal Characteristics," *Journal of Genocide Research* 8 (2006): 153, 158.
6. See Feierstein, "National Security Doctrine in Latin America," 505.
7. W. John Green, *A History of Political Murder in Latin America: Killing the Messengers of Change* (Albany, NY: SUNY Press, 2015), 113.
8. Feierstein, "Political Violence in Argentina and its Genocidal Characteristics," 150.
9. Gabriel Gatti, *Surviving Forced Disappearance in Argentina and Uruguay: Identity and Meaning* (New York, NY: Palgrave Macmillan, 2014), 1.
10. The Report of the Argentine National Commission on the Disappeared, *Nunca Mas* (New York, NY: Farrar Straus Giroux, 1984), 72.
11. Calvin Sims, "Argentine Tells of Dumping 'Dirty War' Captives Into Sea," *The New York Times* (March 13, 1995): A8.
12. Marcelo Brodsky, *Memory Under Construction* (Buenos Aires, Argentina: La Marca Editora, 2005), 243.
13. Gatti, *Surviving Forced Disappearance*, 82.
14. Quoted phrase taken from http://time.com/3096122/ignacio-hurban-argentina/, accessed June 1, 2015. At present, it is not clear whether the family who raised him knew that he had been stolen from his disappeared mother.
15. Accessed June 1, 2015 at http://elpais.com/m/elpais/2014/08/06/inenglish/1407341896_769517.html.
16. Gareth Evans, *The Responsibility to Protect: Ending Mass Atrocity Crimes Once and For All* (Washington, DC: Brookings Institution Press, 2008), 148.
17. International Center for Transitional Justice, accessed June 2, 2015 at https://www.ictj.org/about/transitional-justice.
18. Guillermo O'Donnell, Philippe C. Schmitter, and Laurence Whitehead (eds.), *Transitions from Authoritarian Rule: Tentative Conclusions about Uncertain Democracies* (Baltimore, MD: Johns Hopkins University Press, 1986).
19. Leona Lam, "Velasquez Rodriguez v. Honduras," *Loyola of Los Angeles International and Comparative Law Review* 36 (2014): 1920.
20. Kathleen Daly, "Reparation and Restoration" (2011), accessed June 10, 2015 at http://www.griffith.edu.au/__data/assets/pdf_file/0020/220475/Reparation-and-restoration-as-of-1-Feb-2011.pdf, 37.
21. African Youth Initiative Network, "Victims' Voices . . . on Transitional Justice in Uganda!," accessed June 3, 2015 at http://www.africanyouthinitiative.org/assets/victims-voices-on-transitional-justice--2014-report.pdf, 4.
22. Mthuli Ncube and Basil Jones, "Drivers and Dynamics of Fragility in Africa," *Africa Economic Brief* 4 (2013): 7.
23. The World Bank, *World Development Report 2011* (Washington, DC: The World Bank, 2011), 108.
24. Accessed June 2, 2015 at http://www.insightonconflict.org/2014/03/bosnia-herzegovina-acknowledging-past-crimes/.
25. Roland Paris, "Post-Conflict Peacebuilding," eds. Thomas G. Weiss and Sam Daws, *The Oxford Handbook on the United Nations* (New York, NY: Oxford University Press, 2007), 417.
26. See Alexander Mayer-Rieckh and Serge Rumin, "Confronting an Abusive Past in Security Sector Reform After Conflict: Guidelines for Practitioners," *Initiative for Peacebuilding* (2010).
27. Sean McFate, "Law and Order: Tools for Building State Protection Capacity to Prevent Mass Atrocity Crimes," *Policy Analysis Brief* (December 2013): 1.

28. Accessed June 10, 2015 at https://sites.google.com/site/transitionaljusticedata-base/.
29. Ernesto Verdeja, "Transitional Justice and Genocide," eds. Joyce Apsel and Ernesto Verdeja, *Genocide Matters: Ongoing Issues and Emerging Perspectives* (New York, NY: Routledge, 2013), 176.
30. Verdeja, "Transitional Justice and Genocide," 174–175.
31. Rebecca Wittmann, "Punishment," eds. Peter Hayes and John K. Roth, *The Oxford Handbook of Holocaust Studies* (New York, NY: Oxford University Press, 2010), 525.
32. Martha Minow, *Between Vengeance and Forgiveness: Facing History after Genocide and Mass Violence* (Boston, MA: Beacon Press, 1998), 27.
33. Richard Goldstone, "International Criminal Court and Ad Hoc Tribunals," eds. Weiss and Daws, *The Oxford Handbook on the United Nations*, 467, 468.
34. Minow, *Between Vengeance and Forgiveness*, 30.
35. Ibid, 32, 35.
36. Ibid, 35.
37. Ibid, 31.
38. Ibid, 40.
39. Bernard D. Meltzer, "Remembering Nuremberg," *Occasional Papers from the Law School, University of Chicago* 34 (1995): 7.
40. International Crisis Group, "International Criminal Tribunal for Rwanda: Justice Delayed" (June 7, 2001): iii.
41. Minow, *Between Vengeance and Forgiveness*, 31.
42. Ibid.
43. Ethel Higonnet, "Restructuring Hybrid Courts: Local Empowerment and National Criminal Justice Reform" (2005). Student Scholarship Papers. Paper 6. Accessed June 4, 2015 at http://digitalcommons.law.yale.edu/student_papers/6, 44.
44. Ivana Nizich, "International Tribunals and Their Ability to Provide Adequate Justice: Lessons from the Yugoslav Tribunal," *ILSA Journal of International and Comparative Law* 7 (2001).
45. Charles T. Call, "Is Transitional Justice Really Just?," *Brown Journal of World Affairs* XI (2004): 105.
46. Higonnet, "Restructuring Hybrid Courts," 54.
47. George S. Yacoubian, Jr., "Evaluating the Efficacy of the International Criminal Tribunals for Rwanda and the Former Yugoslavia: Implications for Criminology and International Criminal Law," *World Affairs* 3 (2003): 136, 139.
48. Stuart Ford, "Complexity and Efficiency at International Criminal Courts," *Emory International Law Review* 29 (2014).
49. See https://pcolman.wordpress.com/2014/04/16/rwanda-twenty-years-after-genocide/, accessed June 2, 2015 and Human Rights Watch, "Rwanda: Justice After Genocide––20 Years On" (March 28, 2014), accessed June 2, 2015 at http://www.hrw.org/news/2014/03/28/rwanda-justice-after-genocide-20-years#_ftn8.
50. Verdeja, "Transitional Justice and Genocide," 175.
51. Stephanie A. Barbour, "Making Justice Visible: Bosnia and Herzegovina's Domes War Crimes Trials Outreach," ed. Clara Ramirez-Barat, *Transitional Justice, Culture, and Society* (New York, NY: Social Science Research Council, 2014), 99.
52. Higonnet, "Restructuring Hybrid Courts," 43.
53. Phil Clark, "Do War Crimes Trials Really Help Victims?" (April 28, 2012), accessed June 6, 2015 at http://www.cnn.com/2012/04/26/opinion/charles-taylor-victims/.

54. Ibid, 44.
55. The Office of the Prosecutor is currently conducting preliminary analysis in eight situations: Afghanistan, Colombia, Georgia, Guinea, Iraq, Nigeria, Palestine, and Ukraine.
56. John Mukum Mbaku, "International Justice: The International Criminal Court and Africa," in *Foresight Africa: Top Priorities for the Continent in 2014* (Washington, DC: The Brookings Institution, 2014), 10.
57. Accessed June 5, 2015 at http://www.aljazeera.com/news/africa/2014/02/african-union-urges-united-stand-against-icc-20142111727645567.html.
58. Accessed June 15, 2015 at http://af.reuters.com/article/idAFKBN0OU0NY20150614.
59. Call, "Is Transitional Justice Really Just?," 106.
60. Daniel Donovan, "International Criminal Court: Successes and Failures," accessed June 5, 2015 at http://www.internationalpolicydigest.org/2012/03/23/international-criminal-court-successes-and-failures-of-the-past-and-goals-for-the-future/.
61. Verdeja, "Transitional Justice and Genocide," 177.
62. Kathryn Sikkink, *The Justice Cascade: How Human Rights Prosecutions are Changing World Politics* (New York, NY: W. W. Norton, 2011), 5.
63. Ibid, 26–27.
64. Verdeja, "Transitional Justice and Genocide," 177.
65. Ibid.
66. See Laurel Fletcher and Harvey Weinstein, "Violence and Social Repair: Rethinking the Contribution of Justice to Reconciliation," *Human Rights Quarterly* 24 (2002): 573–639.
67. Laurel Fletcher, "From Indifference to Engagement: Bystanders and International Criminal Justice," *Michigan Journal of International Law* 26 (2004): 1076.
68. Brandon Hamber, "Transitional Justice and Intergroup Conflict," ed. Linda R. Tropp, *The Oxford Handbook of Intergroup Conflict* (New York, NY: Oxford University Press, 2012), 332.
69. Jose Ayala Lasso, keynote speech at Columbia University (May 14, 1996), accessed June 7, 2015 at http://www.columbia.edu/cu/record/archives/vol21/vol21_iss28/record2128.13.html.
70. Minow, *Between Vengeance and Forgiveness*, 51.
71. Sikkink, *The Justice Cascade*, 25.
72. Daly, "Reparation and Restoration," 9.
73. Minow, *Between Vengeance and Forgiveness*, 92.
74. Accessed June 7, 2015 at http://restorativejustice.org/whatisslide/definition.
75. Verdeja, "Transitional Justice and Genocide," 179.
76. Accessed June 7, 2015 at http://www.redress.org/what-is-reparation/what-is-reparation.
77. United Nations Economic and Social Council, "Draft Convention on the Crime of Genocide" (UN Document E/447), June 26, 1947, 9.
78. Ibid, 47.
79. Ibid, 48, 49.
80. Accessed June 7, 2015 at http://www.ohchr.org/EN/ProfessionalInterest/Pages/RemedyAndReparation.aspx.
81. Accessed June 7, 2015 at http://www.ohchr.org/EN/ProfessionalInterest/Pages/IntConventionEnforcedDisappearance.asp.

82. See http://www.trustfundforvictims.org/trust-fund-victims for additional information, accessed June 7, 2015.
83. Aarti Iyer and Craig Blatz, "Apology and Reparation," ed. Tropp, *The Oxford Handbook of Intergroup Conflict*, 317.
84. Verdeja, "Transitional Justice and Genocide," 183.
85. Iyer and Blatz, "Apology and Reparation," 318.
86. Accessed June 7, 2015 at http://en.mercopress.com/2011/08/19/pinochet-s-regime-official-victims-list-increased-by-9.800-to-40.018.
87. Melissa Eddy, "For 60th Year, Germany Honors Duty to Pay Holocaust Victims," *The New York Times* (November 17, 2012).
88. Eduardo Pizarro Leongomez, "Victims and Reparation: The Colombian Experience" (2010), accessed June 10, 2015 at http://www.icc-cpi.int/iccdocs/asp_docs/RC2010/Stocktaking/CNRR-Pizarro.pdf.
89. Edwin Muson, "Genocide Survivors Hopeful of Reparations as ICTR Winds Up," *The New Times* (April 23, 2015), accessed June 7, 2015 at http://www.newtimes.co.rw/section/article/2015-04-23/188122/.
90. Elazar Barkan, *The Guilt of Nations: Restitution and Negotiating Historical Injustices* (New York, NY: Norton, 2000), 168.
91. Dorian Jones, "Turkey: Armenian Church Sues for Lost Property" (May 21, 2015), accessed June 7, 2015 at http://www.eurasianet.org/node/73541.
92. Verdeja, "Transitional Justice and Genocide," 184.
93. Christopher Buck, "'Never Again': Kevin Gover's Apology for the Bureau of Indian Affairs," *Wicazo Sa Review* 21 (2006): 118.
94. Barkan, *The Guilt of Nations*, xix.
95. Nicholas Tavuchis, *Mea Culpa: A Sociology of Apology and Reconciliation* (Palo Alto, CA: Stanford University Press, 1991), 17.
96. Iyer and Blatz, "Apology and Reparation," 313.
97. Barkan, *The Guilt of Nations*, 323.
98. Minow, *Between Vengeance and Forgiveness*, 116.
99. Barkan, *The Guilt of Nations*, 323.
100. Tavuchis, *Mea Culpa*, 8.
101. Damien Short, "When Sorry Isn't Good Enough: Official Remembrance and Reconciliation in Australia," *Memory Studies* 5 (2012): 296.
102. Barkan, *The Guilt of Nations*, 323.
103. Minow, *Between Vengeance and Forgiveness*, 116.
104. Ervin Staub, *Overcoming Evil: Genocide, Violent Conflict, and Terrorism* (New York, NY: Oxford University Press, 2011), 478.
105. Minow, *Between Vengeance and Forgiveness*, 115.
106. Minow, *Between Vengeance and Forgiveness*, 112.
107. The complete text of Gover's speech can be found in the *Journal of American Indian Education* 39 (2000): 4–6.
108. Matt Kelley, "Indian Affairs Head Makes Apology," *The Washington Post* (September 8, 2000).
109. Aaron Lazare, *On Apology* (New York, NY: Oxford University Press, 2004), 83–84.
110. Buck, "'Never Again,'" 99.
111. Accessed June 11, 2015 at https://jimcraven10.wordpress.com/2007/11/22/wbai-interview-with-doug-henwood-61898-genocide-right-here-right-now/.
112. Buck, "'Never Again,'" 109–110.
113. Kelley, "Indian Affairs Head Makes Apology."

114. The U.S. apology came after formal apologies from the Australian and Canadian governments to their indigenous peoples in February 2008 and June 2008, respectively.
115. Accessed June 11, 2015 at https://jimcraven10.wordpress.com/2007/11/22/wbai-interview-with-doug-henwood-61898-genocide-right-here-right-now/.
116. Buck, "'Never Again,'" 115.
117. Iyer and Blatz, "Apology and Reparation," 324.
118. Ibid.
119. Iyer and Blatz, "Apology and Reparation," 321.
120. Fletcher and Weinstein, "Violence and Social Repair," 581.
121. Goran Simic, "Transitional Justice Strategy for Bosnia and Herzegovina: An Overview" (May 7, 2013), accessed June 12, 2015 at http://www.transconflict.com/2013/05/transitional-justice-strategy-for-bosnia-and-herzegovina-an-overview-235/.
122. See, for instance, Richard A. Salem (ed.), *Witness to Genocide: The Children of Rwanda* (New York, NY: Friendship Press, 2000).
123. Muson, "Genocide Survivors Hopeful of Reparations."
124. Fletcher and Weinstein, "Violence and Social Repair," 632.
125. Ervin Staub, "Genocide and Mass Killing: Origins, Prevention, Healing and Reconciliation," *Political Psychology* 21 (2000): 378.
126. Staub, *Overcoming Evil*, 483–487.
127. Verdeja, "Transitional Justice and Genocide," 185.
128. Ibid.
129. Jean-Paul Mugiraneza, "The Rwandan Case: Is It Possible to Truly Compensate Victims of Genocide?," accessed June 7, 2015 at http://www.insightonconflict.org/2013/10/reparations-for-genocide-victims/.
130. Priscilla B. Hayner, *Unspeakable Truths: Transitional Justice and the Challenge of Truth Commissions*, 2nd ed. (New York, NY: Routledge, 2011), 178.
131. Minow, *Between Vengeance and Forgiveness*, 93.
132. Iyer and Blatz, "Apology and Reparation," 319.
133. Hamber, "Transitional Justice and Intergroup Conflict," 332.
134. Alana Poole, "Baraza Justice: A Case Study of Community-Led Conflict Resolution in D.R. Congo" (2014), accessed June 15, 2015 at http://www.peace-direct.org/wp-content/uploads/2014/04/Baraza-Justice.pdf.
135. Republic of Rwanda, "National Service of Gacaca Courts" (June 2012), accessed June 15, 2015 at http://www.minijust.gov.rw/uploads/media/GACACA_COURTS_IN_RWANDA.pdf.
136. BBC News, "Rwanda 'Gacaca' Genocide Courts Finish Work," accessed June 15, 2015 at http://www.bbc.com/news/world-africa-18490348.
137. Larry May, *Genocide: A Normative Account* (New York, NY: Cambridge University Press, 2010), 265.
138. Human Rights Watch, *Justice Compromised: The Legacy of Rwanda's Community-Based Gacaca Courts* (New York, NY: Human Rights Watch, 2011), 1.
139. May, *Genocide: A Normative Account*, 264.
140. Ibid, 266.
141. Hamber, "Transitional Justice and Intergroup Conflict," 333.
142. Daly, "Reparation and Restoration," 6.
143. Accessed June 15, 2015 at http://www.usip.org/sites/default/files/resources/collections/truth_commissions/Chile90-Report/Chile90-Report.pdf, 14.

144. Richard J. Goldstone, "Justice as a Tool for Peace-Making: Truth Commissions and International Criminal Tribunals," *New York University Journal of International Law and Politics* 28 (1995): 491.
145. Dejan Guzina and Branka Marijan, "Strengthening Transitional Justice in Bosnia: Regional Possibilities and Parallel Narratives," *CIGI Policy Brief* (October, 2013): 7.
146. Phil Clark, *The Gacaca Courts, Post-Genocide Justice and Reconciliation in Rwanda: Justice without Lawyers* (New York, NY: Cambridge University Press, 2010).
147. UN Commission on Human Rights, *Human Rights Resolution 2005/66: Right to the Truth* (April 20, 2005), E/CN.4/RES/2005/66, accessed June 17, 2015 at http://www.refworld.org/docid/45377c7d0.html.
148. Hayner, *Unspeakable Truths*, 11–12.
149. Eduardo Gonzalez and Howard Varney (eds.), *Truth Seeking: Elements of Creating an Effective Truth Commission* (Brasilia, Brazil: Amnesty Commission of the Ministry of Justice of Brazil; New York, NY: International Center for Transitional Justice, 2013), 9.
150. Verdeja, "Transitional Justice and Genocide," 179.
151. Accessed June 15, 2015 at http://www.usip.org/publications/truth-commission-digital-collection.
152. A particularly helpful resource is the Truth Commission Digital Collection maintained by the U.S. Institute of Peace, accessed June 15, 2015 at http://www.usip.org/publications/truth-commission-digital-collection.
153. Alexander Dukalskis, "Interactions in Transition: How Truth Commissions and Trials Complement or Constrain Each Other," *International Studies Review* 13 (2011): 436–437.
154. Emilio Crenzel, "Argentina's National Commission on the Disappearances of Persons: Contributions to Transitional Justice," *The International Journal of Transitional Justice* 2 (2008): 179.
155. Ibid.
156. Ibid, 190.
157. The Report of the Argentine National Commission on the Disappeared, *Nunca Mas* (New York, NY: Farrar Straus Giroux, 1986), 1.
158. Ibid, xvi.
159. Hayner, *Unspeakable Truths*, 46.
160. Catoggio, "The Last Military Dictatorship in Argentina," 13.
161. Cited in Alex Boraine, "Alternatives and Adjuncts to Criminal Prosecutions" (1996), accessed June 15, 2015 at http://www.polity.org.za/polity/govdocs/speeches/1996/sp0720.html.
162. Hayner, *Unspeakable Truths*, 18.
163. Ibid, 84.
164. Karen Brouneus, "The Trauma of Truth Telling: Effects of Witnessing in the Rwanda Gacaca Courts on Psychological Health," *Journal of Conflict Resolution* 54 (2010): 429.
165. David Mendeloff, "Truth-Seeking, Truth-Telling, and Postconflict Peacebuilding: Curb the Enthusiasm?," *International Studies Review* 6 (2004): 355.
166. Hamber, "Transitional Justice and Intergroup Conflict," 336.
167. Michael Ignatieff, "Articles of Faith," *Index on Censorship* 25 (1996): 113.
168. Erin Daly, "Truth Skepticism: An Inquiry into the Value of Truth in Times of Transition," *The International Journal of Transitional Justice* 2 (2008): 23.
169. Minow, *Between Vengeance and Forgiveness*, 57.

170. Thomas Buergenthal, "The United Nations Truth Commission for El Salvador," *Vanderbilt Journal of Transnational Law* 27 (1994): 525.

171. Tricia D. Olsen, Leigh A. Payne, and Andrew G. Reiter, "The Justice Balance: When Transitional Justice Improves Human Rights and Democracy," *Human Rights Quarterly* 32 (2010): 980.

172. Gonzalez and Varney (eds.), *Truth Seeking: Elements of Creating an Effective Truth Commission*, 9.

173. Minow, *Between Vengeance and Forgiveness*, 89.

174. Verdeja, "Transitional Justice and Genocide," 180.

175. Call, "Is Transitional Justice Really Just?," 103.

176. Carla de Ycaza and William Schabas, "Transitional Justice and the African Experience," *International Studies Review* 13 (2011): 567.

177. Hayner, *Unspeakable Truths*, 84.

178. Jorge S. Correa, "Dealing with Past Human Rights Violations: The Chilean Case After Dictatorship," *Notre Dame Law Review* 67 (1992): 1480.

179. List drawn from the March 2013 Working Document of the *Transitional Justice Strategy for Bosnia and Herzegovina (2012–2016)*, 20, accessed June 17, 2015 at http://www.nuhanovicfoundation.org/user/file/2013_transitional_justice_strategy_bih_-_new.pdf.

180. "Law on Missing Persons" (2004), accessed June 17, 2015 at http://www.ic-mp.org/wp-content/uploads/2014/08/law-on-missing-persons.pdf.

181. Ibid.

182. Denis Dzidic, "Bosnia Urged to Implement Missing Persons Law" (December 5, 2014), accessed June 17, 2015 at http://www.balkaninsight.com/en/article/bosnia-called-to-implement-law-on-missing-persons.

183. Ibid.

184. The March 2013 Working Document of the *Transitional Justice Strategy for Bosnia and Herzegovina (2012–2016)* was accessed June 17, 2015 at http://www.nuhanovicfoundation.org/user/file/2013_transitional_justice_strategy_bih_-_new.pdf.

185. Ibid, 33.

186. Ibid.

187. Accessed June 17, 2015 at http://www.ic-mp.org/where-we-work/europe/western-balkans/bosnia-and-herzegovina/.

188. Accessed June 17, 2015 at http://www.ic-mp.org/where-we-work/.

189. Accessed June 17, 2015 at http://www.ic-mp.org/wp-content/uploads/2015/03/icmp-dg-945-1-doc-factsheet-bih-missing-persons-from-the-armed-conflicts-of-the-1990s-a-stocktaking.pdf.

190. Dzidic, "Bosnia Urged to Implement Missing Persons Law."

191. Andrew E. Kramer, "Separatists Revise History of Famine in Ukraine," *The New York Times* (April 30, 2015): A4.

192. Karen Murphy, "Facing History: Education's Role in Transitional Justice," accessed June 18, 2015 at http://blog.usaid.gov/2013/06/educations-role-in-transitional-justice/.

193. U.S. Agency for International Development, *USAID Education Strategy* (Washington, DC: USAID, 2011), 1.

194. Clara Ramirez-Barat, *Engaging Children and Youth in Transitional Justice Processes: Guidance for Outreach Programs* (New York, NY: International Center for Transitional Justice, 2012), 3.

195. Ibid.

196. Data in this paragraph were accessed June 18, 2015 at http://www.d.dccam.org/Projects/Genocide/Genocide_Education.htm.
197. Ramirez-Barat, *Engaging Children and Youth in Transitional Justice Processes*, 16.
198. Jelena Subotic, "Remembrance, Public Narratives, and Obstacles to Justice in the Western Balkans," *Studies in Social Justice* 7 (2013): 269.
199. Guzina and Marijan, "Strengthening Transitional Justice in Bosnia: Regional Possibilities and Parallel Narratives," 7.
200. Subotic, "Remembrance, Public Narratives, and Obstacles to Justice in the Western Balkans," 269.
201. USAID, "Fact Sheet: Education for a Just Society in Bosnia and Herzegovina," accessed June 18, 2015 at http://www.usaid.gov/news-information/fact-sheets/education-just-society-bosnia-and-herzegovina.
202. Murphy, "Facing History: Education's Role in Transitional Justice."
203. Luis Bunuel, *My Last Sigh* [translated by Abigail Israel] (New York, NY: Vintage Books, 1984), 4–5.
204. Peter Winn, "'Without Yesterday There Is No Tomorrow': Ricardo Lagos and Chile's Democratic Transition," accessed June 21, 2015 at http://www.asanet.org/footnotes/feb07/indexone.html.
205. UN Document S/2014/30 (January 17, 2014), 3.
206. Ibid, 2.
207. Slavenka Drakulic, *A Guided Tour Through the Museum of Communism* (New York, NY: Penguin, 2011), xiii.
208. Dan Stone, "Genocide and Memory," eds. Donald Bloxham and A. Dirk Moses, *The Oxford Handbook of Genocide Studies* (New York, NY: Oxford University Press, 2010), 103.
209. Ron Eyerman, *Cultural Trauma: Slavery and the Formation of African American Identity* (New York, NY: Cambridge University Press, 2002), 5.
210. Jeffrey K. Olick, Vered Vinitzkyy-Seroussi, and Daniel Levy (eds.), *The Collective Memory Reader* (New York, NY: Oxford University Press, 2011), 16.
211. Stone, "Genocide and Memory," 102, 106.
212. Maurice Halbwachs, *On Collective Memory* [edited by Lewis A. Coser] (Chicago, IL: University of Chicago Press, 1992), 38.
213. Stone, "Genocide and Memory," 103.
214. Eyerman, *Cultural Trauma*, 6.
215. Ziya Meral, "A Duty to Remember? Politics and Morality of Remembering Past Atrocities," *International Political Anthropology* 5 (2012): 30.
216. Stone, "Genocide and Memory," 118.
217. Wulf Kansteiner, "Finding Meaning in Memory: A Methodological Critique of Collective Memory Studies," *History and Theory* 41 (2002): 188.
218. The defining characteristics of an assumptive world are taken from Joan Beder, "Loss of the Assumptive World—How We Deal with Death and Loss," *Omega* 50 (2004–2005): 255–265; quoted material comes from Eyerman, *Cultural Trauma*, 2.
219. Eyerman, *Cultural Trauma*, 6.
220. Victor Roudometof, *Collective Memory, National Identity, and Ethnic Conflict: Greece, Bulgaria, and the Macedonian Question* (Westport, CT: Praeger, 2002), 7.
221. Pierre Nora, "Between Memory and History: Les Lieux de Mémoire," *Representations* 26 (1989): 8.
222. Ronald J. Berger, *The Holocaust, Religion, and the Politics of Collective Memory* (New Brunswick, NJ: Transaction, 2012), 22.

223. George Orwell, *1984*, accessed June 22, 2015 at http://www.planetebook.com/ebooks/1984.pdf, 44.
224. Michael Kammen, *Mystic Chords of Memory: The Transformation of Tradition in American Culture* (New York, NY: Vintage Books, 1991), 3.
225. James E. Young, *The Texture of Memory: Holocaust Memorials and Meaning* (New Haven, CT: Yale University Press, 1993), 2.
226. Katherine Conway, "The Role of Memory in Post-Genocide Rwanda," accessed June 22, 2015 at http://www.insightonconflict.org/2013/08/the-role-of-memory-in-post-genocide-rwanda/.
227. Ibid.
228. Peter Novick, *The Holocaust in American Life* (New York, NY: Houghton Mifflin, 1999), 261.
229. Cited in Julian Borger, "War Is Over—Now Serbs and Bosniaks Fight to Win Control of a Brutal History" (March 23, 2014), accessed June 22, 2015 at http://www.theguardian.com/world/2014/mar/23/war-serbs-bosniaks-history-visegrad.
230. Elvira Jukic, "Dispute Over Visegrad's War Victim's Memorial," accessed June 22, 2015 at http://www.balkaninsight.com/en/article/serbs-bosniaks-dispute-over-Visegrad-victims-monument.
231. Gianluca Mezzofiore, "Bosnian Serbs Remove 'Genocide' from Bosniak's Visegrad Memorial," accessed June 22, 2015 at http://www.ibtimes.co.uk/bosnian-serbs-remove-genocide-bosniaks-visegrad-memorial-video-1433658.
232. UN Document S/2014/30 (January 17, 2014): 2.
233. Ibid.
234. UN Document S/2014/30 (January 17, 2014): 3.
235. Roudometof, *Collective Memory, National Identity, and Ethnic Conflict*, 7.
236. Accessed June 21, 2015 at https://www.ictj.org/sites/default/files/ICTJ-Global-Transitional-Justice-2009-English.pdf.
237. Berger, *The Holocaust, Religion, and the Politics of Collective Memory*, 21.
238. Sara Ahmed, *The Cultural Politics of Emotion* (New York, NY: Routledge, 2004), 201–202.
239. C. Allen Haney, Christina Leimer, and Juliann Lowery, "Spontaneous Memorialization: Violent Death and Emerging Mourning Ritual," *Omega* 35 (1997): 161.
240. Peter Jan Margry and Cristina Sanchez-Carretero, "Memorializing Traumatic Death," *Anthropology Today* 23 (2007): 2.
241. Pamela Roberts, "Encyclopedia of Death and Dying," accessed June 23, 2015 at http://www.deathreference.com/Me-Nu/Memorialization-Spontaneous.html.
242. Maria Tumarkin, *Traumascapes* (Melbourne, Australia: Melbourne University Publishing, 2005).
243. Sara Guyer, "Rwanda's Bones," *Boundary 2* 36 (2009): 157.
244. Clea Koff, *The Bone Woman: A Forensic Anthropologist's Search for Truth in the Mass Graves of Rwanda, Bosnia, Croatia, and Kosovo* (New York, NY: Random House, 2004), 88.
245. Guyer, "Rwanda's Bones," 158–159.
246. Guyer, "Rwanda's Bones," 163.
247. Stone, "Genocide and Memory," 113.
248. Guyer, "Rwanda's Bones," 162.
249. Jon K. Reid, "Impromptu Memorials to the Dead," ed. Clifton D. Bryant, *Handbook of Death and Dying* (Thousand Oaks, CA: Sage, 2003), 716.
250. Margry and Sanchez-Carretero, "Memorializing Traumatic Death," 2.

251. Jack Santino, "Performative Commemoratives, the Personal, and the Public: Spontaneous Shrines, Emergent Ritual, and the Field of Folklore," *Journal of American Folklore* 117 (2004): 369, 370.
252. Ibid, 370.
253. Guyer, "Rwanda's Bones," 161.
254. Filip Reyntjens, "Rwanda Ten Years On: From Genocide to Dictatorship," *African Affairs* 103 (2004): 199.
255. Guyer, "Rwanda's Bones," 159.
256. Reid, "Impromptu Memorials to the Dead," 712.
257. Jason Wells, "'Emotionally Compelling' Teardrop Concept Chosen for Armenian Genocide Memorial in Pasadena" (January 29, 2013), accessed June 28, 2015 at http://www.armeniandiaspora.com/showthread.php?316208-Art-Emotionally-compelling-teardrop-concept-chosen-for-Armenian-g.
258. Quote cited in Kerry Whigham, "Feeling the Past: Practices of Memorialization in Genocide Remembrance," lecture given at Keene State College on September 3, 2014.
259. Accessed June 28, 2015 at http://www.genocidememorials.cga.harvard.edu/.
260. Accessed June 28, 2015 at http://www.memcosoft.com/genocidemuseum/.
261. Erin Kirkpatrick, "Virtual Memorial: Serving Memory or Sabotaging It?" (February 8, 2013), accessed June 28, 2015 at https://thesentinelproject.org/2013/02/08/virtual-memorials-serving-memory-or-sabotaging-it/.
262. James E. Young, *At Memory's Edge: After-Images of the Holocaust in Contemporary Art and Architecture* (New Haven, CT: Yale University Press, 2000), 7.
263. Ibid, 130.
264. Ibid.
265. Ibid.
266. Whigham, "Feeling the Past."
267. Kerry Whigham, "Feeling the Absence: The Re-Embodiment of Sites of Mass Atrocity and the Practices They Generate," *Museum & Society* 12 (2014): 88.
268. Eduardo Maestripieri, "Memory and Landscape," in *Parque de la Memoria: Monumento a las Victimas del Terrorismo de Estado* (Buenos Aires, Argentina: Gobierno de la Ciudad Autonoma de Buenos Aires, 2010), 38.
269. "A Project Not to Forget," in *Parque de la Memoria: Monumento a las Victimas del Terrorismo de Estado* (Buenos Aires, Argentina: Gobierno de la Ciudad Autonoma de Buenos Aires, 2010), 20.
270. Ibid, 24.
271. Ibid.
272. Diana Taylor, *The Archive and the Repertoire: Performing Cultural Memory in the Americas* (Durham, NC: Duke University Press, 2003), 20.
273. Alison Landsberg, *Prosthetic Memory: The Transformation of American Remembrance in the Age of Mass Culture* (New York, NY: Columbia University Press, 2004), 23–24.
274. Ibid, 139.
275. Taylor, *The Archive and the Repertoire*, 19.
276. Olga Gonalez Castaneda, "Scarf of Hope as a Warm and Performative Memorial for the Disappeared in Peru," accessed June 28, 2015 at http://criticalatinoamericana.com/316/.
277. Vladimir Hernandez, "Argentine Mothers Mark 35 Years Marching for Justice," accessed June 29, 2015 at http://www.bbc.com/news/world-latin-america-17847134.

278. Fernando J. Bosco, "The Madres de Plaza de Mayo and Three Decades of Human Rights' Activism: Embeddedness, Emotions, and Social Movements," *Annals of the Association of American Geographers* 96 (2006): 356.
279. Susana Torre, "Constructing Memorials," eds. Okwui Enwezor, Carlos Basualdo, Ute Meta Bauer, Susanne Ghez, Sarat Maharaj, Mark Nash, and Octavio Zaya, *Experiments with Truth: Transitional Justice and the Processes of Truth and Reconciliation* (Berlin, Germany: Hatje Cantz, 2002), 351.
280. Young, *The Texture of Memory*, 6.
281. Ibid, 5.
282. Ibid.
283. Meral, "A Duty to Remember?," 42.
284. The issue of memorials is a key focus in the March 2013 Working Document of the *Transitional Justice Strategy for Bosnia and Herzegovina (2012–2016)*.
285. Mendelof, "Truth-Seeking, Truth-Telling, and Postconflict Peacebuilding," 367.
286. Hayner, *Unspeakable Truths*, 23.
287. Roger I. Simon, "Museums, Civic Life, and the Educative Force of Remembrance," *Journal of Museum Education* 31 (2006): 113.
288. Cited in Duncan Bell (ed.), *Memory, Trauma and World Politics: Reflections on the Relationship between Past and Present* (New York, NY: Palgrave, 2006), v.
289. Meral, "A Duty to Remember?," 44.
290. Subotic, "Remembrance, Public Narratives, and Obstacles to Justice in the Western Balkans," 279.
291. Clara Ramirez-Barat, "The Role of Memorialization in Transitional Justice Processes: An Introductory Approach," paper presented at the international conference titled "Memory: A Pillar of Transitional Justice and Human Rights" (São Paolo, Brazil), November 2014.
292. Gregory H. Stanton, "The Ten Stages of Genocide," accessed June 29, 2015 at http://www.genocidewatch.org/genocide/tenstagesofgenocide.html.
293. Louis Bickford, "Memoryworks/Memory Works," ed. Ramirez-Barat, *Transitional Justice, Culture, and Society*: 499.
294. See http://www.memoriaabierta.org.ar, accessed June 29, 2015.
295. All preceding quoted material in this paragraph is taken from David A. Crocker, "Truth Commission, Transitional Justice, and Civil Society," eds. Robert I. Rotberg and Dennis Thompson, *Truth v. Justice: The Morality of Truth Commissions* (Princeton, NJ: Princeton University Press, 2000), 108.
296. Desmond Mpilo Tutu, "Foreword" to Eric Daily and Jeremy Sarkin, *Reconciliation in Divided Societies: Finding Common Ground* (Philadelphia, PA: University of Pennsylvania Press, 2007), ix–x.
297. All preceding quoted material in this paragraph is taken from Arie Nadler, "Intergroup Reconciliation: Definitions, Processes, and Future Directions, ed. Tropp, *The Oxford Handbook of Intergroup Conflict*, 293–294.
298. Cited in Hayner, *Unspeakable Truths*, 187–188.
299. Cited in Jens Meierhenrich, "Varieties of Reconciliation," *Law & Social Inquiry* 33 (2008): 199.
300. Hayner, *Unspeakable Truths*, 145.
301. Olsen, Payne, and Reiter, "The Justice Balance," 990.

PART III

Never Again?

Conclusion

"Thus Have We Made the World . . .
Thus Have I Made It"

The question of whether we are becoming a more, or less, violent world has become very popular, and often rather contentious, in recent academic debate. Those who believe that war is increasing, or at least remaining stable, use reams of supporting empirical data to counter the reams of contradictory empirical data used by those who believe war is decreasing. As researcher Nils Petter Gleditsch points out, the divisive issues in this robust debate range from nature versus nurture to choice of dataset used to what kinds of violence to study to the use of relative rather than absolute numbers.[1]

Recently, the debate has trended toward the "declinist" side, most popularly articulated in Steven Pinker's 2011 bestseller *The Better Angels of our Nature*.[2] "War appears to be in decline," Pinker argued in a 2013 forum in the *International Studies Review*. He continued: "Wars between states have become extremely rare, and civil wars, after increasing in number from the 1960s through 1990s, have declined in number. The worldwide rate of death from interstate and civil war combined has juddered downward as well, from almost 300 per 100,000 world population during World War II, to almost 30 during the Korean War, to the low teens during the era of the Vietnam War, to single digits in the 1970s and 1980s, to less than 1 in the twenty-first century."[3] Elsewhere, Pinker, joined by Andrew Mack, writes: "By any standard, the world is nowhere near as genocidal as it was during its peak in the 1940s, when Nazi, Soviet, and Japanese mass murders, together with the targeting of civilians by all sides in World War II, resulted in a civilian death rate in the vicinity of 350 per 100,000 per year."[4] Certainly, as Pinker and other declinists argue, there is no better time in human history to be alive—our century is less violent and more peaceful than any previous period of human existence.

We should also recognize, though, that even if a trend toward a reduction in violent or genocidal conflict is verifiable, that is no guarantee that the trend will continue in the future. Even Pinker admits that "only time will tell whether the decline of war is an enduring change in the human condition, rather than a transient lull or statistical fluke."[5] Indeed, as suggested by three independent reports released in June 2015, more than a few scholars see ominous warning signs looming on the horizon that may move the world we aspire to farther away from the world in which we live:

- The CIVICUS Civil Society Watch Report found that democracy was on the retreat and authoritarianism on the rise in more than 96 of the UN's 193 member states. In those countries, CIVICUS found that basic freedoms of expression, association, and peaceful assembly were violated to a significant degree at some point during 2014.[6]
- The well-respected Global Peace Index, issued annually by London's Institute for Economics and Peace, found a divided trend with the world's most peaceful countries enjoying increasing levels of peace and prosperity, while the least peaceful countries spiraled into worsening violence and conflict. Overall, the Index, the world's leading measure of national peacefulness, found that the intensity of armed conflict was increasing dramatically, with the number of people killed in conflicts globally rising more than 3.5 times, from 49,000 in 2010 to 180,000 in 2014. The economic impact of that violence reached a total of US $14.3 trillion, about 13.4% of the world gross domestic product (GDP) and equivalent to the combined economies of Brazil, Canada, France, Germany, Spain, and the United Kingdom.[7]
- The eleventh annual Fragile States Index, published by The Fund for Peace, painted a similar picture of an increasingly divided world in terms of peace and security.[8] In the words of executive director J. J. Messner: "When you see the most fragile countries continuing to worsen and the most stable countries continuing to improve over time, it suggests fragility begets fragility and stability begets stability."[9]

More recently, in January 2016, the latest in a series of annual reports by Freedom House, tellingly titled *Anxious Dictators, Wavering Democracies: Global Freedom under Pressure*, found that—for the tenth year in a row—freedom around the world is declining.[10] While some question the annual reports' biases and methodological problems, the research by Freedom House at least draws our attention to the stressors of economic crises, migration, and terrorism in fueling xenophobia in democracies as well as pushing authoritarian regimes to crack down harder on dissent— both of which place civilians in increasing peril.[11]

As Mary Kaldor has famously argued, declinist arguments also need to be couched in the context of how war is defined.[12] In her opinion, what Pinker and others show is a decline in what she terms "old wars"—wars involving states and characterized by a certain minimum number of battle-related deaths (military as well as civilian). Of more pressing contemporary concern, however, is what Kaldor defines as "new wars"—wars involving networks of state and nonstate actors in which most violence is directed against civilians. For Kaldor, these new wars, born during the last decades of the twentieth century, "are associated with state weakness, extremist identity politics and transnational criminality, and there is a danger that this type of violence will spread as the world faces a growing economic crisis."[13]

Conflict studies scholar Jolle Demmers outlines several distinguishing characteristics of these new wars: they do not have precise beginnings and endings; they are protracted, often lasting for decades; they have different modes of warfare going beyond conventional national armies; their external support typically comes from overseas diaspora, lobby groups, foreign mercenaries, or global networks of trade (legal and illegal); they involve globally dispersed networks of actors and organizations; and they are driven by identity groups, or organizations claiming to represent such groups.[14] In short, the emergence of new war means contemporary war has become democratized; the state has lost the upper hand and nonstate actors play as great, if not a greater, role in civilians being done to death.

To these warning signs—a global democratic recession, a rise in violation of basic freedoms, an increasingly divided world in terms of peace and security, and the advent of new war—can be added a number of potent international and local drivers of conflict that raise additional concern for the future. These intersecting drivers of conflict include economic fragility, mismanagement of natural resources and tensions over equality of access to them, population growth, transnational organized crime, climate change, and the proliferation of violent nonstate actors.[15] These drivers do not respect state borders. They are global "problems without passports" that transcend countries and regions.[16] Taken collectively, all of these factors suggest a tenuously uncertain future, foreshadowed in the echoes of an increasingly violent present.

In February 2016, as I finished this book, civilians found themselves under attack in Chechnya, the Democratic Republic of Congo, Kenya, Ethiopia, Côte d'Ivoire, Kyrgyzstan, Bahrain, Somalia, Yemen, Afghanistan, Nigeria, Zimbabwe, China, the Philippines, Colombia, Macedonia, Pakistan, Libya, North Korea, Ukraine, Tajikistan, and an increasingly wide swath of territory controlled by the Islamic State of Iraq and the Levant (also known as ISIS). Of particular concern are escalating mass atrocity situations in South Sudan (discussed in Chapter 5), Sudan, Burma, Syria, the Central African Republic, Burundi, and Iraq.

From 2003 to 2011, Darfur, the western region of *Sudan*, was wracked with a "slow-motion" genocide by attrition, resulting, according to estimates from activist Eric Reeves, in approximately 500,000 deaths and the displacement of well over two million Darfuris.[17] Camouflaged as a "counterinsurgency strategy" by Sudanese president Omar Hassan al-Bashir (currently under indictment for war crimes, crimes against humanity, and genocide by the International Criminal Court), these indiscriminate scorched-earth attacks, including widespread "torture rapes," more accurately reflect a strategy of ethnic domination and racial subordination. Today, instability in Darfur continues as an estimated 450,000 people were displaced by violence in 2014, and an additional 43,000 in 2015. A total of 2.5 million people are now displaced in Darfur.[18] Every barometer of life has worsened in Darfur with malnutrition above emergency levels, less than 10% of the population having access to clean water and sanitation, and a third of the population reliant on international humanitarian aid.[19] In late 2013, scores were killed in intercommunal clashes in Darfur and in fighting between rebels and government forces from Khartoum.[20] Although UN peacekeeping forces are on the ground, the Sudanese government has succeeded in limiting their sphere of operations, often by direct attacks. In June 2015, despite Bashir's continuing demands for all UN peacekeeping forces to leave Sudan, escalating violence led the UN Security Council to unanimously decide to leave 15,000 peacekeepers in the Darfur region of Sudan for at least another year.

In June 2014, the Sudanese government, with suspected help from Iran, reconstituted the *Janjaweed*, government-sponsored militias responsible for the worst of the genocidal violence in Darfur between 2003 and 2005. Rebranded as "Rapid Support Forces," the militias are better equipped than they were in 2003, are now under central command, and are fully integrated into the state's security apparatus. No longer restricted to the Darfur region, this new iteration of the *Janjaweed* operates with renewed genocidal ambition throughout Sudan, including continuing assaults on civilians in the Nuba Mountains of South Kordofan and Blue Nile, the border region between Sudan and the new Republic of South Sudan. The Enough Project, a U.S.-based monitoring group, has documented widespread atrocities committed by the militias, on government command, including "burning civilian areas to the ground, raping women, and displacing non-Arab civilians from their homes."[21] Emboldened by a culture of impunity granted by Sudanese law, these forces commit war crimes and crimes against humanity under a blanket of legal immunity from prosecution for any acts committed in the course of duty. Since June 2011, the conflict in South Kordofan and the Blue Nile region has led to the internal displacement of over 1.2 million people.[22] At present, "populations in South Kordofan, Blue Nile and Darfur continue to face mass atrocity crimes perpetrated by the Sudanese Armed Forces, affiliated militias and armed rebel groups."[23]

Although *Burma* has seen many democratic reforms after the undoing of more than five decades of military rule and the establishment of a quasicivilian government in 2011, a recent spate of abuses by military and security forces has reawakened concerns for the protection of civilians in certain regions of the country.[24] The Rohingya, a Muslim ethnic minority group in Burma's far west Rakhine State, near the Bangladeshi border, have long been victims of heavy discrimination and persecution in Burma, a predominantly Buddhist country. The Burmese government does not recognize the Rohingya as one of the 135 state-recognized ethnic groups in Burma, Rohingya babies are not issued birth certificates, and Rohingya are subject to laws restricting their marriage and birth rate. Indeed, according to the UN, the Rohingya—an estimated 1.3 million people—are one of the most persecuted minorities in the world.[25] The recent rise of the ultranationalist 969 movement, led by Burmese monk Ashin Wirathu (who appeared on a July 1, 2013 international cover of *Time* magazine labeled "The Face of Buddhist Terror"), has reignited xenophobic fears about the supposed increasing influence of Islam in Burmese society. Incendiary rhetoric and slanderous images from Wirathu, "the Burmese bin Laden," and other hard-line monks in the self-proclaimed "Organization for the Protection of Race, Religion, and Belief," have led to a rapidly worsening situation for the Rohingya. Since June 2012, over 140,000 Rohingya have been displaced, with many fleeing to neighboring countries, and hundreds killed by Burmese security forces. Lack of accountability for these crimes has led to the spread and escalation of anti-Muslim hostility in the region, leaving the broader Muslim community (about 4% of Burma's total population) at risk as well.

At present, President Thein Sein's government remains unwilling to address the endemic, and institutionalized, discrimination against

Rohingya and continues to claim that Rohingya are illegal Bengali immigrants, despite the fact that many have been in the country for generations. The government's recent "Rakhine Action Plan" requires all Rohyingyas to accept ethnic classification as "Bengali" in order to obtain citizenship. Those who refuse to do so will be forced to join the more than 100,000 Rohingya already confined in detention camps. Human Rights Watch has cited the Burmese government and local authorities for engaging "in a campaign of ethnic cleansing against the Rohingya."[26] The Global Centre for the Responsibility to Protect also affirms that "the government's policies regarding the Rohingya suggest that it is attempting to render Arakan/Rakhine state ethnically homogenous through persecution."[27] A February 2014 report by the NGO Fortify Rights, based on leaked government documents from 1993 to 2008, concluded that the Burmese government's maltreatment of the Rohingya is a "crime against humanity" and is punishable under international law.[28] In May 2015, a meeting of several Nobel Peace Prize winners called the situation in Burma "nothing less than genocide."[29] Similarly, an October 2015 investigative report by the International State Crime Initiative at the Queen Mary University of London concluded that the Rohingya are facing the final stages of a genocidal process orchestrated by the highest levels of State and local government.[30] Even during Burma's historic democratic election in November 2015, its first free and fair national parliamentary election since 1990, "Rohingyas were largely disenfranchised in advance of the vote and continue to be denied citizenship and other fundamental human rights by the government."[31] Despite these ongoing issues, the international community continues to reward the Burmese government with increasing diplomatic engagement and direct foreign investment as well as by lifting or suspending sanctions and canceling bilateral debt. As a result, the risk of further human rights abuses and mass atrocity crimes being perpetrated against Muslims in Burma remains high.

In *Syria,* nearly 5 years since the start of their civil war in March 2011, fighting between government and nonstate opposition forces continues to widen in scope and intensity. Civilians allegedly have been subjected to chemical weapons attacks by state security forces and affiliated militia, a clear violation of international humanitarian law and a war crime. The government also stands accused of using explosives and bulldozers to demolish thousands of residential buildings to punish civilians in neighborhoods in which the army has clashed with opposition fighters. In January 2014, an international team of war crimes prosecutors and forensic experts found "clear evidence" of "systematic torture and killing" by al-Assad's regime since the start of the uprising. Their report, which "would support findings of crimes against humanity. . .[and] of war crimes against the current Syrian regime," was based on nearly 27,000 photographs of dead bodies of alleged detainees killed in Syrian government custody.[32] Political scientist Chip Carey maintains that the atrocities committed by the Syrian government, as a matter of state policy, against the Sunni civilian population clearly constitute genocide.[33] Some armed opposition groups—now functionally dominated by foreign-led jihadists—are also committing war crimes and other serious human rights violations in the name of their extremist ideology. Though the government's abuses far outweigh those of the rebels, an October 2013 report by Human Rights Watch did accuse five leading opposition forces of crimes against humanity.[34]

Caught in this unforgiving vise of government and opposition atrocities, over 250,000 people have been killed along with widespread sexual violence amid massive displacement of civilian populations to neighboring Jordan, Turkey, Lebanon, Iraq, and Egypt. The number of Syrian refugees in Lebanon, an unstable country smaller than Connecticut, is documented at 1.2 million, posing a huge burden on the Lebanese government and its people.[35] All told, around 4.4 million Syrian civilians have fled their country to escape the conflict with more than 6.6 million others also believed to be internally displaced in Syria—the largest number of people displaced by any conflict in the world.[36] Ongoing fighting has left at least 13.5 million Syrians in urgent need of humanitarian assistance, 4.5 million of whom remain in inaccessible areas.[37] In the words of Kristalina Georgieva, a humanitarian commissioner for the European Commission: "This is undoubtedly the world's worst refugee crisis in decades, and if we don't get off this slippery slope, it will soon become the largest in our lifetime."[38] Despite consistent calls for the Syrian government to be referred to the International Criminal Court for possible prosecution, the UN Security Council—the only organ that can make such a referral—has failed to take action (largely because of the veto power wielded by Russia and China). A February 2016 UN report did, however, accuse the Syrian government and allied militias "of inhuman actions against Syrian civilians on a scale that amounts to extermination."[39] At present, violence continues to escalate with an increased number of government aerial attacks and waves of Russian airstrikes in civilian-populated areas, prompting retaliatory action by nonstate armed opposition groups.

While the world's attention focused on the crisis in Syria, another human rights and humanitarian crisis was unfolding in the *Central African Republic* (CAR), one of the poorest places on earth. CAR—a landlocked nation of 4.6 million people, 80% of whom are Christian—has witnessed civil strife, pervasive violations of human rights, and political instability for decades. On March 24, 2013, the most recent crisis peaked as Seleka rebels, a coalition comprised largely of fighters from the country's minority Muslim population and backed by powerful neighbor Chad, seized the capital, Bangui, and overthrew the decade-long rule of President Francois Bozize. After grabbing power, Seleka fighters carried out a campaign of executions, indiscriminant killings, village burnings, and rape and sexual violence targeting the country's majority Christian population. In response, there was an activation of Christian self-defense militias—commonly referred to as "anti-balaka" (which means anti-machete in Sango, the local language)—whose revenge attacks were as cruel and abusive as the rebels against which they sought to defend themselves.[40] The interreligious conflict in CAR led to a vicious cycle of massacre and countermassacre with up to 6,000 deaths (including extrajudicial killing of civilians and children being beheaded) as well as pervasive sexual violence, enforced disappearances, arbitrary arrests, detention and torture, and the destruction and looting of property (including hospitals, schools, and places of worship). The sectarian violence dissipated briefly with the arrival of UN-sanctioned French and African forces in December 2013 and the forced resignation, under intense international pressure, of interim president Djotodia the following month. The Seleka rebels have now, however, regrouped in the safe haven of the majority Muslim northeastern corner of CAR, from where they can more safely launch retaliatory attacks against the anti-balaka.

The remaining Muslim communities throughout the rest of CAR remain vulnerable to the reprisals of anti-balaka fighters, as well as to the wrath of the majority Christian population who suffered under the brief period of Seleka rule. Anti-balaka leaders assert that CAR "belongs to Central Africans," whom they define as Christians and traditionalists.[41] To make this vision a reality, the well-structured anti-balaka movement is conducting coordinated and targeted attacks on Muslim neighborhoods throughout CAR, publicly referred to by the anti-balaka as "cleansing operations." According to Peter Bouckaert, emergencies director at Human Rights Watch, "whether the anti-balaka leaders are pursuing a deliberate policy of ethnic cleansing or exacting abusive collective punishment against the Muslim population, the end result is clear: the disappearance of longstanding Muslim communities."[42] The unrest has forced nearly a million people to flee their homes (about half of them children), most of whom are faced with the choiceless choice to "stay in the jungle and die or come back and possibly be killed."[43] A UN Commission of Inquiry estimates that at least 80% of CAR's total Muslim population has been driven out of the country, with about 36,000 Muslim civilians trapped in seven besieged communities throughout the country. There currently are more than 436,000 internally displaced persons in CAR and another 447,000 refugees in neighboring countries. An estimated 2.7 million people, more than half the population of the country, are in need of humanitarian assistance, but the continuing violence makes it impossible to reach them.[44] In a March 14, 2014 briefing to the UN Security Council, Adama Dieng, UN Special Adviser on the Prevention of Genocide, cautioned that the "Central African Republic is on the brink . . . crimes against humanity are being committed and . . . the risk of genocide remains high."[45] Echoing Dieng's caution, another senior UN official—John Ging, director of operations for the Office for the Coordination of Human Affairs—returned from a visit to the CAR "very, very concerned that the seeds of a genocide are being sown."[46] At present, while the country awaits presidential and legislative election results from December 2015, CAR's interim transitional government "requires ongoing and sustained international assistance" to protect its civilian population.[47]

Civilians in *Burundi*, a central African country of 10.4 million people lying east of the Democratic Republic of Congo and directly south of Rwanda, continue to face an imminent risk of mass atrocity crimes. Following the end of the 1993–2005 civil war between a Tutsi-dominated government and Hutu rebels, in which more than 350,000 people were killed and more than 1 million civilians were displaced, Burundi had enjoyed a decade of relative political and social stability. That stability was shaken, though, with the April 25, 2015 announcement by President Pierre Nkurunziza, a former Hutu rebel leader, that he would seek a third term in the upcoming presidential elections. Burundi's Constitutional Court ruled that, because he was elected by the parliament in 2005 and not by voters, Nkurunziza's first term as president did not count. For the political opposition and many civil society groups, however, "President Nkurunziza's candidacy is regarded . . . as being in violation of the constitution and the 2000 Arusha Peace and Reconciliation Agreement."[48] The constitutional crisis prompted by Nkurunziza's announcement led to several weeks of protests throughout Burundi. The political nature of the conflict soon degenerated, once again, in an identity-based conflict between the majority Hutu (85%) and minority Tutsi (15%)—an ethnic duplicate of neighboring Rwanda. Capitalizing on a bitter history of ethnic conflict, Burundian government officials stoked a genocide fear by alleging that the protests were in "Tutsi-dominated areas."[49] The *imbonerakure* (meaning "those who see from afar"), the paramilitary youth wing of the country's ruling party (allegedly trained in eastern Congo by Hutu rebel forces from Rwanda), quickly waged a campaign of ethnic intimidation and violence in support of Nkurunziza's third-term bid.

In May 2015, elements of the Burundian armed forces, led by a former ally of the president, launched an unsuccessful coup against Nkurunziza's government. This has led to deepening fragility and repression in Burundi, as well as fears of regional instability. At present, since the start of the protests, at least 439 people have been killed and scores more wounded by police and security forces, the *imbonerakure*, and anti-Nkurunziza opposition forces. More than 216,000 people—many of whom are Tutsi seeking asylum in Rwanda—have fled Burundi, including one of Burundi's vice-presidents who could not support the third-term bid of President Nkurunziza. Following Nkurunziza's reelection in July 2015, "a systematic policy of targeting members of the opposition, journalists and human rights defenders" has developed.[50] One Burundian Tutsi, living in the Bugendana refugee camp, lamented: "The idea of a genocide has not yet been eradicated, it's still rooted in the heads of these Hutus, who have been killing us since 1993. They still hold the bad dream to exterminate us."[51] Africanist Rene Lemarchand questions if Burundi can be pulled back from the brink of genocide: "The country's rapidly shrinking resource base is bound to further undermine the regime's legitimacy, stimulate wider grievances within the security force, and alienate regional allies."[52]

Finally, ISIS continues to wreak havoc in its self-proclaimed caliphate spanning Syria and Iraq. Since the ouster of Saddam Hussein in 2003, minority communities in *Iraq* have been especially vulnerable to mass atrocities. Christians, in particular, began to leave in large numbers; today, only a third of the 1.5 million Christians who lived in Iraq in 2003 remain. For those unwilling to pay the *jizya* tax or convert to its strict interpretation of Islam, ISIS has vowed their destruction. A September 2015 report by the U.S. Holocaust Memorial Museum "found that IS [Islamic State] targeted civilians based on group identity, committing mass atrocities to control, expel, and exterminate ethnic and religious minorities in areas it seized and sought to hold. IS committed crimes against humanity, war crimes, and ethnic cleansing against. . .communities in Ninewa [province in northern Iraq]. We also assert IS perpetrated genocide against the Yezidi people."[53] A January 2016 report from the Global Centre for the Responsibility to Protect held that ISIS continues to pose ". . .an existential threat to ethnic and religious minorities, who face the risk of further mass atrocities."[54]

On February 4, 2016, the European Parliament broadened the scale of accusations against ISIS by unanimously passing a resolution recognizing ISIS' "systematic killing and persecution of religious minorities in the Middle East as genocide."[55] It was the first time the European Parliament has recognized an ongoing conflict as genocide. Lars Adaktusson, Swedish member of the European Parliament, expressed his hope for the resolution's impact: "It's really important that the Parliament passed it, on a political level and a moral level. The significance is the obligations that follow by such a recognition. The collective obligation to intervene, to stop these atrocities and to stop the persecution in the ongoing discussion about the fight against the Islamic State."[56]

The impact of conflict on civilian populations is not restricted to South Sudan, Sudan, Burma, Syria, the Central African Republic, Burundi, and Iraq. Twenty-five percent of the world's population lives in fragile and conflict-affected settings.[57] A June 2015 UN report revealed that "nearly 60 million people have been driven from their homes by war and persecution, an unprecedented global exodus that has burdened fragile counties with waves of newcomers and littered deserts and seas with the bodies of those who die trying to reach safety."[58] If this number were the population of a country, it would be the world's twenty-fourth largest. Over half of the displaced are children and one in four find refuge in the world's poorest countries, straining the resources of already-fragile states. Every day in 2014, an average of 42,500 people became refugees, internally displaced, or asylum seekers because of conflict or persecution. As a result, today, one in every 122 of us is now either a refugee, internally displaced, or seeking asylum. In 2014, only 126,800 refugees were able to return to their home countries—the lowest such figure in 31 years.[59]

Regardless of whatever language we use to invoke the phrase "never again," our collective response to the protection of civilian populations under duress from violent or genocidal conflict has been far less than adequate. As UN Deputy Secretary-General Jan Eliasson has said: "Repeating the phrase 'never again' is in itself a sign of continued failure."[60] Sali Shetty, Secretary General of Amnesty International, likewise lamented: "The United Nations was established 70 years ago to ensure that we would never again see the horrors witnessed in the Second World War. We are now seeing violence on a mass scale and an enormous refugee crisis caused by that violence. There has been a singular failure to find workable solutions to the most pressing needs of our time."[61] Similarly, in an April 2014 UN Security Council meeting commemorating the Rwandan genocide, Jordanian ambassador Zeid Ra'ad Al Hussein challenged his fellow council members to apply the lessons learned from Rwanda to the ongoing crisis in the Central African Republic: "And ultimately, are we not too late—again? We all care, yes, maybe. But it is equally clear we still do not care enough; not enough to act immediately, overwhelmingly, in those cases where an intervention is needed."[62]

Indeed, it seems that our words of "never again" most often translate into actions leading to "again and again," "ever again," and "here we go again." On our worst of days, our commitment to prevent genocide and mass atrocity can be compromised by a diminishing will, a problem fatigue, or a selfish isolationism. On our best of days, however, we realize that, as Gareth Evans said in a 2012 lecture at Central European University, "genocide, war crimes, ethnic cleansing, and crimes against humanity were not no one else's business, but everyone's business."[63] As this book has attempted to show, in the field of genocide and mass atrocity prevention, there are many actors with many tools. Although they do not always share common interests or utilize the tools for common purposes, the many actors—academics, lawyers, policymakers, and global civil society—can be mobilized to create the political will necessary to prevent genocide and mass atrocity. As Evans writes: "Political will is capable of creation and subject to change: its presence or absence is not a given . . . It has to be painfully and laboriously constructed, case by case, context by context. And all of us have a role in this respect . . . It is also a matter of bottom-up mobilization: making the voices of ordinary concerned citizens heard in the corridors of power, using all the resources and physical and moral energy of civil society organizations all round the world to force the attention of policymakers on what needs to be done, by whom, and when."[64] Juan Mendez concurs with the importance of bottom-up mobilization in which political will "is constructed over time by the force of public opinion that can shame leaders out of their complacency and into effective action."[65] In short, genocide prevention is an achievable goal, but it requires each of us to take our global civic responsibilities seriously in whatever role and in whatever place we find ourselves. As Evans concludes: "You don't get to change the world simply by observing it."[66]

The 1986 dramatic film *The Mission*, directed by Roland Joffee (*The Killing Fields*) and written by Robert Bold (*Man for All Seasons*), depicted a small group of eighteenth-century Spanish Jesuits trying to protect a remote South American mission. A treaty reapportioning the land on which this mission was located was transferred to Portugal and the Portuguese law allowed slavery. Were the mission itself to be transferred to Portugal, the Guarani people in it would be enslaved. The Vatican sends an envoy, Cardinal Altamirano, to decide whether the mission will remain under the protection of the Church or be transferred to Portuguese jurisdiction. Submitting to the political realities, and seeking to appease the Portuguese rulers, Altamirano orders the closure of the mission. A joint Portuguese and Spanish force attacks the mission and slaughters its inhabitants. In a final exchange with Cardinal Altamirano, the Portuguese governor, Don

Hontar, attempts to justify the atrocity: "I did what I had to do . . . We must work in the world. The world is thus." To which Altamirano replies: "No, Señor Hontar. Thus have we made the world . . . thus have I made it."

The world that we have made is not the one for which we must settle. We can be the answer to our own prayers. Each of us has responsibility for the world that we have made and, playing the role of global citizen in the best sense, each of us has our own unique points of leverage to leave an indelible positive impression in the making of a better world. Together, we can commit to taking the collective action necessary to protect civilians from being done to death—by preventing genocide from ever taking place, preventing further atrocities once genocide has begun, and preventing future atrocities once a society has begun to rebuild after genocide.

In 1970, U.S. Southern poet, essayist, and environmentalist Wendell Berry published *The Hidden Wound*, a book-length essay on race and racism. He wrote: "I want to know, as fully and exactly as I can, what the wound is and how much I am suffering from it. And I want to be cured; I want to be free of the wound myself, and I do not want to pass it on to my children. Perhaps this is only wishful thinking; perhaps such a thing is not to be done by one man, or in one generation. Surely a man would have to be almost dangerously proud to think himself capable of it. And so maybe I am really only saying that I feel an obligation to make the attempt, and that I know if I fail to make at least the attempt I forfeit any right to hope that the world will become better than it is now."[67] As challenging as the prevention of genocide seems, let us not, by failing to make at least the attempt, forfeit our dangerously proud right to hope that the world will become better than it is now.

NOTES

1. Nils Petter Gleditsch, "The Decline of War—The Main Issues," *International Studies Review* 15 (2013): 397–399.
2. Steven Pinker, *The Better Angels of Our Nature: Why Violence Has Declined* (New York, NY: Viking, 2011).
3. Steven Pinker, "The Decline of War and Conceptions of Human Nature," *International Studies Review* 15 (2013): 400.
4. Steven Pinker and Andrew Mack, "The World Is Not Falling Apart" (December 22, 2014), accessed June 30, 2015 at http://www.slate.com/articles/news_and_politics/foreigners/2014/12/the_world_is_not_falling_apart_the_trend_lines_reveal_an_increasingly_peaceful.html.
5. Pinker, "The Decline of War and Conceptions of Human Nature," 405.

6. CIVICUS Civil Society Watch Report (June, 2015), accessed June 30, 2015 at http://www.civicus.org/images/CIVICUSCivilSocietyWatchReport2015.pdf.

7. "Global Peace Index," accessed June 30, 2015 at http://www.visionofhumanity. org/#/page/indexes/global-peace-index.

8. "Fragile States Index 2015," accessed June 30, 2015 at http://fsi.fundforpeace. org/.

9. Accessed June 30, 2015 at http://library.fundforpeace.org/fsi15-pressrelease.

10. *Freedom in the World 2016*, accessed February 9, 2016 at https://freedomhouse. org/sites/default/files/FH_FITW_Report_2016.pdf.

11. For one critique, see Jay Ulfelder's blog at https://dartthrowingchimp.word-press.com/2015/01/29/no-democracy-has-not-been-discarded/, accessed February 9, 2016.

12. Mary Kaldor, *New and Old Wars: Organized Violence in a Global Era*, 3rd ed. (Stanford, CA: Stanford University Press, 2012).

13. Ibid, vii.

14. Jolle Demmers, *Theories of Violent Conflict: An Introduction* (New York, NY: Routledge, 2012), 8–9.

15. Clare Castillejo, "Fragile States: An Urgent Challenge for EU Foreign Policy" (FRIDE: February 2015): 2–7.

16. The phrase "problems without passports" is taken from Kofi A. Annan, "Problems Without Passports" (September 1, 2002), accessed January 16, 2014 at http:// www.foreignpolicy.com/articles/2002/09/01/problems_without_passports.

17. Eric Reeves has been writing about greater Sudan for the past 15 years. A catalogue of his work, from which these statistics were drawn, can be found at http://sudanreeves.org/.

18. Global Centre for the Responsibility to Protect, *R2P Monitor* (May 2015): 6.

19. Rick Gladstone, "Number of Darfur's Displaced Surged in 2013," *The New York Times* (January 23, 2014), accessed January 24, 2014 at http://www.nytimes. com/2014/01/24/world/africa/number-of-darfurs-displaced-surged-in-2013. html?emc=edit_tnt_20140123&tntemail0=y&_r=0.

20. Isma'il Kushkush, "Scores Killed in Tribal Clashes in Darfur," *The New York Times* (November 18, 2013), accessed November 20, 2013 at http://www.nytimes. com/2013/11/19/world/africa/scores-killed-in-tribal-clashes-in-darfur. html?emc=edit_tnt_20131118&tntemail0=y&_r=0.

21. Akshaya Kumar and Omer Ismail, "Janjaweed Reincarnate: Sudan's New Army of War Criminals," www.enoughproject.org, June 2014, 1.

22. Global Centre for the Responsibility to Protect, *R2P Monitor* (May 2015): 6.

23. Global Centre for the Responsibility to Protect, *R2P Monitor* (January 2016): 7.

24. The military government changed the name to "Myanmar" in 1989.

25. BBC News Asia (January 24, 2014), accessed January 27, 2014 at http://www. bbc.co.uk/news/world-asia-18395788.

26. Accessed August 21, 2013 at http://www.hrw.org/news/2013/04/22/ burma-end-ethnic-cleansing-rohingya-muslims.

27. Global Centre for the Responsibility to Protect, "Anti-Muslim Violence in Burma/Myanmar and the Responsibility to Protect," January 9, 2014: 2.

28. "Fortify Rights, Policies of Persecution: Ending Abusive State Policies Against Rohingya Muslims in Myanmar," February 2014, accessed March 22, 2014 at http://www.fortifyrights.org.

29. Accessed July 1, 2015 at http://www.theguardian.com/world/2015/may/31/ burma-rejects-unbalanced-rohingya-remarks-by-nobel-prize-winners.

30. Penny Green, Thomas MacManus, and Alicia de la Cour Venning, "Countdown to Annihilation: Genocide in Myanmar" (2015), accessed February 10, 2016 at http://statecrime.org/data/2015/10/ISCI-Rohingya-Report-PUBLISHED-VERSION.pdf.

31. Global Centre for the Responsibility to Protect, *R2P Monitor* (January 2016): 8.

32. "A report into the credibility of certain evidence with regard to Torture and Execution of Persons Incarcerated by the current Syrian regime," prepared for Carter-Ruck and Co. Solicitors of London (January 20, 2014). The report was funded by the Qatari government, an opponent of Syria's government. Quoted material is taken from p. 21.

33. Accessed October 17, 2013 at http://www.worldpolicy.org/blog/2013/09/16/syrias-civil-war-has-become-genocide.

34. Accessed October 17, 2013 at http://www.nytimes.com/2013/10/11/world/middleeast/syrian-civilians-bore-brunt-of-rebels-fury-report-says.html?emc=edit_tnt_20131011&tntemail0=y&_r=0.

35. Global Centre for the Responsibility to Protect, *R2P Monitor* (May 2015): 2.

36. Global Centre for the Responsibility to Protect, *R2P Monitor* (January 2016): 2.

37. Ibid.

38. Mariano Castillo, "Angelina Jolie Turns Spotlight on Syria," accessed June 22, 2013 at http://edition.cnn.com/2013/06/21/world/meast/syria-refugees-angelina-jolie/index.html?hpt=hp_c1.

39. Anne Barnard, "Syrians Desperate to Escape What UN Calls 'Extermination' by Government," *The New York Times* (February 8, 2016), accessed February 9, 2016 at http://www.nytimes.com/2016/02/09/world/middleeast/syria-united-nations-report.html?emc=edit_ee_20160209&nl=todaysheadlines-europe&nlid=33728732&_r=1.

40. See testimony of Philippe Bolopion, accessed November 24, 2013 at http://www.hrw.org/news/2013/11/19/crisis-central-african-republic.

41. Human Rights Watch, "Central African Republic: Muslims Forced to Flee," February 12, 2014, accessed March 22, 2014 at http://www.hrw.org/news/2014/02/12/central-african-republic-muslims-forced-flee.

42. Ibid.

43. Rebecca Hamilton, "Samantha Power in Practice," *Foreign Affairs* (February 3, 2014), accessed February 7, 2014 at http://www.foreignaffairs.com/articles/140709/rebecca-hamilton/samantha-power-in-practice.

44. UN data are taken from Global Centre for the Responsibility to Protect, *R2P Monitor* (May 2015): 9–10.

45. Adama Dieng, "Statement of Under Secretary-General/Special Adviser on the Prevention of Genocide," March 14, 2014.

46. Mick Krever, "'Seeds of Genocide' Sown in Central African Republic, U.N. Official Warns" (November 13, 2013), accessed January 6, 2014 at http://amanpour.blogs.cnn.com/2013/11/13/seeds-of-genocide-sown-in-central-african-republic-u-n-official-warns/.

47. Global Centre for the Responsibility to Protect, *R2P Monitor* (May 2015): 10.

48. Ibid, 14.

49. Elsa Buchanan, "Burundi Genocide Fear: Government Youth Militia Imbonerakure Threatens to Kill Tutsi Refugees" (May 19, 2015), accessed July 1, 2015 at http://www.ibtimes.co.uk/burundi-genocide-fear-government-youth-militia-imbonerakure-threaten-kill-tutsi-refugees-1501869.

50. Global Centre for the Responsibility to Protect, *R2P Monitor* (January 2016): 13.

51. Buchanan, "Burundi Genocide Fear."

52. Rene Lemarchand, "In the Shadow of Genocides Past: Can Burundi be Pulled Back from the Brink?" (January 22, 2016), accessed February 10, 2016 at http://africanarguments.org/2016/01/22/in-the-shadow-of-genocides-past-can-burundi-be-pulled-back-from-the-brink/.

53. U.S. Holocaust Memorial Museum, "'Our Generation is Gone:' The Islamic State's Targeting of Iraqi Minorities in Ninewa" (2015): 2, accessed February 10, 2016 at http://www.ushmm.org/m/pdfs/Iraq-Bearing-Witness-Report-111215.pdf. Yezidis practice a 4,000-year-old religion that contains elements of Zoroastrianism, Judaism, Christianity, and Islam.

54. Global Centre for the Responsibility to Protect, *R2P Monitor* (January 2016): 5.

55. Jack Moore, "European Parliament Recognizes ISIS Killing of Religious Minorities as Genocide" (February 4, 2016), accessed February 10, 2016 at http://www.newsweek.com/european-parliament-recognizes-isis-killing-religious-minorities-genocide-423008.

56. Ibid.

57. Marie Gaarder and Jeannie Annan, "Impact Evaluation of Conflict Prevention and Peacebuilding Interventions," *Independent Evaluation Group*, Policy Research Working Paper 6496 (June 2013): 2.

58. Somini Sengupta, "60 Million People Fleeing Chaotic Lands, U.N. Says," *The New York Times* (June 18, 2015): A1.

59. Data in this paragraph, other than the quoted material, are taken from http://www.unhcr.org/558193896.html, accessed July 1, 2015. A complete copy of the UNHCR report, titled "Global Trends: Forced Displacement in 2014," can be found at http://unhcr.org/556725e69.html#_ga=1.145238644.1300302635.14 35763602.

60. UN News Centre (January 15, 2014), accessed July 1, 2015 at http://www.un.org/apps/news/story.asp?NewsID=46936#.VZRBCRNVhBc.

61. Accessed July 1, 2015 at http://www.amnesty.eu/en/news/press-releases/all/global-response-to-atrocities-by-states-and-armed-groups-shameful-and-ineffective-0858/?preview=fjnxwSdf7cjYui2#.VZRBSBNVhBf.

62. Quote taken from Edith M. Lederer, Associated Press, "Apology for UN Refusal to Stop Rwanda Genocide," *The Washington Times* (April 16, 2014), accessed July 7, 2014 at http://www.washingtontimes.com/news/2014/apr/16/apology-for-un-refusal-to-stop-rwanda-genocide/?page=2. Text of the UN Security Council meeting can be found in UN SC/11356 (April 16, 2014).

63. Accessed July 1, 2015 at https://www.youtube.com/watch?v=ym6BDzUGZ8Q.

64. Evans, *The Responsibility to Protect*, 224.

65. Project for a UN Emergency Peace Service (UNEPS), *Standing for Change in Peacekeeping Operations*, 44.

66. Evans, *The Responsibility to Protect*, 241.

67. Wendell Berry, *The Hidden Wound* (Berkeley, CA: North Point Press, 1970), 4.

INDEX

Abouharb, M. Rodwan, 170
"Acts Constituting a General
    (Transnational) Danger Considered
    as Offences Against the Law of
    Nations," 6–8
Acts of barbarity, 7
Acts of vandalism, 7
Actus reus, 111
Adaktusson, Lars, 362–63
Ad Hoc Committee, 18–19, 65, 69,
    74, 79–80. *see also* Genocide
    Convention
Affordable Care Act, 45–46
Africa, 163, 192, 196–97
African Standby Force (ASF), 257–58
Age of Genocide, x
Ahmed, Sara, 324
Akayesu, Jean-Paul, 59, 62
Al Anfal campaign, 56
Albright, Madeline, xxv, 219
Alexander, Jeffrey, 167
Allport, Gordon, 143
Alvarez, Alex, 11
Ambos, Kai, 67–68
Amnesty International, 81–82, 149
Anaya, James, 63
Anderson, Benedict, 11
Anderton, Charles, 175
Annan, Kofi, xi, xxii–xxiii, 33, 194, 264
Anocracy, 151–52
Apology, 300–303, 343n114
Arendt, Hannah, xiv, 109
Argentina
    education reforms in, 316
    genocide in, x, 82, 279–82, 284, 291
    memorialization in, 330–33
    reconciliation in, 337
    truth commissions in, 309–10

Armenian genocide, x, 5–6, 299, 328–29
Arnado, Gilberto, 23
Arusha Peace and Reconciliation
    Agreement, 361
Asia-Pacific Centre for R2P, 116
Assad, Bashar al, 248, 358–59
Association of Southeast Asian Nations
    (ASEAN), 196
Assumed similarity effect, 142–43
Atrocities definition, 106. *see also* mass
    atrocities
Atrocities Prevention Board, 114
Atrocity crimes definition, 113
Atrocity Forecasting Project, 165
Auschwitz, xiv, xxxii, 15, 61–62
Auschwitz Institute for Peace and
    Reconciliation, 114, 196–97, 316
Austin, Alexander, 148
Australian aborigines, 63–64, 91n121,
    298, 300–301
Authoritarian regimes, 152
Autocracy, 150–52
Axis Rule in Occupied Europe (Lemkin),
    13–14, 17, 296–97

Bangladesh, x, 30–31, 54, 264, 290, 357
Ban Ki-moon, xxiv, 117, 121–22, 223
Baraza peace courts, 305
Barkan, Elazar, 299
Barnett, Michael, 119–20
Bartov, Omar, x, 11–12
Bashir, Omar Hassan al-, 249–50, 294, 356
*Basic Principles and Guidelines on the
    Right to a Remedy and Reparation
    for Victims of Gross Violations of
    International Human Rights and
    Serious Violations of International
    Humanitarian Law*, 297, 303

Battle Groups, 257
Bekele, Daniel, 212
Belfast Guidelines on Amnesty and Accountability, 244
Belgium, 250
Belize, 253
Bellamy, Alex, 115, 138, 216
Bell-Fialkoff, Andrew, 111
Berry, Wendell, 365
Besancon, Marie, 175
The Better Angels of our Nature (Pinker), 353
Bitburg Military Cemetery, 31
Bjorkdahl, Annika, 220
Blatz, Craig, 298, 303
Bloxham, Donald, 55
Blue Helmet of the UN, 258
Bomberger, Kathryne, 313
Bosnia and Herzegovina v. Serbia and Montenegro, 249
Bosnia-Herzegovina. *see also* International Criminal Tribunal for the former Yugoslavia (ICTY); Yugoslavia
    collective memory in, 322–23
    education reforms in, 313–15, 317
    genocide in, xviii, 78, 135–36, 167–68, 285
    memorialization in, 332, 334
    reconciliation projects in, 303–4
    Srebrenica genocide, xxi–xxii, 59–60, 62, 72, 77–78, 112, 135–37, 253–54
Bosnian War, 110
Bouckaert, Peter, 360
Boutros-Ghali, Boutros, 42
Brazil, 76–77
Brewer, Marilynn, 144–45
"Bringing Them Home" report, 91n121
Brouneus, Karen, 310
Brown, Daniel James, 234
Buber, Martin, 46
Budapest Centre, 114
Bureau of Indian Affairs (BIA), 301–2
Burkina Faso, 155
Burma (Myanmar), 182, 228–29, 357–58
Burundi, x, 361–62
Butcher, Charles, 217
Butcher, Thomas, 14

Cambodia
    autogenocide in, 102
    death toll, 100
    education reforms in, 316–17
    forced rustification, 100
    genocide in, x, 99–105
    human rights protections, 100
    Khmer people, 102–3
    Khmer Rouge, 99–102, 125n11, 167, 317
    memorialization in, 330
    military intervention in, 264–65
    perpetrator's intent, determination of, 102
    PTSD rates in, 167
    reconciliation projects in, 304
Canadian aborigines, 63–64, 92n125
Canadian Centre for the Responsibility to Protect, 116
Canadian Museum for Human Rights, 92n125
Canas, Roberto, 310
Caprioli, Mary, 188
Carey, Chip, 359
Carlotto, Estela de, 281–82, 315
Carlotto, Laura de, 281–82
Carter, John, 175
Central African Republic, 257, 258, 359–61
Chadefaux, Thomas, 148
Chalk, Frank, 54
Chekhov's gun, 260
China, 24–25, 100, 107, 119, 221–22, 241, 293–94
Christopher, Warren, 43
Churchill, Winston, 3–4, 287
CIVICUS Civil Society Watch Report, 354
Claes, Jonas, 175
Clandestine detention centers (CDCs), 280–82, 330
Clinton, Hillary Rodham, xi, 238
Clinton, William J., 44, 87n19, 314
Coalition for the Responsibility to Protect, 116
Code of Crimes Against the Peace and Security of Mankind, 84–85
Cohen, William, xxv, 219
Cole, Benjamin, 155, 157, 158
Colombia, 298

Columbine High School, 325
Commission for Historical Clarification, 60, 309
Commission for Reception, Truth and Reconciliation, 309
Committee on the Elimination of Racial Discrimination (CERD), 247
Compaore, Blaise, 155
CONADEP (National Commission on the Disappearance of Persons), 309–10
Conflict history
cultural trauma, 167–68, 171–72
genocides/politicides, prior, 164–66, 171
human rights/international law violations, 170–72
identity-related tension, 163–64, 171
past cultural trauma, 166–68
primary prevention strategies, 171–72
psychological trauma, 166–67
as risk factor, 151, 162–63
vengeance, group grievance legacy, 168–69
Conley-Zilkic, Bridget, 76, 260, 266
Conway, Katherine, 322
Craven, Jim, 303
Crimes against humanity definitions, 108–10, 112
Crocker, David, 336
Cross-race recognition deficit, 199n28

Dallaire, Romeo, 256, 262–63
Daly, Erin, 311
Darfur genocide, xxv–xxvi, 53, 73, 104, 160, 165, 233, 249–50, 294, 356–57, xxivn34
Declaration on the Prevention of Genocide, 247
Declinism in war and conflict, 353–55
Del Ponte, Carla, 66
Demmers, Jolle, 145, 355
Democracy, 150–52
Democratic Republic of Congo, 254
Deng, Francis, 247
Deng, Simon, 266–67
Dieng, Adama, 121, 125, 218, 361
Digital humanitarianism, 238
Dihigo, Ernesto, 16

Dinstein, Yoram, 81
Dolus specialis, 68
"Done to death," ix–x
Donnedieu de Vabres, Henri, 17
Downstream prevention
benefits of, 338
disarmament, demobilization, reintegration (DDR), 285
justice (*see* justice)
justice sector reform (JSR), 285
memory in (*see* memory)
peacebuilding, postconflict, 282–86
reconciliation, 336–38
security sector reform (SSR), 285
state recovery time, 284
strategies, 124, 282–86
transitional justice, 283–86
truth as (*see* truth)
Drakulic, Slavenka, 319
Drost, Pieter, 52
Du Bois, W. E. B., 28
Dubost, Charles, 14
Ducasse-Rogier, Marianne, 119
"Due Obedience" law, 291

Early warning systems, 147–50, 200n54, 218–23, 257–58
East Timor, x
Economic and Social Council, 17, 19–20
Economic conditions
deterioration of, 176–77, 180
development level, 173–74, 179
group-based discrimination, 174–75, 179
informal economies, black market growth, 177–78, 180
macroeconomic stability, 176, 179–80
primary prevention strategies, 178–80
as risk factor, 151, 172–73
Economic preventive response tools
debt relief, increased aid, 237
divestment or aid conditionality, 241–42
freezing/seizing of monetary assets, 240–41
mandatory sanctions, 238–39
new funding, investment, 237–38
sanctions, effectiveness of, 242–43
sanctions/embargoes, lifting, 236–37

Economic preventive response
    tools (*Cont.*)
  targeted financial sanctions, 239
  trade embargoes, 239–40
  trade incentives, 238
ECOWARN, 257–58
ECOWAS, 257
"Education for a Just Society," 317
Eichmann, Adolf, 58, 80–81
Einsatzgruppen, 3–4, 20. *see also*
    Holocaust; Nazis
Eliasson, Jan, 363
Elster, Andrey, 145
Emanuel AME Church, 325
Enough Project, 357
Equity and Reconciliation
    Commission, 309
ESMA, 280–82, 330
Ethnic cleansing definitions,
    110–14, 128n65
Ethnocide, 25, 38n107
European Union, 257
Evans, Gareth, 104, 111, 233–35, 245,
    283, 364
Extraordinary Chambers in the Courts
    of Cambodia (ECCC) for the
    Prosecution of Crimes Committed
    during the Period of Democratic
    Kampuchea, 101–2, 249, 291. *see
    also* Cambodia
Eyerman, Ron, 320

Fabius, Laurent, 223
Feaver, Peter, 237
Feierstein, Daniel, 49, 280
Fein, Helen, 165
Ferencz, Benjamin, 22
Fernandez, Daniel Eduardo, 280
Ficior, Ioan, 55
Finnemore, Martha, 121
Fish, Steven, 189
Fletcher, Laurel, 303
Flights of death, 280, 338
Forced disappearance, 279–84
Forcible transfer of children, 25, 62–65,
    91n121, 92n125
Ford, Stuart, 290
Forum on Early Warning and Early
    Response, 149
Fowler, Jerry, 73

Fragile States Index, 354
Freedom, global, 354–55
"Full Stop" law, 291

Gallie, W. B., 44–45, 87n22
Galtung, Johan, 242
General Assembly Resolution 180, 18
Geneva Conventions, 105, 312
Genocidal mentality, 107, 190–91
Genocide
  acts of destruction, defining
      characteristics, 57–65
  "as such," 69–70
  by attrition, 60–61
  categories of, 17–19
  conceptual blockages, 44–45, 87n23
  cultural, 25, 38n107, 62–63
  decision to exterminate, ix–x
  definitions of, 15–16, 46–47, 50, 51,
      54–56, 103–5, 112–13, 146
  duty to intervene, xxiv
  elements of, 16–17
  evolution of, 8–12
  forcible displacement in, 112
  in geographical area, 78
  global response to, xxi–xxiv
  Gorgon effect, xiii–xiv
  historically, x
  human solution to, xxvii
  intent, inference of, 70–72
  as international crime, 16–17
  Lemkin's conception of, 13–15
  life destruction, 19
  as molecular process, xiv–xv
  motive in, 68–70
  by narcotics, 24–25
  "never again," 363–65
  plea bargaining of, 103–4
  as policy tool, 266
  protected identities, 17, 19
  qualitative measures of, 77–78
  quantitative measures of, 76–77
  study of, xi–xiii, xxiii–xxiv
  term, improper usages of, 45–46
  universal enforcement, 18, 19, 25–26
  universality of, x–xi
  war crimes in relationship to, 106–8
Genocide Convention
  acts defined as criminal, 48, 57–78
  attempt to commit genocide, 76–77

cultural genocide, 25
drafting of, 17–21, 108–9
forcible transfer of children, 25, 62–65, 91n121, 92n125
genocide acts, 24–25
genocide definition in, 21–22
hierarchy of crimes, 103–4
intentionality, 65–74
"in whole or in part," 74–78
jurisdictional responsibility, 25–26, 48, 78–84, 137, 250
member nation interests in, 23
political groups in, 22–24
protected groups in, xxix, 22, 47–57
ratification of, 26–32
reciprocity doctrine, 31
revision of, 84–85
"significant subset," 76
sovereignty package, 31
state sovereignty in, 23, 28–29
Genocide Convention Implementation Act (Proxmire Act), 32, 59, 76
Genocide in International Law (Schabas), 103
Genocide Prevention Task Force, xxv
George, Alexander, 218–19
Gleditsch, Nils Petter, 353
Global Action Against Mass Atrocity Crimes (GAAMAC) initiative, xxiv
Global Centre for R2P, 116
Global Peace Index, 354
Global Responsibility to Protect (GR2P), 116
Goebbels, Joseph, 108
Goeth, Amon, 15
Goldsmith, Benjamin, 152–53, 190, 191, 216
Goldstone, Jack, 152, 158, 165–66, 173, 187
Gomez, Carlos Andres, 45
Gotchev, Atanas, 215
Gover, Kevin, 301–3
Governance
civilian protection, 157, 159–60
corruption, 153–56
human rights, respect for, 162
identity-based polar factionalism, 157–59
inclusiveness in, 161–62
mass protest in, 155

primary prevention strategies, 160–62
regime type, 150–53, 160
as risk factor, 150, 151
rule of law, 156–57
security sector reform, 161
services provision, 155–56, 161, 186–87
state legitimacy deficit, 153–55, 161
state security forces, 153, 191–92
state structure weakness, 155–57
systematic state-led discrimination, 159–60
Gradowski, Zalman, xxxii
Grandmothers of Plaza de Mayo (Abuelas de Plaza de Mayo), 281–82
Greiser, Artur, 15
Gross, Ernest, 24, 84
Guatemala, x, 60, 83, 96n241, 194, 253, 309, 316

Habyarimana, Juvenal, 41, 86n1
Halbwachs, Maurice, 320
Ham, Carter, 252
Hamber, Brandon, 295–96
Hamilton, Rebecca, 233
Harff, Barbara, 56, 152, 153, 158, 159, 165, 176, 190, 216
Hate speech, 181–82
Hayner, Priscilla, 308–9, 312, 334
Hazlett, Chad, 165, 233
Heise, Lori, 189
Helms, Jesse, 31
Hereros, x
Herro, Annie, 258–59
Heydrich, Reinhard, 3
The Hidden Wound, 365
Hiebert, Maureen, 146
Higonnet, Ethel, 292
Hilberg, Raul, x
A History of Democratic Kampuchea, 316–17
Hoess, Rudolf, 15, 61–62
Holl, Jane, 218–19
Holocaust. *see also* Nazis
collective memory and, 322
crimes against humanity, 109
genocide during, x
memorialization of, 330

Holocaust (*Cont.*)
  reparations, 298
  restitution, 299
Homan, Kees, 119
Honduras, 283–84
Howard, John, 91n121
Human Rights Watch, 41, 149
Hun Sen, 101
Hussein, Zeid Ra'ad Al, 319, 363
Hutus. *see* Rwanda

Identicide, 146
Ieng Sary, 101
Ieng Thirith, 101
Ignatieff, Michael, 9, 311
I-identity. *see* social identity
Imbonerakure, 361
India, 25
Indonesia, x, 239
Ingram, Christopher, 170
International Association of Genocide
    Scholars (IAGS), xxiii, xxxivn27
International Commission of Inquiry on
    Darfur, 53, 73, 103
International Commission on
    Intervention and State Sovereignty
    (ICISS), 114, 221
International Commission on Missing
    Persons (ICMP), 314
International Court of Justice,
    111–12, 135–37
International Covenant on Civil and
    Political Rights, 312
International Criminal Court,
    249–50, 292–94
International Criminal Tribunal for
    Rwanda (ICTR)
  crimes against humanity as part of
      jurisdiction, 109
  cultural genocide, 62, 63
  group identity definitions, 51–53
  indictment authority, 249
  intentionality, 66–68, 71
  "members of the group"
      designation, 76
  right of reparation, 297–98
  "serious bodily or mental
      harm," 58–60
  structure, effectiveness of, 287–90
International Criminal Tribunal for the
    former Yugoslavia (ICTY)

crimes against humanity as part of
    jurisdiction, 109
group identity definitions, 52
indictment authority, 249
intentionality, 67, 68, 71–72
"members of the group"
    designation, 76
right of reparation, 297–298
"serious bodily or mental
    harm," 58, 59
Srebrenica genocide ruling, 136
structure, effectiveness of, 287–90
International Crisis Group, 149
International Human Rights
    Covenants, 170
International Military Tribunal at
    Nuremburg, 14–15, 108, 287, 288
International Network of Genocide
    Scholars (INOGS), xxiii, xxxivn27
International War Crimes Tribunal, 30
Iraq, x, 116, 119
ISIS, 362–63
Israel v. Eichmann, 80–81
Iyer, Aarti, 298, 303

Jackson, Robert, 14, 108
Janjaweed militias, 153, 356–57
Jedi religion as protected group, 49
Jelisic, Goran, 76–78
John Paul II (Pope), 41
Jonassohn, Kurt, 54
Jones, Adam, 107
Jones, Basil, 284
Juncker, Jean-Claude, 257
Jurisdictional responsibility, xxix,
    25–26, 48, 78–84, 137, 250
Justice. *see also specific courts and
    tribunals by name*
  economic costs of, 290
  hybrid courts, 291–92
  International Criminal Court,
      249–50, 292–94
  international tribunals, 287–90
  national trials in domestic
      courts, 290–91
  politicization in, 288
  public commemorations, 299–300
  public outreach by, 289
  reparations, 296–307
  restitution, 299
  restorative, 286, 296–307

retributive, 286–96
retroactivity in, 288
selectivity in, 289, 293
tradition-based community
models, 305–7
"Justice and Peace Law" program, 298

Kagame, Paul, 155
Kaing Guek Eav (Duch), 101
Kaldor, Mary, 140, 355
Kammen, Michael, 322
Kaplan, Seth, 183, 192
Kaufman, Stuart, 9
Kaufmann, Daniel, 188
Keating, Colin, 86n12
Kenya, 230–31
Kenyatta, Uhuru, 293
Khieu Samphan, 101–2, 125n11
Khmer Rouge, 99–102, 125n11, 167,
317. *see also* Cambodia
Kiir, Salva, 212
King, Martin Luther Jr., 64
Kopf, David, 107
Kosovo, 187
Krain, Matthew, 235
Kritz, Brian, 49
Krstic, Radislav, 60, 64, 71–72,
77–78, 90n101
Krstic Appeals Chamber, 62
Kuhner, Jeffrey, 45–46
Kulaks, x, 23, 60–61
Kuper, Leo, x
Kuperman, Alan, 265
Kurds, 56

Lachs, Manfred, 61
Lanzmann, Claude, xiv
Latin American Network for
Genocide and Mass Atrocity
Prevention, 114
Lauterpacht, Elihu, 137
Law on Missing Persons, 313–14
Lazare, Aaron, 302
Lebanon, 237, 359
Legal preventive response tools
accountability effect, 251
action by UN organs, appeals
to, 246–48
amnesty/immunity offers, 244–45
compliance monitors, 244
criminal prosecution referral, 249–50

dispute resolution mechanisms
support, 245
existing international law/norms,
references to, 245–46
human rights investigations, 248–49
reconceptualization of, 243
universal jurisdiction, exercise
of, 250
Lemarchand, Rene, 362
Lemkin, Raphael
on education reform, 315
on genocide as crime, 44, 103
Genocide Convention role, 4–8, 12–
21, 24, 29–30, 32–33
on intentionality, 65, 68
on right to reparations, 296–97
Levene, Mark, 10, 54
Levi, Primo, 124
Levy, Daniel, 320
Liberty Lobby, 30
Libya, 240–41
Lie, Trygve, 17
Lieberman, Benjamin, 111
Lin, Justin Yifu, 184
London Charter, 108
Lon Nol, 100
Lorber, Eric, 237
Los desaparecidos, 281
Luttwak, Edward, 185–86

Macedonia, 254
Machar, Riek, 212
Malice Green site, 327
Mancini, Luca, 187
Mann, Michael, 73
Manu, code of, 105
Manuelian, Haig, xii
Markusen, Eric, 107
Marshall, Monty, 155, 157, 158
Mass atrocities
civilian protection, 258
defined, 76, 113–14
peacetime, 138
UN Framework of Analysis, 216–17
warning-response gap, 218–23
windows of atrocity risk, 216, 268n17
Mass Atrocity Response Operations
(MARO) Project, 263
Mass murder. *see* genocide
Mass violence, hierarchy of, 103–4
Masten, Susan, 302

Maxwell-Fyfe, David, 14
May, Brian, 45
May, Larry, 111, 306
Mazower, Mark, 10
McCormick, Ty, 212
McFate, Sean, 285
Meharg, Sarah Jane, 146
Meier, Patrick, 238
Melander, Erik, 188
Memorialization
    collective memory, sustaining, 324
    counter monuments, 329
    performative, 331–33
    site, public space, 330–31
    spontaneous, 325–28
    traditional, 328–29
    transnational justice promotion
        via, 333–35
Memory
    collective, 319–24
    community, social cohesion, 323–24
    forced amnesia, 319
    healthy memory environment, 322
    memorialization, 324–35
    in social identity, 319
    as strategy, 318–19
Menchu, Rigoberta, 83
Mendeloff, David, 310–11, 334
Mendez, Juan, 220–21, 247, 364
Menem, Carlos, 330
Meral, Ziya, 320
Meron, Theodor, 81
Meyer, Christoph, 220
Midlarsky, Manus, 76
Midstream prevention
    accelerants, triggers, 214–18
    basis of conditionality, 225–26
    coercive threats, punishments, 225
    economic preventive response
        tools, 236–43
    legal preventive response
        tools, 243–51
    military intervention,
        118–20, 259–65
    military preventive response
        tools, 251–65
    persuasive process, 219–21
    political preventive response
        tools, 228–36
    preventive response tools,
        223–28, 271n66

rewards, incentives, 224–25
    strategies, 123–24, 213–14, 265–67
    warning–response gap, 218–23
Military preventive response tools
    arms, movements, communications
        restrictions, 255–56
    civilian protection security
        guarantees, 253–54
    civilians, coercive protection
        of, 255–56
    confidence/security-building
        measures, 253
    consensual preventive
        deployment, 254
    cooperative strategies, 255
    credible threat of military
        force, 256–58
    heightened military presence, 256
    military aid, training, 252
    military intervention,
        118–20, 259–65
    strategy for use of, 251–52
Milosevic, Slobodan, 158, 289
Minorities at Risk Project, 148
Minow, Martha, 114, 288, 289, 296
Mironko, Charles, 43
Miskovic, Slavisa, 323
Missing Persons Institute
    (MPI), 314–15
The Mission, 364–65
Modernity thesis, 11–12
Montt, Rios, 83, 96n241, 291
Monument Against Fascism, 329
Monument to the Victims of State
    Terrorism, 331
Moses, Dirk, 10, 29, 44, 72
Moshman, David, 104
Mothers of the Plaza de Mayo (Madres
    de Plaza de Mayo), 332–33
Multidimensional Integrated
    Stabilization Mission in the
    Central African Republic
    (MINUSCA), 258
Murphy, Karen, 315–17
Museveni, Yoweri, 154–55

Nadler, Arie, 336
Naimark, Norman, 61, 111, 128n65
Nation-state lethality, 9–12
The Nature of Prejudice (Allport), 143
Nazis. see also Holocaust

atrocities, 3–4, 14–15
birth prevention by, 61–62
Einsatzgruppen, 3–4, 20
genocide/war relationships, 108
group-based economic
    discrimination, 174–75
group identity definitions, 52
negative violence by, 61
Nuremburg trials, 14–15, 108,
    287, 288
premeditation in actions of,
    73, 94n175
Ncube, Mthuli, 284
Neilsen, Rhiannon, 181
Neurath, Konstantin von, 14
"Never Again" speech, 301–3
Nkunda, Dismas, xiii, xxxiiin18
Nkurunziza, Pierre, 361–62
Norris, John, 252
North Korea, 240
Northern Ireland, 169, 327, 330
Novick, Peter, 322
Nunca Mas ("Never Again"), 309–10
Nuon Chea, 101–2, 125n11
Nuremberg Trials, 14–16, 22, 108

Obama, Barack, 45, 64, 114, 119
Obrenovic, Dragan, ix
Olick, Jeffrey, 320
"On Genocide" (Sartre), 30
Operation Barbarossa, 3
Orwell, George, 321–22

Palomo, Francisco, 291
Paris, Roland, 285
Park of Memory (Parque de la
    Memoria), 330–31
Pasha, Talaat, 5–6
Patterson, William, 28
Peacebuilding Commission, 118,
    129n101
Pella, Vespasian, 17
Peron, Isabel, 279
Perozo, Perez, 69
Peru, 22, 54, 61, 304, 309, 316, 331–32
Petliura, Symon, 6
Petrovic, Drazen, 111
Pillay, Navi, 212
Pinker, Steven, 353, 354
Pinochet, Augusto, 82–83, 96n239
Polish Supreme National Tribunal, 15

Political Instability Task Force
    (PITF), 190
Political preventive response tools
    condemnation (naming and
        shaming), 232–33
    diplomatic disengagement, 235–36
    diplomatic legitimization, recogni-
        tion benefits, 228–29
    diplomatic surge, 235
    human rights promotion/
        support, 231
    political, diplomatic
        sanctions, 231–32
    political and field missions, 229–31
    proscription of individuals/
        organizations, 234–35
    resources for enabling dialogue, 229
    sporting, cultural boycotts, 234
Politicide, 56–57
Pol Pot, 99–101
Posttraumatic stress disorder
    (PTSD), 166–67
Powell, Christopher, 45, 146
Powell, Colin, 104
Power, Samantha, 8, 26, 28, 31
Premeditation in actions, 73, 94n175
Prevention
    downstream (*see* downstream
        prevention)
    importance of, 124–25
    initiatives, xxiv–xxvi, xxivn34
    intent in policymaking, 72–73
    midstream (*see* midstream
        prevention)
    population-based health model, 123
    responsibility to protect (R2P, RtoP),
        114–22, 129n89, 129nn100–102
    strategies generally, 122–24
    upstream (*see* upstream prevention)
    of violent conflict, 138–39
Preventive response tools, 223–28,
    271n66. *see also* economic pre-
    ventive response tools; legal pre-
    ventive response tools; military
    preventive response tools; political
    preventive response tools
Prijedor, 76, 332
Primary prevention. *see* upstream
    prevention
Proportionality doctrine, 262–63
Protected groups, xxix, 22, 47–57

Proxmire, William, 30–31
Proxmire Act (Genocide Convention Implementation Act), 32, 59, 76
Putin, Vladimir, 46
Putzel, James, 216

Qaddafi, Muammar el-, 240–41
Quets, Gail, 55

Racial segregation, 28
Ramirez-Barat, Clara, 316, 335
Raphael Lemkin Seminars for Genocide Prevention, 33
Rapid Support Forces, 356–57
Ratner, Steven, 105
Rawson, David, 43
Reagan, Ronald, 31, 32
"Reconstruction of the portrait of Pablo Miguez," 331
Reeves, Eric, 356
Regime change, 118–20, 190
Regulation 64 Panels in the Courts of Kosovo, 249, 291
Reid, Jon, 328
Reparations
    apology, 300–303, 343n114
    material, 298–99
    psychosocial, 303–5
    right of, 296–98
    symbolic, 299–303
Resolution 96, 16–17, 49, 58, 74, 79. *see also* Genocide Convention
Responsibility to prevent, 115
Responsibility to protect (R2P, RtoP), 114–22, 129n89, 129nn100–102, 261, 264
The Responsibility to Protect (ICISS), 114–15, 120, 122, 261, 264
Responsibility to react, 115, 118, 261
Responsibility to rebuild, 115
Reyntjens, Filip, 327
Rice, Andrew, 163
"Rights Up Front" initiative, 171
Robeson, Paul, 28, 29
Roccas, Sonia, 145
Rohingya, 357–58
Romania, 54–55, 89n72
Romero, Oscar (Archbishop), 308–9
Rome Statute, 66, 85, 105, 109, 112, 293, 294
Roosevelt, Franklin D., 4, 13

Rosenberg, Sheri, 61
Rost, Nicolas, 214
Rothman, Jay, 147
RTLM, 256
Rubenstein, Richard, 11
Ruhashyankiko, Nicodème, 50
Ruhashyankiko report, 75, 81
Rummel, Rudolph, xi
Russell, Bertrand, 30
Russian Federation, 117, 119, 138, 177, 221–22, 293–94, 359
Rutaganda judgment, 63
Rwanda
    apartheid in, 164
    authoritarian tradition in, 62
    birth prevention in, 62
    collective memory control in, 322
    confession, apology in, 301
    economic deterioration in, 177
    economic development level in, 173–74
    education reforms in, 315–16
    ethnic group identity, 51–55
    forcible transfer of children, 62–64
    gacaca courts in, 306–7, 310
    gender rights in, 194
    Genocide Convention, protected groups in, 22, 47–57
    genocide in, x, xiii, xxi–xxii, 26, 41–45, 86n1, 86n12, 87n19, 164
    ICTR (*see* International Criminal Tribunal for Rwanda (ICTR))
    ideologies of antagonism in, 163–64
    intentionality, 65–74
    mental harm *vs.* bodily injury, 59–60
    military intervention in, 262–63
    number of perpetrators in, 123
    numbers killed in, 43
    perpetrators' definition of victim group, 52–54
    polar factionalism in, 158
    psychosocial reparations in, 304, 305
    PTSD rates in, 166–67
    rape, sexual violence, 58–59
    reconciliation in, 337
    refugees/internally displaced persons in, 185–86
    restricted communications in, 256
    spontaneous memorials in, 326–28
    state legitimacy deficit in, 155
Rwandan Patriotic Front (RPF), 41, 43, 86n1

Safe havens, 253–54
Safire, William, 110
Saint Jean, Iberico, 280
Salihovic, Goran, 313
Saloth Sar. *see* Pol Pot
Sandy Hook Elementary School, 325
Santino, Jack, 327
Sartre, Jean-Paul, 8, 30
Satellite Sentinel Project, 248
Save Darfur Coalition, xxv–xxvi, 233,
	xxivn34
Scarf of Hope (Chalina de la
	Esperanza), 331–32
Schabas, William, 52, 54, 62, 65, 66,
	71, 82, 84, 103, 105, 108–9, 111,
	136, 246
Scheffer, David, 113
Scheper-Hughes, Nancy, 12
Schleunes, Karl, 73
Schwarzbard, Shalom, 6
Scilingo, Francisco, 338
Scully, Gerald, 174
Secondary prevention. *see* midstream
	prevention
Sein, Thein, 357–58
Semelin, Jacques, 54
Sentinel Project, 248
Serbia, 135–37, 158, 169
Serious Crimes Panels in the District
	Court of Dili in East Timor,
	249, 291
Shaw, Martin, 11, 54, 107, 110
Shetty, Sali, 363
Short, Damien, 300–301
Sierra Leone, 254, 304, 312, 316
Sikirica, Dusko, 76, 77
Sikkink, Kathryn, 27, 121, 295, 296
Simic, Goran, 285
Sinclair, Murray, 63–64
Sixth Committee/General Assembly,
	19, 23, 25, 50, 58, 65, 69,
	74–75, 80
Sixties Scoop, 63–64
Smith, Alexander, 28
Sobek, David, 170
Social fragmentation
	demographic pressures in,
		183–86, 193
	education access, 187
	gender-based violence, 189
	gender inequalities, 188–89, 194

goods/services access inequalities,
	186–87, 193
identity-based social divisions,
	181–83, 192–93, 280
infant mortality levels, 186–87
neighborhood conflict, 191
political instability, 189–92, 194
primary prevention
	strategies, 192–94
refugees/internally displaced
	persons, 185–86
as risk factor, 151, 180–81
state security forces increase,
	153, 191–92
weapons accessibility, 153, 191–92
youth bulge, 184–85
Social Frameworks of Memory
	(Halbwachs), 320
Social identity
	accentuation effect, 143
	arbitrary, 163–64
	assumed similarity effect, 142–43
	collective memory in, 319–24
	collective trauma in, 167–68
	collectivity in, 7, 49, 55, 146
	conflict-enhancing feedback
		loop, 144–46
	context dependency of, 142
	cultural genocide, 25, 38n107, 62–63
	effects of, 141–42, 146–47
	ethnicity as, 51–55
	group-based, 139–42
	group dynamics, escalatory process
		of, 144–46, 198n24, 199n28
	group identity competition, 144–45
	identity-based social
		divisions, 181–83
	in-group bias, 143–45
	memory in, 319
	nationalism, 8–12
	out-group homogeneity effect, 143
	overview, xxix–xxx, 138–41
	reconfiguration of, 171
	self-esteem in, 144
	as source of conflict, 139–47
	sources of, 141
Social identity theory, 144–45
Softic, Sakib, 136
Sonderkommando revolt, xxxii
South Sudan, 211–13, 230, 231, 234–
	35, 249–50, 266–67, 304, 356–57

Spain, 82–83
Special Adviser on the Prevention of
    Genocide, 247–48
Special Court for Sierra Leone, 249
Special Tribunal for Lebanon, 249
Spencer, Philip, 79
Srebrenica genocide, xxi–xxii, 59–60,
    62, 72, 77–78, 112, 135–37, 253–
    54. see also Bosnia-Herzegovina
Srebrenica-Potocari Memorial
    Center, 330
Sri Lanka, x
Stalin, Joseph, 23, 61, 90n106, 287, 315
Stanton, Gregory, 160
State sovereignty, 6, 8, 14–15, 19, 23,
    79, 114–15
Staub, Ervin, 163, 168, 177,
    192–93, 304
Stefanelli, Joseph, 106
Steinberg, Donald, 42–43
Stockholm Accords on Ethnic
    Cleansing, 111
Subotic, Jelena, 317, 335
Sudan Accountability and Divestment
    Act of 2007 (SADA), 241
Sudjian, Zuart, 299
Sun Tzu, 105
Survival in Auschwitz (Levi), xiv
Syria, 119, 157, 185, 232, 237,
    248, 358–59

Tajfel, Henri, 143–44
Taleb, Nassim Nicholas, 166, 176
Tanzania's National Committee for
    the Prevention and Punishment
    of the Crime of Genocide,War
    Crimes, Crimes Against Humanity
    and All Forms of Discrimination
    (TNC), 196–97
Task Force on the EU Prevention of
    Mass Atrocities, 114
Tavuchis, Nicholas, 300
Taylor, Diana, 331–32
Tehlirian, Soghomon, 5–6
Tertiary prevention. see downstream
    prevention
Thompson, John, 55
Through the Glass Darkly, 329
Tibet, 83
Tokyo War Crimes Trials, 287
Totralita, Lloyd, 302

Track 2 diplomacy, 230
Transitional Justice Data Base
    Project, 286
Transitional Justice Strategy for Bosnia
    and Herzegovina, 303–4, 313–14
Transitions from Authoritarian Rule, 283
Treblinka, 15
Treverton, Gregory, 166, 176
Trial massacres, 215–16
Truth
    commissions, 308–12
    education reform, 315–18
    missing persons fate, resolution of,
        281–82, 312–15
    as postgenocide strategy, 307–8
Truth and Reconciliation Commission
    (Canada), 64
Truth and Reconciliation Commission
    (Chile), 307
Truth and Reconciliation Commission
    (South Africa), 309
Truth Commission Digital Collection,
    344n152
Turner, John, 144
Tutsis. see Rwanda
Tutu, Desmond, 336

U. S. AID, 317
Uganda, 123, 154–55, 230, 308–9
Ukrainian famine, x, 23, 60–61,
    90n106, 315
Ulfelder, Jay, 76
UNAMIR, xxii
UN High Commissioner for
    Refugees, 237
United Nations
    on ethnic cleansing, 112
    genocide role generally,
        xxii–xxiv, 16–17
    R2P role, 116–19
    Rwandan genocide role, 42, 86n12,
        247, 264
United Nations Convention on the
    Prevention and Punishment of the
    Crime of Genocide. see Genocide
    Convention
United Nations Emergency Peace
    Service (UNEPS), 258–59
United States
    confession, apology in, 301–3,
        343n114

forcible transfer of children, 64–65
genocide by, 28–30, 39n125
Genocide Convention role, 18–19,
    23–24, 27–32
genocide prevention by, xxv
National Security Doctrine, 279
Rwandan genocide role, 42–43,
    59, 87n19
sanctions/embargoes, lifting, 237
Somali intervention costs, 260
UN Resolution vetoes by, 221–22
United to End Genocide, xxivn34
Universal Declaration of Human Rights
    (UDHR), 21, 48, 170, 312, xxxiiin1
Universal jurisdiction, 25–26, 48, 78–
    84, 137, 250
Universal punishment, 81, 96n229
Universal repression, 7–8, 78–79, 84
UNPROFOR, xxii
UN Security Council, 42, 116, 119,
    221–23, 232–33, 249, 255, 263–64,
    323, 359
UN Security Council Resolution
    (UNSCR 1325), 194
Upstream prevention
    blended network approach, 149
    conflict history (*see* conflict history)
    early warning systems, 147–50,
        200n54, 218–23, 257–58
    economic conditions (*see* economic
        conditions)
    governance (*see* governance)
    social fragmentation (*see* social
        fragmentation)
    social identity as source of
        conflict, 139–47
    strategies, 123, 137–39, 195–97
Urdal, Henrik, 193
Us-them thinking. *see* social identity

Valentino, Benjamin, 70, 260, 262, 266
Velasquez Rodriguez v. Honduras, 283–84
Verbitsky, Horacio, 337, 338
Verdeja, Ernesto, 67, 73,
    294–96, 311–12
Vietnam War, 30, 99
Vinitzky-Seroussi, Verad, 320
Violent conflict
    collective response to, 363–65
    conflict-enhancing feedback
        loop, 144–46

deaths, statistics, 198n8
declines *vs.* increase in, 353–56
drivers of, 355
early warning systems, 147–50
governance as risk factor (*see*
    governance)
identity group dynamics, escalatory
    process of, 144–46
ideologies of antagonism in, 163–64
impacts of, 356–63
prevention of, 138–39
risk factors for, 147–50
Visegrad genocide, 322–23
Visinescu, Alexandru, 55
Vulliamy, Ed, 158

Waal, Alex de, 76, 165, 266
Wald, Patricia, 104, 109–10
War Crimes Chamber, State Court of
    Bosnia- Herzegovina, 249, 291–92
War crimes definitions, 14, 105–9
Warning-response gap, 218–23
We Charge Genocide
    (organization), 39n125
*We Charge Genocide: The Crime of
    Government Against the Negro
    People*, 28–30, 39n125
We-identity. *see* social identity
Weinstein, Harvey, 303
Weiss, Thomas, 119–20, 223
Whang, Taehee, 242
Whitaker, Benjamin, 50, 85
Whitaker, Forest, 230
Whitaker report, 70, 71, 75, 103
White Armband Day, 332
Wiesel, Elie, 213–14
Wimmer, Andreas, 10
Winter, Jay, 22
Wirathu, Ashin, 182, 357
World Summit Outcome Document, 117

Yacoubian, George, 290
Yemen, 255
Yost, Ned, 46
Young, James, 333–34
Yugoslavia, x, xxi–xxii, 26. *see also*
    Bosnia-Herzegovina; International
    Criminal Tribunal for the former
    Yugoslavia (ICTY)

Zakaria, Fareed, 140

.